COMPUTER-AIDED ENGINEERING DRAWING
Using AutoCAD

COMPUTER-AIDED ENGINEERING DRAWING
Using AutoCAD

Cecil Jensen
Former Technical Director
R. S. McLaughlin Collegiate and Vocational Institute
Oshawa, Ontario, Canada

Jay D. Helsel
Professor
Department of Industrial Arts and Technology
California University of Pennsylvania
California, Pennsylvania

Donald D. Voisinet
Professor of Engineering Technology and Coordinator of
    Design and Drafting
Niagara County Community College
Sanborn, New York

Glencoe/McGraw-Hill
A Macmillan/McGraw-Hill Company

Mission Hills, California ▪ New York, New York

Sponsoring Editor:	Stephen M. Zollo
Editing Supervisor:	Mitsy Kovacs
Design and Art Supervisor:	Joseph Piliero
Production Supervisor:	Albert H. Rihner
Cover Designer:	Caliber Design Planning, Inc.

Library of Congress Cataloging-in-Publication Number: 90 5962

Computer-Aided Engineering Drawing Using AutoCAD

Send all inquiries to:
  Glencoe/McGraw-Hill
  29th floor
  1221 Avenue of the Americas
  New York, NY 10020

ISBN 0-07-067568-6

1 2 3 4 5 6 7 8 9 0   VNHVNH   9 8 7 6 5 4 3 2 1 0

CONTENTS

It all began in the early eighties. We started to implement computer-aided drafting (CAD) into our existing manual drafting or drafting and design programs. CAD was used to "top off" the program since we still taught drafting and design concepts in the traditional manner. At this time, courses included an introduction to CAD at the end. Later, application courses such as "Mechanical Design Using CAD" were developed. These second-level courses were used to develop the student's CAD competency as well as to provide experience with industry-type project applications. Any one of over a hundred different CAD software packages might have been utilized for this purpose. Slowly, but in a most certain fashion, AutoCAD emerged as the market micro CAD leader. It became known as the "industry standard" (and the education standard too).

In the early nineties we are coming to realize that drafting and design concepts can be learned, in a bona fide fashion, directly on a computer. Students learn on CAD all the drafting principles, concepts, and standards that they originally were taught manually on a drafting board. This evolutionary pace is quickening as industry moves closer to the fully CAD-converted drafting and design office.

Computer-Aided Engineering Drawing Using AutoCAD is not simply about learning AutoCAD. It is, instead, about learning all the techniques of developing engineering drawings with the aid of AutoCAD. This means that students will not only learn how to be proficient drafters but that they will simultaneously become CAD competent by understanding how to use and apply the power of AutoCAD. The text uses pictorial representations called *icons* throughout. This makes it easy for the student to recognize where and how to apply each command.

Computer-Aided Engineering Drawing Using AutoCAD is built on a foundation of technical accuracy and comprehensive proven projects. It will prepare students for exciting and rewarding careers in advanced technology industries. The text may be used for one- or two-semester courses in a computer-aided engineering drawing curriculum.

In this new text, the authors have made every effort to translate the most current available technical information into the most usable form from the standpoint of both instructor and student. The latest developments and current CAD practices in all areas of graphic communication, materials representation, shop processes, computer numerical control, true positioning, geometric tolerancing, and metrication have been incorporated into this text in a manner that simplifies and converts complex drafting standards and procedures into understandable instructional units. Author research and visits to CAD facilities through the country have resulted in a presentation that combines current drafting practices with practical techniques to produce the most efficient learning system yet designed for the instruction of computer-aided engineering drawing.

Chapters in the text are divided into a number of single-concept units, each with its own objectives, instructions, examples, review, and assignments. This organization provides the student with a logical sequence of experiences which can be adjusted to individual needs; it also permits maximum efficiency in learning essential concepts. Development of each unit is from the simple to the complex, and from the familiar to the unfamiliar. Checkpoints are included to provide maximum reinforcement at each level.

Although the metric system for drawings has not been adopted by smaller industries to the degree that it has been by the large international companies, it is increasing in use. For this reason all current ANSI standards have also been published in the metric units of size and measurement. In order to prepare students for additional employment options upon graduation, it is recommended that both the International System of Units (SI) and the U.S. Customary System (USCS) units of measurement be included in all technical drawing programs. Both USCS and SI units are used throughout the text and the problems. Thus, the text may be used in completely USCS-oriented courses or in courses that utilize both metric and Customary systems.

The authors would like to thank the many CAD users for their thoughtful and useful comments and to welcome them to this next and crucial stage in the evolution of CAD.

Cecil Jensen
Jay D. Helsel
Donald D. Voisinet

ABOUT THE AUTHORS

CECIL JENSEN is the author or coauthor of many successful technical books, including *Engineering Drawing and Design, Fundamentals of Engineering Drawing, Fundamentals of Engineering Graphics* (formerly called *Drafting Fundamentals*), *Interpreting Engineering Drawings, Architectural Drawing and Design for Residential Construction, Home Planning and Design,* and *Interior Design.* Some of these books are printed in three languages and are used in many countries.

He has twenty-seven years of teaching experience in mechanical and architectural drafting and was a technical director for a large vocational school in Canada.

Before entering the teaching profession, Mr. Jensen gained several years of design experience in the industry. He has also been responsible for the supervision of the teaching of technical courses for General Motors apprentices in Oshawa, Canada.

He is a member of the Canadian Standards Committee (CSA) on Technical Drawings (which includes both mechanical and architectural drawing) and is chairman of the Committee on Dimensioning and Tolerancing. Mr. Jensen is Canada's representative on the American (ANSI) Standards for Dimensioning and Tolerancing and has represented Canada at two world (ISO) conferences in Oslo (Norway) and Paris on the standardization of technical drawings.

He took an early retirement from the teaching profession in order to devote his full attention to writing.

JAY D. HELSEL is a professor of industry and technology at California University of Pennsylvania. He completed his undergraduate work at California State College and was awarded a master's degree from Pennsylvania State University. He has done advanced graduate work at West Virginia and at the University of Pittsburgh, where he completed a doctoral degree in educational communications and technology. In addition, Dr. Helsel holds a certificate in airbrush techniques and technical illustration from the Pittsburgh Art Institute.

He has worked in industry and has taught drafting, metal-working, woodworking, and a variety of laboratory and professional courses at both the secondary and college levels. During the past twenty-five years, he has also worked as a free-lance artist and illustrator. His work appears in many technical publications.

Dr. Helsel is coauthor of *Engineering Drawing and Design, Fundamentals of Engineering Drawing, Programmed Blueprint Reading,* and *Mechanical Drawing.* He is also the author of the series *Mechanical Drawing Film Loops.*

DONALD D. VOISINET is a professor of engineering technology and coordinator of drafting and design at Niagara County Community College (N.C.C.C.). He received his undergraduate (Bachelor of Science, Mechanical Engineering) and masters degrees at the State University of New York at Buffalo (S.U.N.Y.A.B.). Significant industrial experience as a designer and engineer include the Minuteman III Missile program, Energy from Waste (EFW) project, and Chevrolet 396 engine-pattern design.

Mr. Voisinet is the author of many leading-edge CAD texts including *Introduction to CAD,* 2d ed., *Computer-Aided Drafting and Design, AutoCAD Mechanical Laboratory Manual,* and *Mechanical Design Using CADD.* These texts have been translated into three languages and are used in countries throughout the world.

He has over twenty years of experience instructing all phases of mechanical and electrical drafting and design. More recently (since 1983), Mr. Voisinet has concentrated his curriculum effort implementing CAD courses into the programs at N.C.C.C. and at many other institutions across the United States. These have included courses in introduction to CAD and application courses in mechanical design, electrical design, and piping design using CAD as well as advanced-level CAD coursework.

DRAFTING UPDATE (PRESENT DRAWING PRACTICES)

FEATURE		SYMBOL	ANSI PUBLICATION Y14.5M—1982 (EXCEPT WHERE NOTED, REFER TO CLAUSE NO.)
LINES (THREE LINE WIDTHS NOW REPLACED BY TWO LINE WIDTHS.)		▬▬▬ THICK ──── THIN	Y14.2M—1979
LETTERING (TWO APPROVED STYLES. HEIGHT OF LETTERING DEPENDENT ON DRAWING SIZE.)			Y14.2M—1979
MILLIMETER DIMENSIONING PRACTICES			CLAUSE 1.6.1
METRIC LIMITS AND FITS			B 4.2—1978
DIAMETER SYMBOL (NOW PRECEDES THE DIAMETER VALUE. THE SYMBOL REPLACES THE ABBREVIATION DIA)		∅	CLAUSE 1.8.1
RADIUS SYMBOL (NOW PRECEDES THE RADIUS VALUE)		R	CLAUSE 1.8.2
REFERENCE DIMENSION		(8.6)	CLAUSE 1.7.6
SURFACE TEXTURE SYMBOL		√ √ ⟨√⟩ √‾	Y14.36—1978
SPECIFYING REPETITIVE FEATURES		X	CLAUSE 1.9.5
COUNTERBORE OR SPOTFACE		⌴	CLAUSE 3.3.10
COUNTERSINK		⌵	CLAUSE 3.3.11
DEPTH		↧	CLAUSE 3.3.12
CONICAL TAPER		—▷ 0.2 : 1	CLAUSE 2.13
FLAT TAPER		—◁ 0.15 : 1	CLAUSE 2.14
SYMMETRICAL OUTLINES			CLAUSE 1.8.8
ALL AROUND		◯	CLAUSE 3.4.2.3
DIMENSIONING CHORDS, ANGLES, AND ARCS		⊢50⊣ ⊢5̂0⊣ ⟨60°⟩	CLAUSE 1.8.3
NOT TO SCALE DIMENSION		◄─ 120 ─►	CLAUSE 1.7.9
FEATURE CONTROL FRAME (FORMERLY CALLED FEATURE CONTROL SYMBOL ORDER OF SEQUENCE CHANGED)		⊕ ∅ 0.1 A	CLAUSE 3.4.2
DATUM TARGET SYMBOL		∅10 / A 3	CLAUSE 3.3.3 AND 4.5.1
GEOMETRIC CHARACTERISTIC SYMBOLS	STRAIGHTNESS	──	CLAUSE 6.4.1
	FLATNESS	▱	CLAUSE 6.4.2
	PARALLELISM	//	CLAUSE 6.6.3
	SYMMETRY	⊕	CLAUSE 5.12
	CIRCULAR RUNOUT	↗	CLAUSE 6.7.2.1
	TOTAL RUNOUT	↗↗	CLAUSE 6.7.2.2

Basic Drawing Design

1

The Language of Industry

■ UNIT 1-1

The Language of Industry

Since earliest times (Fig. 1-1-1) people have used drawings to communicate and record ideas so that they would not be forgotten. The earliest forms of writing, such as the Egyptian hieroglyphics, were picture forms.

The word *graphic* means dealing with the expression of ideas by lines or marks impressed on a surface. A drawing is a graphic representation of a real thing. Drafting, therefore, is a graphic language, because it uses pictures to communicate thoughts and ideas. Because these pictures are understood by people of different nations, drafting is referred to as a "universal language."

Drawing has developed along two distinct lines, with each form having a different purpose. On the one hand, artistic drawing is concerned mainly with the expression of real or imagined ideas of a cultural nature. Technical drawing, on the other hand, is concerned with the expression of technical ideas or ideas of a practical nature, and it is the method used in all branches of technical industry.

Even highly developed word languages are inadequate for describing the size, shape, and relationship of physical objects. For every manufactured object there are drawings that describe its physical shape completely and accurately, communicating engineering concepts to manufacturing. For this reason, drafting is referred to as the "language of industry."

Drafters translate the ideas, rough sketches, specifications, and calculations of engineers, architects, and designers into working plans which are used in making a product. See Fig. 1-1-2. Drafters may calculate the strength, reliability, and cost of materials. In their drawings and specifications, they describe exactly what materials workers are to use on a particular job. To prepare their drawings, drafters use Computer-Aided Drafting and Design (CADD or CAD) systems.

Drafters are often classified according to their type of work or their level of responsibility. Senior drafters (designers) take the preliminary information provided by engineers and architects to prepare design "layouts" (drawings made to scale of the object to be built). Detailers (junior drafters) make drawings of each part shown on the layout, giving dimensions, material, and any other information necessary to make the detailed drawing clear and complete. Checkers carefully examine drawings for errors in computing or recording sizes and specifications.

Drafters also may specialize in a particular area of specialization such as mechanical, electrical, electronic, aeronautical, structural, piping, or architectural.

DRAWING STANDARDS

Throughout the long history of drafting, many drawing conventions, terms, abbreviations, and practices have come into common use. It is essential

Fig. 1-1-1 Greek architecture.

TYPICAL BRANCHES OF ENGINEERING GRAPHICS	ACTIVITIES	PRODUCTS	SPECIALIZED AREAS
MECHANICAL 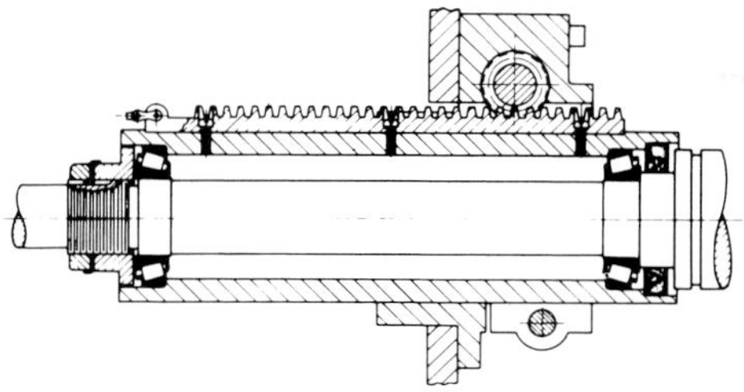 	DESIGNING TESTING MANUFACTURING MAINTENANCE CONSTRUCTION	MATERIALS MACHINES DEVICES	POWER GENERATION TRANSPORTATION MANUFACTURING POWER SERVICES ATOMIC ENERGY MARINE VESSELS
ARCHITECTURAL  	PLANNING DESIGNING SUPERVISING	BUILDINGS ENVIRONMENT LANDSCAPE	COMMERCIAL BUILDINGS RESIDENTIAL BUILDINGS INSTITUTIONAL BUILDINGS ENVIRONMENTAL SPACE FORMS
ELECTRICAL 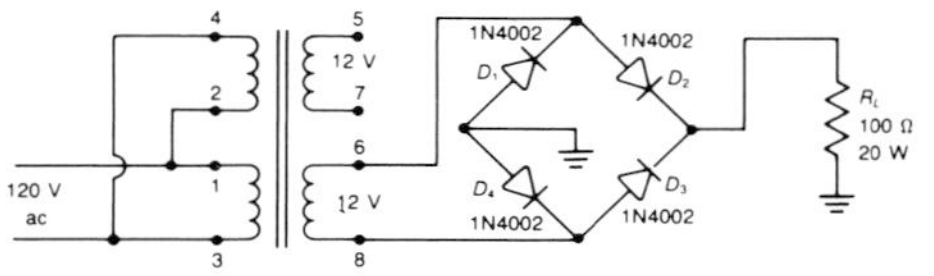 	DESIGNING DEVELOPING SUPERVISING PROGRAMMING	COMPUTERS ELECTRONICS POWER ELECTRICAL	POWER GENERATION POWER APPLICATION TRANSPORTATION ILLUMINATION INDUSTRIAL ELECTRONICS COMMUNICATIONS INSTRUMENTATION MILITARY ELECTRONICS
AEROSPACE 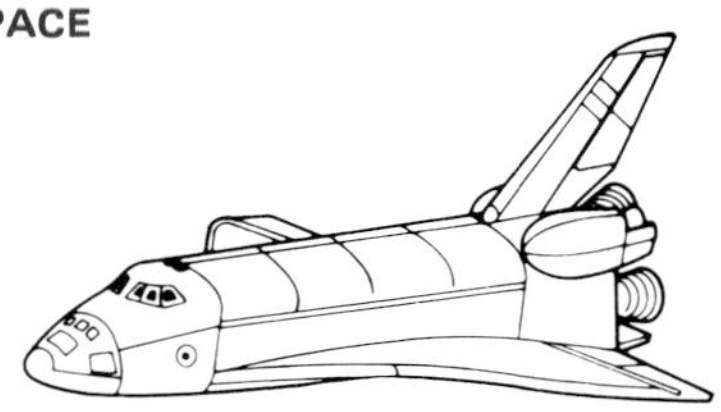 	PLANNING DESIGNING TESTING	MISSILES PLANES SATELLITES ROCKETS	AERODYNAMICS STRUCTURAL DESIGN INSTRUMENTATION PROPULSION SYSTEMS MATERIALS RELIABILITY TESTING PRODUCTION METHODS
TECHNICAL ILLUSTRATING 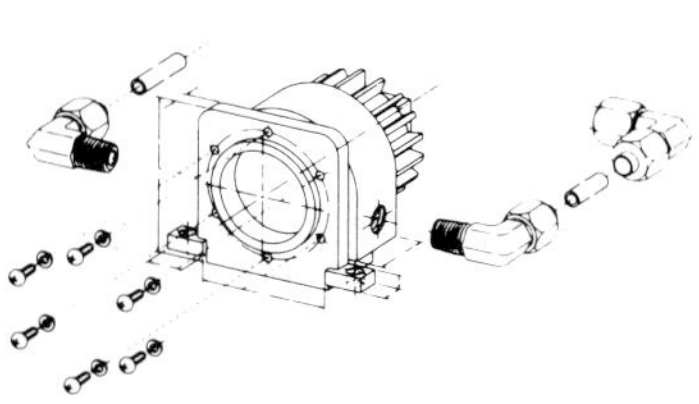 	PROMOTION DESIGNING ILLUSTRATING	CATALOGUES MAGAZINES DISPLAYS	NEW PRODUCTS ASSEMBLY INSTRUCTIONS PRESENTATIONS COMMUNITY PROJECTS RENEWAL PROGRAMS

Fig. 1-1-2 Various fields of drafting.

that different drafters use the same practices if drafting is to serve as a reliable means of communicating technical theories and ideas.

In the interest of efficient communication, the American National Standards Institute (ANSI) has adopted a set of drafting standards which are recommended for drawing practice in all fields of engineering and are used and explained throughout this text. These standards apply primarily to end product drawings, which usually consist of detail or part drawings and assembly or subassembly drawings, and are not intended to fully cover other supplementary drawings such as checklists, item lists, schematic diagrams, electrical diagrams, flowcharts, installation drawings, process drawings, architectural drafting, and pictorial drawing.

The information and illustrations shown in this text reflect current industrial practices in the preparation and handling of engineering documents.

CHANGING TIMES

The last 20 years have brought great changes to the drafting room. Its physical appearance, furnishings, even its drafters and engineers have moved quickly from their battered domain of old into the information age. This era is often referred to as the *technical revolution*.

These changes were brought about largely by the integrated circuit chip. It has, in fact, revolutionized the way we work and play. This era has seen dramatic changes in worldwide communications at all levels—personal, professional, industrial—and in every facet of modern-day life. The circuit chip is on our wrist (quartz digital watches). It is used to help solve math problems (hand-held calculators). It entertains (video games), and helps to run businesses (computers). The technical changes it has launched have affected many careers, and retraining to upgrade job skills has become commonplace. Drafting and design have been at the forefront of the changes. CAD (computer-aided drafting) and CADD (computer-aided drafting and design) are familiar acronyms that have swept through the profession.

Drafting room technology has progressed at the same rapid pace as the economy of our country. Many changes have taken place in the modern drafting room as compared to a typical drafting room scene before CAD as shown in Figure 1-1-3. Not only is there far more equipment, but it is of much higher quality. From automated drafting machines to CADD systems, noteworthy progress has been made and continues to be made as our expanding technology takes giant steps forward in this "advanced" technology.

PLACES OF EMPLOYMENT

There are over 400,000 people working in drafting and design positions in the United States. A significant number now are women. About 9 out of 10 drafters are employed in private industry. Manufacturing industries that employ large numbers are those making machinery, electronic equipment, transportation equipment, and fabricated metal products. Nonmanufacturing industries employing large numbers are engineering and architectural consulting firms, construction companies, and public utilities.

Drafters also work for the government: the majority work for the armed services. Drafters employed by state and local governments work chiefly for highway and public works departments. Several thousand drafters are employed by colleges and universities and by nonprofit organizations.

(A) THE DRAFTING OFFICE AT THE TURN OF THE CENTURY. (Bettman Archive, Inc.)

(B) MANUAL DRAFTING. (Charles Bruning)

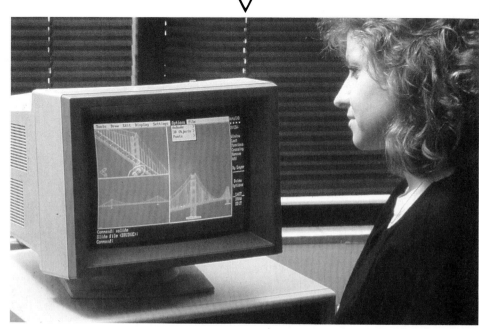

(C) CAD DRAFTING. (Autodesk Inc.)

Fig. 1-1-3 Evolution of the drafting office.

TRAINING, QUALIFICATIONS, ADVANCEMENT

Young people interested in becoming drafters can acquire the necessary education from a number of sources, including technical institutes, junior and community colleges, extension division of universities, and vocational-technical schools. Others may qualify for drafting positions through on-the-job training programs combined with part-time schooling.

The prospective drafter's education in post–high school drafting programs should include courses in mathematics and physical sciences, as well as in CAD and CADD. Studying fabrication practices and learning some technical and design skills also are helpful, since many higher-level drafting jobs require knowledge of manufacturing or construction methods. This is especially true in the mechanical discipline due to the implementation of CAD/CAM (computer-aided drafting/computer-aided manufacturing). Many technical schools offer courses in structural design, strength of materials, physical metallurgy, CAM, and robotics.

As drafters gain skill and experience, they may advance to higher-level positions as checkers, senior drafters, designers, or supervisors of other drafters. See Fig. 1-1-4. Drafters who take additional courses in engineering and mathematics are often able to qualify for engineering positions.

Qualifications for success as a drafter include the ability to visualize objects in three dimensions and the development of problem-solving design techniques. Whether preparing a drawing manually or by CAD, drafting concepts will still be required. The

Courtesy Tektronix

Fig. 1-1-4 Positions within the drafting room.

computer cannot think, draw three-view drawings, dimension, or section a drawing without human interaction. It is the person who has drafting knowledge that will operate the CAD system.

EMPLOYMENT OUTLOOK

The employment opportunities for drafters are expected to be favorable in the future. Prospects will be best for those developing postsecondary CAD and CADD competency, as many industries now regard the two-year post–high school program as a prerequisite for their drafters.

Employment of drafters is expected to rise as a result of the increasingly complex design problems of modern products and processes. In addition, as engineering and scientific occupations continue to grow, more drafters will be needed as support personnel. Also, the use of more efficient CADD equipment has eliminated some of the routine tasks previously performed by drafters. This has reduced the need for some lower-skilled operations.

References

1. Charles Bruning Co.
2. *Occupational Outlook Handbook.*

CHAPTER

2

Drafting Equipment and Drawing Office Practices

■ UNIT 2-1

The CADD Drafting Office

The drafting office is the starting point for all engineering work. Its product, the *engineering drawing*, is the main method of communication between all people concerned with the design and manufacture of parts. Therefore the drafting office must provide accommodations and equipment for the drafters, from designer and checker to detailer; for the personnel who make copies of the drawings; and for the secretarial staff, which assists in the preparation of the drawings.

Few engineering departments still rely on manual drafting. In the majority of cases, CADD is necessary for increased productivity. Equipment for drafting is varied and is steadily being improved. Where a high volume of similar or repetitive work is not necessary, manual equipment does the job adequately and inexpensively.

In recent years, however, companies have turned to automated drafting. The reason is not simply to speed the drafting process. Automated drafting serves as a full partner in the design process, enabling the designer to do jobs that are simply not possible or feasible with manual equipment.

■ UNIT 2-2

Drafting Equipment

COMPONENTS OF A CAD SYSTEM

A CAD system is made up of various combinations of equipment. This holds true for small, medium, and large system applications. The specific package selected largely depends on the needs of the user. Various types of drawings (check print, finished drawing), referred to as *hard copy*, may be preferred by certain companies. Other companies which are fully automated may not require any drawing whatsoever. This means that one company will choose a piece of equipment that prepares a drawing one way. Another company will select equipment that uses another method for preparation of drawings. Still a third company will not utilize any equipment to produce hard copies.

Generally, each piece of equipment can be categorized as one of the following types:

- Processing and storage
- Input
- Output

This chapter will analyze each major piece of equipment within these categories. Figure 2-2-1 shows an overall diagram of a complete micro-

CADD system, including the various pieces of input and output equipment. The purpose and function of each piece as well as its relationship to the complete system will be described. The items shown in Fig. 2-2-1 are typical components found in any system. It would be unlikely, however, to find all of these items in one particular system. The central processing unit (CPU) is considered part of the processing equipment. An alphanumeric (letters and numbers) keyboard is used to manually input data and is normally found with the graphics display monitor as one unit. In combination, a keyboard and graphics display monitor are commonly referred to as a *terminal*. A CPU may be reserved for a single purpose. If so, it is normally with the terminal; this combination is commonly referred to as a *computer*. Thus, a computer is composed of a CPU, alphanumeric keyboard, and graphics display monitor.

The typical system arrangement is interactive. This means that a person must cause the interaction between the CPU and the graphics display shown on the monitor screen. An alphanumeric keyboard or other input equipment will aid this process. After the design and/or drawing on the CAD unit has been completed, the information may be transferred to various output devices.

Figure 2-2-2 illustrates one type of

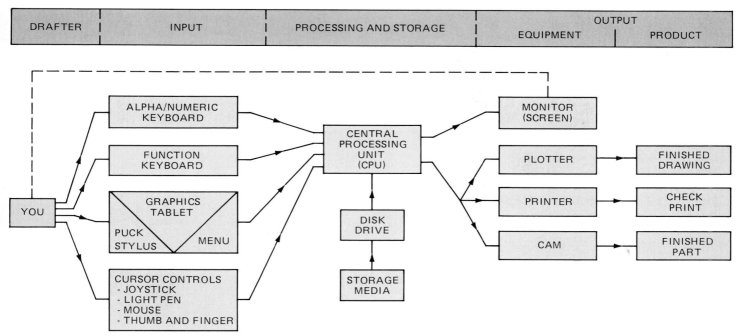

DRAFTER	INPUT	PROCESSING AND STORAGE	OUTPUT	
			EQUIPMENT	PRODUCT

Fig. 2-2-1 Operational flowchart of a CAD system.

system arrangement. To the left is a monitor, the drives, CPU, and a keyboard. In the center are input devices known as a graphics tablet (digitizer), and a joystick. In the background to the right is a plotter.

PROCESSING AND STORAGE EQUIPMENT

The CAD program, drawings, and symbols are stored on disk. The CPU collects input information and places the lines and letters in such a way as to produce the required drawings and data.

Central Processing Unit

Bits and Bytes The CPU is the computing portion of the system. A large number of integrated-circuit (IC) chips are combined into a microprocessor. This is where the number crunching occurs, i.e., the performance of fundamental computations. The number of computations, or the capacity of the unit, is designated by the number of bytes. *Byte* is the base term used by the system manufac-

turers, describing a character of memory containing 8 bits.

A *bit* is a *binary* dig*it*. All messages are digitally sent to a microprocessor by means of the binary code — a two-digit system using the symbols 1 and 0. The digit 1 refers to the presence of a signal (on). The digit 0 refers to the lack of a signal (off). This is similar to a light switch. It is either toggled on (1) to illuminate a lamp or off (0) to plunge a room into darkness.

A signal is transmitted by the opera-

Courtesy Calcomp

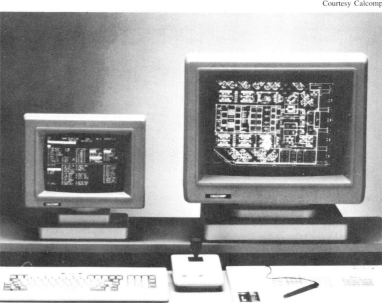

Courtesy IBM

Fig. 2-2-2 CAD system equipment.

tor whenever a key is pressed on the alphanumeric keyboard. For example, the first and third bit of a byte is magnetized to represent the number 5, as illustrated by

$$00000\bullet 0\bullet = 5$$

Each letter of the alphabet (alpha) or number of the base 10 numbering system (numeric) is represented by a byte having a different combination of bits.

The speed at which number crunching occurs is rapidly increasing, as a result of the availability of 16- and 32-bit machines. Eight-bit machines were used exclusively during the early 1980s. Mid-1980 saw the 16-bit microprocessor become the industry standard. Currently, 32-bit machines are common. A 32-bit machine has the ability to process four characters rather than a single character of information instantaneously. A character of information (byte) may be either a letter or a number. A 32-bit machine does not process information four times faster than an 8-bit machine, but many times faster than that. No matter if your unit is in an 8-, a 16-, or a 32-bit type, the basic unit is still the byte. Thus, a 640K-byte unit has a dynamic capacity of approximately 640,000 characters of memory.

The size of the CPU will generally determine the type of CAD system. *Micro* is the term used for small systems; *mini*, for medium systems; and *mainframe*, for large systems.

Micro System The micro unit, which is used for small applications, has a typical user (or dynamic) memory capacity in the 640K- to 4M-byte range. This means there is enough space for about 640,000 to 4 million characters. Due to binary numbering limitations, 1K is not exactly 1K in the computer. It is the closest (1024) multiple. To get a feel for memory size, 640K roughly equals 400 typewritten pages. The term "larger and smaller" has been used to describe micro units. This means that larger and larger capacity is put into smaller and smaller units. The chart shown in Fig. 2-2-3 illustrates the rapid advancement in microcomputing technology. The associated cost per bit (or byte) has fallen at a rate inversely proportional to this increased capacity. As a result, the microcomputer revolution has been launched.

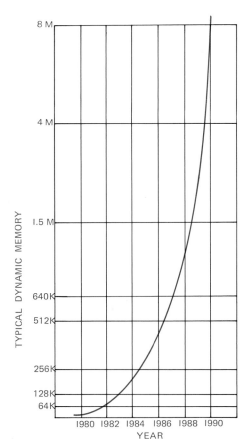

Fig. 2-2-3 Microcomputer dynamic memory (RAM).

A single or dual monitor and alphanumeric keyboard are normally part of a micro unit (shown in Fig. 2-2-4). These units, known as desktop computers, are considered dedicated. When a system is dedicated, it operates for the sole purpose of a single user. Micro systems are economically priced. Consequently, they are readily available and are used for general

drafting applications. Although their capacity is limited, much work can be accomplished with them. Thus, large, expensive systems need not be tied up with basic drafting requirements. The data gathered on the micro unit (or system) can later be "translated" over to a larger system. In this manner, CAD has become accessible to many more designers and drafters.

Mini Systems A mini system is generally a stand-alone, or turnkey, operation. Stand-alone equipment refers to a system that can process information without having to address a separate or mainframe CPU. It is similar to a micro system, but it has added capability. The outstanding feature of a mini is its power. Anything that can be drawn on a traditional drafting board can be created with this type of system. In addition, it can be automatically transformed into three-dimensional (3D) representation and rotated. Thus, prior to the micro-CAD revolution, it constituted the majority of CAD systems. Remember:

Micro systems = accessibility
Mini systems = power

More than one terminal or workstation may be connected to a mini system CPU. This is known as *networking*. The network provides the full power of the system to additional terminals. The result is reduced cost and standardization. Thus, power and accessibility become a reality. The idea of a network is excellent. A single CPU, however, has inherent problems, including downtime and response time, meaning that all the terminals will be inactive until the CPU is operational.

Courtesy Hewlett-Packard Company

Fig. 2-2-4 Sample microcomputers.

Problems in dedicated systems, however, affect only that workstation.

A queue, or response time, means a waiting period. This occurs in a network system when simultaneous requests by several users are made. For example, six individuals request a drawing to be brought up on each of their workstations. This is done sequentially. If your request was made last, you will have to wait for the other five. Processing time has substantially been reduced with the advancement of computer technology, however.

Mainframe A mainframe system has a huge CPU (or host computer). CAD is only one of a multitude of functions which it can execute. Work such as payroll spreadsheets may be part of its operation. Thus, it is not considered stand-alone and is not dedicated to a single user's purpose. It offers even more capability than the micro and mini systems. Mainframes were available long before CAD became popular; consequently, it was the most popular type of computer graphics during the early days of CAD. Mainframe terminals are normally found in a remote location of the workplace and are not combined into a single unit as with the micro system. For example, several terminals, each of which may be in a remote location are still connected to the same processing unit. This is shown schematically in Fig. 2-2-5.

Sometimes it is difficult to determine whether a system is a micro, mini, or mainframe, as the categories are general and tend to overlap. A very large mini, for example, may be considered in either a mainframe or a mini category. Thus, some of the very powerful popular industrial systems are referred to as super-minis.

Software

Program Language Software is the abstract logical concept of a program and what it does. A program is a group of written instructions logically arranged to perform a task. The instructions tell the computer what to do and when to do it. They are used to input information into the system. CAD programs are written in a variety of languages. Common ones are known as LISP (List Processing Language for Symbolic Computing), BASIC (*B*eginners' *a*ll-purpose *s*ymbolic *i*nstruction *c*ode) and C. BASIC is popular since it uses Englishlike and mathlike "easy-to-use" language. The notations are made up of statements rather than sentences.

No matter which language is used, drafters and designers need not necessarily develop a knowledge of it. Some proficiency, however, may be desired, and an introductory programming course may be taken for this purpose.

A drafter or designer will normally serve as the user of programs rather than the developer. Consequently, the programs will be received complete. Software has been extensively developed over the years. A computer programmer will spend thousands of work hours to develop a graphics program. A multitude of complete programs are available for use. The computer explosion has dropped hundreds of CAD software and hardware products onto the market. Never before has industry been confronted by so many choices. The recommendation with software is "Buy—don't build." If the desired software to do the job can be purchased, why invest thousands of work hours to develop a new program? Also, if you build it, it's yours. You must maintain it, update it, etc. This maintenance becomes a waste of time and money. CAD software programs, however, provide an option to write special features into the program. These are referred to as *macros*. Macro capability allows you to customize the system for your particular purpose.

Storage CAD systems will magnetically store programs and drawings on disk. A disk will economically store drawings and programs plus offer speedy retrieval. Only seconds are required to find a program. A program may be found in one of two ways: the sequential method or the random method. Sequential retrieval means that you retrieve information in order, starting at the beginning. The random method allows information to be retrieved or entered immediately. This latter method is commonly referred to as *direct access*. It is accomplished by designating sections on the disk. When you specify the section number, the section is immediately found.

Different types of disks are available. There are hard (fixed) types and flexible (floppy) types. Disks are also single or dual. This means that data storage may be one-sided (single) or that data may be on both sides (dual) of the disk. A flexible disk is similar in appearance to a 45-rpm phonograph record. It is, however, thinner. Also, since it is made from a plastic film, it is more flexible. Hence, the term *floppy disk*. Two standard diameters for floppy disks are 5.25 and 3.50 in. These are illustrated in Fig. 2-2-6. Note the protective covering over the larger disk. Disks must be handled

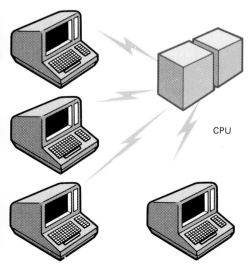

Fig. 2-2-5 **Mainframe network system.**

(A) 5 1/4 IN. COVERED FLOPPY DISK

(B) 5 1/4 IN. UNCOVERED FLOPPY DISK

(C) 3 1/2 IN. DISK

(D) WRITE PROTECT TABS FOR 5 1/4 IN. FLOPPY DISKS

Fig. 2-2-6 **Floppy disks.**

gently. Even a small scratch can ruin the contents of the disk. The cover will protect the disk from dust, dirt, and accidental scratching. It cannot, however, prevent mishandling. A disk, for example, cannot be exposed to heat or magnetic fields. The contents will immediately become damaged.

Notice the small tabs shown in Fig. 2-2-6D. They are used to protect disk contents. It is possible to accidentally write over the data on the disk with new data. The original data is then destroyed. The small tab covers the slot (Fig. 2-2-6D) in order to prevent this. This safety procedure is known as *write protect*.

Hard, or fixed, disks are available in various configurations. See Fig. 2-2-7. They handle a larger amount of data than a floppy disk. It is sealed in a container. Thus, in addition to having a greater capacity, it is also more durable than the floppy. In general, a comparison of the hard to the flexible disk shows that the hard disk:

- Has greater capacity
- Is more durable
- Requires less handling
- Is more expensive

The larger mainframe CAD systems utilize a different software format. The programs are stored on disks and magnetic tapes. They provide extended capability over the small and medium-sized systems. As in all computer instructions, the language of electrical impulses (the binary system) is used. Each portion of a program will normally represent a particular command. Commands are combined to prepare an engineering drawing. For example, one part will instruct the machine to draw a line, another part a circle, and so on.

PROCESSING AND STORAGE UNITS

Additional devices are required to allow input to or output from the processing equipment. Among those required are the drives and memories. The smaller systems, which use floppy disks, require equipment to drive the software. A disk drive as shown in Fig. 2-2-8 receives the floppy disk directly and may be used as permanent storage. The information on the disk may be a program or drawings. When loading a disk into a drive, be certain to insert it correctly. The label is to be up, the slotted portion is placed in first, and the write protect slot is to the left.

Fig. 2-2-8 Floppy disk drive.

Due to CAD software size, micro based systems are now equipped with a hard drive. The floppy drive(s) is used to maintain a permanent record of drawings after they have been developed. The disk drive itself is a piece of hard equipment. *Hardware* is a term that applies to any and all pieces of equipment having a physical entity.

Computers have memory systems to store programs and data. The memory may be either permanent or temporary. Permanent memory is referred to as *read-only memory* (ROM) or on-line storage. ROM may also be referred to as *firmware*. Firmware is software inside of hardware. Temporary memory is referred to as dynamic, user, or *random access memory* (RAM). RAM provides temporary storage locations for entries made by any input device, allowing a drawing to be developed. A complete set of statements (a program), up to system capacity, is stored in RAM. Computers are generally designated by system capacity. A 640K unit, for example, has 640 000 bytes of dynamic memory. The contents in dynamic memory are destroyed when power is lost or when a power surge occurs. Thus, power surge protectors should be used on all systems. In the long run, this will prevent many hours of work from being lost.

The contents stored on a disk are not lost as a result of a power interruption. Remember though not to remove a floppy disk while placing information onto it (writing) or taking information off (reading). A glitch (discontinuity) may result. The drive busy light on the disk drive will be lit when information is being read from or written to the disk. CAD system capability is enhanced by several other peripheral input and output devices. A peripheral is an additional piece of equipment that may be used in conjunction with the computer. Peripherals will be covered in subsequent sections of this chapter.

INPUT EQUIPMENT

The skills in the use and operating of the input equipment replace the skills of manual drafting. This equipment instructs the computer to draw lines and circles of various widths and sizes and to apply such graphics as symbols, dimensions, and notes to a drawing.

Alphanumeric Keyboard

An alphanumeric keyboard allows you to communicate directly with the CPU. It may be used to manually input data for:

Fig. 2-2-7 Fixed hard disk drive.

Nongraphic work
Adding text and notes
Exact coordinate input
Command selection

Every CAD system provides a means to select a part of a program that allows the use of a particular command. One of the ways to effect this is by keying in the appropriate letters (word) after the COMMAND: prompt. For example, LINE may be the command for line creation. To select that part of the program, key in LINE and press the ENTER key.

The keyboard is an extended version of a standard typewriter keyboard, as illustrated in Fig. 2-2-9. The alphanumeric keys are the same. Usually, though, there are additional keys that allow some specialized command options to be quickly accomplished. "Alpha" refers to the keys that input letters of the alphabet. "Numeric" refers to the other keys, each of which inputs a number. The user may type in an alphanumeric instruction. Input is completed by pressing the carriage return (ENTER key). Since computers have become popular, knowledge of the keyboard is indispensable for anyone involved with CAD. The speed of inputing data with the keyboard is a function of the ability to use the keyboard. Thus, users will benefit greatly by taking an introductory keyboard course. Remember, time is valuable.

The alphanumeric keyboard is a separate piece of equipment. It is indispensable and is found on every CAD system.

Fig. 2-2-10 Alphanumeric keyboard, numeric keyboard, and function keys.

Function Keyboard

The function keyboard is a piece of input equipment that is used to retrieve a program or part of a program. (The term program function keyboard is probably more descriptive, but for simplicity, the term function keyboard will be used to describe this input device.) A function keyboard contains several buttons or keys. A part of a program is electronically connected to one of the buttons or keys, and these are operated during the execution of a particular function. A function keyboard is referred to differently by various manufacturers.

The arrangement of the buttons or keys varies with the hardware manufacturer. Some of the smaller dedicated units combine them directly on the alphanumeric board of the computer. An example of this is shown in Fig. 2-2-10. The function keys are located at the left.

Manufacturers of larger minisystems have a completely separate function keyboard, illustrated in Fig. 2-2-11. Each of the particular functions associated with the corresponding button may be identified. The functions vary depending on what is to be accomplished by a particular system. Figure 2-2-11 represents a typical medium-size function keyboard.

Graphics Tablet

The graphics tablet is a flat surface area electronically sensitized beneath

Fig. 2-2-9 Alphanumeric keyboard. (Courtesy Epson)

Fig. 2-2-11 Separate function keyboard.

the surface. When proper contact is made on the surface, electrical impulses are transmitted to the computer. The information that is transmitted provides the programmed instructions to the CPU.

Digitizing

A graphics tablet has become the most popular input device. In terms of graphics creation, it is far more important than the keyboard. Also, it has many purposes. One use is quick and accurate graphic conversion. A rough sketch can be converted to a finished drawing by the transferring of point and line locations to the screen. Information is based on the X-Y (horizontal-vertical) linear coordinate system. It is entered quickly and efficiently into the computer, using this so-called electronic drawing board (the graphics tablet). The result of the input data is graphically displayed on a monitor screen. This method is commonly known as *digitizing*. Consequently, a graphics tablet is also re-

ferred to as a *digitizer*. Other functions such as symbol input may be performed with the aid of a tablet. Figure 2-2-12 shows a graphics tablet menu.

Any selection on the tablet will retrieve a portion of the program corresponding to the desired title or symbol. For example, if you wish to draw lines, select the menu labeled LINE. This will call up the part of the program that allows the creation of lines.

A menu limits the design drafter to only certain types of commands. Both the software and the menu, however, can be changed on many of these systems. One way is to insert a symbol disk or load *Macro* commands. Completely different applications are thus programmed into the unit. A different mask, or overlay, corresponding to a particular program can be used similar to the one shown in Fig. 2-2-13. The

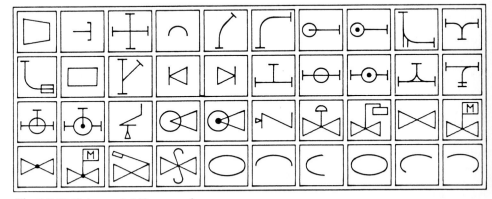

Fig. 2-2-13 Piping symbol library overlay menu.

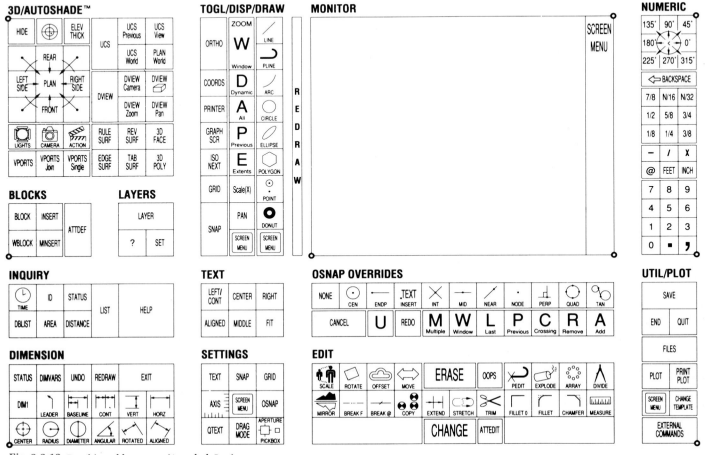

Fig. 2-2-12 Graphics tablet menu. (Autodesk Inc.)

option to switch menus is particularly useful when one wishes to create various schematic diagrams or other standardized graphics.

Several pieces of equipment are used in conjunction with the graphics tablet. These may include a stylus or pen, a push-button cursor or puck, a power module or console, and a menu. The tablet itself is a flat surface and is available in a wide range of sizes. It may vary from a small surface [11 × 11 in. or 279 × 279 millimeters (mm)] to one which exceeds E-size drawing are (36 in. × 48 in. or 910 mm × 1220 mm). Beneath the surface lies a grid pattern of many horizontal and vertical sensors. These lines are used to detect electrical pulses at desired horizontal-vertical coordinate locations using a stylus or puck. Their locations are transferred to the computer. Figure 2-2-14A illustrates a tablet with an associated stylus. Figure 2-2-14B illustrates a tablet using a push-button puck.

Puck and Stylus The position of each desired point of a drawing or sketch on the tablet is sensed by a puck (often called a "mouse" because of its shape) or stylus (electronic pen). Several styles of pucks and styluses are available. Figure 2-2-15 illustrates one puck and two styluses.

Each puck has fine black cross hairs that are used for positioning. Pressing the appropriate button causes horizontal (X) and vertical (Y) data to be accurately sent to the CPU by an electrical signal through an asynchronous (so-called RS232) connection into the series or parallel port in the computer. The result is displayed on the monitor screen as a bright mark. This method of selecting a position and activating the puck is known as digitizing. It is repeated as often as necessary to complete the drawing.

The buttons on a puck may be used for various purposes. This depends on the manner in which the software has been created. A stylus essentially operates the same way as a single-button puck. The position is selected by the tip of the pen. As you move the pen tip across the tablet surface, the position will change correspondingly on the monitor. It will appear as a small bright mark on the monitor. After the desired position has been located, you digitize it by activating the stylus, which usually is accomplished by pressing down on it.

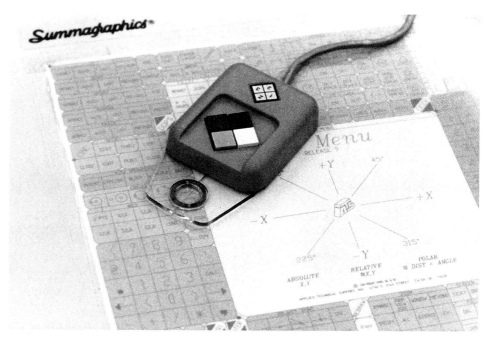

Fig. 2-2-14 Graphics tablet and digitizer.

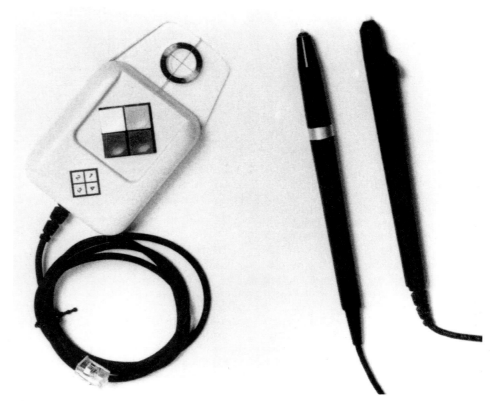

Fig. 2-2-15 Puck and stylus.

Tablet Menu CAD systems are menu-driven. This means that a selection is made from a preprogrammed menu (tablet or screen) by the user to call up a particular part of a program. Graphics tablets are provided with a menu having a variety of options. A menu may appear on the screen, or it may be placed on the tablet surface. A graphics tablet menu is shown in Fig. 2-2-16A. Each of the small boxes, or cells, illustrates the list of available choices. Many of the terms are abbreviated to fit into the box. To make a selection, place and activate the stylus or puck over the desired item, such as the RECTANGLE icon, as shown in Fig. 2-2-16A. An *icon* is a picture (graphical representation) of what something means. To draw lines, for example, digitize within the box or cell labeled LINE. Another standard graphics tablet menu is shown in Fig. 2-2-16B. Many tablet overlays have a double coding to identify a command. Notice both a name and an icon within cells shown in Fig. 2-2-16B. There is an extensive icon (graphical) glossary referred to as the CAD Command Master at the end of this text. Review it to help you more clearly understand the effect of each CAD command.

A menu will normally occupy only a portion of the tablet surface area (Fig. 2-2-16). The location varies with different menus. The main purpose on all systems, however, is rapid data conversion. A symbol also may be generated off the menu by the use of the stylus or puck. You can accomplish this by pointing to the menu item and touching down. Next, digitize the desired position on the graphics tablet. The result is displayed on the screen. The process is repeated until the drawing is finished.

Cursor Controls

Light Pen A light pen is used as a direct-entry input pointing device. It is also considered a digitizer since it can change displayed points and select menu options on the screen. The pen is electronic and contains a photocell sensory element to detect the presence of light. Hence the term light pen. Attached to one end is a cable through which the signal is transmitted. The other end of the pen may be positioned by hand to a desired screen location. After positioning, touch the screen with the tip of the pen. Depressing it causes the pen to become

(A)

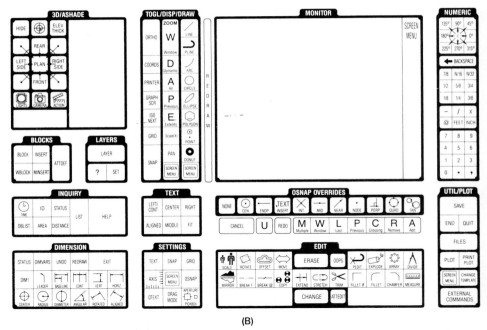

(B)

Fig. 2-2-16 (A) Digitizing a graphics tablet menu item. (B) Graphics tablet menu. (Autodesk Inc.)

activated. Light spots are sensed. A signal is sent to the system, indicating the position. By this method, any element of the graphics display may be identified to the computer. Figure 2-2-17 illustrates a drawing being created using a light pen. One disadvantage of the light pen occurs with prolonged use. After several hours, a drafter may tire from holding the pen. Beyond that, however, the light pen functions quite well.

The light pen is moved about the display screen and indicates the current active position under consideration. The position is illuminated by a blinking character (rectangle, arrow, or cross hair) or an extrabright spot. This indicating position is referred to as a *cursor*. In this text, the term cursor will always refer to the current active position on the screen. This is the same as the pencil point is to a traditional drafter.

Fig. 2-2-17 Creating a drawing using a light pen.

Fig. 2-2-18 Joystick.

cursor is located, press the joystick "fire" button to "set" its position.

Speed Control The rate of speed at which the cursor is moved on the monitor screen is variable. It is proportional to the distance the stick is moved from the vertical position. Another way to think of this is to consider the angle that the stick makes with the horizontal, as seen in an elevation view of the joystick. In the vertical position (90° angle), there is essentially no cursor movement. As the joystick is tilted (less than 90°), the cursor begins to move. The greater the tilt, the smaller the angle with the horizontal and the greater the rate of cursor movement.

Other Input Equipment

Several other pieces of input equipment may be used to position the cursor. They include a thumb and finger wheel, touch pad, mouse, and tracball. While these devices are normally not used, it is possible for one to be found on a particular system. A thumb and finger wheel as shown in Fig. 2-2-19 is used to locate the cursor horizontally (X direction) and vertically (Y direction). Do this by rotating each wheel. The intersection of a horizontal and a vertical line determines the cursor location very accurately.

A tracball or roller ball is seated in a container with a portion of the sphere extended. It is rotated in any direction by the palm of the hand. This rotation

BEFORE   AFTER

AN INDICATING MARK ON THE MONITOR WHICH IS CONTROLLED BY ANY OF SEVERAL TYPES OF INPUT POINTING DEVICES SUCH AS A JOYSTICK, PUCK, OR STYLUS.

being in a 360° circular pattern. Starting with 0 toward the horizontal right (east or three o'clock), the rotation direction is counterclockwise. Thus, to move the cursor position left or right horizontally, tilt the stick either to the left (180°) or to the right (0°). For vertical movement, tilt it either directly up (90°) or directly down (270°). Any combination of horizontal and vertical movements can be made with a corresponding tilt of the stick. Once the

Joystick

Direction Control A joystick is another type of device used to control the cursor. It can be added to many systems, further enhancing CAD capability. The joystick shown in Fig. 2-2-18 is simply an extended version of the type commonly seen with video games. An electrical connection to the computer is made with a cable. The joystick steers a lighted cursor on the monitor screen.

A movement is executed by tilting the joystick lever. This lever extends vertically through the top of the unit shown in Fig. 2-2-18. The tilt angle, looking down on the unit (plan view), determines the direction of cursor movement. Think of the direction as

Courtesy Tektronix, Inc.

(A) Thumb and finger wheel

Courtesy Texas Instruments

(B) Mouse

Fig. 2-2-19 Other input equipment.

causes the cursor to move accordingly. When you arrive at the desired location, simply stop the ball.

OUTPUT EQUIPMENT

The drawings that are being produced are visually observed on the monitor screen. At any time, a print of what is seen on the screen can readily be obtained from a printer or hard copy machine. This print is referred to as a "hard copy" as the drawing reproduces exactly what is shown on the screen. Diagonal lines, circles, and arcs are a combination of vertical and horizontal lines and appear like zigzag or jagged lines. However, this type of drawing is quite useful to check progress while developing the finished design. When the drawing or design is completed, a finished drawing with near perfect lines and lettering is made on a plotter. This is equivalent to the drawing made manually (only better). Prints or microfilm are then produced from this drawing.

If a company has a developed CADD/CAM operation, a drawing may not be required. Instead, a set of instructions in coded form is directly transmitted to the fabricating equipment. The instructions include all location and size information necessary to produce the product.

Monitor

The monitor (or graphics display station) is used to produce the image being drawn onto a screen. The image displays data in either an alphanumeric (written) or a graphical (pictorial) manner. The user can view a picture of the design as the design is being entered into the system. This display can be accomplished in a variety of ways, depending on the type of monitor used.

Cathode-Ray Tube

The most popular monitor is the cathode-ray tube or CRT. The display method is similar to a television screen. A sample screen display is shown in Fig. 2-2-20. The types of CRTs are described here.

Vector The vector-writing CRT is drawn on by an X-Y direction coordinate system. This is similar in principle to the popular Etch a Sketch toy. The

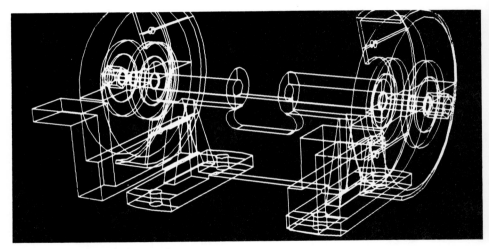

Fig. 2-2-20 High-resolution CRT image.

computer first locates points and then connects the points.

Raster Raster screens have become the dominant type of CRT displays. The raster type uses a grid network to display the image. Each grid is either a dark or a light image that falls within a square area that appears on the screen as a dot (dark) or undot (light). Each dot is known as a *pixel* (picture element). An analogy for how this works is a placard pattern used by fans in the stands of a football game. The cards are used to show a graphical message, and each fan within the pattern holds up either a dark or a light card. At a sufficient distance, the combinations of dark and light spots produce a recognizable image. This phenomenon is shown by the arrow in Fig. 2-2-21.

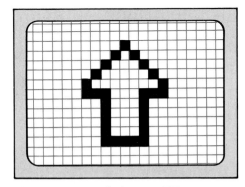

Fig. 2-2-21 Raster display on a CRT.

Another example of pixel representation is shown by the map illustration in Fig. 2-2-22. The horizontal and vertical scan lines are shown so that you can clearly see each pixel. Since the pixels are so large, this would be

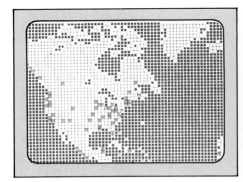

Fig. 2-2-22 Pixel representation.

considered low-resolution. As an analogy, imagine looking at an object through a screened window. Close up, the pixels are large; you can count the number of screened squares (pixels) required to cover the object. As you move farther away, the pixels appear smaller; it takes more pixels to cover the object. There will be more dots (pixels) per unit area. Thus, a higher resolution will result.

The resolution (clearness) of a raster-developed image will depend on the closeness of lines forming the grid pattern. The smaller the pixels, the more resolution the image has. The greater the number of dots per unit area, the greater the resolution. The greater number of dots improves picture quality. For example, an enlarged photograph has a loss in resolution, or clearness, because of the reduced number of dots per unit area.

An example of a low-resolution display is shown in Fig. 2-2-23(A). Notice the unevenness of the top and right-side lines. This is known as "jaggies"

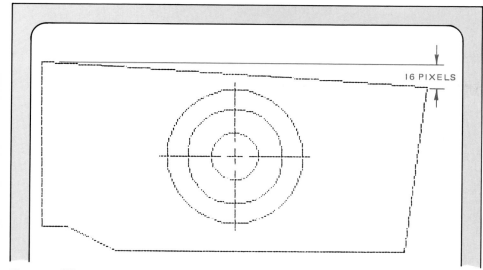

Fig. 2-2-23(A) Low-resolution image.

or "stair stepping." Notice also that the circles have a severe case of the jaggies. The top line actually resembles a stair step, thus the slang terminology. This jagged line will always result on a low-resolution raster screen if the line is inclined. In fact, you can count the stair steps; there are 16 (17 horizontal lines). This means that the right endpoint is 16 raster scan lines (or pixels) lower than the left endpoint.

Significant advancement in raster technology has been achieved in recent years. New techniques enhance resolution. Jaggies appearing on the lines and polygon boundaries have been significantly reduced. Consequently, low resolution is seen only on inexpensive monitors. The improved resolution will more likely be seen in the medium-resolution to "hi-res" (high-resolution) range, as illustrated in the art throughout the text.

Raster display is quickly redrawn. The complete image is redrawn at a rate of speed exceeding the human grasp. The picture is refreshed or scanned, from left to right and from top to bottom very rapidly. When comparing it to the other methods, remember, "Raster does it faster."

Color The types of CRTs mentioned so far produce the image in one color, similar to the black-and-white television. Raster systems are now color-enhanced. This display screen is similar to the color television screen. Each of three electron guns emits one of the primary television colors: red, green, or blue. From a combination of these,

any color pattern may be set up. The vast majority of graphics display stations marketed contain this option. A typical monitor is illustrated in Fig. 2-2-23B.

Other Monitors

There are several other types of monitors. They are less popular and will not be likely to replace the raster CRT.

The first type is plasma. Plasma technique uses a flat, thin panel and the glow from an inert gas to display the image. Neon is the gas commonly used. The gas is ionized to emit visible light in a matrix dot pattern. The plasma technique is potentially popular since it is better for your eyes than the CRT. The CRT has low-level radiation emission and a flicker associated with it. This is eliminated with the plasma panel display which is virtually flicker-free. The primary disadvantage of plasma display is that it produces poor resolution and the size of the panel is small.

Other types of monitors include electroilluminescent, liquid crystal, and projection techniques. Each has its associated problems, and its use is minimal.

Plotters

There are three types of plotters commonly used by industry to produce a finished drawing. They are:

1. Pen plotter
2. Electrostatic plotter
3. Laser plotter

Pen Plotters An impact-line digital pen plotter is an electromechanical graphics output device. Pen plotters (shown in Fig. 2-2-24) are the most popular type used. They move a pen in two dimensions across paper medium. The plotter is used to produce a finished drawing. This can be any combination of lines and alphanumerics. If a CAD system is thought of as an automated drafting machine, the plotter is the part replacing the activity of "laying lead." It produces the finished original drawing that was previously developed and displayed on the monitor. Regardless of screen resolution, a plotter will produce quality lines. There are more addressable dots per unit area. Thus, line quality is excellent and virtually jaggie-free.

Various types of ink pens can be used, such as wet ink, felt tip, or liquid ball. They may be a single color, or multicolor. More importantly, plotter pens offer a variable line width (weight) option, with modern models now offering a pencil option. Different pens are inserted or removed rather quickly. One such pen holder is removed as shown in Fig. 2-2-25A. The desired pen (different width or color) is inserted and the holder returned to the plotter (Fig. 2-2-25B). Pens will draw on various types of media. Most popular are opaque drawing paper, vellum, and polyester film. Being able to match the medium to its purpose is a distinct advantage of the pen plotter. Another advantage is that the drawing produced is of high quality and is uniform and precise. On the other hand, an average D-size pen plot will tie up the plotter for long periods of time. Thus, the plotter should not be used as a print machine. Once the drawing has been finalized, prints may be produced by whiteprinters, photocopy, or microfilm equipment.

The pen plotter is slow compared with other output devices. It will take from several seconds (simple drawing) to several minutes (complex drawing) to produce a drawing—a disadvantage for a user requiring large-scale production. Yet due to cost factors pen plotters will remain the most common output device for low- to medium-volume applications. This still represents a major reduction of time from manual methods of producing these drawings. In fact, a rather complicated D (22 × 34 in.) size drawing, which may have taken a week to create

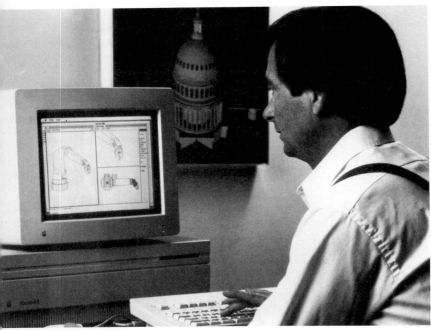

Fig. 2-2-23(B) A typical monitor. (Autodesk Inc.)

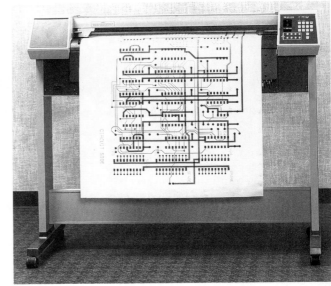

Fig. 2-2-24 Pen plotter. (Hewlett-Packard Company)

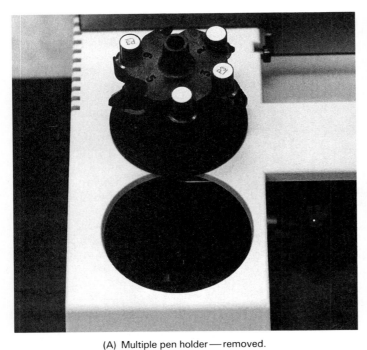

(A) Multiple pen holder — removed.

(B) Multiple pen holder — installed.

Fig. 2-2-25 Using multiple pens for plotting.

on the screen, can be plotted in less than 20 minutes.

Pen plotter technology includes the drum, microgrip, and flatbed types.

Drum. A drum plotter consists of a long cylinder and a pen carriage. The surface area is curved rather than flat and is in the shape of a cylinder. Hence the term drum. The drum rotates to provide one axis of movement. The carriage moves the pen(s) to provide the other axis of movement.

Microgrip. The medium is gripped at the edges with a microgrip plotter. The paper is moved back and forth. High performance is attained at a low cost. A popular microgrip plotter is illustrated in Fig. 2-2-24.

Flatbed. Pen movement occurs in both axes with the flatbed plotter. The pen carriage is controlled in both the X and the Y axes. Motors and cable are used for control. Short digital steps, normally less than .010 in. long, produce the line. The vellum, polyester film, or other medium is held on the bed surface by electrostatic attraction.

The surface area of a pen plot drawing may be as small as an A size and larger than an E-size sheet or drawing format. Also, the size of the drawing to be placed on the paper can vary. You are able to vary the scale of the lines and characters by manually setting the plotting surface area and/or scale.

Electrostatic Plotters Electrostatic plotters will replace pen plotters in applications requiring high production. Plots are made using an ion deposition process at a speed exceeding one inch of paper length per second. This means that a plot can be prepared as much as 20 times quicker. A D size drawing (36 × 24 in.) is plotted in less than a minute with crisp, black lines. The disadvantage of the electrostatic plotter is that it is expensive. As the cost of equipment decreases, however, a wider use is anticipated.

Laser Plotters A laser plotter uses a moving laser beam to alter a point-by-point electrical charge on the surface of a rotating drum. The drum is exposed to dry ink, which adheres to the charged areas of the drum. This is then transferred to a hot roller, where the ink is fused to the medium. Laser plotters, like electrostatic plotters, produce drawings at high speed.

Their disadvantage is that of expense and also that they are large and heavy.

Printers

A print is a preliminary drawing that is produced by a printer. It produces an image of what is seen on the monitor complete with all jagged lines and circles. All lines are shown as one thickness. The print is used to check preliminary stages of the design.

A printer duplicates the screen display quickly and conveniently. The primary advantage of this technique is speed. It produces output much more quickly and less expensively than pen plotting. Complex graphic screen displays may be copied by the PRINT command. Whatever is on the screen will be copied. This includes any combination of graphic and nongraphic (text) display and is called a *screen dump*. The entire process requires but a few seconds. The copy, however, does not approach the level of quality produced by the plotters. If the screen is low-resolution, then so will the copy. Thus, it is used primarily for preliminary "quick-and-dirty" check prints. It is, for example, very useful for a quick preview at various intermediate steps of a design project.

Popular printers include the electrostatic method, the dot-matrix printer, the ink-jet process, and the photoprinter.

- Electrostatic method. The electrostatic method uses a fine array of nibs to electrically charge small dots on the medium. The image is then permanently placed on the charged surface with toner.
- Dot-matrix printer. The newer printers have a much higher resolution than the old style. They do not approach the quality of a plotter, however.
- Ink-jet process. The ink-jet process deposits variously colored ink droplets on the medium. The result is a multiple-color copy. An ink-jet printer is shown in Fig. 2-2-26.
- Photoprinter. A typical photoprinter involves the use of fiber-optics technology to reproduce the image on dry silver paper. The unit produces a small A-size copy that is satisfactory for quick preview during intermediate work steps.

Computer-Aided Manufacturing

Numerical Control Computer-aided manufacturing (CAM) uses the result of a computer-aided design. Combining CAD and CAM has had the effect of radically increasing productivity and accuracy. When CAD is used to prepare the design of a product, the instructions for the manufacture or preparation of that design are sent directly to the factory. One method of

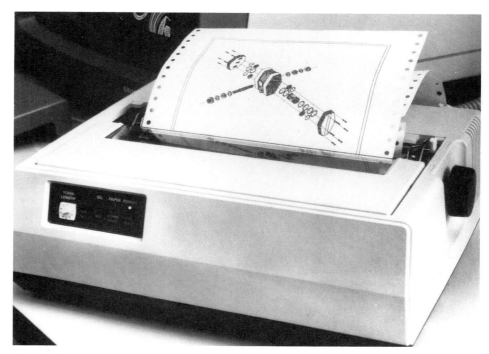

Fig. 2-2-26 Ink-jet printer.

transmitting the information is known as numerical control (NC) or computer numerical control (CNC). NC tapes and equipment can store the designs that are used with a variety of production-related processes without producing an actual engineering drawing. In other words, the information is transmitted directly from one database to another. This process is significantly more sophisticated than the method used to transfer information long distances via phone lines. In that case a standard modulator-demodulator (modem) is used.

True CAD/CAM is the ultimate goal of industry. Many have CAD; many have CAM; few, however, have CAD/CAM. CAD/CAM means that an engineering drawing is no longer produced, since it is a direct hard-wired connection. The output of the CAD system is a drawing stored in a geometric database. This drawing is transmitted directly into the CAM equipment. The result is a finished manufactured part. This means that errors will no longer occur as a machinist will not have to interpret an engineering drawing.

Robotics The other part of CAM is known as robotics. Robot machinery differs from CNC machinery in that movement is now the prime duty. Automatic manipulators are used to perform a variety of materials-handling functions. The robot manipulators are arms and hands. They will grasp, operate, assemble, and handle with great consistency and dependability. They are able to perform tasks that are considered too difficult, dangerous, or monotonous for human workers. This is especially true in environments that are intolerable to human beings. The range of tasks includes:

- Working with metals at extremely high temperatures (e.g., spot welding)
- Working in rooms filled with toxic fumes (e.g., spray painting)
- Exerting great forces (e.g., lifting and moving heavy, awkward products)
- Working with delicate parts (e.g., adjusting electronic systems)

Robots have done each of these tasks superlatively, performing with great consistency, dependability, and (eventually) economy. In addition, they will not pause in their routines for passing wisecracks, taking a break, or filling grievances against the company. Thus, the role of the unskilled factory worker most surely will be diminished.

3

Getting Acquainted With CAD

Prior to learning the fundamentals of drafting, it is recommended that you become familiar with the basics of line and text creation. Also, it will help you to see how easy it is to use a CAD system. Learning these basics will greatly assist in building the confidence and experience necessary to successfully master the drafting program which follows.

■ UNIT 3-1

Startup

PROMPTS

CAD systems guide you through the various aspects of drawing development. Written instruction appears on the screen to accomplish this. The instructions, referred to as *prompts, cues, options, or message lines,* may appear in any location on the screen as shown in Fig. 3-1-1A. Some systems utilize a dual-screen setup. One screen is for the graphics and the other is for status list and inquiry. An example of this is shown in Fig. 3-1-1B. A third method of displaying the prompts is to alternately "toggle" the same screen as illustrated in Fig. 3-1-1C. The display may be automatically "flipped" by pressing function key **F1**. Thus, prompts are found in one of three locations:

- Overlay. Prompts on the same screen as the drawing.

- Dual screen. Separate screens for the drawing and the prompts.
- Toggling. Flip the same screen to alternately display the drawing or the prompts.

You will find any CAD system easier to use if you:

1. Know the location of the prompts.
2. Read and understand each prompt as it is given.
3. Follow the prompt exactly.

In addition to prompts, systems have a HELP option. This is used if further information about a command is sought. At the COMMAND: prompt, key in HELP, press ENTER, and follow the message. You may obtain the command prompt anytime by pressing the CTRL and C keys simultaneously.

START-UP PROCEDURES

Before any graphical data can be displayed on the screen, you must turn on, or "boot up," the system. Each CAD manufacturer has a start-up procedure. For micro and mini systems, this may include checking that each piece of equipment is plugged in (connected) to a convenient outlet (duplex wall receptacle) and power-surge protection device. Both the CPU and the disk drive should have power-surge protection.

Next, you may boot the system by the following procedure:

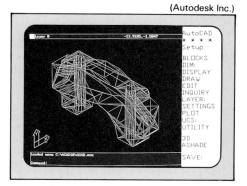

(A) SCREEN MESSAGE OPTIONS

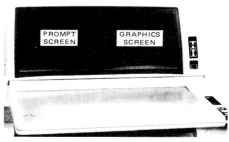

(B) DUAL SCREENS

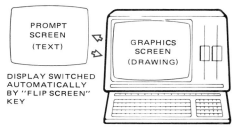

(C) SINGLE FLIP SCREEN

Fig. 3-1-1 Prompt locations.

1. Turn on all peripherals (graphics tablet, monitor, etc.). Power switches may be located on the front, beneath, at either side, or at the rear of the equipment.

2. Normally, the software will be installed on a hard drive. Be certain that a floppy disk is not in the floppy drive(s). A word of caution: Never insert or remove a floppy disk if the red light on the disk drive is lit.

3. The CPU may be turned on by pressing a toggle switch. The switch is purposely located in an inaccessible place. Thus, it is unlikely that the switch will be accidentally toggled off while you are working in the system.

   Now you will have to wait for a brief warm-up period for the program contents to be loaded from the disk into dynamic memory.

4. The contents of the software from the disk are now displayed on the screen. The user may act accordingly by the appropriate selection.

5. Next, make the selection BEGIN A NEW DRAWING, key in a name for the drawing such as CAD1, and press ENTER. Note: You may break communication with the computer at any time by turning off the terminal power switch or a "warm boot" command such as pressing the CTRL, ALT, and DEL keys simultaneously. Caution: when the main power supply is interrupted, all work thus far accomplished will be permanently eliminated if it has not been saved. As a user develops a drawing, he or she should periodically store the drawing (see Unit 4–7), then the work accomplished will not be lost. Work is automatically stored by using the SAVE command, keying in the drawing name, and pressing ENTER.

6. When you SETUP a new drawing, several parameters must be defined. Your choices include drawing scale, units to use, and drawing size. CAD systems are "user-friendly." This means that you will be prompted or instructed each step of the way, as the screen will display a specific message for you to follow. The prompt will be highlighted either directly on the drawing screen or on an adjacent screen. In most cases, the CAD system will tell you what to do next or what you have done wrong. Carefully follow

WHEN BEGINNING A NEW DRAWING, THE PARAMETERS SUCH AS DRAWING SIZE, SCALE, AND UNITS MAY BE SELECTED.

all instructions in the order in which they are given.

After the **NEW DRAWING** option has been selected, either the drawing parameters will be automatically defined by the system or you will have to define each one. The common SETUP parameters are FULL SCALE, INCH, and DECIMAL (for drawings using U.S. customary units). For systems that do not automatically provide this, key in the appropriate numbers corresponding to the preferred UNITS (under SETTINGS). To change only the size of the drawing you are to work on for example, change to a B-size drawing by selecting the submenu option LIMITS under SETTINGS. Key in 0,0 and ENTER; 17,11 and ENTER; and select ZOOM ALL (under SETTINGS).

7. Logging off involves a simple procedure of shutting down, or closing, the "door" to the system. Save the drawing by selecting the UTILITY command END.

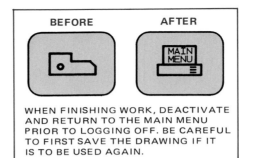

WHEN FINISHING WORK, DEACTIVATE AND RETURN TO THE MAIN MENU PRIOR TO LOGGING OFF. BE CAREFUL TO FIRST SAVE THE DRAWING IF IT IS TO BE USED AGAIN.

Remember, that while start-up procedures may vary, it is accomplished with the aid of prompts. The system will display the instructions or prompts. The above example is typical; however, follow the prompts exactly.

MENUS

CAD systems are "menu-driven." This means you make a selection to call up a particular part of a program to create graphics. For example, the selection of LINE allows line creation to occur. There are two categories of menus: root menu, and submenu. Menu selection is made by either keyboard input, tablet selection, or moving the cursor over the screen menu item and "setting" it. Menu selection on the keyboard is made by typing in the name of the desired command then pressing ENTER. ENTER is an "end-of-statement" command.

Root Menu

A root or master menu for a CAD system is similar in nature to menus found in restaurants. The restaurant master menu lists the foods under different categories: seafood, meat, dessert, and so on. The CAD root menu lists the major drafting commands: DRAW, EDIT, DIMENSION, and so on, as shown in Fig. 3-1-1 (A). To create a particular type of graphics, simply select that menu item. For example, automatic dimensioning may be created by selecting DIM. Because of the length of their names, many of the menu items are abbreviated or shown graphically as icons. Each, however, is easily identifiable.

When a menu item is selected, there will be a time delay. The CAD system must search for that command, so always remember to wait until the unit is ready.

Submenu

Each root menu item has subtasks and/or options also referred to as a submenu. It allows the selection of different types of graphics. Again using the analogy of a restaurant menu, SEAFOOD would have a submenu option list indicating the available selections. A CAD root menu item similarly may have a selection as illustrated in Fig. 3-1-2.

A submenu item may be selected in one of three ways:

Keyboard input. After the COMMAND: prompt enter the name.

Digitizing. Use a stylus or puck to select the item.

Screen selection. Superimpose the cursor over the desired item and select it. Return to the root menu by

ROOT	SUB
SEAFOOD	LOBSTER
MEAT	CRAB LEGS
SALADS	SHRIMP
DESSERTS	SCALLOPS
	HADDOCK

(A) RESTAURANT MENU

ROOT	SUB
DRAW	ARC
EDIT	CIRCLE
DIMENSION	LINE
	TEXT

(B) CAD MENU

Fig. 3-1-2 Similarity between restaurant and CAD menu.

selecting the appropriate item (Auto CAD, for example).

A particular submenu option may, at times, be difficult to locate. Refer to the HELP menu to assist you in determining the name of each available command.

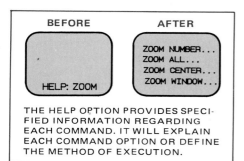

THE HELP OPTION PROVIDES SPECIFIED INFORMATION REGARDING EACH COMMAND. IT WILL EXPLAIN EACH COMMAND OPTION OR DEFINE THE METHOD OF EXECUTION.

ricators and craftsmen who will build and produce the product. The common ways to create horizontal, vertical, and inclined straight lines include:

1. Selection by free input
2. Use of a grid pattern
3. Use of construction lines
4. Keying in distances (coordinate input)

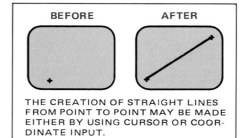

THE CREATION OF STRAIGHT LINES FROM POINT TO POINT MAY BE MADE EITHER BY USING CURSOR OR COORDINATE INPUT.

DRAWING A STRAIGHT LINE BY FREE INPUT

The first graphics to be placed on the screen will usually be in the form of a straight line. Two points (or positions) will determine the endpoints of a line when in the LINE command. Depending on the position of the second point relative to the first, a line may be drawn horizontally, vertically, or inclined. The common methods to accomplish the placement of a line on the monitor follow.

1. To draw select the LINE command. This will be accomplished by one of the following methods.:
   a. Point the cursor to the "on-screen" menu and select it (under DRAW).
   b. Use the appropriate function or alphanumeric keys (e.g., key in the LINE command and press ENTER).
   c. Digitize by activating a stylus or puck within one of the boxes on the graphics tablet as shown in Fig. 3-2-1.
2. Use your input pointing device to select the first line endpoint as shown in Fig. 3-2-2A. When using a joystick, for example, set the cursor by pressing the button on the device. With a graphics tablet, activate the stylus (press down) or puck (press a button) at that location. Any dots (grids) on the screen should be disregarded for the time being.

ASSIGNMENT

See Assignment 1 for Unit 3-1 on page 36.

■ UNIT 3-2

Drawing and Erasing Straight Lines

A line is the fundamental, and perhaps the most important, single entity on an engineering drawing. They are used to help illustrate and describe the shape of objects which later will become the real parts. The lines which you create using a CAD system provide the shape information to the fab-

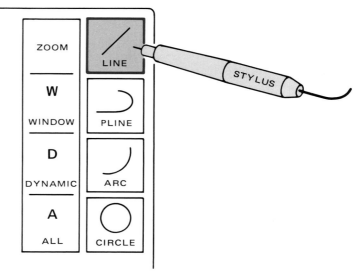

Fig. 3-2-1 LINE command selection from a graphics tablet.

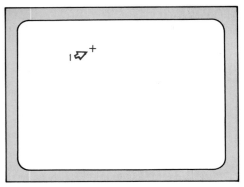

(A) FIRST ENDPOINT

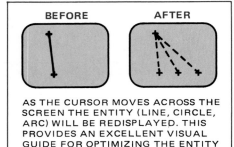

(B) SECOND ENDPOINT AND LINE

Fig. 3-2-2 Drawing a line on the monitor screen.

3. You may see the actual line lengthen as you move the cursor if DRAGMODE is on AUTO. This phenomenon is known as rubberbanding. Select the second line endpoint. A line will appear as shown in Fig. 3-2-2B. The line may have to be set permanently by pressing ENTER.

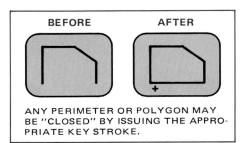

AS THE CURSOR MOVES ACROSS THE SCREEN THE ENTITY (LINE, CIRCLE, ARC) WILL BE REDISPLAYED. THIS PROVIDES AN EXCELLENT VISUAL GUIDE FOR OPTIMIZING THE ENTITY SIZE AND POSITION.

DRAWING CONNECTING LINE SEGMENTS

The outline of any object may be created by using the method as follows:

1. Select the LINE command.
2. Select the first line endpoint at position 1 as shown in Fig. 3-2-3.

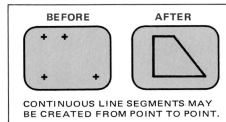

CONTINUOUS LINE SEGMENTS MAY BE CREATED FROM POINT TO POINT.

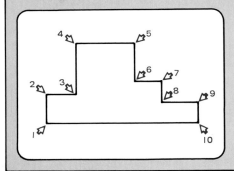

Fig. 3-2-3 Drawing an object.

3. Successively select line endpoints at positions 2, 3, 4, and so on until position 10 is reached.
4. The outline of the object may be completed in one of two ways. Ei-

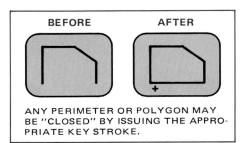

ANY PERIMETER OR POLYGON MAY BE "CLOSED" BY ISSUING THE APPROPRIATE KEY STROKE.

ther reselect position 1 a second time or select the CLOSE (C) option. The object will appear as shown in Fig. 3-2-3. Remember that pressing the ENTER key may be a necessary part of setting the line after reselecting position 1.

DRAWING SEPARATE LINES

You may need to create an additional line, separate from the first. This is

accomplished by moving the cursor to a new position. If the ENTER key was used to place the first line, be certain you are in the LINE command by pressing ENTER again or LINE before you select the beginning location for the next line. Repositioning the cursor location without drawing a line is known as MOVE NEXT POINT. The concept is the same as in manual drafting when the pencil must be lifted off the paper. To create a new and separate line you must lift the pencil to a new position. It is the same with CAD. The cursor is lifted to a new start position with the MOVE NEXT POINT option by pressing ENTER.

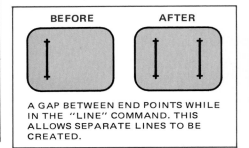

A GAP BETWEEN END POINTS WHILE IN THE "LINE" COMMAND. THIS ALLOWS SEPARATE LINES TO BE CREATED.

Very often you will draw a line that is not required. If this mistake is immediately realized, it is easy to correct. You will quickly learn that CAD systems are very forgiving. Every system has an ERASE LAST command option. It may be called ERASE LAST, OOPS, UNDO, or BACK 1. No matter, the result will be the same. That is, to remove the last command that you have executed.

Suppose you wish to create separate lines. The following procedure will apply:

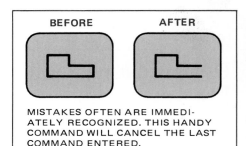

MISTAKES OFTEN ARE IMMEDIATELY RECOGNIZED. THIS HANDY COMMAND WILL CANCEL THE LAST COMMAND ENTERED.

1. Select the LINE command.
2. Locate and set the cursor at position A and then B, as shown in Fig. 3-2-4A. The first line is created as shown.

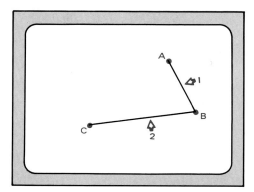

(A) DRAW LINE SEGMENT ABC

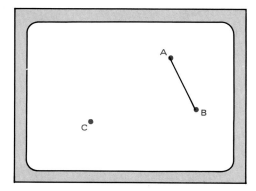

(B) ERASE SEGMENT BC AND MOVE TO NEW POSITION

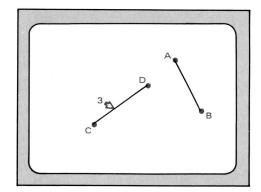

(C) DRAW LINE CD

Fig. 3-2-4 Creating separate lines.

3. Locate and set the cursor at position C (Fig. 3-2-4A). The second line segment is inadvertently created since the MOVE NEXT POINT option was not issued.
4. Immediately select ERASE LAST (under EDIT) and ENTER. The second line will be removed.
5. Select MOVE NEXT POINT. This may be accomplished by selecting the LINE command again

or a key command such as pressing ENTER twice (if in LINE).
6. To begin the second line, locate and set the cursor at position C as shown in Fig. 3-2-4B.
7. Locate and set the cursor at position D as shown in Fig. 3-2-4C. A separate line (3) will be created.
8. Additional separate lines may be created by repeating steps 5, 6, and 7.

DRAWING HORIZONTAL AND VERTICAL LINES

Lines may be created horizontally, vertically, or inclined as previously indicated. CAD systems provide the option to lock onto a horizontal or vertical axis and produce a precise result. This horizontal/vertical constraint, known as ORTHO (short for orthogonalize), will ensure that the lines created will be horizontal or vertical.

This is an important feature since engineering drawings are composed

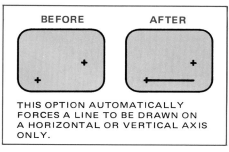

THIS OPTION AUTOMATICALLY FORCES A LINE TO BE DRAWN ON A HORIZONTAL OR VERTICAL AXIS ONLY.

of many such lines. Without it you would have to estimate the second endpoint position. The likely result is shown in Fig. 3-2-5A. Even though the line is nearly horizontal, it is not exact. This will be clearly illustrated on the

monitor as the line will be jagged rather than smooth. The result of locking in on an axis is shown in Fig. 3-2-5B. Notice that the second cursor endpoint location (+) would not have produced the desired result. Since the machine has been commanded to lock in on the axis, however, the resulting horizontal line is exact. This option has the additional advantage of obtaining reference positions from adjacent views when constructing multiview drawings.

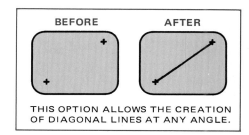

THIS OPTION ALLOWS THE CREATION OF DIAGONAL LINES AT ANY ANGLE.

The method used to accomplish ORTHO is:

1. Select the LINE command.
2. Select the first endpoint.
3. Use the function key **F8** or tablet menu to toggle the ORTHO ON option.
4. Select the second endpoint. The resulting line will be exactly horizontal (or vertical) as shown in Fig. 3-2-5B. Notice also that the length of the line terminates directly above the cursor location.

ERASING TECHNIQUES

Revision or change practice is inherent in the method of preparing engi-

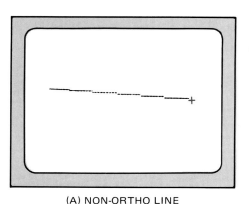

(A) NON-ORTHO LINE

Fig. 3-2-5 Creating a horizontal line.

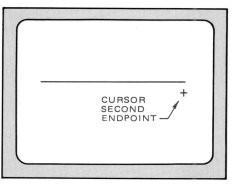

(B) ORTHO LINE

neering drawings. It is much more economical to introduce changes or additions on an original drawing than to re-create the entire drawing. Consequently, a variety of geometry modification or EDIT commands are available. Each is utilized to facilitate the creation of an engineering drawing. One of the most common EDIT commands is ERASE. There are several ways to eliminate various entities from a drawing, including:

1. ERASE LAST entity
2. ERASE ANY entity
3. ERASE by WINDOW
4. ERASE ALL
5. BREAK

ERASE LAST is used the most frequently. Normally, you will recognize an error immediately after it has been made. Whenever this occurs, select the ERASE LAST command and ENTER as previously discussed in this unit under Drawing Separate Lines. The most recently drawn entity will be removed. You can repeat ERASE LAST to "step back" through the drawing. This will erase the most recently drawn entity each time.

To EDIT the screen display, ERASE ALL is used. Like an eraser on a chalkboard, the complete image from the monitor screen is deleted. This function, however, is executed much more quickly than the erasing of a chalkboard. Also, removal is complete, with no trace of the image or erasure remaining. The procedure normally is easy to complete. Usually, just one press of the appropriate button will accomplish complete removal. Since many hours of work may be lost, however, you are given another chance. Immediate selection of the OOPS or UNDO options will restore all entities on the screen that have been removed during ERASE.

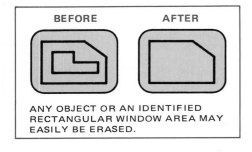

BEFORE　　AFTER

ANY OBJECT OR AN IDENTIFIED RECTANGULAR WINDOW AREA MAY EASILY BE ERASED.

ERASE options also include deletion by WINDOW or area. This would allow you to remove only a selected portion of the object display. Suppose two views of an object have been created and you realize that only one is required. Select the ERASE WINDOW option. By selection of the lower left (LL) and upper right (UR) corners of an imaginary rectangle, any group of entities may be deleted if the complete entity resides fully within the window as shown in Fig. 3-2-6. One always thinks of the ERASE command as removing graphics. CAD systems, however, have the ability to ERASE an ERASE. Suppose you ERASE WINDOW and realize it was a mistake. Immediately select OOPS or UNDO. Since the last entry was a delete execution, the graphics will reappear. ERASE allows you to selectively delete any object regardless of when it was created.

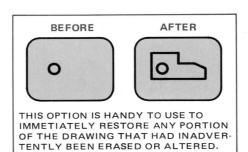

BEFORE　　AFTER

THIS OPTION IS HANDY TO USE TO IMMEDIATELY RESTORE ANY PORTION OF THE DRAWING THAT HAD INADVERTENTLY BEEN ERASED OR ALTERED.

Any portion of a single entity (line, circle, arc) may be edited by using a BREAK (under EDIT) command. This may be accomplished by:

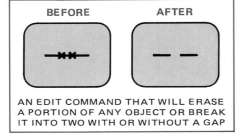

BEFORE　　AFTER

AN EDIT COMMAND THAT WILL ERASE A PORTION OF ANY OBJECT OR BREAK IT INTO TWO WITH OR WITHOUT A GAP

1. Select the BREAK command.
2. Select the line to be edited using gap start point 1 as shown in Fig. 3-2-7A.

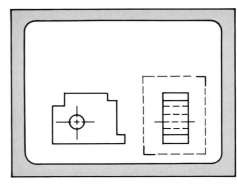

(A) SELECT THE WINDOW

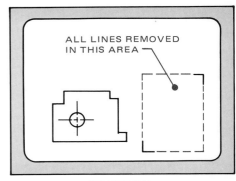

ALL LINES REMOVED IN THIS AREA

(B) RESULT

Fig. 3-2-6 Erase by window.

3. Select the gap distance as shown by point 2 in Fig. 3-2-7A. The result is shown in Fig. 3-2-7B. Note: point 1 is interpreted as the first gap point unless you select F (for FIRST). Then select point 3. Press ENTER.
4. Select the second line to be altered (point 4 in Fig. 3-2-7B) and F.
5. Select point 5 beyond the end of the line (to shorten it).
6. Select point 6 which may be located either on the line to be shortened or the vertical intersecting line if that is where you wish it shortened to. The result is shown in Fig. 3-2-7C.

Data Pack

If the ERASE command has been used extensively on any particular drawing, a significant amount of useless space will be taken on the disk. This can easily be eliminated by the selection of the REGEN command. The drawing will be regenerated removing the space taken on the disk by each ERASE operation.

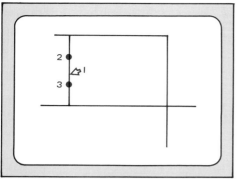

(A) GAP A SEGMENT

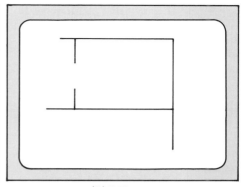

(B) SHORTEN A SEGMENT

(C) RESULT

Fig. 3-2-7 Modify line segments.

ACCUMULATED DELETIONS AND REVISION WORK UTILIZE A SIGNIFICANT AMOUNT OF USELESS DRAWING STORAGE (DISK) SPACE. DATA PACKING WILL DISCARD THIS FROM DRAWING MEMORY, LEAVING MORE ROOM FOR USEFUL WORK.

REDRAW

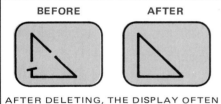

AFTER DELETING, THE DISPLAY OFTEN WILL APPEAR MESSY. REDRAWING WILL REDISPLAY THE OBJECTS ON THE SCREEN, "CLEANING UP" THE DISPLAY.

After erasing a portion of your drawing, the monitor display will not appear as it should. This is due to one pixel being used for two purposes (e.g., a line superimposed over grid dots). Thus, erasing the line will also temporarily erase the grid dots. To "clean up" the display simply issue the REDRAW command.

ASSIGNMENT

See Assignment 2 and 3 for Unit 3-2 on page 36.

See Assignment 2 and 3 for Unit 3-2 on page 36.

■ **UNIT 3-3**

Drawing Lines Using a Grid Pattern

A grid pattern is a valuable asset when learning CAD because it is quick and accurate. An example of a rectangular grid pattern is shown in Fig. 3-3-1. The desired grid pattern size is displayed so that the endpoints of all lines will fall on a grid dot. Grid points are located equidistant (horizontal and vertical) from each other. When it is desired to position points at the nearest grid dot, use the input device to move the cursor. When the cursor appears near a desired point, set it. Depending on your input device, this is accomplished by digitizing, joystick fire button, and so on. The point "snaps" to the nearest dot. This location is determined by both the spacing of the grids and the snap increment. The dot spacing is standard with many

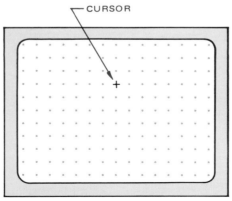

Fig. 3-3-1 Grid pattern and cursor display on monitor screen.

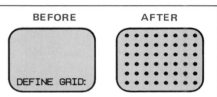

A NETWORK OF EQUALLY SPACED GRID DOTS THAT MAY BE USED FOR REFERENCE. GRID SPACING MAY BE CHANGED BY KEYING IN THE HORIZONTAL AND VERTICAL DISTANCES.

CAD systems. Often, some of the line endpoints will fall between grid dots. The grid pattern may then be reset to a size where the endpoints will fall on grid. For example, set a .25 pattern to create a 4.25 in. long line. The distance between the grid points may be decreased because the spacing is user-definable; that is, the user can change the pattern size at any time. Thus, a different network of points may be used to determine distances within the drawing. Regardless of the spacing, the grid is not part of the drawing and is used for reference (snapping to) only. Employ the following procedure to utilize the GRID SNAP ON option:

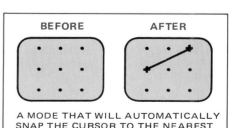

A MODE THAT WILL AUTOMATICALLY SNAP THE CURSOR TO THE NEAREST SNAP INCREMENT. THE SNAP INCREMENT IS OFTEN SET TO THE GRID SPACING OR HALF THE GRID SPACING.

1. Select the GRID (under SET-TINGS) command.
2. Follow the prompts by keying in the desired horizontal and vertical grid interval (e.g., .50 and press ENTER once or twice depending on the software). Grid dots will be displayed .50 inch apart in both the X (horizontal) and Y (vertical) directions as shown in Fig. 3-3-1. *Note:* you will not be able to display a small grid dot spacing of less than .12 in. for B (17 × 11 in.) and C (22 × 17 in.) size drawings. There will be too many grids per unit area. The system will prompt you with a message such as GRID TOO DENSE. To display a smaller grid will require enlarging a portion of the drawing.
3. Select the SNAP command (also a submenu option).
4. Select a value equal to the grid pattern (e.g., .5 and press ENTER). You may now use the grid pattern to snap to the nearest dot. The SNAP option and GRID pattern may readily be turned on or off. A "toggle" command is used for this purpose. A simple function key input F7 and F9 will accomplish this.
5. Select the LINE command.
6. Locate and set the cursor near a dot (point 1). Notice how it snaps to the closest grid dot (point 2) as shown in Fig. 3-3-2A.
7. Locate and set the cursor near a dot (point 3). It snaps to the closest grid dot (point 4) and a line is drawn on the grid pattern (Fig. 3-3-2B).
8. Locate and set the cursor near point 5 and select the CLOSE option. The triangle shown (Fig. 3-3-2C) is created quickly and accurately on the grid pattern. You know that it is exactly 2.00 in. (4 grids) wide and 1.00 in. (2 grids) high. Additional separate lines may be created in a like manner.

The GRID SNAP concept is useful when you are learning to draw with CAD. You are able to create graphics more quickly with great accuracy. Later, as you gain more competency, grids will not be used. Everyone knows that the world is not composed of 1-in. or 10-mm increments. Even though a grid pattern may be changed, it should not be used for all entries, for example, drawing a line 3.456 in. long. (Creating a line to an accurate length will be covered in Unit 3-5.) All CAD

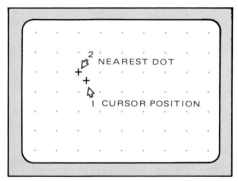

(A) FIRST ENDPOINT GRID SNAP

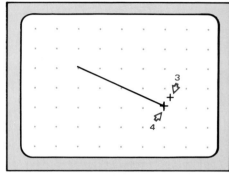

(B) SECOND ENDPOINT GRID SNAP

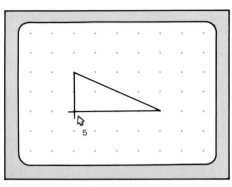

(C) FINISH THE OBJECT USING GRIDS

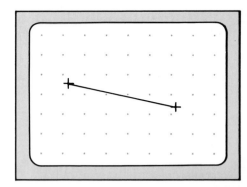

(D) FIRST LINE DRAWN WITH SNAP OFF

Fig. 3-3-2 Lines drawn with and without the SNAP option.

systems have an option to remove the SNAP. Simply select the SNAP OFF option F9. A point can now be located any place on the screen, regardless of the grid pattern. The selection of points 1 and 3 above, for example, would result in a line drawn exactly from the selected cursor positions (Fig. 3-3-2D).

BEFORE	AFTER

A MODE THAT WILL ALLOW ANY POINT TO BE LOCATED AT ANY POSITION ON THE SCREEN REGARD-LESS OF THE GRID PATTERN.

ASSIGNMENTS

See Assignments 4 through 8 for Unit 3-3 starting on page 36.

■ UNIT 3-4

Drawing Lines Using Construction Line Pattern

CREATE THE OBJECT AT FULL SIZE

CAD systems provide a construction line option. Construction lines, like a grid pattern, are used as a guide for constructing the drawing. Thus, they will be displayed differently (e.g., dot or dashed lines) on the monitor. These lines will allow the transferring of information in both the horizontal and vertical directions. This will assist in the creation of lines of uneven length, especially during the preparation of a drawing. The sequence to accomplish this is:

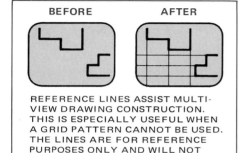

REFERENCE LINES ASSIST MULTI-VIEW DRAWING CONSTRUCTION. THIS IS ESPECIALLY USEFUL WHEN A GRID PATTERN CANNOT BE USED. THE LINES ARE FOR REFERENCE PURPOSES ONLY AND WILL NOT APPEAR ON THE FINISHED PLOT.

1. Determine where the lines are to be located on the monitor as shown in Fig. 3-4-1A. Do not worry about the exact size of the object at this time. Construct it by estimating its proportion.
2. Select LAYER, SET, DOT, press ENTER twice. NOTE: a DOT LAYER must exist.
3. Select the LINE and ORTHO options F8.
4. Place the lines by visually locating and setting the cursor (Fig. 3-4-1B).
5. Select the previous LAYER (SET layer 1, for example) and select LINE.

6. Using the construction lines as a guide, create the outline of an object as shown in Fig. 3-4-1C.
7. The construction lines may now be selectively removed by using ERASE. See Fig. 3-4-1D.

Later you will learn alternate methods of preparing a drawing of this type (e.g.: coordinate input and trimming).

There are more accurate methods that may be used to ensure that the lines of the object actually are on the construction guide lines. One such method includes the magnification of a portion of the screen while creating the outline.

Magnification (ZOOM)

Any portion of the screen may be temporarily enlarged to any desired magnification. This is a tremendous option (not available with manual drafting) to greatly improve drawing accuracy. The command is called ZOOM.

The WINDOW or ZOOM display command is used to change the magnification of an object. You can increase the magnification significantly to more clearly view small details. It will change the size of the display, but it will not change the scale of the drawing. It temporarily enlarges the overall drawing without changing scale. For example, it can be used to double the size of a display so that additional information may then be added to the drawing using the original numeric values. Consequently, it is not the same in concept as the other commands introduced in this section. ZOOM is a tool used for improving accuracy in creating a view.

There are many ways to change the magnification. The alphanumeric keyboard is an important support device. It provides for an exact scale ratio change since you have the option to key in the value. Exact magnification values, however, are normally not important. You will usually magnify the screen enough so that the lines to be drawn will be positioned more closely. Whether the magnification level is 10 times or 11 times probably is not important.

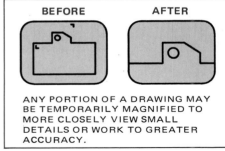

ANY PORTION OF A DRAWING MAY BE TEMPORARILY MAGNIFIED TO MORE CLOSELY VIEW SMALL DETAILS OR WORK TO GREATER ACCURACY.

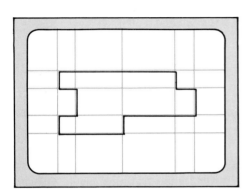

(A) SKETCH OF A PART TO BE DRAWN

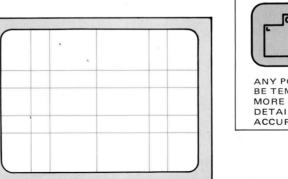

(B) DRAWING CONSTRUCTION LINES

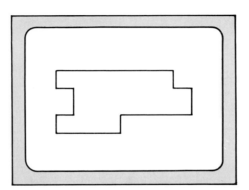

(C) USING CONSTRUCTION LINES AS A GUIDE

(D) CONSTRUCTION LINES REMOVED

Fig. 3-4-1 Use of construction lines.

Changing the window size will require defining limits. The common method is to select lower left and upper right corners of a rectangular area. Refer to Fig. 3-4-2A. This will "trap" an imaginary box around that section of the display to be magnified. The procedure involves selecting ZOOM command and WINDOW option, and following the directions on the screen. To get an idea of the window concept, place yourself in a room and look out the window. You see a rectangular portion of the view. Move closer to the window, and you see a wider area. The original size of the drawing may be recreated by selecting the ZOOM command and ALL option.

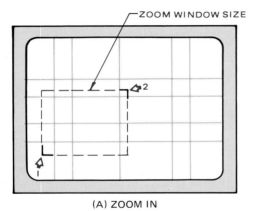

(A) ZOOM IN

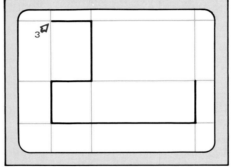

(B) CREATE PORTION OF OBJECT

DISTANCE OF MOVEMENT ON MONITOR

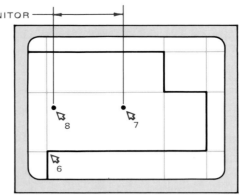

(C) ZOOM ALL AND ZOOM IN TO NEW AREA

(D) CREATE PORTION OF OBJECT AND PAN TO NEW AREA

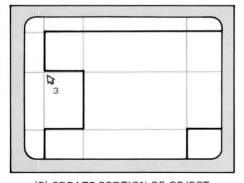

(E) CREATE PORTION OF OBJECT

(F) RESULT OF ZOOM ALL

Fig. 3-4-2 Use of **ZOOM** and **PAN** commands.

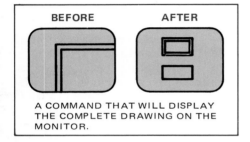

A COMMAND THAT WILL DISPLAY THE COMPLETE DRAWING ON THE MONITOR.

When you are zooming by rectangle, the exact scale magnification is not known. Again, this is unimportant.

Usually, it is desired to enlarge the display so that work may be accomplished more accurately. If the magnification is not great enough, repeat the procedure. Thus, you have the ability to zoom in on a ZOOM. This may be repeated as many times as desired.

Regardless of the number of zoomins, the ZOOM command and ALL or EXTENTS option will always return you to the original size display. Also, it is important to select the rectangular window area in the approximate proportion as the monitor when zooming.

Changing Area of Interest (PAN)

While zooming in it may be desirable to change the area of interest without returning back to the original size. This may be accomplished by the PAN option. PAN enables you to move the zoom window to a different area of concentration without having to return to full window. Thus, it allows access to a part of the drawing outside of the original zoomed-in window area.

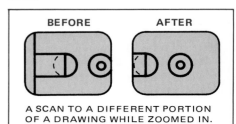

A SCAN TO A DIFFERENT PORTION OF A DRAWING WHILE ZOOMED IN.

Create the Object under Magnification

1. Create the construction as before (Fig. 3-4-1A).
2. Select the ZOOM command and WINDOW option (under DISPLAY).
3. Locate and set the cursor at the lower left (point 1) and upper right (point 2) corners of an imaginary rectangle as shown in Fig. 3-4-2A. This will define the level of magnification. Remember to select the rectangle in approximately the same proportion as the monitor screen.
4. Select the LINE and ORTHO (**F8**) commands.
5. Using the construction lines as a guide, draw the object beginning at point 3 as shown in Fig. 3-4-2B.
6. To return to the original full window, select the ZOOM command and ALL option (under DISPLAY).
7. Select ZOOM command and WINDOW option.
8. Select lower left (point 4) and upper right (point 5) corners as shown in Fig. 3-4-2C.
9. Continue to draw the object from point 6 (Fig. 3-4-2D).
10. Select the PAN (DISPLAY) command.
11. Select points 7 and 8 as shown in Fig. 3-4-2D. Whatever distance and direction you select between the points is the distance that the zoomed-in image will be moved.

In this case the image is panned to the left.

12. Complete the outline of the object. Draw from point 9, returning to the original starting point 3 (Fig. 3-4-2E).

13. Select the ZOOM command and ALL option. The result is shown in Fig. 3-4-2F.

Even though you may not be able to distinguish any difference between Figs. 3-4-1B and 3-4-2F, the latter will be more accurate. For even greater accuracy, zoom in with more magnification.

ASSIGNMENTS

See Assignments 9 and 10 for Unit 3-4 on page 37.

 UNIT 3-5

Coordinate Input

We have seen that a grid pattern is used to great advantage to quickly and accurately create lines. We know, however, that the world is not made up of even increments. What about that 3.456 in. line? How is it drawn? How about a point that must be located accurately on your drawing? This brings us to COORDINATE INPUT.

The alphanumeric keyboard can be used to generate points in exact locations and lines of exact length. There are three methods of coordinate input:

1. Absolute coordinate
2. Relative coordinate
3. Polar coordinate (line length and angle)

Coordinate input is based on the rectangular (horizontal and vertical) measurement system. All absolute distances are described in terms of distance from the drawing origin. Relative and polar coordinates may be described with respect to a particular point (position) on the drawing. This position may lie any place on the drawing and is described by two-dimensional coordinates, horizontal (X) and vertical (Y). The X axis is horizontal and is considered the first and basic reference axis. The Y axis is vertical and is at a 90° angle to the X axis. Any distance to the right of the position is considered a positive X value and any distance to the left a negative X value. Distances above the position are considered positive and distances below, negative values.

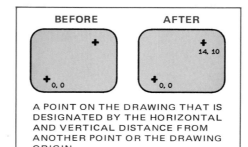

A POINT ON THE DRAWING THAT IS DESIGNATED BY THE HORIZONTAL AND VERTICAL DISTANCE FROM ANOTHER POINT OR THE DRAWING ORIGIN.

ABSOLUTE COORDINATES

An absolute coordinate is placed with respect to the drawing origin. This is normally located to the lower left of the monitor (Fig. 3-5-1) so that all values are positive with respect to the origin. The origin is a base reference point from which all positions on the drawing may be measured. Its dimensions are $X = 0$ and $Y = 0$, referred to as 0, 0. A point (or current access position) may be accurately located with respect to the origin. Its position is referred to as an absolute coordinate.

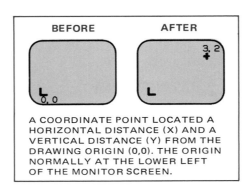

A COORDINATE POINT LOCATED A HORIZONTAL DISTANCE (X) AND A VERTICAL DISTANCE (Y) FROM THE DRAWING ORIGIN (0,0). THE ORIGIN NORMALLY AT THE LOWER LEFT OF THE MONITOR SCREEN.

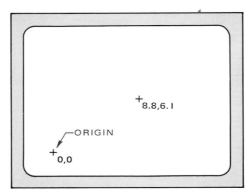

Fig. 3-5-1 Absolute coordinate input.

Placing an Absolute Coordinate Point

The method used to input an absolute coordinate point is:

1. Select the POINT or LINE command.

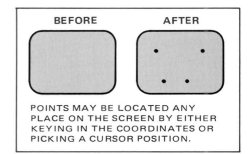

POINTS MAY BE LOCATED ANY PLACE ON THE SCREEN BY EITHER KEYING IN THE COORDINATES OR PICKING A CURSOR POSITION.

2. Use the alphanumeric keyboard to specify the X (horizontal) and Y (vertical) distance from the origin. For example, if you desire a point to be located 8.8 in. to the right and 6.1 in. above the origin, key in 8.8, 6.1 and press ENTER. Remember to specify a comma between the X and Y coordinates. Also, the ENTER key must be used to end the command. You could, for example, key to two decimal places (6.12), three (6.123), and so on. The two coordinates need not be to the same number of decimal places. The absolute coordinate will be located as shown in Fig. 3-5-1. The coordinate values have been shown for reference purpose only and will not be displayed on the monitor although the current access location is identified at the top of the screen.

3. Additional coordinate points may be specified by repeating step 2. Lines would connect each of the coordinate points if you were in the LINE command. Note: The position of any point on the drawing from the origin may be found (determined) using the STATUS command.

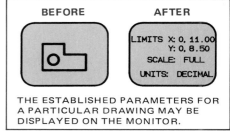

THE ESTABLISHED PARAMETERS FOR A PARTICULAR DRAWING MAY BE DISPLAYED ON THE MONITOR.

RELATIVE COORDINATES

A relative coordinate is located with respect to the current access location (last cursor position selected) rather than the origin (0, 0). That is, with respect to another point on your drawing. Often, both absolute and relative coordinate input are used during drawing preparation. A line may be created by combining these two methods as follows:

1. Select the LINE command.

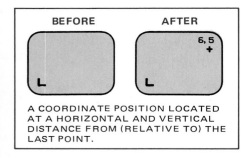

A COORDINATE POSITION LOCATED AT A HORIZONTAL AND VERTICAL DISTANCE FROM (RELATIVE TO) THE LAST POINT.

2. Key in the desired *X* and *Y* values for the first endpoint, e.g., 10.5, 10

and press ENTER. The first endpoint (point 1), which is now the current access location, will be displayed as shown in Fig. 3-5-2A. It is 10.5 in. to the right, and 10 in. above the origin.

3. Select the RELATIVE COORDINATE input option using the @ key.

4. Key in the desired *X* and *Y* values for the second endpoint, e.g., 5.12, 0. It will be located 5.12 in. to the right "relative" to the last point selected as indicated in Fig. 3-5-2B.

5. Press ENTER. The line (2) will appear on the screen at the desired location, as shown in Fig. 3-5-2C. It begins 10.5 units to the right and 10 units up from the origin. It will be horizontal and 5.12 in. long extending right (positive direction).

6. Select the RELATIVE COORDINATE input option @.

7. Key in −5.12, −5. The new position will be 5 in. below and 5.12 in. to the left of the second position. Notice the result of using the minus sign.

8. Press ENTER. The result is shown in Fig. 3-5-2D.

POLAR COORDINATES

A polar coordinate is similar to a relative coordinate since it is positioned with respect to the current access location. A line, however, will be specified according to its actual length and a direction rather than an X, Y coordinate distance. The direction is measured angularly in a counterclockwise direction. Zero degrees is located horizontal to the right (east or 3 o'clock) as shown in Fig. 3-5-3.

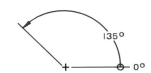

Fig. 3-5-3 Polar coordinate angle.

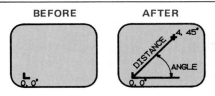

A LINE OR SECOND POINT IS LOCATED BY KEYING ITS DISTANCE AND ANGLE FROM AN EXISTING POINT.

You may create a line with respect to a position using polar coordinate input as follows:

1. Select the LINE command.
2. Locate point 1 as shown in Fig. 3-5-4A.
3. Select the POLAR COORDINATE option and specify the line length and angle (e.g., key in @ 6.5 < 45 and press ENTER). The line, 6.5 in. long, will be created 45° with respect to point 1, as shown in Fig. 3-5-4B.
4. A second line may be created relative to the new current access location (point 2 Fig. 3-5-4B) by repeating Step 3. This time, however, by keying in 6.5 < 315 and pressing ENTER will produce a line having coordinates as shown in Fig. 3-5-4C. The second line is drawn 6.5 in. long and 315° counterclockwise from point 2. The final result is shown in Fig. 3-5-4D.

The identification of the coordinates and angle of these or any lines may easily be checked any time by the

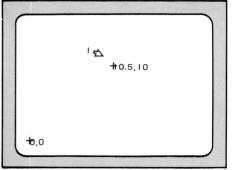

(A) FIRST POSITION (ABSOLUTE COORDINATE)

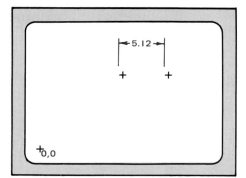

(B) SECOND POSITION (RELATIVE COORDINATE)

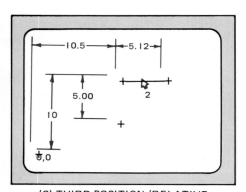

(C) THIRD POSITION (RELATIVE COORDINATE

Fig. 3-5-2 Line creation using coordinate input.

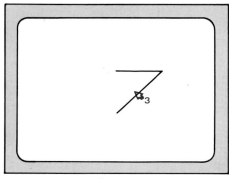

(D) RESULT

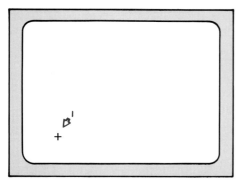

(A) SELECTING A CURRENT ACCESS LOCATION

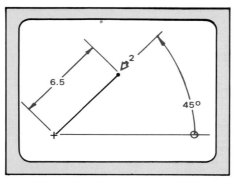

(B) FIRST LINE COORDINATES

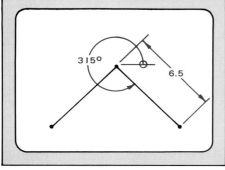

(C) SECOND LINE COORDINATES

Fig. 3-5-4 Polar coordinate input.

(D) RESULT

selection of the DISTANCE (IN-QUIRY) option. Also, the current co-ordinate location is displayed at the top of the monitor and toggled by using function key F6.

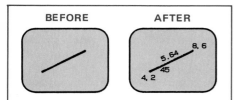

BEFORE   AFTER

DESCRIBES SPATIAL CHARACTER-ISTICS OF A SEGMENT OR BETWEEN TWO POINTS. THE CHARACTERISTICS MAY INCLUDE THE DISTANCE BE-TWEEN END POINTS, ANGLE, THE CHANGE IN HORIZONTAL DISTANCE, THE CHANGE IN VERTICAL DISTANCE, AND LOCATION WITH RESPECT TO THE ORIGIN.

ASSIGNMENTS

See assignments 11 through 15 for Unit 3-5 starting on page 38.

■ UNIT 3-6

Circles and Arcs

Curved lines include the following types: circle, arc, donut (two concentric circles), ellipse, and spline. There are several different methods which may be employed to create each type. This unit will concentrate only on the common methods used in the construction of circles and arcs.

CIRCLES

The common methods used to DRAW circles include:

1. Center and radius
2. Center and diameter
3. Three-point circle
4. Two-point circle
5. Concentric circles

The procedures to accomplish these follow:

Center and Radius (Fig. 3-6-1A)

1. Select the CIRCLE command and CEN, RAD option.

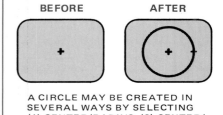

BEFORE   AFTER

A CIRCLE MAY BE CREATED IN SEVERAL WAYS BY SELECTING (1) CENTER/RADIUS, (2) CENTER/KEY THE SIZE, (3) TWO OPPOSITE POINTS ON THE CIRCLE, OR (4) THREE POINTS ON THE CIRCUM-FERENCE.

2. Select a center (point 1).
3. Select the endpoint which is equal to the radius (point 2).

The circle will be created as shown in Fig. 3-6-1A.

Center and Diameter (Fig. 3-6-1B).

1. Select the CIRCLE command and CEN, DIA option.
2. Select a center (point 1).
3. Key in the diameter and press ENTER. The circle will be created. Keying in the size provides the option to accurately create circles of any diameter.

Three-Point Circle (Fig. 3-6-1C)

1. Select the CIRCLE command and THREE POINT option.
2. Select points 1, 2, and 3. The circle will be drawn with the circumference through each point.

Two-Point Circle (Fig. 3-6-1D)

1. Select the CIRCLE command and TWO POINT option.
2. Select points 1 and 2. The circle will be drawn through both points. The distance between the two points is the circle's diameter.

Concentric Circles (Fig. 3-6-2)

1. Draw concentric circles by selecting the DONUT command. Note: Select the FILL option and be sure

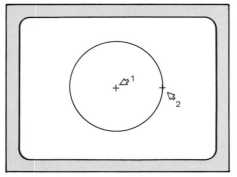

(A) CENTER AND RADIUS

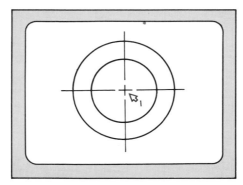

Fig. 3-6-2 Concentric circles.

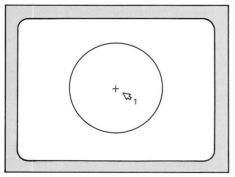

(B) CENTER AND DIAMETER

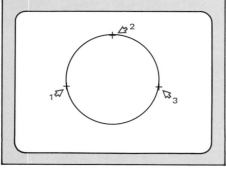

(C) THREE POINT

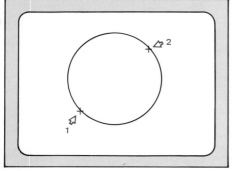

(D) TWO POINT

Fig. 3-6-1 Circle creation methods.

that it is OFF if you do not want the donut to be darkened in.

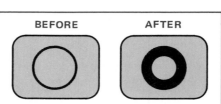

A SOLID (FILLED) CIRCLE, WITH OR WITHOUT A HOLE, MAY BE AUTOMATICALLY CREATED. ELIMINATION OF THE FILL RESULTS IN TWO CIRCLES CONCENTRIC ABOUT A COMMON CENTER.

2. Key in the desired size for the smaller circle and press ENTER.
3. Key in the desired size for the larger circle and press ENTER.
4. Select the center position (point 1).

ARCS

The common methods used to DRAW arcs include:

1. Three points
2. Start, center, and end
3. Start, end, and radius
4. Start, center, and angle

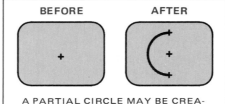

A PARTIAL CIRCLE MAY BE CREATED IN SEVERAL WAYS INCLUDING (1) START/END/ANGLE, (2) START/END/RADIUS, (3) START/MIDPOINT/END, (4) THREE POINTS.

The procedures to accomplish these follow:

Three-Point Arc (Fig. 3-6-3A)

1. Select the ARC command and THREE POINT option.
2. Select three points (1, 2, and 3). The three points will lie on the arc's circumference with the first and third points defining the ends of the arc. The arc will be drawn through each point.

Start, Center, and End (Fig. 3-6-3B)

1. Select the ARC command and START/CENTER/END option.
2. Select the start (point 1).
3. Select the center (point 2).
4. Select the end (point 3). The arc will be drawn concentric to the centerpoint as shown.

Start, End, and Radius (Fig. 3-6-3C)

1. Select the ARC command and START/END/RADIUS option.
2. Select the start (point 1).
3. Select the end (point 2).
4. Key in the desired radius and press ENTER. The arc will be created as shown in Fig. 3-6-2C.

Start, Center, and Angle (Fig. 3-6-3D)

1. Select the ARC and START/CENTER/ANGLE option.
2. Select the start (point 1).
3. Select the center (point 2).
4. Key in an angle (3) such as 120 (for degrees), and press ENTER. The arc will be drawn counterclockwise as shown. To create the arc in the clockwise direction, use a minus sign before keying in the number of degrees.

There are additional methods that may be used to create arcs. The four presented, however, are the most common and may be used to solve practically any arc requirement.

ASSIGNMENTS

See Assignments 16 through 18 for Unit 3-6 starting on page 41.

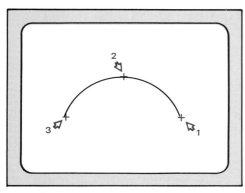

(A) THREE POINT

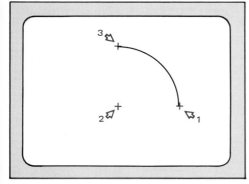

(B) START/CENTER/END

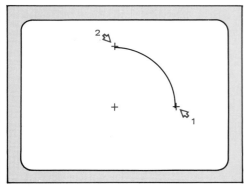

(C) START/END/RADIUS

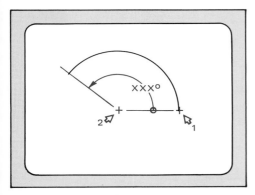

(D) START/CENTER/ANGLE

Fig. 3-6-3 Arc creation methods.

Text

The TEXT command allows you to insert letters, numbers, words, notes, symbols, and messages as required on an engineering drawing. Additionally, it may be utilized for size description (lengths, diameters, etc.) or to provide finishing touches, such as information that cannot be shown graphically on a drawing. The alphanumeric keyboard is an indispensable input device used to specify the text. Text style and height can be altered to suit the drawing requirements. Each letter, number, or symbol is separately keyed in. The basic procedure to accomplish this is:

1. Select the TEXT (DRAW) command.

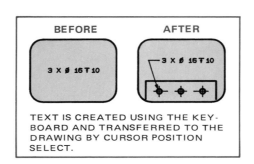

TEXT IS CREATED USING THE KEYBOARD AND TRANSFERRED TO THE DRAWING BY CURSOR POSITION SELECT.

2. The system will prompt you and provide submenu options. If you will be keying more than a single line of text, the system will automatically line up the beginning position for each row of text (left-justified) as shown in Fig. 3-7-1. Select

CENTERED or RIGHT if you desire the text to be lined center-justified or right-justified. Select the ALIGNED option if you desire to place the text parallel at an inclined line.

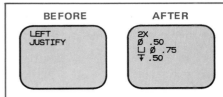

ROWS OF TEXT MAY BE "LINED UP" IN ANY OF SEVERAL ARRANGEMENTS. LEFT JUSTIFY, FOR EXAMPLE, WILL LINE THE STARTING POINT FOR EACH ROW OF TEXT WITH RESPECT TO A VERTICAL LINE.

3. Locate and set the cursor at the start point.
4. From the HEIGHT option, key in the desired text height, and press ENTER.
5. From the ROTATION ANGLE option, key in the desired angle, and press ENTER (e.g., 90° ROTATION).
6. Key in the text and press ENTER. The note will be displayed beginning at the position selected in Step 3.
7. Additional rows of text may be placed by repeating Step 6.

ASSIGNMENTS

See Assignments 19 through 22 for Unit 3-7 starting on page 43.

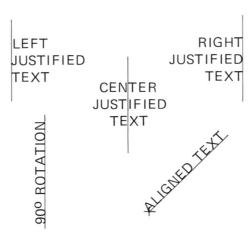

Fig. 3-7-1 Text alignment.

ASSIGNMENTS FOR CHAPTER 3

Assignment for Unit 3-1, Start-up

1. Start up your system from the beginning. SETUP a B-size LIMIT (17 × 11 in.), FULL SCALE, INCH, and DECIMAL drawing. Review the LINE, CIRCLE, ARC, and TEXT commands and subcommands, then proceed to Assignment 2.

Assignments for Unit 3-2, Drawing and Erasing Straight Lines

2. Draw the objects shown in Fig. 3-2-A using the free input LINE option. Drawings need not be created to scale but should be approximately the same proportion as that shown. Any time a mistake is made, use one of the ERASE options to correct it.

3. Redraw the objects shown in Fig. 3-2-A, but this time use the ORTHO line option. Drawings need not be to scale but should be approximately the same proportion as that shown. *Note:* for inclined lines remove the ORTHO option.

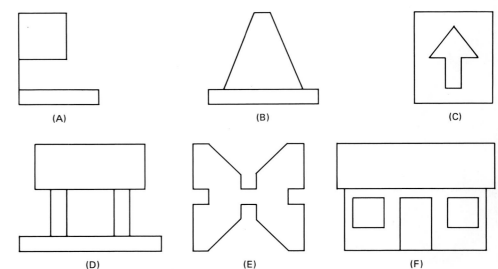

(A) (B) (C)

(D) (E) (F)

Fig. 3-2-A Drawing lines.

1.00 IN. OR 20mm GRID

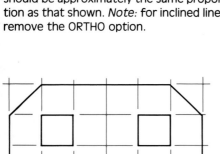
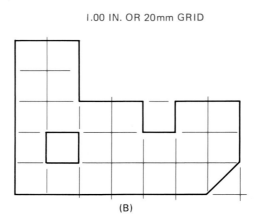
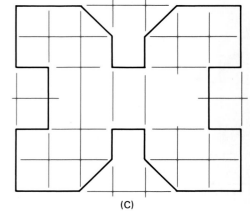

(A) (B) (C)

Fig. 3-3-A Drawing assignment.

Assignments for Unit 3-3, Drawing Lines Using a Grid Pattern

4. On an A3 or B size drawing, draw any two of the objects shown in Fig. 3-3-A. Use either a 1.00 in. or 20 mm grid and snap to create the views. Scale 1 : 1.

5. On an A3 or B size drawing, draw the three objects shown in Fig. 3-3-B. Use either a .50 in. or 10 mm grid and snap to create the views. Scale 1 : 1.

.50 IN. OR 10mm GRID

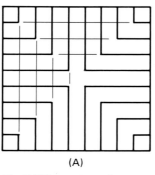
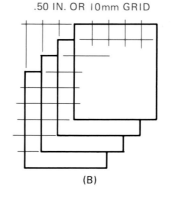
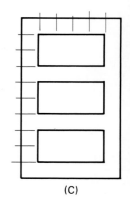

(A) (B) (C)

Fig. 3-3-B Drawing assignment.

6. On an A3 or B size drawing, draw the three objects shown in Fig. 3-3-C. Use either a .50 in. or 10 mm grid and snap to create the views. Scale 1:1.

7. On an A3 or B size drawing, draw the part shown in Fig. 3-3-D. First draw the horizontal and vertical lines as shown in Fig. 3-3-D(A). Using BREAK or TRIM, remove the unwanted portions of the lines as shown by the finished drawing in Fig. 3-3-D(B). Use either a .50 in. or 10 mm grid. Scale 1:1.

8. Same as Assignment 7, except use any of the problems shown in Fig. 3-3-E. Scale 1:1.

Assignments for Unit 3-4, Drawing Lines Using a Construction Line Pattern

9. Same as Assignment 7 except replace the grid with DOT construction lines for Fig. 3-3-D. Scale 1:1.

10. Same as Assignment 8 except replace the grid with DOT construction lines for Fig. 3-3-E. Scale 1:1.

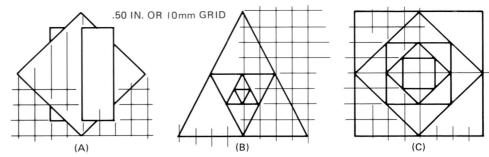

Fig. 3-3-C Drawing assignments.

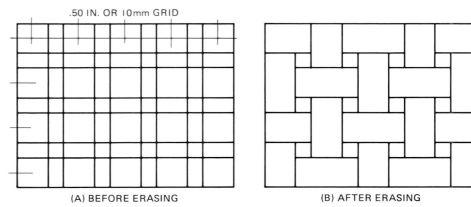

(A) BEFORE ERASING   (B) AFTER ERASING

Fig. 3-3-D Drawing assignments.

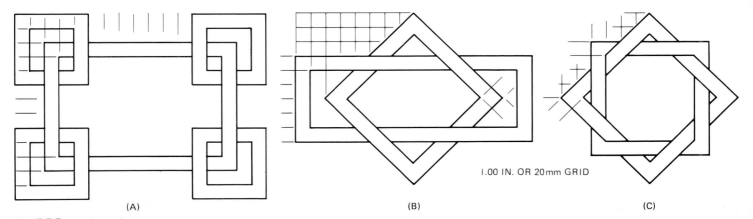

(A)   (B)   (C)

Fig. 3-3-E Drawing assignments.

Assignments for Unit 3-5, Lines Using Coordinate Input

11. On an A3 or B size drawing, draw the parts shown in Fig. 3-5-A and plot the relative coordinates of each of the line intersections. The bottom left-hand corner is the drawing coordinate (absolute) starting point for each part. Move in a clockwise direction. Scale: one grid square equals .50 in. or 12 mm.

12. Same as Assignment 11 except use absolute coordinates.

13. Using absolute coordinates plot Figs. 3-5-B and 3-5-C on a B or A3 size drawing. The bottom left-hand corner of the drawing is the starting point. Scale 1:1.

14. Using relative coordinates plot Figs. 3-5-D and 3-5-E on a B or A3 size drawing. Begin the bottom left-hand corner of the drawing at .50, .50 (10, 10). Scale 1:1.

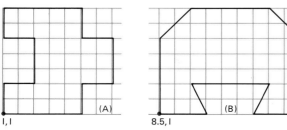

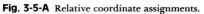

Fig. 3-5-A Relative coordinate assignments.

ABSOLUTE COORDINATES (INCHES)

Point	X Axis	Y Axis
1	.25	.25
2	7.00	.25
3	8.50	1.00
4	8.50	2.25
5	7.00	3.00
6	8.50	3.75
7	8.50	5.25
8	7.00	6.25
9	5.50	6.25
10	5.50	4.50
11	4.75	4.50
12	4.75	6.25
13	3.50	6.25
14	3.50	5.50
15	1.50	5.50
16	1.50	6.25
17	.75	6.25
18	.25	5.5
19	.25	.25
New Start		
20	.75	1.50
21	2.25	3.50
22	.75	3.50
23	.75	1.50
New Start		
24	3.00	2.25
25	5.75	2.25
26	5.75	3.75
27	3.00	3.75
28	3.00	2.25
New Start		
29	2.75	.75
30	6.00	.75
31	5.25	1.50
32	3.50	1.50
33	2.75	.75

Fig. 3-5-B Absolute coordinates (inches) assignment.

ABSOLUTE COORDINATES (MILLIMETERS)		
Point	X Axis	Y Axis
1	10	10
2	50	10
3	50	20
4	120	20
5	120	10
6	150	10
7	180	30
8	220	30
9	220	100
10	160	100
11	160	130
12	140	130
13	140	160
14	110	160
15	120	140
16	90	140
17	70	100
18	40	120
19	60	160
20	40	160
21	10	140
22	10	80
23	20	40
24	10	40
25	10	10
	New Start	
26	40	50
27	160	50
28	120	90
29	40	70
30	40	50

Fig. 3-5-C Absolute coordinates (metric) assignment.

RELATIVE COORDINATES (INCHES)		
Point	X Axis	Y Axis
1	0	0
2	4.50	0
3	0	.75
4	−.75	0
5	0	.75
6	−.75	0
7	0	.75
8	−3.00	0
9	0	−2.25
	New Start—Solid	
10	0	.75
11	3.75	0
	New Start	
12	−.75	.75
13	−3.00	0
	New Start—Solid	
14	0	1.50
15	4.50	0
16	0	2.25
17	−4.50	0
18	0	−2.25
	New Start—Solid	
19	0	.75
20	3.75	0
21	0	1.50
	New Start—Solid	
22	−.75	0
23	0	−.75
24	−3.00	0
	New Start—Solid	
25	5.25	−4.50
26	2.25	0
27	0	2.25
28	−.75	0
29	0	−.75
30	−.75	0
31	0	−.75
32	−.75	0
33	0	−.75
	New Start—Solid	
34	.75	.75
35	1.75	0
	New Start—Solid	
36	0	.75
37	−.75	0

Fig. 3-5-D Relative coordinates (inches) assignment.

RELATIVE COORDINATES (MILLIMETERS)		
Point	X Axis	Y Axis
1	0	0
2	30	0
3	0	10
4	10	0
5	0	−10
6	30	0
7	0	50
8	−10	0
9	0	−15
10	−50	0
11	0	15
12	−10	0
13	0	−50
	New Start—Solid	
14	5	10
15	15	0
16	0	20
17	−15	0
18	0	−20
	New Start—Solid	
19	−45	0
20	15	0
21	0	20
22	−15	0
23	0	−20

Fig. 3-5-E Relative coordinates (metric) assignment.

15. Using both relative and polar coordinates plot Figs. 3-5-F to 3-5-H on a B or A3 size drawing. Scale 1:1.

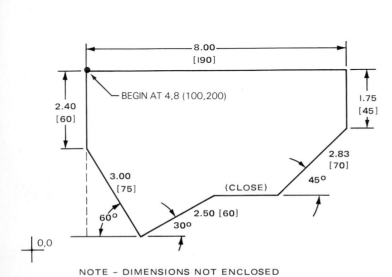

NOTE – DIMENSIONS NOT ENCLOSED IN BRACKETS ARE IN INCHES. DIMENSIONS ENCLOSED IN BRACKETS ARE IN MILLIMETERS.

Fig. 3-5-F Template 1 — polar coordinates.

NOTE - DIMENSIONS NOT ENCLOSED IN BRACKETS ARE IN MILLIMETERS. DIMENSIONS ENCLOSED IN BRACKETS ARE IN INCHES.

Fig. 3-5-G Template 2 — relative or absolute coordinates.

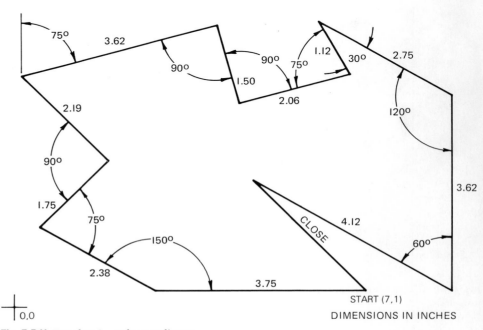

Fig. 3-5-H Template 3 — polar coordinates.

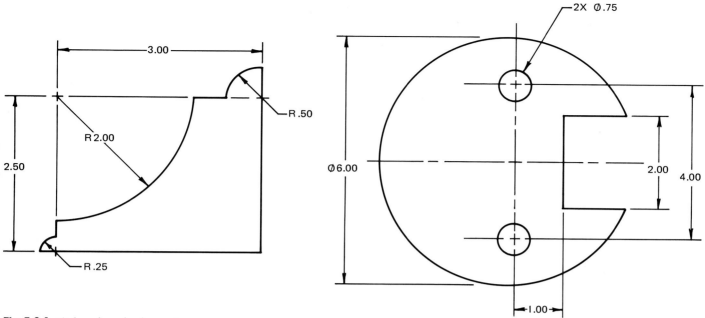

Fig. 3-6-A Circle and arc development.

Assignments for Unit 3-6, Circles and Arcs

16. On an A3 or B size drawing, and using a .50 in. grid, draw the two parts shown in Fig. 3-6-A. Scale 1 : 1. Place both parts next to each other on one sheet. Do not dimension or show center lines.

17. On an A3 or B size drawing, and using a .50 in. grid, draw the two parts shown in Fig. 3-6-B. Scale 1 : 1. Do not dimension or show center lines.

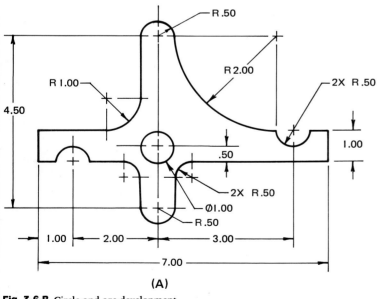

(A)

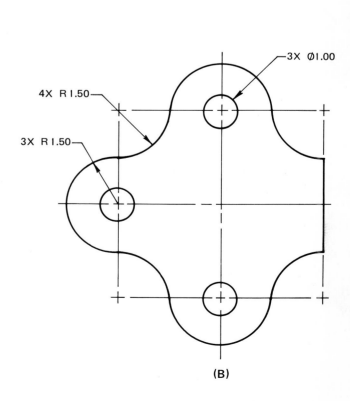

(B)

Fig. 3-6-B Circle and arc development.

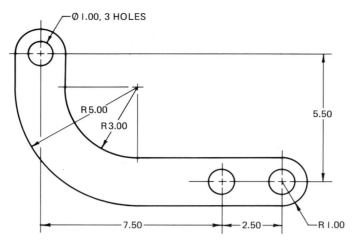

Fig. 3-6-C Rod support.

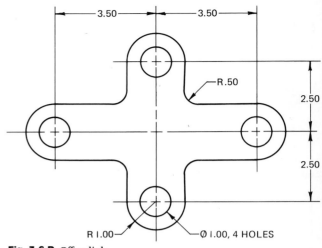

Fig. 3-6-D Offset link.

18. On an A3 or B size drawing and using construction lines or grids, draw any of the parts shown in Figs. 3-6-C to 3-6-E. Show only the object lines. Scale 1 : 1. The dimension and center lines are shown only for reference purpose.

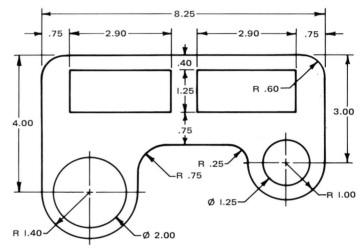

Fig. 3-6-E Template.

Assignments for Unit 3-7, Text

19. On an A3 or B size drawing, draw the dartboard shown in Fig. 3-7-A. Use concentric circles and indicate the number heights and diameters as shown. Plot Scale 1:2. Use LIMITS of 800,570 mm and draw full scale.`

20. On an A3 or B size drawing, draw one-half of the shuffleboard as shown in Fig. 3-7-B. Plot Scale 1:20. Use LIMITS of 8000,5700 mm and draw full scale.

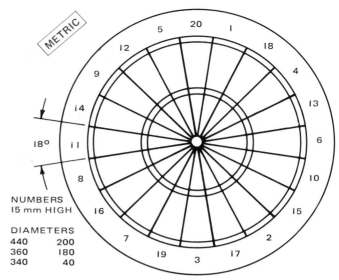

Fig. 3-7-A Dart board.

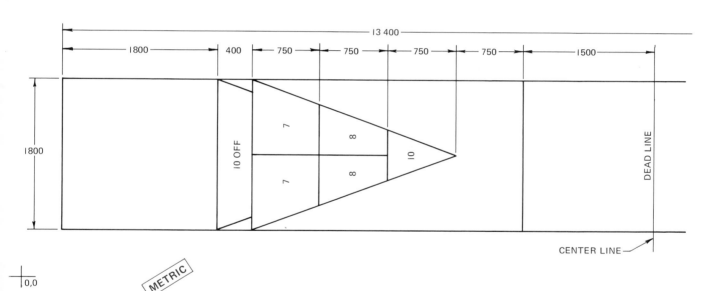

Fig. 3-7-B Shuffleboard.

21. On an A3 or B size drawing, draw the pizza carton development (carton opened up in a flat position) as shown in Fig. 3-7-C and add the folding instructions as shown. Plot Scale 1 : 2. Use LIMITS of 32,20 and draw full scale.

22. Using an A3 or B size drawing, the TEXT command, and different height options, prepare a chart showing the subjects taken each year and semester for the program you are presently enrolled in. Scale 1 : 1. Remember to press the CAPS LOCK key.

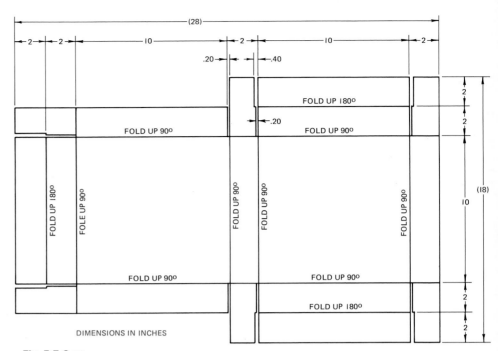

Fig. 3-7-C Pizza carton.

4

Basic Drawing Requirements

Lettering and Line Work

This unit establishes the line and lettering practices for use in the preparation of engineering drawings. Using these practices will ensure that your drawing will meet the requirements for photographic reduction and reproduction as well as the other conventional methods of reproduction.

LETTERING

The most important requirements for lettering on engineering drawings are legibility and reproducibility. These are particularly important because of the use of microforming and photoreproduction, which require optimum clarity and adequate size of all details and lettering.

These requirements are met in the recommended Gothic characters shown in Fig. 4-1-1, or adaptations thereof, which improve reproduction legibility. One such adaptation by the National Microfilm Association is the vertical Gothic-style Microfont alphabet (Fig. 4-1-2) intended for general usage. CAD systems provide the option to place text using any of several text fonts.

STANDARD FONT | ital font

VARIOUS TEXT STYLE OPTIONS ARE AVAILABLE AND MAY BE SELECTED FOR USE ON ANY DRAWING.

Uppercase letters should be used for all lettering on drawings unless lowercase letters are required to conform with other established standards, equipment nomenclature, or marking. The alphanumeric keyboard is used for text input.

The recommended minimum mechanical letter heights for various ap-

ABCDEFGHIJKLMNOP
QRSTUVWXYZ&
1234567890

VERTICAL LETTERS

Fig. 4-1-1 Approved lettering for engineering drawings.

ABCDEFGHIJKLMNO
PQRSTUVWXYZ
1234567890

Fig. 4-1-2 Microfont letters. *(National Microfilm Assoc.)*

USE	INCH	METRIC mm	DRAWING SIZE
DRAWING NUMBER IN TITLE BLOCK	0.24	7	UP TO AND INCLUDING 17 X 22 INCHES
	0.30		LARGER THAN 17 X 22 INCHES
DRAWING TITLE	0.24	7	ALL
SECTION AND TABULATION LETTERS	0.24	7	
ZONE LETTERS AND NUMERALS IN BORDER	0.18	5	
DIMENSION, TOLERANCE, LIMITS, NOTES, SUBTITLES FOR SPECIAL VIEWS, TABLES, REVISIONS, AND ZONE LETTERS FOR THE BODY OF THE DRAWING	0.12	3.5	UP TO AND INCLUDING 17 X 22 INCHES
	0.14	5	LARGER THAN 17 X 22 INCHES

THIS IS AN EXAMPLE OF .125 IN. LETTERING

THIS IS AN EXAMPLE OF .188 IN. LETTERING

THIS IS AN EXAMPLE OF .250 IN. LETTERING

Fig. 4-1-3 Recommended lettering heights. *(ANSI Y14.2M 1979.)*

plications are given in Fig. 4-1-3. The height-to-width ratio is 1.00, although it may be varied for a customized application. Also, lettering height and angle may easily be changed each time the TEXT command is used.

When drawings are being made for microforming, the size of the lettering is an important consideration. The print (a copy of the original drawing) of the original drawing size is made from film which may be reduced as much as 30 times the original size. (Most microform engineering readers and blowback equipment have a magnification of 15×. If a drawing is microformed at 30× reduction, the enlarged blown-back image is 50 percent; at 24×, it is 62 percent of its original size.)

Standards generally do not allow characters smaller than .12 in. (3 mm) for drawings to be reduced 30×, and the trend is toward larger characters. Figure 4-1-4 shows the proportionate size of letters after reduction and enlargement.

Use the STYLE submenu option under TEXT to change a FONT. Select the desired font (GOTHIC, for example) and follow the instructions on the screen.

LINE WORK

The various lines used in drawing form the "alphabet" of the drafting language. Like letters of the alphabet, they are different in appearance. See Fig. 4-1-5. The distinctive features of all lines that form a permanent part of the drawing are the differences in their width and construction. Lines must be clearly visible and stand out in sharp contrast to one another. This line contrast is necessary if the drawing is to be clear and easily understood.

Line Widths

Two widths of lines, thick and thin, as shown in Fig. 4-1-6, are recommended for use on drawings. Thick lines are .030 to 0.38 in. (0.5 to 0.8 mm) wide, thin lines between .015 and .022 in. (0.3 to 0.5 mm) wide. The actual width of each line is governed by the PENS that are used and the plotter holder where each is inserted. All lines of the same type should be uniform throughout the drawing. Spacing between parallel lines should be such that there is no fill-in when the copy is

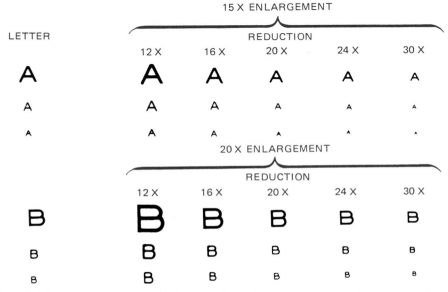

Fig. 4-1-4 Proportionate size of letters after reduction and enlargement. *(National Microfilm Assoc.)*

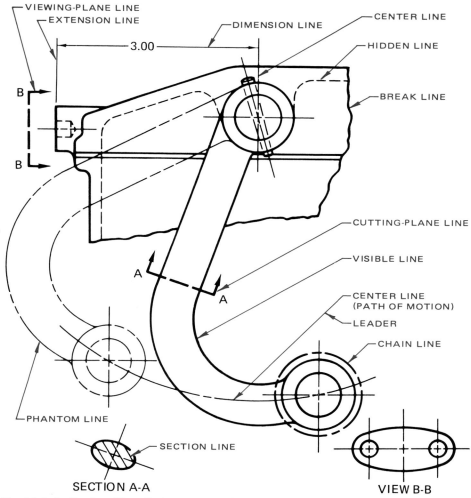

Fig. 4-1-5 Application of lines *(ANSI Y14.2M 1975.)*

Labels in figure:
VIEWING-PLANE LINE
EXTENSION LINE
3.00
DIMENSION LINE
CENTER LINE
HIDDEN LINE
BREAK LINE
B
B
CUTTING-PLANE LINE
VISIBLE LINE
A
A
CENTER LINE (PATH OF MOTION)
LEADER
CHAIN LINE
PHANTOM LINE
SECTION LINE
SECTION A-A
VIEW B-B

THICK
WIDTH .032 IN. (0.7mm)

THIN
WIDTH .016 IN. (0.35mm)

Fig. 4-1-6 Line widths.

reproduced by available photographic methods. Spacing of no less than .12 in. (3 mm) normally meets reproduction requirements.

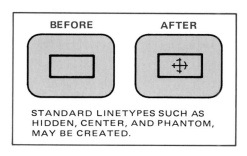

BEFORE   AFTER

STANDARD LINETYPES SUCH AS HIDDEN, CENTER, AND PHANTOM, MAY BE CREATED.

PEN 1   PEN 2

PEN NUMBERS REFER TO THE PLOTTING OF A DRAWING TO PRODUCE DIFFERENT LINE WEIGHTS. A NUMBER 2 PEN SELECTION WILL BE PLOTTED WITH THE PEN THAT HAS BEEN PLACED IN THE NUMBER 2 PLOTTER POSITION.

senting visible edges or contours of objects. Visible lines should be drawn so that the views they outline clearly stand out on the drawing with a definite contrast between these lines and other line types.

Hidden Lines Hidden lines consist of short, evenly spaced thin dashes and are used to show the hidden features of an object. See Fig. 4-1-7. The lengths of the dashes may vary slightly in relation to the size of the drawing. Hidden lines should always begin and end with a dash, except when such a dash would form a continuation of a visible line. Dashes should join at corners, and arcs should start with dashes at tangent points. Hidden lines should be omitted when they are not required for the clarity of the drawing.

All lines are clean-cut, opaque, uniform, and properly spaced for legible reproduction by all commonly used methods, including microforming in accordance with industry and government requirements. Even though lines will appear the same on the monitor there is a distinct contrast between widths of lines on the plot. Standard-thickness plotter pens are available for this purpose.

Types of Lines

The types of lines used in engineering drawings are illustrated in Figs. 4-1-5 through 4-1-11. All lines must be clear and dense to obtain good reproduction. When additions or revisions are made to existing drawings, the line widths and density should match the original work.

Visible Lines The visible lines (continuous thick) should be used for repre-

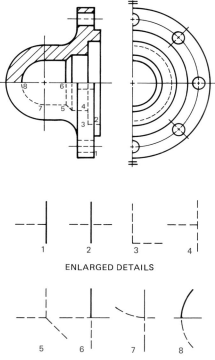

ENLARGED DETAILS

Fig. 4-1-7 Hidden line technique.

Although features located behind transparent materials may be visible, they should be treated as concealed features and shown with hidden lines.

Center Lines Center lines consist of alternating long and short thin dashes

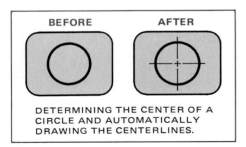

DETERMINING THE CENTER OF A CIRCLE AND AUTOMATICALLY DRAWING THE CENTERLINES.

(Fig. 4-1-8). They are used to represent the axis of symmetrical parts and features, bolt circles, and paths of motion. The long dashes of the center lines may vary in length, depending upon the size of the drawing. Center lines should start and end with long dashes and should intersect with the crossing of the short dashes. Center lines should extend uniformly and distinctly a short distance beyond the object or feature of the drawing unless a longer extension is required for dimensioning or for some other purpose. They should not terminate at other lines of the drawing, nor should they extend through the space between views. Very short center lines may be unbroken if no confusion results with other lines.

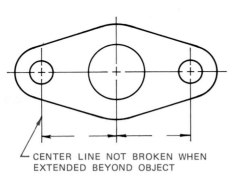

CENTER LINE NOT BROKEN WHEN EXTENDED BEYOND OBJECT

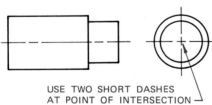

USE TWO SHORT DASHES AT POINT OF INTERSECTION

Fig. 4-1-8 Center line technique.

Extension and Dimension Lines These thin continuous lines are created when dimensioning a drawing and are explained in detail in Chap. 7.

Leaders Leaders are thin continuous lines with an arrowhead or dot at one end. They are used to indicate the part of a drawing to which a note refers. See Chap. 7 for further details.

Cutting-Plane Lines Cutting-plane lines (thick interrupted) are used to show the location of cutting planes for sectional views and are explained in detail in Chap. 8.

Section Lining Section lining is used to show the surface in the section view imagined to be cut along the cutting-plane line. Refer to Chap. 8 for further details.

Symmetry Lines Symmetry lines are center lines used as an axis of symmetry for partial views. The line of symmetry is identified by two thick, short parallel lines drawn at right angles to the center line. Symmetry lines are used when representing partially drawn views and partial sections of symmetrical parts. See Fig. 4-1-9. Symmetrical view visible and hidden lines may extend past the symmetrical line if clarity will be improved.

Viewing-Plane Lines Viewing-plane lines are used to locate the viewing position for removed partial views.

Break Lines Break lines are shown in Fig. 4-1-10. They are used to shorten the view of long uniform sections or when only a partial view is required. Such lines are used on both detail and assembly drawings. The straight thin line with zigzags is recommended for long breaks, the thick irregular line for short breaks, and the jagged line for wood parts. The LINE command may be used for this purpose. Remember to use the proper pen so that you obtain the correct line thickness on the plot.

The special breaks shown for cylindrical and tubular parts are useful when an end view is not shown; otherwise, the thick break line is adequate. To create curved break lines it will be best to use the SPLINE command.

Phantom Lines Phantom lines consist of long thin dashes separated by pairs of short thin dashes. See Fig. 4-1-11. The long dashes may vary in length, depending on the size of the drawing or line type scale (LTSCALE) used.

Phantom lines are used to indicate alternate positions of moving parts, adjacent positions of related parts, and repeated detail. These lines are also used for features such as bosses and lugs (later removed), for delineating machining stock and blanking developments, for piece parts in jigs and fixtures, and for mold lines on drawings or formed metal parts. Phantom lines should start and end with long dashes.

Stitch Lines Two forms of stitch lines are approved for general use as follows:

1. Short thin dashes and spaces of equal lengths
2. Dots approximately .016 in. (0.35 mm) diameter, .12 in. (3 mm) apart

Stitch lines are used for indicating a sewing or stitching process. See Fig. 4-1-9.

Chain Lines Chain lines, as shown in Fig. 4-1-9, consist of thick alternating long and short dashes. This line is used to show that a surface or surface zone is to receive additional treatment or considerations within limits specified on a drawing.

Drawing Line Types

All CAD systems provide the option to create various line types. The most common types that are typically standard include:

Continuous — thick and thin
Hidden or dashed
Center
Phantom
Dot

One method used to create various line types is

1. SET the LAYER and number that correspond to the desired line type; e.g., HIDDEN (This assumes that a layer with a hidden line type is existing. The concept of layers will be discussed in a later section.) Note that the new layer you have set is now displayed on the screen.
2. Select the LINE command.
3. Locate and set the cursor at the first endpoint.
4. Locate and set the cursor at the second endpoint. A hidden line will appear as shown in Fig. 4-1-12.
5. Press ENTER to set the line.
6. For different types of lines select the appropriate layer number that

TYPE OF LINE	APPLICATION	DESCRIPTION
VISIBLE LINE THICK	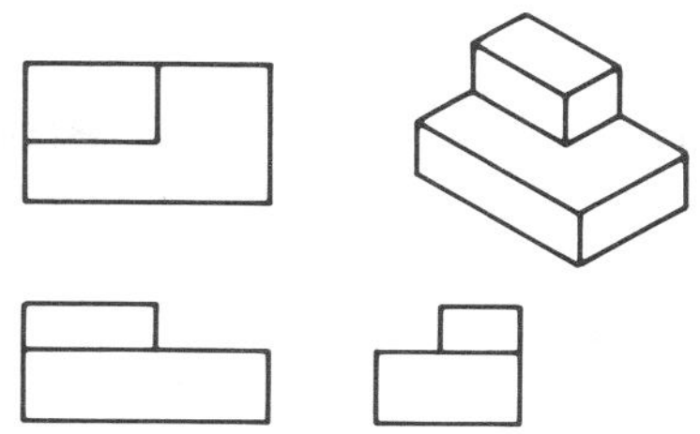	THE VISIBLE LINE IS USED TO INDICATE ALL VISIBLE EDGES OF AN OBJECT. THEY SHOULD STAND OUT CLEARLY IN CONTRAST TO OTHER LINES SO THAT THE SHAPE OF AN OBJECT IS APPARENT TO THE EYE.
HIDDEN LINE THIN	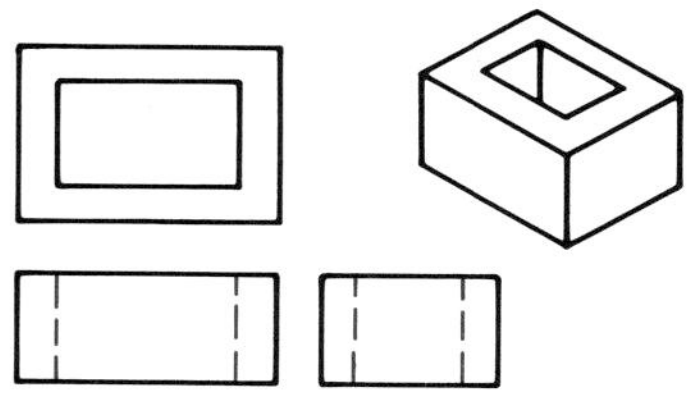	THE HIDDEN OBJECT LINE IS USED TO SHOW SURFACES, EDGES, OR CORNERS OF AN OBJECT THAT ARE HIDDEN FROM VIEW
CENTER LINE THIN ALTERNATE LINE AND SHORT DASHES	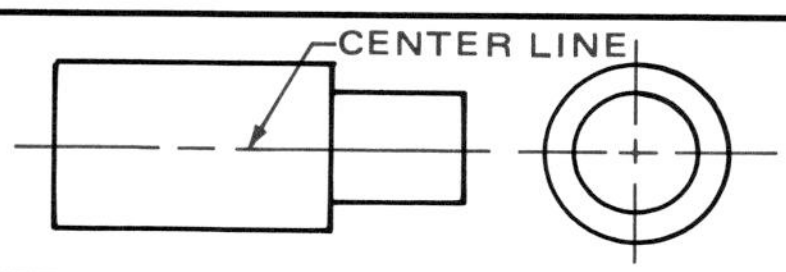 CENTER LINE	CENTER LINES ARE USED TO SHOW THE CENTER OF HOLES AND SYMMETRICAL FEATURES.
SYMMETRY LINE CENTER LINE THICK SHORT LINES	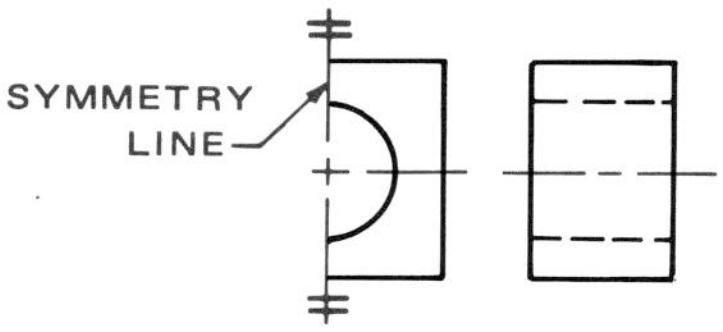 SYMMETRY LINE	SYMMETRY LINES ARE USED WHEN PARTIAL VIEWS OF SYMMETRICAL PARTS ARE DRAWN. IT IS A CENTER LINE WITH TWO THICK SHORT PARALLEL LINES DRAWN AT RIGHT ANGLES TO IT AT BOTH ENDS.
EXTENSION AND DIMENSION LINES THIN DIMENSION LINE EXTENSION LINE	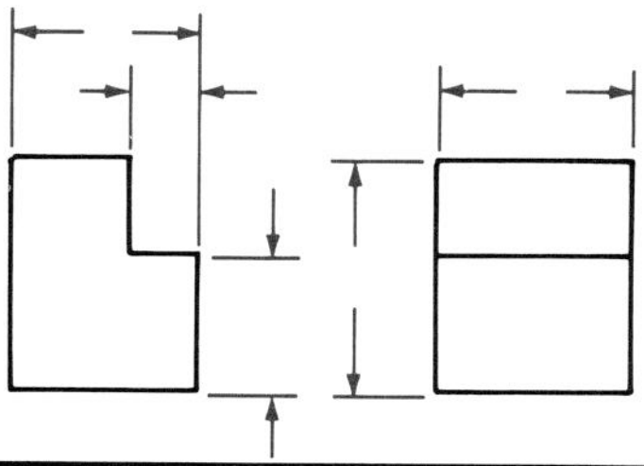	EXTENSION AND DIMENSION LINES ARE USED WHEN DIMENSIONING AN OBJECT.
LEADERS ARROW　　　　　　DOT THIN	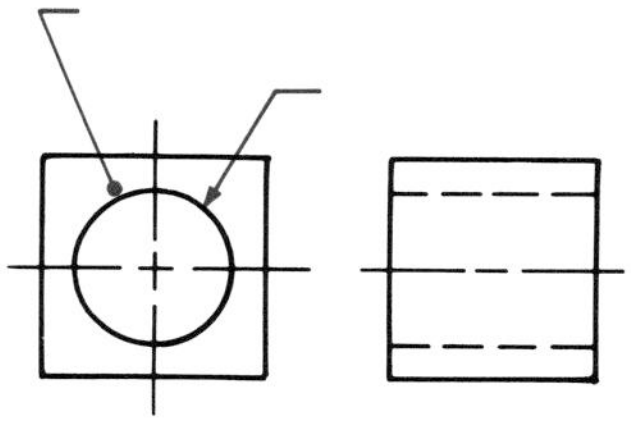	LEADERS ARE USED TO INDICATE THE PART OF THE DRAWING TO WHICH A NOTE REFERS. ARROWHEADS TOUCH THE OBJECT LINES WHILE THE DOT RESTS ON A SURFACE.
BREAK LINES THIN LONG BREAK THICK SHORT BREAK	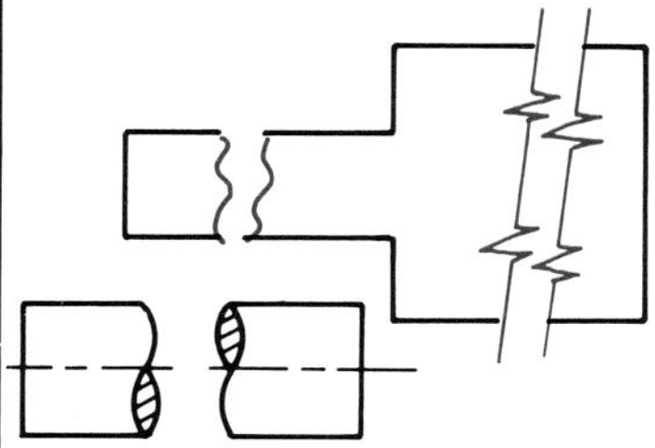	BREAK LINES ARE USED WHEN IT IS DESIRABLE TO SHORTEN THE VIEW OF A LONG PART.

Fig. 4-1-9 Types of lines.

TYPE OF LINE	APPLICATION	DESCRIPTION
CUTTING-PLANE LINE 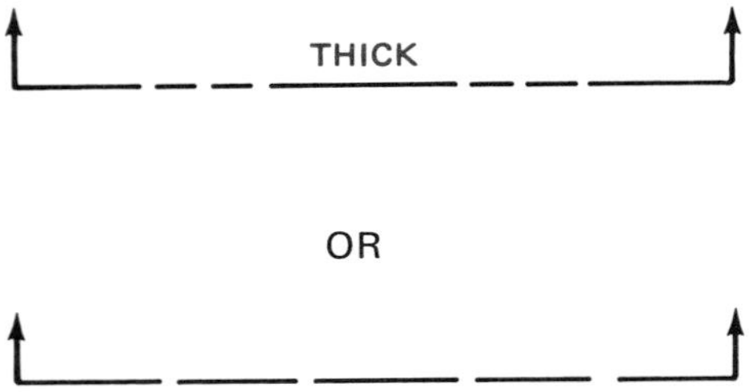 ———— —— — — ———— THICK OR ———— —— —— ———— 	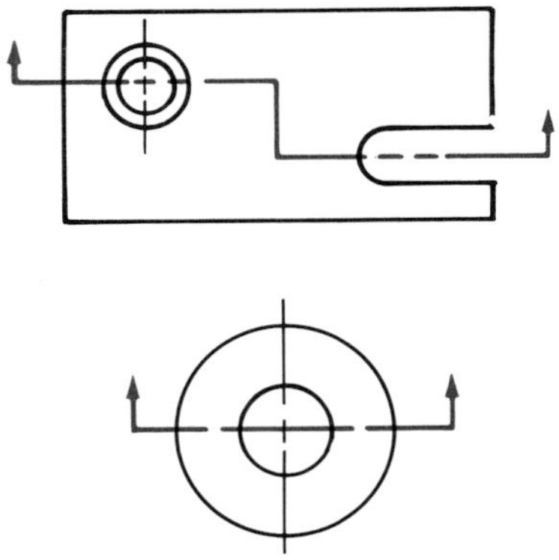	THE CUTTING-PLANE LINE IS USED TO DESIGNATE WHERE AN IMAGINARY CUTTING TOOK PLACE.
SECTION LINES 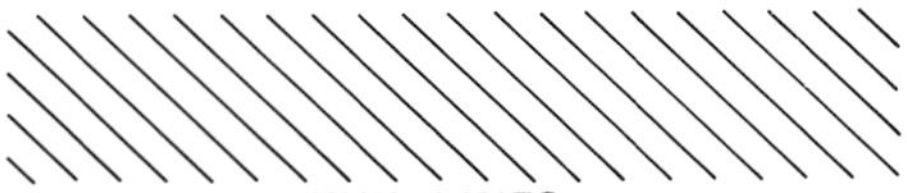 ///////////// THIN LINES	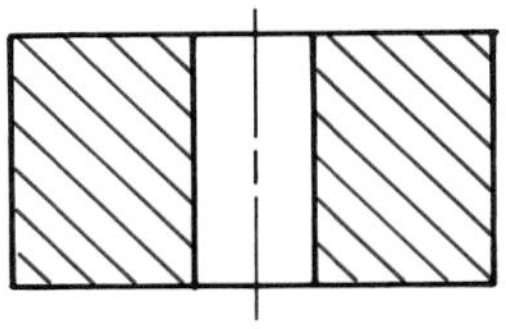	SECTION LINING IS USED TO INDICATE THE SURFACE IN THE SECTION VIEW IMAGINED TO HAVE BEEN CUT ALONG THE CUTTING PLANE LINE.
VIEWING-PLANE LINE 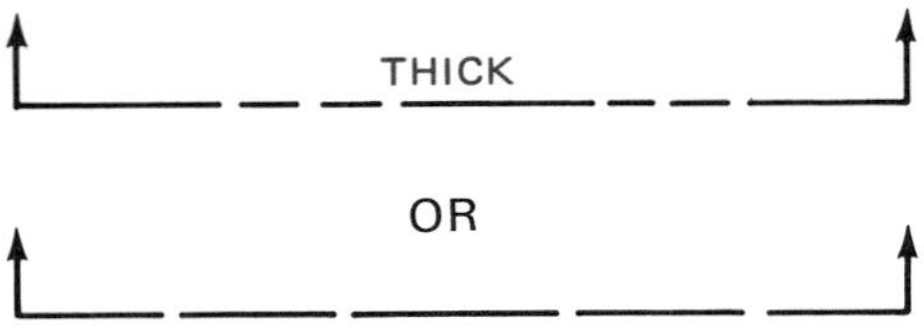 ———— —— — — ———— THICK OR ———— —— —— ———— 	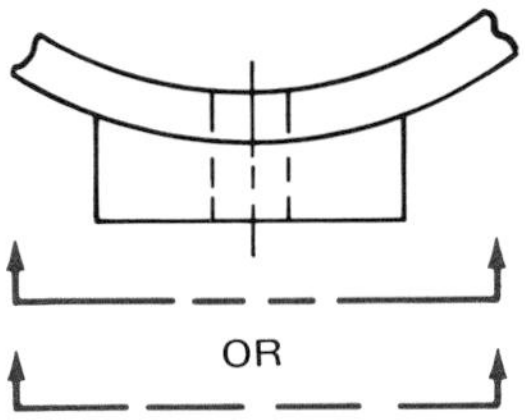	THE VIEWING-PLANE LINE IS USED TO INDICATE DIRECTION OF SIGHT WHEN A PARTIAL VIEW IS USED.
PHANTOM LINE  ———— — — ———— THIN	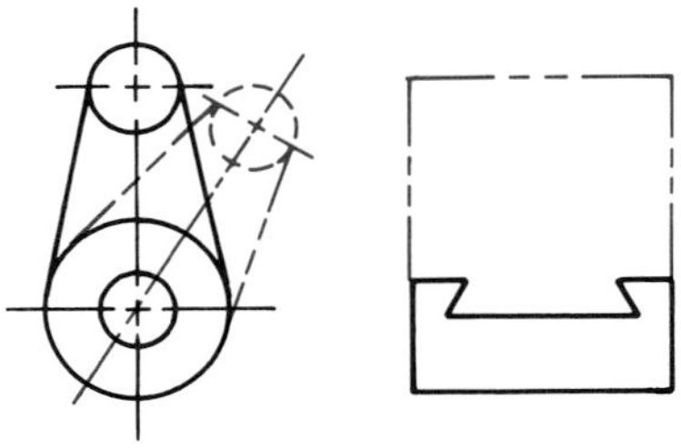	PHANTOM LINES ARE USED TO INDICATE ALTERNATE POSITION OF MOVING PARTS, ADJACENT POSITION OF MOVING PARTS, ADJACENT POSITION OF RELATED PARTS, AND REPETITIVE DETAIL. FOR PHANTOM LINE APPLICATIONS SEE FIGURE 2-6-12.
STITCH LINE 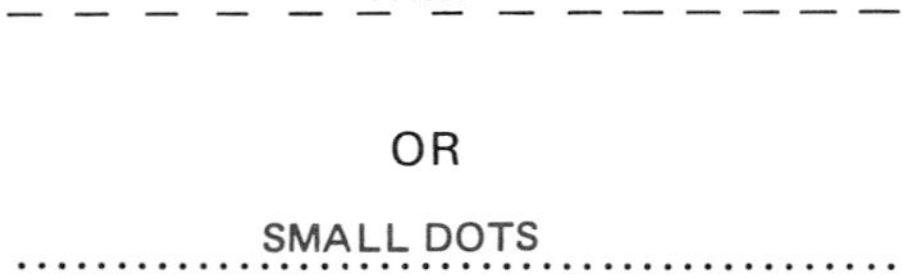 — — — — — — THIN OR ·················· SMALL DOTS	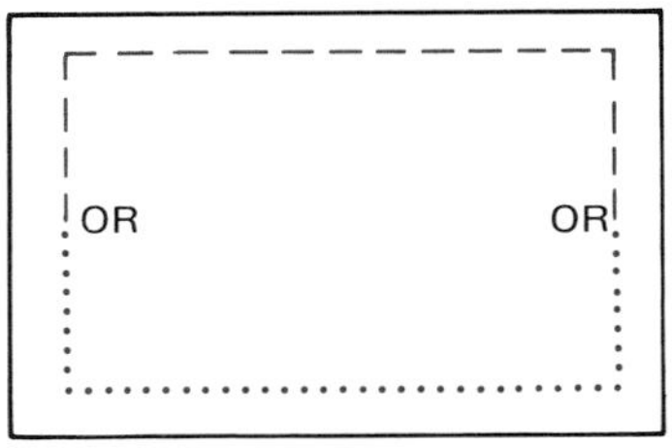	STITCH LINES ARE USED FOR INDICATING A SEWING OR STITCHING PROCESS.
CHAIN LINE 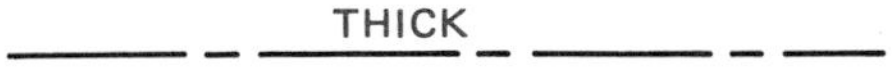 ———— — ———— THICK	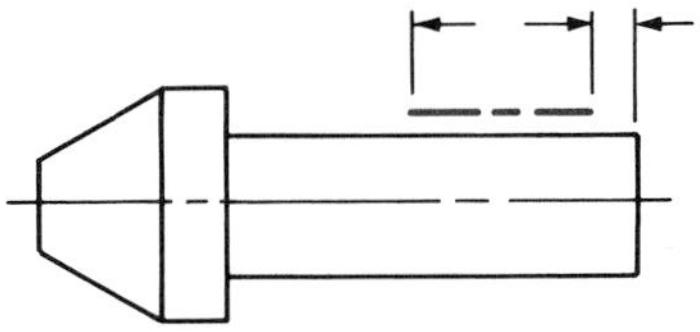	CHAIN LINES ARE USED TO INDICATE THAT A SURFACE OR ZONE IS TO RECEIVE ADDITIONAL TREATMENT OR CONSIDERATIONS.

Fig. 4-1-9 Types of lines *(continued)*.

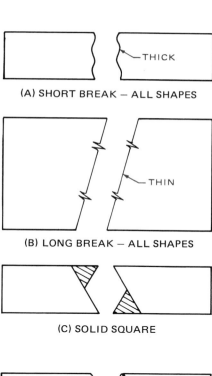

(A) SHORT BREAK — ALL SHAPES

(B) LONG BREAK — ALL SHAPES

(C) SOLID SQUARE

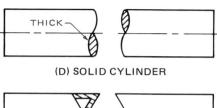

THICK

(D) SOLID CYLINDER

(E) TUBULAR (SQUARE)

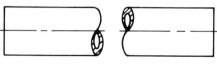

(F) TUBULAR (ROUND)

THIN

(G) WOOD

Fig. 4-1-10 Conventional break lines.

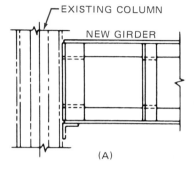

EXISTING COLUMN
NEW GIRDER

(A)

INDICATION OF ADJACENT PARTS

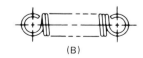

(B)

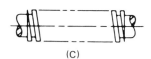

(C)

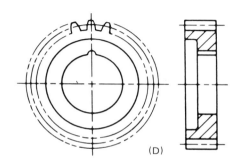

(D)

INDICATION OF REPEATED DETAIL

Fig. 4-1-11 Phantom line applications.

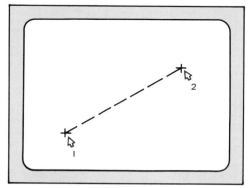

Fig. 4-1-12 Drawing line types.

corresponds to that type and repeat Steps 2 through 5.

The alternate method used to create a different line type is:

1. Select menu and submenu SET-TINGS LINETYPE, and SET.
2. Select the desired line type (e.g., HIDDEN).
3. Select the LINE command.
4. Locate and set the cursor at the first endpoint (point 1).

5. Locate and set the cursor at the second endpoint (point 2). A hidden line will appear as shown in Fig. 4-1-12.
6. For different line types select the desired option in Step 2 (e.g., CENTER).

ASSIGNMENTS

See Assignments 1 and 2 for Unit 4-1 on page 63.

■ UNIT 4-2

Drawing and Layout Form

After booting the CADD system you should set the drawing size LIMITS. This will be determined by the space that the object to be drawn will require (inside border size). For example, to create a full-scale single view of a small object will require only a small drawing size. To prepare a full scale multi-view drawing of a larger object will require a larger drawing size. There are several standard drawing sizes to choose from. At this point, it is best to select the same standard LIMITS on the monitor as the finished drawing plot (inside border size) to be produced. Be sure to use a border smaller than the maximum useful plot sizes given in Fig. 4-2-1.

Standard Drawing Sizes

U.S. Customary (Inches) Drawing sizes in this system are based on dimensions of commercial letterheads, 8.50×11.00 in., and standard rolls of paper or film 36 in. (Architectural) and 34 in. (Engineering) wide. They can be cut from these standard rolls with a minimum of waste. See Fig. 4-2-1.

Metric Metric drawing sizes are based on the AO size, having an area of 1 square meter (m^2) and a length-to-width ratio of $1 : \sqrt{2}$. Each smaller size has an area half of the preceding size, and the length-to-width ratio remains constant. See Fig. 4-2-2.

Drawing Paper Format

A general format for drawing plotter paper is shown in Fig. 4-2-3. It is recommended that a prepared standard border and title block be utilized for each new drawing. This way plots will always fit within the useful plot size.

Zoning System

Drawings larger than B size may be zoned for easy reference by dividing the space between the paper border

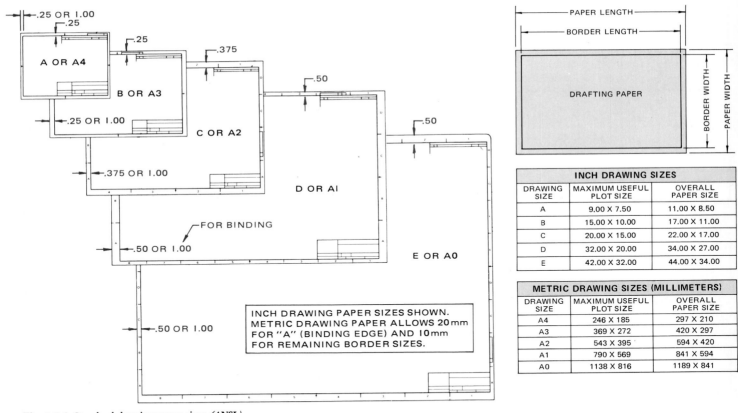

INCH DRAWING SIZES		
DRAWING SIZE	MAXIMUM USEFUL PLOT SIZE	OVERALL PAPER SIZE
A	9.00 X 7.50	11.00 X 8.50
B	15.00 X 10.00	17.00 X 11.00
C	20.00 X 15.00	22.00 X 17.00
D	32.00 X 20.00	34.00 X 27.00
E	42.00 X 32.00	44.00 X 34.00

METRIC DRAWING SIZES (MILLIMETERS)		
DRAWING SIZE	MAXIMUM USEFUL PLOT SIZE	OVERALL PAPER SIZE
A4	246 X 185	297 X 210
A3	369 X 272	420 X 297
A2	543 X 395	594 X 420
A1	790 X 569	841 X 594
A0	1138 X 816	1189 X 841

INCH DRAWING PAPER SIZES SHOWN. METRIC DRAWING PAPER ALLOWS 20 mm FOR "A" (BINDING EDGE) AND 10 mm FOR REMAINING BORDER SIZES.

Fig. 4-2-1 Standard drawing paper sizes. *(ANSI.)*

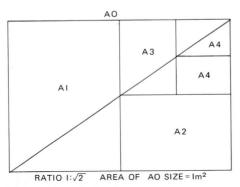

Fig. 4-2-2 Metric drawing paper.

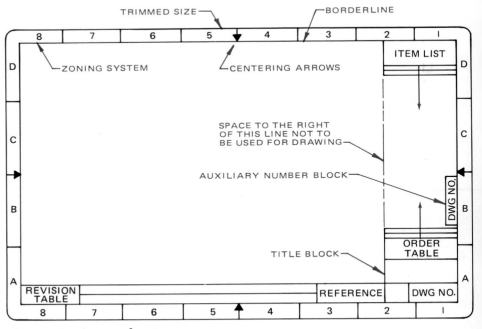

Fig. 4-2-3 Drawing paper format.

and the inside border into zones measuring 4.25×5.50 in. These zones are numbered horizontally and lettered vertically, with uppercase letters, from the lower right-hand corner, as in Fig. 4-2-3, so that any area of the drawing can be identified by a letter and a number, such as B3.

Marginal Marking

In addition to zone identification, the margin may also carry fold marks to enable folding and a graphical scale to

facilitate reproduction to a specific size. It has become common practice to put a centering arrow or mark on at least three sides of the drawing. Most

practices include the arrows on each of the four sides. If three sides are used, the arrows should be on the two sides and on the bottom.

Title Blocks and Tables

Title Block The title block is located in the lower right-hand corner on the monitor and finished plot. The arrangement and size of the title block are optional, but the following information should be included:

1. Drawing number
2. Name of firm or organization
3. Scale
4. Title or description

Provision may also be made within the title block for the date of issue, signatures, approvals, sheet number, drawing size, job, order, or contract number; references to this or other documents; and standard notes such as tolerances or finishes. An example of a typical title block is shown in Fig. 4-2-4. In classrooms, a title strip is often used on A and B size drawings, such as shown in Fig. 4-2-5.

NORDALE MACHINE COMPANY PITTSBURGH, PENNSYLVANIA		
COVER PLATE		
MATERIAL- M S		NO. REQD- 4
SCALE- 1 : 2	DN BY D Scott	A - 7628
DATE- 90-03-06	CH BY [illegible]	

Fig. 4-2-4 Title block.

Item List and Order Table The whole space above the title block, with the exception of the auxiliary number block, should be reserved for tabulating materials, change of order, and revision as shown in Fig. 4-2-6. Drawing in this space should be avoided.

Change or Revision Table All drawings should carry a change or revision table, either down the right-hand side or across the bottom. In addition to the description of drawing changes, provision may be made for recording a revision symbol zone location, issue number, date, and approval of the change. Typical revision tables are shown in Fig. 4-2-7.

Auxiliary Number Blocks An auxiliary number block, approximately 2.00 × .25 in. (50 × 10 mm) is placed above the title block so that when prints are folded, the number will appear close to the top right-hand corner of the print, as in Fig. 4-2-3. This is done to facilitate identification when the folded prints are filed on edge.

Auxiliary number blocks are usually placed within the inside border, but they may be placed in the margin outside the border line if space permits.

AMT	DET	STOCK SIZE	MAT.

NORALE MACHINE CO. PITTSBURGH, PENNSYLVANIA	
MODEL ______	
PART NAME ______	
PART NO. ______	
OPERATION ______	
FOR USE ON ______	
METAL ______	DIE CLEARANCE ______
TOLERANCE: ±0.5mm UNLESS OTHERWISE SPECIFIED	METRIC
LAYOUT ______	DRAWN ______
CHECKED ______	APPROVED ______
SCALE ______	DATE ______
FROM B. P. ______	DATED ______
SHEETS	SHEET	**NO.**

Fig. 4-2-6 Combined title block, order table, and item list.

DRAFTING TECHNOLOGY CALIFORNIA UNIVERSITY OF PENNSYLVANIA CALIFORNIA, PENNSYLVANIA	NAME:	DWG NAME:	DWG NO.
	COURSE:		
	DATE: APPD:	SCALE:	

Fig. 4-2-5 Title strip.

UNIT 4-3

Drawing Media

The families of drafting materials—paper and film—differ sufficiently between and within themselves to provide a wide choice of qualities and characteristics for selection of the best material for the finished drawing plot.

PAPER

Drafting papers come with a wide range of qualities—strength, permanence, translucency, etc. The distinguishing feature between drawing paper (opaque) and vellum is translucency.

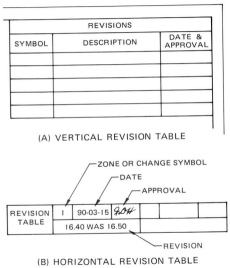

(A) VERTICAL REVISION TABLE

REVISIONS		
SYMBOL	DESCRIPTION	DATE & APPROVAL

ZONE OR CHANGE SYMBOL
DATE
APPROVAL

REVISION TABLE	I	90-03-15	𝓰𝓞𝓗		
	16.40 WAS 16.50				

REVISION

(B) HORIZONTAL REVISION TABLE

Fig. 4-2-7 Revision tables.

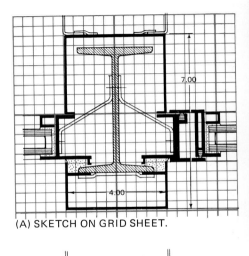

2			
I △		WAS 3.90	90-04-03 𝓰𝓞𝓗
CHANGE	DESCRIPTION		DATE & APPROVAL
REVISIONS			

(C) APPLICATION

(A) SKETCH ON GRID SHEET.

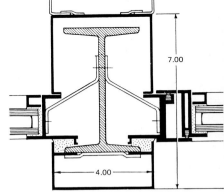

(B) PRINT OF DRAWING SHOWN IN (A).

Fig. 4-3-1 Drawing directly on preprinted grid sheet.

Opaque papers are used primarily as plotter papers due to their low cost. Because of a change in drafting practices, the need for drawing papers today is extensive. Finished plots yielding quality lettering and line work are produced at a moderate cost. If multiple copies of the drawing are necessary, do not use opaque plotting paper. Microfilming and electrostatic reproduction can reproduce prints from drawings on opaque paper; however, if many prints are required, an intermediate drawing is first plotted on a transparent paper.

Vellum is a translucent paper. A plot may be made directly on the translucent medium. This provides an option to reproduce virtually an unlimited number of quick, low-cost copies with a diazo (white) printer. In addition to good translucency, the modern high-grade vellum must be able to withstand considerable handling. The paper will retain these qualities for a long time to avoid the eventual necessity of replotting.

FILM

The most recently developed drafting medium is film. The advantages of polyester film as a drawing material are many. Raw polyester has natural dimensional stability, great tearing strength, high transparency, age and heat resistance, nonsolubility, and waterproofness. The outstanding virtue of film over any other drafting medium is that film is almost indestructi-ble. Its amazing permanence safeguards the important investment in engineering drawings and records. It is permanently translucent and waterproof and is unaffected by aging.

Polyester materials, however, present some problems. The material must be sufficiently dense to avoid reflection from the copyboard when microfilming, but translucent enough for backlighting or contact printing.

SKETCHING PAPER

This type of drawing paper is primarily used for freehand sketches and drawings. It will assist the designer or drafter to formulate his or her design ideas before beginning the CADD master drawing. It may also be used for plotter paper. There may be an occasion to match the screen grid to the finished drawing. The use of a preprinted grid the same size as the one used on the monitor will provide this option. Light cross-sectional guidelines can be preprinted directly on the paper to provide an accurate guide for all drawing work. These cross-sectional lines are available in several grid sizes. The squared and pictorial styles (isometric, perspective, and oblique) are the more common sketching papers used by drafters. Coordinate and isometric sketching paper is shown in Fig. 4-3-1.

For freehand work, grid-line papers are a valuable aid. The cross-sectional patterns serve as ready-made guides for base lines, dimensioning, and angles.

References

1. Keuffel and Esser Co.
2. *Machine Design* and National Microfilm.
3. Eastman Kodak Company.

■ UNIT 4-4

Sketching

Sketching is still a necessary part of drafting because the drafter in industry frequently sketches ideas and designs prior to making CAD drawings. Sketching may be accomplished manually (freehand) or on a CAD monitor using the SKETCH command.

The drafter may also use sketches to explain thoughts and ideas to other people in discussions of mechanical parts and mechanisms. Sketching, therefore, is an important method of communication. Practice in sketching helps the student to develop a good sense of proportion and accuracy of observation. In addition, sketch out each design. It will help determine what drawing size and what plot scale to use.

Freehand Sketching

A fairly soft (HB, F, or H) pencil should be used for preliminary practice. Many types of graph (ordinate) paper are available and can be used to advantage when close accuracy to scale or proportion is desirable. Freehand sketching of lines, circles, and arcs is illustrated in Fig. 4-4-1.

Since the shapes of objects are made up of flat and curved surfaces, the lines forming views of objects will be both straight and curved. Do not attempt to draw long lines with one continuous stroke. First plot points along the desired line path: then connect these points with a series of light strokes.

When you are sketching a view (or views), first lightly sketch the overall size as a rectangular or square shape, estimating its proportions carefully. Then add lines for the details of the shape, and thicken all lines forming the view. See Fig. 4-4-2.

Figure 4-4-3 shows two methods of sketching circles. Figure 4-4-4 illustrates, both pictorially and orthographically, the use of graph paper for the sketching of a machine part. Coordinate and isometric sketching paper are shown in Fig. 4-4-5.

CAD Sketching

Sketching methods are valid for both manual and CAD application. Instead

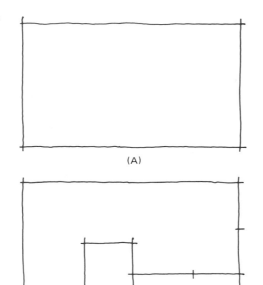

(A)

(B)

(C)

Fig. 4-4-2 Sketching a view having straight lines.

of graph paper, however, use an appropriate size grid (rectilinear or isometric) pattern on the CAD system and:

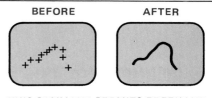

BEFORE   AFTER

THIS COMMAND PERMITS FREEHAND DRAWINGS TO BE CREATED. IT IS USED FOR IRREGULAR SHAPE APPLICATIONS.

1. Select the SKETCH (DRAW) command.
2. Set the spacing (increment) of each sketch line (e.g., .25).
3. Set the cursor at the desired starting point.
4. Move the cursor to create the sketch (curves will be represented by a series of short lines .25 in. each).
5. Issue the END (EXIT) command.
6. Repeat Steps 3, 4, and 5 for each line or curve.
7. Using the ERASE command, remove unwanted sketch lines that have been created.

ASSIGNMENTS

See Assignments 3 and 4 for Unit 4-4 on page 64.

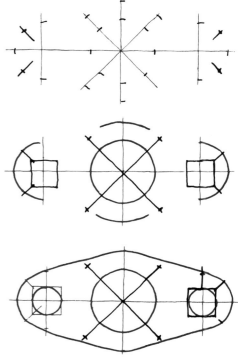

Fig. 4-4-3 Sketching a figure having circles and arcs.

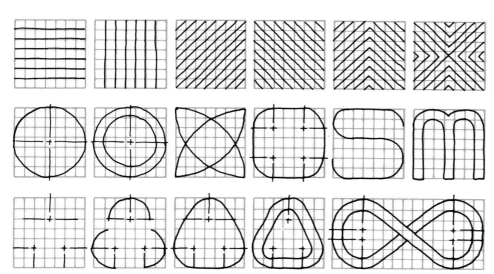

Fig. 4-4-1 Sketching lines, circles, and arcs.

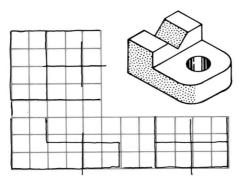

A

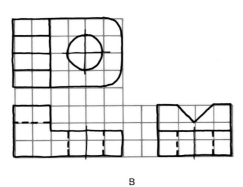

B

Fig. 4-4-4 Usual procedure for sketching three views.

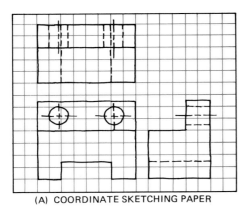

(A) COORDINATE SKETCHING PAPER

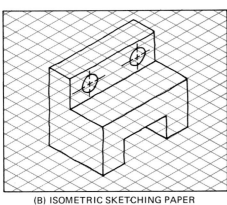

(B) ISOMETRIC SKETCHING PAPER

Fig. 4-4-5 Sketching paper.

Use of Scales

INTERPRETATION

The use of scales (measuring instruments) is not required when using a CAD system since the measurement of all entities is accurately (six decimal places) determined and stored within the microprocessor. Drafters and designers occasionally, however, will be required to measure actual parts. Consequently, an understanding of the use of scales remains a necessity.

Scales are instruments used only for measuring and are not to be used as a straightedge for drawing lines. It is important that drafters measure accurately to scale and understand scale ratios since drawings are not always plotted full scale.

When objects are drawn at their actual size, the drawing is called full scale or scale 1:1. Many objects, however, such as buildings, ships, or airplanes, are too large to be plotted full scale, so they must be plotted to a reduced

---

BEFORE   **AFTER**

Y AXIS
X AXIS

THE X AXIS IS THE HORIZONTAL AXIS ON THE GRAPHICS MONITOR. THE Y AXIS IS THE VERTICAL AXIS ON THE GRAPHICS MONITOR. THE AXES MAY BE MARKED WITH RULER LINES.

---

scale. An example would be the plotted drawing of a house to a scale of ¼ in. = 1 ft. (U.S. Customary) or 1:50 (metric).

Frequently, objects such as small watch parts are plotted larger than their actual size so that their shape can be seen clearly. Such a drawing has been plotted to an enlarged scale. The minute hand of a wristwatch, for example, could be plotted to a scale of 4:1.

Many mechanical parts are plotted to half-inch scale, 1:2; one-fourth-inch scale, 1:4; or metric scale, 1:5. Notice that the scale is expressed as an equation. The left side of the equation represents a unit of the size plotted; on

the right side, a unit of the actual drawing equals two, four, or five units of measurement of the actual object.

Drafting scales are made with a variety of combined scales marked on their surfaces. This combination of scales spares the drafter the necessity of calculating the sizes to be drawn when working to a scale other than full size.

METRIC SCALES

The linear unit of measurement for mechanical drawings is the millimeter. Scale multipliers and divisors of 2 and 5 are recommended, which give the scales shown in Fig. 4-5-1.

The numbers shown indicate the difference in size between the drawing and the actual part. For example, the ratio 10:1 shown on the drawing means that the drawing is 10 times the actual size of the part, whereas a ratio of 1:5 on the drawing means the object is 5 times smaller than shown on the drawing.

The units of measurement for architectural drawings are the meter and millimeter. The same scale multipliers and divisors as used for mechanical drawings are used for architectural drawings.

U.S. CUSTOMARY SCALES

Inch Scales There are three types of scales which show various values that are equal to 1 inch (in.) (Fig. 4-5-2). They are the decimal inch scale, the fractional inch scale, and the scale which has divisions of 10, 20, 30, 40, 50, 60, and 80 parts to the inch. The last scale is known as the civil engineer's scale. It is used for making maps and charts. The divisions or parts of an inch can be used to represent feet, yards, rods, or miles. The decimal inch scale is the scale recommended for engineering drawings when U.S. Customary units are required. The full scale is divided into 50 units to the inch (.02 spacing); the half scale into 20 units to the inch (.10 spacing). See Fig. 4-5-2.

On fractional inch scales, multipliers or divisors of 2, 4, 8, and 16 are used, offering such scales as full size, half size, quarter size, etc.

Foot Scales These scales are used mostly in architectural work. See Fig. 4-5-3. They differ from the inch scales in that each major division represents

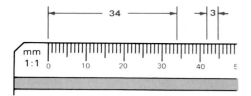

1:1 SCALE (1 mm DIVISIONS)

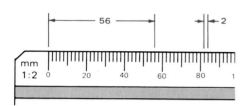

1:2 SCALE (2 mm DIVISIONS)

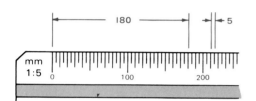

1:5 SCALE (5 mm DIVISIONS)

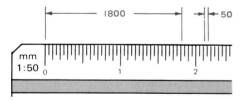

1:50 SCALE (50 mm DIVISIONS)

ENLARGED	SIZE AS	REDUCED
1000 : 1	1 : 1	1 : 2
500 : 1		1 : 5
200 : 1		1 : 10
100 : 1		1 : 20
50 : 1		1 : 50
20 : 1		1 : 100
10 : 1		1 : 200
5 : 1		1 : 500
2 : 1		1 : 1000

Fig. 4-5-1 Metric scales.

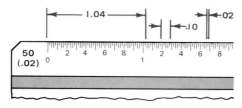

DECIMAL INCH SCALE (FULL SIZE)

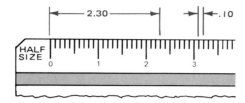

DECIMAL INCH SCALE (HALF SIZE)

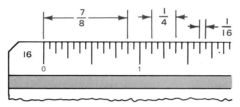

FRACTIONAL INCH SCALE (FULL SIZE)

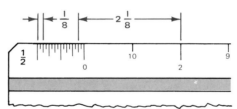

FRACTIONAL INCH SCALE (HALF SIZE)

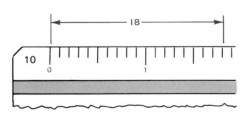

CIVIL ENGINEER SCALE (10 DIVISIONS)

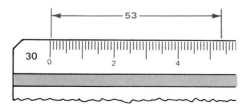

CIVIL ENGINEER SCALE (30 DIVISIONS)

Fig. 4-5-2 Inch scales.

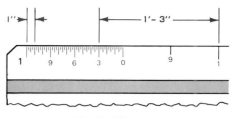

1″ = 1′– 0″ SCALE

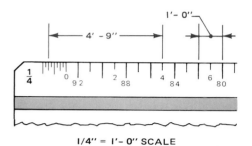

1/4″ = 1′– 0″ SCALE

Fig. 4-5-3 Foot scales.

a foot, not an inch, and the end units are subdivided into inches or parts of an inch. The more common scales are ⅛ in. = 1 ft, ¼ in. = 1 ft, 1 in. = 1 ft, and 3 in. = 1 ft. The most commonly used inch and foot scales are shown in Fig. 4-5-4.

ASSIGNMENTS

See Assignments 5, 6, and 7 for Unit 4-5 starting on page 65.

DECIMALLY DIMENSIONED DRAWINGS	FRACTIONALLY DIMENSIONED DRAWINGS	DIMENSIONED IN FEET AND INCHES	
		SCALE	EQUIVALENT RATIO
10 : 1	8 : 1	6 IN.= 1 FT	1 : 2
5 : 1	4 : 1	3 IN.= 1 FT	1 : 4
2 : 1	2 : 1	1½ IN.= 1 FT	1 : 8
1 : 1	1 : 1	1 IN.= 1 FT	1 : 12
1 : 2	1 : 2	¾ IN.= 1 FT	1 : 16
1 : 5	1 : 4	½ IN.= 1 FT	1 : 24
1 : 10	1 : 8	⅜ IN.= 1 FT	1 : 32
1 : 20	1 : 16	¼ IN.= 1 FT	1 : 48
ETC.	ETC.	3/16 IN.= 1 FT	1 : 64
		⅛ IN.= 1 FT	1 : 96
		1/16 IN.= 1 FT	1:192

Fig. 4-5-4 Commonly used foot and inch scales.

UNIT 4-6

Drawing Plotting and Reproduction

A revolution in reproduction technologies and methods began several decades ago. It brought with it new equipment and supplies which have made quick copying commonplace. The advent of 1980s high-quality, moderate-cost CAD plotters has changed this somewhat. One or two copies of a drawing may readily be produced on plotter paper using the system. If multiple copies are required, however, reproduction equipment will be utilized. One finished drawing plot, on film, vellum, or paper will be used as the master drawing. An unlimited number of low-cost copies ranging from small documents to large engineering drawings (see Fig. 4-6-1) may be produced from it. To try to utilize a plotter as a copying machine would be too slow and costly. A complex engineering drawing, for example, may require nearly a half hour to produce a pen plot. Thus, reproduction equipment will produce copies quicker, at a lower cost, and not tie-up a plotter for long periods of time. The pressures on business and government for greater efficiency, space savings, cost reductions, lower investment costs, and equally important factors provided a fertile field for the reproduction technologies. There is no reason to believe that such pressures will diminish; in fact, as the years go by, it is certain that more and more improvements will occur,

newer and better reproduction and information handling equipment and methods will be discovered, and the advantages which they offer will find ever-widening application.

PLOTTING

As a drawing is in the process of being created, preliminary copies, at various stages, may be required. These are often used for the purpose of checking the progress of the design. A quick copy from a printer (as explained in Chap. 2) will suffice. After the drawing has been completed, however, a finished plot (drawing) is made. The procedure is:

1. Connect the plotter to the CAD workstation and activate it.
   Note: CAD systems are able to plot to many different types of plotters. If more than one plotter is available, you may have to first check that the correct plotter is configured. This means that the CAD system has previously been set for this plotter.
2. Select the PLOT command.

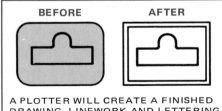

BEFORE   AFTER

A PLOTTER WILL CREATE A FINISHED DRAWING. LINEWORK AND LETTERING OF PROFESSIONAL QUALITY WILL BE PRODUCED.

Note: If the finished plot is extensive and required many hours of drawing effort, it should first be saved (refer to SAVE, Unit 4-7).

3. Questions will now be asked such as:

WHAT TO PLOT?   (e.g., DISPLAY)
ANY CHANGES?   (e.g., SET PENS or Change plot scale)

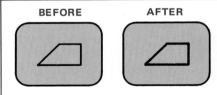

BEFORE   AFTER

A LINE OR CURVE MAY BE WIDENED AFTER THE DESIRED WIDTH HAS BEEN DEFINED BY THE USER. THIS OPTION MAY BE USED TO DISPLAY A THICK LINE ON THE MONITOR.

Remember to *follow the prompts* and issue appropriate responses such as those shown in parentheses. Plotters will not plot the full drawing area. For example, a D (34×22) size will effectively plot only 32×20 in. Remember to draw only within these limits or you will be required to reduce the plot scale. Better yet, use a predrawn stored border. Use the INSERT command to place it.

4. Position the drawing paper and pen(s) in plotter.
5. Issue the CONTINUE (or ENTER) command. The plot will now automatically be created.
   Note: A plot may at any time be terminated by issuing the CTRL and C key command.
6. After the finished drawing has been removed from the plotter remember to:
   a. replace the pen covers to keep the pens from drying out
   b. disconnect plotter from workstation
   c. switch off the plotter

REPRODUCTION EQUIPMENT

Studies of reproduction facilities, existing or proposed, should first consider the nature of the demand for this service, then the processes which best satisfy the demand, and finally the particular machines which employ the processes. Factors to consider at these stages of study include:

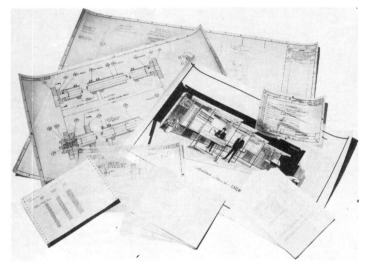

Fig. 4-6-1 Drawing reproduction. *(Eastman Kodak Co.)*

- Input originals—sizes, paper mass, color, artwork
- Quality of output copies—depending on expected use and degree of legibility required
- Size of copies—same size, enlarged, reduced
- Color—copy paper and ink
- Registration—in multiple-color work
- Volume—numbers of orders and copies per order
- Speed—machine productivity, convenient start-stop, and load-unload
- Cost—direct labor, direct material, overhead
- Future requirements—increase on decrease quantities

Two general kinds of reproduction are recognized: *copying* and *duplicating*.

Copying machines are suitable for both line work and pictorials, often on large sheets. They operate at slow speeds, and so the cost per copy is relatively high.

In contrast, duplicating processes are characterized by high speed, high volume, and low cost per copy. They can be used with a wide variety of papers in many sizes, masses, and finishes. Although duplicators—spirit, stencil, and offset—are used in conjunction with copying machines in the engineering and drafting offices, they will not be covered in this text.

Copiers

The principal methods used to produce copies are by the diazo process, photoreproduction, and microforming.

Blueprinting was the classical process for copying engineering drawings. It provided white lines on a blue background. Blueprinting has been replaced, mainly by diazo.

Diazo Process (Whiteprint)

In this process (Figs. 4-6-2 and 4-6-3), paper or film coated with a photosensitive diazonium salt is exposed to light passing through an original of translucent paper or film. The exposed coated sheet is then developed by an alkaline agent such as ammonia vapor. Where the light passes through the clear areas of the master, it decomposes the diazonium salt, leaving a

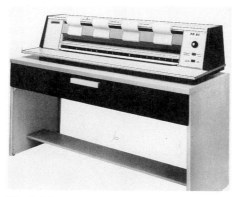

Fig. 4-6-2 A whiteprint machine. *(Bruning.)*

clear area on the copy. Where markings on the original block the light, the ammonia and the unexposed coating produce an opaque dye image of the original markings. A positive original makes a positive copy, and a negative original makes a negative copy. Therefore, the polarity is said to be nonreversing. The three diazo processes currently used differ mainly in the way the ammonia is introduced to the diazo coat. These are ammonia vapor, moist developing, and pressure developing.

Perhaps the most significant characteristic of the diazo process is that it allows reproduction of fine detail. Diazo is a high-contrast process and thus ideal for document reproduction. The diazo process is the most economical method of making prints. The main disadvantages to this process are that only full-size prints can be made and the plot must be made on a transluscent material.

Photoreproduction

Photoreproduction (electrostatic) is one of the newest and most versatile methods for reproducing engineering drawings. There is no need to use transparent originals. It prints on bonds, vellums, and drafting film, in sizes from 8.50×11.00 in. to up to 36.00 in. wide by any manageable length. Each print can be used as another original at any time. It is ideal for cut-and-paste drafting. One such printer offers, in addition to 1 : 1 printing, several reduction settings by which a drawing can be physically reduced in size. See Fig. 4-6-4. Photoreproduction printers can duplicate plotter originals on vellum or polyester for reproduction on diazo (whiteprint) machines.

Photographic

Photography is the process of creating latent images on light-sensitive silver halide material by exposure to light. The images are made visible and permanent by developing and fixing techniques. A camera provides for enlargement or reduction of the image size.

Contact printing and projection printing are the two principal methods of making photographic prints—contact for prints the same size as originals and projection for reduced or enlarged prints.

MICROFORM

Microforming of engineering drawings is now an established practice in many drafting offices. See Fig. 4-6-5.

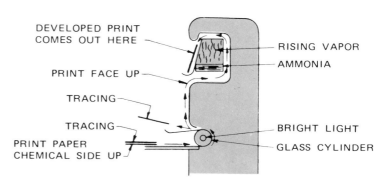

DEVELOPED PRINT COMES OUT HERE — RISING VAPOR
— AMMONIA
PRINT FACE UP
TRACING
TRACING — BRIGHT LIGHT
PRINT PAPER CHEMICAL SIDE UP — GLASS CYLINDER

ROLLERS MOVE THE TRACING AND PRINT AROUND THE LIGHT, AND MOVE THE PRINT PAST THE RISING AMMONIA VAPOR.

Fig. 4-6-3 The diazo process.

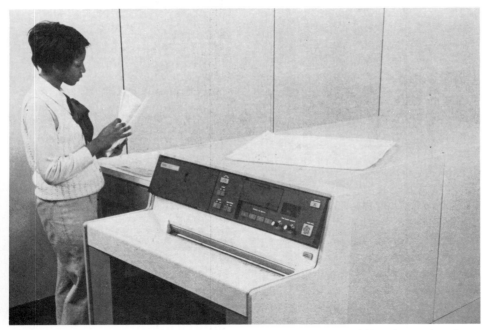

Fig. 4-6-4 Photoreproduction process. This machine will reproduce, reduce, fold, and sort prints. *(Xerox Corp.)*

Fig. 4-6-6 Aperture cards. *(Eastman Kodak Co.)*

Fig. 4-6-5 Microforming. *(3M Co. and American Motors Co.)*

This has come about because of the primary savings in lower transportation, labor, and storage costs of microfilm.

Microform prints are B size, regardless of their original size, and are much easier to handle and store. From the drafting room, drawings are taken to a camera, photographed, and stored in rolls or in cards.

FORMS OF FILM

One way to classify microfilm is according to the physical forms, called *microforms*, in which it is used.

Roll Film This is the form of the film after it has been removed from the camera and developed. Microfilm comes in four different widths — 16, 35, 70, and 105 mm — and is stored in magazines.

Aperture Cards Perhaps the simplest of the flat microforms is finished roll film cut into separate frames, each mounted on a card having a rectangular hole as shown in Fig. 4-6-6. Aperture cards are available in many sizes.

Jackets Jackets are made of thin, clear plastic and have channels into which short strips of microfilm are inserted. They come in a variety of film channel combinations for 16 and/or 35 mm microfilm. Like aperture cards, jackets can be viewed easily.

Microfiche A microfiche is a sheet of clear film containing a number of microimages arranged in rows. A common size, 100×150 mm, frequently is arranged to contain 98 images. Microfiches are especially well suited for quantity distribution of standard information, parts, and service lists.

Readers and Viewers

Microform readers magnify film images large enough to be read and project the images onto a translucent or opaque screen. Some readers accommodate only one microform (rolls, jackets, microfiches, or aperture cards), while others can be used with two or more. Scanning-type readers, having a variable-type magnification, are used when frames containing a large drawing are viewed. Generally, only parts of the drawing can be viewed at one time.

Reader-Printers

Two kinds of equipment are used to make enlarged prints from microform: reader-printers and enlarger-printers. The reader-printer, as illustrated in Fig. 4-6-7, is a reader which incorporates a means of making hard copy from the projected image. The enlarger-printer is designed only for copying and does not include the means for reading.

ASSIGNMENTS

See Assignments 9, 10, and 11 for Unit 4-6 on page 65.

Fig. 4-6-7 Reader-printer. *(Eastman Kodak Co.)*

References

1. National Microfilming Association.
2. *Machine Design*, July 1971.

■ UNIT 4-7

Filing Systems

One of the most common and difficult problems facing an engineering department is how to set up and maintain an efficient engineering filing area. Normal office file methods are not considered satisfactory for engineering drawings. To properly serve its function, an engineering filing area must meet two important criteria: accessibility of information and protection of valuable documentation.

For this kind of system to be effective, drawings must be readily accessible. The degree of accessibility is dependent on whether drawings are considered active, semiactive, or inactive.

The filing of CAD drawings can be divided into two areas: the filing of the original drawing made by the plotter, and the filing of the original drawing in the computer.

FILING ORIGINAL PLOT DRAWINGS

Although an original drawing may be replotted from disk storage, it is not economical to tie up the plotter every time a drawing is required. It is better to store the original drawing and produce prints from it as future requirements dictate.

Unless a company has developed a full microforming system, the original drawings which the drafter produced must be kept and filed for future use

or reference. Unlike the prints, the originals must not be folded to avoid crease lines, which would appear in copies. They are filed in either a flat or rolled position. See Fig. 4-7-1.

In determining what type of equipment to use for engineering files, it should be remembered that different types of drawings require different kinds of files. Also, in planning a filing system, keep in mind that filing requirements are always increasing; unlike normal office files that can be purged each year, the more drawings produced, the more need to be stored. Therefore, any filing system must have the flexibility of being easily expanded, and generally in a minimum of space.

FILING DRAWINGS ON HARD DRIVE OR FLOPPY DISK

Once a drawing has been completed on a CAD system, it may be magnetically stored on disk. To accomplish this, first issue the SAVE command. Follow the prompts keying in the name for the drawing you wish to save. The drawing will be saved on the hard drive filing directory. When working

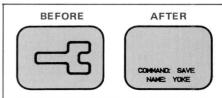

IT IS DESIRABLE TO PERIODICALLY UPDATE THE DRAWING FILE TO DISK. THIS WAY IN THE EVENT OF A POWER FAILURE OR LOCK UP, ONLY WORK SINCE THE LAST SAVE WILL BE LOST.

on a complex drawing, it is advisable to save the drawing every so often (e.g. after 45 minutes). This way, in the event of a malfunction, such as a power interruption or lockup, only work accomplished since the last save will be lost.

Drawings saved to the hard drive are filed by the name used to save it. All drawings on file may be on the screen by issuing LIST DRAWING FILES option under the FILES command on the FILE UTILITIES main menu.

Drawings may be permanently filed by "off-loading" to a floppy disk. In this case a previously formatted floppy must be placed into the floppy drive (e.g., drive A). After issuing the SAVE command, key in the drive destination and a colon before the drawing name A: CAD1, for example, and press ENTER. Remove the floppy. It is then taken to a safe storage area and filed, by project number. At the user's discretion, it may be retrieved and re-loaded back into any compatible CAD system. When the prompt requests the NAME OF DRAWING TO EDIT, key in A: CAD1 and press ENTER. The drawing will reappear on the screen to be used by the CAD drafter.

AFTER A DRAWING IS COMPLETE, IT MAY BE PERMANENTLY STORED. A COMMON FILING PROCEDURE INVOLVES "OFF-LOADING" THE CONTENTS ONTO A FLOPPY DISK PRIOR TO STORAGE.

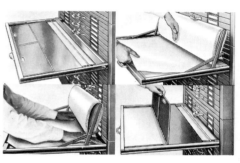

Fig. 4-7-1 Filing systems. (A) Vertical filing. *(Ulrick Plan File.)* (B) Horizontal filing. *(A.M. Bruning.)*

A new disk may easily be formatted using the SHELL command or by exiting to the disk operating system (DOS). In either case properly insert the floppy disk (Fig. 2-2-8B) in drive A, key in FORMAT A: and press ENTER twice. Other disk manipulation (DELETE, RENAME, COPY) are conducted under the FILE UTILITIES menu.

MICROFORM FILING SYSTEMS

It seems logical that reducing drawings to tiny images on film would make them even more difficult to locate. However, this is not the case, for while they are reduced in size, they are made more uniform. This results in improved file arrangements.

Roll Film Roll film can be coded in several ways for visual or automatic retrieval. The more common methods used are flash cards, code lines, sequential numbering image control, and binary code patterns.

Aperture Cards In many respects, aperture cards have the same filing and retrieval capabilities as jackets and microfiches. However, there is one important difference. It is possible to use aperture cards in machine records handling systems. They can be printed, punched, and sorted by machine.

Jackets and Microfiches Both these microforms are basically the same with respect to retrieval. See Fig. 4-7-2. Each has a title header for identifying numbers and titles. Each jacket or microfiche contains a group of images arranged in a logical sequence so that the particular images can be readily found.

Fig. 4-7-2 Microfilm jacket. *(Eastman Kodak Co.)*

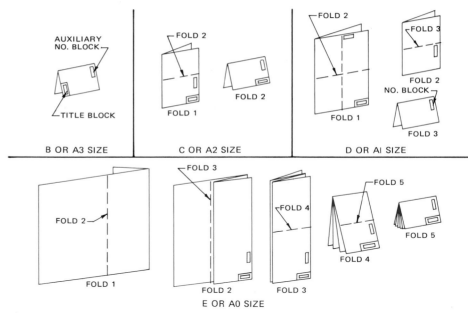

Fig. 4-7-3 Folding prints.

FOLDING OF PRINTS

To facilitate handling, mailing, and filing, prints made from the drawing should be folded to letter size, 8.5 × 11 in. (210 × 297 mm), in such a way that the title block and auxiliary number always appear on the front face and the last fold is always at the top. In filing, this prevents other drawings from being pushed into the folds of filed prints.

Recommended methods of folding standard-size prints are illustrated in Fig. 4-7-3.

On preprinted forms, it is recommended that fold marks be included in the margin of the drawings on size B and larger and be identified by number, for example, "fold 1," "fold 2." In zoned prints, the fold lines will coincide with zone boundaries; but they should, nevertheless, be identified.

To avoid loss of clarity by frequent folding, important details should not be placed close to fold areas.

Reference

1. Eastman Kodak Company and "Setting Up and Maintaining an Effective Drafting Filing System." *Reprographics*, March 1975.

ASSIGNMENTS FOR CHAPTER 4

Assignments for Unit 4-1, Lettering and Line Work

1. Text assignment. Set up an A3 or B size drawing similar to that shown in Fig. 4-1-A.

Using uppercase lettering shown in Fig. 4-1-A complete each line. Each letter and number is to be keyed several times. Vary each height as shown (bracketed dimensions are in millimeters).

2. Set up an A3 or B size having a .25 in. grid pattern. Create the line type drawing as shown in Fig. 4-1-B. Plot the drawing using a thick pen for the continuous, cutting plane, and leader line. Use a thin pen for the center and hidden lines.

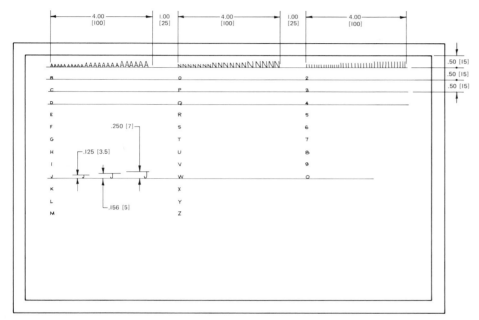

Fig. 4-1-A Text assignment.

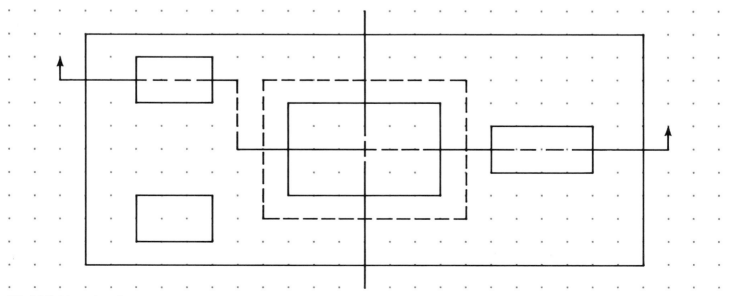

Fig. 4-1-B Line style assignment.

Assignments for Unit 4-4, Sketching

3. On an A3 or B size drawing, create the line graph shown in Fig. 4-4-A. Use a .50 in. grid and the SKETCH command to construct the curved graph line.

4. On an A3 or B size, lay out the pattern for the table leg shown in Fig. 4-4-B. Plot Scale 1:2. Select the appropriate Limits and draw full scale.

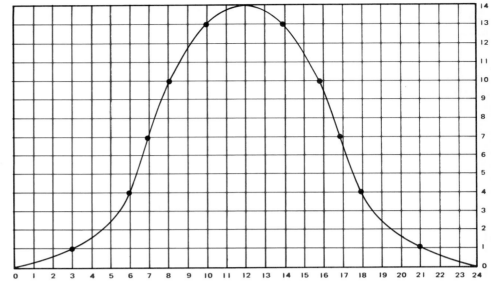

Fig. 4-4-A Line graph.

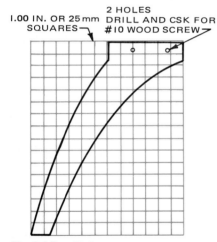

Fig. 4-4-B Table leg.

Assignments for Unit 4-5, Use of Scales

5. Using the scales shown in Fig. 4-5-A determine lengths A to K.

6. Inch measurement assignment. With reference to Fig. 4-5-B and using the scale:

Half-size decimal inch scale measure distances A–F

Half-size fractional inch scale measure distances G–M

Full-size decimal inch scale measure distances N–T

Full-size fractional inch scale measure distances U–Z

7. Metric measurement assignment. With reference to Fig. 4-5-B and using the scale:

1:1	measure distances A–E
1:2	measure distances F–K
1:5	measure distances L–P
1:10	measure distances Q–U
1:50	measure distances V–Z

8. Foot and inch measurement assignment. With reference to Fig. 4-5-B and using the scale:

1″ = 1′–0″ measure distances A–F

3″ = 1′–0″ measure distances G–M

¼″ = 1′–0″ measure distances N–T

⅜″ = 1′–0″ measure distances U–Z

Assignments for Unit 4-6, Drawing Plotting and Reproduction

9. Plot the drawing prepared in Assignment 2 for Unit 4-1.

10. Plot the drawing prepared in Assignment 3 for Unit 4-4.

11. Plot drawings as assigned by your instructor from unit assignments in Chap. 3.

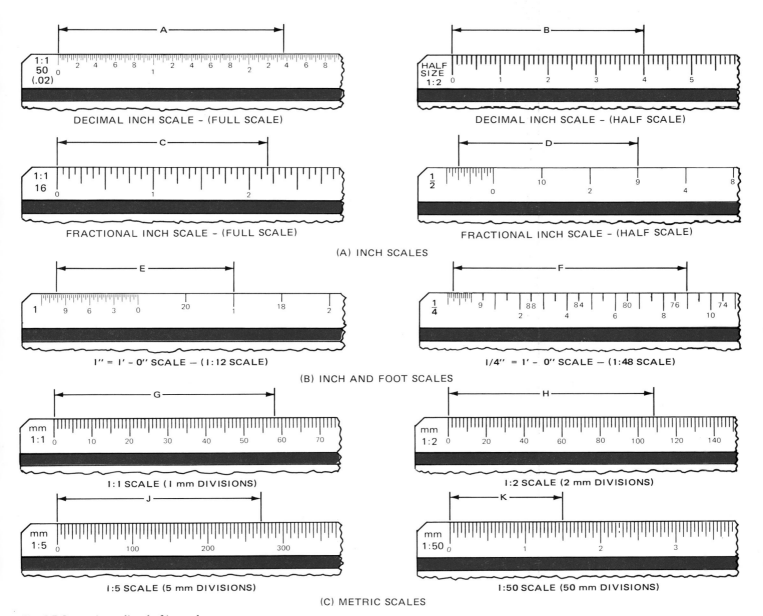

Fig. 4-5-A Test in reading drafting scales.

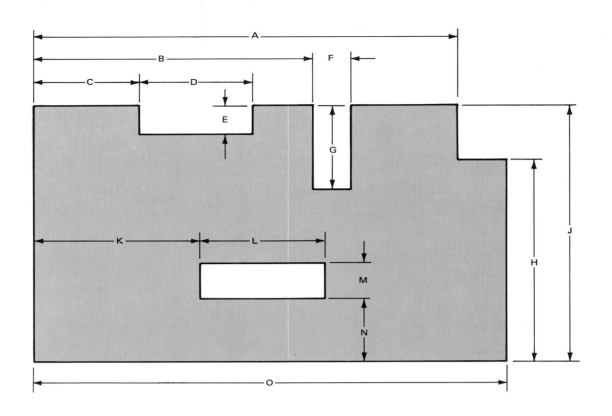

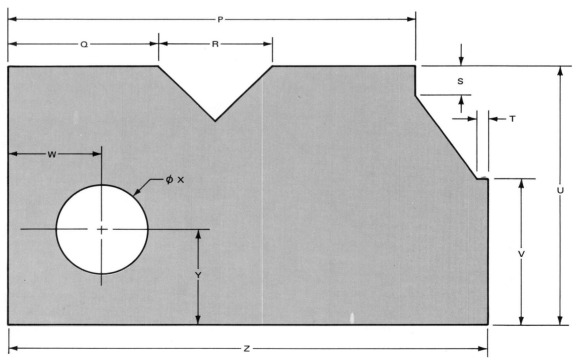

Fig. 4-5-B Scale measurement assignment.

C H A P T E R

5

Theory of Shape Description

UNIT 5-1

Theory of Shape Description

Chapter 3 illustrated many simple parts that required only one view to completely describe them. However, in industry, the parts that have to be drawn are more complicated than those previously described. More than one view of the object is required to show all the construction features.

Pictorial (three-dimensional) drawings of objects are sometimes used, but mainly the drawings used in mechanical drafting and design for completely describing an object are multiview drawings as shown under the heading "orthographic projection" in Fig. 5-1-1.

Pictorial projections, such as axonometric, oblique, and perspective projections, are useful for illustrative purposes and are frequently employed in installation and maintenance drawings and design sketches. See Fig. 5-1-2A.

As a result of CAD capability, pictorial drawings are becoming a popular form of communication, especially with people not trained to read engineering drawings. Practically all drawings of do-it-yourself projects for the general public or of assembly-line instructions for nontechnical personnel are done in pictorial form. After a multiview drawing has been prepared with all data stored in the CAD system,

an option to automatically generate the pictorial view may be executed. This view may then be plotted on the drawing medium.

SHAPE DESCRIPTION BY VIEWS

When looking at objects, we normally see them as three-dimensional, having *width, depth,* and *height,* or *length, width,* and *height.* The choice of terms used depends on the shape and proportions of the object.

Spherical shapes, such as a basketball, are described as having a certain *diameter* (one term).

Cylindrical shapes, such as a baseball bat, have *diameter* and *length.* However, a hockey puck would have *diameter* and *thickness* (two terms).

Objects which are not spherical or cylindrical require three terms to describe their overall shape. The terms used for a car would probably be length, width, and height; for a filing cabinet, width, height, and depth; for a sheet of drawing paper, length, width, and thickness. These terms are used interchangeably according to the *proportions* of the object being described, and the *position* it is in when being viewed. For example, a telephone pole lying on the ground would be described as having diameter and length, but when placed in a vertical position, its dimensions would be diameter and height.

In general, distances from left to right are referred to as width or length, distances from front to back as depth or width, and vertical distances (except when very small in proportion to the others) as height. On drawings, the multidimensional shape is represented by a view or views on the flat surface of the drawing paper.

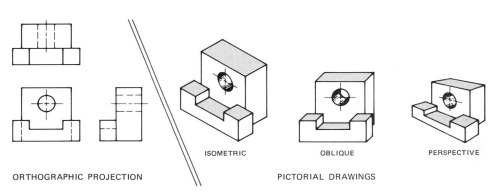

ORTHOGRAPHIC PROJECTION   ISOMETRIC   OBLIQUE   PERSPECTIVE

PICTORIAL DRAWINGS

Fig. 5-1-1 Types of projections used in drafting.

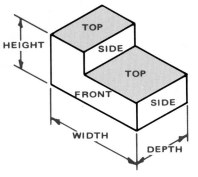

(A) PICTORIAL DRAWING (ISOMETRIC)

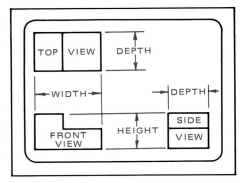

(B) ORTHOGRAPHIC PROJECTION DRAWING (THIRD ANGLE)

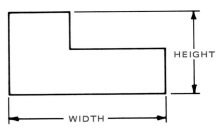

(C) ORTHOGRAPHIC FRONT VIEW

Fig. 5-1-2 A simple object shown in pictorial and orthographic projection.

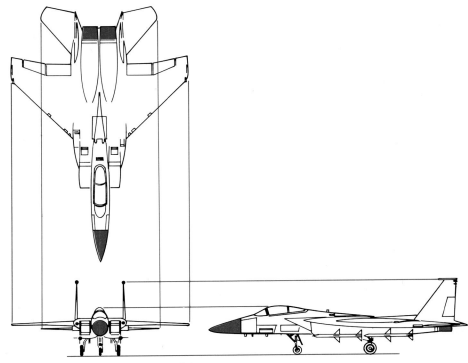

Fig. 5-1-3 Systematic arrangement of views.

ORTHOGRAPHIC PROJECTION

The drafter must represent the part which appears as three-dimensional (width, height, depth) to the eye on the flat plane of the monitor or print. Different views of the object—front, side, and top views—are systematically arranged on the monitor to convey the necessary information to the reader (Fig. 5-1-2B and 5-1-3). Features are projected from one view to another. This type of drawing is called an *orthographic projection*. The word *orthographic* is derived from two Greek words: *orthos,* meaning straight, correct, at right angles to; and *graphikos,* meaning to write or describe by drawing lines.

An orthographic view is what you would see looking directly at one side or "face" of the object. When looking directly at the front face, you would see width and height (two dimensions) but not the third dimension, depth. Each orthographic view gives two of the three major dimensions.

Orthographic Systems

The principles of orthographic projection can be applied in four different "angles" or systems: first-, second-, third-, and fourth-angle projection (Fig. 5-1-4).

However, only two systems—first- and third-angle projection—are used. Third-angle projection is used in the United States, Canada, and many other countries throughout the world. First-angle projection is used mainly in many European and Asiatic countries.

ISO Projection Symbol

With two types of projection being used on engineering drawings, a method of identifying the type of projection is necessary. The International Standards Organization, known as ISO, has recommended that the symbol shown in Fig. 5-1-5 be shown on all drawings and located preferably in the lower right-hand corner of the drawing, adjacent to the title block (Fig. 5-1-6). The ISO symbol will indicate the type of projection used. Notice that the two-view positions are interchanged. The appropriate symbol indicates how the views will appear for that type of projection.

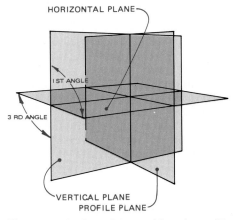

Fig. 5-1-4 The three planes used in orthographic projection.

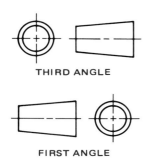

THIRD ANGLE

FIRST ANGLE

Fig. 5-1-5 ISO projection symbol.

TITLE BLOCK

Fig. 5-1-6 Locating ISO symbol on drawing paper.

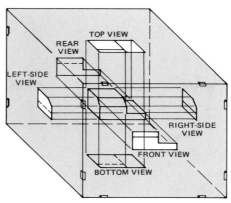

Fig. 5-1-7 Relationship of object with viewing planes in third-angle projection.

Third-Angle Projection

In third-angle projection, the object is positioned in the third-angle quad-rant, as shown in Fig. 5-1-7. The person viewing the object does so from six different positions, namely, from the top, front, right side, left side, rear, and bottom. The views or pictures seen from these positions are then recorded or drawn on the plane located between the viewer and the object. These six viewing planes are then rotated or positioned so that they lie in a single plane, as shown in Fig. 5-1-8. Rarely are all six views used. Only the views which are necessary to fully describe the object are drawn. Simple objects, such as a gasket, can be described sufficiently by one view alone. However, in mechanical drafting two- or three-view drawings of objects are more common, the rear, bottom, and one of the two side views being rarely used. Figure 5-1-9 shows simple objects drawn in orthographic and pictorial form.

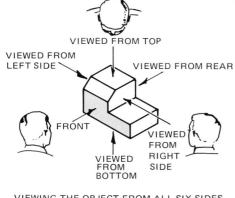

VIEWING THE OBJECT FROM ALL SIX SIDES

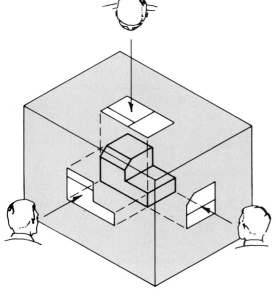

OBJECT ENCLOSED IN GLASS BOX

Fig. 5-1-8 Systematic arrangement of views.

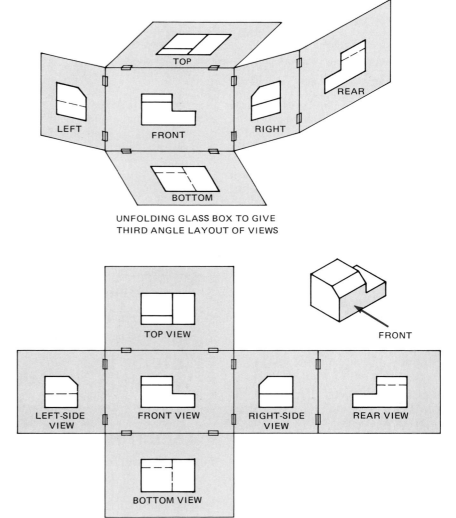

UNFOLDING GLASS BOX TO GIVE THIRD ANGLE LAYOUT OF VIEWS

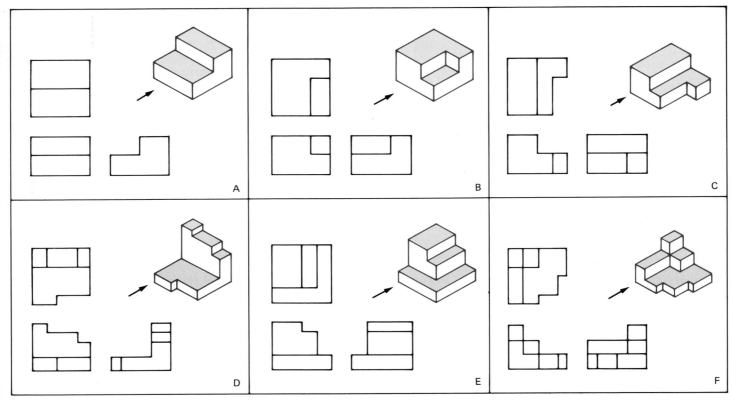

NOTE: ARROWS INDICATE DIRECTION OF SIGHT WHEN LOOKING AT THE FRONT VIEW.

Fig. 5-1-9 Illustrations of objects drawn in third-angle orthographic projection.

To fully appreciate the shape and detail of views drawn in third-angle orthographic projection, the units for this chapter have been designed according to the types of surfaces generally found on objects. These surfaces can be divided into flat surfaces parallel to the viewing planes with and without hidden features; flat surfaces which appear inclined in one plane and parallel to the other two principal reference planes (called *inclined* surfaces); flat surfaces which are inclined in all three reference planes (called *oblique* surfaces); and surfaces which have diameters or radii. These drawings are so designed that only the top, front, and right side views are required.

ALL SURFACES PARALLEL TO THE VIEWING PLANES AND ALL EDGES AND LINES VISIBLE

When a surface is parallel to the viewing planes, that surface will show as a surface on one view and a line on the other views. The lengths of these lines are the same as the lines shown on the surface view. The drawing has been made showing each side to represent the exact shape and size of the object and the relationship of the three views to one another.

ASSIGNMENTS

See Assignment 1 for Unit 5-1 on page 80.

■ UNIT 5-2

Spacing of Views and Use of a Grid Pattern to Construct a Multiview Drawing

SPACING OF VIEWS

It is important for clarity and good appearance that the views be well balanced on the finished drawing, whether the drawing shows one, two, three, or more views. The drafter must anticipate the approximate space required. This is determined from the size of the object to be drawn, the number of views, the finished drawing size selected, the scale used, and the space between views. Ample space should be provided between views to permit placement of dimensions on the drawing without crowding. Space should also be allotted so that notes can be added without crowding. However, space between views should not be excessive. Once the drawing size, scale, and number of views are established, the balancing of the three views on the monitor is relatively simple. A simple method of positioning the views is shown in Fig. 5-2-1. In this example, a distance of 1.50 in. (40 mm) is left between views. For the beginning drafter, between 1.20 to 1.50 in. (30 to 40 mm) is recommended for the distance between views.

USING A GRID PATTERN TO CONSTRUCT A MULTIVIEW DRAWING

The use of a grid pattern provides a quick and accurate method of creating a multiview drawing. It may be used

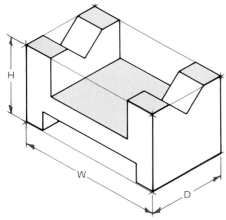

(A) DECIDING THE VIEWS TO BE DRAWN AND THE SCALE TO BE USED.

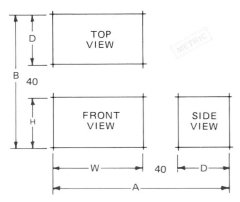

(B) CALCULATING DISTANCES A AND B

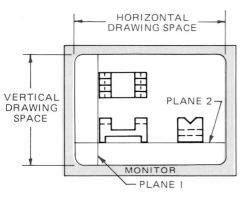

(C) ESTABLISHING LOCATION OF PLANES I and 2

Fig. 5-2-1 Balancing the drawing on the monitor.

any time the size of the object is consistent with a convenient pattern. For example, if the smallest dimension multiple on the size is .25 in., a .25 in. grid may be used. By activating the grid SNAP command, each object line will be created by "snapping" to the closest .25 in. increment.

Sequence

1. Given the pictorial, top, and front views (Fig. 5-2-2A), activate, or boot, the system by switching it on, selecting NEW drawing, keying in a drawing name (PART 1) and pressing ENTER.
2. Select the drawing LIMITS of 0,0 (lower left) and 17, 11 (upper right). Select ZOOM ALL. Select UNITS (SETTINGS) of DECIMAL, 2 place, DECIMAL DEGREES, and 2 place. Toggle back to the drawing using F1.
3. Select GRID. Key in a value equal to the smallest dimensional increment (.50) and press ENTER twice.
4. Select the SNAP increment equal to the grid value.

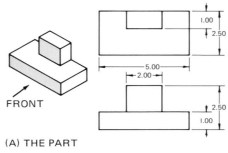

(A) THE PART

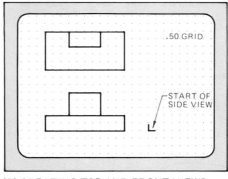

(B) CREATING TOP AND FRONT VIEWS

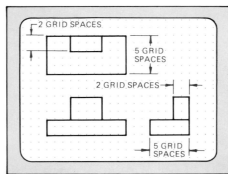

(C) CREATING SIDE VIEW

Fig. 5-2-2 Creating a multiview drawing using a grid pattern.

5. Allowing 1.50 in. (three grid spaces) between views, create the front and top views using the continuous LINE command. Since the outline of the views is comprised of several line segments, each is thought of as a *multisegment poly line*. The result is shown in Fig. 5-2-2B. To begin a new line, remember to MOVE NEXT POINT (ENTER twice) and reselect the LINE command again.
6. To create the side view: start the side view 1.50 in. (three grid spaces) from the front view.
7. Determine the depth of the object from the top view (five grid spaces). Select the LINE command. Draw the side view of the object. First, count grid spaces, then locate and set the cursor beginning at the indicated position. It will SNAP to the closest grid. Continue until the outline is complete.
8. Draw the horizontal line (two grid spaces long) inside the outline.

This completes the orthographic projection to create a three-view drawing by the grid method using the SNAP option.

ASSIGNMENT

See assignments 2 through 5 for Unit 5-2 starting on page 81.

■ UNIT 5-3

All Surfaces Parallel to the Viewing Planes with Some Edges and Surfaces Hidden

Objects drawn in engineering offices are more complicated than the ones shown in Fig. 5-3-1. Many features (lines, holes, etc.) cannot be seen when viewed from outside the piece. These hidden edges are shown with hidden lines and are normally required on the drawing to show the true shape of the object. Hidden lines consist of short, evenly spaced dashes, the length of dashes varying slightly in relation to the size of the drawing. Hidden lines begin and end with a dash except when

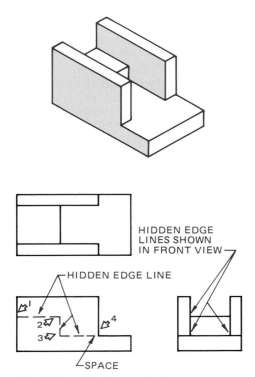

HIDDEN EDGE LINES SHOWN IN FRONT VIEW

HIDDEN EDGE LINE

SPACE

Fig. 5-3-1 Hidden line application.

The HIDDEN (or DASH) option will be located either on a submenu or a layer established for that purpose. The procedure to accomplish this is:

1. Select the HIDDEN line type. If the layer method is used, select LAYER, SET, the number corresponding to hidden lines and press ENTER twice. When plotting, a thinner pen will be used to draw the hidden lines.
2. Select the LINE command.
3. Referring to Fig. 5-3-1, locate and set the cursor at the first endpoint (point 1) of the line.
4. Locate and set the cursor at the other end (point 2). A hidden line will be drawn.
5. Locate and set the cursor two more times (points 3, 4) to produce the result shown in Fig. 5-3-1.

ASSIGNMENTS

See Assignments 7 through 10 for Unit 5-3 starting on page 82.

■ UNIT 5-4

Inclined Surfaces and Use of Construction Lines to Construct a Multiview Drawing

If the surfaces of an object lie in either a horizontal or a vertical position, the surfaces appear in their true shapes in one of the three views, and these surfaces appear as a line in the other two views.

When a surface is inclined or sloped in only one direction, then that surface is not seen in its true shape in the top, front, or side view. It is, however, seen in two views as a distorted surface. On the third view it appears as a line.

The true length of surfaces A and B in Fig. 5-4-1 is represented by a line and seen in the front view only. In the top and side views, only the width of surfaces A and B appears in its true size. The length of these surfaces is "foreshortened."

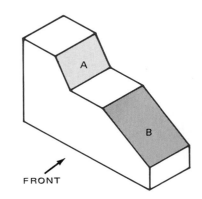

FRONT

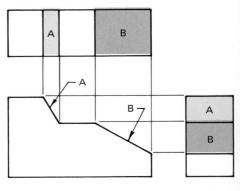

NOTE: THE TRUE SHAPE OF SURFACES A AND B DO NOT APPEAR ON THE TOP OR SIDE VIEWS.

Fig. 5-4-1 Sloping surfaces.

the dash would form a continuation of a visible line. Dashes should join at corners. Figure 5-3-2 shows additional examples of objects requiring hidden lines.

CAD systems will generally have the dash length and spacing established. Thus, when the HIDDEN LINE LAYER is SET, the dash lengths will automatically be created. This "built-in" result is referred to as a *default*. It is, however, possible to vary the length of the dash by changing the line-type scale (LTSCALE). Also, the CAD system may provide more than one dash option within the LINETYPE command.

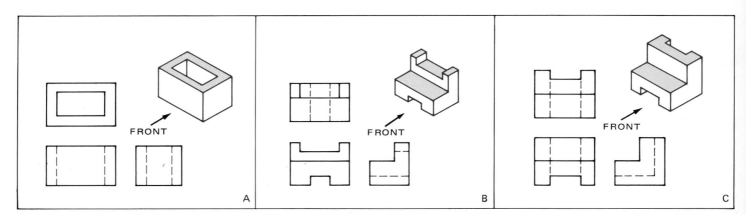

FRONT

FRONT

FRONT

A

B

C

Fig. 5-3-2 Illustrations of objects having hidden features.

Where an inclined surface has important features that must be shown clearly and without distortion, an auxiliary or helper view must be used. This type of view will be discussed in detail in Chap. 16. Figure 5-4-2 shows additional examples of objects having inclined surfaces.

USING CONSTRUCTION LINES TO CONSTRUCT A MULTIVIEW DRAWING

Constructing a multiview drawing with inclined planes is more complicated than with normal surfaces. Points and edges are not always easy to locate. Several commands must be applied to complete the drawing. Various methods such as CLOSE or TRIM are available to accomplish this. The method used in this section will involve the use of TRIM. TRIM is a handy command to know. It will "trim" (or modify) the length of two line segments back to their point of intersection. Thus, in the profile view the edge of two intersecting planes is represented as lines. Their point of intersection may be established with the use of the TRIM command.

The commands that will be used to achieve the construction of a multiview drawing involving an inclined plane (Fig. 5-4-3A) are:

LINE-CONTINUOUS
POLAR COORDINATE INPUT
TRIM
LINE-HIDDEN
ORTHO
CONSTRUCTION LINES—DOT
RELATIVE COORDINATE INPUT
ERASE

Sequence

Note: ENTER must be pressed to be able to execute many operations. Since you are now well aware of this, it will not always be stated henceforth.

1. Begin a NEW drawing using the procedure previously outlined.
2. Set LIMITS of 17,11; UNITS of DECIMAL and 2 place; .50 GRID and .50 SNAP.
3. Select the LINE command.
4. Draw the outline of the object by locating and setting the cursor at positions 1,2,3,4, and 5 as shown in Fig. 5-4-3B. Since the exact intersection at the top of the inclined surface is not known, purposefully select point 5 so that it is beyond the intersection point.
5. MOVE NEXT POINT by pressing ENTER twice (or reselect LINE) and select position 1 with the cursor.
6. To draw the inclined line that represents the inclined surface edge,

select the POLAR COORDINATE INPUT command.
7. Key in @ 3 < 120 and press ENTER. A line (from point 1) 3.00 in. long at an angle of 120° counterclockwise from the horizontal right (east) will be created as shown in Fig. 5-4-3C. Notice that the line has been drawn longer than necessary.
8. Toggle SNAP OFF (F9), and select TRIM (EDIT).

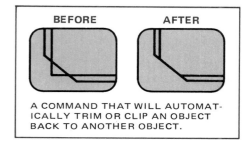

A COMMAND THAT WILL AUTOMATICALLY TRIM OR CLIP AN OBJECT BACK TO ANOTHER OBJECT.

9. Use the cursor to select the top horizontal line 6, as shown in Fig. 3-4-3D and press ENTER.
10. Select position 7, above horizontal line 6. The line will automatically be trimmed to the point of intersection as shown by position 8 in Fig. 5-4-3D. Reverse this procedure to trim the inclined line.

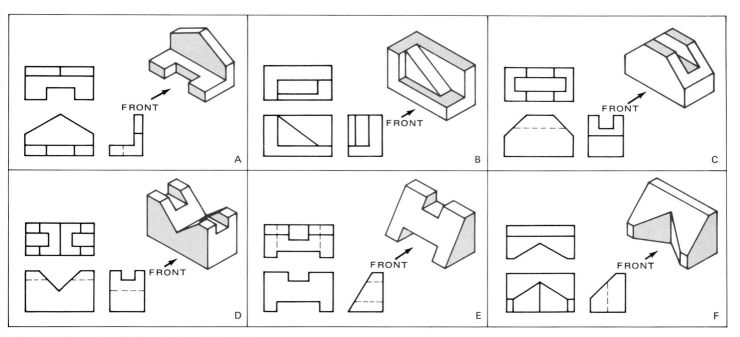

Fig. 5-4-2 Illustrations of objects having sloping surfaces.

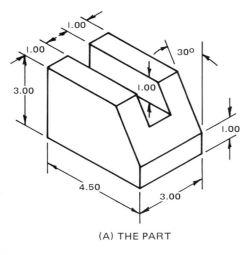

(A) THE PART

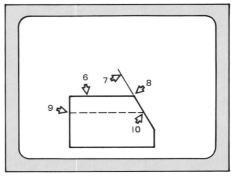

(D) TRIMMING THE LINES

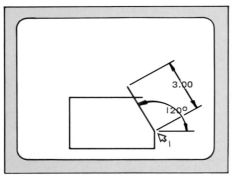

(B) CREATE THE OUTLINE ON GRID

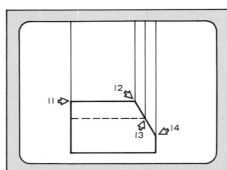

(E) ADDING CONSTRUCTION LINES TO CREATE THE TOP VIEW

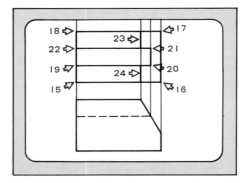

(C) POLAR COORDINATE INPUT

(F) CREATE THE TOP VIEW

Fig. 5-4-3 Creating two views of an object with a sloping surface.

11. Select HIDDEN LAYER, SNAP ON, and LINE.
12. Locate and set the cursor at the left endpoint 9, of the hidden line to be drawn.
13. Turn the GRIDS and SNAP off, and ORTHO on, by pressing function keys F7 , F8, and F9.
14. Locate and set the cursor at the right endpoint 10. Using OSNAP (****) NEAREST touch as closely as possible to the sloped line. If you miss, however, don't worry. Simply select UNDO (or

key U) and repick the point. The result will be as shown in Fig. 5-4-3D.
15. Select the CONTINUOUS LINE LAYER, LINE, and ORTHO-ON (F8) to assist vertical construction line creation.
16. Select object snap (**** INTERSECTION) each time you locate and set the cursor at positions 11,12,13, and 14 in Fig. 5-4-3E. The result will appear as shown.
17. SET the CONTINUOUS LINE LAYER, and LINE to create the

top view. Since ORTHO is on, all lines will be created horizontally or vertically only. Begin at position 15 in Fig. 5-4-3F.
18. Locate and set the cursor at the right construction line position 16. Line 15-16 is created.
19. Select RELATIVE COORDINATE (@), key 0,3 and press ENTER. Line 16 – 17 is created.
20. Locate and set the cursor at the left construction line position 18. Line 17-18 is created.
21. Select the CLOSE option and line 18 – 15 will be created.
22. Toggle the GRIDS and SNAP temporarily on. Select LINE and position 19. Toggle the SNAP OFF.
23. Locate and set the cursor on the construction line position 20. Line 19-20 is created.
24. Select RELATIVE COORDINATE, key @0.1 and press ENTER. Line 20-21 is created.
25. Locate and set the cursor on the left construction line position 22. Line 21-22 is created.
26. The final two 1.00 in. vertical lines may be drawn using the remaining construction line. Select TRIM, the four horizontal lines in the top view and press ENTER. Select above the top, below the bottom, and between the two middle lines leaving only segments 23 and 24. The completed object will be as shown in Fig. 5-4-3F.
27. The construction lines may be removed by selecting ERASE, the three lines (between the views), ENTER, and REDRAW (DISPLAY).

As you gain experience and CAD competency, you will develop alternate methods for multiview projection. For example, you could use TRIM to eliminate all the construction line segments.

ASSIGNMENTS

See Assignments 11 through 13 for Unit 5-4 starting on page 85.

■ UNIT 5-5

Circular Features

Typical parts with circular features are illustrated in Fig. 5-5-1. Note that the circular feature appears circular in

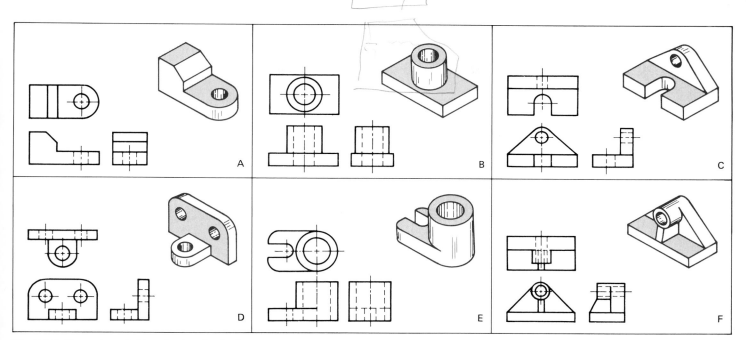

Fig. 5-5-1 Illustrations of objects having circular features.

one view only and that no line is used to show where a curved surface joins a flat surface. Hidden circles, like hidden flat surfaces, are represented on drawings by hidden lines equal to its diameter.

Center Lines

A center line is a thin, broken line of long and short dashes, spaced alternately. Such lines may be used to locate center points, axes of cylindrical parts, and axes of symmetry, as shown in Fig. 5-5-2. Solid center lines are often used when the circular features are small. Center lines should project for a short distance beyond the outline of the part or feature to which they refer. They must be extended for use as extension lines for dimensioning

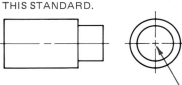

NOTE: AT TIME OF WRITING, CAD SYSTEMS DO NOT COMFORM TO THIS STANDARD.

TWO SHORT INTERSECTING DASHES AT CENTER OF CURVED SURFACE

Fig. 5-5-2 Center line application.

purposes, but in this case the extended portion is not broken.

On views showing the circular features, the point of intersection of the two center lines should be shown by the two intersecting short dashes.

The object shown in Fig. 5-5-2 may be created by using the following commands:

GRID
SNAP ON
CIRCLE-CEN,RAD
LINE-CONTINUOUS
CENTER LINE
ORTHO

Sequence

1. If the object has common decimal sizes, a grid pattern may be used to assist construction. The small diameter is 2.00×1.50 lg. and the large diameter is 3.00×4.50 lg. Thus, for Fig. 5-5-2, a .50 in. grid with the same snap increment can be used.
2. Select the CIRCLE command and submenu option CEN,RAD.
3. Locate and set the cursor at the center of the circle and at a point 1.00 in. (two grids) away. The small circle will be drawn.
4. Locate and set the cursor at the same center, and at a point 1.50 in.

(three grids) away. The large circle will be drawn.
5. SET the CENTER LINE LAYER command and DRAW the two centerlines. Be sure ORTHO is ON (F8) and SNAP is OFF (F9). Draw the center lines a short distance beyond each side of the circle. The horizontal and vertical center lines will be created as shown in the right side view as shown in Fig. 5-5-2. If the length of the long and short dashes is not suitable, select LTSCALE and try some different scale factors (e.g., .5, .25).
6. Select the CONTINUOUS LINE LAYER, SNAP ON, and LINE command.
7. Use the grid pattern (or construction lines if the sizes are uncommon values) to assist in creating the outline of the object in the front view.
8. SET the CENTER LINE LAYER, ORTHO ON, and LINE commands and turn the SNAP OFF.
9. Draw the center line by locating both ends a short distance beyond the outline of the part. The completed object will be as shown in Fig. 5-5-2.

ASSIGNMENTS

See Assignments 14 through 17 for Unit 5-5 starting on page 87.

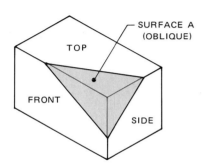

SURFACE A
(OBLIQUE)

TOP

FRONT

SIDE

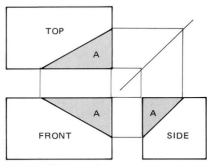

TOP

A

FRONT

A

SIDE

A

Fig. 5-6-1 Oblique surface A is not its true shape in any of the three views.

■ **UNIT 5-6**

Oblique Surfaces

When a surface is sloped so that it is not perpendicular to any of the three viewing planes, it will appear as a surface in all three views but never in its true shape. This is referred to as an *oblique surface* (Fig. 5-6-1). Since the oblique surface is not perpendicular to the viewing planes, it cannot be parallel to them and consequently appears foreshortened. If a true view is required for this surface, two auxiliary views—a primary and a secondary view—need to be drawn. This is discussed in detail under Secondary Auxiliary Views in Unit 16-4. Figure 5-6-2 shows additional examples of objects having oblique surfaces.

As with inclined surface application, the location of some corners of oblique surfaces are found by projecting points and lines from other views. For such cases, the use of construction lines, as shown in Fig. 5-6-2, and object

snap will greatly assist in the construction of views.

ASSIGNMENTS

See Assignments 18 and 19 for Unit 5-6 starting on page 90.

■ **UNIT 5-7**

One- and Two-View Drawings

VIEW SELECTION

Views should be chosen that will best describe the object to be shown. Only the minimum number of views that will completely portray the size and shape of the part should be used. They should also be chosen to avoid hidden feature lines whenever possible, as shown in Fig. 5-7-1.

Except for complex objects of irregular shape, it is seldom necessary to show more than three views. For rep-

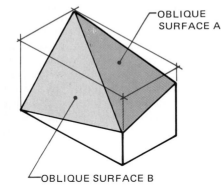

OBLIQUE SURFACE A

OBLIQUE SURFACE B

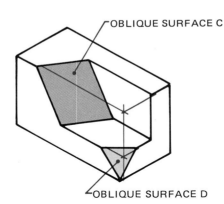

OBLIQUE SURFACE C

OBLIQUE SURFACE D

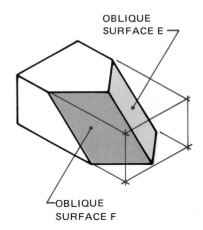

OBLIQUE SURFACE E

OBLIQUE SURFACE F

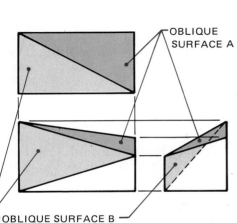

OBLIQUE SURFACE A

OBLIQUE SURFACE B

EXAMPLE 1

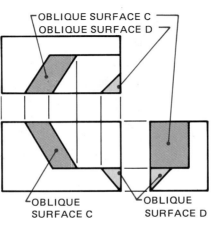

OBLIQUE SURFACE C
OBLIQUE SURFACE D

OBLIQUE SURFACE C

OBLIQUE SURFACE D

EXAMPLE 2

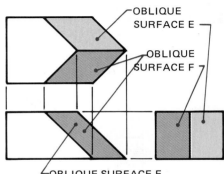

OBLIQUE SURFACE E

OBLIQUE SURFACE F

OBLIQUE SURFACE E DIRECTLY BEHIND OBLIQUE SURFACE F

EXAMPLE 3

Fig. 5-6-2 Examples of objects having oblique surfaces.

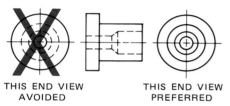

THIS END VIEW   THIS END VIEW
AVOIDED   PREFERRED

Fig. 5-7-1 Avoidance of hidden-line features.

resenting simple parts, one- or two-view drawings will often be adequate.

ONE-VIEW DRAWINGS

In one-view drawings, the third dimension, such as thickness, may be expressed by a note or by symbols or abbreviations, such as ϕ, R, T, HEX, or CSK. See Table 8 of Appendix B and refer to Fig. 5-7-2. Standard symbols will be included in the CAD software. They will normally be stored in a symbol library. Later, you will learn how to locate and use these time-saving options. For now, however, speed and productivity are not as important as learning the proper application of multiview projection.

When cylindrically shaped surfaces include special features such as a key seat, a side view (often called an end view) is required.

TWO-VIEW DRAWINGS

Frequently the drafter will decide that only two views are necessary to explain

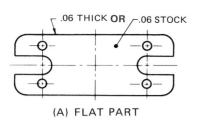

.06 THICK OR .06 STOCK

(A) FLAT PART

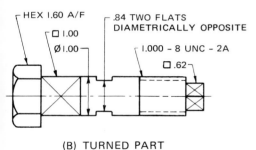

HEX 1.60 A/F
□ 1.00
Ø1.00
.84 TWO FLATS
DIAMETRICALLY OPPOSITE
1.000 – 8 UNC – 2A
□ .62

(B) TURNED PART

Fig. 5-7-2 One-view drawings.

fully the shape of an object (Fig. 5-7-3). For this reason, some drawings consist of two adjacent views, such as the top and front views only, or front and right side views only. Two views are usually sufficient to explain fully the shape of cylindrical objects; if

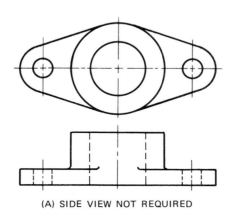

(A) SIDE VIEW NOT REQUIRED

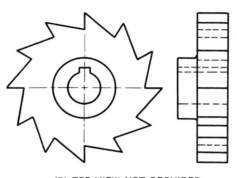

(B) TOP VIEW NOT REQUIRED

Fig. 5-7-3 Two-view drawings.

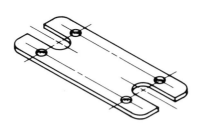

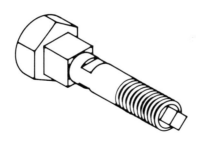

three views were used, two of them would be identical, depending on the detail structure of the part.

ASSIGNMENT

See Assignment 20 for Unit 5-7 starting on page 91.

■ UNIT 5-8

Symmetrical and Partial Views

Symmetrical objects may often be adequately portrayed by half views (Fig. 5-8-1A). A center line is used to show the axis of symmetry. Two short thick lines, above and below the view of the object, are shown at right angles to and on the center line to indicate the line of symmetry.

Partial views, which show only a limited portion of the object with remote details omitted, should be used, when necessary, to clarify the meaning of the drawing (Fig. 5-8-1B). Such views are used to avoid the necessity of drawing many hidden features. The break line shown on the object may be constructed using the SKETCH command. As an alternate, the other break line (shown to the right) may be used. This type may be constructed by using LINE and SNAP OFF.

On drawings of objects where two side views can be used to better advantage than one, each need not be complete if together they depict the shape. Show only the hidden lines of features immediately behind the view (Fig. 5-8-1C).

ASSIGNMENT

See Assignment 21 for Unit 5-8 on page 92.

■ UNIT 5-9

Enlarged, Opposite-Hand, and Rear Views

PLACEMENT OF VIEWS

When views are placed in the relative positions shown in Fig. 5-1-8, it is

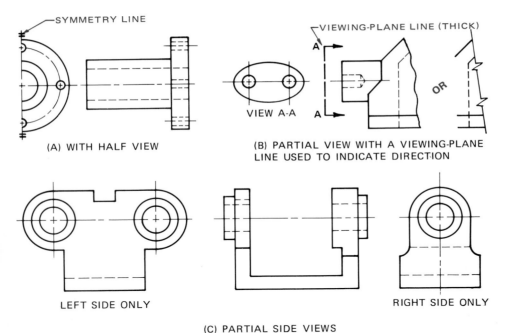

(A) WITH HALF VIEW

(B) PARTIAL VIEW WITH A VIEWING-PLANE LINE USED TO INDICATE DIRECTION

LEFT SIDE ONLY

RIGHT SIDE ONLY

(C) PARTIAL SIDE VIEWS

Fig. 5-8-1 Partial views.

rarely necessary to identify them. When they are placed in other than the regular projected position, the removed view must be clearly identified.

Whenever appropriate, the orientation of the main view on a detail drawing should be the same as on the assembly drawing. To avoid the crowding of dimensions and notes, ample space must be provided between views.

ENLARGED VIEWS

Enlarged views are used when it is desirable to show a feature in greater detail or to eliminate the crowding of details or dimensions (Fig. 5-9-1). This is similar in concept to a road map. An entire state may be represented over the map's drawing surface area. Major cities, however, will be enlarged and illustrated at another location. The main streets of a city may then be distinguished. This would not be possible on the view of the entire state. The enlarged view on an engineering drawing should be oriented in the same manner as the main view and identified as shown by any of the three methods in Fig. 5-9-1. However, if an enlarged view is rotated, state the direction and the amount of rotation of the detail. The view itself is rotated by selecting the ROTATE (EDIT) command, identifying what it is you wish rotated, and keying in the number of degrees of rotation.

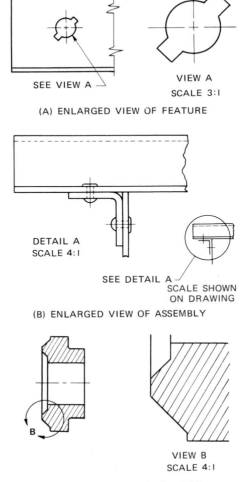

(A) ENLARGED VIEW OF FEATURE

VIEW A
SCALE 3:1

SEE VIEW A

DETAIL A
SCALE 4:1

SEE DETAIL A
SCALE SHOWN ON DRAWING

(B) ENLARGED VIEW OF ASSEMBLY

VIEW B
SCALE 4:1

(C) ENLARGED REMOVED VIEW

Fig. 5-9-1 Enlarged views.

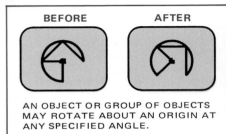

AN OBJECT OR GROUP OF OBJECTS MAY ROTATE ABOUT AN ORIGIN AT ANY SPECIFIED ANGLE.

Creation of enlarged views as shown in Fig. 5-9-1A is easy to accomplish using CAD. The commands to use are BLOCK and INSERT or SCALE (EDIT). A block will group any number of entities (lines, circles, arcs, etc.) together. A CAD system will subsequently deal with the group of entities as if they were one. Any change to one will result in the same change to all. For example, deleting one entity will delete the entire block. Once an assembly is blocked it is easy to insert any number of copies at any magnification. The procedure to block a group of entities is:

1. Select the BLOCK command.

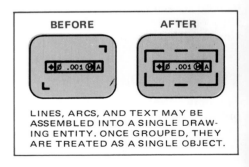

LINES, ARCS, AND TEXT MAY BE ASSEMBLED INTO A SINGLE DRAWING ENTITY. ONCE GROUPED, THEY ARE TREATED AS A SINGLE OBJECT.

2. Key in a name for the block (e.g., SLOT), press ENTER, and select a base point.
3. You may select each entity separately or group them by a WINDOW (W) option. If WINDOW is used, each entity must reside fully within the imaginary box as defined by lower left and upper right corners and press ENTER. The object will disappear.

Any block may be returned to its original state. That is, back to separate entities. Simply select the EXPLODE command and select the block you wish to explode. If you are not sure of the block's name, select BLOCK and LIST. All blocks will be presented in a list form on the monitor.

The block may now be rescaled to more clearly view the details by:

1. Select the INSERT (BLOCKS) command.

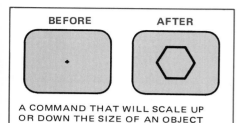

A COMMAND THAT WILL SCALE UP OR DOWN THE SIZE OF AN OBJECT OR BLOCK OF ENTITIES TO BE COPIED.

2. Select the name to be rescaled.
3. Select the location to place the feature. It will be placed with respect to a particular point on the drawing called the origin or *base point*.

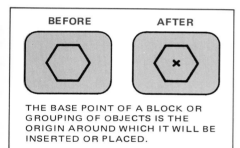

THE BASE POINT OF A BLOCK OR GROUPING OF OBJECTS IS THE ORIGIN AROUND WHICH IT WILL BE INSERTED OR PLACED.

4. In the SCALE option, key the magnification factor (e.g., 3) and 0°.

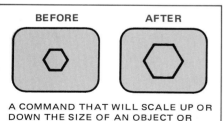

A COMMAND THAT WILL SCALE UP OR DOWN THE SIZE OF AN OBJECT OR GROUP OF OBJECTS WHEN SPECIFYING ANY SCALE FACTOR.

5. Select the TEXT command.
6. Key in the identification of the view (e.g., VIEW A and SCALE 3:1). The result will appear as shown in Fig. 5-9-1A.

If the view has been located incorrectly, it may be easily remedied by:

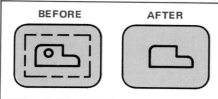

MULTIPLE ENTITIES BLOCKED INTO A SINGLE OBJECT, AS WELL AS DIMENSIONS, MAY LATER BE BROKEN APART. INDIVIDUAL ENTITIES MAY THEN BE ALTERED WITHOUT AFFECTING THE OTHERS.

1. Select the MOVE command.

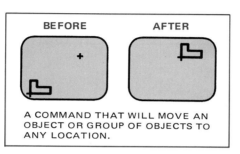

A COMMAND THAT WILL MOVE AN OBJECT OR GROUP OF OBJECTS TO ANY LOCATION.

2. Select either the block to be moved or the WINDOW option. If the WINDOW option is used, select lower left and upper right corners such that the entire view to be moved falls within the rectangle.
3. Select the BASE (initial) location.
4. Select the new location. If the DRAG option is on, you will see the object move across the screen as the cursor is moved. This will help you to better position it.

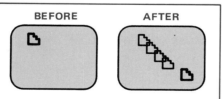

DRAGGING PROVIDES VISUAL MOVEMENT OF AN OBJECT. EACH TIME THE CURSOR IS MOVED (DRAGGED), THE OBJECT WILL BE REDISPLAYED AT THE NEW POSITION.

OPPOSITE-HAND VIEWS

Where parts are symmetrically opposite, such as for right- and left-hand usage, a MIRROR command will be used. Both parts may be shown on the same drawing. This may be accomplished by:

1. Draw PT1 as shown to the left of Fig. 5-9-2.

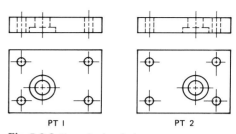

Fig. 5-9-2 Opposite-hand views.

2. Select the MIRROR command.

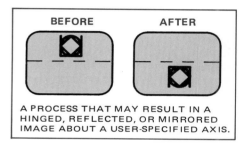

A PROCESS THAT MAY RESULT IN A HINGED, REFLECTED, OR MIRRORED IMAGE ABOUT A USER-SPECIFIED AXIS.

3. Select the WINDOW option [or as an alternate, BLOCK the part (PT1) prior to selecting the MIRROR command].
4. Select PT1 either by lower left and upper right rectangle corners or by picking any place on the block.
5. Select the axis to mirror about, in this case the *Y* axis.
6. Indicate that you wish to save the original view.
7. Select the TEXT command and key in PT2. The result will appear as shown in Fig. 5-9-2.

Mirror is useful any time there is an axis of symmetry. If, for example, an object is symmetrical about the *X* (horizontal) and *Y* (vertical) axes as shown in Fig. 5-7-2A, you only need to draw one-quarter (quadrant) of the object. The object may then be mirrored about the *Y* axis to create the second quadrant. Both quadrants will then be mirrored about the *X* axis to create the complete object. As you can see, much of a CAD drawing may be "built" rather than drawn. This helps to make CAD a much more productive tool than manual drafting.

REAR VIEWS

Rear views are normally mirrored to the right or left about a vertical *(Y)* axis. When this projection is not practical, because of the length of the part, particularly for panels and mounting plates, the rear view must not be mirrored about the horizontal *(X)* axis. Doing so would result in the part being shown upside down. Instead, the view should be shown as if it were projected to the side but located in some other position, by using MIRROR and

MOVE. It should be clearly labeled REAR VIEW REMOVED (Fig. 5-9-3).

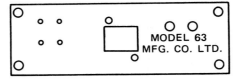

FRONT VIEW

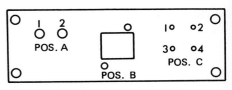

REAR VIEW REMOVED

Fig. 5-9-3 Removed rear view.

ASSIGNMENT

See Assignments 22, 23, and 24 for Unit 5-9 starting on page 93.

ASSIGNMENTS FOR CHAPTER 5

When attempting to solve engineering drawing problems, remember that CAD provides many useful commands to make every job easier. Be sure to use these commands. Some of the more basic ones which will be helpful on almost any drawing you create include: ZOOM, ERASE (ALL, WINDOW, LAST OBJECT), REDRAW, GRID (ON/OFF), SNAP (ON/OFF), and MOVE NEXT POINT. For example, if a mistake has just been made, ERASE LAST. It will be immediately erased and nothing will be lost. Also, if you cannot make out a detail, ZOOM by WINDOW to view it better. This will improve accuracy.

Assignment for Unit 5-1, Theory of Shape Description

1. On two A size sheets of preprinted grid paper (.25 in. or 10 mm grids), sketch three views of each of the objects shown in Fig. 5-1-A and 5-1-B. Sketch three objects on each sheet. Each square shown on the objects represents one square on the grid paper. Allow one grid space between views and a minimum of two grid spaces between objects. Identify the type of projection used by placing the appropriate ISO projection symbol at the bottom of the drawing.

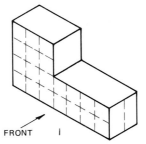
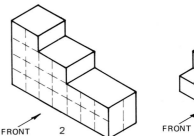
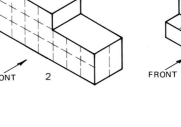
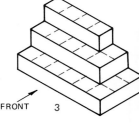

FRONT 1   FRONT 2   FRONT 3

Fig. 5-1-A Sketching assignment.

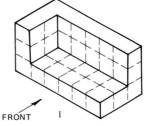
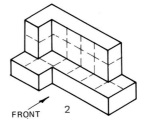
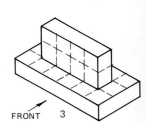

FRONT 1   FRONT 2   FRONT 3

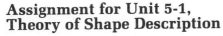

Fig. 5-1-B Sketching assignment.

Assignments for Unit 5-2, Spacing the Views and Use of a Grid Pattern to Construct a Multiview Drawing

Use an A4 or A size drawing for each of the following assignments.

2. Create a drawing similar to Fig. 5-2-2 given the following:

- Size of object—width 4.00 in., depth 2.00 in., height 1.50 in.
- Space between views—1.50 in. (40 mm)
- Space between grid dots—.50 in.
- Scale 1:1. Do not dimension.

3. Create a drawing similar to Fig. 5-2-2 given the following:

- Size of object—width 140 mm, depth 60 mm, height 40 mm

- Space between views—40 mm (1.50 in.)
- Space between grid dots—20 mm
- Scale 1:1. Do not dimension.

4. Using a grid background on the monitor, create a three-view drawing of one of the parts shown in Fig. 5-2-A to 5-2-D. Allow 1.25 in. or 30 mm between views. Use a .25 in. or 10 mm grid. Scale 1:1. Do not dimension.

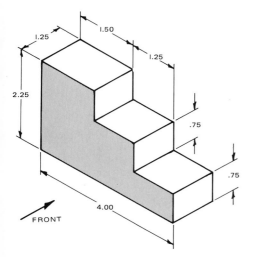

Fig. 5-2-A Step support.

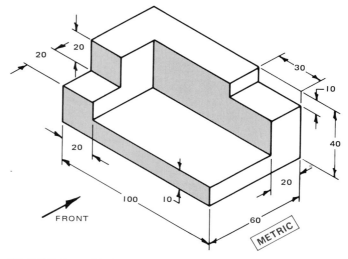

Fig. 5-2-B Corner block.

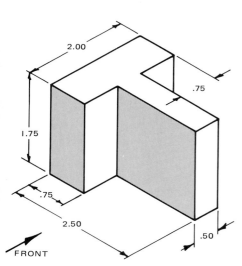

Fig. 5-2-C T bracket.

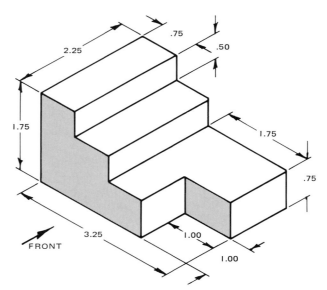

Fig. 5-2-D Angle step bracket.

5. Spacer, Fig. 5-2-E, scale 1:1. Create a three-view drawing using a .20 grid pattern to complete the right side view. Space between views to be 1.40 in. (40 mm). Do not dimension.

6. Bracket, Fig. 5-2-F, scale 1:1. Create a three-view drawing using a grid pattern to complete the top view. Space between views to be 40 mm (1.50 in.). Do not dimension.

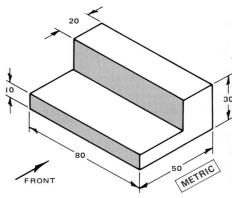

Fig. 5-2-F Bracket.

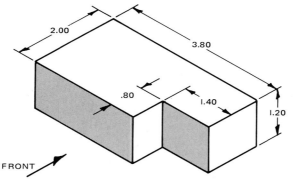

Fig. 5-2-E Spacer.

Assignments for Unit 5-3, All Surfaces Parallel to the Viewing Plane with Some Edges and Surfaces Hidden

7. Using an A3 or B size drawing and a grid background on the monitor, make three-view drawings of each of the objects shown in Figs. 5-3-A and 5-3-B. Each square shown on the objects represents one grid space. Allow one grid space between views and a minimum of two grid spaces between objects. Identify the type of projection used by placing the appropriate ISO projection symbol at the bottom of the drawing.

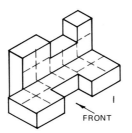
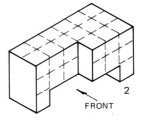
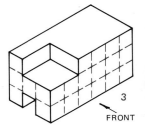

Fig. 5-3-A Hidden line assignments.

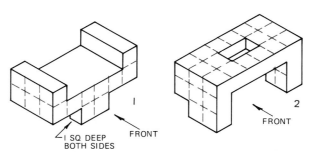
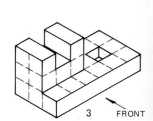

Fig. 5-3-B Hidden line assignments.

8. On an A3 or B size drawing, make three-view drawings similar to Assignment 7 of the parts shown in Fig. 5-3-C.

9. On an A4 or A size drawing, make a three-view drawing of one of the parts shown in Figs. 5-3-D to 5-3-G. Scale 1:1. Select and use the appropriate grid pattern. Allow 1.50 in. (40 mm) between views.

10. Matching test. Match the pictorial drawings to the orthographic drawings shown in Fig. 5-3-H.

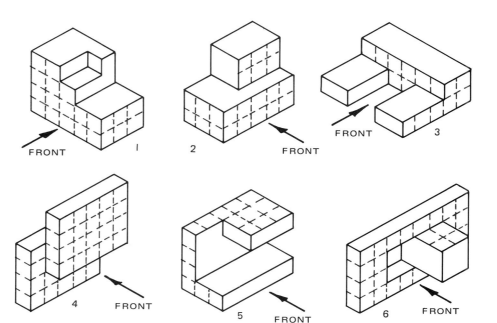

Fig. 5-3-C Hidden line assignments.

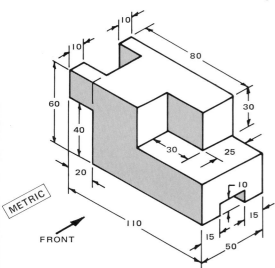

Fig. 5-3-D Adapter.

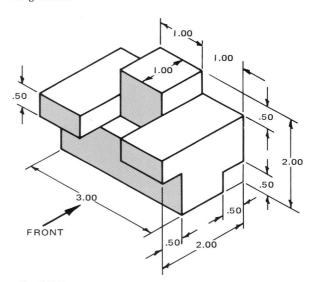

Fig. 5-3-E Link.

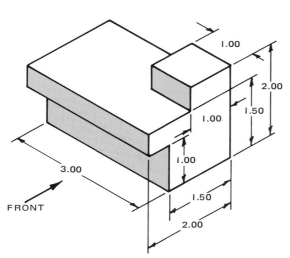

Fig. 5-3-F Bracket.

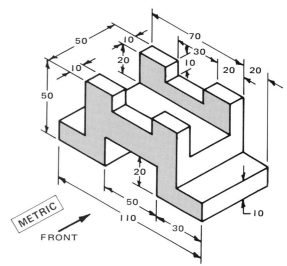

Fig. 5-3-G Guide block.

Fig. 5-3-H Match pictorial drawings A through M with orthographic drawings.

Assignments for Unit 5-4, Inclined Surfaces

11. Use an A4 or A size drawing and a grid background on the monitor to create the front view of each of the objects shown in Figs. 5-4-A and 5-4-B. Each square shown on the objects represents one grid space. Create the top and right side views rather than using grids practice construction lines. The sloped (inclined) surfaces on each of the three objects are identified by a letter. Identify the sloped surfaces on each of the three views with a corresponding letter. Identify the type of projection used by placing the appropriate ISO projection symbol at the bottom of the drawing.

12. On an A3 or B size use construction lines to create a three-view drawing of one of the parts shown in Figs. 5-4C to 5-4F. Allow 1.50 in. (40 mm) between views. Do not dimension. Scale 1:1.

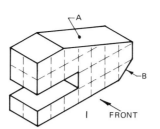
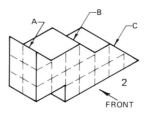
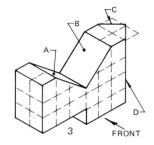

Fig. 5-4-A Inclined surface assignments.

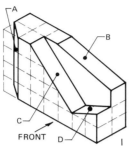
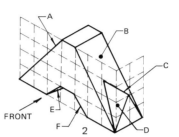
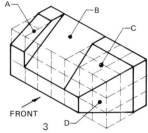

Fig. 5-4-B Inclined surface assignments.

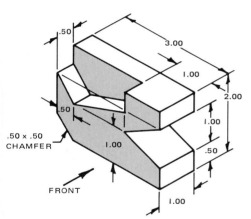

Fig. 5-4-C Slide bar.

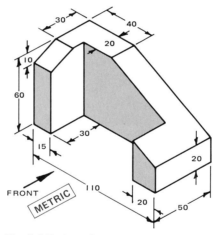

Fig. 5-4-D Flanged support.

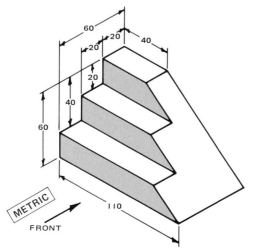

Fig. 5-4-E Adjusting guide.

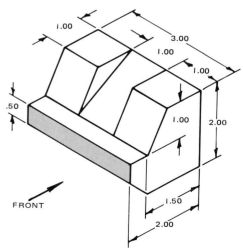

Fig. 5-4-F Separator.

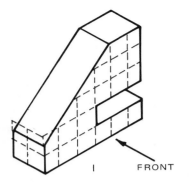

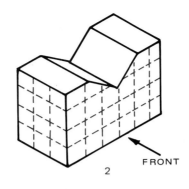

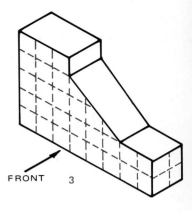

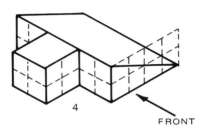

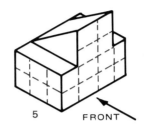

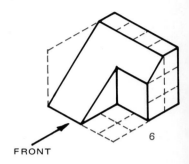

Fig. 5-4-G Inclined surface assignments.

13. Repeat problem 11 for the parts shown in Figs. 5-4G to 5-4J.

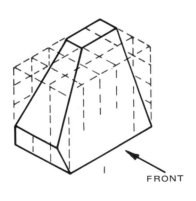

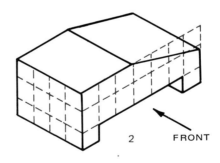

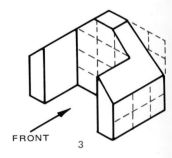

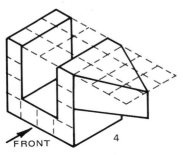

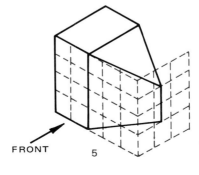

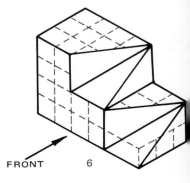

Fig. 5-4-H Inclined surface assignments.

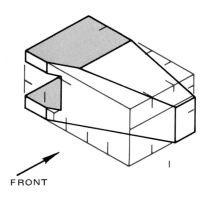

FRONT

1

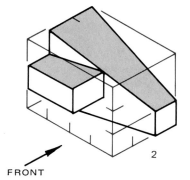

FRONT

2

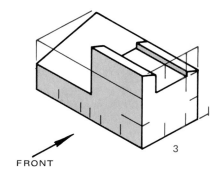

FRONT

3

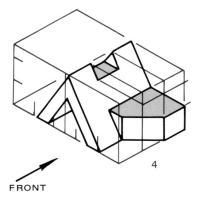

FRONT

4

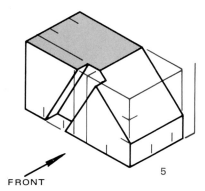

FRONT

5

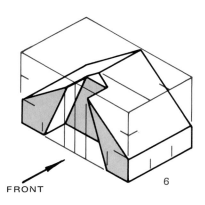

FRONT

6

Fig. 5-4-I Inclined surface assignments.

Assignments for Unit 5-5, Circular Features

14. Use an A3 or B size drawing and a grid background on the monitor to make three-view drawings of each of the objects shown in Figs. 5-5-A and 5-5-B. Each square shown on the objects represents one grid space. Allow one grid space between views and a minimum of two grid spaces between objects.

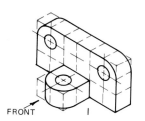

FRONT 1

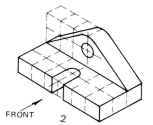

FRONT 2

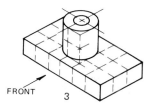

FRONT 3

Fig. 5-5-A Circular feature assignments.

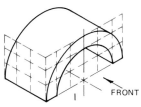

FRONT 1

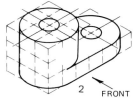

2 FRONT

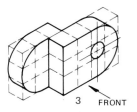

3 FRONT

Fig. 5-5-B Circular fealture assignments.

15. On an A3 or B size drawing, make a three-view drawing of one of the parts shown in Figs. 5-5-C to 5-5-F. Allow 1.50 in. (40 mm) between views. Do not dimension. Scale 1 : 1.

16. Repeat problem 14 for the parts shown in Fig. 5-5-G.

17. Show the views needed for a multiview drawing for the parts shown in Fig. 5-5-H. Choose your own sizes and estimate proportions.

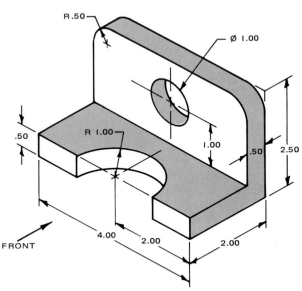

Fig. 5-5-C Rod support.

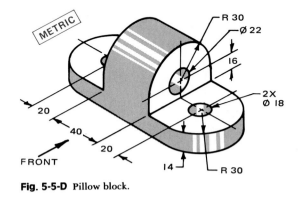

Fig. 5-5-D Pillow block.

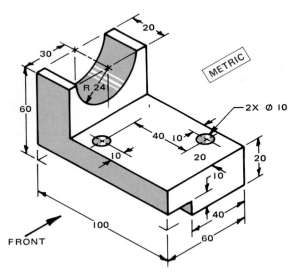

Fig. 5-5-E Cradle support.

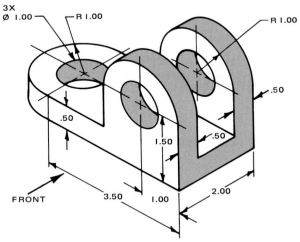

Fig. 5-5-F Rocker arm.

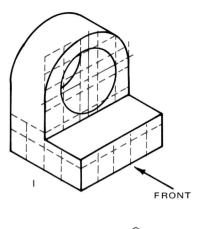

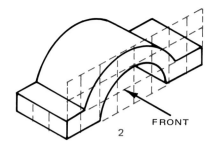

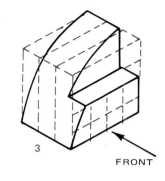

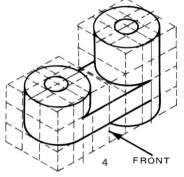

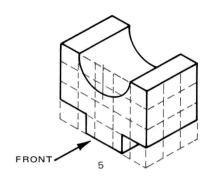

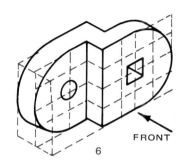

Fig. 5-5-G Circular feature assignments.

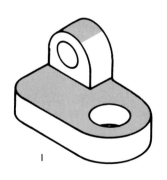

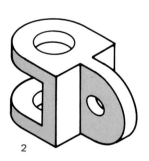

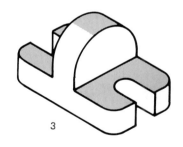

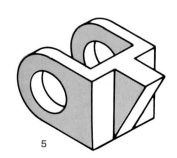

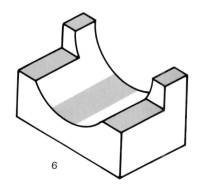

Fig. 5-5-H Circular feature assignments.

Assignments for Unit 5-6, Oblique Surfaces

18. Using an A3 or B size drawing and a grid background on the monitor, make three-view drawings of each of the objects shown in Figs. 5-6-A to 5-6-C. Each square on the objects represents one grid space. Allow one grid space between views and a minimum of two grid spaces between objects. The oblique surfaces on the objects are identified by a letter. Identify the oblique surfaces on each of the three views with a corresponding letter. Also identify the type of projection used by placing the appropriate ISO symbol at the bottom of the drawing.

19. Using an A4 or A size drawing, make a three-view drawing of one of the parts shown in Figs. 5-6-D to 5-6-G. Allow 1.25 in. (30 mm) between views. Do not dimension. As necessary, use construction lines to assist view projection.

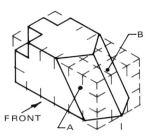 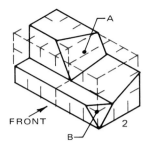 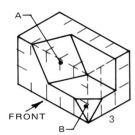

Fig. 5-6-A Oblique surface assignments.

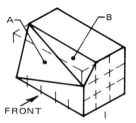 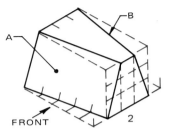 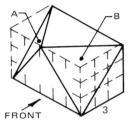

Fig. 5-6-B Oblique surface assignments.

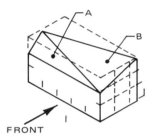 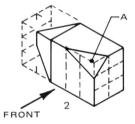 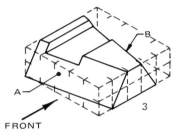

Fig. 5-6-C Oblique surface assignments.

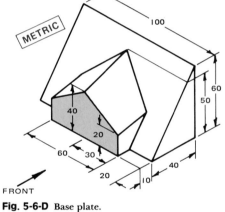

Fig. 5-6-D Base plate.

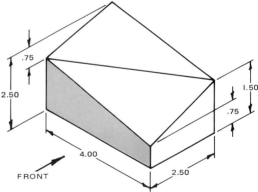

Fig. 5-6-E Angle brace.

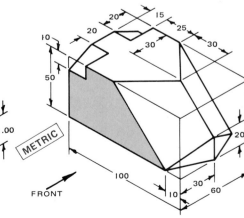

Fig. 5-6-F Support

Fig. 5-6-G Locking base.

Assignment for Unit 5-7, One- and Two-View Drawings

20. Use an A3 or B size drawing, select any four of the objects shown in Figs. 5-7-A or 5-7-B and show only the necessary views in orthographic third-angle projection which will completely describe each part. Use symbols or abbreviations as shown in Table 8 of Appendix B where possible. The drawings need not be to scale but should be drawn in proportion to the illustrations shown.

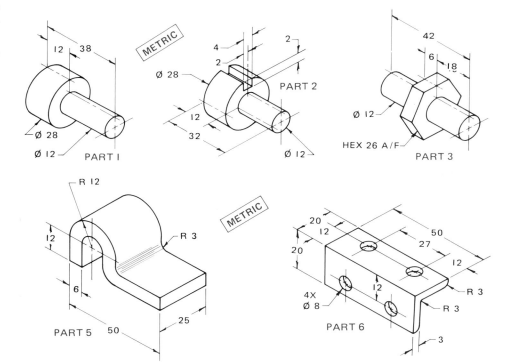

Fig. 5-7-A One- and two-view drawing assignments.

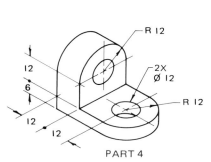

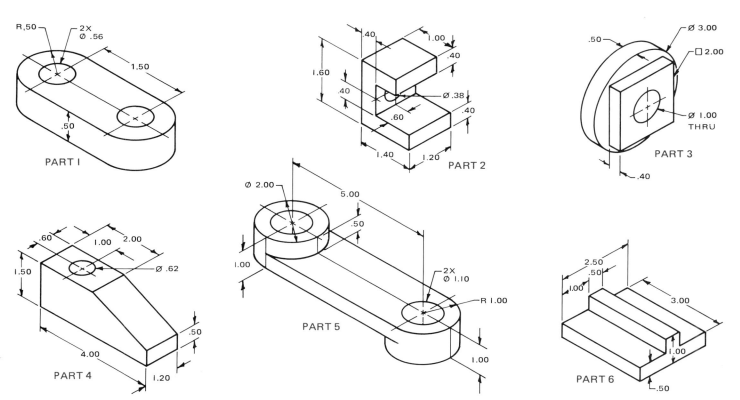

Fig. 5-7-B One- and two-view drawing assignments.

Assignment for Unit 5-8, Partial Views

21. Use an A3 or B size drawing, select any one of the objects shown in Figs. 5-8-A and 5-8-B and draw only the necessary views (full and partial) which will completely describe each part.

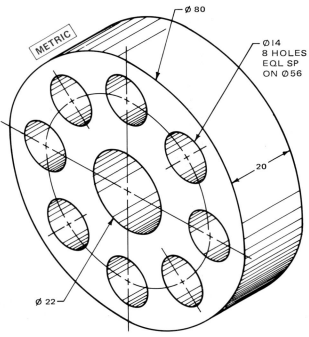

Fig. 5-8-A Round flange.

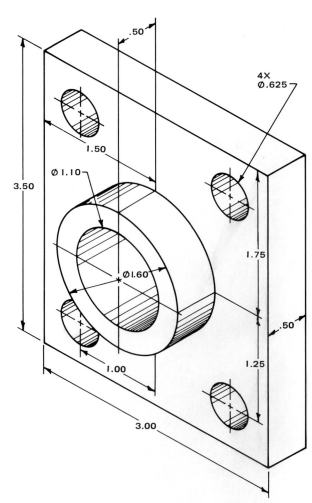

Fig. 5-8-B Square flange.

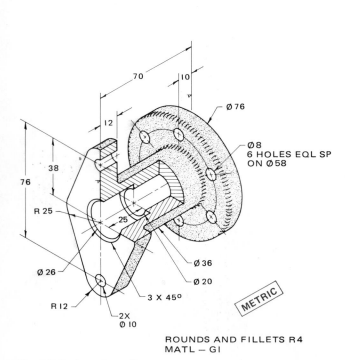

Fig. 5-8-C Flanged coupling.

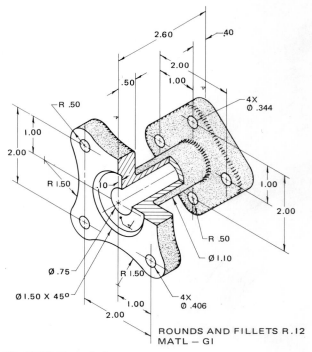

Fig. 5-8-D Flanged adapter.

Assignment for Unit 5-9, Enlarged, Opposite-Hand, and Rear Views

22. Use an A3 or B size drawing to create the truss shown in Fig. 5-9-A. Use BLOCK and RESCALE to create the gusset details A and D as shown. Plot Scale 1 : 24. Use LIMITS of 400 × 260 and draw full scale. Label the detail views.

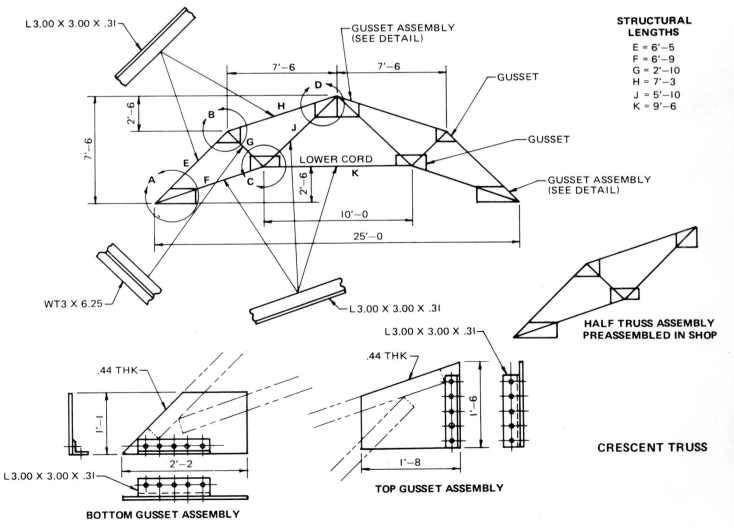

STRUCTURAL LENGTHS

E = 6'−5
F = 6'−9
G = 2'−10
H = 7'−3
J = 5'−10
K = 9'−6

L 3.00 × 3.00 × .31

GUSSET ASSEMBLY (SEE DETAIL)

GUSSET

GUSSET

GUSSET ASSEMBLY (SEE DETAIL)

7'−6   7'−6

2'−6

7'−6

LOWER CORD

2'−6

10'−0

25'−0

WT3 × 6.25

L 3.00 × 3.00 × .31

HALF TRUSS ASSEMBLY PREASSEMBLED IN SHOP

L 3.00 × 3.00 × .31

.44 THK

1'−1

2'−2

L 3.00 × 3.00 × .31

BOTTOM GUSSET ASSEMBLY

.44 THK

1'−6

1'−8

TOP GUSSET ASSEMBLY

CRESCENT TRUSS

Fig. 5-9-A Crescent truss.

23. Create the object shown in Fig. 5-9-B by drawing one quadrant and using the MIRROR command to create the others.

24. Use an A3 or B size drawing to create the front view of the panel shown in Fig. 5-9-C. Do not dimension. Mirror about a *Y* axis to obtain the rear view. Panels such as this, where labeling is used to identify the terminals, are used extensively in the electrical and electronics industry. Add the labeling last.

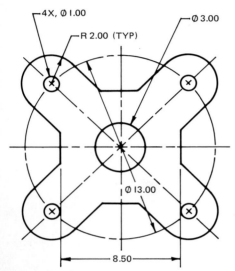

Fig. 5-9-B Pattern.

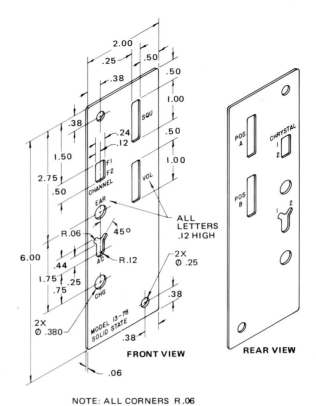

FRONT VIEW

REAR VIEW

NOTE: ALL CORNERS R .06

Fig. 5-9-C Transceiver cover plate.

CHAPTER

6

Applied Geometry and Drawing Conventions

■ UNIT 6-1

Straight Lines

Most of the lines forming the views on engineering drawings can be created using the basic drawing CAD commands described in Chaps. 3 through 5. Geometric constructions, however, have important uses, both in making drawings and in solving problems with graphs and diagrams.

TO DRAW A LINE OR LINES PERPENDICULAR TO A GIVEN LINE

1. Given line A–B (Fig. 6-1-1A), select the LINE and PERPENDICULAR option under OSNAP. **Note:** At this point use the AutoCAD menu or key in the appropriate

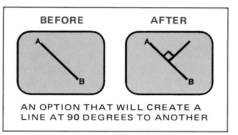

BEFORE   AFTER

AN OPTION THAT WILL CREATE A LINE AT 90 DEGREES TO ANOTHER

command rather than use the pull-down menu.

2. Pick the line A – B (point 1) that you wish the perpendicular line to be drawn from.
3. Pick the location for the perpendicular line (point 2). It will appear as shown by C – D.

TO DRAW A LINE OR LINES PARALLEL TO A GIVEN LINE

1. Given line A – B (Fig. 6-1-1B), se-

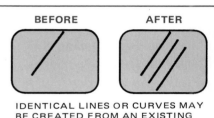

BEFORE   AFTER

IDENTICAL LINES OR CURVES MAY BE CREATED FROM AN EXISTING LINE OR CURVE AT ANY OFFSET DISTANCE.

lect the OFFSET (DRAW) command.

2. Key in the offset distance and press ENTER.
3. Pick the line (A – B).
4. Pick the side (arrow 1) for the parallel line. An identical line of equal length will appear as shown by E – F in Fig. 6-1-1B.

As an alternate, a parallel line may be created using the TRACE (DRAW)

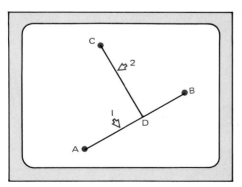

(A) PERPENDICULAR

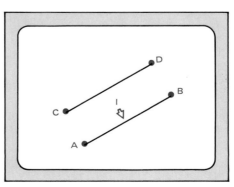

(B) PARALLEL

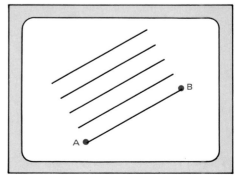

(C) MULTIPLE PARALLEL

Fig. 6-1-1 Drawing perpendicular and parallel lines.

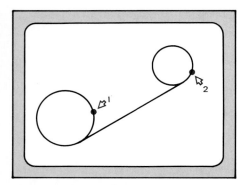

Fig. 6-1-2 Drawing a line tangent to two arcs.

command and FILL OFF option. Use the cursor to select the offset distance. A parallel line of equal length is quickly created, however, not as accurately as the keyed in specified distance. CAD systems provide an additional option to create multiple parallel lines at the specified distance as shown in Fig. 6-1-1C. This is accomplished by selecting the last line drawn each time. The new parallel line (3rd, 4th, etc.) will be created at the same OFFSET distance.

TO DRAW A LINE TANGENT TO TWO ARCS

1. Given two circles (Fig. 6-1-2) select the LINE command and TANGENT OBJECT SNAP option prior to picking each point.

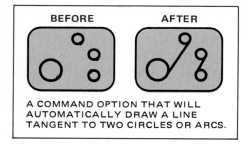

A COMMAND OPTION THAT WILL AUTOMATICALLY DRAW A LINE TANGENT TO TWO CIRCLES OR ARCS.

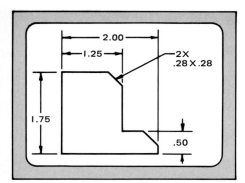

(A) FINISHED OBJECT

Fig. 6-1-3 Automatic chamfers.

2. Pick points (1 and 2) on the circumference of each circle. A line tangent to both circles will be automatically created as shown in Fig. 6-1-2. Select each point near the location of the desired tangent line. If you make a selection too high on the circle (beyond halfway up), the line will be drawn tangent at the upper portion of the circle.

TO CHAMFER (OR BEVEL) AN EDGE

It will often be necessary to draw an inclined line. Only the X and Y distances, as shown in Fig. 6-1-3A (.28 × .28 in.), or one distance with an included angle (45° × .28 in.) may be given. This is sufficient information to mathematically calculate the length by the use of trigonometry. It would be quicker and more accurate, however, to use a CHAMFER command. This will avoid the necessity to make trigonometric calculations.

1. Using the GRID command display a .25 in. pattern and activate the SNAP option.

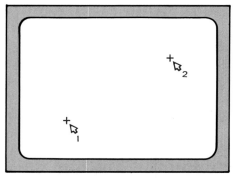

(A) PICKING DIAGONAL CORNERS

Fig. 6-1-4 Automatic rectangles.

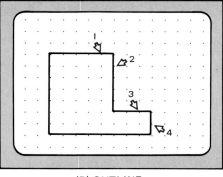

(B) OUTLINE

2. Use the LINE command to create the outline of the object shown in Fig. 6-1-3A but neglecting the inclined lines. The result is shown in Fig. 6-1-3B.

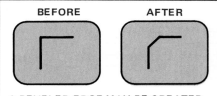

A BEVELED EDGE MAY BE CREATED AFTER THE OBJECT HAS BEEN DRAWN. THIS COMMAND MAY BE USED TO CREATE A HYPOTENUSE (BEVELED EDGE) WHEN ITS LENGTH IS NOT KNOWN.

3. Select the CHAMFER (EDIT) command.
4. Select DISTANCE and key in the desired X,Y chamfer distances .28,ENTER,.28,ENTER.
5. Select the two lines (1 and 2 in Fig. 6-1-3B).
6. Select CHAMFER two lines (3 and 4 in Fig. 6-1-3B). The chamfers will

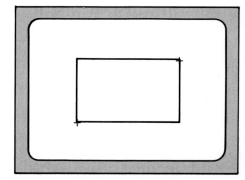

(B) RECTANGLE

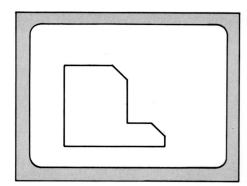

(C) CHAMFER

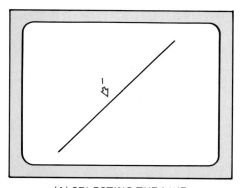

(A) SELECTING THE LINE

Fig. 6-1-5 Dividing a line into equal parts.

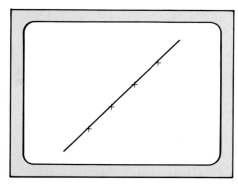

(B) DIVIDE INTO FIVE PARTS

automatically be created as shown in Fig. 6-1-3C.

TO CREATE A RECTANGLE

A rectangle (or square) may be created by drawing four connecting lines. CAD systems provide an option to automatically create a rectangle with less effort as follows:

1. Select the RECTANGLE command (if a MACRO exists).

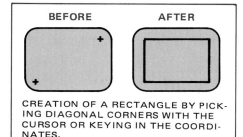

CREATION OF A RECTANGLE BY PICKING DIAGONAL CORNERS WITH THE CURSOR OR KEYING IN THE COORDINATES.

2. Pick the lower left (point 1) and upper right (point 2) corners of the desired rectangle as shown in Fig. 6-1-4A. The result is shown in Fig.

6-1-4B. As an alternate, you may create squares using the POLYGON command (Unit 6-3).

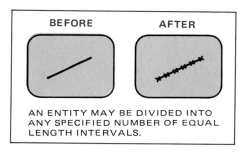

AN ENTITY MAY BE DIVIDED INTO ANY SPECIFIED NUMBER OF EQUAL LENGTH INTERVALS.

TO DIVIDE A LINE INTO EQUAL PARTS

1. Given a line (Fig. 6-1-5A), select the DIVIDE (EDIT) command.
2. Select any place on line 1 (1).
3. Key in the number of divisions you wish to divide the line into (e.g., 5) and press ENTER. This line is not actually divided into five separate lines. The divisions may be illustrated with different markings by setting PDMODE (POINT) to 2 or

3 and REGEN. The result will appear as shown in Fig. 6-1-5B.

The DIVIDE procedure will also work for circles and arcs. If you desire to measure an object into segments of a specified length, use the MEASURE option.

ASSIGNMENT

See Assignment 1 for Unit 6-1 on page 106.

■ UNIT 6-2

Arcs and Circles

TO DRAW AN ARC TANGENT TO TWO LINES (FILLET)

This geometric construction is often better known as the FILLET command. The option to automatically create fillets and rounds is a useful drafting application, especially in designs that involve casting drawings. All corners of a casting are rounded. In manual drafting, each arc (fillet or round) must carefully be drawn tangent to two lines. The same is true for CAD applications not using a FILLET command. Each line has to be drawn foreshortened, and the arc then has to "fit" in. CAD systems, however, have the capability of automatically creating fillets after two intersecting lines have been drawn.

1. Create the object outline (Fig. 6-2-1A) using the LINE command. Draw each line. If SNAP and CLOSE are used, the object will be created rapidly and accurately.
2. Select the FILLET (EDIT) command.

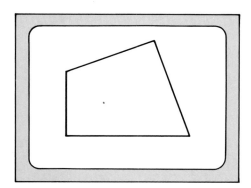

(A) OUTLINE

Fig. 6-2-1 Arc tangent to two lines (fillet).

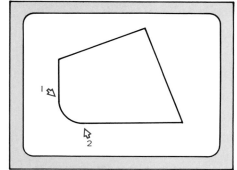

(B) FIRST FILLET

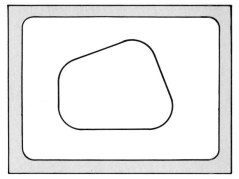

(C) REMAINING FILLETS

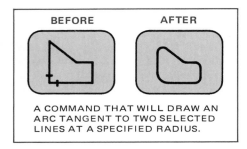

A COMMAND THAT WILL DRAW AN ARC TANGENT TO TWO SELECTED LINES AT A SPECIFIED RADIUS.

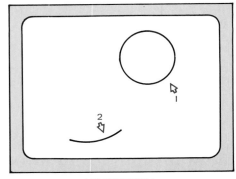

(A) ORIGINAL

Fig. 6-2-2 Extending an arc.

3. Change the fillet radius as desired by selecting RADIUS and keying in the value. Since this is an open-ended command, remember to press ENTER.
4. Locate and set the cursor on the first line segment (1) in Fig. 6-2-1B.
5. Locate and set the cursor on the second line segment (2). The round will appear as shown in Fig. 6-2-1B. Notice that both of these lines have been altered. Each line segment is "trimmed" back to a point of tangency with the round. This automatic function is handy since you do not have to edit each line: the system does it for you.
6. Select FILLET and two lines for each corner. The completed object will appear as shown in Fig. 6-2-1C.

TO LENGTHEN AN ARC

Any arc or line may be shortened by applying the TRIM command. Conversely, any arc or line may be lengthened by the application of an EXTEND command as follows:

1. Given the circle and arc of sufficient radius as shown in Fig. 6-2-2A, EDIT with the EXTEND command.
2. Select where you wish the arc to be

extended to. For example, to the circle (1) and press ENTER.
3. Select the arc (point 2) to be extended. The result will appear as shown in Fig. 6-2-2B.

TO DRAW A CIRCLE OR ARC TANGENT TO TWO CIRCLES

1. Given two circles (Fig. 6-2-3A) select the START/END/RADIUS ARC option.
2. Select the Arc TANGENT (OSNAP) option prior to setting the cursor at points 1 and 2 on the side the tangent arc is to be drawn.

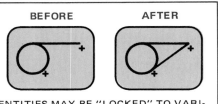

BEFORE   AFTER

ENTITIES MAY BE "LOCKED" TO VARIOUS POSITIONS OF AN OBJECT. COMMON POSITIONS INCLUDE: ENDPOINTS, MIDPOINTS, TANGENT, CENTER, NEAREST, QUADRANT, AND PERPENDICULAR.

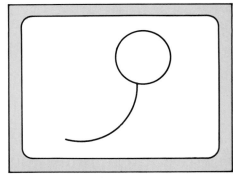

(B) RESULT

3. Select the side (point 3) where the center of the arc is to be placed or key in the desired arc radius and press ENTER. The circle or arc will be created as shown in Fig. 6-3-3B (if the system default is clockwise). Be certain the radius is great enough to span the distance between the circles. If not, you will receive an error message.

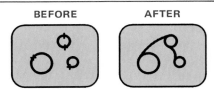

BEFORE   AFTER

A COMMAND OPTION THAT WILL AUTOMATICALLY CREATE AN ARC TANGENT TO TWO OTHER ARCS OR CIRCLES.

4. For a different circle or arc tangent to the same two circles, locate and set the cursor at points 4 and 5. After selecting the center (side where center is to be located) or

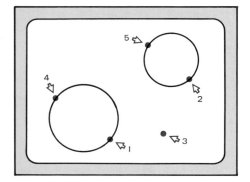

(A) SELECTING THE ARCS

Fig. 6-2-3 Arc tangent to two circles.

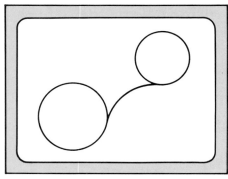

(B) FIRST RESULT

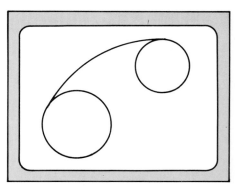

(C) ALTERNATE RESULT

keying the appropriate radius it will appear as shown in Fig. 6-2-3C.

Two alternate procedures to create an arc tangent to two arcs or circles are by using the CONTIN (ARC) or TTR (CIRCLE) options.

ASSIGNMENTS

See Assignments 2 and 3 for Unit 6-2 starting on page 106.

■ UNIT 6-3

Polygons

A regular polygon is a plane figure bounded by straight lines of equal length and containing angles of equal size. The POLYGON command may be used to produce a polygon consisting of any number of sides (greater than 3).

TO DRAW A HEXAGON GIVEN THE DISTANCE ACROSS THE FLATS (Fig. 6-3-1)

1. Select the POLYGON (DRAW) command.

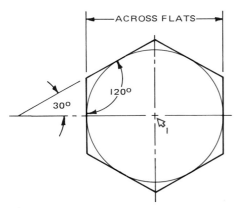

Fig. 6-3-1 Constructing a hexagon, given distance across flats.

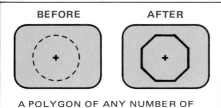

A POLYGON OF ANY NUMBER OF SIDES (GREATER THAN 2) MAY BE INSCRIBED OR CIRCUMSCRIBED ABOUT A CIRCLE OF ANY RADIUS.

2. Key in 6 for the number of sides and press ENTER.
3. Select the center location for the polygon (point 1).
4. Select option CIRCUMSCRIBED (C).
5. Key in the desired radius and press ENTER. The hexagon will be created in the current default rotation angle. The circle and angles are illustrated for reference only and will not actually appear on the screen.

TO DRAW A HEXAGON GIVEN THE DISTANCE ACROSS THE CORNERS (Fig. 6-3-2)

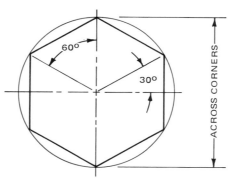

Fig. 6-3-2 Constructing a hexagon, given distance across corners.

1. Select the POLYGON command.
2. Key in 6 for the number of sides and press ENTER.
3. Select the center location for the polygon.
4. Select option INSCRIBED (I).
5. Key in the desired radius and press ENTER. The hexagon will be created in the current rotation angle. The circle and angles are illustrated for reference only.

TO DRAW AN OCTAGON GIVEN THE DISTANCE ACROSS THE FLATS (Fig. 6-3-3)

1. Select the POLYGON command.
2. Key in 8 for the number of sides and press ENTER.
3. Select the center location for the polygon.
4. Select option CIRCUMSCRIBED.
5. Key in the desired radius and press ENTER. The octagon will be created.

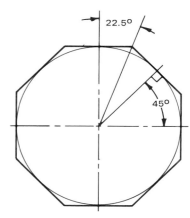

Fig. 6-3-3 Constructing an octagon, given distance across flats.

TO DRAW AN OCTAGON GIVEN THE DISTANCE ACROSS THE CORNERS (Fig. 6-3-4)

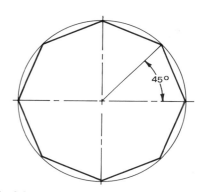

Fig. 6-3-4 Constructing an octagon, given distance across corners.

1. Select the POLYGON command.
2. Key in 8 for the number of sides and press ENTER.
3. Select the center location for the polygon.
4. Select option INSCRIBED.
5. Key in the desired radius and press ENTER. The octagon will be created.

ASSIGNMENT

See Assignment 4 for Unit 6-3 on page 107.

■ UNIT 6-4

Ellipse

An *ellipse* is the plane curve generated by a point moving so that the sum of the distances from any point on the curve to two fixed points, called foci, is a constant. Often a drafter is called upon to draw oblique and inclined holes and surfaces which take the form of an ellipse.

One general procedure to construct an ellipse is:

1. Select the ELLIPSE (DRAW) command and ISO or DIAMETER option.
2. If using ISO, an ISO grid must be displayed. Select the desired isometric plane (e.g., RIGHT) by pressing CTRL and E.

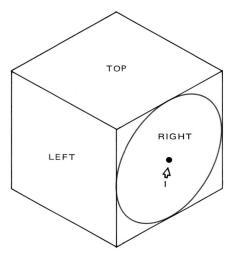

Fig. 6-4-1 Isometric ellipse.

3. Select the center (point 1).
4. Select the axis endpoint. The result appears in Fig. 6-4-1. The angles and outline are shown for reference only.

Since an important application of an ellipse is on isometric drawings, command options available include the ability to "fit" the ellipse on one of three major isometric planes. This will be applied in Chapter 17, Pictorial Drawings.

Another procedure to create an ellipse includes keying in the second axis distance. This generally does not provide sufficient accuracy for application on isometric drawings, however.

ASSIGNMENT

See Assignment 5 for Unit 6-4 on page 108.

■ UNIT 6-5

Spline, Helix, Parabola, and Offset Curve

SPLINE

An irregular curve is a nonconcentric, nonstraight line drawn smoothly through a series of points. It is commonly referred to as *spline*. Other nomenclature includes pline, curve, and fit curve. Often, nonconcentric curves are desired. One common application is the construction of a plate cam profile (Fig. 6-5-1). The methods and procedures involve selecting several points and automatically blending a curve through them. At least three points, not in a straight line, must be selected.

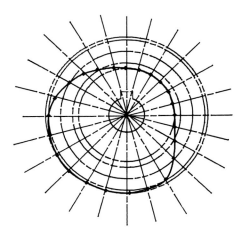

Fig. 6-5-1 Spline application.

1. Select the PLINE command. Instructions will be displayed on the monitor. The location of a point is requested.

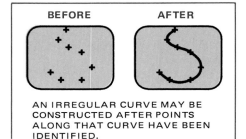

AN IRREGULAR CURVE MAY BE CONSTRUCTED AFTER POINTS ALONG THAT CURVE HAVE BEEN IDENTIFIED.

2. Key the X and Y coordinate values for the first point on the curve or use an input device to locate and set the cursor. A point appears on the screen similar to Fig. 6-5-2A.
3. Repeat Step 2 for the second point. A second point appears on the screen, as shown in Fig. 6-5-2B.
4. Repeat Step 2 for the third point, as shown in Fig. 6-5-2C. Sufficient information to construct a curve is now available. Additional points, however, as required to increase accuracy, may be defined, as shown.
5. After all the points are defined, select PEDIT, the line, ENTER, and FIT CURVE. The curve tangent to each point will be displayed as shown in Fig. 6-5-2D. To "fair a curve," that is, create the curve at an appropriate distance between points, select SPLINE rather than FIT CURVE.

A graphics tablet may be used to quickly trace a spline. You may accomplish this with the SKETCH command.

1. Select the SKETCH (DRAW) command, key in the increment value, and press ENTER.
2. Depress the stylus, on the graphics tablet, at the location of the start of the curve. This point may be digitized from a rough sketch or perhaps from grid paper on the surface of the tablet. The graphics tablet electrical network understructure senses the location.
3. Next, trace the shape of the curve with the stylus or puck. This may be done either freehand or with the aid of a drawing instrument. The shape is duplicated and appears on the screen. Press ENTER.

This method constructs an irregular curve as rapidly as the user can input points. Its limitation, however, is inaccuracy. It is only as accurate as the user's hand and eye. This accuracy, however, is all that drawings produced by manual drafting could ever attain.

HELIX

The *helix* is the curve generated by a point that revolves uniformly around and up or down the surface of a cylinder. The lead is the vertical distance that the point rises or drops in one complete revolution.

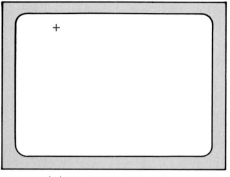

(A) SELECT FIRST POINT

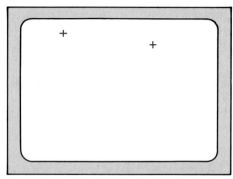

(B) SELECT SECOND POINT

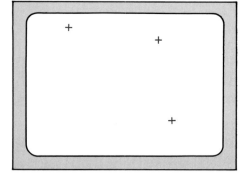

(C) SELECT THIRD POINT

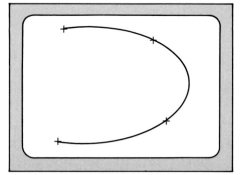

(D) END OPERATION

Fig. 6-5-2 Constructing a spline.

To Draw A Helix

1. Given the diameter of the cylinder and the lead (Fig. 6-5-3), draw the top and front views.
2. DIVIDE the circumference (top view) into a convenient number of parts (use 12) and label them using TEXT. Be sure the PDMODE is set.
3. Project LINES down to the front view using the ORTHO-ON. Use NODE (OSNAP) for the exact location of each divide point with the circle.
4. DIVIDE the circumference into the same number of equal parts and label them as shown. Project lines over to the front view.

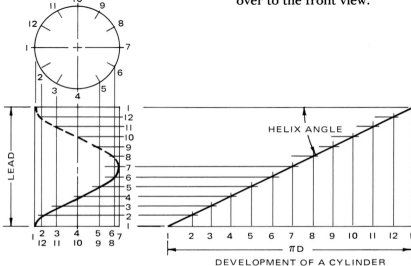

Fig. 6-5-3 Drawing a cylindrical helix.

5. The points of intersection of lines with corresponding numbers in the front view lie on the helix. Select the PLINE command, pick each point, and press ENTER. *Note:* Since points 8 to 12 lie on the back portion of the cylinder, the helix curve starting at point 7 and passing through points 8, 9, 10, 11, 12 to point 1 should appear as a hidden line. Use the HIDDEN LAYER for this. Create the spline using FIT CURVE (PEDIT).
6. If the development of the cylinder is drawn, the helix will appear as a straight line on the development.

PARABOLA

The *parabola* is a plane curve generated by a point that moves along a path equidistant from a fixed line (directrix) and a fixed point (focus).

To Construct a Parabola — Parallelogram Method

1. Given the sizes of the enclosing rectangle, distances A–B and A–C (Fig. 6-5-4A), construct a parallelogram.

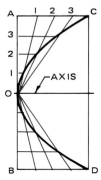

PARALLELOGRAM METHOD

Fig. 6-5-4 Common method used to construct a parabola.

2. DIVIDE distance A–C into a number of equal parts. Divide distance A–O into the same number of equal parts. Use TEXT to label the points as shown.
3. DRAW a LINE from 0 to point 1 on line A–C. Use the OFFSET (PARALLEL) LINE option to draw a line parallel to the axis through point 1 on line A–O, intersecting the previous line O–1. The point of intersection will be one point on the parabola.

4. Proceed in the same manner to find other points on the parabola.
5. Select the PLINE command, pick each point. Use PEDIT and FIT CURVE.

OFFSET CURVE

As with parallel lines, curve may be created at a specified distance from the original curve.

1. Select the PLINE command.
2. Pick cursor points 1, 2, 3, 4, 5, 6 on (Fig. 6-5-5) and use FIT CURVE (PEDIT). The first curve will be created.

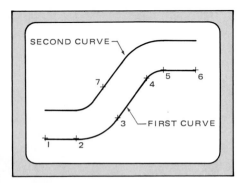

Fig. 6-5-5 Creating an offset curve.

3. Select the OFFSET command.
4. Select the offset distance by keying in the value (distance to 7).
5. Pick the curve to offset and the side to offset (above).

ASSIGNMENTS

See Assignments 6 through 8 for Unit 6-5 starting on page 108.

■ **UNIT 6-6**

Conventional Representation of Common Features (Copy and Array)

REPETITIVE FEATURES

Common features are simplified by a number of conventional drafting practices. Many conventions are used to save drafting time and simplify drawing, making it easier to interpret.

For example, repetitive features, such as gear and spline teeth, are shown by drawing a partial view, showing two or three of these features, with a phantom line or lines to indicate the extent of the remaining features. See Fig. 6-6-1A and B. Other conventions and deviations from true projection are used for the purpose of clarity. For example, square sections on shafts and similar parts may be illustrated by thin, crossed, diagonal lines, as shown in Fig. 6-6-1C.

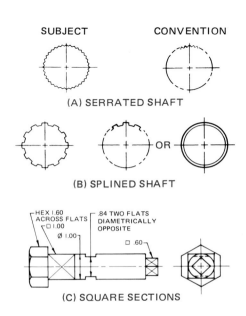

(A) SERRATED SHAFT

(B) SPLINED SHAFT

(C) SQUARE SECTIONS

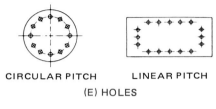

DIAMOND

STRAIGHT

(D) KNURLS

CIRCULAR PITCH   LINEAR PITCH

(E) HOLES

PARTS   DETAILS

(F) REPETITIVE FEATURES

Fig. 6-6-1 Conventional representation of common features.

Knurls

Knurling is an operation which puts patterned indentations in the surface of a metal part to provide a good finger grip. See Fig. 6-6-1D. Commonly used types of knurls are straight, diagonal, spiral, convex, raised diamond, depressed diamond, and radial. The pitch refers to the distance between corresponding indentations, and it may be a straight pitch, a circular pitch, or a diametral pitch. For cylindrical surfaces, the latter is preferred. The pitch of the teeth for coarse knurls (measured parallel to the axis of the work) is 15 teeth per inch (TPI) or about 2 mm; for medium knurls, 20 TPI or about 1.2 mm; and for fine knurls, 33 TPI or 0.8 mm. The medium-pitch knurl is the most commonly used.

On detail drawings the knurl is not usually shown, but is identified by a note on the drawing. The knurl symbol is often shown on assembly and drawings made for catalogs.

Repetitive Features

Repetitive features may include any identical details from holes (Fig. 6-6-1E), to parts (Fig. 6-6-1F). CAD has made it easy to illustrate repetitive features on a drawing. Several COPY options are used including:

- Copy — single entity
- Copy — a block
- Copy — by window
- Copy repeat — rectangular array
- Copy repeat — circular array

Copy a Single Entity Any entity may be duplicated at any distance from the original. This command may also be used to quickly copy many identical entities any place on the screen.

1. Select the COPY (EDIT) command.

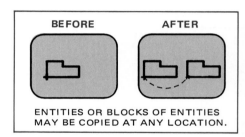

BEFORE   AFTER

ENTITIES OR BLOCKS OF ENTITIES MAY BE COPIED AT ANY LOCATION.

2. Select the entity to be copied (point 1 on Fig. 6-6-2A) and press ENTER.

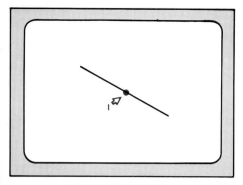

(A) SELECT ENTITY

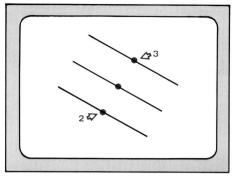

(B) SELECT COPY LOCATION(S)

Fig. 6-6-2 Copying an entity.

3. Select the base position (e.g., point 1), and desired copy position (point 2, Fig. 6-6-2B).
4. Repeat Steps 2 and 3 for additional copies as shown by point 3 in Fig. 6-6-2B.

Copy by WINDOW (or BLOCK)
Any portion (or all) of a drawing may be copied. This is done by either selecting a rectangle, or if previously blocked, selecting the block.

1. Select the COPY command.
2. Select the WINDOW option (or the BLOCK to copy).
3. Pick lower left and upper right rectangle corners (Fig. 6-6-3A). Be sure all entities fully reside within the rectangle.
4. Select the base position (point 1).
5. Pick the location for the copy (point 2) and it will automatically be placed (Fig. 6-6-3B). The distance between the point 1 (base position) and point 2 is the displacement of the copy.

Array — Rectangular

1. Select the ARRAY (EDIT) command.
2. Choose object 1 (Fig. 6-6-4A) by WINDOW and press ENTER.

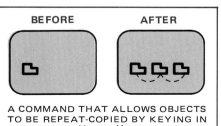

BEFORE   AFTER

A COMMAND THAT ALLOWS OBJECTS TO BE REPEAT-COPIED BY KEYING IN A SPECIFIED *X* AND *Y* DISTANCE (OR ANGLE) AND NUMBER OF COPIES. THE PATTERN MAY BE EITHER RECTANGULAR OR POLAR (CIRCULAR).

3. Select RECTANGLE (R) option.
4. Key in number of horizontal (———)rows (e.g., 3) and press ENTER.
5. Key in number of vertical (III) columns (e.g., 4) and press ENTER.
6. Key in unit distance between rows (e.g., 2.5) and press ENTER.
7. Key in distance between columns (e.g., 3) and press ENTER.
8. Objects will be arrayed in rectangular form as shown Fig. 6-6-4B.

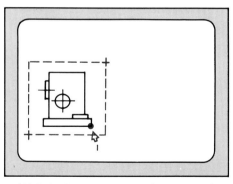

(A) SELECT RECTANGLE (OR BLOCK) AND BASE POINT

Fig. 6-6-3 Copy by rectangle.

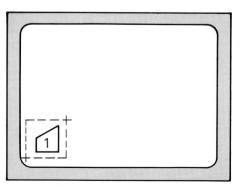

(A) CHOOSE OBJECT TO BE DUPLICATED

Fig. 6-6-4 Rectangular array.

Note: Giving a negative number for row distance will result in the array going down. A negative number for column distance will result in the array going to the left.

Array — Polar

1. DRAW object 1 (Fig. 6-6-5). Create the horizontal line by using LINE command, OSNAP, and QUADRANT options.
2. Select ARRAY.
3. Choose object 1 to be arrayed by WINDOW.
4. Select the POLAR (P) option.
5. Select the center rotational point of the array (2).
6. Key in the number of objects (e.g., 8 for a complete circular pattern) and press ENTER.
7. Key in angle to array (e.g., 360) and press ENTER.
8. Respond to the prompt to rotate objects as they are copied. One keystroke will array the object as shown in the pattern. For a partial pattern (Fig. 6-6-5B), key in a smaller number of objects (e.g., 6) in Step 6 and smaller angle in Step 7

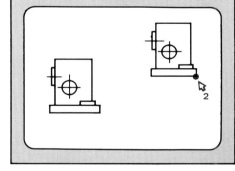

(B) SELECT COPY LOCATION

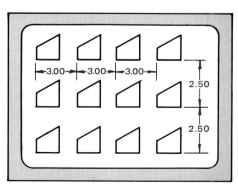

(B) RESULT

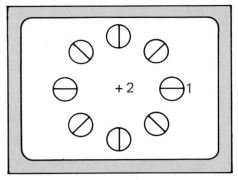

(A) FULL PATTERN

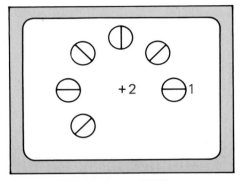

(B) PARTIAL PATTERN

Fig. 6-6-5 Circular array.

(e.g., 225). To change direction of the copies, key in a minus angle in Step 7.

Additional representations of common features are covered in the remaining units in this chapter and other chapters throughout this text.

ASSIGNMENTS

See Assignments 10 through 13 for Unit 6-6 starting on page 110.

■ UNIT 6-7

Conventional Breaks

Long, simple parts such as shafts, bars, tubes, and arms need not be drawn to their entire length. Conventional breaks located at a convenient position may be used and the true length indicated by a dimension. See Fig. 6-7-1. The breaks shown in Fig. 6-7-1A, B, and C are general in nature and are preferred in many cases. The breaks shown in Fig. 6-7-1C to F are used for specific shapes. Often a part can be

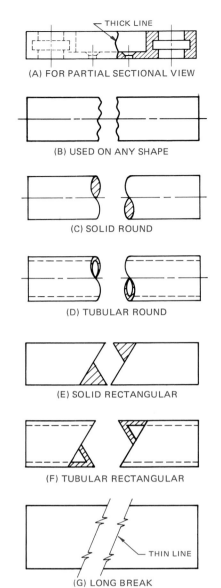

THICK LINE

(A) FOR PARTIAL SECTIONAL VIEW

(B) USED ON ANY SHAPE

(C) SOLID ROUND

(D) TUBULAR ROUND

(E) SOLID RECTANGULAR

(F) TUBULAR RECTANGULAR

THIN LINE

(G) LONG BREAK

Fig. 6-7-1 Conventional breaks.

drawn to a larger scale to produce a clearer drawing if a conventional break is used. One type of break line used for round objects is known as the

S break (Figs 6-7-1C and D). It may be drawn with the ARC, PLINE, or SKETCH command.

A break line is also used to indicate the cutaway location on partial section views. See Fig. 6-7-1A.

ASSIGNMENTS

See Assignments 14 and 15 for Unit 6-7 on page 111.

■ UNIT 6-8

Cylindrical Intersections

The intersections of rectangular and circular contours, unless they are very large, are shown conventionally as in Figs. 6-8-1 and 6-8-2. The same convention may be used to show the intersection of two cylindrical contours, or the curve of intersection may be shown as a circular arc. Conventional representation is not only more appealing in appearance (Fig. 6-8-2) but is also easier to construct and interpret.

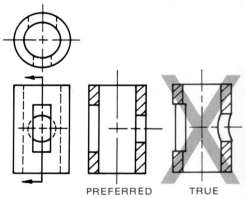

PREFERRED   TRUE

Fig. 6-8-2 Conventional representation of cylindrical intersections.

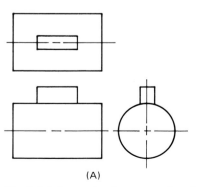

(A)

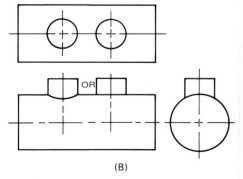

OR

(B)

Fig. 6-8-1 Conventional representation of external intersections.

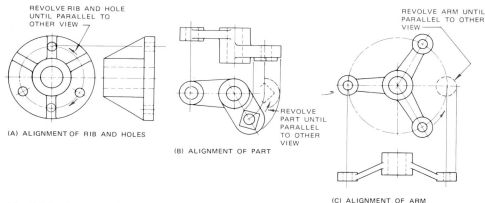

Fig. 6-9-1 Alignment of parts and holes to show true relationship.

(A) ALIGNMENT OF RIB AND HOLES

(B) ALIGNMENT OF PART

(C) ALIGNMENT OF ARM

jection. Note that in each example the true projection would be misleading. In the case of the large radius, such as shown in Fig. 6-10-1C, no line is drawn. Members such as ribs and arms that blend into other features terminate in curves called *runouts*. Runouts are drawn using the ARC or SKETCH command. See Fig. 6-10-2.

ASSIGNMENT

See Assignment 18 for Unit 6-10 on page 112.

ASSIGNMENT

See Assignment 16 for Unit 6-8 on page 112.

 UNIT 6-9

Foreshortened Projection

When the true projection of a feature would result in confusing foreshortening, it should be rotated until it is parallel to the line of the section or projection. See Fig. 6-9-1.

Holes Revolved to Show True Distance from Center

Drilled flanges should show the holes at their true distance from the center rather than the true projection.

ASSIGNMENT

See Assignment 17 for Unit 6-9 on page 112.

UNIT 6-10

Intersections of Unfinished Surfaces

The intersections of unfinished surfaces that are rounded or filleted may be indicated conventionally by a line coinciding with the theoretical line of intersection. The need for this convention is demonstrated by the examples shown in Fig. 6-10-1, where the upper top views are shown in true pro-

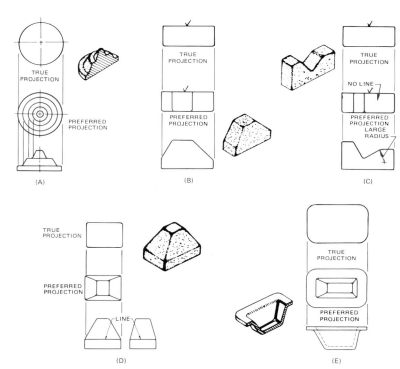

Fig. 6-10-1 Conventional representation of rounds and fillets.

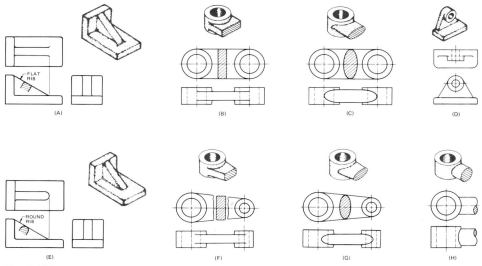

Fig. 6-10-2 Conventional representation of runouts.

ASSIGNMENTS FOR CHAPTER 6

Assignments for Unit 6-1, Straight Lines

1. Divide an A3 or B size drawing as shown in Fig. 6-1-A. In the designated areas perform the geometric constructions.

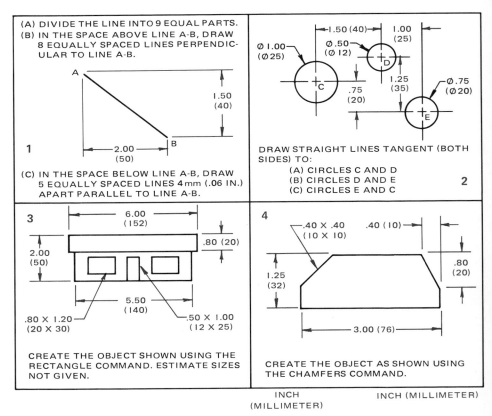

Fig. 6-1-A (1) and (2) Straight-line construction. (3) Create the object as shown using the **RECTANGLE** command. (4) Create the objects as shown using the **CHAMFERS** command.

Assignments for Unit 6-2, Arcs and Circles

2. Divide an A3 or B size drawing as shown in Fig. 6-2-A. In the designated areas perform the geometric constructions.

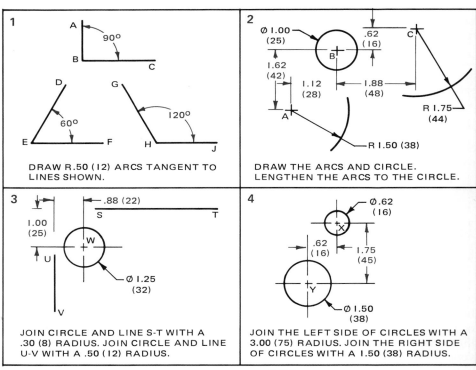

Fig. 6-2-A Drawing assignments.

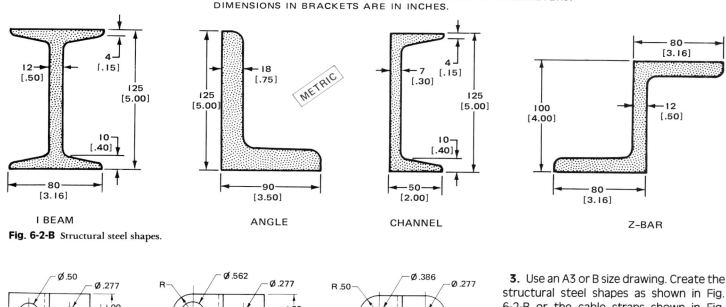

NOTE — DIMENSIONS NOT ENCLOSED IN BRACKETS ARE IN MILLIMETERS.
DIMENSIONS IN BRACKETS ARE IN INCHES.

I BEAM   ANGLE   CHANNEL   Z–BAR

Fig. 6-2-B Structural steel shapes.

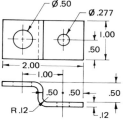 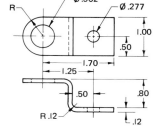 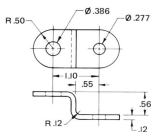

Fig. 6-2-C Cable straps.

3. Use an A3 or B size drawing. Create the structural steel shapes as shown in Fig. 6-2-B or the cable straps shown in Fig. 6-2-C. Use a 12 mm (.50 in.) fillet for the angle and a 4 mm (.12 in.) fillet for the I-beam, channel, and 8-mm (30-in.) Z-bar in Fig. 6-2-B.

Assignment for Unit 6-3, Polygons

4. Divide an A3 or B size drawing as shown in Fig. 6-3-A. In the designated areas, perform the geometric constructions.

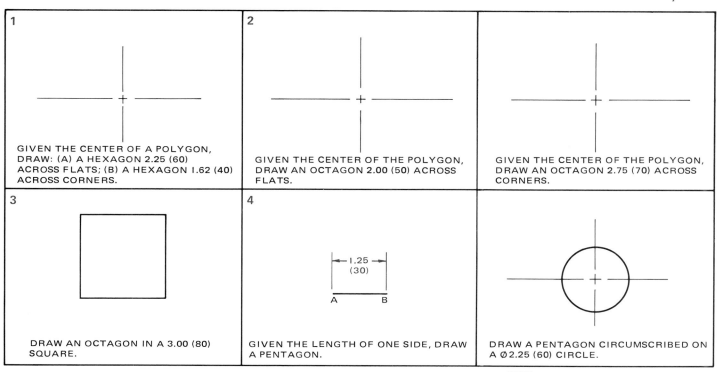

1 GIVEN THE CENTER OF A POLYGON, DRAW: (A) A HEXAGON 2.25 (60) ACROSS FLATS; (B) A HEXAGON 1.62 (40) ACROSS CORNERS.

2 GIVEN THE CENTER OF THE POLYGON, DRAW AN OCTAGON 2.00 (50) ACROSS FLATS.

GIVEN THE CENTER OF THE POLYGON, DRAW AN OCTAGON 2.75 (70) ACROSS CORNERS.

3 DRAW AN OCTAGON IN A 3.00 (80) SQUARE.

4 GIVEN THE LENGTH OF ONE SIDE, DRAW A PENTAGON.

DRAW A PENTAGON CIRCUMSCRIBED ON A Ø2.25 (60) CIRCLE.

INCH (MILLIMETER)   INCH (MILLIMETER)

Fig. 6-3-A Drawing assignment.

Assignment for Unit 6-4, Ellipse

5. Divide an A3 or B size drawing and create the isometric ellipses on the faces as shown in Fig. 6-4-A.

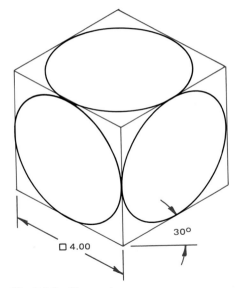

Fig. 6-4-A Ellipse assignment.

Assignment for Unit 6-5, Spline, Helix, Parabola, and Offset Curve

6. Create the line graph shown in Fig. 6-5-A using the (S)PLINE and FIT CURVE option on an A3 or B size drawing. Use a 50-in. (10-mm) grid.

7. Create a template for the table leg shown in Fig. 6-5-B. Use an A3 or B size drawing.

8. Divide an A3 or B drawing size as shown in Fig. 6-5-C. In the designated areas, draw the geometric constructions.

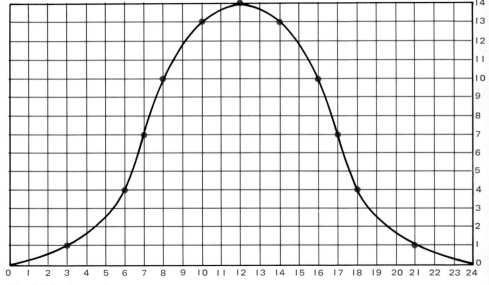

Fig. 6-5-A Line graph.

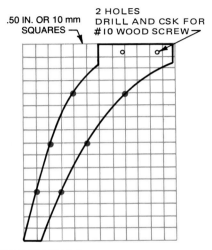

Fig. 6-5-B Table leg.

108 BASIC DRAWING DESIGN

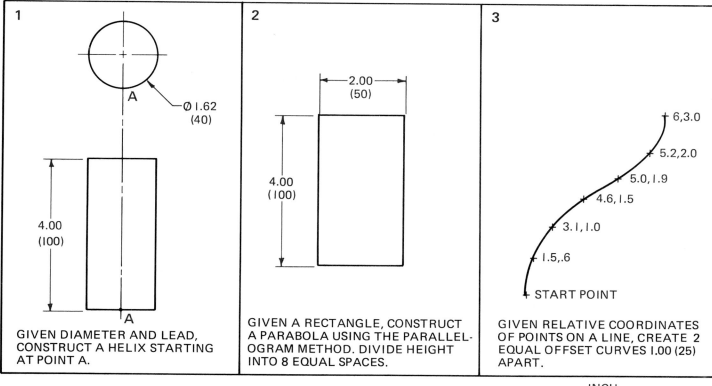

Fig. 6-5-C Drawing assignment.

Review Assignments for Units 6-1 to 6-5

9. On an A3 or B size drawing, create one of the parts shown in Figs. 6-5-D to 6-5-G. Scale 1 : 1. Do not dimension.

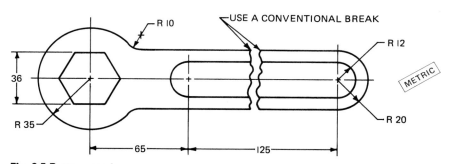

Fig. 6-5-D Hex wrench.

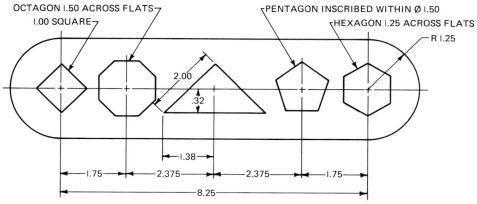

Fig. 6-5-E Template.

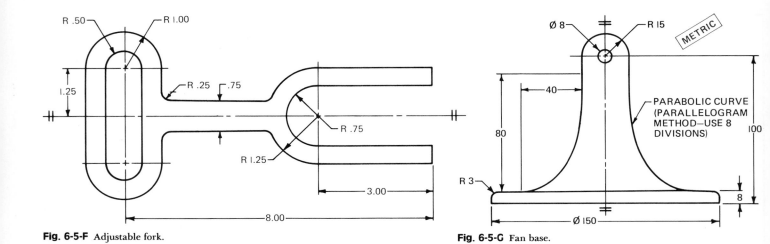

Fig. 6-5-F Adjustable fork.

Fig. 6-5-G Fan base.

Assignments for Unit 6-6, Conventional Representation of Common Features

10. On an A3 or B size drawing, create one of the lines shown in Fig. 6-6-A. Use the COPY command to create the remaining lines.

11. On an A3 or B size drawing, create one of the parts shown in Fig. 6-6-B. Use the COPY by WINDOW command to create several other identical parts.

12. On an A3 or B size drawing, create the drawing shown in Fig. 6-6-C. Use a rectangular array (size to suit).

13. On an A3 or B size drawing, prepare a drawing of one of the parts shown in Fig. 6-6-D or Fig. 6-6-E. Use a polar array to create the teeth and hole patterns. Do not dimension.

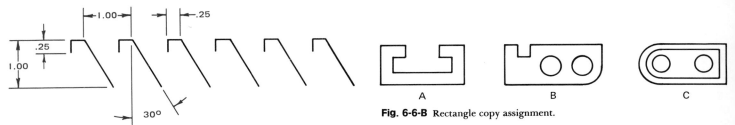

Fig. 6-6-A Copy assignment.

Fig. 6-6-B Rectangle copy assignment.

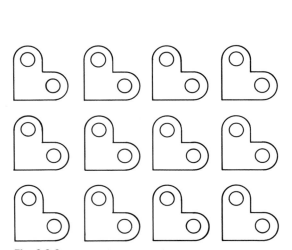

Fig. 6-6-C Rectangular array assignment.

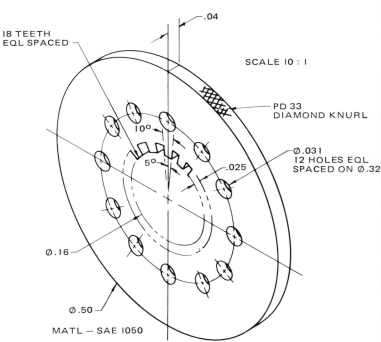

Fig. 6-6-D Adjustable locking plate.

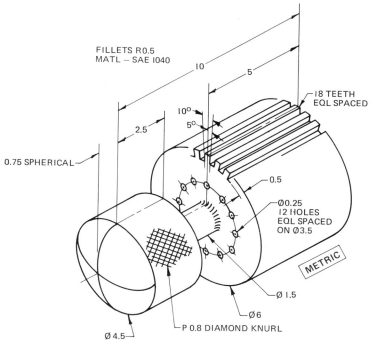

FILLETS R0.5
MATL — SAE 1040

10

5

2.5

10°
5°

0.75 SPHERICAL

18 TEETH
EQL SPACED

0.5

Ø0.25
12 HOLES
EQL SPACED
ON Ø3.5

METRIC

Ø 1.5

Ø6

Ø 4.5

P 0.8 DIAMOND KNURL

Fig. 6-6-E Clock stem.

Assignment for Unit 6-7, Conventional Breaks

14. On a B or A3 size drawing, prepare a drawing of the part shown in Fig. 6-7-A. Use conventional breaks to shorten the part's length. Use your judgment for the size of the part.

15. On a B or A3 size drawing, prepare a drawing of one of the parts shown in Fig. 6-7-B or 6-7-C. Use conventional breaks to shorten the length of the part. An enlarged view is also recommended where the detail cannot be clearly shown at full scale. Scale is 1:1.

Fig. 6-7-A Plate.

.06

45°

.12

14.00

45° X .12
CHAM

6.00

HEX 1.12 ACROSS
CORNERS

R .18

2.00

1.00

Ø .75

1.00

.12

FINISH — HEAT TREAT
MATL — SAE 1080

Fig. 6-7-B Hand chisel.

4X M6

R 6

Ø 10 SLOT

254

76

38

127

6

50

25

25

25

SLOT 1.5 WIDE
X 2 DEEP
HEX 12 AF
BOTH
SIDES

12

2X Ø12

13

25

10

12

26

12

354

METRIC

HEX AND SLOT TO BE
ROUNDS AND FILLETS R 2
MATL — CAST STEEL
FINISH — HEAT TREAT

Fig. 6-7-C Fixture base.

Assignment for Unit 6-8, Cylindrical Intersections

16. On an A3 or B size drawing, prepare a drawing of the part shown in Fig. 6-8-A. Use your judgment for all sizes and in selecting the number of views required.

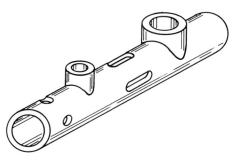

Fig. 6-8-A Cylindrical intersections.

Assignment for Unit 6-9, Foreshortened Projection

17. On an A3 or B size drawing, prepare a detail drawing of the part shown in Fig. 6-9-A. Where required, rotate the features to show their true distances from the centers and edges. Scale is 1:1.

Assignment for Unit 6-10, Intersections of Unfinished Surfaces

18. On an A3 or B size drawing, make a two-view detail drawing of one of the parts shown in Figs. 6-10-A or 6-10-B. Scale is 1:1.

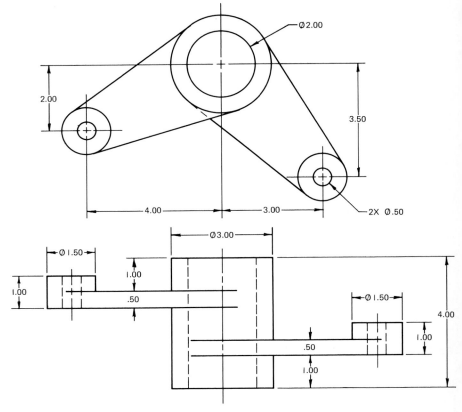

Fig. 6-9-A Crank.

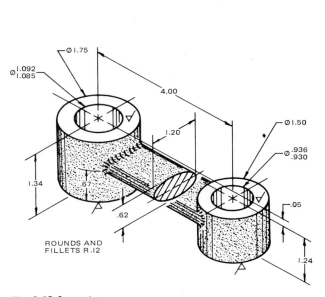

Fig. 6-10-A Casting.

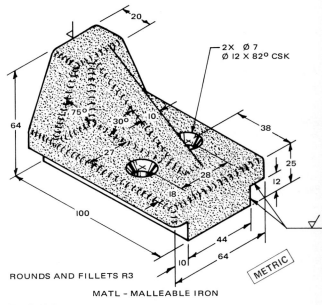

Fig. 6-10-B Sparker bracket.

7

Basic Dimensioning

■ UNIT 7-1

Dimensioning Techniques

A working drawing is one from which a fabricator can produce a part. The drawing must be a complete set of instructions, so that it will not be necessary to give further information to the people fabricating the product. A working drawing, then, consists of the views necessary to explain the shape and size as needed by the fabricator, and required specifications, such as material and quantity needed. The latter information may be found in the notes on the drawing, or it may be located in the title block.

DIMENSIONING

Dimensions are indicated on drawings by extension lines, dimension lines, leaders, arrowheads, figures, notes, and symbols. Much of this is automatically performed by the CAD software. They define geometric characteristics such as lengths, diameters, angles, and locations. See Fig. 7-1-1. The lines used in dimensioning are thin in contrast to the outline of the object. Thus, if a pen plotter is used, these lines are to be made with a thinner pen. The dimensions must be clear and concise and permit only one interpretation. Deviations from the approved rules for dimensioning should be made only

in exceptional cases, when they will improve the clarity of the dimensions. An exception to these rules is for arrowless and tabular dimensioning, which is discussed in Unit 7-4.

In general, each surface, line, or point is located by only one set of dimensions. These dimensions are not duplicated in other views, except for

the purpose of identification, the improvement of clarity, or both.

Drawings for industry require some form of tolerancing on dimensions so that components can be properly assembled and manufacturing and production requirements can be met. This chapter deals only with basic dimensioning and tolerancing tech-

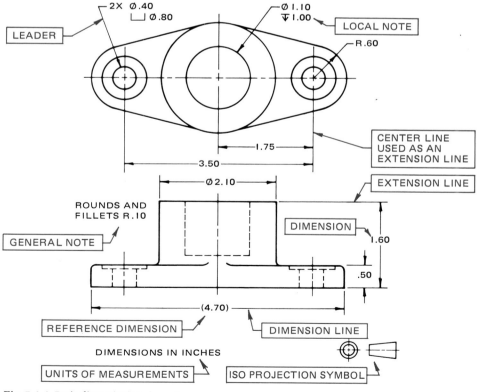

Fig. 7-1-1 Basic dimensioning elements.

niques. Modern engineering tolerancing, such as true positioning and tolerance of form, is covered in detail in Chap. 15.

Dimension and Extension Lines

Dimension lines are used to determine the extent and direction of dimensions, and they are normally terminated by uniform arrowheads, as shown in Fig. 7-1-2. The recommended length and width of arrowheads should be in a ratio of 3 : 1 (Fig. 7-1-3B). The length of the arrowhead should be equal to the height of the dimension numerals. A single style of arrowhead should be used throughout the drawing.

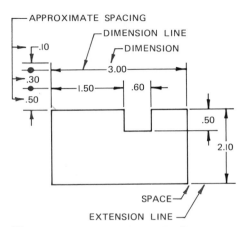

Fig. 7-1-2 Dimension and extension lines.

An industrial practice is, where space is limited, to use a small circle in lieu of an arrowhead (Fig. 7-1-3D).

Preferably, dimension lines should be broken for insertion of the dimension which indicates the distance between the extension lines. Where dimension lines are not broken, the dimension is placed above the dimension line. When several dimension lines are directly above or next to one another, it is good practice to stagger the dimensions in order to improve the clarity of the drawing. The spacing suitable for most drawings between parallel dimension lines is .30 in. (6 mm), and the spacing between the outline of the object and the nearest dimension line should be .38 to .50 in. (10 to 12 mm). When the space between the extension lines is too small to permit the placing of the dimension line complete with arrowheads and di-

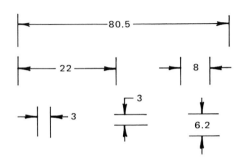

(A) PLACEMENT OF DIMENSIONS

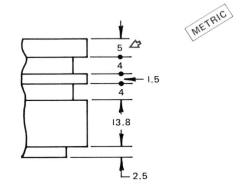

METRIC

A SMALL CIRCULAR DOT MAY BE USED IN LIEU OF ARROWHEADS WHERE SPACE IS RESTRICTED.

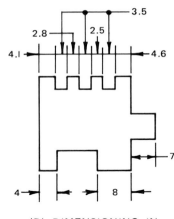

(D) DIMENSIONING IN RESTRICTED AREAS

Fig. 7-1-3 Dimension lines.

mension, then the alternate option of placing the dimension line, dimension, or both outside the extension lines will be executed. See Fig. 7-1-3D. Center line (type) should never be used for dimension lines. Every effort should be made to avoid crossing dimension lines by placing the shortest dimension closest to the outline (Fig. 7-1-3E). Avoid dimensioning to hidden lines. In order to do so, it may be necessary to use a sectional view or a broken-out section. When the termination for a dimension is not included, as when

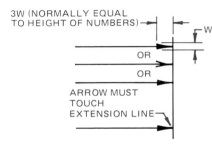

(B) ARROWHEAD SIZE AND STYLES

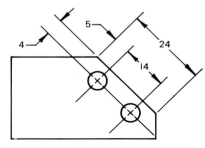

(C) OBLIQUE DIMENSIONING

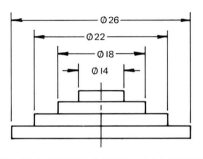

(E) SHORTEST DIMENSION CLOSEST

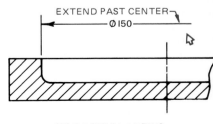

(F) PARTIAL VIEWS

used on partial or sectional views, the dimension line should extend beyond the center of the feature being dimensioned and shown with only one arrowhead (Fig. 7-1-3F).

Dimension lines should be placed outside the view where possible and should extend to extension lines rather than visible lines. However, when readability is improved by avoiding either extra-long extension lines (Fig. 7-1-4) or the crowding of dimensions, placing of dimensions on views is permissible.

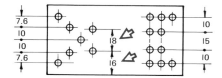

(A) IMPROVING READABILITY OF DRAWING

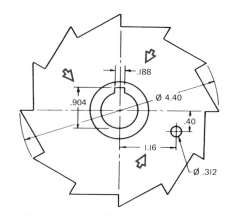

(B) AVOIDING LONG EXTENSION LINES

Fig. 7-1-4 Placing dimensions on view.

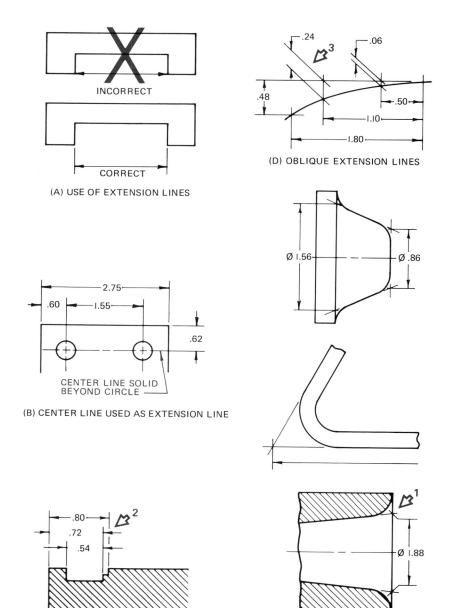

(A) USE OF EXTENSION LINES

(B) CENTER LINE USED AS EXTENSION LINE

(C) BREAK IN EXTENSION LINES

Fig. 7-1-5 Extension (projection) lines.

(D) OBLIQUE EXTENSION LINES

(E) EXTENSION LINE FROM POINTS

Extension (projection) lines are used to indicate the point or line on the drawing to which the dimension applies. See Fig. 7-1-5. A small gap is left between the extension line and the outline to which it refers, and the extension line extends about .10 in. (3 mm) beyond the outermost dimension line. However, when extension lines refer to points, as in Fig. 7-1-5E, they should extend through the intersection (1). Extension lines are usually drawn perpendicular to dimension lines. However, to improve clarity or when there is overcrowding, extension lines may be drawn at an oblique angle (3) as long as clarity is maintained.

Center lines may be used as extension lines in dimensioning. In this case you may wish to suppress (not draw) the extension line that would normally be automatically drawn. The portion of the center line extending past the circle is not broken, as in Fig. 7-1-5B.

Where extension lines cross other extension lines, dimension lines, or visible lines, they are not broken. However, if extension lines cross arrowheads or dimension lines close to arrowheads, a break in the extension line is recommended. (See 2 Fig. 7-1-5C).

When using the DIMENSION (DIM) command, CAD systems automatically place the dimension, extension lines, dimension lines, and arrows. If any item is incorrectly placed or is not standard, it may easily be rectified. Select the DIMENSION STATUS option. Look at the default values (Fig. 7-1-6) and make the appropriate change. For example, if the plot scale is to be reduced to 1 : 12, select DIMSCALE and key in a new factor of 12. LTSCALE also must be changed. In this case use 5 or 6. Select REGEN to complete the change.

Leaders

Leaders are used to direct notes, dimensions, symbols, or item numbers to features on the drawing. See Fig. 7-1-7. A leader should generally be a single straight inclined line (not vertical or horizontal) except for a short horizontal portion extending to the center of the height of the first or last letter or digit of the note. The leader is terminated by an arrowhead or a dot of at least .06 in. (1.5 mm) in diameter. The arrowhead size, DIMASZ (DIM) may be changed to suit any particular application. Arrowheads should always terminate on a line; dots should be used within the outline of the object and rest on a surface. Leaders should not be bent in any way unless it is unavoidable. Leaders should not cross one another, and two or more leaders adjacent to one another should be

1.0000	DIMSCALE	Overall scale factor
0.1800	DIMASZ	Arrow size
0.0900	DIMCEN	Center mark size
0.0625	DIMEXO	Extension line origin offset
0.3800	DIMDLI	Dimension line increment for continuation
0.1800	DIMEXE	Extension above dimension line
0.0000	DIMTP	Plus tolerance
0.0000	DIMTM	Minus tolerance
0.1800	DIMTXT	Text height
0.0000	DIMTSZ	Tick size
Off	DIMTOL	Generate dimension tolerances
Off	DIMLIM	Generate dimension limits
On	DIMTIH	Text inside extensions is horizontal
On	DIMTOH	Text outside extensions is horizontal
Off	DIMSE1	Suppress the first extension line
Off	DIMSE2	Suppress the second extension line
Off	DIMTAD	Place text above the dimension line

Fig. 7-1-6 Dimension variable option (Autodesk, Inc.)

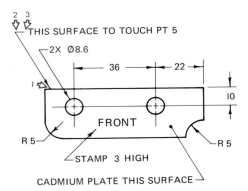

Fig. 7-1-7 Leaders.

drawn parallel if practical. It is better to repeat dimensions or references than to use long leaders.

Where a leader is directed to a circle or circular arc, its direction should point to the center of the arc or circle. Regardless of the reading direction used, aligned or unidirectional, all notes and dimensions used with leaders are placed in a horizontal position. To place a leader and subsequent note:

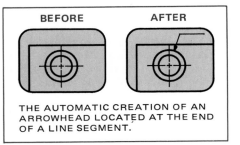

THE AUTOMATIC CREATION OF AN ARROWHEAD LOCATED AT THE END OF A LINE SEGMENT.

1. Select the LEADER (DIM) command.
2. Select points 1, 2, 3 (Fig. 7-1-7), and press ENTER.
3. Key in the desired note — THIS SURFACE TO TOUCH PT 5 and press ENTER. Be sure the CAPS LOCK key is down.

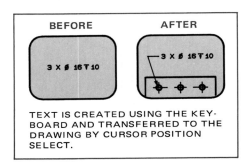

TEXT IS CREATED USING THE KEYBOARD AND TRANSFERRED TO THE DRAWING BY CURSOR POSITION SELECT.

Notes

Notes are used to simplify or complement dimensioning by giving information on the drawing in a condensed and systematic manner. They may be general or local notes, and should be in the present or future tense. Notes will normally be placed by the TEXT or DTEXT command (refer to Unit 3-7). Although it is not recommended for engineering drawings, different STYLES (e.g., italic) may be selected by changing the fonts.

General Notes These refer to the part or the drawing as a whole. They

should be shown in a central position below the view to which they apply or placed in a general note column. Typical examples of this type of note are:

FINISH ALL OVER
ROUNDS AND FILLETS R .06
REMOVE ALL SHARP EDGES

Local Notes These apply to local requirements only and are connected by a leader to the point to which the note applies.

Repetitive features and dimensions may be specified in the local note by the use of an "✕" in conjunction with the numeral to indicate the number of times or places they are required. See Figs. 7-1-1 and 7-1-7. A full space is left between the ✕ and the feature dimension. For additional information refer to Unit 7-3.

Typical local note examples are:

.40 ✕ .06
.20 ✕ 45°
ϕ 3.00
M12 ✕ 1.25

UNITS OF MEASUREMENTS

Although the metric system of dimensioning is becoming the official international standard of measurement, most drawings in the United States are still dimensioned in inches or feet and inches. For this reason, drafters should be familiar with all the dimensioning systems which they may encounter. The dimensions used in this book are primarily decimal inch. However, metric and dual dimensions are shown on some problems in this text.

On drawings where all dimensions are either in inches or millimeters, individual identification of linear units is not required. However, the drawing should contain a note stating the units of measurement.

Where some inch dimensions, such as nominal pipe sizes, are shown on a millimeter-dimensioned drawing, the abbreviation IN must follow the inch values.

Inch Units of Measurement

Decimal-Inch System (U.S. Customary Linear Units) Parts are designed in basic decimal increments, preferably .02 in., and are expressed with a minimum of two figures to the right of the decimal point. See Fig. 7-1-8. When you set up UNITS for a new drawing, select the DECIMAL units and 2 PLACE decimals variable. Using the .02 in. module, the second decimal place (hundredths) is an even number or zero. By using the design modules having an even number for the last digit, dimensions can be halved for center distances without increasing the number of decimal places. Decimal dimensions which are not multiples of .02, such as .01, .03, and .15 should be used only when it is essential to meet design requirements such as to provide clearance, strength, smooth curves, etc. The DIMENSION command, which automatically determines the length of a segment, may yield an odd number. This may easily be overridden by the user. When greater accuracy is required, sizes are expressed as three- or four-place decimal numbers, for example, 1.875. Se-

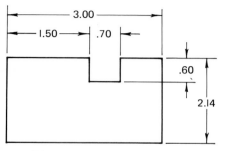

(A) DECIMAL INCH

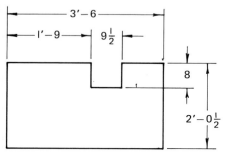

(B) FEET AND INCHES

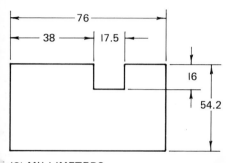

(C) MILLIMETERS

Fig. 7-1-8 Dimensioning units.

lect the DECIMAL UNITS, key 3 or 4, and press ENTER.

Whole dimensions will show a minimum of two zeros to the right of the decimal point.

24.00 *not* 24

In cases where parts have to be aligned with existing parts or commercial products, which are dimensioned in fractions, it may be necessary to use decimal equivalents of fractional dimensions.

Fractional Inch System In this system, parts are designed in basic units of common fractions down to 1/64 in. Decimal dimensions are used when finer divisions than 1/64 in. must be made. Common fractions may be used for specifying the size of holes that are produced by drills ordinarily stocked in fraction sizes and for the sizes of standard screw threads.

When common fractions are used on drawings, the fraction bar must not be omitted and should be horizontal except when applied with an alphanumeric keyboard which does not have a horizontal fraction bar. Since mechanical drawings seldom use fractions, mechanical drafters will normally not use this selection. The option will be used with architectural applications.

When a dimension intermediate between 1/64 increments is necessary, it is expressed in decimals, such as .30, .257, or .2575 in.

The inch marks (″) should not be shown with the dimensions. A note such as

DIMENSIONS ARE IN INCHES

should be clearly shown on the drawing. The exception is when the dimension "1 in." is shown on the drawing. The 1 should then be followed by the inch marks: 1″, not 1.

Foot and Inch System Feet and inches are often used for installation drawings, drawings of large objects, and floor plans associated with architectural work. When beginning a new drawing, select the ARCHITECTURAL (UNITS) option. In this case, all dimensions 12 in. or greater are specified in feet and inches. For example, 24 in. is expressed as 2′-0, and 27 in. is expressed as 2′-3. Parts of an inch are usually expressed as common fractions rather than as decimals.

When the inch marks (″) are not shown on the drawings. The drawing should carry a note such as

DIMENSIONS ARE IN FEET AND INCHES UNLESS OTHERWISE SPECIFIED

A hyphen and space should be left between the foot and inch values. For example, 1′-3, not 1′3.

SI Metric Units of Measurement

The standard metric units on engineering drawings are the millimeter (mm) for linear measure and micrometer (μm) for surface roughness. See Fig. 7-1-8. When beginning a new drawing, select the DECIMAL (UNITS) option. Select the SIZE UNITS option MILLIMETERS when plotting.

Whole numbers from 1 to 9 are shown without a zero to the left of the number or a zero to the right of the decimal point.

2 *not* 02 or 2.0

A millimeter value of less than 1 is shown with a zero to the left of the decimal point.

0.2 *not* .2 or .20
0.26 *not* .26

Decimal points are uniform and large enough to be clearly visible on reduced-size plots or prints. They are placed in line with the bottom of the associated digits and be given adequate space.

Neither commas nor spaces are used to separate digits into groups in specifying millimeter dimensions on drawings.

32545 *not* 32,545 or 32 545

Identification A metric drawing should include a general note, such as

UNLESS OTHERWISE SPECIFIED DIMENSIONS ARE IN MILLIMETERS

and be identified by the word METRIC prominently displayed near the title block.

Units Common to Both Systems

Some measurements can be stated so that the callout will satisfy the units of both systems. For example, tapers such as .006 in. per inch and 0.006 mm per millimeter can both be expressed simply as the ratio 0.006 : 1 or in a note such as TAPER 0.006 : 1. Angular dimensions are also specified the same in both inch and metric systems.

Standard Items

Fasteners and Threads Either inch or metric fasteners and threads may be used. Refer to Appendix B and Chapters 9 and 10 for additional information.

Hole Sizes Tables showing standard inch and metric drill sizes are shown in Appendix B.

Placing Linear Dimensions on Drawings

A part (Fig. 7-1-9A) may easily be automatically dimensioned. When beginning the drawing select the UNITS of DECIMAL and 2 PLACE.

1. Select the DIMENSION and LINEAR commands and the HORIZONTAL option.

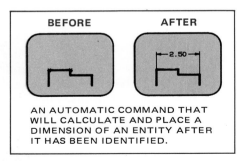

BEFORE   AFTER

AN AUTOMATIC COMMAND THAT WILL CALCULATE AND PLACE A DIMENSION OF AN ENTITY AFTER IT HAS BEEN IDENTIFIED.

2. Pick points 1 and 2 (Fig. 7-1-9B). Dimensions that fall off the grid pattern may be correctly specified by using the OBJECT SNAP ENDPOINT option.
3. Pick location point 3 (Fig. 7-1-9B).
4. You now have the option to override the size measured by the system. If it is correct, press ENTER. The result appears in Fig. 7-1-9C.
5. Repeat Steps 2, 3, and 4 for the remaining dimensions.

Select the VERTICAL option before placing the vertical dimensions. One vertical dimension is created by selecting points 4, 5, and 6 (Fig. 7-1-9B).

If the resulting dimensions do not appear as shown, change the appropriate dimension variable. For example, there will be times when you will not

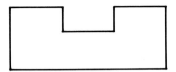

(A) THE PART

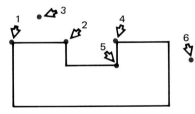

(B) FIRST DIMENSION

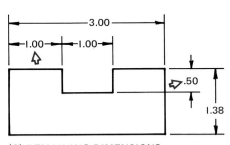

(C) REMAINING DIMENSIONS

Fig. 7-1-9 Linear dimensioning.

wish the extension lines to be drawn (suppressed), or you may wish to have the dimension placed outside the extension lines, and so on. First select the STATUS command to list on the monitor, the current status of all variables. To change any, select DIMENSION VARIABLES, the name of the variable to change (e.g., DIMSE1 for the first extension line), and key in the change (e.g., ON to suppress it). An

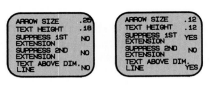

THE VALUES WHICH DETERMINE THE MANNER IN WHICH SYSTEM DIMENSIONS ARE PLACED ON THE DRAWING MAY BE VARIED.

alternate method which automatically suppresses extension lines on LINEAR dimensions is to use the BASELINE and CONTINUE options (Unit 7-4).

Layers

The term *layer* had been mentioned in previous chapters when reference to line types was made. The default layer, usually #1, will be used for general drafting work. It is common, however, to place different line types on different layers. A layer is to a CAD system what a sheet of vellum is to manual drafting. Different sheets may be "stacked-up" (superimposed) on top of each other. Since the vellum is transparent, the information presented on each individual sheet is seen all at once. Any sheet may be removed, or inserted, at the user's discretion. This concept is the same with CAD with the layers normally preset into the program.

Common industrial use of layering is to prepare different portions of a drawing on different levels. When you want to edit the drawing, call up only that layer where the changes are to be made. This will provide you with a much less cluttered drawing. The changes will be made more easily, and redrawing will be quicker. This is especially useful in mechanical design drafting applications. In fact, for consistency, many designers use a "layer table." This means placing the same type of information on the same layer. For example, notes may be placed on layer 10 for every drawing, dimensions on layer 2, and so on.

The procedure to preset your own particular layers is easy and consists of the following steps.

1. Select the LAYER command.

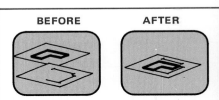

BEFORE   AFTER

DIFFERENT PORTIONS OF A DRAWING MAY BE CREATED ON DIFFERENT LAYERS (OR INVISIBLE PLANES). LAYERS MAY BE "SWITCHED" ON OR OFF, ALLOWING VARIOUS COMBINATIONS OF A DRAWING TO BE DISPLAYED OR PLOTTED.

2. To create another layer select the NEW option.
3. Key in the desired number or name for the new layer to be created and press ENTER.
4. Repeat Steps 2 and 3 for any number of additional layers.

You may create graphics on the new layer of your choice by selecting LAYER, SET, the layer name, and ENTER twice. The name of the layer you are drawing on will be displayed on the monitor and will not change until you SET a different layer. The graphics created on different layers will likely be displayed in different colors assuming of course that you have a colored monitor. This will assist you in interpreting various features of the drawing.

Different layers may be displayed at your discretion by:

1. Select the LAYER command.
2. Select the OFF (or ON) option.
3. Key in the layer name to turn off (or on) and press ENTER twice.

You may at any time check to see what layers have been set for a particular drawing by selecting the LAYER command and ? option. Information regarding the existing layers will be displayed on the monitor. If you have a single-screen system, remember that a simple toggle command (F1) will return you to the graphics display.

ANGULAR UNITS

Angles are measured in degrees although the UNITS command provides several options. The decimal degree is now preferred over the use of degrees, minutes, and seconds. For example, the use of 60.5° is preferred to the use of 60° 30′. Where only minutes or seconds are specified, the number of minutes or seconds is preceded by 0°, or 0° 0′, as applicable. Some examples follow.

DECIMAL DEGREE	DEGREES, MINUTES, AND SECONDS
10°+0.5°	10°±0°30′
0.75°	0° 45′
0.004°	0° 0′15″
90°±1.0°	90°±1°
25.6°±0.2°	25°36′±0° 12′
25.51°	25° 30′36″

The dimension line of an angle is an arc drawn with the apex of the angle as the center point for the arc, wherever practical. The position of the dimension varies according to the size of the angle and appears in a horizontal position. Recommended arrangements are shown in Fig. 7-1-10. There may not be sufficient space for the dimension and/or dimension lines to be placed inside the extension lines. The system will automatically adjust to this by placing some or all (top two illustra-

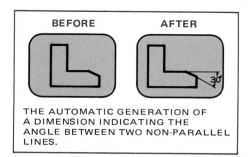

THE AUTOMATIC GENERATION OF A DIMENSION INDICATING THE ANGLE BETWEEN TWO NON-PARALLEL LINES.

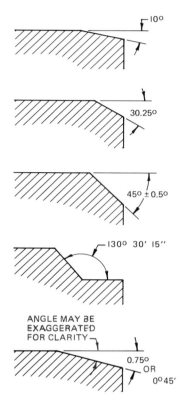

Fig. 7-1-10 Angular units.

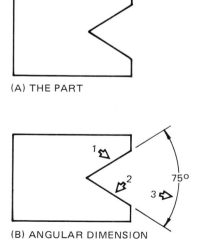

(A) THE PART

(B) ANGULAR DIMENSION

Fig. 7-1-11 Angular dimensioning.

tions in Fig. 7-1-10) to the outside. Dimension the angle (Fig. 7-1-11A) by:

1. Select the DIMENSION and ANGULAR commands.
2. Pick lines 1 and 2 (Fig. 7-1-11B) on the first and second line.
3. Pick location 3.
4. If desired, override the measured angle or press ENTER twice. The result appears in Fig. 7-1-11B.

READING DIRECTION

Dimensions and notes should be placed to be read from the bottom of the drawing for engineering drawings (unidirectional system). For architectural and structural drawings the aligned system of dimensioning is used. See Fig. 7-1-12. Be sure to set the appropriate DIM VARIABLE (DIMEXE and DIMTIH).

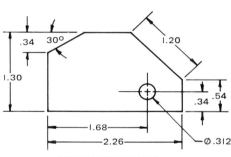

UNIDIRECTIONAL
USED ON ENGINEERING DRAWINGS

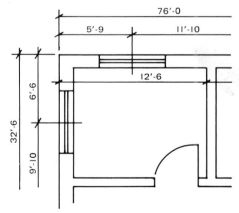

ALIGNED
USED ON ARCHITECTURAL AND STRUCTURAL DRAWINGS

Fig. 7-1-12 Reading direction of dimensions.

In both methods, angular dimensions and dimensions and notes shown with leaders should be aligned with the bottom of the drawing.

BASIC RULES FOR DIMENSIONING

Refer to Fig. 7-1-13.

- Place dimensions between the views when possible.
- Place the dimension line for the shortest length, width, or height nearest the outline of the object. Parallel dimension lines are placed in order of their size, making the longest dimension line the outermost.
- Place dimensions with the view that best shows the characteristic contour or shape of the object. In following this rule, dimensions will not always be between views.
- On large views, dimensions of features near the center can be placed on the view to improve clarity.
- Dimensions should be selected so that it will not be necessary to add or subtract dimensions in order to define or locate a feature.

SYMMETRICAL OUTLINES

Partial views are often drawn for the sake of economy or space. When only one-half the outline of a symmetrically shaped part is drawn, symmetry is indicated by applying the symmetry symbol (point 1 in Fig. 7-1-14) to the center line on both sides of the part. It requires little effort to duplicate the other half using a MIRROR command. Space constraints, however, may preclude this possibility. See Fig. 7-1-14.

REFERENCE DIMENSIONS

A reference dimension is shown for information only, and it is not required for manufacturing or inspection purposes. It is enclosed in parentheses, as shown in Fig. 7-1-15. The parentheses may be added when the DIMENSION TEXT prompt option appears. Formerly the abbreviation REF was used to indicate a reference dimension.

NOT-TO-SCALE DIMENSIONS

When a dimension on a drawing is altered, making it not to scale, it should be underlined (underscored) with a straight, thick line (Fig. 7-1-16), except when the condition is clearly shown by break lines. The underscoring toggle mode (% % u) is available in the TEXT command.

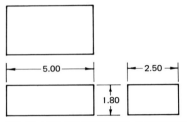

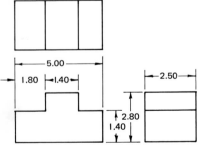

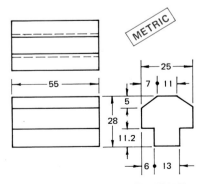

Fig. 7-1-13 Basic dimensioning rules.

(A) PLACE DIMENSIONS BETWEEN VIEWS

(B) PLACE SMALLEST DIMENSION NEAREST THE VIEW BEING DIMENSIONED

(C) DIMENSION THE VIEW THAT BEST SHOWS THE SHAPE

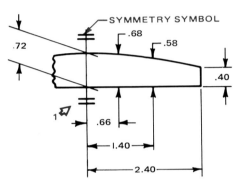

Fig. 7-1-14 Dimensioning symmetrical outlines or features.

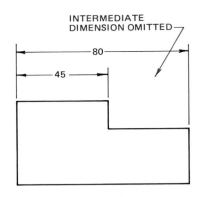

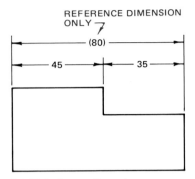

Fig. 7-1-15 Reference dimensions.

Fig. 7-1-16 Not-to-scale dimensions.

OPERATIONAL NAMES

The use of operational names with dimensions, such as turn, bore, grind, ream, tap, and thread, should be avoided. While the drafter should be aware of the methods by which a part can be produced, the method of manufacture is better left to the fabricator. If the completed part is adequately dimensioned and has surface texture symbols showing finish quality desired, it remains a shop problem to meet the drawing specifications.

ABBREVIATIONS

Abbreviations and symbols are used on drawings to conserve space and time, but used only where their meanings are quite clear. Therefore, only commonly accepted abbreviations such as those shown in the Appendix should be used on drawings.

References

1. ANSI Y14.5M, *Dimensioning and Tolerancing.*

ASSIGNMENTS

See Assignments 1 through 3 for Unit 7-1 starting on page 146.

■ UNIT 7-2

Dimensioning Circular Features

DIAMETERS

The diameter symbol (Ø) precedes all diametrical values. Where the diameter of a single or the diameters of a number of concentric cylindrical features are to be specified, it is recommended that they be shown on the longitudinal view. See Fig. 7-2-1. The dimensional representation of holes is shown in the view where the hole is visible.

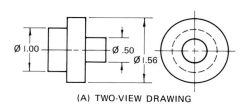

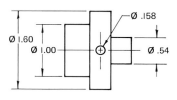

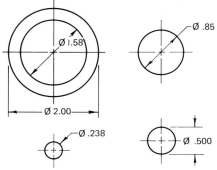

Fig. 7-2-1 Diameters.

The hole in the part shown in Fig. 7-2-2A may be easily dimensioned:

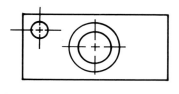

(A) THE PART

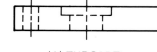

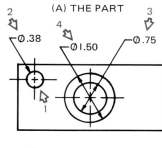

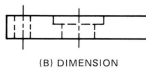

(B) DIMENSION

Fig. 7-2-2 Diameter dimensioning.

1. Select the DIMENSION and DIAMETER commands.
2. Select the arc or circle (point 1).

3. Override or accept the dimension.
4. Select the location of text (2). On larger holes the dimension line or dimension and dimension line may appear within the circle (3 or 4). It will appear as shown in Fig. 7-2-2B.

RADII

The general method of dimensioning a circular arc is by giving its radius. A radius dimension line passes through, or is in line with, the radius center and terminates with an arrowhead touching the arc. See Fig. 7-2-3. An arrowhead is never used at the radius center. The size of the dimension is preceded by the abbreviation R for both U.S. Customary and metric dimensioning. Where space is limited, as for a small radius, the radial dimension line may extend through the radius center. Where it is inconvenient to place the arrowhead between the radius center and the arc, it may be placed outside the arc, or a LEADER may be used (Fig. 7-2-3A).

Where a dimension is given to the center of the radius, a small cross should be drawn at the center (Figs. 7-2-3B and 7-2-3C) by selecting CENTER (DIM) and the arc. Where

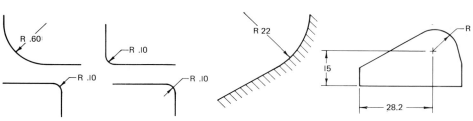

(A) RADII WHICH NEED NOT HAVE THEIR CENTERS LOCATED

(B) LOCATING RADIUS CENTER

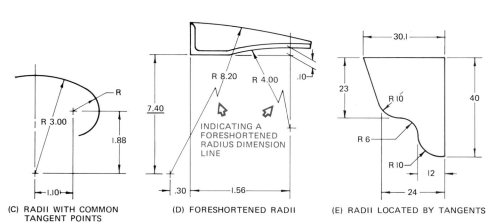

(C) RADII WITH COMMON TANGENT POINTS

(D) FORESHORTENED RADII

(E) RADII LOCATED BY TANGENTS

Fig. 7-2-3 Radii.

the location of the center is unimportant, a radial arc may be located by tangent lines (Fig. 7-2-3E).

Where the center of a radius is outside the drawing or interferes with another view, the radius dimension line may be foreshortened (Fig. 7-2-3D). The portion of the dimension line next to the arrowhead should be radial relative to the curved line. Where the radius dimension line is foreshortened and the center is located by coordinate dimensions, the dimensions locating the center should be shown as foreshortened or the dimension shown as not to scale.

Simple fillet and corner radii may also be dimensioned by use of a general note, such as

UNLESS OTHER SPECIFIED ALL ROUNDS AND FILLETS R.12 or ALL RADII R.12

The arcs shown on the part (Fig. 7-2-4A) may be dimensioned by:

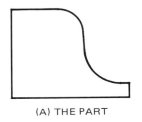

(A) THE PART

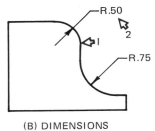

(B) DIMENSIONS

Fig. 7-2-4 Radius dimensioning.

1. Select the DIMENSION and RADIUS commands.

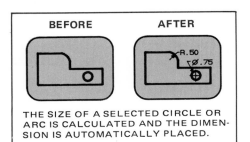

THE SIZE OF A SELECTED CIRCLE OR ARC IS CALCULATED AND THE DIMENSION IS AUTOMATICALLY PLACED.

2. Select the arc or circle (1).
3. Override or accept the dimension.
4. Select the location of the dimension (2). It will appear as shown in Fig. 7-2-4B.
5. Repeat Steps 2, 3, and 4 for the other arc. On larger arcs the dimension will appear within the arc as shown in Fig. 5-2-3 (C).

Where a radius is dimensioned in a view that does not show the true shape of the radius, TRUE R is added before the radius dimension, as illustrated in Fig. 7-2-5.

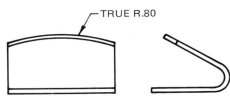

Fig. 7-2-5 Indicating true radius.

ROUNDED ENDS

Overall dimensions should be used for parts or features having rounded ends. For fully rounded ends, the number of rounded ends (2X) and the radius (R) are shown but the size is not (Fig. 7-2-6A). (For dimensioning repetitive features see Unit 7-3.) For parts with partially rounded ends, the

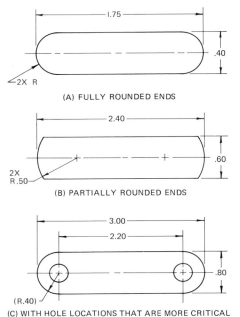

(A) FULLY ROUNDED ENDS

(B) PARTIALLY ROUNDED ENDS

(C) WITH HOLE LOCATIONS THAT ARE MORE CRITICAL

Fig. 7-2-6 External surfaces with rounded ends.

radius is dimensioned (Fig. 7-2-6B). Where a hole and radius have the same center and the hole location is more critical than the location of a radius, then either the radius or the overall length should be shown as a reference dimension (Fig. 7-2-6C). When executing the DIMENSION and RADIUS commands you will be prompted with the option to override or accept the dimension. The 2X and ( ) may be included by overriding rather than accepting the dimension. Do this by keying in the necessary information and pressing ENTER.

Dimensioning Chords, Arcs, and Angles

The difference in dimensioning chords, arcs, and angles is shown in Fig. 7-2-7.

Spherical Features

Spherical surfaces may be dimensioned as diameters or radii, but preceding the dimension should be abbreviation SR or SØ. See Fig. 7-2-8.

Cylindrical Holes

Plain, round holes are dimensioned in various ways, depending upon design and manufacturing requirements (Fig. 7-2-9). However, the leader is the method most commonly used. When a

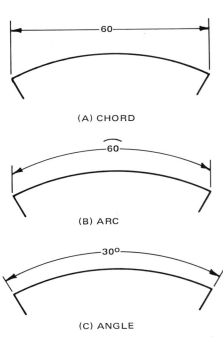

(A) CHORD

(B) ARC

(C) ANGLE

Fig. 7-2-7 Dimensioning chords, arcs, and angles.

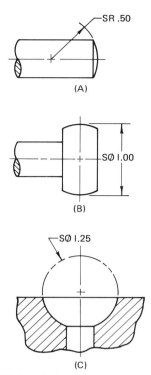

(A)

(B)

(C)

Fig. 7-2-8 Spherical surfaces.

leader is used to specify diameter sizes, as with small holes, the dimension is identified as a diameter by preceding the numerical value with the diameter symbol Ø. When overriding the calculated size use % % c to place the symbol.

The size, quantity, and depth may be shown on a single line, or on several lines. For through holes, the abbreviation THRU should follow the dimension if the drawing does not make this clear. The depth dimension of a blind hole is the depth of the full diameter and is normally included as part of the dimensioning note. The symbolic means of indicating where a dimension applies to the depth of a feature is to precede that dimension with the depth symbol, as shown in Fig. 7-2-9B.

Minimizing Leaders

If too many leaders would impair the legibility of a drawing, letters or symbols as shown in Fig. 7-2-10 should be used to identify the features.

Slotted Holes

Elongated holes and slots are used to compensate for inaccuracies in manufacturing and to provide for adjustment. See Fig. 7-2-11. The method selected to locate the slot would depend on how the slot was made. The method shown in Fig. 7-2-11B is used when the slot is punched out and the location of the punch is given. Figure 7-2-11A shows the dimensioning method used when the slot is machined out.

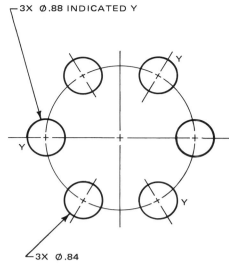

Fig. 7-2-10 Minimizing leaders.

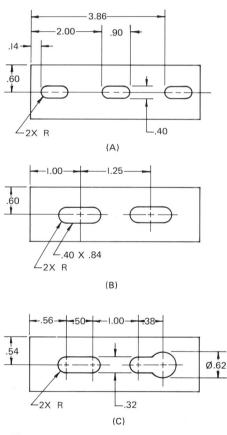

Fig. 7-2-11 Slotted holes.

Counterbores, Spotfaces, and Countersinks

Counterbores, spotfaces, and countersinks are specified on drawings by means of dimension symbols or abbreviations, the symbols being preferred.

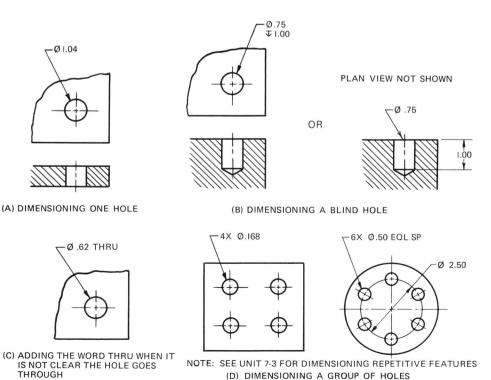

(A) DIMENSIONING ONE HOLE

(B) DIMENSIONING A BLIND HOLE

PLAN VIEW NOT SHOWN

OR

(C) ADDING THE WORD THRU WHEN IT IS NOT CLEAR THE HOLE GOES THROUGH

Fig. 7-2-9 Cylindrical holes.

NOTE: SEE UNIT 7-3 FOR DIMENSIONING REPETITIVE FEATURES
(D) DIMENSIONING A GROUP OF HOLES

If the symbols are not standard library items, it would be wise to prepare a symbol library.

The terms counterbore, spotface, and countersink indicate the form of the surface only and do not restrict the methods used to produce that form.

A **counterbore** is a flat-bottomed, cylindrical recess which permits the head of a fastening device, such as a bolt, to lie recessed into the part. The diameter, depth, and corner radius are specified in a note. In some cases, the thickness of the remaining stock may be dimensioned rather than the depth of the counterbore.

A **spotface** is an area where the surface is machined just enough to provide smooth, level seating for a bolt head, nut, or washer. The diameter of the faced area and either the depth of the spotface or the remaining thickness are given. A spotface may be specified by a general note and not delineated on the drawing. If no depth or remaining thickness is specified, it is implied that the spot-facing is the minimum depth necessary to clean up the surface to the specified diameter.

A **countersink** is an angular-sided recess to accommodate the head of flathead screws, rivets, and similar items. The diameter at the surface and the included angle are given. When the depth of the tapered section of the countersink is critical, this depth is specified in the note or by a dimension. For counterdrilled holes, the diameter, depth, and included angle of the counterdrill are given.

The symbols for counterbore or spotface, countersink, and depth are shown in Figs. 7-2-12 and 7-2-13. In each case the symbol precedes the dimension.

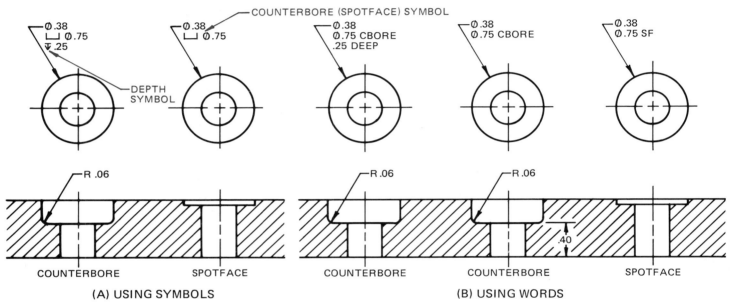

Fig. 7-2-12 Counterbored and spotfaced holes.

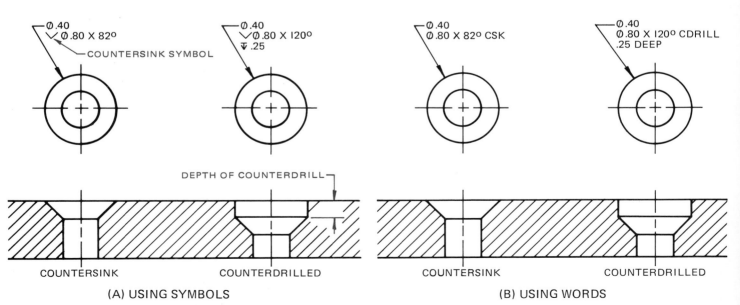

Fig. 7-2-13 Countersunk and counterdrilled holes.

Symbol Library Creation

The concept of a library is important when using standard parts or symbols. There are a great number of standard parts used by several industries. CAD systems offer users a variety of pre-drawn symbols. Normally, several symbols (e.g., all fasteners) are grouped together on a floppy disk. There are many standardized libraries. In the mechanical discipline common ones include:

- Dimension symbols
- Fasteners
- Welds
- Geometric tolerancing

Libraries are especially valuable for the development of schematic diagrams, since many identical symbols are required on the same drawing. Some examples of other standard symbol libraries include:

- Piping
- Architectural
- Electronic
- Electrical

Advantages to the use of a library are several. First, tremendous productivity gains are experienced. It is, in fact, common to outpace the manual development of schematics by a factor of 20 to 1.

Second, since the human factor is eliminated, accuracy is improved. If the size of the symbol in the library is correct, every subsequent symbol will be correct because each is an exact copy. Also, if each symbol must be created directly on the drawing, it will increase the required file size on the disk. Thus, the use of standardized libraries produces a better result with less effort and disk space. Remember, whenever possible "build drawings" don't "draw drawings."

Generally, libraries are used in one of two ways. Commonly, they are combined with menus (screen or tablet) for standard applications. If a graphics tablet is used, each symbol may easily be "pulled off" a menu cell (box). Digitize within the appropriate cell for the symbol you wish to have automatically created. The other methods is to key in the name of the desired symbol and follow the prompts.

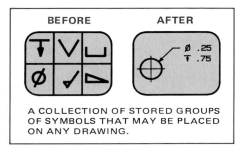

A COLLECTION OF STORED GROUPS OF SYMBOLS THAT MAY BE PLACED ON ANY DRAWING.

If a dimension symbol library does not exist, it will be wise to prepare it yourself and it will always be available for future use. First, however, the meaning of each symbol will be defined.

The procedure to prepare a symbol library consisting of the three symbols (counterbore, countersink, and depth) is:

1. Draw the counterbore (or spotface) symbol using the LINE command.
2. Issue the command to create a symbol library (e.g., WBLOCK).
3. Key in a name for the symbol, CBORE, and press ENTER twice.
4. Select an insertion point (where it is to be placed).
5. Select each entity (line) that describes the symbol and press ENTER.
6. Select SAVE and store the symbol on disk by following the prompts.
7. Repeat Steps 1 through 6 for the remaining symbols.

If it is desired to store symbols on a floppy disk, insert a pre-formatted floppy into drive A (Unit 2-2) and key A: prior to the name you are saving under.

The symbol library has now been prepared and may be used on any drawing over and over again. To do this:

1. Select the command to INSERT a previously defined symbol.
2. Key in the symbol name (CBORE) and press ENTER. Remember to use A: if it is on a floppy in drive A.
3. Select the insertion point by indicating where it is to be placed.
4. Follow the prompts to key in a different symbol size and rotation angle if desired. The symbol will appear.

5. Repeat Steps 1 through 4. The symbols will appear as shown in Fig. 7-2-14.

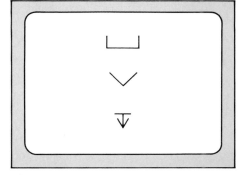

Fig. 7-2-14

References and Source Materials

1. ANSI Y14.5M *Dimensioning and Tolerancing.*

ASSIGNMENTS

See Assignments 4 and 5 for Unit 7-2 starting on page 148.

■ UNIT 7-3

Dimensioning Common Features

Repetitive Features and Dimensions

Repetitive features and dimensions may be specified on a drawing by the use of a X in conjunction with the numeral to indicate the number of times or places they are required. (See Fig. 7-3-1). A space is shown between the X and the dimension. This will either be keyed in using the TEXT command overriding when executing the DIMENSION command.

Symmetrical Outlines

Symmetrical outlines may be dimensioned on one side of the axis of symmetry only. See Fig. 7-3-2. Where only part of the outline is shown, because the size of the part or space limitations, symmetrical shapes may be shown by only one-half of the outline, and the symmetry is indicated by applying the symbol for part symmetry to the

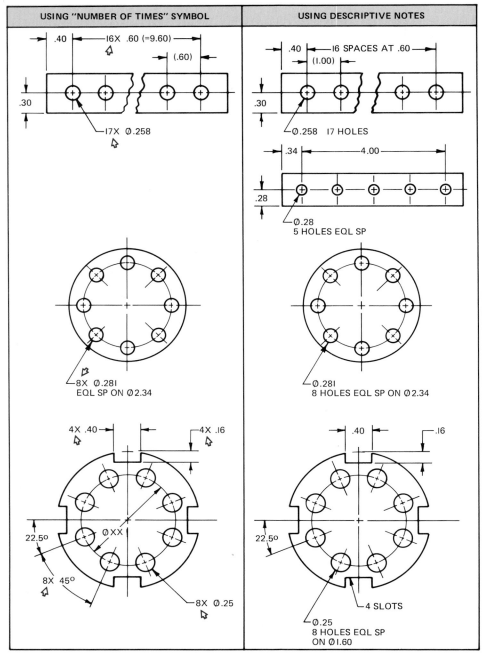

USING "NUMBER OF TIMES" SYMBOL	USING DESCRIPTIVE NOTES

Fig. 7-3-1 Dimensioning repetitive features.

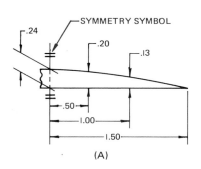

(A)

Fig. 7-3-2 Dimensioning symmetrical features.

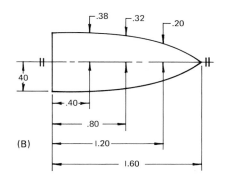

(B)

center line. In such cases, the outline of the part should extend slightly beyond the center line and terminate with a break line. Note the dimensioning method of extending the dimension lines to act as extension lines for the perpendicular dimensions.

Chamfers

The process of chamfering, that is, cutting away the inside or outside piece, is done to facilitate assembly. Chamfers are normally dimensioned by giving their angle and linear length using the LEADER, or LEADER and TEXT commands. See Fig. 7-3-3. When the chamfer is 45°, it may be specified as a note.

When a very small chamfer is permissible, primarily to break a sharp corner, it may be dimensioned but not

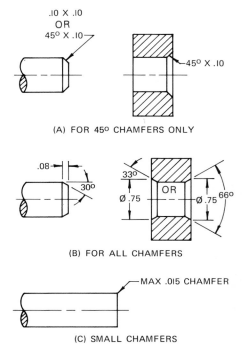

(A) FOR 45° CHAMFERS ONLY

(B) FOR ALL CHAMFERS

(C) SMALL CHAMFERS

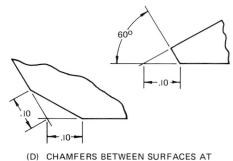

(D) CHAMFERS BETWEEN SURFACES AT OTHER THAN 90°

Fig. 7-3-3 Dimensioning chamfers.

drawn, as in Fig. 7-3-3C. If not otherwise specified, an angle of 45° is understood.

Internal chamfers may be dimensioned in the same manner, but it is often desirable to give the diameter over the chamfer. The angle may also be given as the included angle using the ANGULAR DIMENSION command (Fig. 7-3-3B) if this is a design requirement. This type of dimensioning is generally necessary for larger diameters, especially those over 2 in. (50 mm), whereas chamfers on small holes are usually expressed as countersinks. Chamfers are never measured along the angular surface.

Slopes and Tapers

Slope A slope is the inclination of the line representing an inclined surface. It is expressed as a ratio of the difference in the heights at right angles to the base line, at a specified distance apart. See Fig. 7-3-4A through D. Figure 7-3-4D is the preferred method of dimensioning slopes on architectural and structural drawings.

The following dimensions and symbol may be used, in different combinations, to define the slope of a line or flat surface:

- The slope specified as a ratio combined with the slope symbol (Fig. 7-3-4A)
- The slope specified by an angle (Fig. 7-3-4B)
- The dimensions showing the difference in the heights of two points from the base line and the distance between them (Fig. 7-3-4C)

Taper A taper is the ratio of the difference in the diameters of two sections (perpendicular to the axis) of a cone to the distance between these two

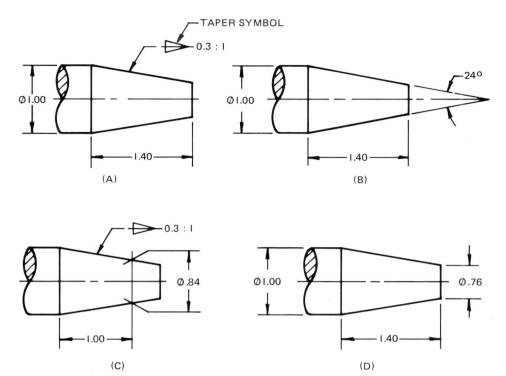

Fig. 7-3-5 Dimensioning tapers.

sections. See Fig. 7-3-5. When the taper symbol is used, the vertical leg is always shown on the left and precedes the ratio figures. The following dimensions may be used, in suitable combinations, to define the size and form of tapered features:

- The diameter at one end of the tapered feature
- The length of the tapered feature
- The rate of taper
- The included angle
- The taper ratio
- The diameter at a selected cross section
- The dimension locating the cross section

Knurls

Knurling is specified by keying in the type, pitch, and diameter before and after knurling. See Fig. 7-3-6. The pitch follows the pitch number. Where control is not required, the diameter after knurling is omitted. Where only portions of a feature require knurling, axial dimensions must be provided. Commonly used types of knurls are straight, diagonal, spiral, convex, raised diamond, depressed diamond, and radial. Where required to provide a press fit between parts, knurling is specified by a note on the drawing which includes the type of knurl required, the pitch, the toleranced diam-

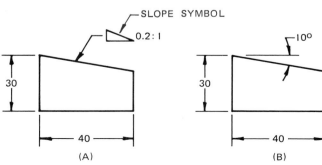

Fig. 7-3-4 Dimensioning slopes.

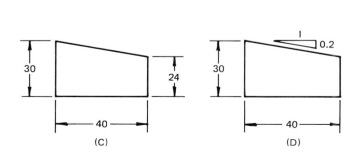

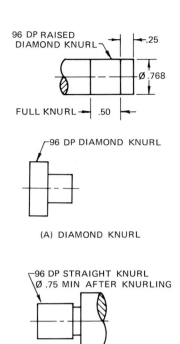

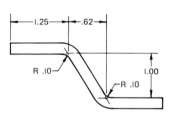

(A) DIAMOND KNURL

(B) STRAIGHT KNURL

Fig. 7-3-6 Dimensioning knurls.

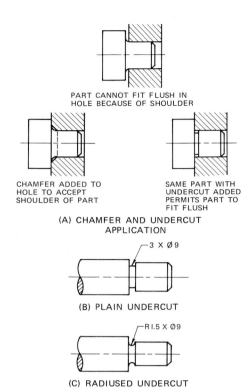

(A) CHAMFER AND UNDERCUT APPLICATION

(B) PLAIN UNDERCUT

(C) RADIUSED UNDERCUT

Fig. 7-3-8 Dimensioning undercuts.

the same side if possible. Dimensions apply to the side on which the dimensions are shown unless otherwise specified. See Fig. 7-3-7. The LINEAR DIMENSIONS are accurately created by using OSNAP INTERSECTION when picking the extension line locations.

Undercuts

The operation of undercutting or necking, that is, cutting a recess in a diameter, is done to permit two parts to come together, as illustrated in Fig. 7-3-8A. It is indicated on the drawing by the LEADER command indicating the width and then the diameter. If the radius is shown at the bottom of the undercut, it will be assumed that the radius is equal to one-half the width unless otherwise specified, and the diameter will apply to the center of the undercut. When the size of the undercut is unimportant, the dimension may be left off the drawing.

Fig. 7-3-7 Dimensioning theoretical points of intersection.

eter of the feature prior to knurling, and the minimum acceptable diameter after knurling. The pitch is usually expressed in terms of teeth per inch or millimeter and may be the straight pitch, circular pitch, or diametral pitch. For cylindrical surfaces, the latter is preferred. Although it is no longer common to illustrate a knurl, CAD systems have a "double hatch" option (see Unit 8-1). This allows the effortless creation of a knurl.

Formed Parts

In dimensioning formed parts, the inside radius is usually specified, rather than the outside radius, but all forming dimensions should be shown on

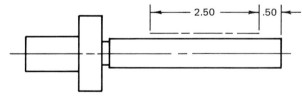

(A) LENGTH OF SURFACE

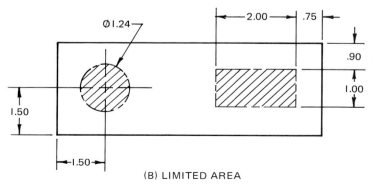

(B) LIMITED AREA

Fig. 7-3-9 Dimensioning limited lengths and areas.

Limited Lengths and Areas

Sometimes it is necessary to dimension a limited length or area of a surface to indicate a special condition. In such instances, the area or lengths is indicated by a chain line (Fig. 7-3-9A). When indicating a length of surface, the chain line is drawn parallel and adjacent to the surface. When indicating an area of surface, the area is cross-hatched (see Unit 8-1) within the chain line boundary. See Fig. 7-3-9B.

Wire, Sheet Metal, and Drill Rod

Wire, sheet metal, and drill rod, which are manufactured to gage or code sizes, should be shown by their decimal dimensions, but gage numbers, drill letters, etc., may be shown in parentheses following those dimensions.

EXAMPLES

Sheet — .141 (No. 10 USS GA)
— .081 (No. 12 B & S GA)

References

1. ANSI Y14.5M, *Dimensioning and Tolerancing.*

ASSIGNMENTS

See Assignments 6 through 10 for Unit 7-3 starting on page 150.

■ UNIT 7-4

Dimensioning Methods

The choice of the most suitable dimensions and dimensioning methods will depend, to some extent, on how the part will be produced and whether the drawings are intended for unit or mass production.

Unit production refers to cases where each part is to be made separately, using general-purpose tools and machines.

Mass production refers to parts produced in quantity, where special tools and gages are usually provided.

Either linear or angular dimensions may locate features with respect to one another (point-to-point) or from a datum. Point-to-point dimensions may be adequate for describing simple parts. Dimensions from a datum plane

may be necessary if a part with more than one critical dimension must assemble with another part. CAD systems provide the datum plane technique, referred to as *baseline* dimensioning.

The following systems of dimensioning are used more commonly for engineering drawings.

Rectangular Coordinate Dimensioning

This is a method for indicating distance, location, and size by means of linear dimensions measured parallel or perpendicular to reference axes or datum planes that are perpendicular to one another.

Coordinate dimensioning with dimension lines must clearly identify the datum plane from which the dimensions originate. See Fig. 7-4-1. Be sure to select the BASELINE submenu option immediately after the smallest dimension is placed. Select the second extension line location for the next largest dimension and press ENTER. Repeat the procedure.

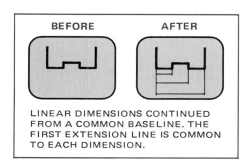

LINEAR DIMENSIONS CONTINUED FROM A COMMON BASELINE. THE FIRST EXTENSION LINE IS COMMON TO EACH DIMENSION.

Rectangular Coordinates for Arbitrary Points Coordinates for arbitrary points of reference without a grid appear adjacent to each point (See Fig. 7-4-2) or in tabular form. See Fig. 7-4-3. The CAD system will automatically display the X, Y position of any point coordinate by toggling the COORDINATE option. Simply move the cursor to the desired position and read the result on the monitor screen.

Rectangular Coordinate Dimensioning Without Dimension Lines (Arrowless Dimensioning) Dimensions may be shown on extension lines without the use of dimension lines and arrowheads. The base lines may be zero coordinates or they may be labeled *X, Y,* and *Z.* See Figs. 7-4-4 and 7-4-5.

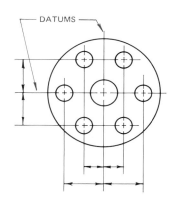

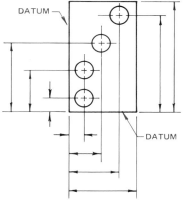

Fig. 7-4-1 Rectangular coordinate dimensioning.

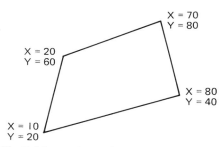

Fig. 7-4-2 Coordinates for arbitrary points.

This type can be obtained by using TEXT to key in the dimension and placing the dimension near each extension line.

Tabular Dimensioning

Tabular dimensioning is a type of coordinate dimensioning in which dimensions from mutually perpendicular planes are listed in a table on the drawing rather than on the pictorial delineation. This method is used on drawings which require the location of

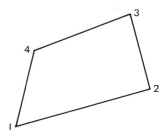

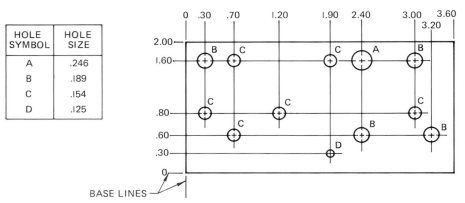

POINT	X	Y
1	10	20
2	80	40
3	70	80
4	20	60

Fig. 7-4-3 Coordinates for arbitrary points in tabular form.

HOLE SYMBOL	HOLE SIZE
A	.246
B	.189
C	.154
D	.125

Fig. 7-4-4 Rectangular coordinate dimensioning (arrowless dimensioning).

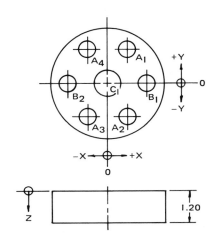

HOLE DIA	HOLE SYMBOL	LOCATION		
		X	Y	Z
.375	A_1	.50	.75	THRU
	A_2	.50	−.75	THRU
	A_3	−.50	−.75	THRU
	A_4	−.50	.75	THRU
.250	B_1	1.00	0	.60
	B_2	−1.00	0	.60
.500	C_1	0	0	THRU

Fig. 7-4-6 Rectangular coordinate dimensioning in tabular form with base (zero) line located at center of part.

HOLE DIA	HOLE SYMBOL	LOCATION		
		X	Y	Z
5.6	A_1	60	40	18
4.8	B_1	10	40	THRU
	B_2	75	40	THRU
	B_3	60	16	THRU
	B_4	80	16	THRU
4	C_1	18	40	THRU
	C_2	55	40	THRU
	C_3	10	20	THRU
	C_4	30	20	THRU
	C_5	75	20	THRU
	C_6	18	16	THRU
3.2	D_1	55	8	12
8.1	E_1	42	20	12

Fig. 7-4-5 Tabular dimensioning.

a larger number of similarly shaped features. See Figs. 7-4-5 and 7-4-6.

Polar Coordinate Dimensioning

Polar coordinate dimensioning is commonly used in circular planes or circular configurations of features. It is a method of indicating the position of a point, line, or surface by means of an ANGULAR dimension or both a LINEAR and an ANGULAR dimension. See Fig. 7-4-7.

Chordal Dimensioning

The chordal dimensioning system may also be used for the spacing of points on the circumference of a circle relative to a datum, where manufacturing methods indicate that this will be more convenient. See Fig. 7-4-8. The ALIGNED (LINEAR) dimensioning option would be used for this purpose and executed using the standard linear dimension procedure.

True Position Dimensioning

True position dimensioning has many advantages over the coordinate dimensioning system. See Fig. 7-4-9. Because of its scope, it is covered as a complete topic in Chap. 15.

Chain Dimensioning

When a series of dimensions is applied on a point-to-point basis, it is called chain dimensioning. See Fig. 7-4-10. Immediately following placement of the 1.80 dimension select CONTINUOUS, the next extension line location, and press ENTER. Continue the procedure for remaining dimensions. Each dimension continues from the second extension line of the previous

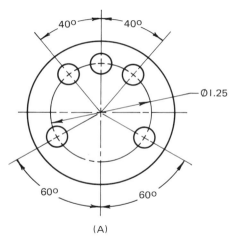

Fig. 7-4-7 Polar coordinate dimensioning.

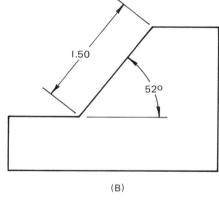

(B)

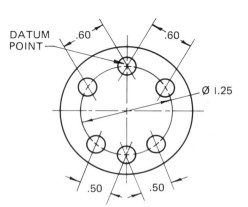

Fig. 7-4-8 Chordal dimensioning.

dimension. A disadvantage of this system is that it may result in an undesirable accumulation of tolerances between individual features. (See Unit 7-5.) Also it is difficult to execute when one of the dimensions is small.

Datum, Common-Point, or Baseline Dimensioning

When several dimensions begin at a common reference point, line, or plane, the method is called datum,

(A) PARALLEL METHOD

(B) SUPERIMPOSED METHOD

Fig. 7-4-11 Common point (baseline) dimensioning.

common-point, or baseline dimensioning. Dimensioning from reference lines may be executed as parallel dimensioning or as a superimposed running dimensioning. See Fig. 7-4-11. To obtain the datum dimensioning result as shown in Fig. 7-4-11A, use the

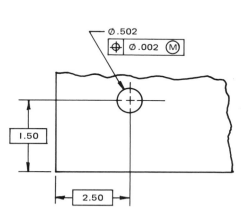

Fig. 7-4-9 True position dimensioning.

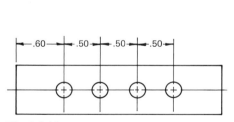

Fig. 7-4-10 Chain dimensioning.

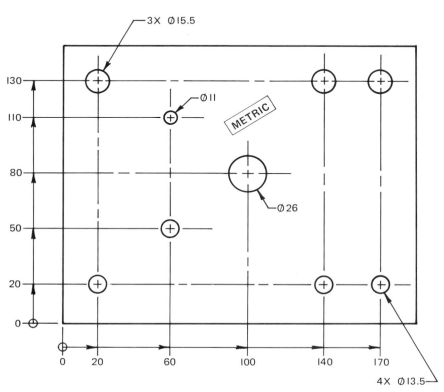

Fig. 7-4-12 Superimposed running dimensioning in two directions.

BASELINE dimension linear submenu option. Due to space limitations smaller dimensions will not place the text within the extension lines.

Superimposed running dimensioning is simplified parallel dimensioning and may be used where there are space problems. Dimensions should be placed near the arrowhead, in line with the corresponding extension line as shown in Fig. 7-4-11B.

The origin is indicated by a circle and the opposite end of each LEADER is terminated with an arrowhead. Dimensions are placed near the arrowhead 90° rotated TEXT.

It may be advantageous to use datum, common-point, or baseline dimensions in two directions. In such cases, the origins may be shown as in Fig. 7-4-12, or at the center of a hole, or other feature.

References

1. ANSI Y14.5M, *Dimensioning and Tolerancing.*

ASSIGNMENTS

See Assignments 11 through 14 for Unit 7-4 starting on page 151.

■ **UNIT 7-5**

Limits and Tolerances

In the 6000 years of the history of technical drawing as a means for the communication of engineering information, it seems inconceivable that such an elementary practice as the tolerancing of dimensions, which we take so much for granted today, was introduced for the first time about 70 years ago.

Apparently, engineers and fabricators came in a very gradual manner to the realization that exact dimensions and shapes could not be attained in the manufacture of materials and products.

The skilled tradespeople of old prided themselves on being able to work to exact dimensions. What they really meant was that they dimensioned objects with a degree of accuracy greater than that with which they could measure. The use of modern measuring instruments would have shown the deviations from the sizes which they called exact.

As soon as it was realized that variations in the sizes of parts had always been present, that such variations could be restricted but not avoided, and also that slight variations in the size which a part was originally intended to have could be tolerated without its correct functioning being impaired, it was evident that interchangeable parts need not be identical parts, but that it would be sufficient if the significant sizes which controlled their fits lay between definite limits. Accordingly, the problem of interchangeable manufacture evolved from the making of parts to a would-be exact size, to the holding of parts between two limiting sizes lying so closely together that any intermediate size would be acceptable.

Tolerances are the permissible variations in the specified form, size, or location of individual features of a part from that shown on the drawing. The finished form and size into which material is to be fabricated are defined on a drawing by various geometric shapes and dimensions.

As mentioned previously, the worker cannot be expected to produce the exact size of parts as indicated by the dimensions on a drawing; so a certain amount of variation on each dimension must be tolerated. For example, a dimension given as 1.500 ± .004 in. means that the manufactured part can be anywhere between 1.496 and 1.504 in. and that the

tolerance sizes (1.504 and 1.496 in., respectively) are known as the *limits.*

Greater accuracy costs more money, and since economy in manufacturing would not permit all dimensions to be held to the same accuracy, a system for dimensioning must be used. See Fig. 7-5-1. Generally, most parts require only a few dimensions to be accurate.

In order that assembled parts may function properly and to allow for interchangeable manufacturing, it is necessary to permit only a certain amount of tolerance on each of the mating parts and a certain amount of allowance between them.

In order to calculate limit dimensions, the following definitions should be clearly understood (refer to Fig. 7-5-2).

BASIC SIZE	1.500
BASIC SIZE WITH TOLERANCE ADDED	1.500± .004
HALF OF TOTAL TOLERANCE ⟋	
LIMITS—LARGEST AND SMALLEST SIZES PERMITTED	1.504 1.496
TOLERANCE— DIFFERENCE BETWEEN MIN AND MAX LIMITS	.008

Fig. 7-5-2 Limit and tolerance terminology.

Basic Size The *basic size* of a dimension is the theoretical size from which the limits for that dimension are derived, by the application of the allowance and tolerance.

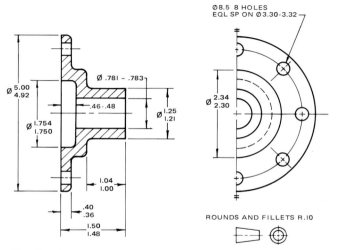

Fig. 7-5-1 A working drawing.

Limits of Size These limits are the maximum and minimum sizes permissible for a specific dimension.

Tolerance The *tolerance* on a dimension is the total permissible variation in its size. The tolerance is the difference between the limits of size.

Maximum Material Size The *maximum material size* is that limit of size of a feature which results in the part containing the maximum amount of material. Thus it is the maximum limit of size for a shaft or an external feature, or the minimum limit of size for a hole or internal feature.

TOLERANCING

All dimensions required in the manufacture of a product have a tolerance, except those identified as reference, maximum, minimum, or stock. Tolerances may be expressed in one of the following ways:

- As specified limits of tolerances shown directly on the drawing for a specified dimension
- In a general tolerance note, referring to all dimensions on the drawing for which tolerances are not otherwise specified
- In the form of a note referring to specific dimensions

Tolerances on dimensions that locate features may be applied directly to the locating dimensions or by the positional tolerancing method covered in Chapter 15. Tolerancing applicable to the control of form and runout is also covered in detail in Chapter 15 and is referred to as geometric tolerancing.

Direct Tolerancing Methods

A tolerance applied directly to a dimension may be expressed in two ways.

Limit Dimensioning (Refer to Figs. 7-5-3 and 7-5-4). For this method, the high limit (maximum value) is placed above the low limit (minimum value). When it is expressed in a single line, the low limit precedes the high limit and they are separated by a dash.

Where limit dimensions are used and where either the maximum or minimum dimension has digits to the right of the decimal point, the other value should have the zeros added so that both the limits of size are ex-

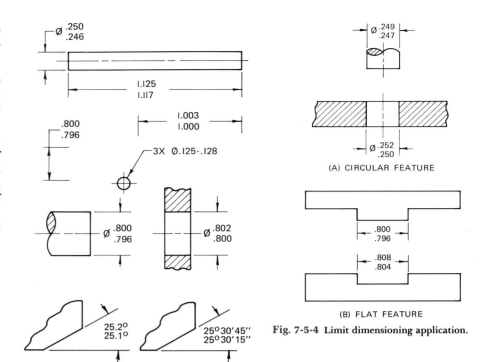

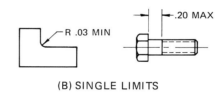

(A) TWO LIMITS

R .03 MIN .20 MAX

(B) SINGLE LIMITS

Fig. 7-5-3 Limit dimensioning.

(A) CIRCULAR FEATURE

(B) FLAT FEATURE

Fig. 7-5-4 Limit dimensioning application.

pressed to the same number of decimal places. This applies to both U.S. Customary and metric drawings. For example:

30.75		30.75
30.00	*not*	30
.750		.75
.748	*not*	.748

Plus and Minus Tolerancing (Refer to Fig. 7-5-5). For this method the dimension of the specified size is given

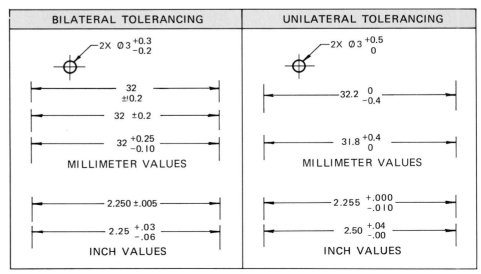

Fig. 7-5-5 Plus and minus tolerancing.

first and is followed by a plus or minus expression of tolerancing. The plus value is placed above the minus value. This type of tolerancing can be broken down into bilateral and unilateral tolerancing. See Figs. 7-5-6 and 7-5-7.

Metric Tolerancing

In the metric system (millimeter) the dimension need not be shown to the

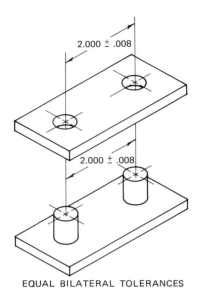

EQUAL BILATERAL TOLERANCES

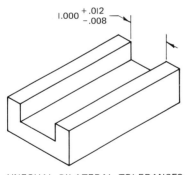

UNEQUAL BILATERAL TOLERANCES

Fig. 7-5-6 Application of bilateral tolerances.

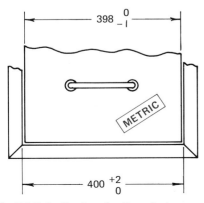

Fig. 7-5-7 Application of unilateral tolerances.

same number of decimal places as its tolerance. For example:

$$1.5 \pm 0.04 \quad not \quad 1.50 \pm 0.04$$
$$10 \pm 0.1 \quad not \quad 10.0 \pm 0.1$$

Where bilateral tolerancing is used both the plus and minus values have the same number of decimal places, using zeros where necessary. For example:

$$30 \begin{array}{l} +0.15 \\ -0.10 \end{array} \quad not \quad 30 \begin{array}{l} +0.15 \\ -0.1 \end{array}$$

Where unilateral tolerancing is used and either the plus or minus value is nil, a single zero is shown without a plus or minus sign. For example:

$$40 \begin{array}{l} 0 \\ -0.15 \end{array} \quad or \quad 40 \begin{array}{l} +0.15 \\ 0 \end{array}$$

Inch Tolerancing

In the U.S. Customary system (inch), both the plus and minus tolerance and its dimension are expressed with the same number of decimal places. For example:

Bilateral:

$$.500 \pm .004 \quad not \quad .50 \pm .004$$

Unilateral:

$$.750 \begin{array}{l} +.005 \\ -.000 \end{array} \quad not \quad .750 \begin{array}{l} +.005 \\ -0 \end{array}$$

bilateral:

$$30.0° \pm .2° \quad not \quad 30° \pm .2°$$

Conversion charts for tolerances are shown in Fig. 7-5-8.

Either bilateral or unilateral tolerances may be readily added to any dimension.

1. Set the tolerance (DIMTOL) to ON and then select the PLUS TOLERANCE (DIMPT) from the DIMENSION VARIABLE submenu.

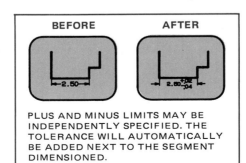

PLUS AND MINUS LIMITS MAY BE INDEPENDENTLY SPECIFIED. THE TOLERANCE WILL AUTOMATICALLY BE ADDED NEXT TO THE SEGMENT DIMENSIONED.

2. Key in the desired value (e.g., .04) and press ENTER.

TOTAL TOLERANCE IN INCHES		MILLIMETER CONVERSION ROUNDED TO
AT LEAST	LESS THAN	
.00004	.0004	4 DECIMAL PLACES
.0004	.004	3 DECIMAL PLACES
.004	.04	2 DECIMAL PLACES
.04	.4	1 DECIMAL PLACE
.4 AND OVER		WHOLE mm

TOTAL TOLERANCE IN MILLIMETERS		INCH CONVERSION ROUNDED TO
AT LEAST	LESS THAN	
0.002	0.02	5 DECIMAL PLACES
0.02	0.2	4 DECIMAL PLACES
0.2	2	3 DECIMAL PLACES
2 AND OVER		2 DECIMAL PLACES

Fig. 7-5-8 Conversion charts for tolerances.

3. Select the MINUS TOLERANCE (DIMTM) from the DIMENSION VARIABLE submenu.
4. Key in the desired value (e.g., .02) and press ENTER.
5. Select the F1 and the HORIZONTAL (LINEAR) DIMENSION command.
6. Select the end positions (points 1 and 2) of the desired segment as shown in Fig. 7-5-9A. Use OSNAP ENDPOINT.
7. Select location for the dimension and accept it (ENTER). The dimension and tolerance will automatically be created as shown in Fig. 7-5-9B.

General Tolerance Notes The use of general tolerance notes using the TEXT command greatly simplifies the drawing and saves much layout in its preparation. The following examples illustrate the wide field of application of this system. The values given in the examples are typical.

EXAMPLE 1 (METRIC)
EXCEPT WHERE STATED OTHERWISE, TOLERANCES ON FINISHED DECIMAL DIMENSIONS ±0.1.

EXAMPLE 2
EXCEPT WHERE STATED OTHERWISE, TOLERANCES ON FINISHED DIMENSIONS TO BE AS FOLLOWS:

Dimension (in.)	Tolerance
Up to 4.00	±.004
From 4.01 to 12.00	±.003
from 12.01 to 24.00	±.02
Over 24.00	±.04

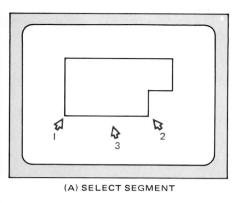

(A) SELECT SEGMENT

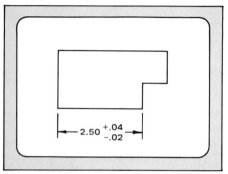

(B) PLACE DIMENSION WITH TOLERANCE

Fig. 7-5-9 Tolerancing method.

A comparison between the tolerancing methods described is shown in Fig. 7-5-10.

Tolerance Accumulation

It is necessary also to consider the effect of each tolerance with respect to other tolerances, and not to permit a chain of tolerances to build up a cumulative tolerance between surfaces or points that have an important rela-

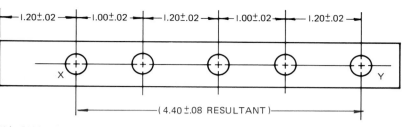

(A) CHAIN DIMENSIONING (GREATEST TOLERANCE ACCUMULATION)

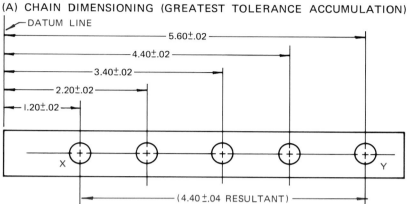

(B) DATUM DIMENSIONING (LESSER TOLERANCE ACCUMULATION)

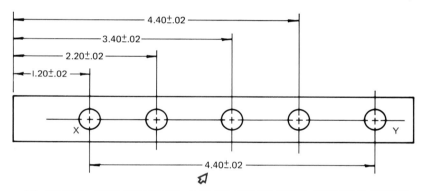

(C) DIRECT DIMENSIONING (LEAST TOLERANCE ACCUMULATION)

Fig. 7-5-11 Dimensioning method comparison.

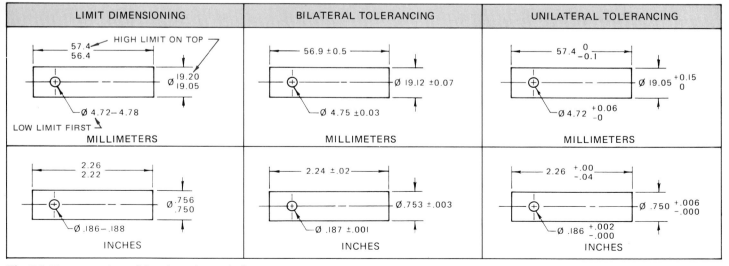

Fig. 7-5-10 A comparison of the tolerancing methods.

tion to one another. Where the position of a surface in any one direction is controlled by more than one tolerance, then the tolerances are cumulative. Figure 7-5-11 compares the tolerance accumulation resulting from three different methods of dimensioning.

Chain Dimensioning The maximum variation between any two features is equal to the sum of the tolerances on the intermediate distances. This results in the greatest tolerance accumulation, as illustrated by the ±.08 variation between holes X and Y, as shown in Fig. 7-5-11A.

Datum Dimensioning The maximum variation between any two features is equal to the sum of the tolerances on the two dimensions from the datum to the feature. This reduces the tolerance accumulation, as illustrated by the ±.04 variation between holes X and Y, as shown in Fig. 7-5-11B.

Direct Dimensioning The maximum variation between any two features is controlled by the tolerance on the dimension between the features. This results in the least tolerance accumulation, as illustrated by the ±.02 variation between holes X and Y as shown in Fig. 7-5-11C.

References

1. ANSI Y14.5M, *Dimensioning and Tolerancing.*

ASSIGNMENT

See Assignment 15 for Unit 7-5 on page 153.

■ UNIT 7-6

Fits and Allowances

In order that assembled parts may function properly and to allow for interchangeable manufacturing it is necessary to permit only a certain amount of tolerance on each of the mating parts and a certain amount of allowance between them.

Fits

The fit between two mating parts is the relationship between them with respect to the amount of clearance or interference present when they are assembled.

There are three basic types of fits: clearance, interference, and transition.

Clearance Fit A fit between mating parts having limits of size so prescribed that a clearance always results in assembly.

Interference Fit A fit between mating parts having limits of size so prescribed that an interference always results in assembly.

Transition Fit A fit between mating parts having limits of size so prescribed as to partially or wholly overlap, so that either a clearance or interference may result in assembly.

Allowance

An allowance is an intentional difference in correlated dimensions of mating parts. It is the minimum clearance (positive allowance) or maximum interference (negative allowance) between such parts.

The most important terms relating to limits and fits are shown in Fig. 7-6-1. The terms are defined as follows:

Basic Size The size to which limits or deviations are assigned. The basic size is the same for both members of a fit.

Deviation The algebraic difference between a size and the corresponding basic size.

Upper Deviation The algebraic difference between the maximum limit of size and the corresponding basic size.

Lower Deviation The algebraic difference between the minimum limit of size and the corresponding basic size.

Tolerance The difference between the maximum and minimum size limits on a part.

Tolerance Zone A zone representing the tolerance and its position in relation to the basic size.

Fundamental Deviation The deviation closest to the basic size.

DESCRIPTION OF FITS
Running and Sliding Fits

These fits, for which tolerances and clearances are given in the Appendix, represent a special type of clearance fit. These are intended to provide a similar running performance, with suitable lubrication allowance, throughout the range of sizes.

Locational Fits

Locational fits are intended to determine only the location of the mating parts; they may provide rigid or accurate location, as with interference fits, or some freedom of location, as with

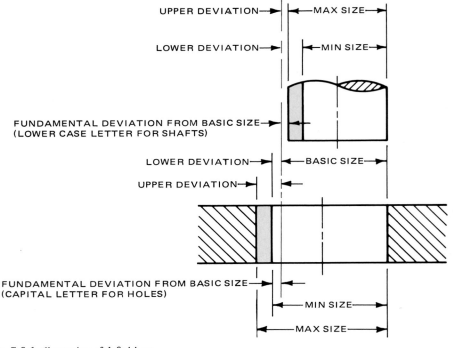

Fig. 7-6-1 Illustration of definitions.

clearance fits. Accordingly, they are divided into three groups: clearance fits, transition fits, and interference fits.

Locational clearance fits are intended for parts which are normally stationary but which can be freely assembled or disassembled. They run from snug fits for parts requiring accuracy of location, through the medium clearance fits for parts such as ball, race, and housing, to the looser fastener fits where freedom of assembly is of prime importance.

Locational transition fits are a compromise between clearance and interference fits, for application where accuracy of location is important but a small amount of either clearance or interference is permissible.

Locational interference fits are used where accuracy of location is of prime importance and for parts requiring rigidity and alignment with no special requirements for bore pressure. Such fits are not intended for parts designed to transmit frictional loads from one part to another by virtue of the tightness of fit; these conditions are covered by force fits.

Drive and Force Fits

Drive and force fits constitute a special type of interference fit, normally characterized by maintenance of constant bore pressures throughout the range of sizes. The interference therefore varies almost directly with diameter, and the difference between its minimum and maximum values is small, to maintain the resulting pressures within reasonable limits.

Interchangeability of Parts

Increased demand for manufactured products led to the development of new production techniques. Interchangeability of parts became the basis for mass-production, low-cost manufacturing, and it brought about the refinement of machinery, machine tools, and measuring devices. Today it is possible and generally practical to design for 100 percent interchangeability.

No part can be manufactured to exact dimensions. Tool wear, machine variations, and the human factor all contribute to some degree of deviation from perfection. It is therefore necessary to determine the deviation and permissible clearance, or interfer-

ence, to produce the desired fit between parts.

Modern industry has adopted three basic approaches to manufacturing.

1. *The completely interchangeable assembly.* Any and all mating parts of a design are toleranced to permit them to assemble and function properly without the need for machining or fitting at assembly.
2. *The fitted assembly.* Mating features of a design are fabricated either simultaneously or with respect to one another. Individual members of mating features are not interchangeable.
3. *The selected assembly.* All parts are mass-produced, but members of mating features are individually selected to provide the required relationship with one another.

STANDARD INCH FITS

Standard fits are designated for design purposes in specifications and on design sketches by means of the symbols as shown in Fig. 7-6-2. These symbols, however, are not intended to be shown directly on shop drawings; instead the actual limits of size shall be determined, and the limits shall be specified on the drawings.

The letter symbols used are as follows:

RC   Running and sliding fit
LC   Locational clearance fit
LT   Locational transition fit
LN   Locational interference fit
FN   Force or shrink fit

These letter symbols are used in conjunction with numbers representing the class of fit; for example, FN4 represents a class 4, force fit.

Each of these symbols (two letters and a number) represents a complete fit, for which the minimum and maximum clearance or interference, and the limits of size for the mating parts, are given directly in Appendix B tables 47 through 51. See Fig. 7-6-3.

Running and Sliding Fits

RC1 Precision Sliding Fit This fit is intended for the accurate location of parts which must assemble without perceptible play, for high precision work such as gages.

RC2 Sliding Fit This fit is intended for accurate location, but with greater maximum clearance than class RC1.

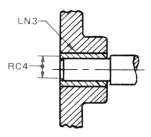

(A) SHAFT IN BUSHED HOLE

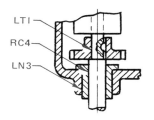

(B) GEAR AND SHAFT IN BUSHED BEARING

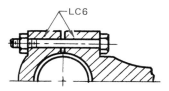

(C) CONNECTING-ROD BOLT

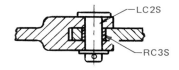

(D) LINK PIN (SHAFT BASIS FITS)

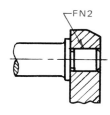

(E) CRANK PIN IN CAST IRON

Fig. 7-6-2 Typical design sketches showing classes of fits.

Parts made to this fit move and turn easily but are not intended to run freely, and in the larger sizes may seize with small temperature changes.

Note: LC1 and LC2 locational clearance fits may also be used as sliding fits with greater tolerances.

RC3 Precision Running Fit This fit is about the closest fit which can be expected to run freely, and is intended for precision work for oil-lubricated bearings at slow speeds and light journal pressures, but is not suitable where

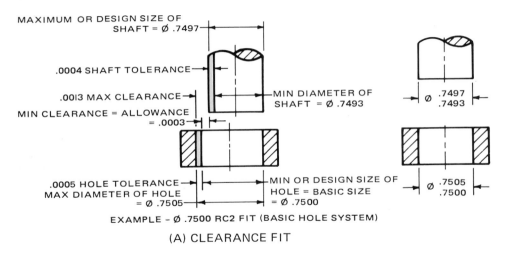

(A) CLEARANCE FIT

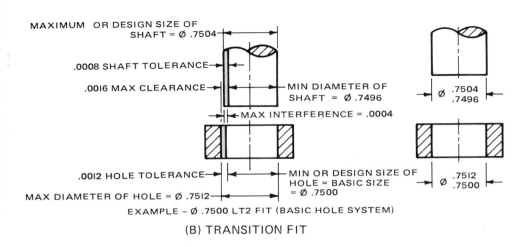

(B) TRANSITION FIT

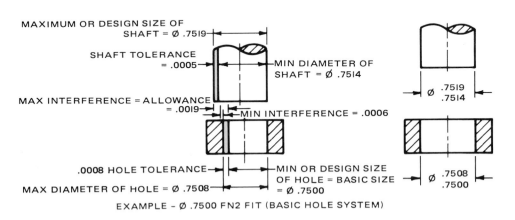

(C) INTERFERENCE FIT

Fig. 7-6-3 Types of inch fits.

appreciable temperature differences are likely to be encountered.

RC4 Close Running Fit This fit is intended chiefly as a running fit for grease or oil-lubricated bearings on accurate machinery with moderate surface speeds and journal pressures, where accurate location and minimum play are desired.

RC5 and RC6 Medium Running Fits These fits are intended for higher running speeds and/or where temperature variations are likely to be encountered.

RC7 Free Running Fit This fit is intended for use where accuracy is not essential, and/or where large temperature variations are likely to be encountered.

RC8 and RC9 Loose Running Fits These fits are intended for use where materials made to commercial tolerances are involved such as cold-rolled shafting, tubing, etc.

Locational Clearance Fits

Locational clearance fits are intended for parts which are normally stationary, but which can be freely assembled or disassembled. They run from snug fits for parts requiring accuracy of location, through the medium clearance fits for parts such as spigots, etc., to the looser fastener fits where freedom of assembly is of prime importance.

These are classified as follows:

LC1 to LC4 These fits have a minimum zero clearance, but in practice the probability is that the fit will always have a clearance. These fits are suitable for location of nonrunning parts and spigots, although classes LC1 and LC2 may also be used for sliding fits.

LC5 and LC6 These fits have a small minimum clearance, intended for close location fits for nonrunning parts. LC5 can also be used in place of RC2 as a free-slide fit, and LC6 may be used as a medium running fit having greater tolerances than RC5 and RC6.

LC7 to LC11 These fits have progressively larger clearances and tolerances, and are useful for various loose clearances for assembly of bolts and similar parts.

Locational Transition Fits

Locational transition fits are a compromise between clearance and interference fits, for application where accuracy of location is important, but either a small amount of clearance or interference is permissible.

These are classified as follows:

LT1 and LT2 These fits average a slight clearance, giving a light push fit, and are intended for use where the maximum clearance must be less than for the LC1 to LC3 fits, and where slight interference can be tolerated for assembly by pressure or light hammer blows.

LT3 and LT4 These fits average virtually no clearance, and are for use where some interference can be tolerated, for example: to eliminate vibration. These are sometimes referred to as an easy keying fit, and are used for shaft keys and ball race fits. Assembly is generally by pressure or hammer blows.

LT5 and LT6 These fits average a slight interference, although appreciable assembly force will be required when extreme limits are encountered, and selective assembly may be desirable. These fits are useful for heavy keying, for ball race fits subject to heavy duty and vibration, and as light press fits for steel parts.

Locational Interference Fits

Locational interference fits are used where accuracy of location is of prime importance, and for parts requiring rigidity and alignment with no special requirements for bore pressure. Such fits are not intended for parts designed to transmit frictional loads from one part to another by virtue of the tightness of fit, as these conditions are covered by force fits.

These are classified as follows:

LN1 and LN2 These are light press fits, with very small minimum interference, suitable for parts such as dowel pins, which are assembled with an arbor press in steel, cast iron, or brass. Parts can normally be dismantled and reassembled, as the interference is not likely to overstrain the parts, but the interference is too small for satisfactory fits in elastic materials or light alloys.

LN3 This is suitable as a heavy press fit in steel and brass, or a light press fit in more elastic materials and light alloys.

LN4 to LN6 While LN4 can be used for permanent assembly of steel parts, these fits are primarily intended as press fits for more elastic or soft materials, such as light alloys and the more rigid plastics.

Force or Shrink Fits

Force or shrink fits constitute a special type of interference fit, normally characterized by maintenance of constant bore pressures throughout the range of sizes. The interference therefore varies almost directly with diameter, and the difference between its minimum and maximum values is small to maintain the resulting pressures within reasonable limits.

These fits may be described briefly as follows:

FN1 Light Drive Fit Requires light assembly pressure, and produces more or less permanent assemblies. It is suitable for thin sections or long fits, or in cast-iron external members.

FN2 Medium Drive Fit Suitable for ordinary steel parts, or as a shrink fit on light sections. It is about the tightest fit that can be used with high-grade cast-iron external members.

FN3 Heavy Drive Fit Suitable for heavier steel parts or as a shrink fit in medium sections.

FN4 and FN5 Force Fits Suitable for parts which can be highly stressed, and/or for shrink fits where the heavy pressing forces required are impractical.

Basic Hole System

In the basic hole system, which is recommended for general use, the basic size will be the design size for the hole, and the tolerance will be plus. The design size for the shaft will be the basic size minus the minimum clearance, or plus the maximum interference, and the tolerance will be minus, as given in the tables in the Appendix. For example, (see Table 47) for a 1 in. RC7 fit, values of +.0020, .0025, and −.0012 are given; hence, limits will be

$$\text{Hole } \varnothing\ 1.0000\ \begin{matrix} +\ .0020 \\ -\ .0000 \end{matrix}$$

$$\text{Shaft } \varnothing\ .9975\ \begin{matrix} +\ .0000 \\ -\ .0012 \end{matrix}$$

Basic Shaft System

Fits are sometimes required on a basic shaft system, especially in cases where two or more fits are required on the same shaft. This is designated for design purposes by a letter S following the fit symbol; for example, RC7S.

Tolerances for holes and shaft are identical with those for a basic hole system, but the basic size becomes the design size for the shaft and the design size for the hole is found by adding the minimum clearance or subtracting the maximum interference from the basic size.

For example, for a 1-in. RC7S fit, values of +.0020, .0025, and −.0012 are given; therefore, limits will be

$$\text{Hole } \varnothing\ 1.0025\ \begin{matrix} +\ .0020 \\ -\ .0000 \end{matrix}$$

$$\text{Shaft } \varnothing\ 1.000\ \begin{matrix} +\ .0000 \\ -\ .0012 \end{matrix}$$

Tolerances are easily placed for either the basic hole or basic shaft system. Simply set the plus and minus tolerance accordingly. Dimension the part using the OVERRIDE option to key in the uneven design size (e.g., 1.0025).

PREFERRED METRIC LIMITS AND FITS

The ISO system of limits and fits for mating parts is approved and adopted for general use in the United States. It establishes the designation symbols used to define specific dimensional limits on drawings.

The general terms "hole" and "shaft" can also be taken as referring to the space containing or contained by two parallel faces of any part, such as the width of slot, or the thickness of a key.

An "International Tolerance grade" establishes the magnitude of the tolerance zone or the amount of part size variation allowed for internal and external dimensions alike. See Table 44 Appendix B. There are eighteen tolerance grades which are identified by the prefix IT, such as IT6; IT11, etc. The smaller the grade number the smaller the tolerance zone. For general applications of IT grades see Fig. 7-6-4.

Grades 1 to 4 are very precise grades intended primarily for gage making and similar precision work, although grade 4 can also be used for very precise production work.

Grades 5 to 16 represent a progressive series suitable for cutting operations, such as turning, boring, grinding, milling, and sawing. Grade 5 is the most precise grade, obtainable by fine grinding and lapping, while 16 is the coarsest grade for rough sawing and machining.

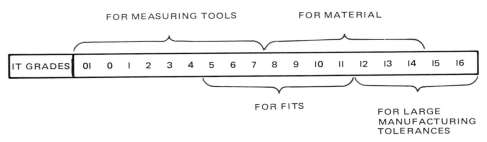

Fig. 7-6-4 Applications of International Tolerance (IT) grades.

Grades 12 to 16 are intended for manufacturing operations such as cold heading, pressing, rolling, and other forming operations.

As a guide to the selection of tolerances, Fig. 7-6-5 has been prepared to show grades which may be expected to be held by various manufacturing processes for work in metals. For work in other materials, such as plastics, it may be necessary to use coarser tolerance grades for the same process.

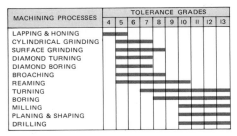

Fig. 7-6-5 Tolerancing grades for machining processes.

A fundamental deviation establishes the position of the tolerance zone with respect to the basic size. Fundamental deviations are expressed by "tolerance position letters." Capital letters are used for internal dimensions, and lower case letters for external dimensions.

Symbols

Tolerance Symbol For metric application of limits and fits, the tolerance may be indicated by a basic size and tolerance symbol. By combining the IT grade number and the tolerance position letter, the tolerance symbol is established which identifies the actual maximum and minimum limits of the part. The toleranced sizes are thus defined by the basic size of the part followed by the symbol composed of a letter and a number. See Fig. 7-6-6.

Preferred Tolerance Zones

The preferred tolerance zones are shown in Table 43 of Appendix B. The encircled tolerance zones (13 each) are first choice, the framed tolerance zones are second choice, and the open tolerance zones are third choice.

Hole Basis Fits System

In the hole basis fits system (see Tables 45 and 52 of the Appendix) the basic size will be the minimum size of the hole. For example, for a ∅ 25 H8/f7 fit, which is a Preferred Hole Basis Clearance Fit, the limits for the hole and shaft will be as follows:

Refer to Tables 44 and 51 of Appendix B.
Hole limits = ∅ 25.000 − ∅ 25.033
Shaft limits = ∅ 24.959 − ∅ 24.980
Minimum clearance = 0.020
Maximum clearance = 0.074

If a ∅ 25 H7/s6 Preferred Hole

Basis Interference Fit is required, the limits for the hole and shaft will be as follows:

Refer to Tables 45 and 52 of Appendix B.
Hole limits = ∅ 25.000 − ∅ 25.021
Shaft limits = ∅ 25.035 − ∅ 25.048
Minimum interference = −0.014
Maximum interference = −0.048

Shaft Basis Fits System

Where more than two fits are required on the same shaft, the shaft basis fits system is recommended. Tolerances for holes and shaft are identical with those for a basic hole system. However, the basic size becomes the maximum shaft size. For example for a ∅ 16 C11/h11 fit, which is a Preferred Shaft Basis Clearance Fit, the limits for the hole and shaft will be as follows:

Refer to Tables 46 and 53 of Appendix B.
Hole limits = ∅ 16.095 − ∅ 16.205
Shaft limits = ∅ 15.890 − ∅ 16.000
Minimum clearance 0.095
Maximum clearance 0.315

References

1. ANSI B4.2, *Preferred Metric Limits and Fits.*

ASSIGNMENTS

See Assignments 16 through 18 for Unit 7-6 starting on page 153.

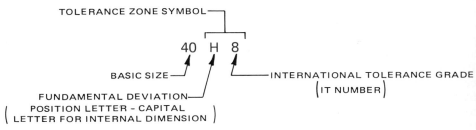

Fig. 7-6-6 Metric tolerance symbol.

Surface Texture

Modern development of high-speed machines has resulted in higher loadings and increased speeds of moving parts. To withstand these more severe operating conditions with minimum friction and wear, a particular surface finish is often essential, making it necessary for the designer to accurately describe the required finish to the persons who are actually making the parts.

For accurate machines it is no longer sufficient to indicate the surface finish by various grind marks, such as "g," "f," or "fg." It becomes necessary to define surface finish and take it out of the opinion or guesswork class.

All surface finish control starts in the drafting room. The designer has the responsibility of specifying the right surface to give maximum performance and service life at the lowest cost. In selecting the required surface finish for any particular part, the designer bases her or his decision on past experience with similar parts, on field service data, or on engineering tests. Such factors as size and function of the parts, type of loading, speed and direction of movement, operating conditions, physical characteristics of both materials on contact, whether they are subjected to stress reversals, type and amount of lubricant, contaminants, temperature, etc., influence the choice.

There are two principal reasons for surface finish control:

1. To reduce friction
2. To control wear

Whenever a film of lubricant must be maintained between two moving parts, the surface irregularities must be small enough so they will not penetrate the oil film under the most severe operating conditions. Bearings, journals, cylinder bores, piston pins, bushings, pad bearings, helical and worm gears, seal surfaces, machine ways, and so forth, are examples where this condition must be fulfilled.

Surface finish is also important to the wear of certain pieces which are subject to dry friction, such as machine tool bits, threading dies, stamping dies, rolls, clutch plates, brake drums, etc.

Smooth finishes are essential on certain high-precision pieces. In mechanisms such as injectors and high-pressure cylinders, smoothness and lack of waviness are essential to accuracy and pressure-retaining ability.

Surfaces, in general, are very complex in character. Only the height, width, and direction of surface irregularities will be covered in this section since these are of practical importance in specific applications.

Surface Texture Characteristics

Refer to Fig. 7-7-1.

Microinch A microinch is one millionth of an inch (.000 001 in.). For written specifications or reference to surface roughness requirements, microinches may be abbreviated as μin.

Micrometer A micrometer is one millionth of a meter (0.000 001 m). For written specifications or reference to surface roughness requirements, micrometer may be abbreviated as μm.

Roughness Roughness consists of the finer irregularities in the surface texture usually including those which result from the inherent action of the production process. These are considered to include traverse feed marks and other irregularities within the limits of the roughness-width cutoff.

Roughness-Height Value Roughness-height value is rated as the arithmetic average (AA) deviation expressed in microinches or micrometers measured normal to the center line. ISO and many European countries use the term CLA (center line average) in lieu of AA. Both have the same meaning.

Roughness Spacing Roughness spacing is the distance parallel to the nominal surface between successive peaks or ridges which constitute the predominant pattern of the roughness. Roughness spacing is rated in inches or millimeters.

Roughness-Width Cutoff The greatest spacing of repetitive surface irregularities is included in the measurement of average roughness height. Roughness-width cutoff is rated in inches or millimeters and must always be greater than the roughness width in order to obtain the total roughness height rating.

Waviness Waviness is the usually widely spaced component of surface texture and is generally of wider spacing than the roughness-width cutoff. Waviness may result from such factors as machine or work deflections, vibration, chatter, heat treatment, or warping strains. Roughness may be considered as superimposed on a "wavy" surface. Although waviness is not currently in ISO Standards, it is included as part of the surface texture symbol to follow present industrial practices in the United States.

Lay The direction of the predominant surface pattern, ordinarily determined by the production method used, is the *lay*. Lay symbols are specified as shown in Fig. 7-7-2.

Flaws Flaws are irregularities which occur at one place or at relatively infrequent or widely varying intervals in a surface. Flaws include such defects as cracks, blow holes, checks, ridges,

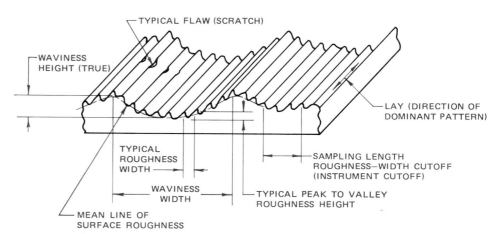

Fig. 7-7-1 Surface texture characteristics.

Fig. 7-7-2 Location of notes and symbols on surface texture symbols.

PRESENT SYMBOLS VALUES SHOWN IN CUSTOMARY OR METRIC		FORMER SYMBOLS VALUES SHOWN IN MICROINCHES AND INCHES	
BASIC SURFACE TEXTURE SYMBOL	√	√	BASIC SURFACE TEXTURE SYMBOL
ROUGHNESS HEIGHT RATING IN MICROINCHES OR MICROMETERS AND N SERIES ROUGHNESS NUMBERS	63 √ N8 √	63 √	ROUGHNESS HEIGHT RATING IN MICROINCHES.
MAXIMUM AND MINIMUM ROUGHNESS HEIGHT IN MICROINCHES OR MICROMETERS	63/32 √	63/32 √	MAXIMUM AND MINIMUM ROUGHNESS HEIGHT RATINGS IN MICROINCHES
WAVINESS HEIGHT IN INCHES OR MILLIMETERS (F)	63/32 √ F	63/32 √ .002	WAVINESS HEIGHT IN INCHES
WAVINESS SPACING IN INCHES OR MILLIMETERS (G)	63/32 √ F−G	63/32 √ .002−1	WAVINESS WIDTH IN INCHES
LAY SYMBOL (D)	63/32 √⊥	63/32 √⊥	LAY SYMBOL
MAXIMUM ROUGHNESS SPACING IN INCHES OR MILLIMETERS (B)	63/32 √⊥ B	√⊥ .002−1 .008	SURFACE ROUGHNESS WIDTH IN INCHES
ROUGHNESS SAMPLING LENGTH OR CUT OFF RATING IN INCHES OR MILLIMETERS (C)	63/32 √⊥ C	√⊥ .002−1 .030 .008	ROUGHNESS WIDTH CUTOFF IN INCHES

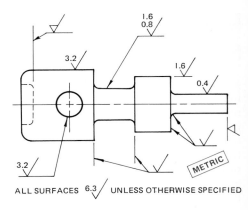

ALL SURFACES 6.3 √ UNLESS OTHERWISE SPECIFIED

NOTE: VALUES SHOWN ARE IN MICROMETERS

Fig. 7-7-4 Application of surface texture symbols and notes.

pany the symbol, the symbol should be in an upright position in order to be readable from the bottom. This means that the long leg and extension line are always on the right. Select the TEXT command, key in the required size, and place the numbers in the proper location. When no numerical values are shown on the symbol, the symbol may also be positioned to be readable from the right side. If necessary, the

scratches, etc. Unless otherwise specified, the effect of flaws is not included in the roughness-height measurements.

Surface Texture Symbol

Surface characteristics of roughness, waviness, and lay may be controlled by applying the desired values to the surface texture symbol, shown in Figs. 7-7-2 and 7-7-3. DRAW each required symbol once. COPY by window or COPY and ROTATE as many additional symbols as necessary. In Unit 7-2 the procedure to store this symbol

in a library so that you will never have to draw it again was covered. Where only the roughness value is indicated, the horizontal extension line on the symbol may be omitted. The horizontal bar is used whenever any surface characteristics are placed above the bar or to the right of the symbol. The point of the symbol should be located on the line indicating the surface, on an extension line from the surface, or on a leader pointing to the surface or extension line. See Fig. 7-7-4. To accomplish this, combine the LEADER command with the COPY of the symbol. When numerical values accom-

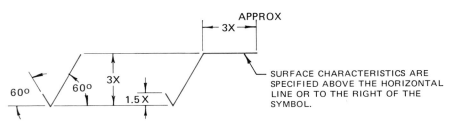

APPROX

X = FIGURE HEIGHT OF VALUES.
HORIZONTAL EXTENSION BAR REQUIRED WHEN WAVINESS RATINGS ARE SHOWN.

SURFACE CHARACTERISTICS ARE SPECIFIED ABOVE THE HORIZONTAL LINE OR TO THE RIGHT OF THE SYMBOL.

Fig. 7-7-3 Basic surface texture symbol.

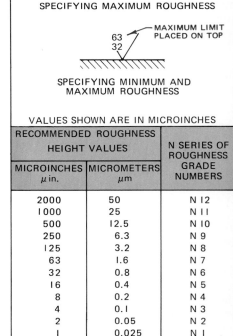

63 √

SPECIFYING MAXIMUM ROUGHNESS

63/32 √

MAXIMUM LIMIT PLACED ON TOP

SPECIFYING MINIMUM AND MAXIMUM ROUGHNESS

VALUES SHOWN ARE IN MICROINCHES

RECOMMENDED ROUGHNESS HEIGHT VALUES		N SERIES OF ROUGHNESS GRADE NUMBERS
MICROINCHES μ in.	MICROMETERS μm	
2000	50	N 12
1000	25	N 11
500	12.5	N 10
250	6.3	N 9
125	3.2	N 8
63	1.6	N 7
32	0.8	N 6
16	0.4	N 5
8	0.2	N 4
4	0.1	N 3
2	0.05	N 2
1	0.025	N 1

Fig. 7-7-5 Roughness height ratings.

MICROINCHES AA RATING	MICROMETERS AA RATING	APPLICATION
1000	25.2	ROUGH, LOW GRADE SURFACE RESULTING FROM SAND CASTING, TORCH OR SAW CUTTING, CHIPPING OR ROUGH FORGING. MACHINE OPERATIONS ARE NOT REQUIRED AS APPEARANCE IS NOT OBJECTIONABLE. THIS SURFACE, RARELY SPECIFIED, IS SUITABLE FOR UNMACHINED CLEARANCE AREAS ON ROUGH CONSTRUCTION ITEMS.
500	12.5	ROUGH, LOW GRADE SURFACE RESULTING FROM HEAVY CUTS AND COARSE FEEDS IN MILLING TURNING, SHAPING, BORING, AND ROUGH FILING, DISC GRINDING AND SNAGGING. IT IS SUITABLE FOR CLEARANCE AREAS ON MACHINERY, JIGS, AND FIXTURES. SAND CASTING OR ROUGH FORGING PRODUCES THIS SURFACE.
250	6.3	COARSE PRODUCTION SURFACES, FOR UNIMPORTANT CLEARANCE AND CLEANUP OPERATIONS, RESULTING FROM COARSE SURFACE GRIND, ROUGH FILE, DISC GRIND, RAPID FEEDS IN TURNING, MILLING, SHAPING, DRILLING, BORING, GRINDING, ETC., WHERE TOOL MARKS ARE NOT OBJECTIONABLE. THE NATURAL SURFACES OF FORGINGS, PERMANENT MOLD CASTINGS, EXTRUSIONS, AND ROLLED SURFACES ALSO PRODUCE THIS ROUGHNESS. IT CAN BE PRODUCED ECONOMICALLY AND IS USED ON PARTS WHERE STRESS REQUIREMENTS, APPEARANCE, AND CONDITIONS OF OPERATIONS AND DESIGN PERMIT.
125	3.2	THE ROUGHEST SURFACE RECOMMENDED FOR PARTS SUBJECT TO LOADS, VIBRATION, AND HIGH STRESS. IT IS ALSO PERMITTED FOR BEARING SURFACES WHEN MOTION IS SLOW AND LOADS LIGHT OR INFREQUENT. IT IS A MEDIUM COMMERCIAL MACHINE FINISH PRODUCED BY RELATIVELY HIGH SPEEDS AND FINE FEEDS TAKING LIGHT CUTS WITH SHARP TOOLS. IT MAY BE ECONOMICALLY PRODUCED ON LATHES, MILLING MACHINES, SHAPERS, GRINDERS, ETC., OR ON PERMANENT MOLD CASTINGS, DIE CASTINGS, EXTRUSION, AND ROLLED SURFACES.
63	1.6	A GOOD MACHINE FINISH PRODUCED UNDER CONTROLLED CONDITIONS USING RELATIVELY HIGH SPEEDS AND FINE FEEDS TO TAKE LIGHT CUTS WITH SHARP CUTTERS. IT MAY BE SPECIFIED FOR CLOSE FITS AND USED FOR ALL STRESSED PARTS, EXCEPT FAST ROTATING SHAFTS, AXLES, AND PARTS SUBJECT TO SEVERE VIBRATION OR EXTREME TENSION. IT IS SATISFACTORY FOR BEARING SURFACES WHEN MOTION IS SLOW AND LOADS LIGHT OR INFREQUENT. IT MAY ALSO BE OBTAINED ON EXTRUSIONS, ROLLED SURFACES, DIE CASTINGS AND PERMANENT MOLD CASTINGS WHEN RIGIDLY CONTROLLED.
32	0.8	A HIGH-GRADE MACHINE FINISH REQUIRING CLOSE CONTROL WHEN PRODUCED BY LATHES, SHAPERS, MILLING MACHINES, ETC., BUT RELATIVELY EASY TO PRODUCE BY CENTERLESS, CYLINDRICAL OR SURFACE GRINDERS. ALSO, EXTRUDING, ROLLING, OR DIE CASTING MAY PRODUCE A COMPARABLE SURFACE WHEN RIGIDLY CONTROLLED. THIS SURFACE MAY BE SPECIFIED IN PARTS WHERE STRESS CONCENTRATION IS PRESENT. IT IS USED FOR BEARINGS WHEN MOTION IS NOT CONTINUOUS AND LOADS ARE LIGHT. WHEN FINER FINISHES ARE SPECIFIED, PRODUCTION COSTS RISE RAPIDLY; THEREFORE, SUCH FINISHES MUST BE ANALYZED CAREFULLY.
16	0.4	A HIGH QUALITY SURFACE PRODUCED BY FINE CYLINDRICAL GRINDING, EMERY BUFFING, COARSE HONING OR LAPPING. IT IS SPECIFIED WHERE SMOOTHNESS IS OF PRIMARY IMPORTANCE, SUCH AS RAPIDLY ROTATING SHAFT BEARINGS, HEAVILY LOADED BEARINGS AND EXTREME TENSION MEMBERS.
8	0.2	A FINE SURFACE PRODUCED BY HONING, LAPPING, OR BUFFING. IT IS SPECIFIED WHERE PACKINGS AND RINGS MUST SLIDE ACROSS THE DIRECTION OF THE SURFACE GRAIN, MAINTAINING OR WITHSTANDING PRESSURES, OR FOR INTERIOR HONED SURFACES OF HYDRAULIC CYLINDERS. IT MAY ALSO BE REQUIRED IN PRECISION GAGES AND INSTRUMENT WORK, OR SENSITIVE VALUE SURFACES, OR ON RAPIDLY ROTATING SHAFTS AND ON BEARINGS WHERE LUBRICATION IS NOT DEPENDABLE.
4	0.1	A COSTLY REFINED SURFACE PRODUCED BY HONING, LAPPING, AND BUFFING. IT IS SPECIFIED ONLY WHEN THE REQUIREMENTS OF DESIGN MAKE IT MANDATORY. IT IS REQUIRED IN INSTRUMENT WORK, GAGE WORK, AND WHERE PACKINGS AND RINGS MUST SLIDE ACROSS THE DIRECTION OF SURFACE GRAIN SUCH AS ON CHROME-PLATED PISTON RODS, ETC., WHERE LUBRICATION IS NOT DEPENDABLE.
2 1	0.05 0.025	COSTLY REFINED SURFACES PRODUCED ONLY BY THE FINEST OF MODERN HONING, LAPPING, BUFFING, AND SUPERFINISHING EQUIPMENT. THESE SURFACES MAY HAVE A SATIN OR HIGHLY POLISHED APPEARANCE DEPENDING ON THE FINISHING OPERATION AND MATERIAL. THESE SURFACES ARE SPECIFIED ONLY WHEN DESIGN REQUIREMENTS MAKE IT MANDATORY. THEY ARE SPECIFIED ON FINE OR SENSITIVE INSTRUMENT PARTS OR OTHER LABORATORY ITEMS, AND CERTAIN GAGE SURFACES, SUCH AS ON PRECISION GAGE BLOCKS.

Fig. 7-7-6 Typical surface roughness height applications.

symbol may be connected to the surface by a leader line terminating in an arrow. The symbol applies to the entire surface, unless otherwise specified. The symbol for the same surface should not be duplicated on other views.

Application

Plain (Unplated or Uncoated) Surfaces Surface texture values specified on plain surfaces apply to the completed surface unless otherwise noted.

Plated or Coated Surfaces Drawings or specifications for plated or coated parts must indicate whether the surface texture value applies before, after, or both before and after plating or coating.

Surface Texture Ratings The roughness value rating is indicated at the left of the long leg of the symbol. See Fig. 7-7-4. The specification of only one rating indicates the maximum value, and any lesser value is acceptable. The specification of two ratings indicates the minimum and maximum values, and anything lying within that range is acceptable. See Fig. 7-7-5 on page 135. The maximum value is placed over the minimum.

Typical surface roughness-height applications are shown in Fig. 7-7-6.

The surface roughness range for common production methods is shown in Fig. 7-7-7.

Waviness-height rating is specified in inches or millimeters and is located above the horizontal extension of the symbol (Fig. 7-7-3). Any lesser value is acceptable.

Waviness spacing is indicated in inches or millimeters and is located above the horizontal extension and to the right, separated from the waviness-height rating by a dash (Fig. 7-7-3). Any lesser value is acceptable. If the waviness value is a minimum, the abbreviation MIN should be placed after the value.

MACHINED SURFACES

In preparing working drawings or parts to be cast, molded, or forged, the drafter must indicate the surfaces on the drawing which will require machining or finishing. The symbol √ identifies those surfaces which are produced by machining operations.

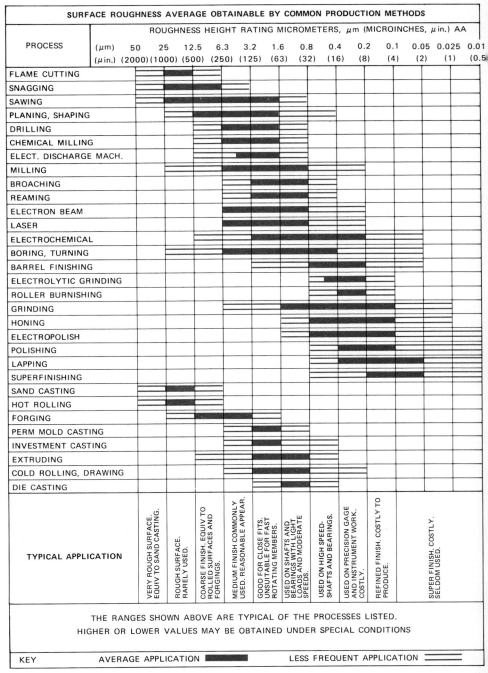

Fig. 7-7-7 Surface roughness range common production.

REMOVAL OF MATERIAL BY MACHINING IS

OPTIONAL   OBLIGATORY

Fig. 7-7-8 Indicating the removal of material on the surface texture symbol.

See Fig. 7-7-8. It indicates that material is to be provided for removal by machining. Where all the surfaces are to be machined, a general note such as FINISH ALL OVER may be used, and the symbols on the drawing may be omitted. Where space is restricted, the machining symbol may be placed on an extension line.

Machining symbols, like dimensions, are not normally duplicated. They should be used on the same view as the dimensions that give the size or

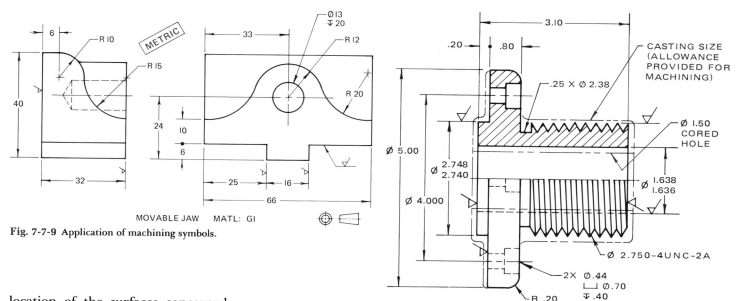

Fig. 7-7-9 Application of machining symbols.

MOVABLE JAW   MATL: GI

Fig. 7-7-10 Extra metal allowance for machined surfaces.

location of the surfaces concerned. The symbol is placed on the line representing the surface or, where desirable, on the extension line locating the surface. Figures 7-7-9 and 7-7-10 show examples of the use of machining symbols.

Material Removal Allowance

When it is desirable to indicate the amount of material to be removed, the amount of material in inches or millimeters is shown to the left of the symbol. Illustrations showing material removal allowance are shown in Figs. 7-7-11 and 7-7-12.

Material Removal Prohibited

When it is necessary to indicate that a surface must be produced without material removal, the machining prohibited symbol shown in Fig. 7-7-13 must be used.

Former Machining Symbols

Former machining symbols, as shown in Fig. 7-7-14, may be found on many

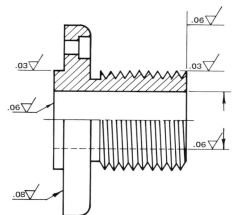

Fig. 7-7-12 Indicating machining allowance on drawings.

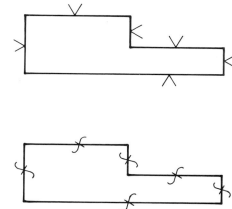

Fig. 7-7-14 Former machining symbols.

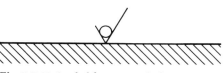

Fig. 7-7-13 Symbol for "removal of material not permitted."

drawings in use today. When called upon to make changes or revisions to a drawing already in existence, a drafter must adhere to the drawing conventions shown on that drawing.

References and Source Materials

1. ANSI Y14.36, *Surface Texture Symbols.*
2. GAR.
3. General Motors.

ASSIGNMENTS

See Assignments 19 through 22 for Unit 7-7 starting on page 155.

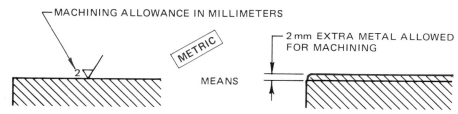

Fig. 7-7-11 Indication of machining allowance.

ASSIGNMENTS FOR CHAPTER 7

For all assignments in this chapter, set up an A3 or B size drawing or as assigned by your instructor. Use the appropriate drawing LIMITS for plot scales other than 1:1. The mirror command may be used to help create all symmetrical slopes.

Assignments for Unit 7-1, Dimensioning Techniques

1. Select one of the template drawings (Figs. 7-1-A or 7-1-B) and make a one-view drawing, complete with dimensions, of the part. Scale 1:1.

2. Select one of the parts shown in Figs. 7-1-C to 7-1-F and make a three-view drawing, complete with dimensions, of the part. Scale 1:1.

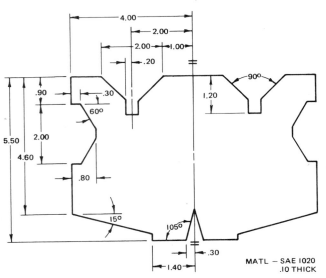

Fig. 7-1-A Template no. 1.

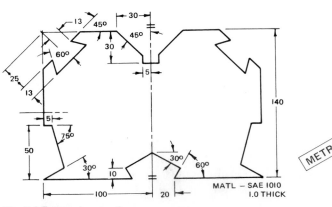

Fig. 7-1-B Template no. 2.

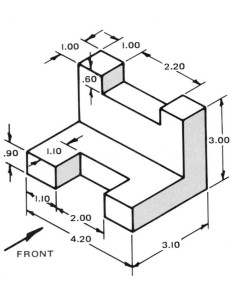

Fig. 7-1-C Cross slide.

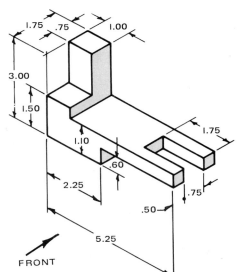

Fig. 7-1-D Notched block.

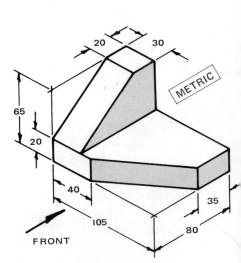

Fig. 7-1-E Angle plate.

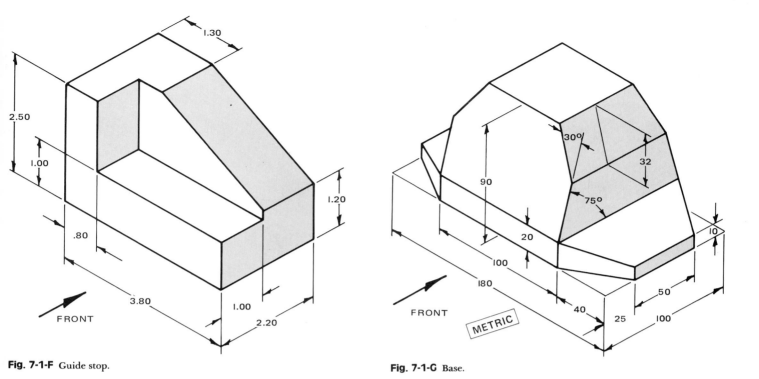

Fig. 7-1-F Guide stop.

Fig. 7-1-G Base.

3. Select one of the parts shown in Figs. 7-1-G to 7-1-J and make a three-view drawing, complete with dimensions, of the part.

Show the dimensions with the view which best shows the shape of the part or feature. Scale 1 : 1.

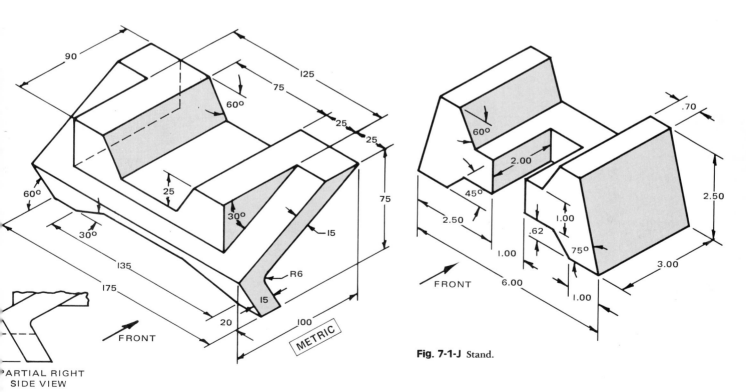

Fig. 7-1-H Separator.

PARTIAL RIGHT
SIDE VIEW

Fig. 7-1-J Stand.

Assignments for Unit 7-2, Dimensioning Circular Features

4. Select one of the problems shown in Figs. 7-2-A to 7-2-D and make a one-view drawing, complete with dimensions, of the part. Scale 1:1.

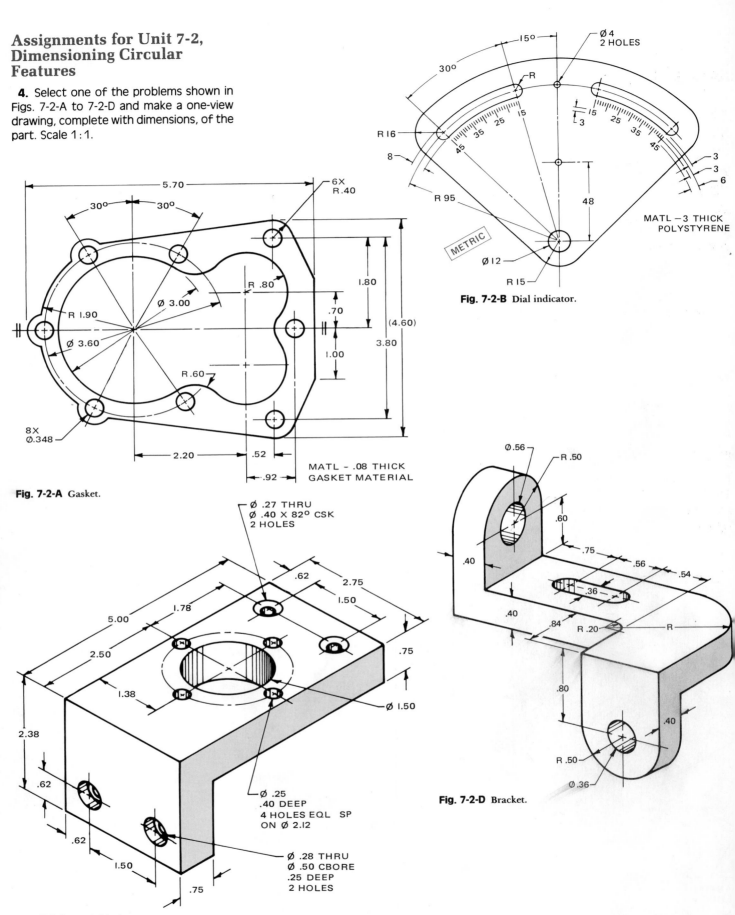

Fig. 7-2-A Gasket.

MATL – .08 THICK GASKET MATERIAL

Fig. 7-2-B Dial indicator.

MATL – 3 THICK POLYSTYRENE

METRIC

Fig. 7-2-C Guide block.

Ø .27 THRU
Ø .40 X 82° CSK
2 HOLES

Ø .25
.40 DEEP
4 HOLES EQL SP
ON Ø 2.12

Ø .28 THRU
Ø .50 CBORE
.25 DEEP
2 HOLES

Fig. 7-2-D Bracket.

5. Select one of the parts shown in Figs. 7-2-E to 7-2-G and make a three-view drawing, complete with the dimensions, of the part. Scale 1:1.

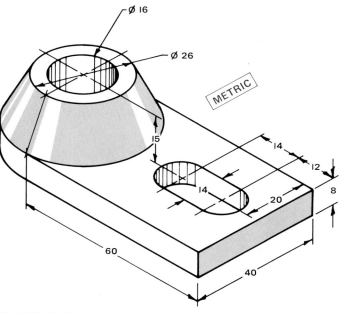

Fig. 7-2-E Shaft support.

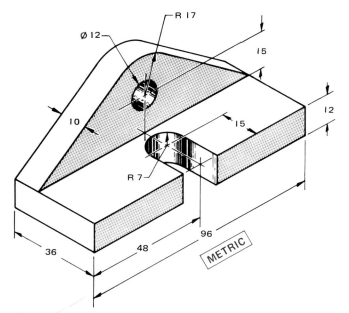

Fig. 7-2-F Offset plate.

Fig. 7-2-G Yoke.

Assignments for Unit 7-3, Dimensioning Common Features

6. Redraw the handle shown in Fig. 7-3-A. Scale 1:1. The following feaures are to be added and dimensioned:

a. 45° × .10 chamfer
b. 33DP diamond knurl for 1.20 in. starting .80 in. from left end
c. 1:8 taper for 1.20 in. length on right end of φ 1.25
d. .16 × φ .54 in. undercut on φ .75
e. φ .189 × .25 in. deep, 4 holes equally spaced
f. 30 degrees × .10 chamfer. The .10 in. dimension taken horizontally along the shaft.

7. Redraw the selector shaft shown in Fig. 7-3-B and dimension. Scale the drawing for sizes.

8. Make a one-view drawing (plus a partial view of the blade), with dimensions, of the screwdriver shown in Fig. 7-3-C. Scale 1:1.

9. Make a one-view drawing with dimensions of the indicator rod shown in Fig. 7-3-D. Scale 1:1.

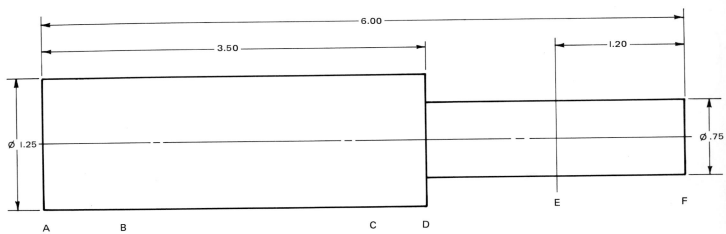

Fig. 7-3-A Handle.

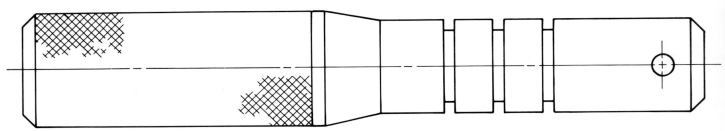

Fig. 7-3-B Selector shaft.

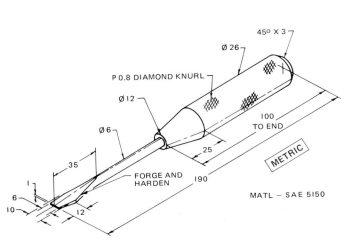

Fig. 7-3-C Screwdriver.

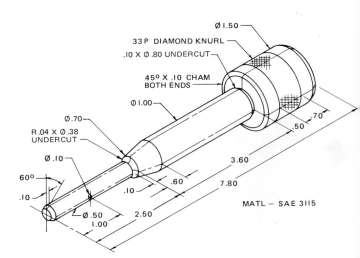

Fig. 7-3-D Indicator rod.

10. Make a half-view drawing of one of the parts shown in Fig. 7-3-E to 7-3-F. Use the MIRROR command, add the symmetry symbol to the drawing, and dimension. Use symbolic dimensioning wherever possible. Plot Scale 1:1 for 7-3-E and 10:1 for 7-3-F.

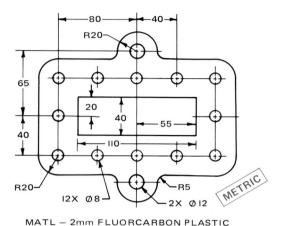

MATL — 2mm FLUORCARBON PLASTIC

Fig. 7-3-E Gasket.

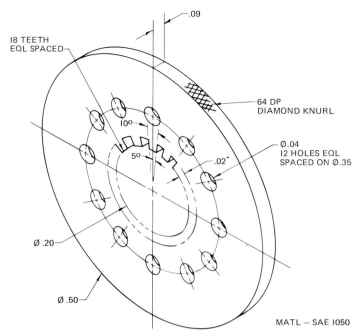

18 TEETH EQL SPACED

64 DP DIAMOND KNURL

Ø.04 12 HOLES EQL SPACED ON Ø.35

Ø .20

Ø .50

MATL — SAE 1050

Fig. 7-3-F Adjusting locking plate.

Assignments for Unit 7-4, Dimensioning Methods

11. Select one of the problems shown in Figs. 7-4-A and 7-4-B, and make a working drawing of the part. The arrowless dimensioning shown is to be replaced with rectangular coordinates or datum dimensioning and has the following dimensioning changes. For Fig. 7-4-A:

• Holes A, E, and D are located from the zero coordinates

• Holes B are located from center of hole E

• Holes C are located from center of hole D

For Fig. 7-4-B:

• Holes E and D are located from left and bottom edges

• Holes A and C are located from center of hole D

• Holes B are located from center of hole E

For the sake of clarity, some dimensions may best be shown on the part. Scale 1:1.

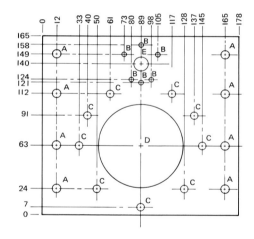

HOLE	DIA
A	8
B	4
C	5
D	76
E	12

MATL — SAE 1006
3mm THICK

Fig. 7-4-A Cover plate.

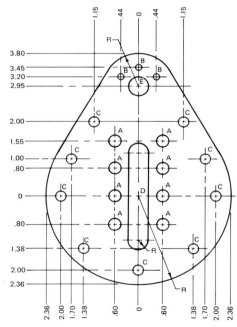

HOLE	SIZE
A	.30
B	.16
C	.24
D	.40 X 2.80
E	.50

MATL — SAE 1008
.12 THICK

Fig. 7-4-B Transmission cover.

12. The adapter plate shown in Fig. 7-4-C is to be shown four times. Different methods of dimensioning are to be used for each drawing. The methods are rectangular co-ordinate, chordal, arrowless, and tabular. Scale 1 : 1.

13. Select one of the parts shown in Figs. 7-4-D or 7-4-E and redimension the part using arrowless or tabular dimensioning. For Fig. 7-4-D use the bottom and left-hand edge for the datum surfaces. For Fig. 7-4-E use the bottom and the center of the part for the datum surfaces. Use the MIRROR command to create the views. Plot Scale 1 : 2.

14. Redraw the terminal board shown in Fig. 7-4-F using tabular dimensioning. Scale 1 : 1. Use the bottom left edge for the datum surface.

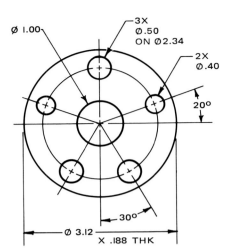

Fig. 7-4-C Adapter plate.

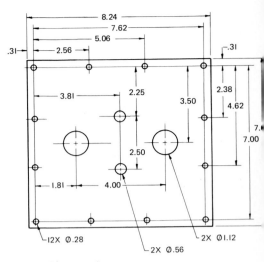

Fig. 7-4-D Cover plate.

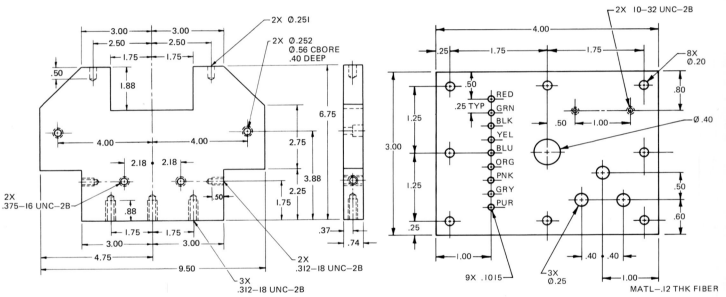

Fig. 7-4-E Back plate.

Fig. 7-4-F Terminal board.

Assignment for Unit 7-5, Limits and Tolerances

15. Calculate the sizes and tolerances for the drawings shown in Figs. 7-5-A and 7-5-B.

Assignments for Unit 7-6, Fits and Allowances

16. Using the tables of fits located in Appendix B, calculate the missing dimensions in any of the four charts shown in Figs. 7-6-A and 7-6-B.

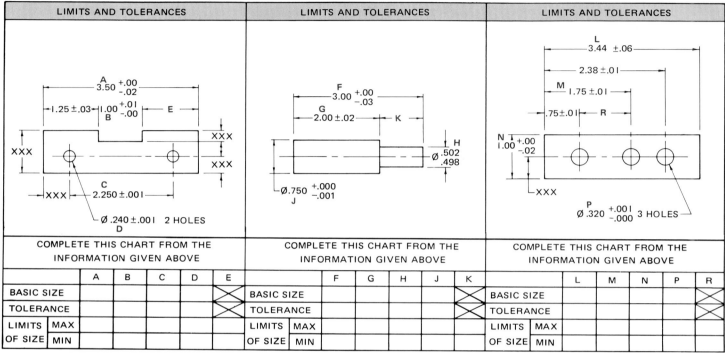

Fig. 7-5-A Inch limits and tolerances.

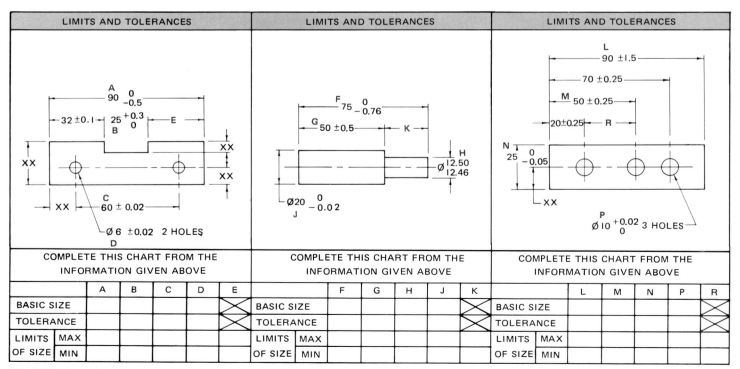

Fig. 7-5-B Metric limits and tolerances.

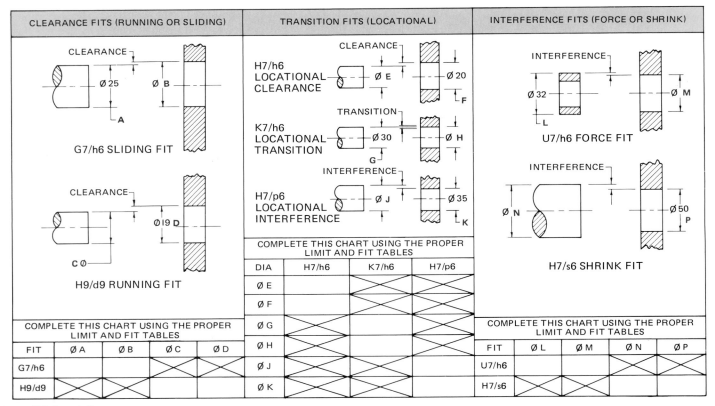

Fig. 7-6-A Inch fits.

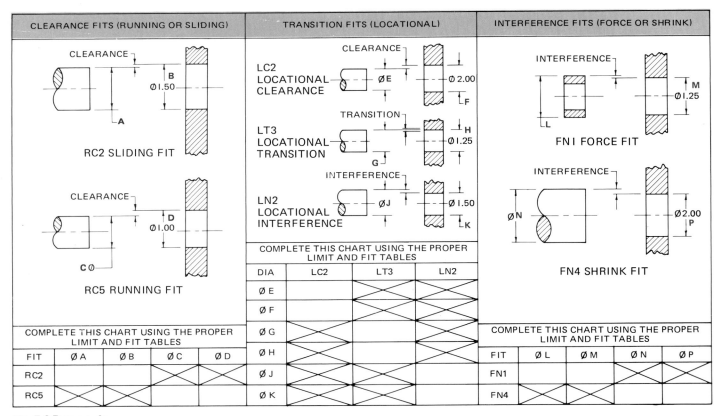

Fig. 7-6-B Metric fits.

17. Make a detail drawing of the roller guide base shown in Fig. 7-6-C. Scale the drawing for sizes using one of the scales shown with the drawing. Other considerations are:

• Keyseat to be for standard square key and limits on the hole controlled by either an H9/d9 (metric) or RC6 (inch) fit.

• Control critical machine surfaces to 0.8 μm or 32 μin.

• Dimension in metric or decimal inch.

18. Make a detail drawing of the spindle shown in Fig. 7-6-D. Scale the drawing for sizes using the scales shown with the drawing. Other considerations are:

• "A" diameter to have an LC3 (inch) or H7/h6 (metric) fit.

• "B" diameter requires a 96 diamond knurl or its equivalent.

• "C" diameter to have an LT3 (inch) or H7/K6 (metric) fit.

• "D" diameter to be a minimum relief (undercut).

• "E" to be a standard No. 807 Woodruff key in center of segment and the diameter to be controlled by an RC3 (inch) or H7/g6 (metric) fit.

• "F" to be undercut for a standard retaining ring and controlled form to manufacturer's specifications.

• Dimensions in decimal inch or metric.

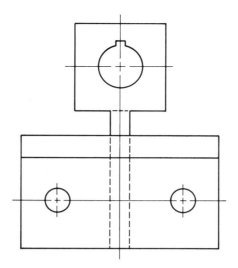
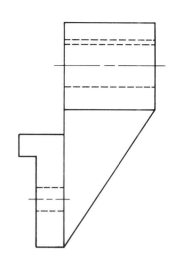

Fig. 7-6-C Roller guide base.

INCHES

MILLIMETERS

SCALES FOR FIGURES 7—6—C AND 7—6—D

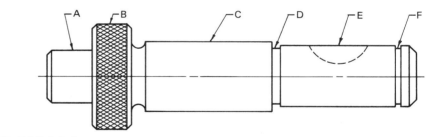

Fig. 7-6-D Spindle.

Assignments for Unit 7-7, Surface Texture

19. Make a detail drawing of the cross slide shown in Fig. 7-7-A. Scale 1:1. The following surface texture information is to be added to the drawing:

• The dovetail slot is to have a maximum roughness value of 3.2 μm and a machining allowance of 2 mm.

• The ends of the shaft support are to have maximum and minimum roughness values of 1.6 and 0.8 μm and a machining allowance of 2 mm.

• The hole is to have an H8 tolerance.

20. Make a working drawing of the column bracket shown in Fig. 7-7-B. Scale 1:1. The following surface texture information is to be added to the drawing:

• The bottom of the base is to have a maximum roughness value of 125 μin. and a machining allowance of .06 in.

• The tops of the bosses are to have a maximum roughness value of 250 μin. and a machining allowance of .04 in.

• The end surfaces of the hubs supporting the shafts are to have maximum

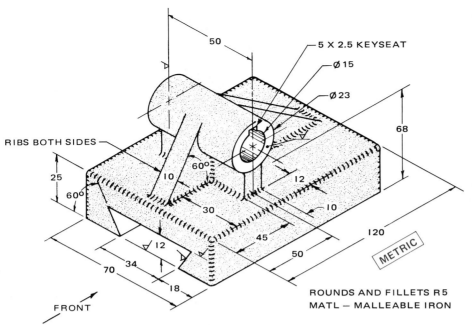

Fig. 7-7-A Cross slide.

- 5 X 2.5 KEYSEAT
- Ø 15
- Ø 23
- RIBS BOTH SIDES
- 50
- 68
- 25
- 60°
- 60°
- 10
- 30
- 45
- 12
- 10
- 120
- 50
- 70
- 34
- 18
- 12
- METRIC
- FRONT
- ROUNDS AND FILLETS R5
- MATL – MALLEABLE IRON

and minimum roughness values of 63 and 32 μin. and a machining allowance of .04 in.

• The large hole is to be dimensioned for an RC4 fit. The small hole is to be dimensioned for an LN3 fit for plain bearings.

21. Make a detail drawing of the adjustable base plate shown in Fig. 7-7-C. The amount of material to be removed on the surfaces requiring machining is 2 mm. The center hole is to be dimensioned having an H8 tolerance. Scale 1:1.

22. Make a detail drawing of the link shown in Fig. 7-7-D. The amount of material to be removed from the end surfaces of the hub is .09 in. and .06 in. on the bosses and bottom of the vertical hub. The two large holes are to have an LN3 fit for journal bearings. Scale 1:1.

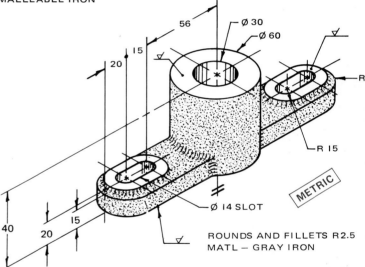

- 56
- 15
- 20
- Ø 30
- Ø 60
- R
- R 15
- 40
- 20
- 15
- Ø 14 SLOT
- METRIC
- ROUNDS AND FILLETS R2.5
- MATL – GRAY IRON

Fig. 7-7-C Adjustable base plate.

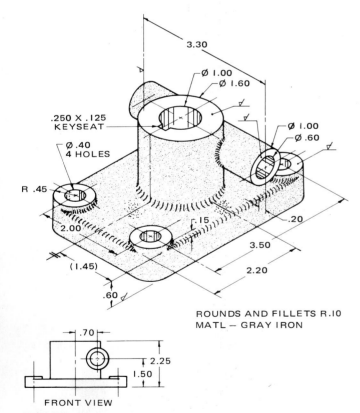

- 3.30
- Ø 1.00
- Ø 1.60
- .250 X .125 KEYSEAT
- Ø .40 4 HOLES
- Ø 1.00
- Ø .60
- R .45
- 2.00
- .15
- .20
- 3.50
- 2.20
- (1.45)
- .60
- ROUNDS AND FILLETS R.10
- MATL – GRAY IRON

- .70
- 2.25
- 1.50
- FRONT VIEW

Fig. 7-7-B Column bracket.

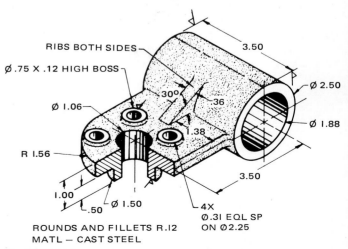

- RIBS BOTH SIDES
- Ø .75 X .12 HIGH BOSS
- 3.50
- Ø 2.50
- Ø 1.06
- 30°
- 36
- Ø 1.88
- R 1.56
- 1.38
- 3.50
- 1.00
- .50
- Ø 1.50
- 4X Ø.31 EQL SP ON Ø2.25
- ROUNDS AND FILLETS R.12
- MATL – CAST STEEL

Fig. 7-7-D Link.

8

Section Drawings

■ UNIT 8-1

Sectional Views

Sectional views, commonly called *sections*, are used to show interior detail that is too complicated to be shown clearly by regular views containing many hidden lines. For some assembly drawings, they show a difference in materials. A sectional view is an illustration of the interior of an object as if it were cut away (e.g. imagined to be cut in half). The exposed or cut surfaces are identified by section lining or cross-hatching. Hidden lines and details behind the cutting-plane line are usually omitted unless they are required for clarity or dimensioning. It should be understood that only in the sectional view is any part of the object shown as having been removed.

A sectional view frequently replaces one of the regular views. For example, a regular front view is replaced by a front view in section, as shown in Fig. 8-1-1.

Whenever practical, except for revolved sections, sectional views should be projected perpendicular to the cutting plane and be placed in the normal position for third-angle projection.

When the preferred placement is not practical, the sectional view may be removed to some other convenient position on the drawing, but it must be clearly identified, usually by two capital letters, and labeled.

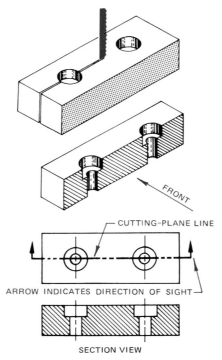

Fig. 8-1-1 A full-section drawing.

Cutting-Plane Lines

Cutting-plane lines (Fig. 8-1-2) are used to indicate the location of cutting planes for sectional views and the viewing position for removed partial views. Two forms of cutting-plane lines are approved for general use.

The first form consists of evenly spaced, thick dashes with arrowheads. The second form consists of alternat-

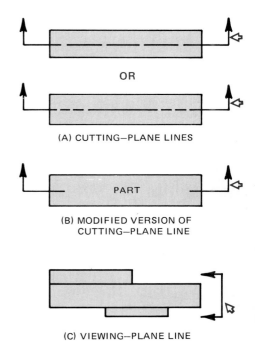

Fig. 8-1-2 Cutting-plane and viewing-plane lines.

ing long dashes and pairs of short dashes. The long dashes may vary in length, depending on the size of the drawing. These lengths may, at any time, be changed by using a LINE TYPE SCALE (LTSCALE) option for that purpose. Cutting-plane lines may be created by selecting the LAYER command and SET the PHANTOM linetype layer from the submenu. The layer number corresponding to phantom lines must be keyed in. Select

LINE, ORTHO ON, and draw the line. The ends of the lines are bent at 90° and terminated by bold arrowheads to indicate the direction of sight for viewing the section. Arrows may be placed at each end by the LEADER command. The arrow size may be increased by changing the DIMENSION VARIABLE DIMASZ. Create the leader on a LAYER that will plot with the same pen as the phantom line.

Cutting-plane lines should be drawn to stand out clearly on the drawing. Change the layer number prior to creating the line(s). This way either a thicker plotting pen may be used or a line thickness (offset) option may be employed if a pen plotter is not to be used.

The cutting-plane line can be omitted when it corresponds to the center line of the part and it is obvious where the cutting plane lies. On drawings with a high density of line work and for offset sections (see Unit 8-6), cutting-plane lines may be modified by omitting the dashes between the line ends for the purpose of obtaining clarity, as shown in Fig. 8-1-2B. In this instance, a phantom line is not used. Use the LEADER command at each end. Remember to first change the layer number to plot with a thicker pen.

Full Sections

When the cutting plane extends entirely through the object in a straight line and the front half of the object is theoretically removed, a full section is obtained. See Figs. 8-1-3 and 8-1-4. This type of section is used for both detail and assembly drawings. When the section is on an axis of symmetry, it is not necessary to indicate its locations. See Fig. 8-1-5. However, it may be identified and indicated in the normal manner to increase clarity, if so desired.

Section Lining

Section lining, referred to as *hatching*, can serve a double purpose. It indicates the surface that has been theoretically cut and makes it stand out clearly, thus helping the observer to understand the shape of the object. Section lining may also indicate the material from which the object is to be made, when the section lining symbols shown in Fig. 8-1-6 are used. CAD sys-

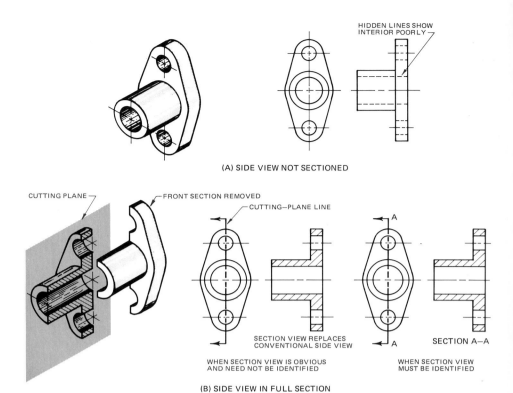

(A) SIDE VIEW NOT SECTIONED

(B) SIDE VIEW IN FULL SECTION

Fig. 8-1-3 Full-section view.

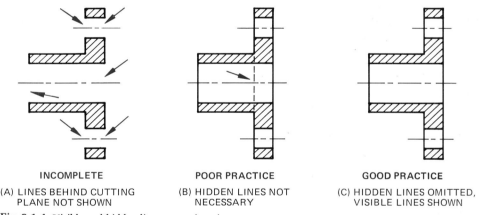

INCOMPLETE

(A) LINES BEHIND CUTTING PLANE NOT SHOWN

POOR PRACTICE

(B) HIDDEN LINES NOT NECESSARY

GOOD PRACTICE

(C) HIDDEN LINES OMITTED, VISIBLE LINES SHOWN

Fig. 8-1-4 Visible and hidden lines on section views.

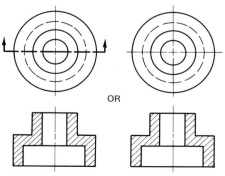

Fig. 8-1-5 Cutting-plane line may be omitted when it corresponds with the center line.

tems provide the option to use different section lining. The selection available on a particular system, however, will not be exactly the same as Fig. 8-1-6.

Section Lining for Detail Drawings Since the exact material specifications for a part are usually given elsewhere on the drawing, the general-purpose section lining symbol is recommended for most detail drawings. An exception may be made for wood when it is desirable to show the direction of the grain.

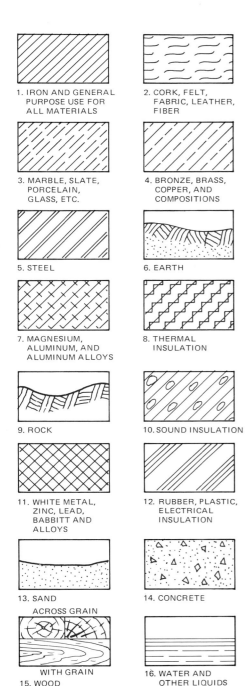

1. IRON AND GENERAL PURPOSE FOR ALL MATERIALS

2. CORK, FELT, FABRIC, LEATHER, FIBER

3. MARBLE, SLATE, PORCELAIN, GLASS, ETC.

4. BRONZE, BRASS, COPPER, AND COMPOSITIONS

5. STEEL

6. EARTH

7. MAGNESIUM, ALUMINUM, AND ALUMINUM ALLOYS

8. THERMAL INSULATION

9. ROCK

10. SOUND INSULATION

11. WHITE METAL, ZINC, LEAD, BABBITT AND ALLOYS

12. RUBBER, PLASTIC, ELECTRICAL INSULATION

13. SAND

14. CONCRETE

ACROSS GRAIN
WITH GRAIN
15. WOOD

16. WATER AND OTHER LIQUIDS

Fig. 8-1-6 Symbolic section lining.

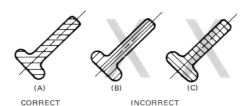

CORRECT   INCORRECT

Fig. 8-1-7 Direction of section lining.

ing. The pitch, or distance between lines, normally varies between .03 and .12 in. (1 and 3 mm) depending on the size of the area to be sectioned. This also may be changed when executing the command.

Formally, large, manually drafted areas shown in section were not entirely section-lined. See Fig. 8-1-8. Section lining around the outline provided sufficient clarity while saving a good deal of time. Automatic sectioning using CAD, however, has made this technique trivial. The entire area, described by you, is completely sectioned effortlessly.

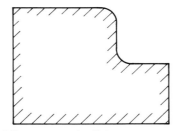

Fig. 8-1-8 Outline section lining.

Dimensions or other lettering should not be placed in sectioned areas. When this is unavoidable, the section lining should be omitted for the numerals or lettering. See Fig. 8-1-9. Some systems have a "cut and

The lines for section lining are thin and are usually drawn at an angle of 45° to the major outline of the object. The same angle is used for the whole "cut" surface of the object. If the part shape would cause section lines to be parallel, or nearly so, to one of the sides of the part, then some angle other than 45° should be chosen when executing the command. See Fig. 8-1-7. The spacing of the hatching lines should be reasonably uniform to give a good appearance to the draw-

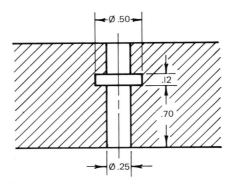

Fig. 8-1-9 Section lining omitted to accommodate dimensions.

paste" command that may be used for this purpose.

Sections which are too thin for effective section lining, such as sheet-metal items, packing, and gaskets, may be shown without section lining; or the area may be filled in completely by reducing the distance between the hatch lines to a small value such as .02 in. (0.5 mm). See Fig. 8-1-10.

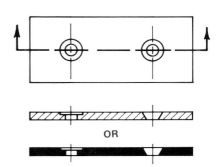

OR

Fig. 8-1-10 Thin parts in section.

Procedure There are two ways to automatically section. The hatch pattern can be determined by selecting:

- Each entity (line, arc)
- Entire perimeter by window

To section by entity, you must do the following:

1. Create the outline of the part to be sectioned (Fig. 8-1-11A). Create the center lines after completing the hatch sequence.
2. Select the HATCH (DRAW) command.

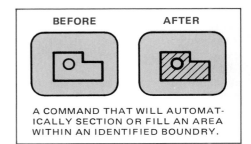

BEFORE   AFTER

A COMMAND THAT WILL AUTOMATICALLY SECTION OR FILL AN AREA WITHIN AN IDENTIFIED BOUNDRY.

3. Key in the name of the hatch pattern or select U or U, O for the general purpose pattern. Key ? to list the available patterns.
4. Key in the desired angle for cross-hatch lines (e.g., 45) and press ENTER.
5. Key in the spacing between lines (e.g., .12), press ENTER, and indi-

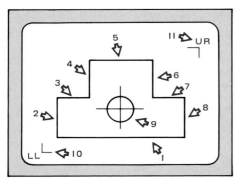

(A) DEFINING SECTION BOUNDARY

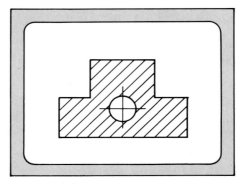

(B) SECTION COMPLETE

Fig. 8-1-11 Automatic sectioning.

cate if you desire a double hatch pattern (e.g., NO).

6. Locate and set the cursor on lines 1 through 9 (Fig. 8-1-11A). Be careful of this if any of the segments extend beyond the perimeter of the area to be sectioned. A CAD system at times gets confused here by your instructions and results in quite a strange pattern. This problem may be resolved by BREAKing the line at the outline boundary.

7. Select the ENTER. The area will be automatically sectioned as shown in Fig. 8-1-11B.

If an area fill (Fig. 8-1-10) had been desired, simply reduce the spacing between lines (Step 4).

It is often more convenient to section by a window or rectangle since it is less work. In this case, repeat the above procedure except for Step 6. Here you will select the W (window) option. Then select the lower left (LL) and upper right (UR) corners (points 10 and 11 in Fig. 8-1-11A). Be sure all entities reside fully within the area. The result will be exactly the same as using the section-by-entity method (Fig. 8-1-11B).

As an alternative, the EDIT pull down menu may be used to select HATCH. In this case, however, the spacing (scale) is built-in as a standard default. Press ENTER to accept it. The remaining sequence varies slightly.

ASSIGNMENT

See Assignment 1 for Unit 8-1 on page 168.

See Assignment 1 for Unit 8-1 on page 168.

UNIT 8-2

Two or More Sectional Views on One Drawing

If two or more sections appear on the same drawing, the cutting-plane lines are identified by two identical large letters, one at each end of the line, placed behind the arrowhead so that the arrow points away from the letter. Use the TEXT command and increase the lettering HEIGHT. Identify each sectional view beginning alphabetically with A-A, B-B, and so on. The identification letters should not include I, O, Q, and Z. See Fig. 8-2-1.

Sectional view subtitles are given when identification letters are used and appear directly below the view, incorporating the letters at each end of the cutting-plane line thus: SECTION A-A, or abbreviated, SECT. B-B. When the scale is different from the main view, it is stated below the subtitle thus

SECTION A-A
SCALE 1:4

ASSIGNMENT

See Assignment 2 for Unit 8-2 on page 168.

See Assignment 2 for Unit 8-2 on page 168.

UNIT 8-3

Half-Sections

A half-section is a view of an assembly or object, usually symmetrical, showing one-half of the view in section. See Figs. 8-3-1 and 8-3-2. Two cutting-plane lines, perpendicular to each other, extend halfway through the view, and one-quarter of the view is considered removed with the interior exposed to view.

Similar to the practice followed for full-section drawings, the cutting-plane line need not be drawn for half-sections when it is obvious where the cutting took place. Instead, center lines may be used. When a cutting plane is used, the common practice is to show only one end of the cutting-plane line, terminating with an arrow to show the direction of sight for viewing the section.

On the sectional view a center line or a visible object line may be used to divide the sectioned half from the un-

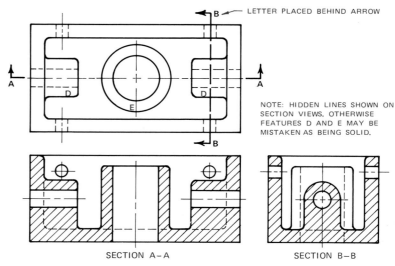

LETTER PLACED BEHIND ARROW

NOTE: HIDDEN LINES SHOWN ON SECTION VIEWS, OTHERWISE FEATURES D AND E MAY BE MISTAKEN AS BEING SOLID.

SECTION A-A

SECTION B-B

Fig. 8-2-1 Detail drawing having two section views.

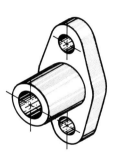

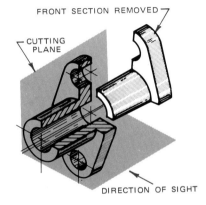

FRONT SECTION REMOVED

CUTTING PLANE

DIRECTION OF SIGHT

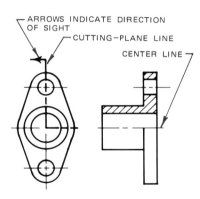

ARROWS INDICATE DIRECTION OF SIGHT

CUTTING-PLANE LINE

CENTER LINE

Fig. 8-3-1 A half-section drawing.

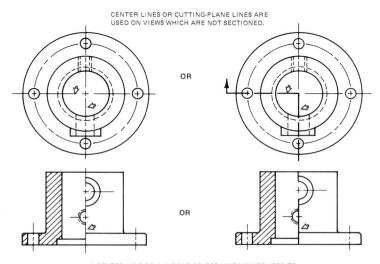

CENTER LINES OR CUTTING-PLANE LINES ARE USED ON VIEWS WHICH ARE NOT SECTIONED.

OR

OR

A CENTER LINE OR A VISIBLE OBJECT LINE MAY BE USED TO DIVIDE THE SECTIONED HALF FROM THE UNSECTIONED HALF

Fig. 8-3-2 Half-section views.

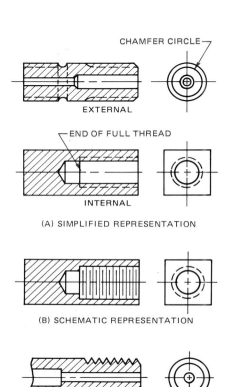

CHAMFER CIRCLE

EXTERNAL

END OF FULL THREAD

INTERNAL

(A) SIMPLIFIED REPRESENTATION

(B) SCHEMATIC REPRESENTATION

EXTERNAL

PREFERRED

ALTERNATE

(C) DETAILED REPRESENTATION

Fig. 8-4-1 Threads in section.

sectioned half of the drawing. This type of sectional drawing is best suited for assembly drawings where both internal and external construction is shown on one view and where only overall and center-to-center dimensions are required. The main disadvantage of using this type of sectional drawing for detail drawings is the difficulty in dimensioning internal features without adding hidden lines. However, hidden lines may be added for dimensioning, as shown in Fig. 8-3-3. In such instances, you may wish to revert to a full section. It will be easy to create since only one-half needs to be drawn. Prior to HATCH, BLOCK the half and MIRROR about a Y axis, the other half is automatically produced.

ASSIGNMENT

See Assignment 3 for Unit 8-3 on page 169.

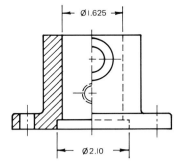

Ø1.625

Ø2.10

HIDDEN LINES ADDED FOR DIMENSIONING

Fig. 8-3-3 Dimensioning half-section view.

■ UNIT 8-4

Threads in Section

True representation of a screw thread is seldom provided on working drawings. A symbolic representation of threads is now standard practice.

Three types of conventions are in general use for screw thread representation. See Fig. 8-4-1. These are known as *detailed, schematic,* and *sim-*

plified representations. Simplified representation should be used whenever it will clearly portray the requirements. Schematic and detailed representations require more drafting time, but are sometimes necessary to avoid confusion with other parallel lines or to more clearly portray particular aspects of the threads. For drawings requiring multiple representations of the same size thread, remember to draw only one. Use COPY by WINDOW (or BLOCK and INSERT for different size threads).

THREADED ASSEMBLIES

Any of the thread conventions shown here may be used for assemblies of threaded parts, and two or more methods may be used on the same drawing, as shown in Fig. 8-4-2. In sectional views, the externally threaded part is always shown covering the internally threaded part, as illustrated in Fig. 8-4-3.

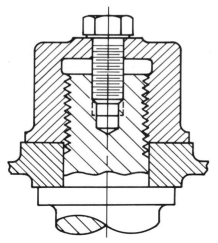

Fig. 8-4-2 Threaded assembly.

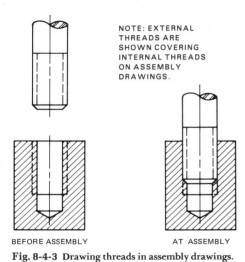

NOTE: EXTERNAL THREADS ARE SHOWN COVERING INTERNAL THREADS ON ASSEMBLY DRAWINGS.

BEFORE ASSEMBLY   AT ASSEMBLY

Fig. 8-4-3 Drawing threads in assembly drawings.

ASSIGNMENT

See Assignment 4 for Unit 8-4 on page 169.

■ UNIT 8-5

Assemblies in Section

SECTION LINING ON ASSEMBLY DRAWINGS

General-purpose section lining is recommended for most assembly drawings, especially if the detail is small. The method of sectioning a single part by selecting each line bounding the perimeter, as described in Unit 8-1, may be extended to all parts of a section assembly drawing.

The general-purpose section lining should be drawn at an angle of 45° with the main outlines of the view. On

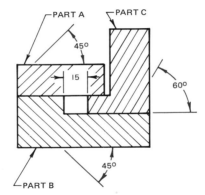

Fig. 8-5-1 Direction of section lining.

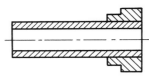

(A) ADJACENT PARTS

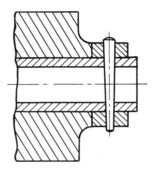

(B) ANGLE AND SPACING OF SECTION LINING

Fig. 8-5-2 Arrangement of section lining.

adjacent parts, the section lines should be drawn in the opposite direction by keying in 135 for the desired angle as shown in Figs. 8-5-1 and 8-5-2.

For additional adjacent parts, any suitable angle and spacing may be used to make each part stand out separately and clearly.

When two or more thin adjacent parts are filled in using a small incremental spacing (or use TRACE and FILL ON), a space is left between them, as shown in Fig. 8-5-3.

STEEL PLATES

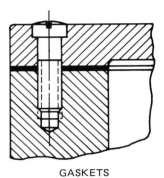

GASKETS

Fig. 8-5-3 Assembly of thin parts in section.

Symbolic section lining is used on special-purpose assembly drawings such as illustrations for parts catalogs, display assemblies, promotional materials, etc., when it is desirable to distinguish between different materials (Fig. 8-1-6).

All assemblies and subassemblies pertaining to one particular set of drawings should use the same symbolic conventions.

SHAFTS, BOLTS, PINS, KEYSEATS, AND SIMILAR SOLID PARTS, IN SECTION

Shafts, bolts, nuts, rods, rivets, keys, pins, and similar solid parts, the axes of which lie in the cutting plane, should not be sectioned except that a broken-out section of the shaft may be used to describe more clearly the key, keyseat, or pin. See Fig. 8-5-4.

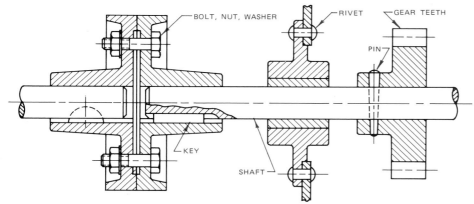

Fig. 8-5-4 Parts that are not section-lined even though the cutting plane passes through them.

ASSIGNMENT

See Assignment 5 for Unit 8-5 starting on page 169.

■ UNIT 8-6

Offset Sections

In order to include features that are not in a straight line, the cutting plane may be offset or bent, so as to include several planes or curved surfaces. Re-member to toggle the ORTHO ON option so the lines will be locked into the horizontal and vertical axis. See points 1 through 6 in Fig. 8-6-1. Figure 8-6-2 shows the modified version of the cutting-plane lines used to represent offset sections. Toggle ORTHO off.

An offset section is similar to a full section in that the cutting-plane line extends through the object from one side to the other. The change in direction of the cutting-plane line is not shown in the sectional view.

ASSIGNMENT

See Assignment 6 for Unit 8-6 on page 171.

■ UNIT 8-7

Ribs, Holes, and Lugs in Section

RIBS IN SECTIONS

A true-projection sectional view of a part, such as shown in Fig. 8-7-1, would be misleading when the cutting plane passes longitudinally through the center of the rib. To avoid this impression of solidity, a section not showing the ribs section-lined is preferred. When there is an odd number of ribs, such as those shown in Fig. 8-7-1B, the top rib is aligned with the bottom rib to show its true relationship with the hub and flange. If the rib is not aligned or revolved, it would appear distorted on the sectional view and would therefore be misleading.

At times it may be necessary to use an alternative method of identifying ribs in a sectional view. Figure 8-7-2

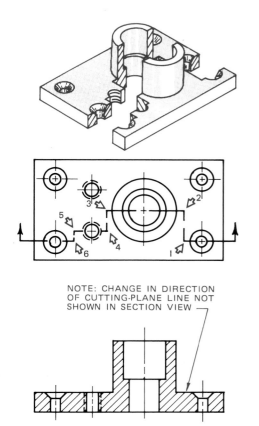

Fig. 8-6-1 An offset section.

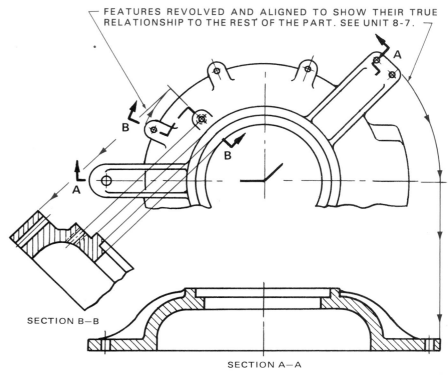

Fig. 8-6-2 Positioning offset sections.

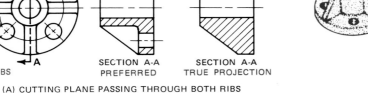

HOLES ARE ROTATED TO CUTTING PLANE TO SHOW THEIR
TRUE RELATIONSHIP WITH THE REST OF THE ELEMENT

RIBS ARE NOT SECTIONED

SECTION A-A
PREFERRED

SECTION A-A
TRUE PROJECTION

4 RIBS

(A) CUTTING PLANE PASSING THROUGH BOTH RIBS

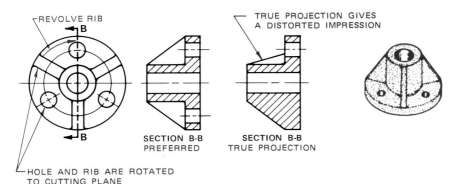

REVOLVE RIB

TRUE PROJECTION GIVES
A DISTORTED IMPRESSION

SECTION B-B
PREFERRED

SECTION B-B
TRUE PROJECTION

HOLE AND RIB ARE ROTATED
TO CUTTING PLANE

(B) CUTTING PLANE PASSING THROUGH ONE RIB AND ONE HOLE

Fig. 8-7-1 Preferred and true projection through ribs and holes.

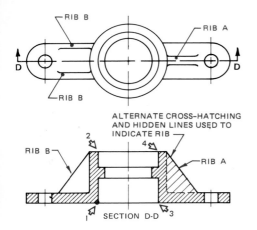

RIB B

RIB A

RIB B

ALTERNATE CROSS-HATCHING
AND HIDDEN LINES USED TO
INDICATE RIB

RIB B

RIB A

SECTION D-D

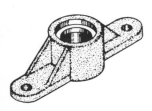

(A) BASE

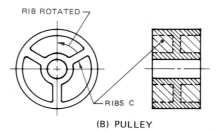

RIB ROTATED

RIBS C

(B) PULLEY

Fig. 8-7-2 Alternate method of showing ribs in section.

shows a base and a pulley in section. If rib A of the base was not sectioned as previously mentioned, it would appear exactly like rib B in the sectional view and would be misleading. Similarly, rib C shown on the pulley may be overlooked. To clearly show the rela-

tionship of the ribs with the other solid features on the base and pulley, alternate sectional lining on the ribs is used. The line between the rib and solid portions is shown as a broken line. Section each area by the entity method (Unit 8-1) or block the area of the outline you wish sectioned. Often some lines of an object are drawn such that they are part of different section outlines. In these cases you may have to EDIT the line into segments as shown by points 1 through 4 in Fig. 8-7-2A. Use BREAK and a gap distance of nearly zero (or FILLET with a radius of 0) so that the object lines still appear to be continuous.

HOLES IN SECTIONS

Holes, like ribs, are aligned as shown in Fig. 8-7-1 to show their true relationship to the rest of the part.

LUGS IN SECTION

Lugs, like ribs and holes, are also aligned to show their true relationship to the rest of the part, because true projection may be misleading. Figure 8-7-3 shows several examples of lugs in section. Note how the cutting-plane line is bent or offset so that the features may be clearly shown in the sectional view.

Some lugs are shown in section and some are not. When the cutting plane passes through the lug crosswise, the lug is sectioned; otherwise, the lugs are treated in the same manner as ribs. Notice that many of the line segments extend beyond the hatched area. Whenever possible, create the outline to be hatched, then create the remainder of the view separately. This means you will be drawing more, shorter lines. Otherwise, use the BREAK command (Fig. 8-7-2).

ASSIGNMENT

See Assignment 7 for Unit 8-7 on page 172.

See Assignment 7 for Unit 8-7 on page 172.

■ UNIT 8-8

Revolved and Removed Sections

Revolved and removed sections are used to show the cross-sectional shape of ribs, spokes, or arms when the shape is not obvious in the regular views. See

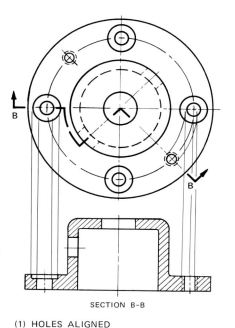

SECTION B-B

(1) HOLES ALIGNED

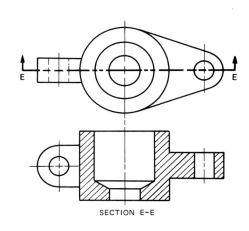

SECTION C-C

(2) LUGS ALIGNED AND SECTIONED

SECTION D-D

(3) LUGS ALIGNED AND SECTIONED

SECTION E-E

(4) LUG NOT SECTIONED

Fig. 8-7-3 Aligning holes and lugs in section drawings.

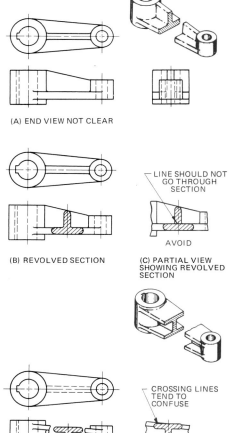

(A) END VIEW NOT CLEAR

(B) REVOLVED SECTION

LINE SHOULD NOT GO THROUGH SECTION

AVOID

(C) PARTIAL VIEW SHOWING REVOLVED SECTION

CROSSING LINES TEND TO CONFUSE

AVOID

(D) REVOLVED SECTION WITH MAIN VIEW BROKEN FOR CLARITY

(E) PARTIAL VIEW SHOWING REVOLVED SECTION

Fig. 8-8-1 Revolved sections.

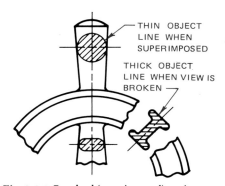

THIN OBJECT LINE WHEN SUPERIMPOSED

THICK OBJECT LINE WHEN VIEW IS BROKEN

Fig. 8-8-2 Revolved (superimposed) sections.

Figs. 8-8-1 to 8-8-3. Often end views are not needed when a revolved section is used. For a revolved section, imagine a plane cutting through the object to be described, then imagine the part rotated 90°, so that the cut surface would be seen clearly. See Figs. 8-8-1 and 8-8-2. If the revolved section does not interfere with the view on which it is revolved, then the view is not broken unless it would provide for clearer dimensioning. When the revolved section interferes or passes through lines on the view on which it is revolved, then the general practice is to break the view (Fig. 8-8-2). Often the break is used to shorten the length of the object. In no

circumstances should the lines on the view pass through the section. When superimposed on the view, draw the outline of the revolved section using a different layer to produce a thin, continuous line on the plot.

The removed section differs in that the section, instead of being drawn right on the view, is removed to an open area on the drawing (Fig. 8-8-3). Frequently the removed section is drawn to an enlarged scale for clarification and easier dimensioning. Removed sections of symmetrical parts should be placed, whenever possible, on the extension of the center line (Fig. 8-8-3B). SCALE, ROTATE, and MOVE by WINDOW commands will

assist in the placement of removed sections.

On complicated drawings where the placement of the removed view may be some distance from the cutting plane, auxiliary information, such as the reference zone location (Fig. 8-8-4), may be helpful.

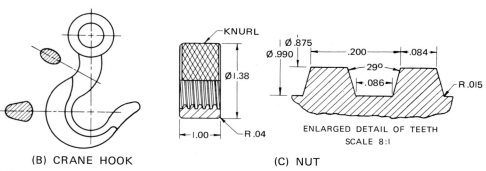

SECTION A-A
DOUBLE SIZE

SECTION B-B
DOUBLE SIZE

SECTION C-C
DOUBLE SIZE

VIEW D-D
DOUBLE SIZE

(A) REMOVED SECTIONS AND REMOVED VIEW

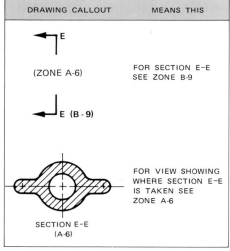

(B) CRANE HOOK

KNURL

Ø1.38

1.00

R.04

Ø.875
Ø.990

.200

.084

29°

.086

R.015

ENLARGED DETAIL OF TEETH
SCALE 8:1

(C) NUT

Fig. 8-8-3 Removed sections.

DRAWING CALLOUT	MEANS THIS
E (ZONE A-6)	FOR SECTION E-E SEE ZONE B-9
E (B-9)	FOR VIEW SHOWING WHERE SECTION E-E IS TAKEN SEE ZONE A-6
SECTION E-E (A-6)	

Fig. 8-8-4 Reference zone location.

PLACEMENT OF REMOVED SECTIONAL VIEWS

Whenever practical, sectional views should be projected perpendicular to the cutting plane and be placed in the normal position for third-angle projection. See Fig. 8-8-5.

When the preferred placement is not practical, the sectional view may be removed to some other convenient position on the drawing, but it must be clearly identified, usually by two capital letters, and be labeled.

ASSIGNMENT

See Assignment 8 for Unit 8-8 on page 172.

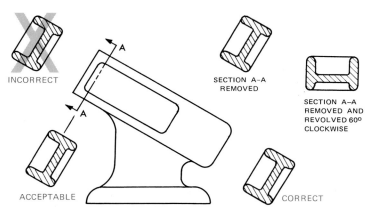

INCORRECT

ACCEPTABLE

SECTION A-A
REMOVED

SECTION A-A
REMOVED AND
REVOLVED 60°
CLOCKWISE

CORRECT

Fig. 8-8-5 Placement of sectional views.

Spokes and Arms in Section

A comparison of the true projection of a wheel with spokes and a wheel with a web is made in Figs. 8-9-1A and B. This comparison shows that a preferred section for the wheel and spokes is desirable so that it will not appear to be a wheel with a solid web. In preferred sectioning, any part that is not solid or continuous around the hub is drawn without the section lining, even though the cutting plane passes through the spoke. When there is an odd number of spokes, as shown in Fig. 8-9-1C, the bottom spoke is aligned with the top spoke to show its true relationship to the wheel and to the hub. If the spoke were not revolved or aligned, it would appear distorted in the sectional view.

ASSIGNMENT

See Assignment 9 for Unit 8-9 on page 173.

Partial or Broken-Out Sections

Where a sectional view of only a portion of the object is needed, partial sections may be used. See Fig. 8-10-1. An irregular break line using the SKETCH option shows the extent of the section. With this type of section, a

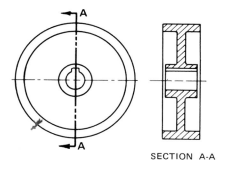

(A) FLAT PULLEY WITH WEB

SECTION A-A

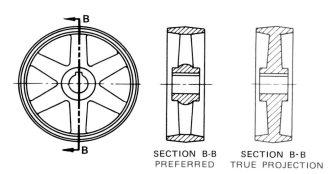

(B) HANDWHEEL WITH EVEN NUMBER OF SPOKES

SECTION B-B
PREFERRED

SECTION B-B
TRUE PROJECTION

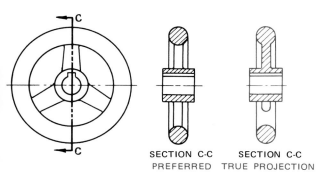

SECTION C-C
PREFERRED

SECTION C-C
TRUE PROJECTION

(C) HANDWHEEL WITH ODD NUMBER OF SPOKES

SECTION D-D
PREFERRED

SECTION D-D
TRUE PROJECTION

(D) HANDWHEEL WITH ODD NUMBER OF OFFSET SPOKES

Fig. 8-9-1 Preferred and true projection through spokes.

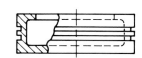

EXAMPLE 1

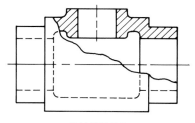

EXAMPLE 2

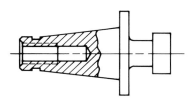

EXAMPLE 3

Fig. 8-10-1 Broken-out or partial sections.

cutting-plane line is not required. The visible lines forming the outline extend beyond the break line. It is best to BREAK (gap of zero length) the segments at the irregular break prior to sectioning.

ASSIGNMENT

See Assignment 10 for Unit 8-10 on page 173.

■ UNIT 8-11

Phantom or Hidden Sections

A phantom section is used to show the typical interior shapes of an object in one view when the part is not truly symmetrical in shape, as well as to show mating parts in an assembly drawing. See Fig. 8-11-1. It is a sectional view superimposed on the regular view without the removal of the front portion of the object. The sec-

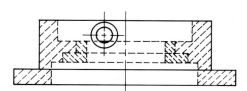

Fig. 8-11-1 Phantom or hidden section.

tion lining used for phantom sections consists of thin, evenly spaced, broken lines. Use the DASH hatch pattern.

ASSIGNMENT

See Assignment 11 for Unit 8-11 on page 174.

■ UNIT 8-12

Sectional Drawing Review

In Units 8-1 through 8-11 the different types of sectional views have been explained and drawing problems have been assigned with each type of section drawing.

In the drafting office, it is the drafter who must decide which views are required to fully explain the part to be made. In addition, the drafter must select the proper scale(s) which will show the features clearly.

This unit has been designed to review the sectional-view options open to the drafter.

Remember, when the resulting section is not what was expected, it probably is due to the system not understanding what boundary you have defined. You may have to redraw it so that none of the visible lines extend beyond the boundary or BREAK the lines into segments (at the boundary).

ASSIGNMENT

See Assignment 12 for Unit 8-12 on page 175.

ASSIGNMENTS FOR CHAPTER 8

Assignment for Unit 8-1, Sectional Views

1. Select one of the problems shown in Fig. 8-1-A or 8-1-B, and on a B or A3 size drawing make a two-view working drawing of the part, showing one of the views in full section. Use symbolic dimensioning wherever possible. Scale 1:1.

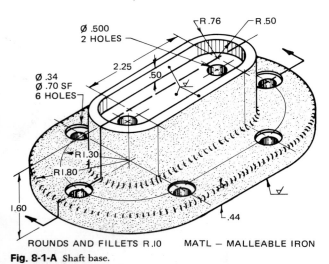

Fig. 8-1-A Shaft base.

Fig. 8-1-B Flanged elbow.

Assignment for Unit 8-2, Two or More Sectional Views on One Drawing

2. Select one of the problems shown in Fig. 8-2-A or 8-2-B and on a B or A3 size make a working drawing of the part showing the appropriate views in sections. Refer to the Appendix for taper sizes. Use symbolic dimensioning wherever possible. Scale 1:1.

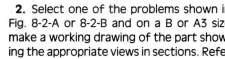

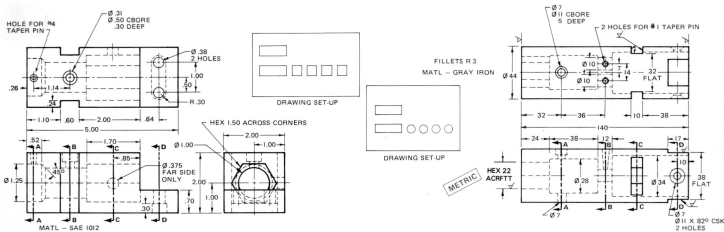

Fig. 8-2-A Casting.

Fig. 8-2-B Housing.

Assignment for Unit 8-3, Half-Sections

3. Select one of the problems shown in Fig. 8-3-A or 8-3-B. On a B or A3 size drawing, make a two-view working drawing of the part showing the side view in half-section. Redimension the keyseat as per the method in Chap. 10. Scale 1 : 1.

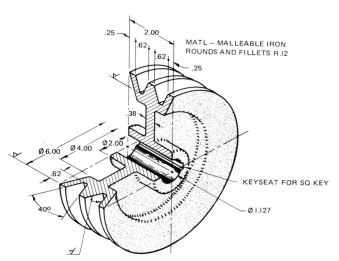

Fig. 8-3-A Double-V pulley.

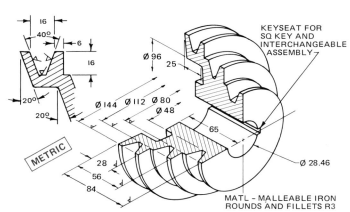

Fig. 8-3-B Step-V pulley.

Assignment for Unit 8-4, Threads in Section

4. Select one of the problems shown in Fig. 8-4-A or 8-4-B. On a B or A3 size drawing, make a working drawing of the part. Determine the number of views and the best type of section which will clearly describe the part. Use symbolic dimensioning wherever possible and add undercut sizes. Scale 1 : 1.

Assignment for Unit 8-5, Assemblies in Section

5. On an A3 or B size drawing, make a one-view section assembly drawing of one of the problems shown in Fig. 8-5-A or 8-5-B. Assuming that this drawing will be used in a catalog, place on the drawing the dimensions and information required by the potential buyer. Scale 1 : 1.

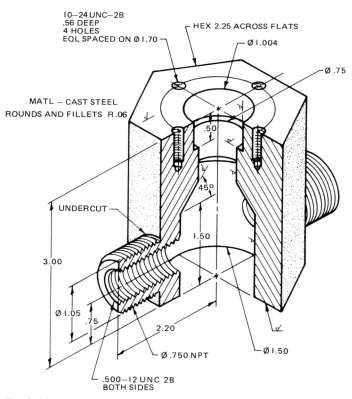

Fig. 8-4-A Valve body.

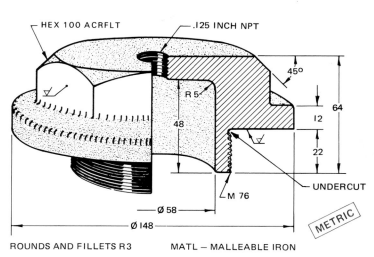

Fig. 8-4-B Pipe plug.

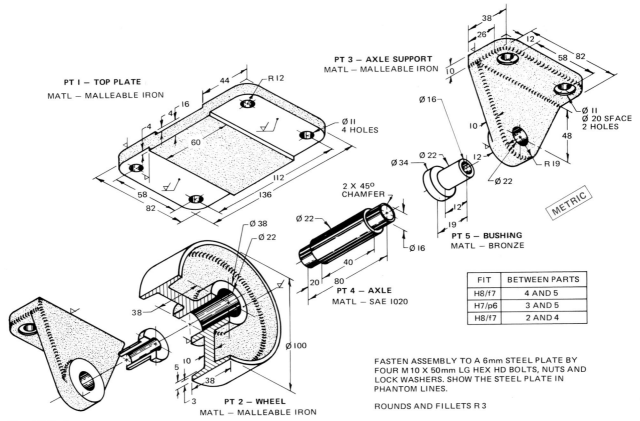

PT 1 — TOP PLATE
MATL — MALLEABLE IRON

PT 3 — AXLE SUPPORT
MATL — MALLEABLE IRON

PT 5 — BUSHING
MATL — BRONZE

PT 4 — AXLE
MATL — SAE 1020

PT 2 — WHEEL
MATL — MALLEABLE IRON

METRIC

FIT	BETWEEN PARTS
H8/f7	4 AND 5
H7/p6	3 AND 5
H8/f7	2 AND 4

FASTEN ASSEMBLY TO A 6mm STEEL PLATE BY
FOUR M 10 X 50mm LG HEX HD BOLTS, NUTS AND
LOCK WASHERS. SHOW THE STEEL PLATE IN
PHANTOM LINES.

ROUNDS AND FILLETS R 3

Fig. 8-5-A Caster.

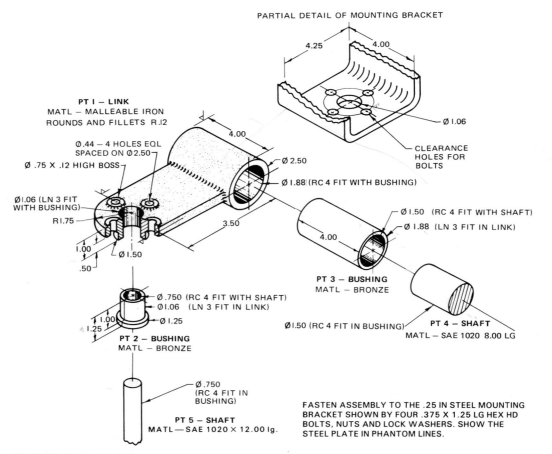

PARTIAL DETAIL OF MOUNTING BRACKET

PT 1 — LINK
MATL — MALLEABLE IRON
ROUNDS AND FILLETS R .12

CLEARANCE
HOLES FOR
BOLTS

PT 3 — BUSHING
MATL — BRONZE

PT 4 — SHAFT
MATL — SAE 1020 8.00 LG

PT 2 — BUSHING
MATL — BRONZE

PT 5 — SHAFT
MATL — SAE 1020 × 12.00 lg.

FASTEN ASSEMBLY TO THE .25 IN STEEL MOUNTING
BRACKET SHOWN BY FOUR .375 X 1.25 LG HEX HD
BOLTS, NUTS AND LOCK WASHERS. SHOW THE
STEEL PLATE IN PHANTOM LINES.

Fig. 8-5-B Connecting link.

Assignment for Unit 8-6, Offset Sections

6. Select one of the problems shown in Fig. 8-6-A or 8-6-B. On a B or A3 size drawing make a working drawing of the part. Scale 1:1.

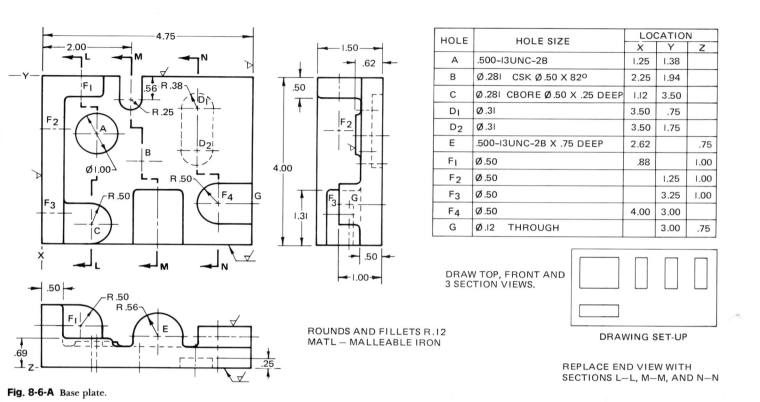

HOLE	HOLE SIZE	LOCATION		
		X	Y	Z
A	.500–13UNC–2B	1.25	1.38	
B	Ø.281 CSK Ø.50 X 82°	2.25	1.94	
C	Ø.281 CBORE Ø.50 X .25 DEEP	1.12	3.50	
D₁	Ø.31	3.50	.75	
D₂	Ø.31	3.50	1.75	
E	.500–13UNC–2B X .75 DEEP	2.62		.75
F₁	Ø.50	.88		1.00
F₂	Ø.50		1.25	1.00
F₃	Ø.50		3.25	1.00
F₄	Ø.50	4.00	3.00	
G	Ø.12 THROUGH		3.00	.75

DRAW TOP, FRONT AND 3 SECTION VIEWS.

ROUNDS AND FILLETS R.12
MATL – MALLEABLE IRON

DRAWING SET-UP

REPLACE END VIEW WITH
SECTIONS L–L, M–M, AND N–N

Fig. 8-6-A Base plate.

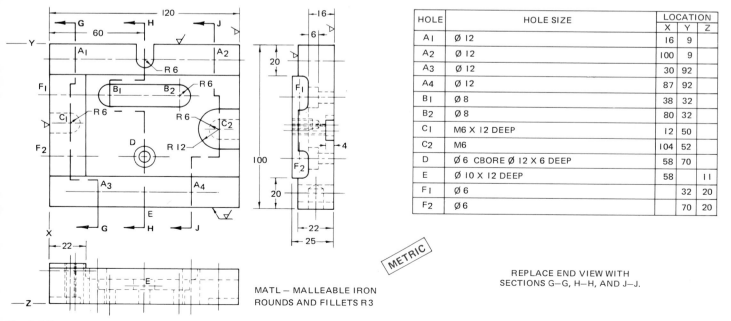

HOLE	HOLE SIZE	LOCATION		
		X	Y	Z
A₁	Ø 12	16	9	
A₂	Ø 12	100	9	
A₃	Ø 12	30	92	
A₄	Ø 12	87	92	
B₁	Ø 8	38	32	
B₂	Ø 8	80	32	
C₁	M6 X 12 DEEP	12	50	
C₂	M6	104	52	
D	Ø 6 CBORE Ø 12 X 6 DEEP	58	70	
E	Ø 10 X 12 DEEP	58		11
F₁	Ø 6		32	20
F₂	Ø 6		70	20

METRIC

MATL – MALLEABLE IRON
ROUNDS AND FILLETS R3

REPLACE END VIEW WITH
SECTIONS G–G, H–H, AND J–J.

Fig. 8-6-B Mounting plate.

Assignment for Unit 8-7, Ribs, Holes, and Lugs in Section

7. Select one of the problems shown in Fig. 8-7-A or 8-7-B. On a B or A3 size drawing, make a three-view working drawing of the part showing the front and side views in section. Both parts are to be used here and abroad, so a dual dimensioning system must be used. Scale 1:1.

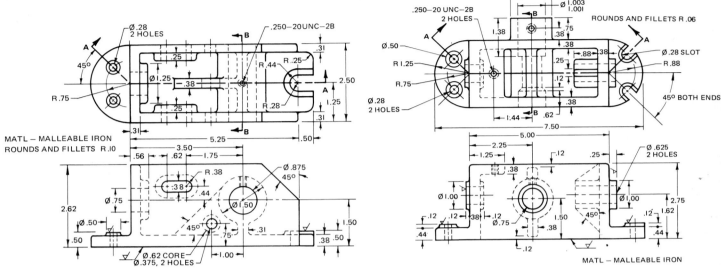

Fig. 8-7-A Bracket bearing.

Fig. 8-7-B Shaft support.

Assignment for Unit 8-8, Revolved and Removed Sections

8. Select one of the problems shown in Fig. 8-8-A or 8-8-B and on a B or A3 size drawing make a working drawing of the part. For clarity it is recommended that an enlarged removed view be used to show the detail of the inclined hole. Use symbolic dimensioning wherever possible. Scale is 1:1.

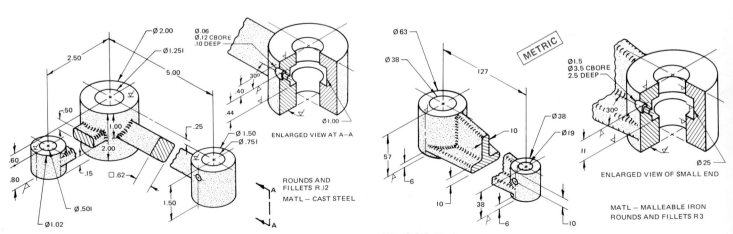

Fig. 8-8-A Idler support.

Fig. 8-8-B Shaft support.

Assignment for Unit 8-9, Spokes and Arms in Section

9. Select one of the problems shown in Fig. 8-9-A or 8-9-B and on a B or A3 size drawing, make a two-view working drawing. Draw the side view in full section, and show a revolved section of the spoke in the front view. Scale 1:1.

Assignment for Unit 8-10, Partial or Broken-Out Sections

10. Select one of the problems shown in Fig. 8-10-A or 8-10-B and make a two-view working drawing on a B or A3 size drawing. Use partial sections where clarity of drawing can be achieved. Scale 1:1.

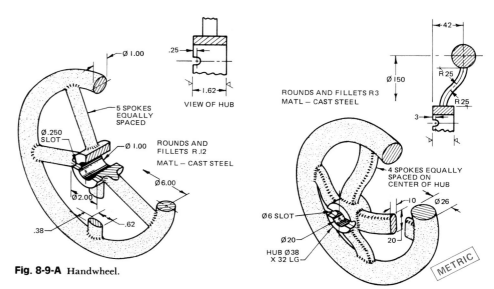

Fig. 8-9-A Handwheel.

Fig. 8-9-B Offset handwheel.

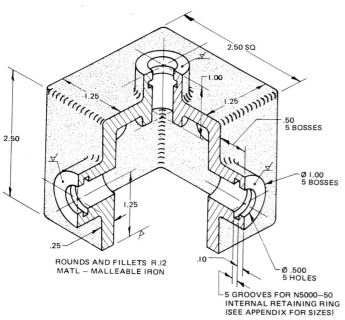

Fig. 8-10-A Tumble box.

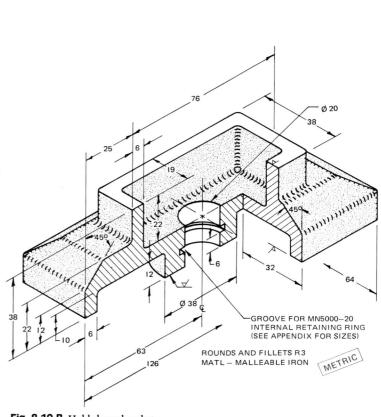

Fig. 8-10-B Hold-down bracket.

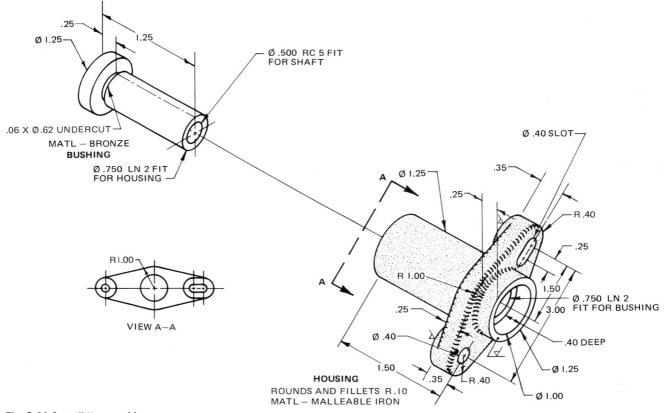

Fig. 8-11-A Drill-jig assembly.

On the shaft/bushing (upper left):
Ø 1.25
.25
1.25
Ø .500 RC 5 FIT FOR SHAFT
.06 X Ø .62 UNDERCUT
MATL — BRONZE
BUSHING
Ø .750 LN 2 FIT FOR HOUSING

VIEW A—A
R1.00

On the housing:
A
A
Ø 1.25
.25
.35
Ø .40 SLOT
R .40
.25
R 1.00
1.50
3.00
Ø .750 LN 2 FIT FOR BUSHING
.40 DEEP
Ø 1.25
Ø 1.00
.25
Ø .40
1.50
.35
R .40
HOUSING
ROUNDS AND FILLETS R .10
MATL — MALLEABLE IRON

Assignment for Unit 8-11, Phantom or Hidden Sections

11. On an A3 or B size drawing make a two-view assembly drawing of one of the assemblies shown in Fig. 8-11-A or 8-11-B. The front view is to be drawn as a phantom section drawing. Show only the hole and shaft sizes for the fits shown. Scale is 1 : 1.

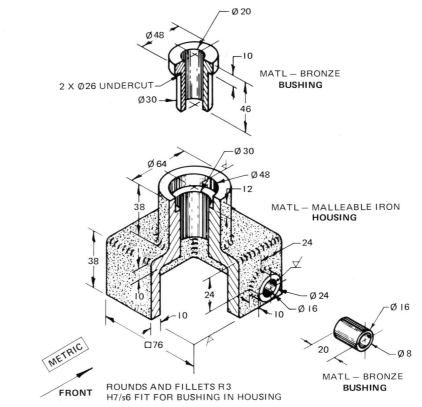

Bushing (upper):
Ø 20
Ø 48
10
MATL — BRONZE
BUSHING
2 X Ø26 UNDERCUT
Ø30
46

Housing (lower):
Ø 30
Ø 64
Ø 48
12
38
38
10
24
24
10
10
Ø 24
Ø 16
MATL — MALLEABLE IRON
HOUSING
□ 76
METRIC
FRONT
ROUNDS AND FILLETS R3
H7/s6 FIT FOR BUSHING IN HOUSING

Bushing (lower right):
Ø 16
20
Ø 8
MATL — BRONZE
BUSHING

Fig. 8-11-B Housing.

174 BASIC DRAWING DESIGN

Assignment for Unit 8-12, Sectional Drawing Review

12. On a B or A3 size drawing make a three-view working drawing of one of the parts shown in Fig. 8-12-A or 8-12-B. From the information on section drawings found in Units 8-1 to 8-11, select appropriate sectional views which will improve the clarity of the drawing. Scale 1:1.

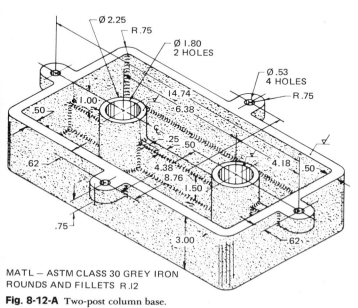

Fig. 8-12-A Two-post column base.

MATL — ASTM CLASS 30 GREY IRON
ROUNDS AND FILLETS R .12

Ø 2.25
R .75
Ø 1.80 2 HOLES
Ø .53 4 HOLES
R .75
14.74
6.38
.50
1.00
.25
.50
4.18
.62
4.38
8.76
1.50
.50
.75
3.00
.62

Fig. 8-12-B Shaft support base.

ROUNDS AND FILLETS R 3
MATL — MALLEABLE IRON

Ø 16.1 2 HOLES SYMMETRICAL ABOUT CENTER LINE
70
Ø 25
Ø 5 THRU 2 HOLES
22
R 40
176
146
10
Ø 35
3 mm HIGH BOSS
8
25
16
15
R 11
R 120
58
10
80
53
Ø 10.5 4 SLOTS
11
METRIC
RIBS 8 mm THICK LOCATED ON CENTER LINES

PART 2

Fasteners, Materials, and Forming Processes

CHAPTER 9

Threaded Fasteners

■ UNIT 9-1

Simplified Thread Representation

Fastening devices are important in the construction of manufactured products, in the machines and devices used in manufacturing processes, and in the construction of all types of buildings. Fastening devices are used in the smallest watch to the largest ocean liner. See Fig. 9-1-1.

There are two basic kinds of fasteners: permanent and removable. Rivets and welds are permanent fasteners. Bolts, screws, studs, nuts, pins, rings, and keys are removable fasteners. As industry progressed, fastening devices became standardized, and they developed definite characteristics and names. A thorough knowledge of the design and graphic representation of the more common fasteners is an essential part of drafting.

The cost of fastening, once considered only incidental, is fast becoming recognized as a critical factor in total product cost. "It's the in-place cost that counts, not the fastener cost" is an old saying of fastener design. The art of holding down fastener cost is not learned simply by scanning a parts catalog. More subtly, it entails weighing such factors as standardization, automatic assembly, tailored fasteners, and joint preparation.

Standardization A favorite cost-reducing method, standardization not

Fig. 9-1-1 Fasteners.

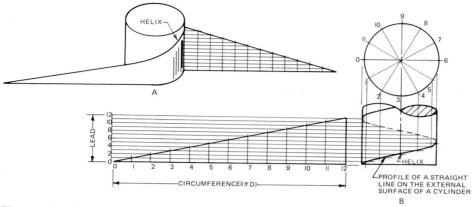

Fig. 9-1-2 The helix.

SCREW THREADS

A screw thread is a ridge of uniform section in the form of a helix on the external or internal surface of a cylinder. See. Fig. 9-1-2. The helix of a square thread is shown in Fig. 9-1-3.

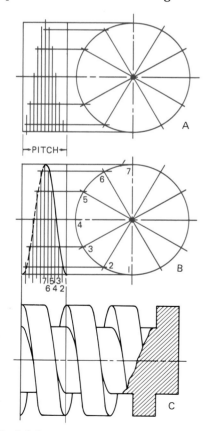

Fig. 9-1-3 The helix of a square thread.

only cuts the cost of parts but also reduces paperwork and simplifies inventory and quality control. By standardizing on type and size, it may be possible to reach the level of usage required to make power tools or automatic assembly feasible.

The pitch P of a thread is the distance from a point on the thread form to the corresponding point on the next form, measured parallel to the axis. See. Fig. 9-1-4. The lead L is the dis-

tance the threaded part would move parallel to the axis during one complete rotation in relation to a fixed mating part (the distance a screw would enter a threaded hole in one turn).

THREAD FORMS

Figure 9-1-5 shows some of the more common thread forms in use today. The ISO metric thread will eventually replace all the V-shaped metric and inch threads. As for the other thread forms shown, the proportions will be the same for both metric- and inch-size threads.

The knuckle thread is usually rolled or cast. A familiar example of this form is seen on electric light bulbs and sockets. See Fig. 9-1-6. The square and acme forms are designed to trans-

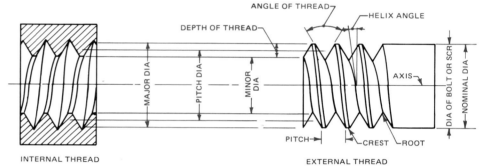

Fig. 9-1-4 Screw thread terms.

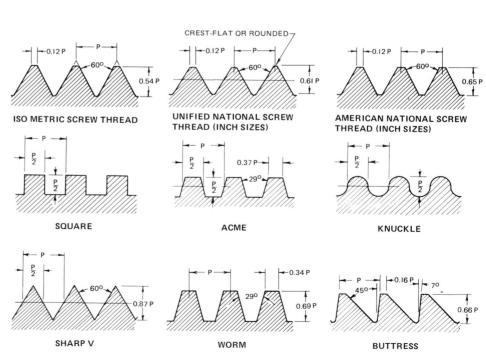

Fig. 9-1-5 Common thread forms and proportions.

Fig. 9-1-6 Application of a knuckle thread.

mit motion or power, as on the lead screw of a lathe. The buttress thread takes pressure in only one direction — against the surface perpendicular to the axis.

THREAD REPRESENTATION

True representation of a screw thread is seldom used on working drawings. Symbolic representation of threads are now standard practice. There are three types of conventions in general use for screw thread representation. These are known as simplified, detailed, and schematic. See Fig. 9-1-7. Simplified representation should be used whenever it will clearly portray the requirements. Detailed representation is used to show the detail of a screw thread, especially for dimensioning in enlarged views, layouts, and

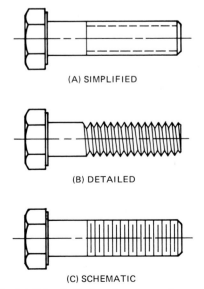

(A) SIMPLIFIED

(B) DETAILED

(C) SCHEMATIC

Fig. 9-1-7 Symbolic thread representation.

assemblies. Creating detailed representation of threads requires considerable time and effort. Once a thread form has been detailed it should be saved so that it may be copied when needed again. The schematic representation is nearly as effective as the detailed representation and is much easier to draw. This representation has given way to the simplified representation (Fig. 9-1-7), and as such, has been discarded as a thread symbol by most countries.

RIGHT- AND LEFT-HAND THREADS

Unless designated otherwise, threads are assumed to be right-hand. A bolt being threaded into a tapped hole would be turned in a right-hand (clockwise) direction. See Fig. 9-1-8. For some special applications, such as turnbuckles, left-hand threads are required. When such a thread is necessary, the letters LH are added after the thread designation.

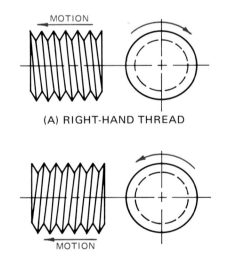

(A) RIGHT-HAND THREAD

(B) LEFT-HAND THREAD

Fig. 9-1-8 Right- and left-hand threads.

SINGLE AND MULTIPLE THREADS

Most screws have single threads. It is understood that unless the thread is designated otherwise, it is a single thread. The single thread has a single ridge in the form of a helix (Fig. 9-1-9). The lead of a thread is the distance traveled parallel to the axis in one rotation of a part in relation to a fixed mating part (the distance a nut would

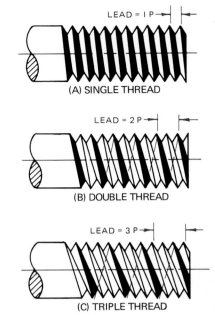

(A) SINGLE THREAD

(B) DOUBLE THREAD

(C) TRIPLE THREAD

Fig. 9-1-9 Single and multiple threads.

travel along the axis of a bolt with one rotation of the nut). In single threads, the lead is equal to the pitch. A double thread has two ridges, started 180° apart, in the form of helices; and the lead is twice the pitch. A triple thread has three ridges, started 120° apart, in the form of helices, and the lead is 3 times the pitch. Multiple threads are used where fast movement is desired with a minimum number of rotations, such as on threaded mechanisms for opening and closing windows.

SIMPLIFIED THREAD REPRESENTATION

In this system the thread crests, except in hidden views, are represented by a thick outline and the thread roots by a thin broken line. See Fig. 9-1-10. Remember to change layers when drawing the roots. The end of the full-form thread is indicated by a thick line across the part, and imperfect or run-out threads are shown beyond this line by running the root line at an angle to meet the crest line. If the length of runout threads is unimportant, this portion of the convention may be omitted.

THREADED ASSEMBLIES

For general use, the simplified representation for assemblies of threaded parts is recommended. See Fig.

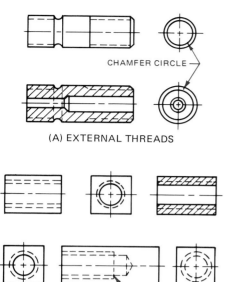

(A) EXTERNAL THREADS

(B) INTERNAL THREADS

CHAMFER CIRCLE

END OF FULL THREAD

Fig. 9-1-10 Simplified thread convention.

9-1-11. In sectional views, the externally threaded part is always shown covering the internally threaded part.

INCH THREADS

In the United States a great number of threaded assemblies are still designed using inch-sized threads. In this system the pitch is equal to

$$\frac{1}{\text{Number of threads per inch}}$$

The number of threads per inch is set for different diameters in what is called a thread series. For the Unified National system there is the coarse-thread series (UNC) and the fine-thread series (UNF). See Table 11 of Appendix B.

In addition, there is an extra-fine-thread series. UNEF, for use where a small pitch is desirable, such as on thin-walled tubing. For special work and for diameters larger than those specified in the coarse and fine series, the Unified Thread system has three series that provide for the same number of threads per inch regardless of the diameter. These are the 8-thread series, the 12-thread series, and the 16-thread series. These are called *constant-pitch threads*.

Thread Class

Three classes of external thread (classes 1A, 2A, and 3A) and three classes of internal thread (classes 1B, 2B, and 3B) are provided. These classes differ in the amount of allowances and tolerances provided in each class.

The general characteristics and uses of the various classes are as follows.

Classes 1A and 1B These classes produce the loosest fit, that is, the greatest amount of play in assembly. They are useful for work where ease of assembly and disassembly is essential, such as for stove bolts and other rough bolts and nuts.

Classes 2A and 2B These classes are designed for the ordinary good grade of commercial products, such as machine screws and fasteners, and for most interchangeable parts.

Classes 3A and 3B These classes are intended for exceptionally high-grade commercial products, where a particu-larly close or snug fit is essential and the high cost of precision tools and machines is warranted.

Thread Designation

Thread designation for inch threads, whether external or internal, is expressed in this order: diameter (nominal or major diameter in decimal form with a minimum of three, or a maximum of four decimal places), number of threads per inch, thread form and series, and class of fit (number and letter). See Fig. 9-1-12. These may be added using the LEADER command.

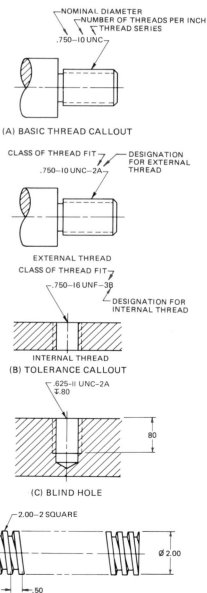

NOMINAL DIAMETER
NUMBER OF THREADS PER INCH
THREAD SERIES
.750—10 UNC

(A) BASIC THREAD CALLOUT

CLASS OF THREAD FIT
.750—10 UNC—2A

DESIGNATION FOR EXTERNAL THREAD

EXTERNAL THREAD
CLASS OF THREAD FIT
.750—16 UNF—3B
DESIGNATION FOR INTERNAL THREAD

INTERNAL THREAD
(B) TOLERANCE CALLOUT

.625—11 UNC—2A
↧.80

80

(C) BLIND HOLE

2.00—2 SQUARE

Ø 2.00

.50

(D) MISCELLANEOUS THREAD FORMS

Fig. 9-1-12 Thread specifications for inch-size threads.

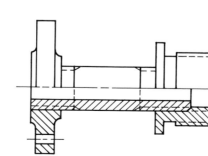

Fig. 9-1-11 Simplified representation of threads in assembly drawings.

METRIC THREADS

Metric threads are grouped into diameter-pitch combinations distinguished from one another by the pitch applied to specific diameters. See Fig. 9-1-13. The *pitch* for metric threads is the distance between corresponding points on adjacent teeth. In addition to a coarse- and fine-pitch series, a series of constant pitches is available. See Table 12 of Appendix B.

Coarse-Thread Series This series is intended for use in general engineering work and commercial applications.

Fine-Thread Series The fine-thread series is for general use where a finer thread than the coarse-thread series is desirable. In comparison with a coarse-thread screw, the fine-thread screw is stronger in both tensile and torsional strength and is less likely to loosen under vibration.

Thread Grades and Classes The *fit* of a screw thread is the amount of clearance between the internal and external threads when they are assembled.

For each of the two main thread elements—pitch diameter and crest diameter—a number of tolerance grades have been established. The number of the tolerance grades reflects the size of the tolerance. For example, grade 4 tolerances are smaller than grade 6 tolerances, and grade 8 tolerances are larger than grade 6 tolerances.

In each case, grade 6 tolerances should be used for medium-quality length-of-engagement applications. The tolerance grades below grade 6 are intended for applications involving fine quality and/or short lengths of engagement. Tolerance grades above grade 6 are intended for coarse quality and/or long lengths of engagement.

In addition to the tolerance grade, a positional tolerance is required. This tolerance defines the maximum-material limits of the pitch and crest diameters of the external and internal threads and indicates their relationship to the basic profile.

In conformance with current coating (or plating) thickness requirements and the demand for ease of assembly, a series of tolerance positions reflecting the application of varying amounts of allowance has been established as follows:

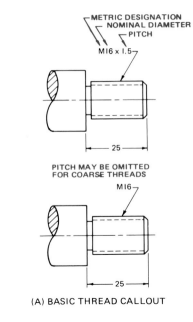

PITCH MAY BE OMITTED FOR COARSE THREADS

(A) BASIC THREAD CALLOUT

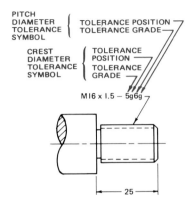

(B) TOLERANCE CALLOUT

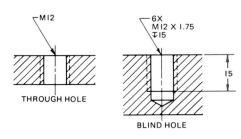

(C) INTERNAL THREAD CALLOUT

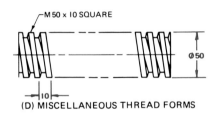

(D) MISCELLANEOUS THREAD FORMS

Fig. 9-1-13 Thread specifications for metric threads.

For external threads:

- Tolerance position e (large allowance)
- Tolerance position g (small allowance)
- Tolerance position h (no allowance)

For internal threads:

- Tolerance position G (small allowance)
- Tolerance position H (no allowance)

Thread Designation

ISO metric screw threads are defined by the nominal size (basic major diameter) and pitch, both expressed in millimeters. An "M" specifying an ISO metric screw thread precedes the nominal size, and an "X" separates the nominal size from the pitch. See Fig. 9-1-13. For the coarse-thread series only, the pitch is not shown unless the dimension for the length of the thread is required. In specifying the length of thread, an X is used to separate the length of thread from the rest of the designations. For external threads, the length or depth of thread may be given as a dimension on the drawing.

For example, a 10 mm diameter, 1.25 pitch, fine-thread series is expressed as M10 × 1.25. A 10 mm diameter, 1.5 pitch, coarse-thread series is expressed as M10; the pitch is not shown unless the length of thread is required. If the latter thread were 25 mm long and this information was required on the drawing, then the thread callout would be M10 × 1.5 × 25.

A complete designation for an ISO metric screw thread comprises, in addition to the basic designation, an identification for the tolerance class. The tolerance class designation is separated from the basic designation by a dash and includes the symbol for the pitch diameter tolerance followed immediately by the symbol for crest diameter tolerance. Each of these symbols consists of a numeral indicating the grade tolerance followed by a letter representing the tolerance position (a capital letter for internal threads and a lowercase letter for external threads). Where the pitch and crest diameter symbols are identical, the symbol need be given only once.

For external threads, the length of thread may be given as a dimension on the drawing. The length given is to be the minimum length of full thread.

For threaded holes that go all the way through the part, the term THRU is sometimes added to the note. If no depth is given, the hole is assumed to go all the way through. For threaded holes that do not go all the way through, the depth (in conjunction with the depth symbol or word) is given in the note, for example, M12 × 1.75 × 20 DEEP. The depth given is the minimum depth of full thread.

Neither the chamfer shown at the beginning of a thread, nor the undercut at the end of a thread where a small diameter meets a larger diameter is required to be dimensioned, as shown in Fig. 9-1-14. A comparison of customary and metric thread sizes is shown in Fig. 9-1-15.

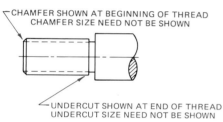

Fig. 9-1-14 Omission of thread information on detail drawings.

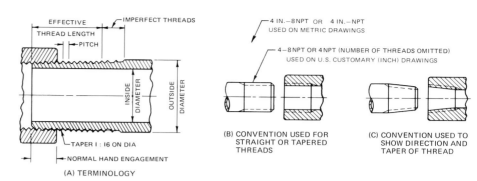

Fig. 9-1-16 Pipe thread terminology and conventions.

used is similar to that for screw threads. When calling for a pipe thread on a metric drawing, the abbreviation "IN." follows the pipe size. See Fig. 9-1-16.

EXAMPLE 1

$$4 \times 8NPT$$

where 4 = nominal diameter of pipe, in inches
8 = number of threads per inch
N = American Standard
P = pipe
T = taper thread

References and Source Material

1. ANSI Y14.6, *Screw Thread Representation*.

ASSIGNMENTS

See Assignments 1 through 4 for Unit 9-1 on page 194.

■ UNIT 9-2

Detailed and Schematic Representation of Threads

DETAILED REPRESENTATION

Detailed representation of threads is a close approximation of the actual appearance of a screw thread. The form of the thread is simplified by showing the helices as straight lines and the truncated crests and roots as sharp Vs. It is used when a more realistic thread representation is required. See Fig. 9-2-1.

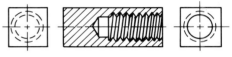

Fig. 9-2-1 Detailed representation of threads.

Detailed Representation of V Threads

The detailed representation for V-shaped threads uses the sharp-V profile. Straight lines are used to represent the helices of the crest and root lines.

The order of drawing the screw threads is shown in Fig. 9-2-2. The pitch is seldom drawn to scale; generally it is approximated. Lay off the pitch P and the half-pitch P/2, as shown in Fig. 9-2-2A. Add the crest lines, root line, and 60°V's. Complete the thread profile (Fig. 9-2-2B) by using a RECTANGULAR ARRAY with ONE row, NINE columns, and column SPACING equal to the pitch. EXPLODE (EDIT) the thread and ERASE lines on both ends as shown in Fig. 9-2-2C. At D, add the root lines, which complete the detailed representation of the threads.

Detailed Representation of Square Threads

The depth of the square thread is one-half the pitch. In Fig. 9-2-3A, lay off lines equal to P/2 along the diameter. Create one thread (Fig. 9-2-3B). Use RECTANGULAR ARRAY with

PIPE THREADS

The pipe universally used is the inch-sized pipe. When pipe is ordered, the outside diameter and wall thickness (in inches or millimeters) are given. In calling for the size of thread, the note

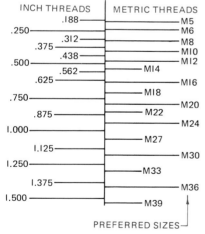

Fig. 9-1-15 Comparison of thread sizes.

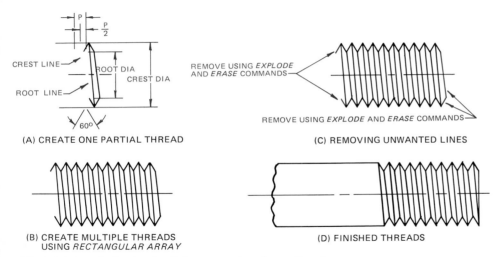

(A) CREATE ONE PARTIAL THREAD

(C) REMOVING UNWANTED LINES

(B) CREATE MULTIPLE THREADS USING *RECTANGULAR ARRAY*

(D) FINISHED THREADS

Fig. 9-2-2 Steps in drawing detailed representation of screw threads.

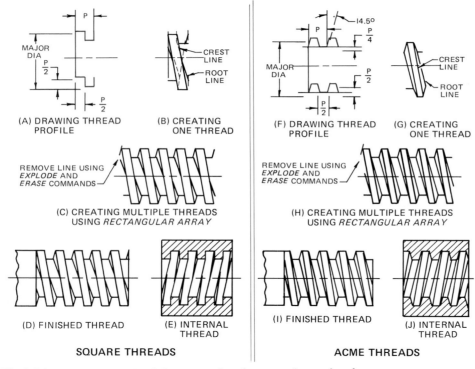

(A) DRAWING THREAD PROFILE

(B) CREATING ONE THREAD

(C) CREATING MULTIPLE THREADS USING *RECTANGULAR ARRAY*

(D) FINISHED THREAD

(E) INTERNAL THREAD

SQUARE THREADS

(F) DRAWING THREAD PROFILE

(G) CREATING ONE THREAD

(H) CREATING MULTIPLE THREADS USING *RECTANGULAR ARRAY*

(I) FINISHED THREAD

(J) INTERNAL THREAD

ACME THREADS

Fig. 9-2-3 Steps in drawing detailed representation of square and acme threads.

ONE row, FIVE columns, and column spacing equal to the pitch. EXPLODE the thread and ERASE lines as shown in Fig. 9-2-3C. At D the internal square thread is shown in section. Note the MIRROR image of the crest and root lines.

Detailed Representation of Acme Threads

The depth of the acme thread is one-half the pitch. See Fig. 9-2-3F through

J. The stages in drawing acme threads are shown at F and G. The pitch diameter is midway between the outside diameter and the root diameter and locates the pitch line. On the pitch line, lay off half-pitch spaces and add the root lines to complete the view.

Sectional views of an internal acme thread are shown at H, I, and J. Showing the root and crest lines on sectional views is optional.

Creating detailed representation of threads requires considerable time

and effort. Once a thread form has been detailed, BLOCK or WBLOCK it so that you may INSERT it when needed again. Also, because it may be *scaled* up or down, it need only be drawn one time.

THREADED ASSEMBLIES

It is often desirable to show threaded assembly drawings in detailed form, e.g., in presentation or catalog drawings. Hidden lines are normally omitted on these drawings, as they do nothing to add to the clarity of the drawing. See Fig. 9-2-4.

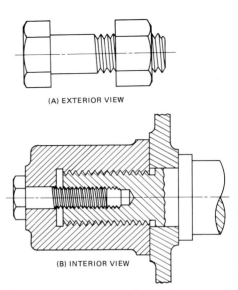

(A) EXTERIOR VIEW

(B) INTERIOR VIEW

Fig. 9-2-4 Detailed threaded assembly.

SCHEMATIC REPRESENTATION

Schematic representation is nearly as effective as the detailed representation and is easier to draw. The staggered lines, symbolic of the thread roots and crests, are normally drawn perpendicular to the axis of the thread. For certain applications these lines may be shown slanted to the approximate angle of the thread helix. The schematic representation should not be used for hidden internal threads or sections of external threads. See Fig. 9-2-5.

References and Source Material

1. ANSI Y14.6, *Screw Thread Representation*.

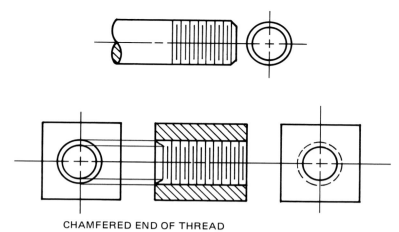

CHAMFERED END OF THREAD

Fig. 9-2-5 Schematic representation of threads.

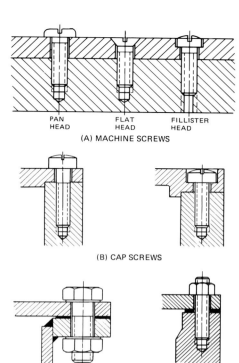

Fig. 9-3-2 Fastener applications.

2. *Machine Design,* Materials reference issue, March 1981.

ASSIGNMENTS

See Assignments 5 and 6 for Unit 9-2 starting on page 195.

■ UNIT 9-3

Common Threaded Fasteners

FASTENER SELECTION

Fastener manufacturers agree that product selection must begin at the design stage. For it is here, when a product is still a figment of someone's imagination, that the best interests of the designer, production manager, and purchasing agent can be served. Designers, naturally, want optimum performance; production people are interested in the ease and economics of assembly; purchasing agents are keen to minimize initial costs and stocking costs.

The answer, pure and simple, is to determine the objectives of the particular fastening job and then consult fastener suppliers. These technical experts can often shed light on the situation and then recommend the right item at the best in-place cost.

Machine screws are among the most common fasteners in industry. See Figs. 9-3-1 and 9-3-2. They are the easiest to install and remove. They are also among the least understood. To obtain maximum machine-screw effi-

ciency, thorough knowledge of the properties of both the screw and the materials to be fastened together is required.

For a given application, a designer should know the load which the screw must withstand, whether the load is one of tension or shear, and whether the assembly will be subject to impact shock or vibration. Once these factors have been determined, then the size, strength, head shape, and thread type can be selected.

The threads and fasteners series has been standardized. This means that the same size thread or fastener will appear identical on all drawings. A .25 in. standard hexagon nut, for example, will look the same on any of thousands of applications. Consequently, common threads and fasteners are created by using pre-drawn BLOCKS and INSERT at the desired scale factor.

FASTENER DEFINITIONS

Machine Screws *Machine screws* have either fine or coarse threads and are available in a variety of heads. They may be used in tapped holes as shown in Fig. 9-3-2A, or with nuts.

Cap Screws A *cap screw* is a threaded fastener which joins two or more parts by passing through a clearance hole in one part and screwing into a tapped hole in the other, Fig. 9-3-2B. A cap screw is tightened or released by torquing the head. Cap screws range

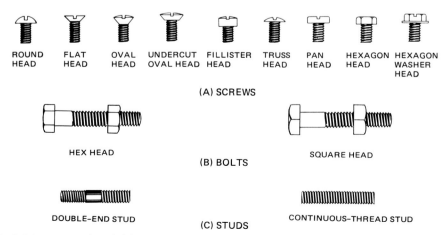

Fig. 9-3-1 Common threaded fasteners.

in size from .25 in. (6 mm) in diameter and are available in five basic types of head.

Captive Screws *Captive screws* are those that remain attached to the panel or parent material even when disengaged from the mating part. They are used to meet military requirements, to prevent screws from being lost, to speed assembly and disassembly operations, and to prevent damage from loose screws falling into moving parts or electrical circuits.

Tapping Screws *Tapping screws* cut or form a mating thread when driven into preformed holes.

Bolts A *bolt* is a threaded fastener which passes through clearance holes in assembled parts and threads into a nut, Fig. 9-3-2C. Bolts and nuts are available in a variety of shapes and sizes. The square and hexagon head are the two most popular designs.

Studs *Studs* are shafts threaded at both ends, and they are used in assemblies. One end of the stud is threaded into one of the parts being assembled; and the other assembly parts, such as washers and covers, are guided over the studs through clearance holes and are held together by means of a nut which is threaded over the exposed end of the stud. See Fig. 9-3-2D.

Explanatory Data

A bolt is designed for assembly with a nut. A screw has features in its design which make it capable of being used in a tapped or other preformed hole in the work. Because of basic design, it is possible to use certain types of screws in combination with a nut.

THE CHANGE TO METRIC FASTENERS

In the United States, the Industrial Fasteners Institute (IFI) has undertaken a major compilation of standards in its *Metric Fastener Standards* book.

FASTENER CONFIGURATION

Head Styles

Which of the various head configurations to specify depends on the type of driving equipment used (screwdriver, socket wrench, etc.), the type of joint

load, and the external appearance desired. The head styles shown in Fig. 9-3-3 can be used for both bolts and screws but are most commonly identified with the fastener category called machine screw or cap screw.

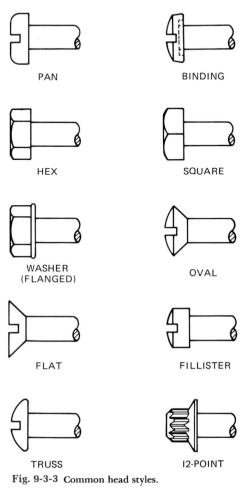

Fig. 9-3-3 Common head styles.

Hex and Square The hex head is the most commonly used head style. The hex head design offers greater strength, ease of torque input, and area than the square head.

Pan This head combines the qualities of the truss, binding, and round head types.

Binding This type of head is commonly used in electrical connections because its undercut prevents fraying of stranded wire.

Washer (flanged) This configuration eliminates the need for a separate assembly step when a washer is required, increases the bearing areas of the head, and protects the material finish during assembly.

Oval Characteristics of this head type are similar to those of the flat head but it is sometimes preferred because of its neat appearance.

Flat Available with various head angles, this fastener centers well and provides a flush surface.

Fillister The deep slot and small head allow a high torque to be applied during assembly.

Truss This head covers a large area. It is used where extra holding power is required, holes are oversize, or the material is soft.

12-Point This twelve-sided head is normally used on aircraft-grade fasteners. Multiple sides allow for a very sure grip and high torque during assembly.

Drive Configurations

Figure 9-3-4 shows sixteen different driving designs.

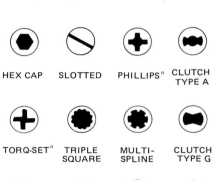

Fig. 9-3-4 Drive configuration.

Shoulders and Necks

The shoulder of a fastener is the enlarged portion of the body of a threaded fastener or the shank of an unthreaded fastener. See Fig. 9-3-5.

Point Styles

The point of a fastener is the configuration of the end of the shank of a headed or a headless fastener. Stan-

OVAL SHOULDER   ROUND SHOULDER

FIN NECK   SQUARE (CARRIAGE) NECK

Fig. 9-3-5 Shoulder and necks.

CUP   FLAT   CONE

OVAL   HALF DOG

Fig. 9-3-6 Point styles.

dard point styles are shown in Fig. 9-3-6.

Cup Most widely used when the cutting-in action of point is not objectionable.

Flat Used when frequent resetting of a part is required. Particularly suited for use against hardened steel shafts. This point is preferred where walls are thin or the threaded member is a soft material.

Cone Used for permanent location of parts. Usually spotted in a hole to half its length.

Oval Used when frequent adjustment is necessary or for seating against angular surfaces.

Half Dog Normally applied where permanent location of one part in relation to another is desired.

PROPERTY CLASSES OF FASTENERS

Inch Fasteners

The strength of customary fasteners for most common uses is determined by the size of the fastener and the material from which it is made. Property classes are defined by the Society of Automotive Engineers (SAE), or the American Society for Testing and Materials (ASTM).

Figure 9-3-7 lists the mechanical requirements of inch-sized fasteners and their identification patterns.

Metric Fasteners

For mechanical and material requirements, metric fasteners are classified under a number of property classes. Bolts, screws, and studs have seven property classes of steel suitable for general engineering applications. The property classes are designated by numbers where increasing numbers generally represent increasing tensile strengths. The designation symbol consists of two parts: the first numeral of a two-digit symbol or the first two numerals of a three-digit symbol approximates one-hundredth of the minimum tensile strength in megapascals; and the last numeral approximates one-tenth of the ratio expressed as a percentage of minimum yield strength and minimum tensile strength.

EXAMPLE 1 A property class 4.8 fastener (see Fig. 9-3-8) has a minimum tensile strength of 420 MPa and a minimum yield strength of 340 MPa. One percent of 420 is 4.2. The first digit is 4. The minimum yield strength of 340 MPa is equal to approximately 80 percent of the minimum tensile strength of 420 MPa. One-tenth of 80 percent is 8. The last digit of the property class is 8.

EXAMPLE 2 A property class 10.9 fastener (see Fig. 9-3-8) has a minimum tensile strength of 1040 MPa and a minimum yield strength of 940 MPa. One percent of 1040 is 10.4 The first two numerals of the three-digit symbol are 10. The minimum yield strength of 940 MPa is equal to approximately 90 percent of the minimum tensile strength of 1040 MPa. One-tenth of 90 percent is 9. The last digit of the property class is 9.

Machine screws are normally available only in classes 4.8 and 9.8; other bolts, screws, and studs are available in all classes within the specified product size limitations given in Fig. 9-3-7.

For guidance purposes only, to assist designers in selecting a property class, the following information may be used.

- Class 4.6 is approximately equivalent to SAE grade 1 and ASTM A 307, grade A.
- Class 5.8 is approximately equivalent to SAE grade 2.
- Class 8.8 is approximately equivalent to SAE grade 5 and ASTM A 449.
- Class 9.8 has properties approximately 9 percent stronger than SAE grade 5 and ASTM A 449.
- Class 10.9 is approximately equivalent to SAE grade 8 and ASTM A 354 grade BD.

PROPERTY CLASS ∠	NOMINAL DIAMETER	MINIMUM TENSILE STRENGTH MPa	MINIMUM YEILD STRENGTH MPa
4.6	M5 THRU M36	400	240
4.8	M1.6 THRU M16	420	340
5.8	M5 THRU M24	520	420
8.8	M16 THRU M36	830	660
9.8	M1.6 THRU M16	900	720
10.9	M5 THRU M36	1040	940
12.9	M1.6 THRU M36	1220	1100

Fig. 9-3-8 Mechanical requirements for metric bolts, screws, and studs.

HEAD DESIGNATION					
GRADE	GRADES 0, I, 2	GRADE 3	GRADE 5	GRADE 7	GRADE 8
MINIMUM TENSILE STRENGTH KIPS	0—NO REQUIREMENTS 1—55 2—69 64 55	110 100	120 115 105	133	150

Fig. 9-3-7 Mechanical requirements for inch-size threaded fasteners.

Fastener Markings

Slotted and crossed recessed screws of all sizes and other screws and bolts of sizes .25 in. or M4 and smaller need not be marked. All other bolts and screws of sizes .25 in. or M5 and larger are marked to identify their strength. The property class symbols for metric fasteners are shown in Fig. 9-3-9. The symbol is located on the top of the bolt head or screw. Alternatively, for hex-head products, the markings may be indented on the side of the head.

PROPERTY CLASS	IDENTIFICATION SYMBOL	
	BOLTS, SCREWS AND STUDS	STUDS SMALLER THAN M12
4.6	4.6	—
4.8	4.8	—
5.8	5.8	—
8.8 (1)	8.8	○
9.8 (1)	9.8	+
10.9 (1)	10.9	□
12.9	12.9	△

NOTE 1: PRODUCTS MADE OF LOW CARBON MARTENSITE STEEL SHALL BE ADDITIONALLY IDENTIFIED BY UNDERLINING THE NUMERALS.

Fig. 9-3-9 Metric property class identification symbols for bolts, screws, and studs.

All studs of size .25 in. or M5 and larger are identified by the property class symbol. The marking is located on the extreme end of the stud. For studs with an interference fit thread the markings are located at the nut end.

Nuts

The customary terms *regular* and *thick* for describing nut thicknesses have been replaced by the terms *style 1* and *style 2* for metric nuts. The design of style 1 and 2 steel nuts shown in Fig. 9-3-10 is based on providing sufficient nut strength to reduce the possibility of thread stripping. There are three property classes of steel nuts available. See Fig. 9-3-11.

PROPERTY CLASS	NOMINAL NUT SIZE	SUGGESTED PROPERTY CLASS OF MATING BOLT, SCREW OR STUD
5	M5 THRU M36	4.6, 4.8, 5.8
9	M5 THRU M16 M20 THRU M36	5.8, 9.8 5.8, 8.8
10	M6.3 THRU M36	10.9

Fig. 9-3-11 Metric nut selection for bolts, screws, and studs.

Hex Flanged Nuts These nuts are intended for general use in applications requiring a large bearing contact area. The two styles of flanged hex nuts differ dimensionally in thickness only. The standard property classes for hex flanged nuts are identical to the hex nuts. All metric nuts are marked to identify their property class.

DRAWING A BOLT OR NUT

On assembly drawings it may be necessary to draw a nut and bolt if a fastener symbol library is not available. Approximate nut and bolt sizes are shown in Fig. 9-3-12. Actual sizes are found in Appendix B. Conventional drawing practice is to show the nuts and bolt heads in the across-corners position in all views. If a fastener symbol library is available, however, you will not have

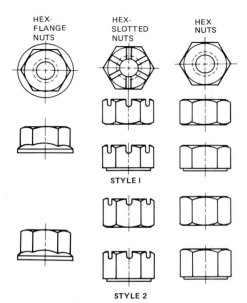

Fig. 9-3-10 Hex-nut styles.

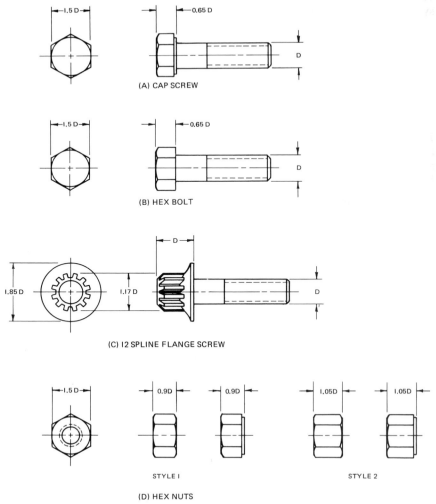

Fig. 9-3-12 Approximate head proportions for hex-head cap screws, bolts, and nuts.

to draw any nut or bolt. The one you need may be "pulled out" of the library for use on any drawing by using INSERT. It may be scaled up or down as necessary for the application.

If a standard library is not available, draw the nut or bolt to actual size using the LINE and ARC commands. If other similar nuts or bolts are required for the same drawing, BLOCK (or WBLOCK) the original one. Use INSERT (or COPY by WINDOW or re-SCALE) to place new ones. By this method, new fasteners, of any size, may be placed on the drawing. At this point, you will want to file the original symbols for future use (see Unit 7-2). Remember you may SAVE all WBLOCK symbols on a pre-formatted floppy disk using the drive designation prefix (e.g. A:).

To reuse a symbol on a different drawing:

1. Be certain first that the originals are existing, on disk, in the system you are using. Direct access to any symbol is made by issuing the command (WBLOCK) for that purpose.
2. Key in the name for the symbol, HEX NUT and press ENTER.
3. Pick the symbol location.
4. If the size is to be different from unity (the size in the library), specify this.
5. If the symbol is to be placed at an angle, key in the number of degrees and ENTER. It will automatically be placed (see Fig. 9-3-2C).

CAD systems offer additional options. One option includes adding text next to the symbol as it is being inserted. Use the ATTRIBUTE DEFINITION (ATTDEF) command for this purpose. Another option allows you to vary certain parameters such as selecting the thread (e.g., simplified) you wish to display. Using MACROS or LISP are a step into the world of "parametric design." This means that you do not draw anything. You depict what you wish to have drawn by specifying the parameters. The system will respond by automatically accomplishing all of the drawing activity.

INCH THREADS
Studs

Studs, as shown in Fig. 9-3-13, are still used in large quantities to best fulfill

(A) DOUBLE END

(B) CONTINUOUS THREAD

Fig. 9-3-13 Studs.

the needs of certain design functions and for overall economy.

Double-End Studs These studs are designated in the following sequence: Type and name; nominal size; thread information; stud length; material, including grade identification; and finish (plating or coating) if required.

EXAMPLE
TYPE 2 DOUBLE-END STUD, .500 — 13 UNC — 2A × 4.00, CADMIUM PLATED

Continuous-Thread Studs These studs are designated in the following sequence: Product name, nominal size, thread information, stud length, material and finish (plating or coating) if required.

EXAMPLE
TYPE 3 CONTINUOUS THREAD STUD, M24 × 3 × 200, STEEL CLASS ZINC PHOSPHATE AND OIL

WASHERS

Washers are one of the most common forms of hardware and perform many varied functions in mechanically fastened assemblies. They may only be required to span an oversize clearance hole, to give better bearing for nuts or screw faces, or to distribute loads over a greater area. Often, they serve as locking devices for threaded fasteners. They are also used to maintain a spring-resistance pressure, to guard surfaces against marring, and to provide a seal.

Classification of Washers

Washers are commonly the elements which are added to screw systems to keep them tight, but not all washers are locking types. Many washers serve other functions, such as surface pro-

tection, insulation, sealing, electrical connection, and spring-tension take-up devices.

Flat Washers Plain, or flat, washers are used primarily to provide a bearing surface for a nut or a screw head, to cover large clearance holes, and to distribute fastener loads over a larger area — particularly on soft materials such as aluminum or wood. See Fig. 9-3-14.

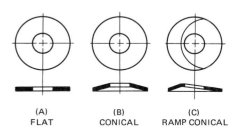

(A)
FLAT

(B)
CONICAL

(C)
RAMP CONICAL

Fig. 9-3-14 Flat and conical washers.

Conical Washers These washers are used with screws to effectively add spring take-up to the screw elongation.

Helical Spring Washers These washers are made of slightly trapezoidal wire formed into a helix of one coil so that the free height is approximately twice the thickness of the washer section. See Fig. 9-3-15.

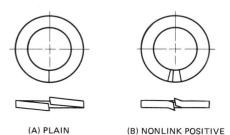

(A) PLAIN

(B) NONLINK POSITIVE

Fig. 9-3-15 Helical spring washers.

Tooth Lock Washers Made of hardened carbon steel, a tooth lock washer has teeth that are twisted or bent out of the plane of the washer face so that sharp cutting edges are presented to both the workpiece and the bearing face of the screw head or nut. See Fig. 9-3-16.

Spring Washers There are no standard designs for spring washers. See Fig. 9-3-17. They are made in a great variety of sizes and shapes and are usually selected from a manufacturer's catalog for some specific purpose.

EXTERNAL TYPE

INTERNAL TYPE

HEAVY DUTY INTERNAL TYPE

COUNTERSUNK TYPE

EXTERNAL—INTERNAL TYPE

DOME TYPE

DISHED TYPE

PYRAMIDAL TYPE

Fig. 9-3-16 Tooth lock washers.

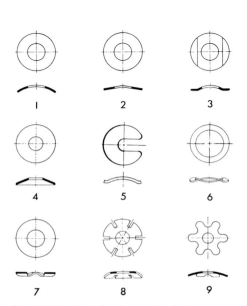

Fig. 9-3-17 Typical spring washer design.

Special-Purpose Washers Molded or stamped nonmetallic washers are available in many materials and may be used as seals, electrical insulators, or for protection of the surface of assembled parts.

Many plain, cone, or tooth washers are available with special mastic sealing compounds firmly attached to the washer. These washers are used for sealing and vibration isolation in high-production industries.

Terms Related to Threaded Fasteners

The *tap drill size* for a threaded (tapped) hole is a diameter equal to the minor diameter of the thread. The *clearance drill size,* which permits the free passage of a bolt, is a diameter slightly greater than the major diameter of the bolt. See Fig. 9-3-18. A *counterbored hole* is a circular, flat-bottomed recess that permits the head of

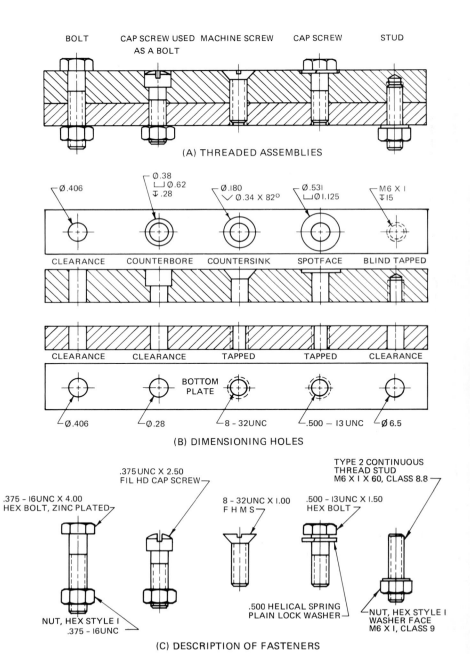

Fig. 9-3-18 Specifying threaded fasteners and holes.

a bolt or cap screw to rest below the surface of the part. A *countersunk hole* is an angular-sided recess that accommodates the shape of a flat-head cap screw or machine screw or an oval-head machine screw. *Spot-facing* is a machine operation that provides a smooth, flat surface where a bolt head or a nut will rest.

SPECIFYING FASTENERS

In order for the purchasing department to properly order the fastening device which has been selected in the design, the following information is required. (*Note:* The information listed will not apply to all types of fasteners):

1. Type of fastener
2. Thread specifications
3. Fastener length
4. Material
5. Head style
6. Type of driving recess
7. Point type (setscrews only)
8. Property class
9. Finish

EXAMPLES

.375 — 16 UNC — 2A × 4.00 HEX BOLT, ZINC PLATED

M10 × 1.5 × 50, 9.8 12-SPLINE FLANGE SCREW, CADMIUM PLATED

TYPE 2 DOUBLE-END STUD, M10 × 1.5 × 100, STEEL CLASS 9.8, CADMIUM PLATED

NUT, HEX, STYLE 1, .500 UNC STEEL

MACH SCREW, PHILLIPS ROUND HD, 8 — 32 UNC × 1.00, BRASS

WASHER, FLAT 8.4 ID × 17 OD × 2 THK, STEEL HELICAL SPRING.

References and Source Material

1. *Machine Design*, Fastening and joining reference issue, Nov. 1981.
2. *Design Engineering* and staff of Stelco's "Fastener Facts."

ASSIGNMENTS

See Assignments 7 and 8 for Unit 9-3 on page 196.

■ **UNIT 9-4**

Special Fasteners

SETSCREWS

Setscrews are used as semipermanent fasteners to hold a collar, sheave, or gear on a shaft against rotational or translational forces. In contrast to most fastening devices, the setscrew is essentially a compression device. Forces developed by the screw point on tightening produce a strong clamping action that resists relative motion between assembled parts. The basic problem in setscrew selection is to find the best combination of setscrew form, size, and point style that provides the required holding power.

Setscrews can be categorized in two ways: by their head style and by the point style desired. See Fig. 9-4-1. Each setscrew style is available in any one of five point styles.

Setscrews and Keyseats When a setscrew is used in combination with a key, the screw diameter should be equal to the width of the key. In this combination the setscrew is locating the parts in an axial direction only. The torsional load on the parts is carried by the key.

The key should be tight-fitting, so that no motion is transmitted to the screw. Key design will be further covered in Chap. 10.

KEEPING FASTENERS TIGHT

Fasteners are inexpensive, but the cost of installing them can be substantial. Probably the simplest way to cut assembly costs is to make sure that, once installed, fasteners stay tight.

The American National Standards Institute has identified three basic locking methods: free-spinning, prevailing-torque, and chemical locking. Each has its own advantages and disadvantages. See Fig. 9-4-2.

Free-spinning fastening devices include toothed and spring lockwashers and screws and bolts with washerlike heads. With these arrangements, the fasteners spin free in the clamping direction, which makes them easy to assemble, and the break-loose torque is greater than the seating torque. However, once break-loose torque is exceeded, free-spinning washers have no

STANDARD POINTS	
	CUP Most generally used. Suitable for quick and semipermanent location of parts on soft shafts, where cutting in of edges of cup shape on shaft is not objectionable.
	FLAT Used where frequent resetting is required, on hard steel shafts, and where minimum damage to shafts is necessary. Flat is usually ground on shaft for better contact.
	CONICAL For setting machine parts permanently on shaft, which should be spotted to receive cone point. Also used as a pivot or hanger.
	SPHERICAL Should be used against shafts spotted, splined or grooved to receive it. Sometimes substituted for cup point.
	HALF DOG For permanent location of machine parts, although cone point is usually preferred for this purpose. Point should fit closely to dia. of drilled hole in shaft. Sometimes used in place of a dowel pin.
STANDARD HEADS	
	HEXAGON SOCKET Standard size range: No. 0 to 1.0 in. (2 to 24mm), threaded entire length of screw in .06 in. (2mm) increments from .25 to .62 in. (6 to 16mm), .12 in. (3mm) increments from .62 to 1.0 in. (16 to 24mm). Coarse or fine thread series.
	SLOTTED Standard size range: No. 5 to .75 in. (3 to 20mm) threaded entire length of screw. Coarse or fine thread series.
	FLUTED SOCKET Same as hexagon socket. No. 0 and 1 (2 to 3mm) have four flutes. All others have six flutes.
	SQUARE HEAD Standard size range: No. 10 to 1.50 in. (5 to 36mm). Entire body is threaded. Coarse or fine-thread series. Sizes .25 in. (6mm) and larger are normally available in coarse threads only.

Fig. 9-4-1 Setscrews

prevailing torque to prevent further loosening.

Prevailing-torque methods make use of increased friction between nut and bolt. Metallic types usually have deformed threads or contoured thread profiles that jam the threads on assembly. Nonmetallic types make use of nylon or polyester insert elements that produce interference fits on assembly.

Chemical locking is achieved by coating the fastener with an adhesive.

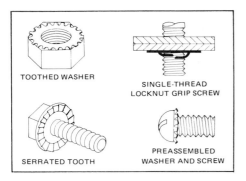

TOOTHED WASHER

SINGLE-THREAD LOCKNUT GRIP SCREW

SERRATED TOOTH

PREASSEMBLED WASHER AND SCREW

(A) FREE-SPINNING

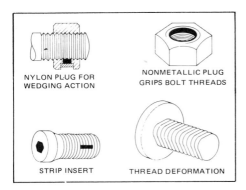

NYLON PLUG FOR WEDGING ACTION

NONMETALLIC PLUG GRIPS BOLT THREADS

STRIP INSERT

THREAD DEFORMATION

(B) PREVAILING TORQUE

Fig. 9-4-2 Typical setscrew installation locking fasteners.

LOCKNUTS

A *locknut* is a nut with special internal means for gripping a threaded fastener to prevent rotation. Generally it has the dimensions, mechanical requirements, and other specifications of a standard nut, but with a locking feature added.

Locknuts are divided into two general classifications: prevailing-torque and free-spinning types. These are shown in Fig. 9-4-3.

Prevailing-Torque Locknuts

Prevailing-torque locknuts spin freely for a few turns, and then must be wrenched to final position. The maximum holding and locking power is reached as soon as the threads and the locking feature are engaged. Locking action is maintained until the nut is removed. Prevailing-torque locknuts are classified by basic design principles:

1. Thread deflection causes friction to develop when the threads are mated; thus the nut resists loosening.

(A) PREVAILING TORQUE LOCKNUTS

NONMETALLIC COLLAR CLAMPED IN THE TOP OF THIS NUT PRODUCES LOCKING ACTION.

THREADED ELLIPTICAL SPRING-STEEL INSERT GRIPS THE BOLT AND PREVENTS TURNING.

SLOTTED SECTION OF THIS PREVAILING-TORQUE NUT FORMS BEAMS WHICH ARE DEFLECTED INWARD AND GRIP THE BOLT.

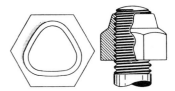

THREE SECTORS OF TAPERED CONE, PREFORMED INWARDLY, ARE ELASTICALLY RETURNED TO CIRCU-FORM WHEN THE NUT IS APPLIED.

(B) FREE-SPINNING LOCKNUTS

DEFORMED BEARING SURFACE. TEETH ON THE BEARING SURFACE "BITE" INTO WORK TO PROVIDE A RATCHET LOCKING ACTION.

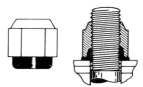

NYLON INSERT FLOWS AROUND THE BOLT RATHER THAN BEING CUT BY THE BOLT THREADS TO PROVIDE LOCKING ACTION AND AN EFFECTIVE SEAL.

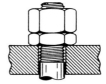

JAM NUT, APPLIED UNDER A LARGE REGULAR NUT, IS ELASTICALLY DEFORMED AGAINST BOLT THREADS WHEN THE LARGE NUT IS TIGHTENED.

NUT WITH A CAPTIVE-TOOTHED WASHER. WHEN TIGHTENED, THE CAPTIVE WASHER PROVIDES THE LOCKING MEANS WITH SPRING ACTION BETWEEN THE NUT AND WORKING SURFACE.

(C) OTHER LOCKNUT TYPES

SLOTTED NUT USES A COTTER PIN THROUGH A HOLE IN THE BOLT FOR LOCKING ACTION.

SINGLE-THREAD LOCKNUT, WHICH IS SPEEDILY APPLIED, LOCK BY GRIP OF ARCHED PRONGS WHEN BOLT OR SCREW IS TIGHTENED.

Fig. 9-4-3 Locknuts.

2. The out-of-round top portion of the tapped nut grips the bolt threads and resists rotation.
3. The slotted section of locknut is pressed inward to provide a spring frictional grip on the bolt.
4. Inserts, either nonmetallic or of soft metal, are plastically deformed by the bolt threads to produce a frictional interference fit.
5. A spring wire or pin engages the bolt threads to produce a wedging or ratchet-locking action.

Free-Spinning Locknuts

Free-spinning locknuts are free to spin on the bolt until seated. Additional tightening locks the nuts.

Since most free-spinning locknuts depend on clamping force for their locking action, they are usually not recommended for joints that might relax through plastic deformation or for fastening materials that might crack or crumble.

Other Locknut Types

Jam nuts are thin nuts used under full-sized nuts to develop locking action. The large nut has sufficient strength to elastically deform the lead threads of the bolt and jam nut. Thus, a considerable resistance against loosening is built up. The use of jam nuts is decreasing; a one-piece, prevailing-torque locknut usually is used instead at a savings in assembled cost.

Slotted and castle nuts have slots which receive a cotter pin that passes

through a drilled hole in the bolt and thus serves as the locking member. Castle nuts differ from slotted nuts in that they have a circular crown of a reduced diameter.

Single-thread locknuts are spring steel fasteners which may be speedily applied. Locking action is provided by the grip of the thread-engaging prongs and the reaction of the arched base. Their use is limited to nonstructural assemblies and usually to screw

FOR HOLDING A MOTOR MOUNTING SECURELY IN POSITION.

USE OF LOCKNUT ON A SPRING CLAMP.

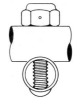
USE OF LOCKNUT FOR TUBULAR FASTENING.

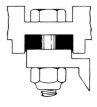
FOR RUBBER-INSULATED AND CUSHION MOUNTINGS WHERE THE NUT MUST REMAIN STATIONARY.

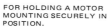
USE OF LOCKNUT ON A BOLTED CONNECTION THAT REQUIRES PRE-DETERMINED PLAY.

FOR AN EXTRUDED PART ASSEMBLY.

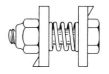
FOR SPRING-MOUNTED CONNECTIONS WHERE THE NUT MUST REMAIN STATIONARY OR IS SUBJECT TO ADJUSTMENT.

USE OF LOCKNUT WHERE ASSEMBLY OR CYCLIC MOTIONS THAT COULD CAUSE LOOSENING.

Fig. 9-4-4 Typical locknut applications.

sizes below 6 mm in diameter. See Fig. 9-4-4 for typical uses of locknuts.

References and Source Material

1. *Machine Design*, Fastening and joining reference issue, Nov. 1981.

ASSIGNMENTS

See Assignments 9 and 10 for Unit 9-4 on page 197.

ASSIGNMENTS FOR CHAPTER 9

Assignments for Unit 9-1, Simplified Thread Representation

1. Make a two-view assembly drawing of the parallel clamps shown in Fig. 9-1-A. Use simplified thread conventions and call for all the parts. The only dimension required on the drawing is the maximum opening of the jaws. Identify the parts on the assembly. Scale 1:1.

2. Make detail drawings of the parts shown in Fig. 9-1-A. Scale 1:1. Use your judgment for the number of views required for each part.

3. Make a one-view assembly drawing of the turnbuckle shown in Fig. 9-1-B. Show the assembly in its shortest length and also include the maximum position shown in phantom lines. The only dimensions required are the minimum and maximum distances between the eye centers. Scale 1:1.

4. Make detail drawings of the parts shown in Fig. 9-1-B. Scale 1:1.

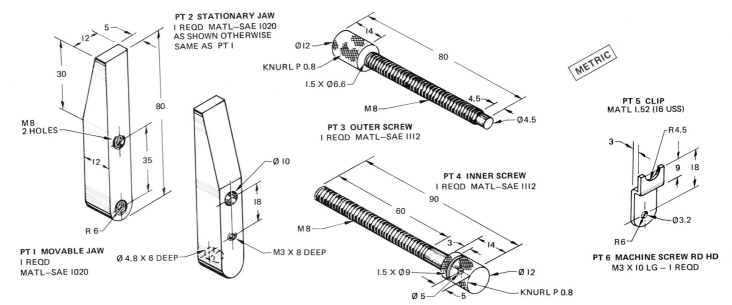

Fig. 9-1-A Parallel clamps.

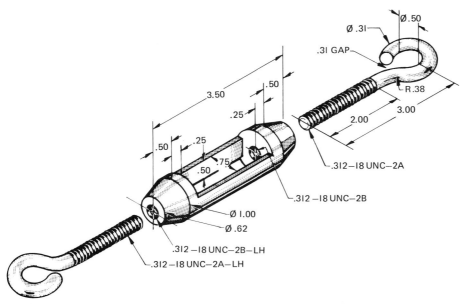

Fig. 9-1-B Turnbuckle.

Assignments for Unit 9-2, Detailed and Schematic Thread Representation

5. Make one-view drawings of the parts shown in Fig. 9-2-A or 9-2-B. Use detailed representation for the threads. Use conventional breaks to shorten the lengths of the guide rod and jack screw.

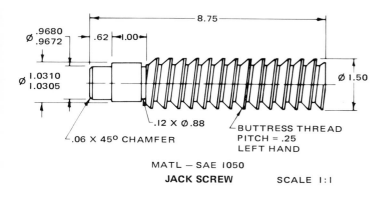

Ø .9680 / .9672
.62 — 1.00 — 8.75
Ø 1.0310 / 1.0305
Ø 1.50
.12 X Ø .88
.06 X 45° CHAMFER
BUTTRESS THREAD
PITCH = .25
LEFT HAND

MATL — SAE 1050

JACK SCREW   SCALE 1:1

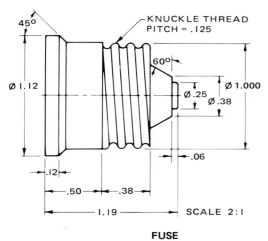

45°
KNUCKLE THREAD
PITCH = .125
60°
Ø 1.12
Ø .25
Ø .38
Ø 1.000
.06
.12
.50
.38
1.19   SCALE 2:1

FUSE

Fig. 9-2-A Jack screw and fuse.

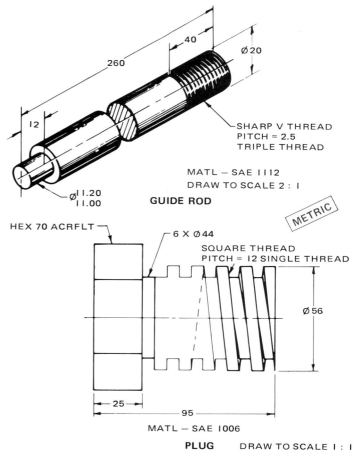

260
40
Ø 20
12
SHARP V THREAD
PITCH = 2.5
TRIPLE THREAD
Ø 11.20 / 11.00

MATL — SAE 1112
DRAW TO SCALE 2 : 1

GUIDE ROD

HEX 70 ACRFLT
6 X Ø 44
SQUARE THREAD
PITCH = 12 SINGLE THREAD
Ø 56
25
95

MATL — SAE 1006

PLUG   DRAW TO SCALE 1 : 1

Fig. 9-2-B Guide rod and plug.

METRIC

6. Prepare an assembly drawing for either Fig. 9-2-C or 9-2-D showing the connector threads engaging 1.00 in. (25mm) of the end rod threads. The end rods are to be drawn in section. Scale 1:1.

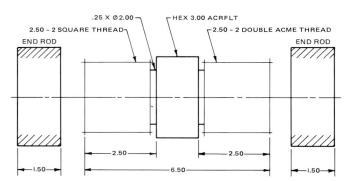

Fig. 9-2-C Connector and supports.

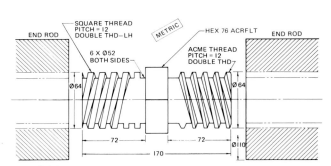

Fig. 9-2-D Connector and supports.

Assignments for Unit 9-3, Common Threaded Fasteners

7. Prepare drawings of the four fastener assemblies shown in Fig. 9-3-A. If available, use a fasteners symbol library. Dimension both the clearance and the threaded holes. A partial top view may be shown if desired. Scale 1:1.

8. Prepare full section assembly drawings of the five fastener assemblies shown in Fig. 9-3-B. If available, use a fasteners symbol library and use simplified thread symbols. Scale 1:1. Dimension both the clearance and the threaded holes. If desired, a top view of the fasteners may be shown.

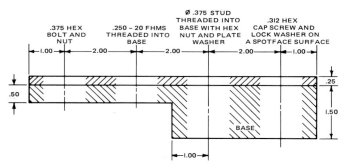

Fig. 9-3-A Threaded fasteners.

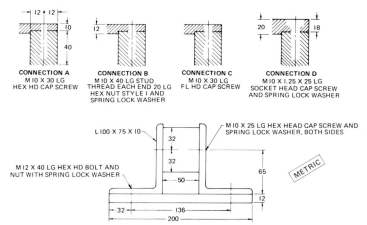

Fig. 9-3-B Standard fasteners.

Assignments for Unit 9-4, Special Fasteners

9. Make a one-view assembly drawing of the flexible coupling shown in Fig. 9-4-A. The shafts, which are coupled, are 1.50 in. in diameter and are to be shown in the assembly. They are to extend beyond the coupling for approximately 2.00 in. and end with a conventional break. Show the setscrews and keys in position. Scale 1:1.

10. Make a one-view assembly drawing of the adjustable shaft support shown in Fig. 9-4-B. Show the base in full section. A broken-out section is recommended to clearly show the setscrews in the yoke. Add part numbers to the assembly drawing. Do not dimension. Scale 1:1.

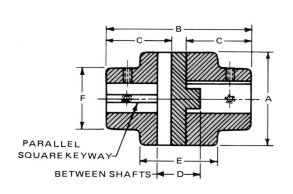

Fig. 9-4-A Flexible coupling.

MAXIMUM BORE	A	B	C	D	E	F
.9375	3.00	3.75	1.75	.88	1.50	2.38
1.1875	3.50	4.69	2.19	1.06	1.81	2.75
1.4375	4.00	5.62	2.62	1.25	2.12	3.12
1.6875	5.00	6.56	3.06	1.44	2.44	3.50
1.9375	5.50	7.50	3.50	1.50	2.50	4.00
2.1875	6.00	8.44	3.94	1.81	3.06	4.38

DIMENSIONS SHOWN ARE IN INCHES

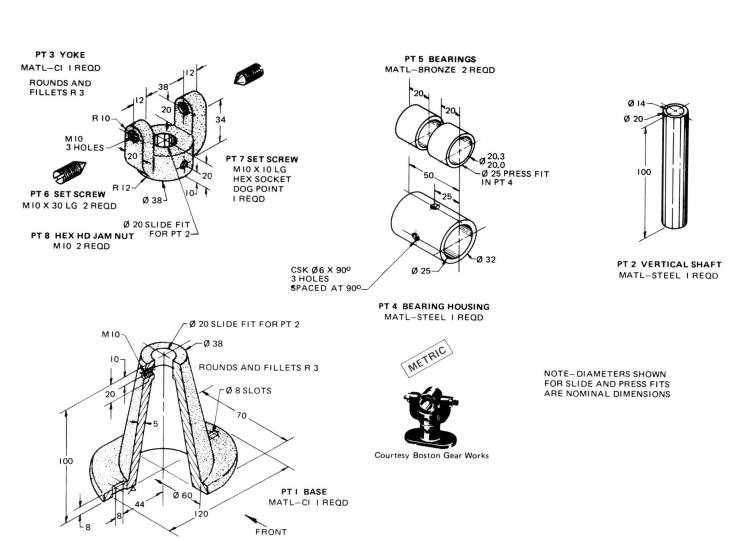

Fig. 9-4-B Adjustable shaft support.

10

Miscellaneous Types of Fasteners

UNIT 10-1

Keys, Splines, and Serrations

KEYS

A *key* is a piece of steel lying partly in a groove in the shaft and extending into another groove in the hub. These grooves are called keyseats. See boxes 6 and 8 in Fig. 10-1-1. A key is used to secure gears, pulleys, cranks, handles, and similar machine parts to shafts, so that the motion of the part is transmitted to the shaft, or the motion of the shaft to the part, without slippage. The key may also act in a safety capacity; its size is generally calculated so that when overloading takes place, the key will shear or break before the part or shaft breaks.

There are many kinds of keys. The most common types are shown in Fig. 10-1-2. Square and flat keys are widely used in industry. The width of the square and flat key should be approximately one-quarter the shaft diameter, but for proper key selection refer to tables 25-28, Appendix B. These keys are also available with a 1 : 100 taper on their top surfaces and are then known as *square taper* or *flat tapered* keys. The keyseat in the hub is tapered to accommodate the taper on the key.

The gibhead key is the same as the square or flat tapered key but has a head added for easy removal.

The Pratt and Whitney key is rectangular with rounded ends. Two-thirds of this key sits in the shaft, one-third sits in the hub.

The Woodruff key is semicircular and fits into a semicircular keyseat in the shaft and a rectangular keyseat in the hub. The width of the key should be approximately one-quarter the diameter of the shaft, and its diameter should approximate the diameter of the shaft. Half the width of the key extends above the shaft and into the hub. Refer to Appendix B for exact sizes. Woodruff keys are identified by a number which gives the nominal dimensions of the key. The numbering system, which originated many years ago, is identified with the fractional-inch system of measurement. The last two digits of the number give the normal diameter in eighths of an inch, and the digits preceding the last two give the nominal width in thirty-seconds of an inch. For example, a No. 1210 Woodruff key indicates a key $^{12}\!/_{32}$ ×

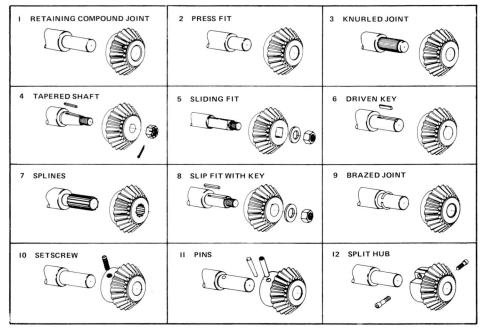

1 RETAINING COMPOUND JOINT	2 PRESS FIT	3 KNURLED JOINT
4 TAPERED SHAFT	5 SLIDING FIT	6 DRIVEN KEY
7 SPLINES	8 SLIP FIT WITH KEY	9 BRAZED JOINT
10 SETSCREW	11 PINS	12 SPLIT HUB

Fig. 10-1-1 Miscellaneous types of fasteners.

Fig. 10-1-2 Common keys.

TYPE OF KEY	ASSEMBLY SHOWING KEY, SHAFT AND HUB	SPECIFICATION
SQUARE		.25 SQUARE KEY, 1.25 LG OR .25 SQUARE TAPERED KEY, 1.25 LG
FLAT		.188 X .125 FLAT KEY, 1.00 LG OR .188 X .125 FLAT TAPERED KEY, 1.00 LG
GIB-HEAD		.375 SQUARE GIB-HEAD KEY, 2.00 LG
PRATT AND WHITNEY		NO. 15 PRATT AND WHITNEY KEY
WOODRUFF		NO. 1210 WOODRUFF KEY

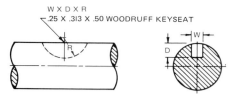

Fig. 10-1-4 Alternative method of detailing a Woodruff keyseat.

for square and flat keys, specifying first the width and then the depth.

ASSIGNMENT

See Assignment 1 for Unit 10-1 on page 206.

■ UNIT 10-2

Pin Fasteners

Pin fasteners are an inexpensive and effective approach to assembly where loading is primarily in shear. They can be separated into two groups: *semipermanent* and *quick-release*.

SEMIPERMANENT PINS

Semipermanent pin fasteners require application of pressure or the aid of tools for installation or removal. The two basic types are machine pins and radial-locking pins.

The following general design rules apply to all types of semipermanent pins:

- Avoid conditions where the direction of vibration parallels the axis of the pin.
- Keep the shear plane of the pin a minimum distance of one diameter from the end of the pin.
- In applications where engaged length is at a minimum and appearance is not critical, allow pins to protrude the length of the chamfer at each end for maximum locking effect.

MACHINE PINS

Four types are generally considered to be most important: *hardened and ground dowel pins and commercial straight pins, taper pins, clevis pins,* and

---

1⅝ in., or a ⅜ × 1¼ (.38 × 1.25) in. key.

In specifying keys on the item list, only the information shown in the column "Specifications" in Fig. 10-1-2 need be given.

Dimensioning of Keyseats

Keyseats are dimensioned by width, depth, location, and, if required, length. The depth is dimensioned from the opposite side of the shaft or hole. See Fig. 10-1-3. Set the TOLER-ANCE (DIMTOL) DIMVARS to ON and the DIMTP, DIMTM limits accordingly.

Tapered Keyseats The depth of tapered keyseats in hubs, which is shown on the drawing, is the nominal depth $H/2$ minus an allowance. This is always the depth at the large end of the tapered keyseat and is indicated on the drawing by the abbreviation LE.

The radii of fillets, when required, must be dimensioned on the drawing.

Since standard milling cutters for Woodruff keys have the same appropriate number, it is possible to call for a Woodruff keyseat by the number only.

Where it is desirable to detail Woodruff keyseats on a drawing, all dimensions use LEADER with a note in the following order: width, depth, and radius of cutter. See Fig. 10-1-4.

Woodruff keyseats may alternately be dimensioned in the same manner as

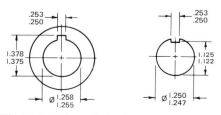

Fig. 10-1-3 Dimensioning keyseats.

HARDENED AND GROUND DOWEL PIN	TAPER PIN	CLEVIS PIN	COTTER PIN
Standardized in nominal diameters ranging from .12 to .88 in. (3 to 22 mm). 1. Holding laminated sections together with surfaces either drawn up tight or separated in some fixed relationship. 2. fastening machine parts where accuracy of alignment is a primary consideration. 3. locking components on shafts, in the form of transverse pin key.	Standard pins have a taper of 1:48 measured on the diameter. Basic dimension is the diameter of the large end. Used for light duty service in the attachment of wheels, levers and similar components to shafts. Torque capacity is determined on the basis of double shear, using the average diameter along the tapered section in the shaft for area calculations.	Standard nominal diameters for clevis pins range from .19 to 1.00 in. (5 to 25mm). Basic function of the clevis pin is to connect mating yoke, or fork, and eye members in knuckle-joint assemblies. Held in place by a small cotter pin or other fastening means, it provides a mobile joint construction, which can be readily disconnected for adjustment or maintenance.	Sizes have been standardized in nominal diameters ranging from .03 to .75 in. (1 to 20mm). Locking device for other fasteners. Used with a castle or slotted nut on bolt, screws, or studs, it provides a convenient, low-cost locknut assembly. Hold standard clevis pins in place. Can be used with or without a plain washer as an artificial shoulder to lock parts in position on shafts.

Fig. 10-2-1 Machine pins.

standard cotter pins. Descriptive data and recommended assembly practices for these four traditional types of machine pins are presented in Fig. 10-2-1. For proper size selection of cotter pins, refer to Fig. 10-2-2.

NOMINAL THREAD SIZE in. (mm)	NOMINAL COTTER PIN SIZE in. (mm)	COTTER PIN HOLE in. (mm)	END CLEARANCE* in. (mm)
.250 (6)	.062 (1.5)	.078 (1.9)	.11 (3)
.312 (8)	.078 (2)	.094 (2.4)	.11 (3)
.375 (10)	.094 (2.5)	.109 (2.8)	.14 (4)
.500 (12)	.125 (3)	.141 (3.4)	.17 (5)
.625 (14)	.156 (3)	.172 (3.4)	.23 (5)
.750 (20)	.156 (4)	.172 (4.5)	.27 (7)
1.000 (24)	.188 (5)	.203 (5.6)	.31 (8)
1.125 (27)	.188 (5)	.203 (5.6)	.39 (8)
1.250 (30)	.219 (6)	.234 (6.3)	.41 (10)
1.375 (36)	.219 (6)	.234 (6.3)	.44 (11)
1.500 (42)	.250 (6)	.266 (6.3)	.48 (12)
1.750 (48)	.312 (8)	.312 (8.5)	.55 (14)

*DISTANCE FROM EXTREME POINT OF BOLT OR SCREW TO CENTER OF COTTER PIN HOLE.

Fig. 10-2-2 Recommended cotter pin sizes.

Radial Locking Pins

Two basic pin forms are employed: *solid with grooved surfaces* and *hollow spring pins,* which may be either slotted or spiral-wrapped.

Grooved Straight Pins Locking action of the grooved pin is provided by parallel, longitudinal grooves uniformly spaced around the pin surface. Rolled or pressed into solid pin stock, the grooves expand the effective pin diameter. When the pin is driven into a drilled hole corresponding in size to nominal pin diameter, elastic deformation of the raised groove edges produces a secure force-fit with the hole wall. Figure 10-2-3 shows six of the

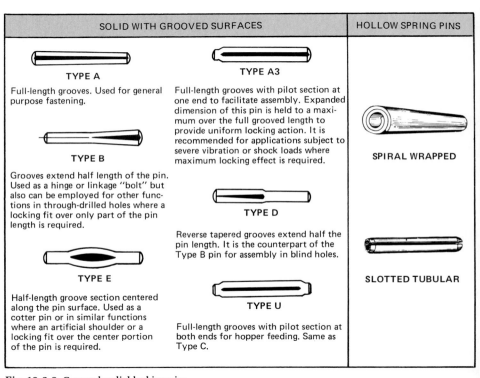

SOLID WITH GROOVED SURFACES		HOLLOW SPRING PINS
TYPE A Full-length grooves. Used for general purpose fastening.	**TYPE A3** Full-length grooves with pilot section at one end to facilitate assembly. Expanded dimension of this pin is held to a maximum over the full grooved length to provide uniform locking action. It is recommended for applications subject to severe vibration or shock loads where maximum locking effect is required.	**SPIRAL WRAPPED**
TYPE B Grooves extend half length of the pin. Used as a hinge or linkage "bolt" but also can be employed for other functions in through-drilled holes where a locking fit over only part of the pin length is required.	**TYPE D** Reverse tapered grooves extend half the pin length. It is the counterpart of the Type B pin for assembly in blind holes.	
TYPE E Half-length groove section centered along the pin surface. Used as a cotter pin or in similar functions where an artificial shoulder or a locking fit over the center portion of the pin is required.	**TYPE U** Full-length grooves with pilot section at both ends for hopper feeding. Same as Type C.	**SLOTTED TUBULAR**

Fig. 10-2-3 Grooved radial locking pins.

grooved-pin constructions that have been standardized. For typical grooved pin size selection, refer to Fig. 10-2-4.

Reference and Source Material

1. *Machine Design,* Fastening and joining reference issue, Nov. 1981.

ASSIGNMENTS

See Assignments 2 through 5 for Unit 10-2 starting on page 206.

SHAFT DIA in. (mm)	TRANSVERSE KEY		LONGITUDINAL KEY
	PIN DIA in. (mm)	TAPER PIN NO.	PIN DIA in. (mm)
.375 (10)	.125 (3)	3/0	.094 (2.5)
.438 (12)	.156 (4)	0	.125 (3)
.500 (14)	.156 (5)	0	.125 (4)
.562 (16)	.188 (5)	2	.156 (4)
.625 (18)	.188 (6)	2	.156 (5)
.750 (20)	.250 (6)	4	.156 (5)
.875 (22)	.250 (6)	4	.219 (6)
1.000 (24)	.312 (8)	6	.250 (6)
1.062 (26)	.312 (8)	6	—
1.125 (28)	.375 (10)	7	—
1.188 (30)	.375 (10)	7	—
1.250 (32)	.375 (10)	7	.312 (8)
1.375 (34)	.438 (11)	7	.375 (10)
1.438 (36)	.438 (11)	7	—
1.500 (38)	.500 (12)	8	.438 (11)

Fig. 10-2-4 Recommended groove pin sizes.

UNIT 10-3

Retaining Rings

Retaining rings, or *snap rings,* are used to provide a removable shoulder to accurately locate, retain, or lock components on shafts and in bores of housings. Figure 10-3-1 illustrates how they are represented on a drawing. The darkened portion is created by filling the area with the aid of the HATCH command, using a small increment spacing between the general pattern lines. They are easily installed and removed, and since they are usually made of spring steel, retaining rings have a high shear strength and impact capacity. In addition to fastening and positioning, a number of rings are designed for taking up end play caused by accumulated tolerances or wear in the parts being retained. In general, these devices can be placed into three categories which describe the type and method of fabrication: stamped retaining rings, wire-formed rings, and spiral-wound retaining rings.

STAMPED RETAINING RINGS

Stamped retaining rings, in contrast to wire-formed rings with their uniform cross-sectional area, have a tapered radial width which decreases symmetrically from the center section to the free ends. The tapered construction permits the rings to remain circular when they are expanded for assembly over a shaft or contracted for insertion into a bore or housing. This constant circularity ensures maximum contact surface with the bottom of the groove.

Stamped retaining rings can be classified into three groups: axially assembled rings, radially assembled rings, and self-locking rings which do not require grooves. *Axially assembled rings* slip over the ends of shafts or down into bores, while *radially assembled rings* have side openings which permit the rings to be snapped directly into grooves on a shaft.

Commonly used types of stamped retaining rings are illustrated and compared in Fig. 10-3-2.

WIRE-FORMED RETAINING RINGS

The *wire-formed retaining ring* is a split ring formed and cut from spring wire of uniform cross-sectional size and shape. The wire is cold-drawn or rolled into shape from a continuous coil or bar. Then the gap ends are cut into various configurations for ease of application and removal.

Rings are available in many cross-sectional shapes, but the most commonly used are the rectangular and circular cross sections.

SPIRAL-WOUND RETAINING RINGS

Spiral-wound retaining rings consist of two or more turns of rectangular material, wound on edge to provide a continuous crimped or uncrimped coil.

Reference and Source Material

1. *Machine Design,* Fastening and joining reference issue, Nov. 1981.

ASSIGNMENT

See Assignment 6 for Unit 10-3 on page 208.

UNIT 10-4

Rivets

STANDARD RIVETS

Riveting is a popular method of fastening and joining, primarily because of its simplicity, dependability, and low cost. A myriad of manufactured products and structures, both small and large, are held together by these fasteners. Rivets are classified as permanent fastenings, as distinguished from removable fasteners, such as bolts and screws.

Basically, a *rivet* is a ductile metal pin which is inserted through holes in two or more parts, and the ends are formed over to securely hold the parts.

Another important reason for riveting is versatility, with respect to both the properties of rivets as fasteners and the method of clinching.

- Part materials: Rivets can be used to

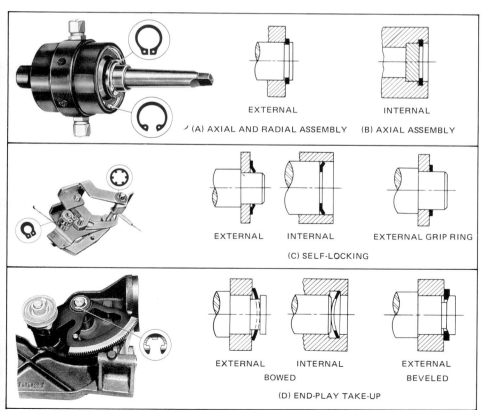

Fig. 10-3-1 Retaining ring applications.

EXTERNAL INTERNAL
(A) AXIAL AND RADIAL ASSEMBLY (B) AXIAL ASSEMBLY

EXTERNAL INTERNAL EXTERNAL GRIP RING
(C) SELF-LOCKING

EXTERNAL INTERNAL EXTERNAL
BOWED BEVELED
(D) END-PLAY TAKE-UP

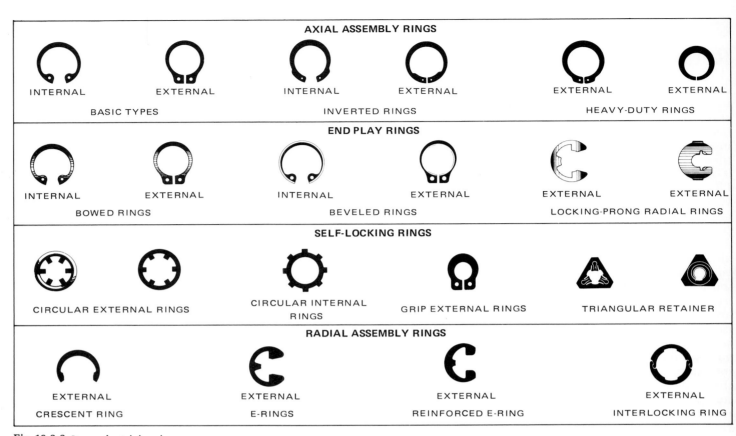

Fig. 10-3-2 Stamped retaining rings.

join dissimilar materials, metallic or nonmetallic, in various thicknesses.

- Multiple functions: Rivets can serve as fasteners, pivot shafts, spacers, electric contacts, stops, or inserts.
- Fastening finished parts: Rivets can be used to fasten parts that have already received a final painting or other finishing.

Riveted joints are neither watertight nor airtight, although such a joint may be attained at some added cost by using a sealing compound. The riveted parts cannot be disassembled for maintenance or replacement without knocking the rivet out and clinching a new one in place for reassembly. Common riveted joints are shown in Fig. 10-4-1.

Large Rivets

Large rivets are used in structural work of buildings and bridges. Today, however, high-strength bolts have almost completely replaced rivets in field connections because of cost, strength, and the noise factor. Rivet joints are of two types: butt and

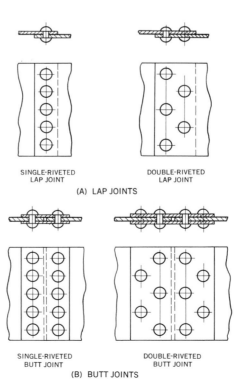

SINGLE-RIVETED LAP JOINT   DOUBLE-RIVETED LAP JOINT

(A) LAP JOINTS

SINGLE-RIVETED BUTT JOINT   DOUBLE-RIVETED BUTT JOINT

(B) BUTT JOINTS

Fig. 10-4-1 Common riveted joints.

lapped. The more common types of large rivets are shown in Fig. 10-4-2. In order to show the difference between *shop rivets* (rivets that are put in the structure at the shop) and *field rivets* (rivets that are used on the site), two types of symbols are used. In drawing shop rivets, the diameter of the rivet head is shown on the drawings. For field rivets, the shaft diame-

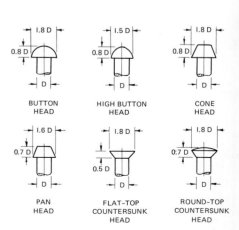

BUTTON HEAD   HIGH BUTTON HEAD   CONE HEAD

PAN HEAD   FLAT-TOP COUNTERSUNK HEAD   ROUND-TOP COUNTERSUNK HEAD

Fig. 10-4-2 Approximate sizes and types of large rivets .50 in. (12 mm) and up.

ter is used. Figure 10-4-3 shows the conventional rivet symbols adopted by the American and Canadian Institutes of Steel Construction. If you are going to be working extensively with rivets, it would be advisable to prepare your own symbol library (see Unit 7-2).

Small Rivets

Design of small rivet assemblies is influenced by two major considerations:

1. The joint itself, its strength, appearance, and configuration
2. The final riveting operation, in terms of equipment capabilities and production sequence.

Types of Small Rivets (Fig. 10-4-4)

Semitubular This is the most widely used type of small rivet. The depth of the hole in the rivet, measured along the wall, does not exceed 112 percent of the mean shank diameter. The hole may be extruded (straight or tapered) or drilled (straight), depending on the manufacturer and/or rivet size.

Full Tubular This rivet has a drilled shank with a hole depth more than 112 percent of the mean shank diameter. It can be used to punch its own hole in fabric, some plastic sheets, and other soft materials, eliminating a preliminary punching or drilling operation.

Bifurcated (Split) The rivet body is sawed or punched to produce a

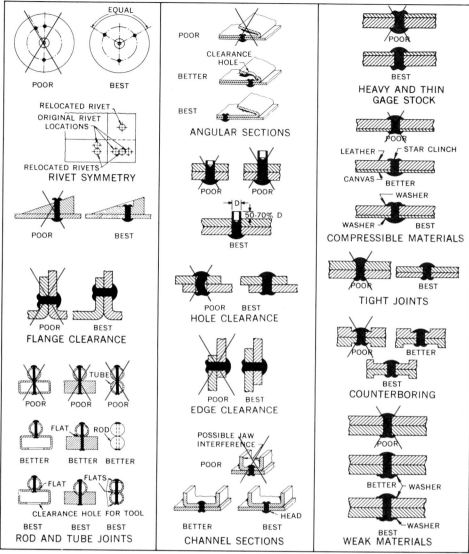

Fig. 10-4-5 Small rivet design data.

pronged shank that punches its own hole through fiber, wood, or plastic.

Compression This rivet consists of two elements: the solid or blank rivet and the deep-drilled tubular member. Pressed together, these form an interference fit.

Design Recommendations (Fig. 10-4-5)

Select the Right Rivets Basic types are covered in Fig. 10-4-4. Rivet standards for all types but compression rivets have been published by the Tubular and Split Rivet Council.

Rivet Diameters The optimum rivet diameter is determined not by performance requirements but by economics — the costs of the rivet and the

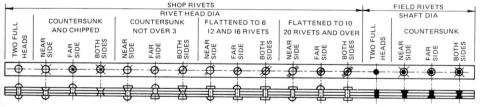

Fig. 10-4-3 Conventional rivet symbols.

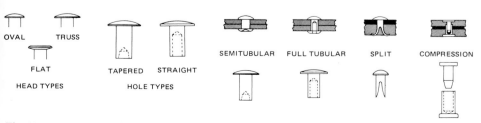

Fig. 10-4-4 Basic types of small rivets.

labor to install it. The rivet length-to-diameter ratio should not exceed 6:1.

Rivet Positioning The location of the rivet in the assembled product influences both joint strength and clinching requirements. The important dimensions are edge distance and pitch distance.

Edge distance is the interval between the edge of the part and the center line of the rivet.

The recommended edge distance for plastic materials, either solid or laminated, is between 2 and 3 diameters, depending on the thickness and inherent strength of the material.

Pitch distance — the interval between center lines of adjacent rivets — should not be too small. Unnecessarily high stress concentrations in the riveted material and buckling and adjacent empty holes can result if the pitch distance is less than 3 times the diameter of the largest rivet in the assembly (metal parts) or 5 times the diameter (plastic parts).

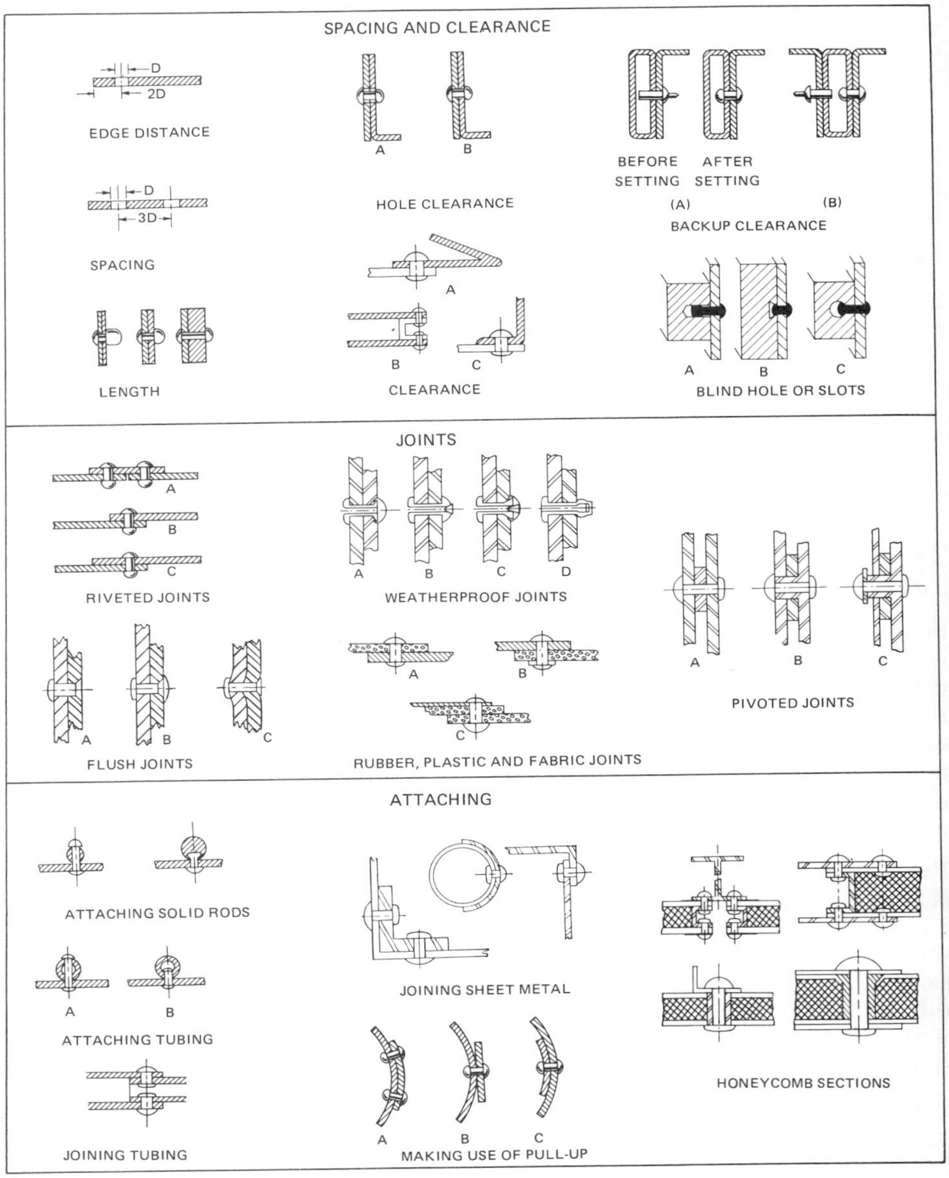

BLIND RIVETS

Blind riveting is a technique for setting a rivet without access to the reverse side of the joint. However, blind rivets may also be used in applications in which both sides of the joint are actually accessible.

Blind rivets are classified according to the methods with which they are set: pull-mandrel, drive-pin, and chemically expanded. See Fig. 10-4-6.

Design Considerations (Fig. 10-4-7)

Type of Rivet Selection depends on a number of factors, such as speed of assembly, clamping capacity, available sizes, adaptability to the assembly, ease of removal, cost, and structural integrity of the joint.

Fig. 10-4-7 Blind rivet design data.

Joint Design Factors that must be known include allowable tolerances of rivet length versus assembly thickness, hole clearance, joint configuration, and type of loading.

Speed of Installation The fastest, most efficient installation is done with power tools — air, hydraulic, or electric. Manual tools, such as special pliers, can be used efficiently with practically no training.

In-Place Costs Blind rivets often have lower in-place costs than solid rivets or tapping screws.

Loading A blind-rivet joint is usually in compression or shear.

Material Thickness Some rivets can

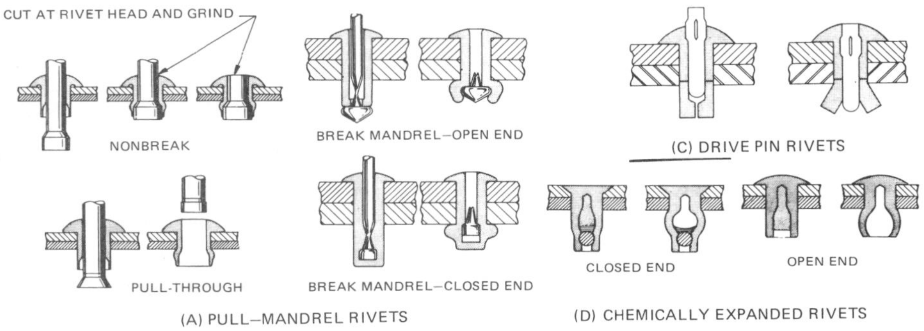

Fig. 10-4-6 Basic types of blind rivets and methods of setting.

be set in materials as thin as .02 in. (0.5 mm). Also, if one component is of compressible material, rivets with extra-large head diameter should be used.

Edge Distance The average recommended edge distance (Fig. 10-4-7, top) is twice the diameter of the rivet.

Spacing Rivet pitch (Fig. 10-4-7, top) should be 3 times the diameter of the rivet.

Length The amount of length needed (Fig. 10-4-7, top) for clinching action varies greatly. Most rivet manufacturers provide data on grip ranges of their rivets.

Back-Up Clearance Full entry of the rivet is essential for tightly clinched joints. Sufficient back-up clearance (Fig. 10-4-7, top) must be provided to accommodate the full length of the unclinched rivet, A.

Blind Holes or Slots A useful application of a blind rivet is in fastening members in a blind hole (Fig. 10-4-7, top). At A, the formed head bears against the side of the hole only. This joint is not as strong as the other two (B and C).

Riveted Joints Riveted cleat or batten holds a butt joint, A. The simple lap joint, B, must have sufficient material beyond the hole for strength. Excessive material beyond rivet hole C may curl up or vibrate or cause interference problems, depending on the installation (Fig. 10-4-7, middle).

Flush Joints Generally, flush joints are made by countersinking one of the sections and using a rivet with a countersunk head, A.

Weatherproof Joints A hollow-core rivet can be sealed by capping it, A; by plugging it, B; or by using both a cap and a plug, C. To obtain a true seal, however, a gasket or mastic should be used between the sections and perhaps under the rivet head. An ideal solution is to use a closed-end rivet, D (Fig. 10-4-7, middle).

Rubber, Plastic, and Fabric Joints Some plastics, such as reinforced molded Fiberglass, or polystyrene, which are reasonably rigid, present no problem for most small rivets. However, when the material is very flexible or is a fabric, set the rivet as shown at A or B, with the upset head against the solid member. If this practice is not possible, use a back-up strip as shown at C (Fig. 10-4-7, middle).

Pivoted Joints There are a number of ways of producing a pivoted assembly. Three are shown in Fig. 10-4-7, middle.

Attaching Solid Rod When attaching a rod to other members, the usual practice is to pass the rivet completely through the rod (Fig. 10-4-7, bottom).

Attaching Tubing Attaching tubing is an application for which the blind rivet is ideally suited.

Joining Tubing This tubing joint is a common form of blind riveting (Fig. 10-4-7, bottom).

Making Use of Pull-Up By judicious positioning of rivets and parts that are to be assembled with rivets, the setting force can sometimes be used to pull together unlike parts (Fig. 10-4-7, bottom).

Honeycomb Sections Inserts should be employed to strengthen the section and provide a strong joint.

References and Source Material

1. *Machine Design*, Fastening and joining reference issue, Nov. 1981.

ASSIGNMENT

See Assignment 8 for Unit 10-4 on page 209.

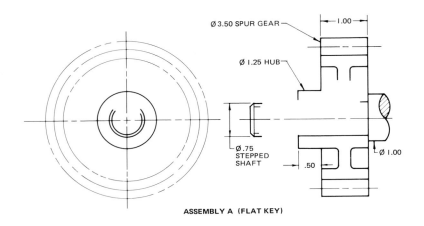

ASSEMBLY A (FLAT KEY)

Ø 3.50 SPUR GEAR
Ø 1.25 HUB
Ø .75 STEPPED SHAFT
1.00
.50
Ø 1.00

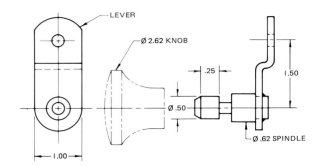

ASSEMBLY B (SQUARE KEY)

LEVER
Ø 2.62 KNOB
Ø .50
Ø .62 SPINDLE
.25
1.50
1.00

Fig. 10-1-A Key and serration fasteners.

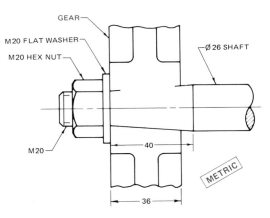

ASSEMBLY A (WOODRUFF KEY)

GEAR
M20 FLAT WASHER
M20 HEX NUT
M20
Ø 26 SHAFT
40
36
METRIC

Fig. 10-1-B Key fasteners.

Assignment for Unit 10-1, Keys, Splines, and Serrations

1. Lay out the two fastener assemblies shown in Fig. 10-1-A or 10-1-B. The following fasteners are used:

For Fig. 10-1-A
- *Assembly A:* flat key
- *Assembly B:* square key
For Fig. 10-1-B
- *Assembly A:* Woodruff key

Refer to the Appendix and manufacturers' catalogs for sizes and use your judgment for dimensions not shown. Show the dimensions for the keyseats. Scale 1 : 1.

Assignments for Unit 10-2, Pin Fasteners

2. Complete the pin assemblies shown in Fig. 10-2-A or 10-2-B, given the following information:

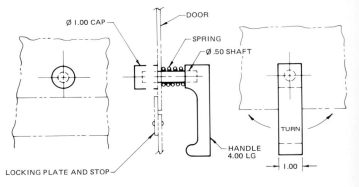

Ø 1.00 CAP
DOOR
SPRING
Ø .50 SHAFT
TURN
HANDLE 4.00 LG
1.00
LOCKING PLATE AND STOP

ASSEMBLY A (CABINET HANDLE)

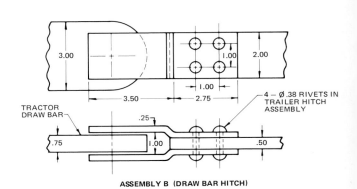

3.00
3.50
1.00
2.00
1.00
2.75
.25
.75
1.00
.50
4 – Ø .38 RIVETS IN TRAILER HITCH ASSEMBLY
TRACTOR DRAW BAR

ASSEMBLY B (DRAW BAR HITCH)

Fig. 10-2-A Pin fasteners.

For Fig. 10-2-A
- *Assembly A.* Pins are used to fasten the cap and handle to the shaft. Scale 1:2.
- *Assembly B.* A pin whose area is equal to the four rivets is used to fasten the trailer hitch to the tractor draw bar. Scale 1:2.

For Fig. 10-2-B
- *Assembly A.* A type E grooved pin holds the roller to the bracket. A washer and cotter pin are used to fasten the bracket to the pushrod. Scale 1:1.
- *Assembly B.* A type A3 grooved pin holds the V-belt pulley to the shaft. Scale 1:1.

Refer to manufacturers' catalogs for pin sizes and provide the complete information to order each fastener.

3. Prepare detail drawings of the parts shown in Fig. 10-2-C. Use your judgment for the scale and selection of views. Include an item list.

4. Make a two-view assembly drawing of the crane hook shown in Fig. 10-2-D. The hook is to be held to the U-frame with a slotted locknut. A clevis pin is inserted through the locknut slots to prevent the nut from turning. A clevis pin with washer and cotter pin holds the pulley to the frame. Scale 1:1.

5. Prepare detail drawings of the parts in assignment 4. Use your judgment for the scale and selection of views.

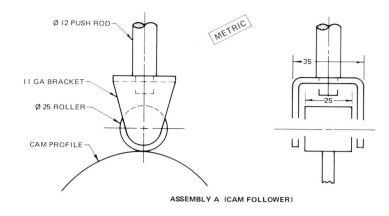

ASSEMBLY A (CAM FOLLOWER)

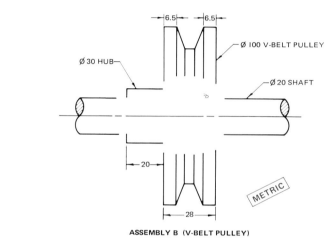

ASSEMBLY B (V-BELT PULLEY)

Fig. 10-2-B Pin fasteners.

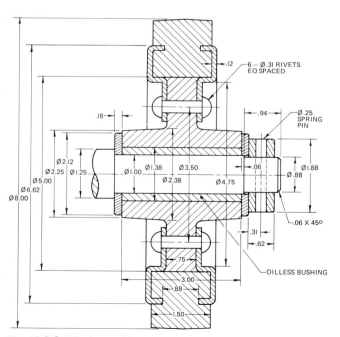

Fig. 10-2-C Wheel assembly.

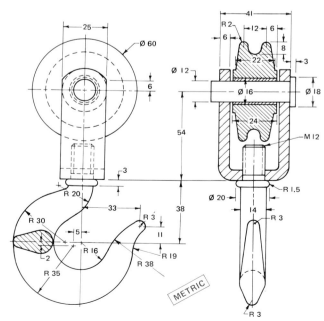

Fig. 10-2-D Crane hook.

Assignments for Unit 10-3, Retaining Rings

6. Complete the assemblies shown in Fig. 10-3-A or 10-3-B by adding suitable retaining rings as per the information supplied below. Refer to manufacturers' catalogs and show on the drawing the catalog number for the retaining ring. Add ring and groove sizes. Scale 1 : 1. Use your judgment for dimensions not shown.

For Fig. 10-3-A
- *Assembly A.* An external radial retaining ring mounted on the shaft is to act as a shoulder for the shaft support. An external axial retaining ring is required to hold the gear on the shaft.
- *Assembly B.* The plunger and punch are held into the punch holder by internal retaining rings.

For Fig. 10-3-B
- *Assembly A.* External self-locking retaining rings hold the roller shaft in position on the bracket.
- *Assembly B.* An external self-locking ring holds the plastic housing to the viewer case. An internal self-locking ring holds the lens in position.

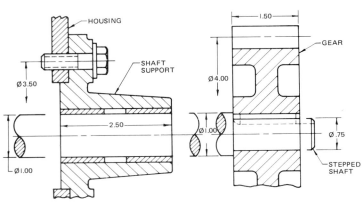

ASSEMBLY A (EXTERNAL RETAINING RINGS)

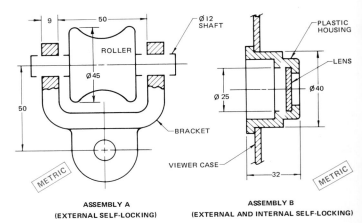

ASSEMBLY A
(EXTERNAL SELF-LOCKING)

ASSEMBLY B
(EXTERNAL AND INTERNAL SELF-LOCKING)

Fig 10-3-B Retaining ring fasteners.

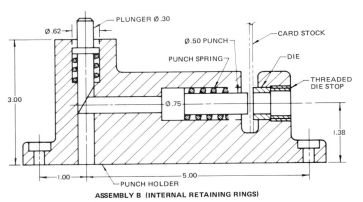

ASSEMBLY B (INTERNAL RETAINING RINGS)

Fig. 10-3-A Retaining ring fasteners.

Assignment for Unit 10-4, Rivets

8. Complete the two assembly drawings shown in Fig. 10-4-A or 10-4-B from the information supplied below. Refer to manufacturers' catalogs for rivet type and sizes, and on each assembly show the callout for the rivets. Use your judgment for sizes not given.

For Fig. 10-4-A
- *Assembly A.* Padlock brackets are riveted to the locker door and door frame with two blind rivets in each bracket. Scale 1:1.
- *Assembly B.* The roof truss is assembled in the shop with five evenly spaced Ø .50-in. (12-mm) rivets in each angle. Scale 1:4.

For Fig. 10-4-B
- *Assembly A.* The grill is held to the panel by four truss-head full tubular rivets. Scale 1:1.
- *Assembly B.* The support is held to the plywood panel by blind rivets uniformly spaced on the gage lines. Two rivets hold the bracket to the support. Scale 1:1.

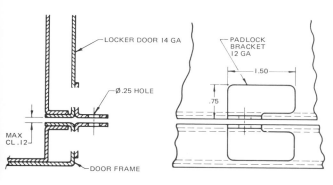

ASSEMBLY A (BLIND RIVETS)

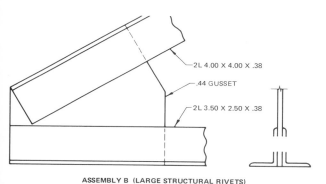

ASSEMBLY B (LARGE STRUCTURAL RIVETS)

Fig. 10-4-A Rivet fasteners.

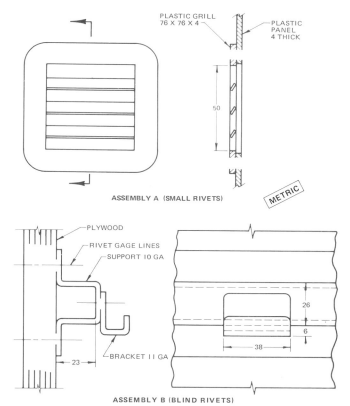

Fig. 10-4-B Rivet fasteners.

CHAPTER 11 Casting Processes

UNIT 11-1

Metal Castings

FORMING PROCESSES

When a component of a machine takes shape on the monitor of the designer, the method of its manufacture may still be entirely open. The number of possible manufacturing processes is increasing day by day, and the optimum process is found only by carefully weighing technological advantages and drawbacks in relation to the economy of production.

The choice of the manufacturing process depends on the quantity, size, and shape of the component. Manufacturing processes are therefore important to the engineer and drafter in order to properly design a part. They must be familiar with the advantages, disadvantages, costs, and machines necessary for manufacturing. Since the cost of the part is influenced by the production method, such as welding or casting, the designer must be able to choose wisely the method which will reduce the cost. In some cases it may be necessary to recommend the purchase of a new or different machine in order to produce the part at a competitive price.

This means the designer should design the part for the process as well as for the function. Most of all, unnecessarily close tolerances on nonfunctional dimensions should be avoided.

This chapter covers the casting process. Forming by means of welding is covered in Chap. 12.

CASTING PROCESSES

Casting is the process whereby parts are produced by pouring molten metal into a mold. A typical cast part is shown in Fig. 11-1-1. Casting pro-

Fig. 11-1-1 Typical cast part.

cesses for metals can be classified by either the type of mold or pattern or the pressure or force used to fill the mold. Conventional sand, shell, and plaster molds utilize a permanent pattern, but the mold is used only once. Permanent molds and die-casting dies are machined in metal or graphite sections and are employed for a large number of castings. Investment casting and the relatively new full-mold and an expendable pattern.

Casting metals are usually alloys or compounds of two or more metals. They are generally classed as ferrous or nonferrous metals. *Ferrous* metals are those which contain iron, the most common being gray iron, steel, and malleable iron. *Nonferrous* alloys, which contain no iron, are those containing metals such as aluminum, magnesium, and copper.

SAND MOLD CASTING

The most widely used casting process for metals uses a permanent pattern of metal or wood that shapes the mold cavity when loose molding material is compacted around the pattern. This material consists of a relatively fine sand, which serves as the refractory aggregate, plus a binder.

A typical sand mold, with the various provisions for pouring the molten metal and compensating for contraction of the solidifying metal, and a sand core for forming a cavity in the casting are shown in Fig. 11-1-2. Sand molds consist of two or more sections: bottom (*drag*), top (*cope*), and intermediate sections (*cheeks*) when required. The sand is contained in flasks equipped with pins and plates to ensure the alignment of the cope and drag.

Molten metal is poured into the sprue, and connecting runners provide flow channels for the metal to enter the mold cavity through gates. Riser cavities are located over the

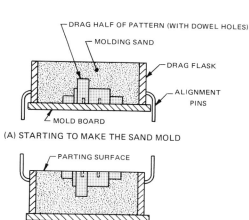

(A) STARTING TO MAKE THE SAND MOLD

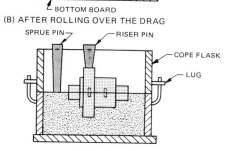

(B) AFTER ROLLING OVER THE DRAG

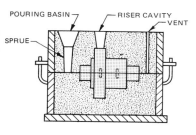

(C) PREPARING TO RAM MOLDING SAND IN COPE

(D) REMOVING RISER AND GATE SPRUE PINS AND ADDING POURING BASIN

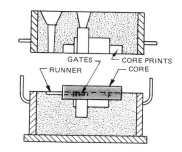

(E) PARTING FLASKS TO REMOVE PATTERN AND TO ADD CORE AND RUNNER

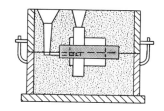

(F) SAND MOLD READY FOR POURING

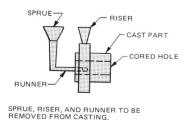

SPRUE, RISER, AND RUNNER TO BE REMOVED FROM CASTING.

(G) CASTING AS REMOVED FROM THE MOLD

Fig. 11-1-2 Sequence in preparing a sand casting.

heavier sections of the casting. A vent is usually added to permit the escape of gases which are formed during the pouring of metal.

When a hollow casting is required, a form called a *core* is usually used. Cores occupy that part of the mold which is intended to be hollow in the casting. Cores, like molds, are formed of sand and placed in the supporting impressions or *core prints* in the molds. The core prints ensure positive location of the core in the mold and, as such, should be placed so that they support the mass of the core uniformly to prevent shifting or sagging. Metal core supports called *chaplets,* which are used in the mold cavity and which fuse into the casting, are sometimes used by the foundry in addition to core prints. See Fig. 11-1-3. Chaplets and their lo-

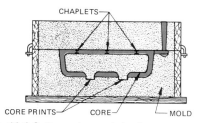

Fig. 11-1-3 Core prints and chaplets.

cations are not usually specified on drawings.

In producing sand molds, a metal or wooden pattern must first be made. The pattern, normally made in two parts, is slightly larger in every dimension than the part to be cast, to allow for shrinkage when the casting cools. This is known as *shrinkage allowance,*

and the pattern maker allows for it by using a shrink rule for each of the cast metals.

Drafts or slight tapers (1° or 2°) are also placed on the pattern to allow for easy withdrawal from the sand mold. The parting line location and amount of draft are very important considerations in the design process.

In the construction of patterns for castings in which various points on the surface of the casting must be machined, sufficient excess metal should be provided for all machined surfaces. Allowance depends on the metal used, the shape and size of the part, the tendency to warp, the machining method, and setup.

The molten metal is poured into the pouring basin and runs down the sprue to a runner and into the mold cavity.

When the metal has hardened, the sand mold is broken and the casting removed. Next the excess metal, gates, and risers are removed and remelted.

Shell Mold Casting

The refractory sand used in shell molding is bonded by a thermostable resin that forms a relatively thin shell mold. A heated, reusable metal pattern plate (Fig. 11-1-4) is used to form each half of the mold by either dumping a sand-resin mixture on top of the heated pattern or by blowing resin-coated sand under air pressure against the pattern.

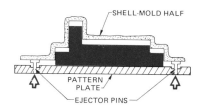

Fig. 11-1-4 Shell mold being stripped from pattern.

Plaster Mold Casting

Plaster of Paris and fillers are mixed with water and setting-control agents to form a *slurry.* This slurry is poured around a reusable metal or rubber pattern and sets to form a gypsum mold. See Fig. 11-1-5. The molds are then dried, assembled, and filled with molten (nonferrous) metals. Plaster mold casting is ideal for producing thin, sound walls. As in sand mold

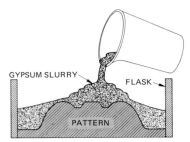

GYPSUM SLURRY

FLASK

PATTERN

Fig. 11-1-5 Pouring slurry over a plaster mold pattern.

(1) THE DIE

(2) THE WAX PATTERN

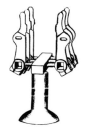

(3) THE CLUSTER ASSEMBLY

casting, a new mold is required for each casting. Castings made by this process have smoother finish, finer detail, and greater dimensional accuracy than sand castings.

Permanent Mold Casting

This process makes use of a metal mold, similar to a die, which is utilized to produce many castings from each mold. See Fig. 11-1-6. It is used to produce some ferrous alloy castings, but due to rapid deterioration of the mold caused by the high pouring temperatures of these alloys, and the high mold cost, the process is confined largely to production of nonferrous alloy castings.

Investment Mold Casting

Investment castings have been better known in the past by the term *lost wax castings*. The term *investment* refers to the refractory material used to encase the wax patterns.

This process uses both an expendable pattern and an expendable mold. Patterns of wax, plaster, or frozen mercury are cast in metal dies. The molds are formed either by pouring a slurry of a refractory material around the pattern positioned in a flask or by building a thick layer of shell refractory on the pattern by repeated dip-

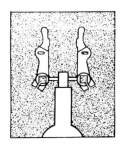

(4) REFRACTORY MOLD

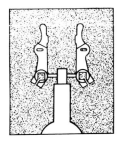

(5) FIRED MOLD

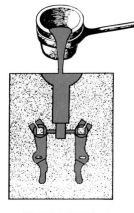

(6) THE CASTING

Fig. 11-1-7 Investment mold casting.

ping into slurries and drying. The arrangement of the wax patterns in the flask method is shown in Fig. 11-1-7.

Full Mold Casting

The characteristic feature of the full mold process is the use of consumable patterns made of foamed plastic. These are not extracted from the mold, but are vaporized by the molten metal.

The full mold process is suitable for individual castings. The advantages it offers are obvious: it is very economical and reduces the delivery time required for prototypes, articles urgently needed for repair jobs, or individual large machine parts.

Centrifugal Casting

In the centrifugal casting process, commonly applied to cylindrical casting of either ferrous or nonferrous alloys, a permanent mold is rotated rapidly about the axis of the casting while a measured amount of molten metal is poured into the mold cavity. See Fig. 11-1-8. The centrifugal force is used to hold the metal against the outer walls of the mold with the volume of metal poured determining the wall thickness of the casting. Rotation speed is rapid enough to form the central hole without a core. Castings made by this method are smooth, sound, and clean on the outside.

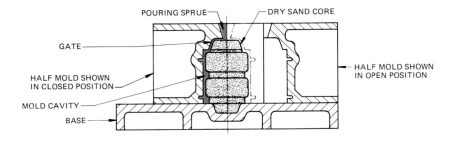

POURING SPRUE

DRY SAND CORE

GATE

HALF MOLD SHOWN IN CLOSED POSITION

MOLD CAVITY

BASE

HALF MOLD SHOWN IN OPEN POSITION

Fig. 11-1-6 Permanent mold.

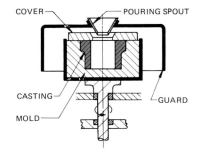

COVER

POURING SPOUT

CASTING

MOLD

GUARD

Fig. 11-1-8 Centrifugal mold equipment.

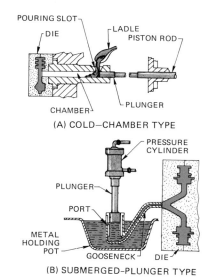

POURING SLOT
DIE
LADLE
PISTON ROD

CHAMBER
PLUNGER

(A) COLD—CHAMBER TYPE

PRESSURE
CYLINDER

PLUNGER
PORT

METAL
HOLDING
POT
GOOSENECK
DIE

(B) SUBMERGED-PLUNGER TYPE

Fig. 11-1-9 Die-casting machines.

Continuous Casting

Continuous casting produces semi-finished shapes such as uniform section rounds, ovals, squares, rectangles, and plates. These shapes are cast from nearly all ferrous and nonferrous metals by continuously pouring the molten metal into a water-jacketed mold. The metal solidifies in the mold, and the solid billet exits continuously into a water spray. These sections are processed further by rolling, drawing, or extruding into smaller, more intricate shapes. Iron bars cast by this process are finished by machining.

Die Casting

One of the least expensive, fastest, and most efficient processes used in the production of metal parts is die casting. Die castings are made by forcing molten metal into a die or mold. Large quantities, accurately cast, can be produced with a die-casting die, thus eliminating or reducing machining costs. Many parts are completely finished when taken from a die. Since die castings can be accurate to within .001 in. (0.02 mm) of size, internal and external threads, gear teeth, and lugs can readily be cast.

Die casting has its limitations. Only nonferrous alloys can be die-cast economically because of the lack of a suitable die material to withstand the higher temperatures required for steel and iron.

Die-casting machines are of two types: the *submerged-plunger* type for low-melting alloys containing zinc, tin, lead, etc., and the *cold-chamber* type for high-melting nonferrous alloys containing aluminum and magnesium. See Fig. 11-1-9.

SELECTION OF PROCESS

Selection of the most feasible casting process for a given part requires an evaluation of the type of metal, the number of castings required, their shape and size, the dimensional accuracy required, and the casting finish required. When the casting can be produced by a number of methods, selection of the process is based on the most economical production of the total requirement. Since final cost of the part, rather than price of the rough casting, is the significant factor, the number of finishing operations necessary on the casting is also considered. Those processes that provide the closest dimensions, the best surface finish, and the most intricate detail generally require the smallest number of finishing operations.

A direct comparison of the capabilities, production characteristics, and limitations of several processes is indicated in Fig. 11-1-10.

DESIGN CONSIDERATIONS

The advantages of using castings for engineering components are well appreciated by designers. Of major importance is the fact that they can produce shapes of any degree of complexity and of virtually any size.

PROCESS	METALS CAST	USUAL WEIGHT (MASS) RANGE	MINIMUM PRODUCTION QUANTITIES	RELATIVE SETUP COST	CASTING DETAIL FEASIBLE	MINIMUM THICKNESS in. (mm)	DIMENSIONAL TOLERANCES in. (mm)	SURFACE FINISH, RMS (μ in.)
SAND (Green, Dry, and Core) CO₂ Sand	All ferrous and nonferrous	Less than 1 lb. (0.5 kg) to several tons	3, without mechanization	Very low to high depending on mechanization	Fair	.12 to .25 (3 to 6) / .10 to .25 (2.5 to 6)	± .03 (0.8) / ± .02 (0.5)	350 / 250
SHELL	All ferrous and nonferrous	0.5 to 30 lb. (0.2 to 15 kg)	50	Moderate to high depending on mechanization	Fair to good	.03 to .10 (0.8 to 2.5)	± .015 (0.4)	200
PLASTER	Al, Mg, Cu, and Zn alloys	Less than 1 lb. to 3000 lb. (0.5 to 1350 kg)	1	Moderate	Excellent	.03 to .08 (0.8 to 2)	± .01 (0.2)	100
INVESTMENT	All ferrous and nonferrous	Less than 1 oz. to 50 lb. (30 g to 25 kg)	25	Moderate	Excellent	0.2 to .06 (0.5 to 1.5)	± .005 (0.1)	80
PERMANENT MOLD Metal Mold	Nonferrous and cast iron	1 to 40 lb. (0.5 to 20 kg)	100	Moderate to high	Poor	.18 to .25 (4.5 to 6)	± .02 (0.5)	200
Graphite Mold	Steel	5 to 300 lb. (2 to 150 kg)	100			.25 (6)	± .03 (0.8)	200
DIE	Sn, Pb, Zn, Al, Mg, and Cu alloys	Less than 1 lb. to 20 lb. (0.5 to 10 kg)	1000	High	Excellent	.05 to .08 (1.2 to 2)	± .002 (0.5)	60

* Values listed are primarily for aluminum alloys, but data applies generally to other metals also.

† Depends on surface area.   Double if dimension is across parting line.

Fig. 11-1-10 General characteristics of casting processes.

Solidification of Metal in a Mold

While this is not the first step in the sequence of events, it is of such fundamental importance that it forms the most logical point to begin understanding the making of a casting.

Consider a few simple shapes transformed into mold cavities and filled with molten metal.

In a sphere, heat dissipates from the surface through the mold while solidification commences from the outside and proceeds progressively inward, in a series of layers. As liquid metal solidifies, it contracts in volume, and unless feed metal is supplied, a shrinkage cavity may form in the center. See Fig. 11-1-11.

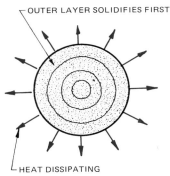

Fig. 11-1-11 Circular mold cavity filled with molten metal.

The designer must realize that a shrinkage problem exists and that the foundry worker must attach risers to the casting or resort to other means to overcome it.

When the simple sphere has solidified further, it continues to contract in volume, so that the final casting is smaller than the mold cavity.

Consider a shape with a square cross section such as the one shown in Fig. 11-1-12A. Here again, cooling proceeds at right angles to the surface and is necessarily faster at the corners of the casting. Thus, solidification proceeds more rapidly at the corners.

The resulting hot spot prolongs solidification, promoting solidification shrinkage and lack of density in this area. The only logical solution, from the designer's viewpoint, is the provision of very generous fillets or radii at the corners. Additionally, the relative size or shape of the two sections forming the corner is of importance. If they are materially different, as in Fig.

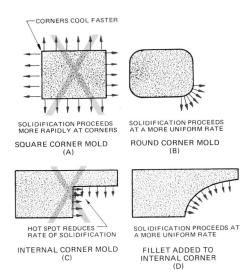

Fig. 11-1-12 Cooling effect on mold cavities filled with molten metal.

11-1-12D, contraction in the lighter member will occur at a different rate from that in the heavier member. Differential contraction is the major cause of casting stress, warping, and cracking.

General Design Rules

Design for Casting Soundness See Fig. 11-1-13. Most metals and alloys shrink when they solidify. Therefore, the design must be such that all members of the parts increase in dimension progressively to one or more suitable locations where feeder heads can be placed to offset liquid shrinkage.

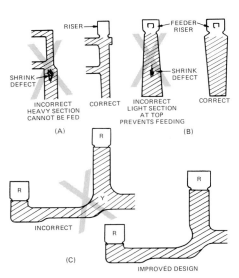

Fig. 11-1-13 Design members so that all parts increase progressively to feeder risers.

Fillet All-Sharp Angles See Fig. 11-1-14. Fillets have three functional purposes: to reduce stress concentration in the casting in service; to eliminate cracks, tears, and draws at reentry angles; and to make corners more moldable to eliminate hot spots.

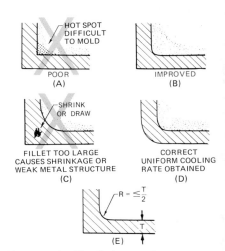

Fig. 11-1-14 Fillet all sharp angles.

Bring the Minimum Number of Adjoining Sections Together See Fig. 11-1-15. A well-designed casting brings the minimum number of sections together and avoids acute angles.

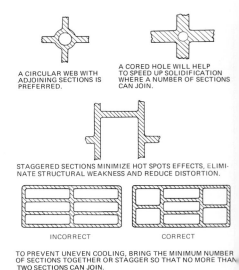

Fig. 11-1-15 Bringing the minimum number of adjoining sections together.

Design All Sections as Nearly Uniform in Thickness as Possible Shrink defects and casting strains existed in the casting illustrated in Fig

11-1-16. Redesigning eliminated excessive metal and resulted in a casting that was free from defects, was lighter in weight (mass), and prevented the development of casting strains in the light radial veins.

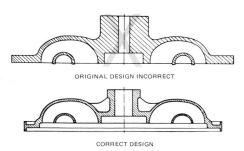

Fig. 11-1-16 Design all sections as nearly uniform in thickness as possible.

Avoid Abrupt Section Changes — Eliminate Sharp Corners at Adjoining Sections

See Fig. 11-1-17. The difference in the relative thickness of adjoining sections should be a minimum and not exceed a 2:1 ratio.

When a change of thickness must be less than 2:1, it may take the form of a fillet; where the difference must be greater, the form recommended is that of a wedge.

Wedge-shaped changes in wall thickness are to be designated with a taper not exceeding 1 in 4.

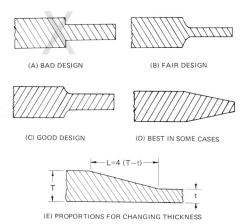

Fig. 11-1-17 Avoid abrupt changes.

Design Ribs for Maximum Effectiveness

See Fig. 11-1-18. Ribs have two functions: to increase stiffness and to reduce the mass. If too shallow in depth or too widely spaced, they are ineffectual.

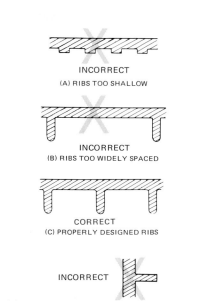

(A) RIBS TOO SHALLOW — INCORRECT

(B) RIBS TOO WIDELY SPACED — INCORRECT

(C) PROPERLY DESIGNED RIBS — CORRECT

(D) THIN RIBS SHOULD BE AVOIDED WHEN JOINED TO A HEAVY SECTION. OTHERWISE, THEY WILL LEAD TO HIGH STRESSES AND CRACKING. — INCORRECT

(E) AS FAR AS POSSIBLE, JUNCTION BETWEEN RIBS AND MAIN CASTING SHOULD PREVENT ANY LOCAL ACCUMULATION OF METAL. — INCORRECT

(F) RIBS SHOULD SOLIDIFY BEFORE THE CASTING SECTION THEY ADJOIN. — CORRECT

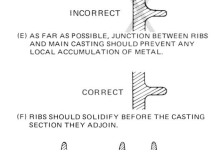

(G) T- AND H-SHAPED RIBBED DESIGNS HAVE THE ADVANTAGE OF UNIFORM METAL SECTIONS AND HENCE UNIFORM COOLING.

THICKNESS OF RIBS SHOULD APPROXIMATE 0.8 CASTING THICKNESS.

Fig. 11-1-18 Design ribs for maximum effectiveness.

Bosses and Pads Should Not Be Used Unless Absolutely Necessary

Bosses and pads increase metal thickness, create hot spots, and cause open grain or draws. Blend these into the casting by tapering or flattening the fillets. Bosses should not be included in casting design when the surface to support bolts, etc., may be obtained by milling or countersinking.

Spoked Wheels

See Fig. 11-1-19. A curved spoke is preferred to a straight one. It will tend to straighten slightly, thereby offsetting the dangers of cracking.

Use an Odd Number of Spokes

A wheel having an odd number of spokes will not have the same direct tensile

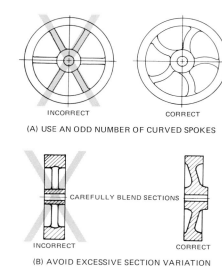

(A) USE AN ODD NUMBER OF CURVED SPOKES — INCORRECT / CORRECT

(B) AVOID EXCESSIVE SECTION VARIATION — INCORRECT (CAREFULLY BLEND SECTIONS) / CORRECT

Fig. 11-1-19 Spoked-wheel design.

stress along the arms as one having an even number and will have more resiliency to casting stresses.

Wall Thicknesses

Walls should be of minimum thickness, consistent with good foundry practice, and should provide adequate strength and stiffness. Wall thicknesses for different materials are as follows:

1. Walls of gray-iron castings and aluminum sand castings should not be less than .16 in. (4 mm) thick.
2. Walls of malleable iron and steel castings should not be less than .18 in. (5 mm) thick.
3. Walls of bronze, brass, or magnesium castings should not be less than .10 in. (2.4 mm) thick.

Parting Lines

A *parting line* is a line along which the pattern is divided for molding, or along which the sections of a mold separate. Selection of a parting line depends on a number of factors:

- Shape of the casting
- Elimination of machining on draft surfaces
- Method of supporting cores
- Location of gates and feeders.

Holes in Castings

Small holes usually are drilled and not cored.

Drafting Practices

It is important that a detail drawing give complete information on all cast parts, e.g.:

- Machining allowances

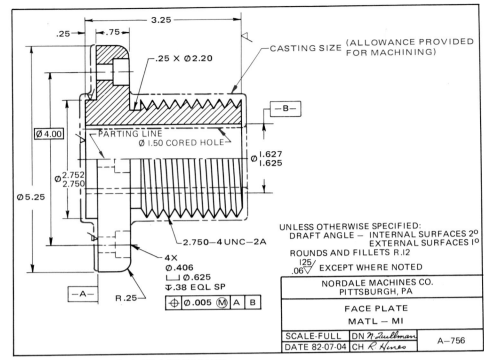

(A) WORKING DRAWING OF A CAST PART

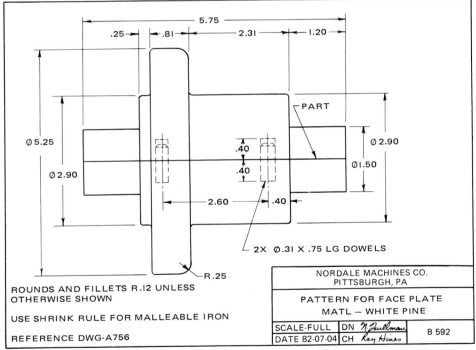

(B) PATTERN DRAWING FOR THE CAST PART SHOWN IN (A)

Fig. 11-1-20 Cast part drawings.

- Surface texture
- Draft angles
- Limits on cast surfaces that must be controlled
- Locating points
- Parting lines

On small, simple parts all casting information is included on the finished drawing. See Fig. 11-1-20. On more complicated parts, it may be necessary to show additional casting views and sections to completely illustrate the construction of the casting. These additional views should show the rough casting outline using the PHANTOM LINE LAYER LINES and the finished contour in CONTINUOUS LINE LAYER LINES.

Material In the selection of material for any particular application, the designer is influenced primarily by the physical characteristics such as strength, hardness, density, resistance to wear, mass, antifrictional properties, conductivity, corrosion resistance, shrinkage, and melting point.

Machining Allowance In the construction of patterns for castings in which various points on the surface of the casting must be machined, sufficient excess metal should be provided for all machined surfaces. Unless otherwise specified; Fig. 11-1-21 may be used as a guide to machine finish allowance.

CASTING ALLOY	DIMENSIONS WITHIN THIS RANGE	CASTING ALLOWANCE
CAST IRON, ALUMINUM, BRONZE, ETC. SAND CASTINGS	UP TO 8.00 8.00 TO 16.00 16.00 TO 24.00 24.00 TO 32.00 OVER 32.00	.06 .09 .12 .18 .25
PEARLITIC, MALLEABLE, AND STEEL SAND CASTINGS	UP TO 8.00 8.00 TO 16.00 16.00 TO 24.00 OVER 24.00	.06 .09 .18 .25
PERMANENT AND SEMIPERMANENT MOLD CASTINGS	UP TO 12.00 12.00 TO 24.00 OVER 24.00	.06 .09 .18
PLASTER MOLD CASTINGS	UP TO 8.00 8.00 TO 12.00 OVER 12.00	.03 .06 .10

Fig. 11-1-21 Guide to machining allowance for castings.

Fillets and Radii Generous fillets and radii (rounds) should be provided on cast corners and specified on the drawing.

These are easily created. First use a GRID with SNAP ON to DRAW each LINE without rounds. Using the FILLET command, select and key in the desired RADIUS, and pick two intersecting lines. Every fillet and round is quickly and accurately created using this procedure.

Casting Tolerances A great many factors contribute to the dimensional variations of castings. However, the standard drawing tolerances specified in Fig. 11-1-22 can be satisfactorily attained in the production of castings. Remember to set the appropriate DIMENSION VARIABLES prior to DIMENSIONING.

TYPE OF CASTING	DIMENSIONS WITHIN THIS RANGE	STANDARD DRAWING TOLERANCE (±)
IRON AND ALUMINUM SAND CASTINGS	UP TO 8.00 8.00 TO 16.00 16.00 TO 24.00 24.00 TO 32.00 OVER 32.00	.03 .06 .07 .09 .12
PEARLITIC, MALLEABLE IRON AND STEEL SAND CASTINGS	UP TO 8.00 8.00 TO 16.00 16.00 TO 24.00 OVER 24.00	.03 .06 .09 .12
PERMANENT MOLD CASTING (SEMIPERMANENT MOLD CASTING)	UP TO 5.00 5.00 TO 12.00 12.00 TO 24.00 OVER 24.00	.03 .03 .06 .09
PLASTER MOLD CASTING	UP TO 4.00 4.00 TO 8.00 8.00 TO 12.00 OVER 12.00	.02 .02 .03 .06
CENTRIFUGAL PRECISION CASTING	UP TO .50 .50 TO 5.00 OVER 5.00	.02 .02 .02

Fig. 11-1-22 Guide to casting tolerances.

Draft All casting methods require a draft or taper on all surfaces perpendicular to the parting line, to facilitate removal of the pattern and ejection of the casting. The permissible draft must be specified on the drawing, in either degrees of taper for each surface, inches of taper per inch of length, or millimeters of taper per millimeter of length.

Suitable draft angles for general use, for both sand and die castings, are 1° for external surfaces and 2° for internal surfaces, as shown in Fig. 11-1-23.

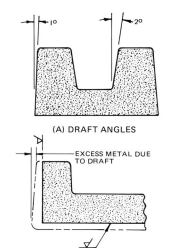

(A) DRAFT ANGLES

(B) DRAFT AND MACHINING ALLOWANCE

Fig. 11-1-23 Draft for removal of pattern from mold.

The drawing must always clearly indicate whether the draft should be added to, or subtracted from, the casting dimensions.

CASTING DATUMS

It is recognized that in many cases a drawing is made of the fully machined end product; and casting dimensions, draft, and machining allowances are left entirely to the patternmaker or foundry worker. However, for mass-production purposes it is generally advisable to make a separate casting drawing, with carefully selected datums, to ensure that parts will fit into machining jigs and fixtures and will meet final requirements after machining. Under these circumstances, dimensioning requires the selection of two sets of datum surfaces, lines, or points—one for the casting and one for the machining—to provide common reference points for measuring, machining, and assembly. To select suitable datums, it will be necessary to know how the casting is to be made, where the parting line or lines are to be, and how the part is going to fit into machining jigs and fixtures.

The first step in dimensioning is to select a primary datum surface for the casting, which is sometimes referred to as the *base* surface, and to identify it as datum A. See Fig. 11-1-24. This primary datum should be a surface which meets the following criteria as closely as possible:

1. It must be a surface, or datum targets on a surface (see Fig. 11-1-25), which can be used as the basis for measuring the casting and which can later be used for mounting and locating the part in a jig or fixture, for the purpose of machining the finished part.
2. It should be a surface which will not be removed by machining, so that control of material to be removed is

not lost, and can be checked at final inspection.

3. It should be parallel with the top of the mold, or parting line; that is, a surface which has no draft or taper.
4. It should be integral with the main body of the casting, so that measurements from it to the main surfaces of the casting will be least affected by cored surfaces, parting lines, or gated surfaces.
5. It should be a surface, or target areas on a surface, on which the part can be clamped without causing any distortion, so that the casting will not be under a distortional stress for the first machining operation.
6. It should be a surface which will provide locating points as far apart as possible, so that the effect of any flatness error will be minimized.

The second step is to select two other planes to serve as secondary and tertiary surfaces. These planes should be at right angles to one another and to the primary datum surface. They probably will not coincide with actual surfaces, because of taper or draft, except at one point, usually a point adjacent to the primary datum surface. These are identified as datum B and datum C, respectively, as shown in Fig. 11-1-26.

In the case of a circular part, the end-view center lines may be selected as secondary and tertiary datums, as shown in Fig. 11-1-27. In this case, unless otherwise specified, the center lines represent the center of the outside or overall diameter of the part.

MACHINING DATUMS

The first step in dimensioning the machined or finished part is to select a primary datum surface for machining and to identify it as datum D. This surface is the first surface on the casting to be machined and is thereafter used as

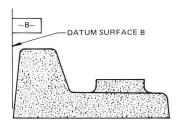

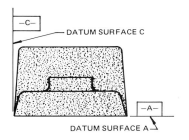

Fig. 11-1-24 Casting datums.

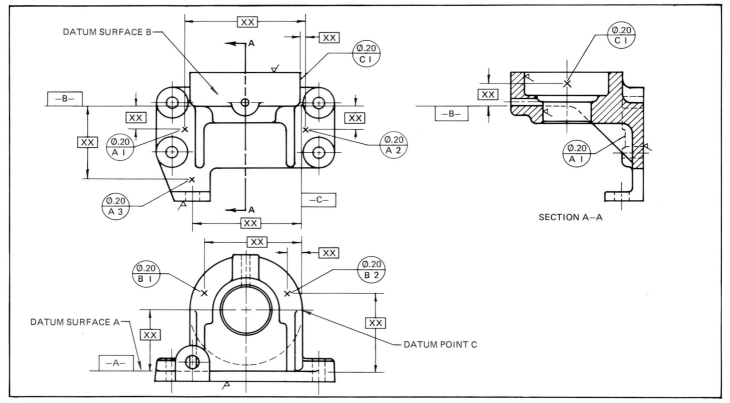

Fig. 11-1-25 Machined cast drawing illustrating datum lines, setup points, and surface finish.

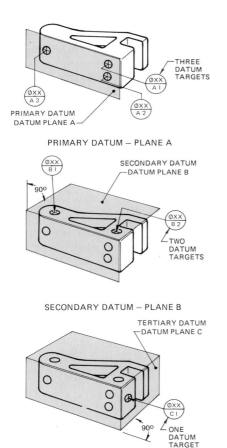

PRIMARY DATUM — PLANE A

SECONDARY DATUM — PLANE B

TERTIARY DATUM — PLANE C

Fig. 11-1-26 Datum planes and datum targets.

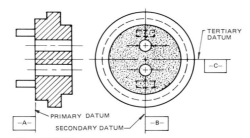

Fig. 11-1-27 Datums for circular casting.

the datum surface for all other machining operations. It should be selected to meet the following criteria:

1. It is generally preferable, though not essential, that it be a surface which is parallel to the primary casting datum surface.
2. It may be a large, flat, machined surface or several small areas of surfaces in the same or parallel planes.
3. If the primary casting datum surface is smooth and does not require machining, as in die castings, or if suitable target areas have been selected, the same surface may be used as the machining datum surface.

4. If the primary casting datum surface of sand castings appears to be the only suitable surface, it is recommended that three or four pads be provided, which can be machined to form the machining datum surface, as shown in Fig. 11-1-28.

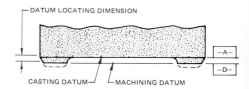

Fig. 11-1-28 Primary machining datums.

5. When pads or small target areas are selected, they should be placed as far apart as possible and located where the part can be readily clamped in jigs or fixtures without distorting it or interfering with other machining operations.

The second step is to select two other surfaces to serve as secondary and tertiary datums. If these datum surfaces are required only for locating and dimensioning purposes, and not for clamping in a jig or fixture, some suitable datums other than flat, machined surfaces may be chosen. These could be the same datums as used for casting, if the locating point in each case is clearly defined and is not removed in machining. For circular parts, a hole drilled in the center, or a turned diameter other than the outside diameter, may provide suitable center lines for use as secondary datum surfaces, as shown in Fig. 11-1-29.

The third step is to specify the *datum-locating dimension*, that is, DIMENSION between each casting datum surface and the corresponding machining datum surface. See Fig. 11-1-28. There is never more than one such dimension from each casting datum surface.

Dimensions

When suitable datum surfaces have been selected, with datum-locating di-

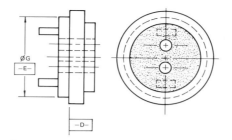

Fig. 11-1-29 Machining datums for circular parts.

mensions for the machined casting drawing, dimensioning may proceed, with dimensions being specified directly from the datums to all main surfaces. However, where it is necessary to maintain a particular relationship between two or more surfaces or features, the use of CONTINUOUS LINEAR DIMENSIONS is usually

the preferred method. This will generally include all such items as thickness of ribs, height of bosses, projections, depth of grooves, most diameters and radii, and center distances between holes and similar features. Whenever possible, specify dimensions to surfaces or surface intersections, rather than to radii centers or nonexistent center lines.

Dimensions given on the casting drawing should not be repeated, except as reference dimensions, on the machined part drawing.

References and Source Material

1. American Iron and Steel Institute, "Principles of Forging Design."
2. General Motors Corporation.
3. Meehanite Metal Corporation.

ASSIGNMENTS

See Assignments 1 through 3 for Unit 11-1 starting on page 219.

ASSIGNMENTS FOR CHAPTER 11

Assignments for Unit 11-1, Castings

1. Complete the detail drawing of the base for the adjustable shaft support assembly shown in Fig. 11-1-A. Cored holes are to be used for the shaft holes. Scale 1:1.

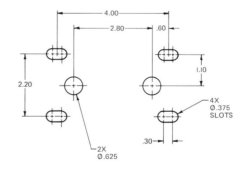

Fig. 11-1-A Adjustable shaft support.

2. Complete the detail drawing of the fork for the hinged pipe vise assembly shown in Fig. 11-1-B. Use your judgment for dimensions not given. Scale is 1:1.

3. Prepare both the casting and the machining drawings for the connector shown in Fig. 11-1-C. Draw a one-view full section, complete with the necessary dimensions for each drawing. Scale 1:1.

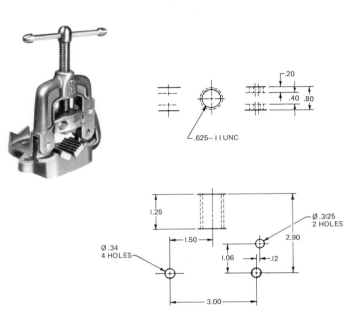

Fig. 11-1-B Pipe vise.

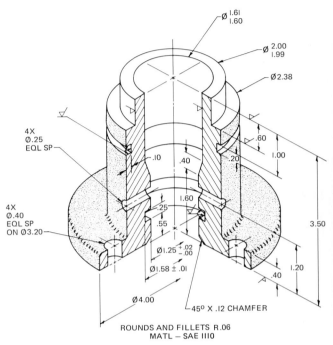

Fig. 11-1-C Connector.

12 Welding Drawings

UNIT 12-1

Designing for Welding

The primary importance of welding is to unite various pieces of metal so that they will operate as a unit structure to support the loads to be carried. In order to design such a structure, which will be both economical and efficient, the drafter must have a knowledge of the basic principles of welding practice and an understanding of the advantages and limitations of the process.

In order to produce an economical and pleasing design, the designer should endeavor to utilize the method of construction which is clearly the most advantageous for the application under consideration. This may mean a combination of welding and bolting, or even the incorporation of pressings, forgings, or even castings where they may be advantageous. The possibility of using structural steel shapes and tubes should also be kept in mind. See Fig. 12-1-1.

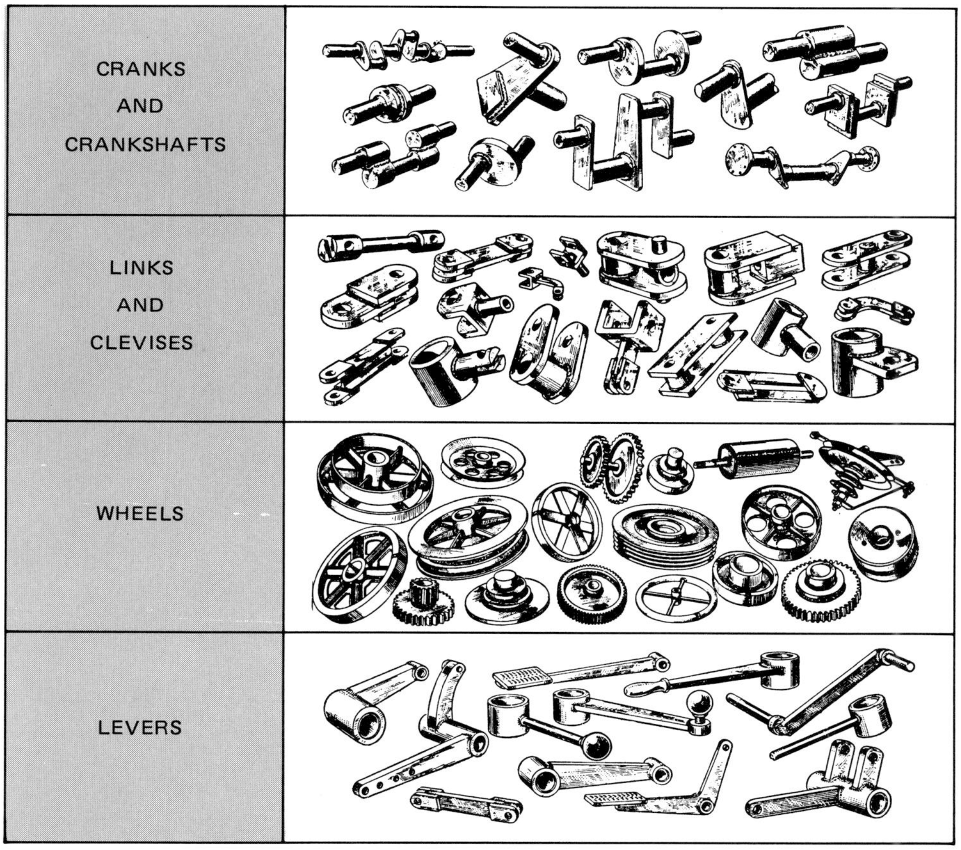

Welding Processes Of more than 40 welding processes used in industry today, only a few are industrially important. Arc welding, gas welding, and resistance welding are the three most important types of welding.

The workpieces are melted along a common edge or surface so that their molten metal—and usually a filler metal also—is allowed to form a com-

CRANKS AND CRANKSHAFTS	
LINKS AND CLEVISES	
WHEELS	
LEVERS	

Fig. 12-1-1 A variety of weldments.

mon pool or puddle. The pieces are fused when the puddle solidifies. See Figs. 12-1-2 and 12-1-3.

Gas welding, the most common form of which is oxyacetylene welding, gets its heat from the burning of

flammable gases. This process is slow compared to other modern welding methods, so gas welding is normally confined to repair and maintenance work rather than being a major mass-production technique.

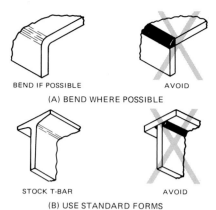

BEND IF POSSIBLE   AVOID

(A) BEND WHERE POSSIBLE

STOCK T-BAR   AVOID

(B) USE STANDARD FORMS

Fig. 12-1-2 Preferred welding design.

References and Source Material

1. American Welding Society.

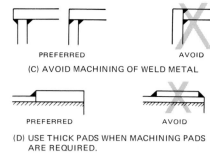

PREFERRED   AVOID

(C) AVOID MACHINING OF WELD METAL

PREFERRED   AVOID

(D) USE THICK PADS WHEN MACHINING PADS ARE REQUIRED.

2. *Machine Design,* Fastening and joining reference issue, Nov. 1981.

ASSIGNMENT

See Assignment 1 for Unit 12-1 on page 235.

Welding Symbols

The introduction of welding symbols enables the designer to indicate clearly the type and size of weld required to meet design requirements, and it is becoming increasingly important for the designer to specify the required type of weld correctly. Points which must be made clear are the type of weld, the joint preparation, the weld size, and the root opening (if any). These points can be clearly indicated on the drawing by the welding symbol. See Fig. 12-2-1.

Welding symbols are a shorthand language. They save time and money and, if used correctly, ensure under-

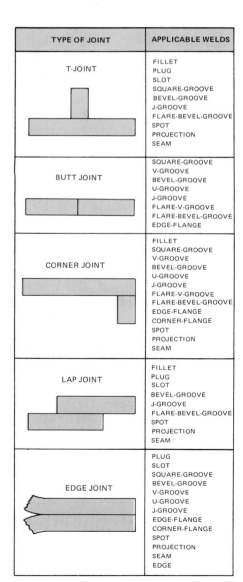

TYPE OF JOINT	APPLICABLE WELDS
T-JOINT	FILLET PLUG SLOT SQUARE-GROOVE BEVEL-GROOVE J-GROOVE FLARE-BEVEL-GROOVE SPOT PROJECTION SEAM
BUTT JOINT	SQUARE-GROOVE V-GROOVE BEVEL-GROOVE U-GROOVE J-GROOVE FLARE-V-GROOVE FLARE-BEVEL-GROOVE EDGE-FLANGE
CORNER JOINT	FILLET SQUARE-GROOVE V-GROOVE BEVEL-GROOVE U-GROOVE J-GROOVE FLARE-V-GROOVE FLARE-BEVEL-GROOVE EDGE-FLANGE CORNER-FLANGE SPOT PROJECTION SEAM
LAP JOINT	FILLET PLUG SLOT BEVEL-GROOVE J-GROOVE FLARE-BEVEL-GROOVE SPOT PROJECTION SEAM
EDGE JOINT	PLUG SLOT SQUARE-GROOVE BEVEL-GROOVE V-GROOVE U-GROOVE J-GROOVE EDGE-FLANGE CORNER-FLANGE SPOT PROJECTION SEAM EDGE

Fig. 12-1-3 Basic welding joints.

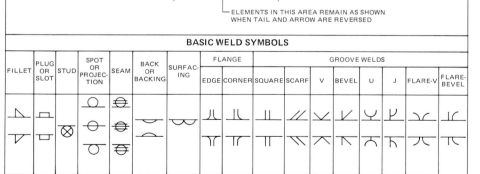

SUPPLEMENTARY SYMBOLS

	CONTOUR		BACKING OR SPACER (RECTANGULAR)	CONSUMABLE INSERT (SQUARE)	MELT THROUGH	WELD ALL AROUND	FIELD WELD
FLAT	CONVEX	CONCAVE					

FINISH SYMBOL
CONTOUR SYMBOL
GROOVE ANGLE; INCLUDED ANGLE OF COUNTERSINK FOR PLUG WELDS
GROOVE WELD SIZE
DEPTH OF PREPARATION OR SIZE OR STRENGTH FOR CERTAIN WELDS
SPECIFICATION, PROCESS, OR OTHER REFERENCE
TAIL
REFERENCE LINE
BASIC WELD SYMBOL OR DETAIL REFERENCE
NUMBER OF SPOT, STUD, OR PROJECTION WELDS

ROOT OPENING; DEPTH OF FILLING FOR PLUG AND SLOT WELDS
LENGTH OF WELD
FIELD WELD SYMBOL
WELD-ALL-AROUND SYMBOL
ARROW CONNECTING REFERENCE LINE TO ARROW SIDE MEMBER OF JOINT OR ARROW SIDE OF JOINT
PITCH (CENTER-TO-CENTER SPACING) OF WELDS

F
A
R
S(E)
T
(N)
BOTH SIDES
OTHER SIDE
ARROW SIDE
L—P

ELEMENTS IN THIS AREA REMAIN AS SHOWN WHEN TAIL AND ARROW ARE REVERSED

BASIC WELD SYMBOLS

FILLET	PLUG OR SLOT	STUD	SPOT OR PROJEC-TION	SEAM	BACK OR BACKING	SURFAC-ING	FLANGE		GROOVE WELDS						
							EDGE	CORNER	SQUARE	SCARF	V	BEVEL	U	J	FLARE-V	FLARE-BEVEL

NOTE: SIZE, WELD SYMBOL, LENGTH OF WELD AND SPACING MUST READ IN THAT ORDER FROM LEFT TO RIGHT ALONG THE REFERENCE LINE. NEITHER ORIENTATION OR REFERENCE LINE NOR LOCATION ALTER THIS RULE. THE PERPENDICULAR LEG OR ⌐V,⌐ WELD SYMBOLS MUST BE AT LEFT. SYMBOLS APPLY BETWEEN ABRUPT CHANGES IN DIRECTION OF WELDING UNLESS GOVERNED BY THE "ALL-AROUND" SYMBOL OR OTHERWISE DIMENSIONED.

Fig. 12-2-1 Welding symbols.

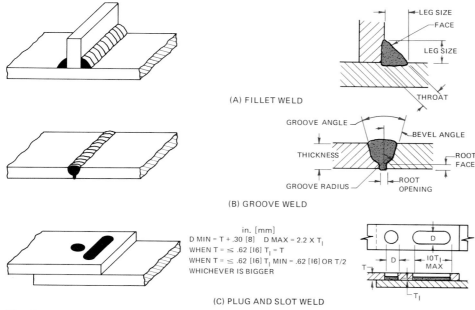

(A) FILLET WELD

GROOVE ANGLE
BEVEL ANGLE
THICKNESS
ROOT FACE
GROOVE RADIUS
ROOT OPENING

(B) GROOVE WELD

in. [mm]
D MIN = T + .30 [8]   D MAX = 2.2 X T_I
WHEN T = ≤ .62 [16] T_I = T
WHEN T = ≤ .62 [16] T_I MIN = .62 [16] OR T/2
WHICHEVER IS BIGGER

(C) PLUG AND SLOT WELD

Fig. 12-2-2 Weld terminology.

	SINGLE	DOUBLE
FILLET		
SQUARE		
BEVEL GROOVE		
V GROOVE		
J GROOVE		
U GROOVE		
FLARE-BEVEL GROOVE		
FLARE-V GROOVE		

Fig. 12-2-3 Fillet and groove welds.

mentary information and consists of the following eight elements. Not all elements need be used unless required for clarity.

1. Reference line
2. Arrow
3. Basic weld symbol
4. Dimensions and other data
5. Supplementary symbols
6. Finish symbols
7. Tail
8. Specification, process or other reference

The use of the words *far side* and *near side* in the past has led to confusion because when joints are shown in section, all welds are equally distant from the reader, and the words *near* and *far* are meaningless.

In the present system the joint is the basis of reference. Any joint, the welding of which is indicated by a symbol, will usually have an arrow side and another side. Accordingly, the words *arrow side, other side,* and *both sides* are used here to locate the weld with respect to the joint. See Fig. 12-2-4.

The tail of the symbol is used for designating the welding specifications, procedures, or other supplementary information to be used in the making of the weld. See Fig. 12-2-5.

The use of letters can designate different welding and cutting processes. See Figs. 12-2-6 and 12-2-7.

standing and accuracy. It is desirable that they should be a universal language; and for this reason the symbols of the American Welding Society, which are already well established, have been adopted. See Figs. 12-2-2 and 12-2-3.

A distinction between the terms *weld symbol* and *welding symbol* should be understood. The weld symbol indicates the type of weld. The welding symbol is a method of representing the weld on drawings. It includes supple-

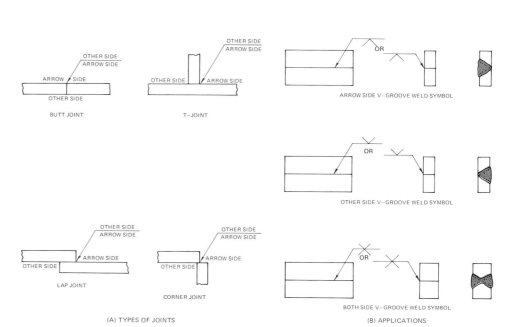

(A) TYPES OF JOINTS

BUTT JOINT
T-JOINT
LAP JOINT
CORNER JOINT

ARROW SIDE V—GROOVE WELD SYMBOL
OTHER SIDE V—GROOVE WELD SYMBOL
BOTH SIDE V—GROOVE WELD SYMBOL

(B) APPLICATIONS

Fig. 12-2-4 Arrow side and other side of joint.

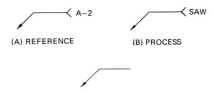

Fig. 12-2-5 Location of reference and processes on welding symbols.

DESIGNATION	WELDING PROCESS
CAW	Carbon-Arc Welding
CW	Cold Welding
DB	Dip Brazing
DFW	Diffusion Welding
EBW	Electron Beam Welding
ESW	Electroslag Welding
EXW	Explosion Welding
FB	Furnace Brazing
FCAW	Flux Cored Arc Welding
FOW	Forge Welding
FRW	Friction Welding
FW	Flash Welding
GMAW.	Gas Metal Arc Welding
GTAW	Gas Tungsten Arc Welding
IB	Induction Brazing
IRB.	Infrared Brazing
IW.	Induction Welding
LBW	Laser Beam Welding
OAW.	Oxyacetylene Welding
OHW	Oxyhydrogen Welding
PAW	Plasma Arc Welding
PEW	Percussion Welding
PGW	Pressure Gas Welding
PW	Projection Welding
RB	Resistance Brazing
RSEW	Resistance Seam Welding
RSW	Resistance Spot Welding
SAW	Submerged Arc Welding
SMAW	Shielded Metal Arc Welding
SW	Stud Welding
TB	Torch Brazing
TW	Thermit Welding
USW	Ultrasonic Welding
UW	Upset Welding

Fig. 12-2-6 Designation of welding processes by letters.

DESIGNATION	CUTTING PROCESS
AAC	Air-Carbon Arc Carbon
AC	Arc Cutting
AOC	Oxygen Arc Cutting
CAC	Carbon Arc Cutting
FOC	Chemical Flux Cutting
MAC	Metal-Arc Cutting
OC	Oxygen Cutting
PAC	Plasma Arc Cutting
POC	Metal Powder Cutting

Fig. 12-2-7 Designation of cutting processes by letters.

Location Significance of Arrow

1. In the case of fillet, groove, and flanged weld symbols, the arrow connects the welding symbol refer-ence line to one side of the joint, and this side is considered the *arrow side* of the joint. The side opposite the arrow side of the joint is considered the *other side* of the joint.
2. When a joint is depicted by a single line on the drawing and the arrow of a welding symbol is directed to this line, the arrow side of the joint is considered the *near side* of the joint.
3. In the case of plug, slot, spot, projection and seam weld symbols, the arrow connects the welding symbol reference line to the outer surface of one of the members of the joints at the center line of the desired weld. The member to which the arrow points is the *arrow-side* member. The remaining member of the joint is considered the *other-side* member.

Symbols with No Side Significance Some weld symbols have no arrow side or other side significance, although supplementary symbols used in conjunction with them may have such significance.

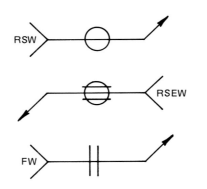

Orientation of Specific Weld Symbols Fillet, bevel-groove, J-groove, flare-bevel-groove, and corner-flange weld symbols are drawn with the perpendicular leg always to the left.

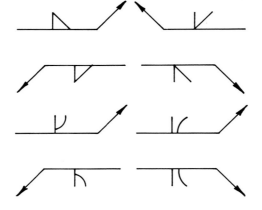

Break in Arrow When only one member of a joint is to be prepared, the arrow shall have a break, and point toward that member. See Fig. 12-2-8. If it is obvious which member is to be prepared, or there is no preference as to which member is to be prepared, the arrow need not be broken.

Location of Weld Symbol with Respect to Joint

1. Welds on the arrow side of the joint are shown by placing the weld symbol below the reference line.

2. Welds on the other side of the joint are shown by placing the weld symbol above the reference line.

3. Welds on both sides of the joint are shown by placing the weld symbol on both sides of the reference line.

Use of Weld-All-Around Symbol

A weld extending completely around a joint is indicated by means of a weld-all-around symbol placed at the intersection of the reference line and the arrow. See Fig. 12-2-9, examples 1 and 2.

Welds extending around the circumference of a pipe are excluded from the requirement regarding changes in direction and do not require the weld-all-around symbol to specify a continuous weld. See Fig. 12-2-9, example 3.

Use of Field Weld Symbol

Field welds (welds not made in a shop or at the place of initial construction) are indicated by means of the field weld symbol placed at the intersection of the reference line and the arrow. The flag is placed above and at right angles to the reference line and always points toward the tail of the arrow. See Fig. 12-2-10.

DRAWING CALLOUT	INTERPRETATION

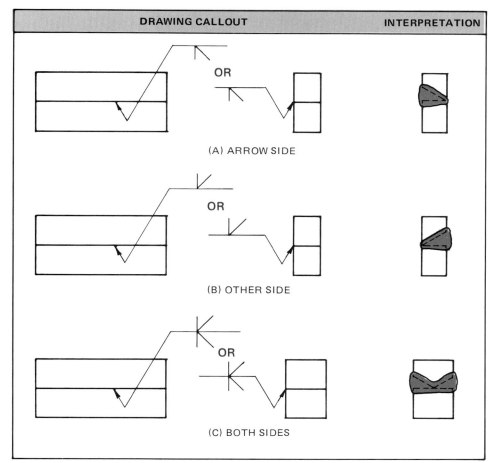

(A) ARROW SIDE

(B) OTHER SIDE

(C) BOTH SIDES

Fig. 12-2-8 Application of break in arrow of welding symbol.

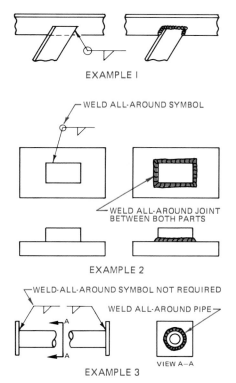

EXAMPLE I

WELD ALL-AROUND SYMBOL

WELD ALL-AROUND JOINT BETWEEN BOTH PARTS

EXAMPLE 2

WELD-ALL-AROUND SYMBOL NOT REQUIRED

WELD ALL-AROUND PIPE

VIEW A–A

DRAWING CALLOUT   DESIRED WELD

Fig. 12-2-9 Application of weld all-around.

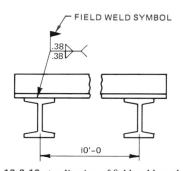

FIELD WELD SYMBOL

Fig. 12-2-10 Application of field weld symbols.

Combined Weld Symbols

For joints having more than one weld, a symbol is shown for each weld. See Fig. 12-2-11.

Contours Obtained by Welding

Welds that are to be welded with approximately flush or convex faces without postweld finishing are specified by adding the flush or convex

contour symbol to the welding symbol.

FLAT   CONVEX   CONCAVE

Finishing of Welds

Welds whose faces are to be finished flush or convex by postweld finishing are specified by adding both the appropriate contour and finishing symbol to the welding symbol.

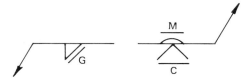

The following finishing symbols may be used to specify the method of finishing, but not the degree of finishing:

C = Chipping
G = Grinding
M = Machining
R = Rolling
H = Hammering

An application of a weld requiring postweld finishing is shown in Fig. 12-2-12.

Multiple Reference Lines

Two or more reference lines may be used to indicate a sequence of operations. The first operation is specified

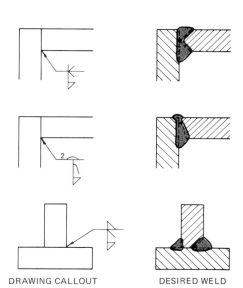

DRAWING CALLOUT   DESIRED WELD

Fig. 12-2-11 Combined welding symbols.

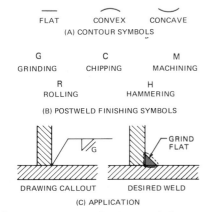

FLAT CONVEX CONCAVE
(A) CONTOUR SYMBOLS

G   C   M
GRINDING CHIPPING MACHINING

R   H
ROLLING   HAMMERING

(B) POSTWELD FINISHING SYMBOLS

DRAWING CALLOUT   DESIRED WELD

(C) APPLICATION

GRIND FLAT

Fig. 12-2-12 Welding finishing symbols.

on the reference line nearest the arrow. Subsequent operations are specified sequentially on other reference lines.

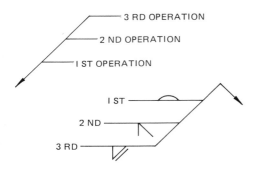

3 RD OPERATION
2 ND OPERATION
I ST OPERATION

I ST
2 ND
3 RD

Tail of Welding Symbol

The welding and allied process to be used may be specified by placing the appropriate letter designations from Figs. 12-2-6 and 12-2-7 in the tail of the welding symbol.

The tail of additional reference lines may be used to specify data supplementary to welding symbol information.

When no references are required, the tail may be omitted from the welding symbol.

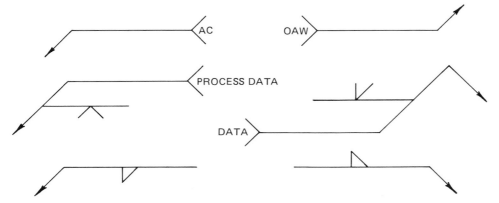

AC

OAW

PROCESS DATA

DATA

THE DESIGN OF WELDED JOINTS

Since loads are transferred from one member to another through the welds on a fabricated assembly, the type of joint and weld is specified by the designer. Figure 12-2-4 shows basic joint and weld types. Specifying the joint does not by itself describe the type of weld to be used. Several types of welds may be used for making a joint.

The fillet weld, requiring no groove preparation, is one of the most commonly used welds. Corner welds are also widely used in machine design. The corner-to-corner joint, shown in Fig. 12-2-13A, is difficult to assemble because neither plate can be supported by the other. The joint also requires a larger amount of weld than the other joints illustrated. The corner joint shown in Fig. 12-2-13B is easy to assemble and requires half the amount of weld metal as the joint in Fig. 12-2-13A. However, by using half the weld size, but placing two welds, one on each side, as in Fig. 12-2-13C, it is possible to obtain the same total throat as with the first weld. Only half the weld metal is required.

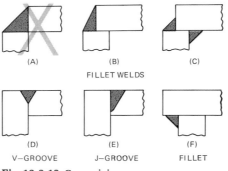

(A)   (B)   (C)

FILLET WELDS

(D)   (E)   (F)

V–GROOVE   J–GROOVE   FILLET

Fig. 12-2-13 Corner joints.

With thick plates, a partial-penetration groove joint, as in Fig. 12-2-13D, is used. This requires beveling. For a deeper joint, a J preparation, as in Fig. 12-2-13E, may be used in preference to a bevel. The fillet weld in Fig. 12-2-13F is out of sight and makes a neat and economical corner.

The size of the weld should always be designed with reference to the size of the thinner member. The joint cannot be made any stronger by using the thicker member for the weld size, and much more weld metal may be required, as illustrated in Fig. 12-2-14.

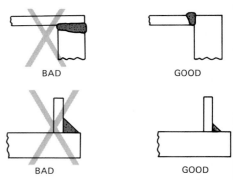

BAD   GOOD

BAD   GOOD

Fig. 12-2-14 Size of weld determined by thinner member.

The designer is frequently faced with the question of whether to use fillet or groove welds. Here cost becomes a major consideration. The fillet welds in Fig. 12-2-15A are easy to apply and require no special plate preparation.

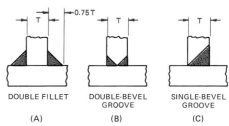

0.75 T   T   T

DOUBLE FILLET DOUBLE-BEVEL   SINGLE-BEVEL
                GROOVE   GROOVE
(A)   (B)   (C)

Fig. 12-2-15 Comparison between fillet and groove welds.

In comparison, the double-bevel groove weld in Fig. 12-2-15B has about one-half the weld area of the fillet welds. However, it requires extra preparation and the use of smaller-diameter electrodes with lower welding currents to place the initial pass without burning through. As plate thickness increases, this initial low-deposition region becomes a less important factor, and the higher cost factor decreases in significance.

Refer to Fig. 12-2-15C. It will be noted that the single-bevel groove weld requires about the same amount of weld metal as the fillet welds deposited in Fig. 12-2-15A. Thus, there is no apparent economic advantage. There are some disadvantages, though. The single-bevel joint requires bevel preparation and initially a lower deposit rate at the root of the joint. From a design standpoint, however, it offers a direct transfer of force through the joint, which means that it is probably better under fatigue loading. Although the illustrated full-strength fillet welds, having leg sizes equal to 75 percent of the plate thickness, would be sufficient, some codes have higher allowable limits for fillet welds and may require a leg size equal to the plate thickness. In this case, the cost of the fillet-welded joint may exceed the cost of a single-bevel groove in thicker plates. Also, if the joint is so positioned that the weld can be made in a flat position, a single-bevel groove weld would be less expensive than if the fillet welds were specified. As can be seen in Fig. 12-2-16, one of the fillets would have to be made in the overhead position—a costly operation.

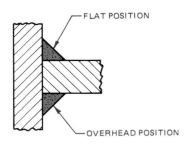

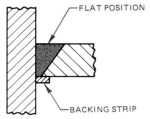

Fig. 12-2-16 In the flat position, a single-groove joint is less expensive than two fillet welds.

SYMBOL LIBRARY

Industries involved in the manufacture of mechanical products will likely have a predrawn weld symbol library available. This way the symbols never need to be drawn. They are selected from the library by specifying the appropriate command and may be placed on any drawing as often as desired.

Companies may obtain the symbol libraries from an outside source, referred to as "third-party software." This being the case, the libraries may not perform exactly the way you require for your particular application. You will want to modify the library to suit your specific needs. Consequently, knowing how to customize a library becomes important. If companies do not obtain libraries from an outside source, they must create their own. In this case you may not only need to know how to modify a library but also the procedure required to create one.

To create a library, first decide which symbols you want in it. The applications in this chapter will require the following weld symbols (Fig. 12-2-1):

Fillet
Groove (common types)

In addition, the weld-all-around, field weld, flush, convex, and concave supplementary symbols may be prepared. Before beginning, review all units in this chapter. Study the illustrations. Pay particular attention to the way each symbol appears as it is applied on a drawing. The basic symbols to be placed in the library are illustrated in Figs. 12-3-1 and 12-4-1. There are several ways to prepare the library. Each symbol, for example, may be drawn twice. One with the leader line pointing to the left and the other to the right. Another method is to draw the symbols once (except the fillet) and mirror or rotate it into position, as desired. A fillet-weld symbol is always shown with the vertical line to the left side. Thus, a mirror or rotate operation would result in it being incorrectly illustrated. A third method is to utilize the macro and parametric capability of the CADD system. This way you input the parameters for the type of symbol you want. Parametric design is beyond the scope of this text, so use one of the first two methods.

The concept of a symbol is similar to a block except more use can be made of a symbol. Symbols are created using standard commands (LINE, CIRCLE, LEADER, and so on). Instead of grouping them into a block, however, place them into a custom library (write block). This means that any symbol can be placed on any drawing. With standard blocks, the group of entities is placed or copied on only the drawing you are working with. The procedure to create a welding symbol library is:

1. Select a symbol you wish to be placed into the library (e.g., fillet weld—arrow side). Use the LEADER and LINE commands to create the symbol (See Fig. 12-3-1 top).
2. Select the WBLOCK (write block) command.
3. Key in a name for the symbol (e.g., FILLETA) and press ENTER twice.
4. Select the insertion point and each entity of the symbol.

Continue to add additional symbols into the welding library by repeating Steps 1 through 4. Remember each time to substitute the correct symbol name (Step 3). Select symbols, as necessary, from the standard tables. If you do not have a particular symbol in the library, it can be added at a later time by using this procedure. Also, if an existing symbol is incorrect, it may, at any time, be deleted and replaced with the correct one. Do this by first drawing the correct symbol. Select the LIBRARY or WBLOCK command and key in the existing name. The system will indicate that this symbol already exists. Follow the prompts to replace it with the newly drawn symbol. After the work is finished, remember to save it to disk. The symbols now stored into a library may be used as often as desired on any drawing. Insert each one, calling it up by name, selecting the desired location (insertion point), and scale. Remember hard disk space may be conserved by storing the weld symbols on a single floppy disk.

Labels may be placed on the symbols by using ATTDEF (BLOCKS). Follow the prompts to accept all defaults except for TAG and NAME (key in desired label). Next, select a point on the drawing near the symbol and key in text height & angle. When INSERTING the block by the tag it will be placed; you can add any identification at that time. These attributes may be edited using ATTEDIT.

References and Source Material

1. American Welding Society.
2. The Lincoln Electric Company.

ASSIGNMENTS

See Assignments 2 through 4 for Unit 12-2 on page 234.

UNIT 12-3

Fillet Welds

FILLET WELD SYMBOLS

Figure 12-3-1 shows the fillet weld symbol and its relative position on the reference line.

LOCATION SIGNIFICANCE	SYMBOL
ARROW SIDE	
OTHER SIDE	
BOTH SIDES	

Fig. 12-3-1 Fillet weld symbol and its location significance.

1. Dimensions of fillet welds are shown on the same side of the reference line as the weld symbol and shown to the left of the weld symbol.

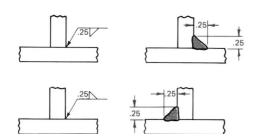

2. The dimensions of fillet welds on both sides of a joint are specified whether the dimensions are identical or different.

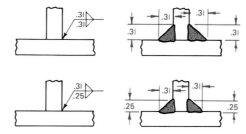

3. When there appears on a drawing a general note governing the dimension of fillet welds, such as ALL FILLET WELDS .25 IN. UNLESS OTHERWISE NOTED, and all the welds have dimensions governed by the note, the dimension need not be shown on the welding symbols.

4. When the dimensions of either arrow side or other side or both welds differ from the dimensions given in the general note, both welds are dimensioned.

5. The size of a fillet weld with unequal legs is shown to the left of the weld symbol. Weld orientation is not shown by the symbol. It is shown on the drawing when necessary.

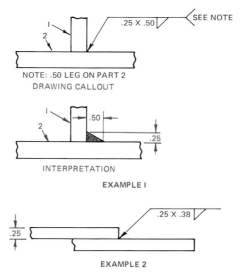

6. The length of a fillet weld, when indicated on the welding symbol, is shown to the right of the weld symbol.

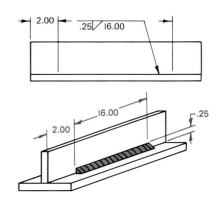

7. Specific lengths of fillet welds may be indicated by symbols in conjunction with dimension lines.

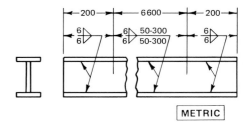

8. The pitch (center-to-center spacing) of intermittent fillet welds is shown as the distance between centers of increments on one side of the joint. It is shown to the right of the length dimension, following a hyphen.

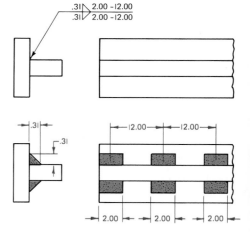

9. Staggered intermittent fillet welds are shown with the weld symbols staggered.

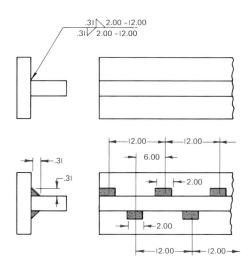

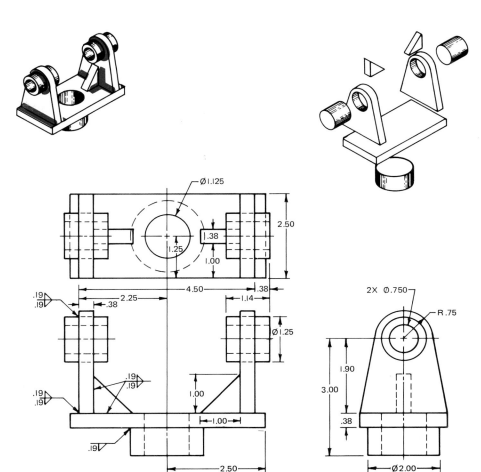

Fig. 12-3-2 Welded-steel shaft support.

10. Fillet welds that are to be welded with approximately flat, convex, or concave faces without postweld finishing are specified by adding the flat, convex, or concave contour symbol to the weld symbol.

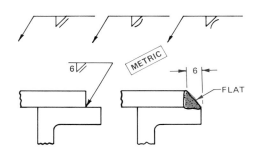

11. Fillet welds that are to be made flat-faced by mechanical means are shown by adding both the flush-contour symbol and the user's standard finish symbol.

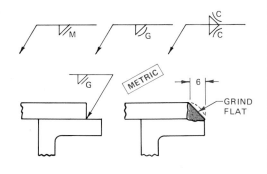

A weld assembly example is shown in Fig. 12-3-2.

SIZE OF FILLET WELDS

Figure 12-3-3 gives the sizing of fillet welds for rigidity designs at various strengths and plate thicknesses, where the strength of the weld metal matches the plate.

In machine design work, where the

DIMENSIONS IN INCHES				DIMENSIONS IN MILLIMETERS			
	Strength Design	Rigidity Design			Strength Design	Rigidity Design	
Plate Thickness	Full-strength Weld	50% Full-strength Weld	33% of Full-strength Weld	Plate Thickness	Full-strength Weld	50% Full-strength Weld	33% of Full-strength Weld
Up to .25	.12	.12	.12	Up to 6	3	3	3
.25	.19	.19	.19	6	5	5	5
.31	.25	.19	.19	8	6	5	5
.38	.31	.19	.19	10	8	5	5
.44	.38	.19	.19	11	10	5	5
.50	.38	.19	.19	12	10	5	5
.56	.44	.25	.25	14	11	6	6
.62	.50	.25	.25	16	12	6	6
.75	.56	.31	.25	20	14	8	6
.88	.62	.38	.31	22	16	10	8
1.00	.62	.38	.31	25	16	10	8
1.12	.88	.44	.31	28	22	11	8
1.25	1.00	.50	.31	32	25	12	8
1.38	1.00	.50	.38	35	25	12	10
1.50	1.12	.56	.38	38	28	14	10

Fig. 12-3-3 Rule-of-thumb fillet weld sizes where the strength of the weld metal matches the plate.

primary design requirement is rigidity, members are often made with extra-heavy sections, so that improvement under load would be within very close tolerances. The question arises of how to determine the weld size for these types of rigidity designs.

A very practical method is to design the weld for the thinner plate, making it sufficient to carry one-third to one-half the carrying capacity of the plate. This means that if the plate were stressed one-third to one-half its usual value, the weld would be of sufficient size. Most rigidity designs are stressed much below these values. However, any reduction in weld size below one-third the full-strength value would give a weld too small in appearance for general acceptance.

EXAMPLE 1 What size fillet weld is required to match the strength of the fabricated design shown in Fig. 12-3-4A?

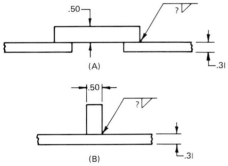

Fig. 12-3-4 Calculating fillet weld size.

SOLUTION With reference to Fig. 12-3-3, a full-strength weld is required. Thinner plate = .31 in. Fillet weld required = .25 in.

EXAMPLE 2 What size fillet weld is required to hold the rib to the plate shown in Fig. 12-3-4B? Weld design is for rigidity only, and only 33 percent of full-strength weld is required.

SOLUTION Thinner plate = .31 in. With reference to Fig. 12-3-3, the weld size under rigidity design, 33 percent across from .31 in., is .19 in.

Figure 12-3-5 illustrates a cast part which has been redesigned using welded steel members of equal strength and rigidity. The thickness of the ribs and base were reduced by approximately 50 percent due to the strength of the steel used. However, certain dimensions must not be al-

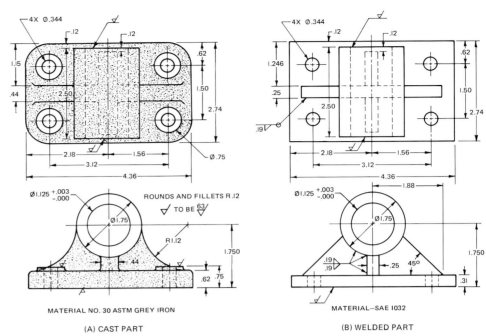

Fig. 12-3-5 Comparison of a cast shaft support with a welded-steel shaft support.

tered because the welded steel design may be used as a replacement for the cast-iron shaft support. The 1.750 in. is an example of a dimension that should not be altered.

Figure 12-3-6 shows the application

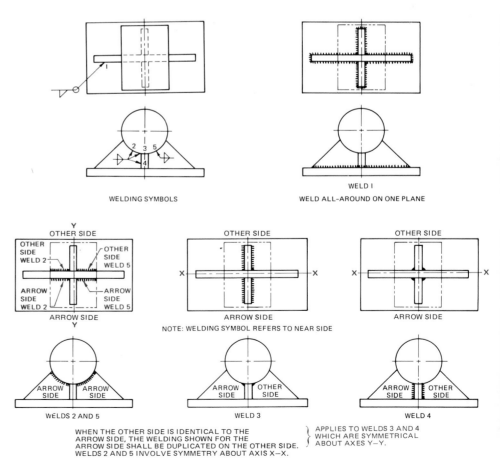

Fig. 12-3-6 Application of fillet weld for shaft support shown in Fig. 12-3-5B.

of the fillet welds for the shaft support shown in Fig. 12-3-5.

References and Source Material

1. American Welding Society.
2. The Lincoln Electric Company.

ASSIGNMENT

See Assignments 5 and 6 for Unit 12-3 starting on page 237.

 UNIT 12-4

Groove Welds

USE OF BREAK IN ARROW OF BEVEL AND J-GROOVE WELDING SYMBOLS

When a bevel or J-groove weld symbol is used, the arrow points with a definite break toward the member which is to be chamfered. In cases where the member to be chamfered is obvious,

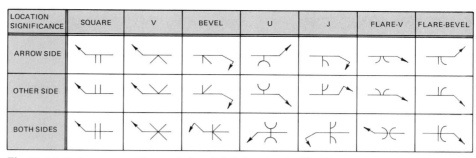

LOCATION SIGNIFICANCE	SQUARE	V	BEVEL	U	J	FLARE-V	FLARE-BEVEL
ARROW SIDE							
OTHER SIDE							
BOTH SIDES							

Fig. 12-4-1 Basic groove welding symbols and their location significance.

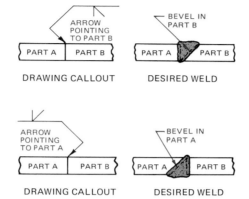

DRAWING CALLOUT — ARROW POINTING TO PART B

DESIRED WELD — BEVEL IN PART B

DRAWING CALLOUT — ARROW POINTING TO PART A

DESIRED WELD — BEVEL IN PART A

Fig. 12-4-2 Use of break in arrow.

the break in the arrow may be omitted. See Figs. 12-4-1 through 12-4-3.

GROOVE WELD SYMBOLS

1. Dimensions of groove welds are shown on the same side of the reference line as the weld symbol.

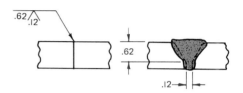

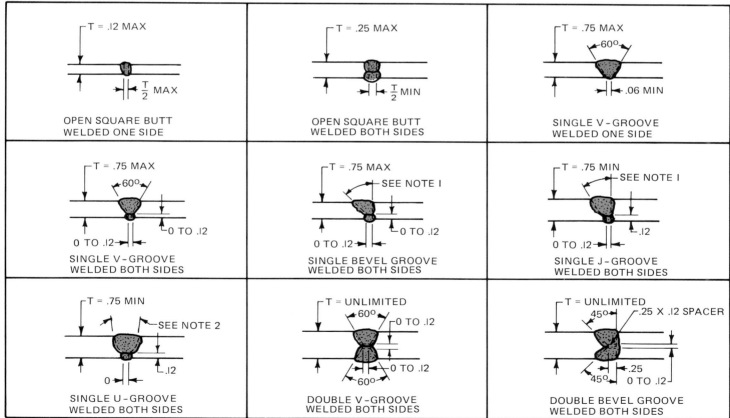

NOTE 1 – 45° ALL POSITIONS, 30° FLAT AND OVERHEAD ONLY
NOTE 2 – 45° ALL POSITIONS, 20° FLAT AND OVERHEAD ONLY

Fig. 12-4-3 Shaping and material thickness for common butt joints.

2. The dimensions of groove welds on both sides of a joint are specified whether the dimensions are the same or different. However, the root opening need appear only once.

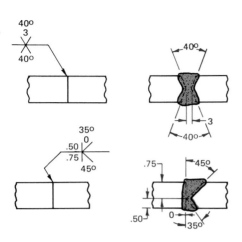

3. When there appears on the drawing a general note governing the dimensions of groove welds, such as ALL V-GROOVE WELDS ARE TO HAVE A 60° ANGLE UNLESS OTHERWISE NOTED, groove welds need not be dimensioned.

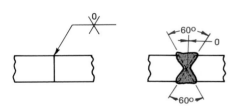

4. For bevel and groove welds, the arrow points with a definite break toward the member being beveled.

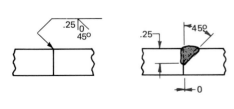

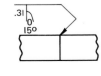 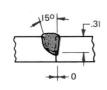

5. When the dimensions of one or both welds differ from the dimensions given in the general note, both welds are dimensioned.

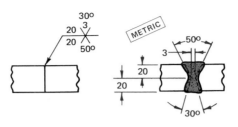

6. The size of groove welds is shown to the left of the weld symbol.

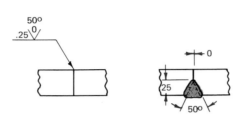

7. When the single-groove and symmetrical double-groove welds extend completely through the member or members being joined, the size of the weld need not be shown on the welding symbol.

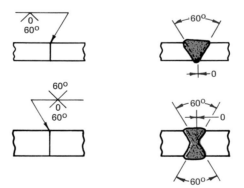

8. When the groove welds extend only partly through the member being joined, the size of the weld is shown on the welding symbol.

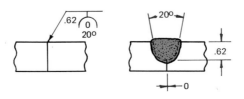

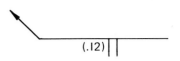

9. The depth of groove preparation and size of a groove weld (shown in brackets), when specified, are placed to the left of the weld symbol. Either or both maybe shown. See Fig. 12-4-4. Only the groove weld size is shown for square-groove welds.

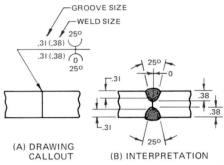

(A) DRAWING CALLOUT   (B) INTERPRETATION

Fig. 12-4-4 Groove weld symbol showing use of combined dimensions.

10. The size of flare-groove welds is considered as extending only to the tangent points. The extension beyond the point of tangency is treated as an edge or lap joint. See Fig. 12-4-5.

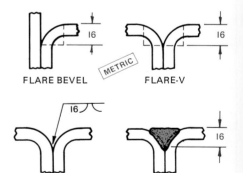

FLARE BEVEL   METRIC   FLARE-V

11. Root opening of groove welds is the user's standard unless otherwise indicated. Root opening of groove welds, when not the user's standard, is shown inside the weld symbol.

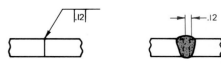

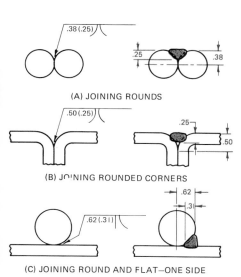

(A) JOINING ROUNDS

(B) JOINING ROUNDED CORNERS

(C) JOINING ROUND AND FLAT—ONE SIDE

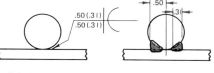

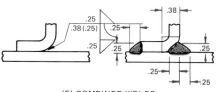

(D) JOINING ROUND AND FLAT—BOTH SIDES

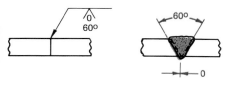

(E) COMBINED WELDS

Fig. 12-4-5 Application of flare-V and flare-bevel welds.

12. Groove angle of groove welds is the user's standard, unless otherwise indicated. Groove angle of groove welds, when not the user's standard, is shown.

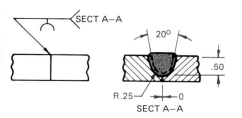

13. The groove radii and root faces of U- and J-groove welds are specified by a cross section, detail, or other data, with reference thereto in the tail of the welding symbol.

14. Groove welds that are to be welded with approximately flush or convex faces without postweld finishing are specified by adding the flush or convex contour symbol to the welding symbol.

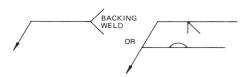

15. Groove welds whose faces are to be finished flush or convex by postweld finishing are specified by adding both the appropriate contour and finishing symbol to the welding symbol. Welds that require a flat but not flush surface, require an explanatory note in the tail of the welding symbol. Standard finishing symbols are: C = chipping, G = grinding, M = machining, R = rolling, H = hammering.

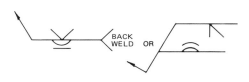

Back and Backing Welds

The back or backing weld symbol is used to indicate bead-type back or backing welds of single-groove welds.

The back and backing weld symbols are identical. The sequence of welding determines which designation applies. The back weld is made after the groove weld and the backing weld is made before the groove weld.

1. The back weld symbol is placed on the side of the reference line opposite a groove weld symbol. When a single reference line is used, "Back weld" is specified in the tail of the symbol. Alternately, if a multiple reference line is used, the back weld symbol is placed on a reference line subsequent to the reference line specifying the groove weld. See Fig. 12-4-6(A).

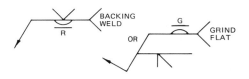

2. The backing weld symbol is placed on the side of the reference line opposite the groove weld symbol. When a single reference line is used, "backing weld" is specified in the tail of the arrow. If a multiple reference line is used, the backing-weld symbol is placed on a reference line prior to that specifying the groove weld. See Figs. 12-4-6B and C.

3. Back or backing welds that are to be welded with approximately flush or convex faces without postweld finishing are specified by adding the flush or convex contour symbol to the back or backing weld symbol.

4. Back or backing welds that are finished approximately flush or convex by postweld finishing are specified by adding the appropriate contour and finishing symbols to the back or backing weld symbol. Welds that require a flat but not flush surface require an explanatory note in the tail of the symbol.

5. A joint with backing is specified by placing the backing symbol on the side of the reference line opposite the groove-weld symbol. If the backing is to be removed after the welding, an R is placed in the backing symbol. Material and dimensions of backing are specified in the tail symbol or on the drawing. See Fig. 12-4-7A.

WELDING DRAWINGS **233**

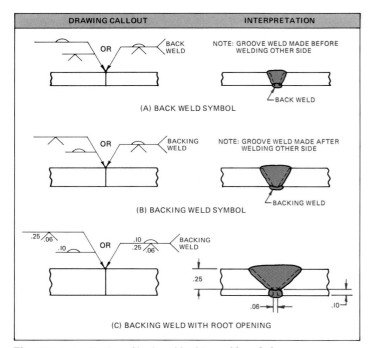

Fig. 12-4-6 Application of back and backing weld symbols.

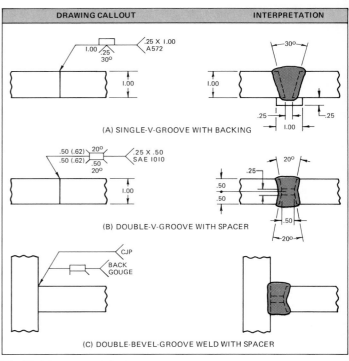

Fig. 12-4-7 Joints with backing and spacers.

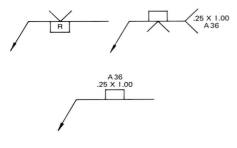

DOUBLE-V   DOUBLE-BEVEL

DOUBLE-U   DOUBLE-J

7. Consumable inserts are specified by placing the consumable insert

symbol on the side of the reference line opposite the groove weld symbol. The consumable insert class is placed in the tail of the symbol.

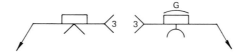

A joint requiring complete penetration involving back gouging may be specified using either a single or multiple reference line symbol. That welding symbol includes a reference to back gouging in its tail and (1) in the case of assymetrical groove welds, must show the depth of preparation from each side (see Fig. 12-4-8A and B), together with groove angles and root openings; or (2) in the case of symmetrical groove welds, need not include any other information except the weld symbol (see Fig. 12-4-8C), with groove angles and root opening.

GROOVE JOINT DESIGN

Figure 12-4-9 indicates that the root opening R is the separation between the members to be formed. A root opening is used for electrode accessibility to the base or root of the joint.

The smaller the angle of bevel, the larger the root opening must be to get good fusion at the root. If the root opening is too small, root fusion is more difficult to obtain and smaller electrodes must be used, thus slowing down the welding process.

Figure 12-4-10 indicates how the root opening must be increased as the included angle of the bevel is decreased. Backup strips are used on larger root openings. All three preparations are acceptable; all are conducive to good welding procedure and good weld quality. Selection, therefore, is usually based on cost.

Root opening and joint preparation will directly affect weld cost, and selection should be made with this in mind. Joint preparation involves the work required on plate edges prior to welding and includes beveling and providing a root face.

Using a double-groove joint in preference to a single-groove, as in Fig. 12-4-11, halves the amount of welding. This reduces distortion and makes possible alternating the weld passes on each side of the joint, again reducing distortion.

References and Source Material

1. American Welding Society.
2. Lincoln Electric Company.

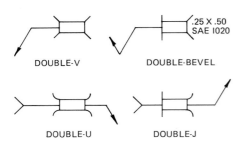

6. A joint with a required spacer is specified with the groove weld symbol modified to show a rectangle within it, (Fig. 12-4-7B). In case of multiple reference lines, the rectangle need only appear on the reference line nearest the arrow. See Fig. 12-4-7C. Material and dimensions of the spacer are specified in the tail of the symbol or on the drawing.

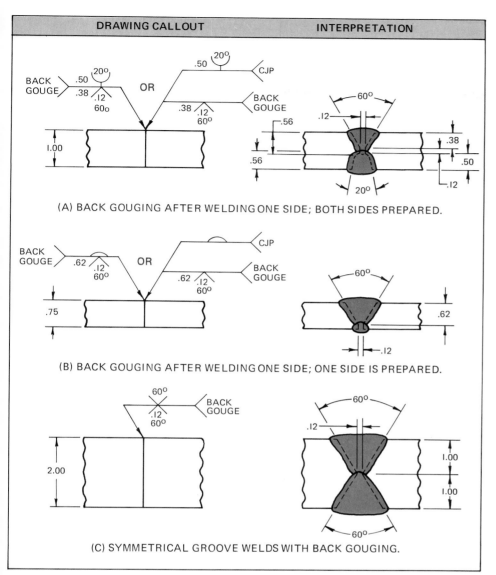

DRAWING CALLOUT — **INTERPRETATION**

(A) BACK GOUGING AFTER WELDING ONE SIDE; BOTH SIDES PREPARED.

(B) BACK GOUGING AFTER WELDING ONE SIDE; ONE SIDE IS PREPARED.

(C) SYMMETRICAL GROOVE WELDS WITH BACK GOUGING.

Fig. 12-4-8 Groove welds with back gauging.

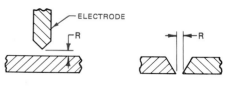

Fig. 12-4-9 Root openings.

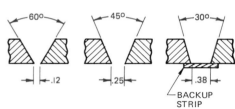

Fig. 12-4-10 Root opening increases as the angle decreases.

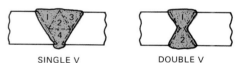

SINGLE V — DOUBLE V

Fig. 12-4-11 Single-V weld uses twice as much weld material as double-V weld.

ASSIGNMENT

See Assignments 7 and 8 for Unit 12-4 starting on page 239.

ASSIGNMENTS FOR CHAPTER 12

Assignment for Unit 12-1, Designing for Welding

1. Redesign one of the cast parts shown in Fig. 12-1-A or 12-1-B for fabrication by welding, using standard metal sizes and shapes. Make a detail assembly drawing. Welding symbols or sizes are not required. Include on the drawing the identity of each part on the assembly. Scale 1:1.

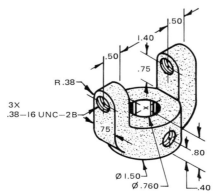

Fig. 12-1-A Pivot arm.

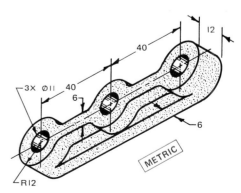

Fig. 12-1-B Link.

Assignments for Unit 12-2, Welding Symbols

2. Complete the enlarged views of the welded joints for the drawing callouts shown in Fig. 12-2-A. Use notes to explain any additional welding requirements.

3. Add the information shown above Fig. 12-2-B to the seven welding symbols shown in this figure.

4. Create a weld symbol library. Select symbols, as assigned by your instructor, from Figs. 12-3-1 and 12-4-1. Save the library on a floppy disk so it may be used in later assignments.

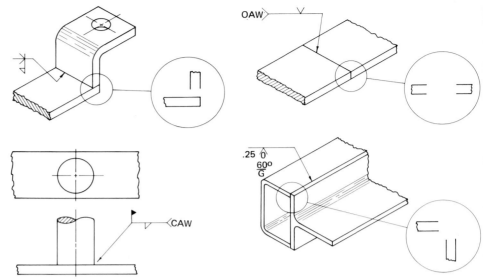

Fig. 12-2-A Showing weld type and proportion on drawings.

Weld	Welding Process Required	Type of Weld	Additional Requirements
1	Carbon-Arc Welding	Bevel	
2	Oxyacetylene Welding	Double Fillet	Both Sides Field Weld
3	Oxyacetylene Welding	Fillet	Both Sides
4	No Specifications Required	J Groove	
5	Carbon-Arc Welding	Fillet	All Around
6	Carbon-Arc Welding	Fillet	All Around Field Weld
7	Gas Metal-Arc Welding	Double V-Groove	

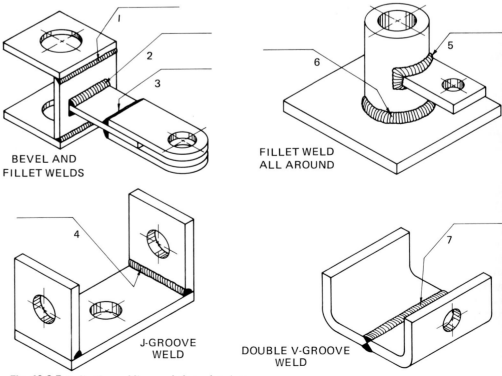

Fig. 12-2-B Indicating welding symbols on drawings.

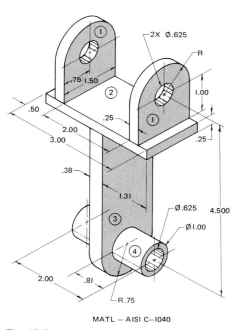

Fig. 12-3-A Swing bracket.

MATL — AISI C—1040

Assignment for Unit 12-3, Fillet Welds

5. Select one of the problems shown in Figs. 12-3-A to 12-3-D and make a two-view working drawing complete with dimensions and welding symbols. Include on the drawing an item list and identify each part on the assembly. Use full-strength welds. Scale 1:1.

6. With reference to Fig. 12-3-E, complete the welding symbols shown to the right of the desired welds.

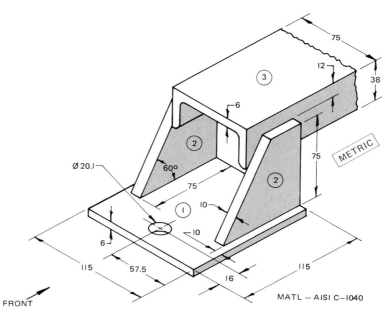

FRONT

Fig. 12-3-B Step bracket.

MATL — AISI C—1040

METRIC

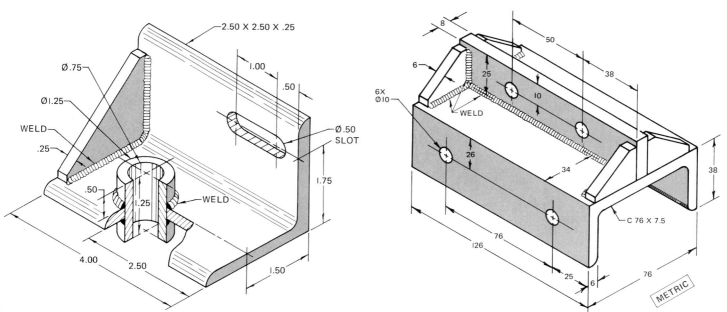

Fig. 12-3-C Slide bracket.

Fig. 12-3-D Caster frame.

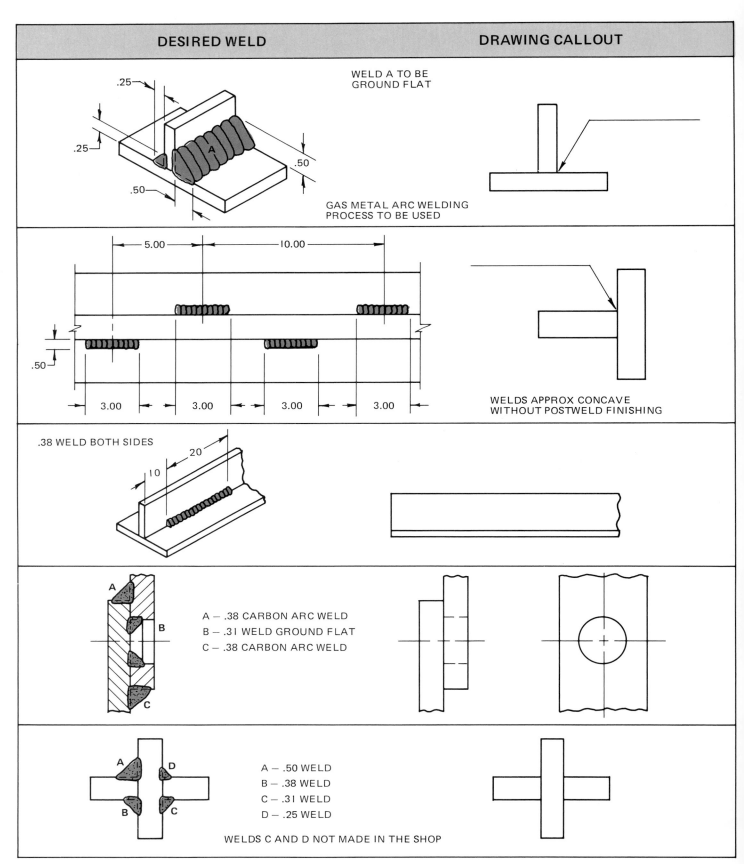

DESIRED WELD	DRAWING CALLOUT

WELD A TO BE
GROUND FLAT

.25

.25

.50

.50

GAS METAL ARC WELDING
PROCESS TO BE USED

5.00   10.00

.50

3.00   3.00   3.00   3.00

WELDS APPROX CONCAVE
WITHOUT POSTWELD FINISHING

.38 WELD BOTH SIDES

20

10

A — .38 CARBON ARC WELD
B — .31 WELD GROUND FLAT
C — .38 CARBON ARC WELD

A — .50 WELD
B — .38 WELD
C — .31 WELD
D — .25 WELD

WELDS C AND D NOT MADE IN THE SHOP

Fig. 12-3-E Fillet weld symbols.

Assignment for Unit 12-4, Groove Welds

7. Select one of the problems shown in Figs. 12-4-A through 12-4-D and make a working drawing complete with dimensions and welding symbols. Include on the drawing the identity of each part on the assembly. Use full-strength welds. Scale 1:1, or as shown. A comparison of a cast and welded steel part is shown in Fig. 12-3-5. For Fig. 12-4-A dimension the keyseat to the opposite side of the hole as shown in Table 24, Appendix B.

8. With reference to Fig. 12-4-E, prepare detailed sketches of the groove welds from the information shown.

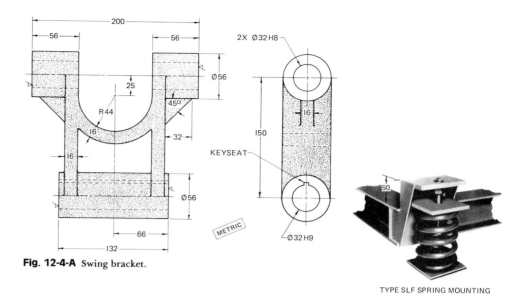

Fig. 12-4-A Swing bracket.

TYPE SLF SPRING MOUNTING

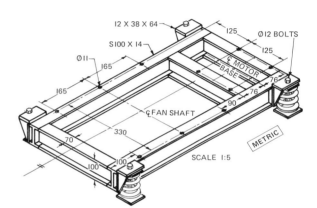

Fig. 12-4-B Connecting link.

Fig. 12-4-C Fan and motor base.

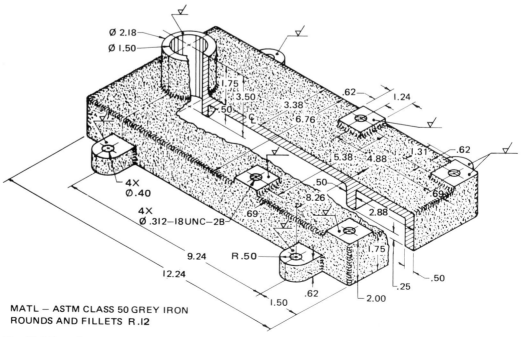

MATL — ASTM CLASS 50 GREY IRON
ROUNDS AND FILLETS R.12

Fig. 12-4-D Drill press base.

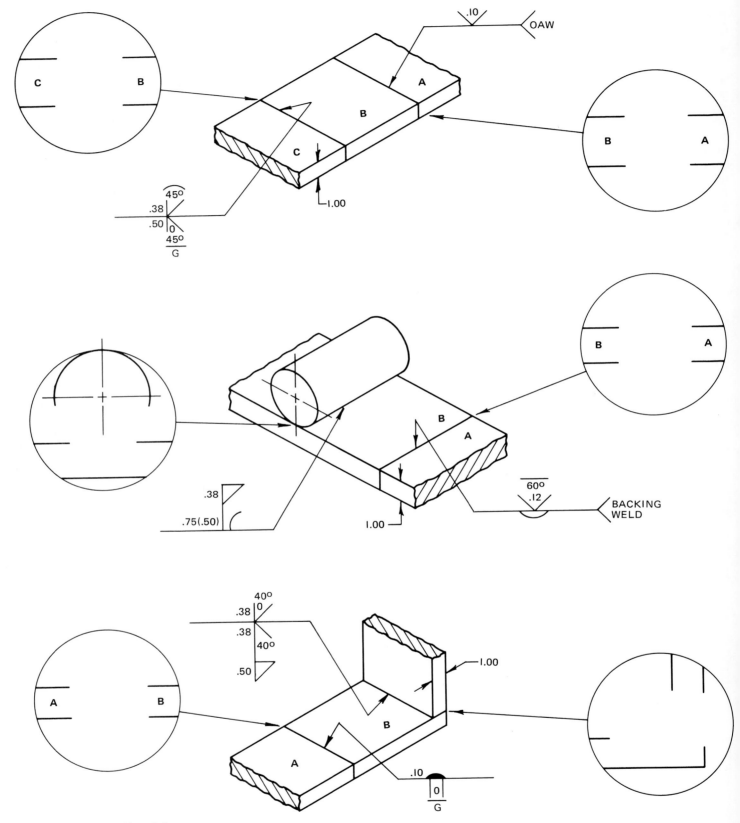

Fig. 12-4-E Groove weld symbols.

Working Drawings and Design

CHAPTER

13

Detail and Assembly Drawings

■ UNIT 13-1

Detail Drawings

A *working drawing* is a drawing that supplies information and instructions for the manufacture or construction of machines or structures. Generally, working drawings may be classified into two groups: detail drawings, which provide the necessary information for the manufacture of the parts, and assembly drawings, which supply the necessary information for their assembly.

Since working drawings may be sent to other companies to make or assemble the parts, the drawings should conform with the drawing standards of that company. For this reason, most companies follow the drawing standards of their country. The drawing standards recommended by the American National Standards Institute (ANSI) have been adopted by the majority of industries in the United States.

DETAIL DRAWINGS

A detail drawing (Fig. 13-1-1) must supply the complete information for the construction of a part. This information may be classified under three headings: shape description, size description, and specifications.

Shape Description This term refers to the selection and number of views to show or describe the shape of the part. The part may be shown in either pictorial or orthographic projection, the latter being used more frequently. Sectional views, auxiliary views, and enlarged detail views may be added to the drawing in order to provide a clearer image of the part. A multitude of CAD commands must be combined to produce the shape of a complicated detail. The sequence of execution must be effectively developed for full CAD competency.

There are other SETTINGS avail-

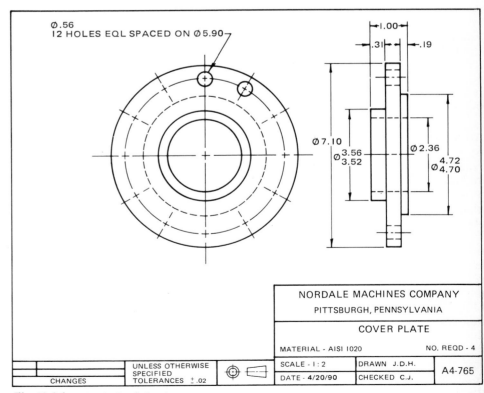

Fig. 13-1-1 A simple detail drawing.

NORDALE MACHINES COMPANY
PITTSBURGH, PENNSYLVANIA
COVER PLATE
MATERIAL - AISI 1020   NO. REQD - 4
UNLESS OTHERWISE SPECIFIED TOLERANCES ±.02
CHANGES
SCALE - 1 : 2   DRAWN J.D.H.
DATE - 4/20/90   CHECKED C.J.
A4-765

able which may facilitate development. While they are not widely used each one may be helpful for a particular application. These SETTINGS options include:

- DDEMODES (DDLMODES)—The selection will provide a dialogue box to edit: COLOR, LAYER, LINETYPE, ELEVATION, THICKNESS
- DDRMODES—Changes—GRID, SNAP, AXIS, ISOPLANE toggles—BLIP, ORTHO, AXIS, GRID, SNAP
- AXIS—By keying in an increment it will add X and Y ruler marks for reference
- UCS/KON—Toggle OFF to remove screen axis marker

Size Description Dimensions which show the size and location of the shape features are then added to the drawing. The manufacturing process will influence the selection of some dimensions, such as datum features. Tolerances are then selected for each dimension. Be sure to set the DIMVARS to tolerance ON when setting upper and lower tolerance limits.

Specifications This term refers to general notes, material, heat treatment, finish, general tolerances, and number required. This information is located on or near the title block or strip. Use a TEXT HEIGHT multiple equal to the reciprical of the plot scale reduction, e.g. use .50 in. for 1:4 reduction and DIMSCALE of 4.

Additional Drawing Information In addition to the information pertaining to the part, a detail drawing includes additional information such as drawing number, scale, method of projection, date, name of part or parts, and the drafter's name.

The selection of plot scale is determined by the number of views selected, the number of general notes required, and the drawing LIMITS used. If the drawing is to be microfilmed, then the lettering size and dimscale would be readjusted. The drawing number usually carries a prefix or suffix number or letter to indicate the sheet size of the plot such as A-571 or 4-571; the letter A indicates that it is made on an 11.00 × 8.50 in.

sheet, and the number 4 indicates that the drawing is made on a 297 × 210 mm sheet.

DRAWING CHECKLIST

As an added precaution against errors occurring on a drawing, many companies have provided checklists for drafters to follow before a drawing is issued to the shop. A typical checklist may be as follows:

1. *Dimensions.* Is the part fully dimensioned, and are the dimensions clearly positioned? Is the drawing dimensioned to avoid unnecessary shop calculations?
2. *Scale.* Is the drawing to scale? What will the plot scale be? Is it shown?
3. *Tolerances.* Are the clearances and tolerances specified by the linear and angular dimensions and by local, general, or title block notes suitable for proper functioning? Are they realistic? Can they be liberalized?
4. *Standards.* Have standard parts, design, materials, processes, or other items been used where possible?
5. *Surface Texture.* Have surface roughness values been shown where required? Are the values shown compatible with overall design requirements?
6. *Material.* Have proper material and heat treatment been specified?
7. *Inquiry.* You may wish to determine some information from the drawing data base. The INQUIRY options that you may use for this purpose include:

- AREA—Select each perimeter vertex for AREA and PERIMETER. Helpful in ordering the correct amount of material (e.g., pattern)
- LIST—Select object(s) for information. Various coordinate locations may be useful for CAD/CAM applications (Chapter 14).
- DBLIST—All coordinate information for every entity will be scrolled on screen.
- DIST—Select the length of any line—All coordinate information (X, Y, Z, length, and angle) will be displayed.

- ID—Select any point using an OSNAP option (e.g., NODE]. Coordinate location (X, Y, Z) will be displayed.
- STATUS and TIME—Displays drawing parameters and time expenditure.

Qualifications of a Detail CAD Drafter

The CAD drafter or detailer should have a thorough understanding of materials, shop processes, and operations in order to properly dimension the part and call for the correct finish and material. In addition, the detailer must have a thorough knowledge of how the part functions in order to provide the correct data and tolerances for each dimension.

The detailer may be called upon to work from a complete set of instructions and drawings, or he or she may be required to make working drawings of parts which involve the design of the part.

The detailer must know how to "preplan the drawing." Proper preplanning will unleash the power of CAD to be utilized to its fullest advantage. Detailers know that drawings "are built," not drawn. Fully using the sophistication of CAD to build drawings qualifies you as a competent CAD detail drafter.

MANUFACTURING METHODS

The type of manufacturing process will influence the selection of material and detailed feature of a part. See Fig. 13-1-2. For example, if the part is to be cast, rounds and fillets using FILLETS will be added. Additional material will also be required where surfaces are to be finished.

The more common manufacturing processes are machining from standard stock; prefabrication which includes welding, riveting, soldering, brazing; casting; and forging. The latter two processes are justifiable only when large quantities are required and for specially designed parts. All these processes have been described in detail in other chapters.

Several drawings may be made for the same part, each one giving only the

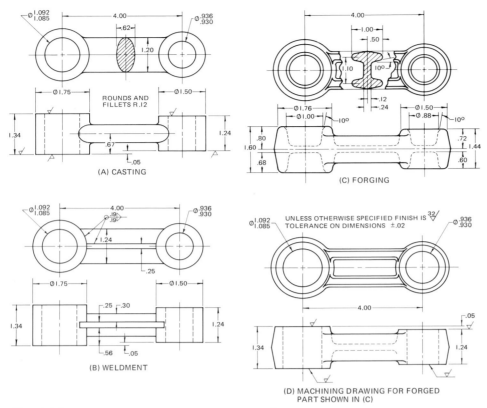

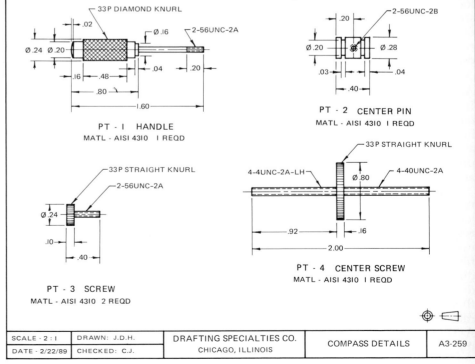

Three separate detail sheets — one for wood parts, one for fiber parts, and the third for the metal parts — may be drawn. These parts would be made in the different shops and sent to another area for assembly. In order to facilitate assembly, each part is given an identification part number which is shown on the assembly drawing. A typical detail drawing showing multiple parts is illustrated in Fig. 13-2-1.

If the details are few, the assembly drawing may appear on the same sheet. Often, for clarity, it is desired to illustrate details at a larger scale. One method to achieve this is to create and dimension the detail at full scale, BLOCK it, and INSERT it at the desired magnification. When using enlarged details preplan and prepare a "mock-up" sketch prior to starting the CAD drawing. The sketch will show the assembly and all details (at their enlargement). This will determine if the limits and plot scale are correctly made.

ASSIGNMENT

See Assignment 5 and 6 for Unit 13-2 on page 249.

Fig. 13-1-2 Manufacturing process influences the shape of the part.

information necessary for a particular step in the manufacture of the part. A part which is to be produced by forging, for example, may have one drawing showing the original rough forged part and one detail of the finished forged part. See Figs. 13-1-2C and 13-1-2D.

ASSIGNMENTS

See Assignments 1 through 4 for Unit 13-1 starting on page 244.

■ UNIT 13-2

Multiple Detail Drawings

Detail drawings may be shown on separate sheets, or they may be grouped on one or more large sheets.

Often the detailing of parts is grouped according to the department in which they are made. For example, wood, fiber, and metal parts are used in the assembly of a transformer.

Fig. 13-2-1 Detail drawing containing many details on one sheet.

UNIT 13-3

Drawing Revisions

Revisions are made to an existing drawing when manufacturing methods are improved, to reduce cost, to correct errors, and to improve design. A clear record of these revisions must be registered on the drawing.

All drawings must carry a change or revision table, either down the right-hand side or across the bottom of the drawing. In addition to a description of drawing changes, provision may be made for recording a revision symbol, a zone location, an issue number, a date, and the approval of the change. Should the drawing revision cause a dimension or dimensions to be other than the scale indicated on the drawing, then the dimensions that are not to scale should be indicated by the method shown in Fig. 7-1-16. Typical revision tables are shown in Fig. 13-3-1.

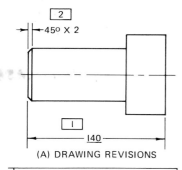

(A) DRAWING REVISIONS

REVISIONS		
SYMBOL	DESCRIPTION	DATE & APPROVAL
1	LENGTH WAS 150	J. Helsel 3-4-88
2	CHAMFER ADDED	F. Newman 2-2-89

(B) VERTICAL REVISION BLOCK

REVISION TABLE	DESCRIPTION				

(C) HORIZONTAL REVISION BLOCK

Fig. 13-3-1 Drawing revisions.

Formerly, with manual drafting, when a large number of revisions were to be made, it was more economical to make a new drawing. When this was done, the words REDRAWN and REVISED would appear in the revision column of the new drawing. A new

date was also shown for updating old prints. CAD, however, has many powerful on-screen editing options available. Any entity (line or arc) incorrectly created no longer must be erased and then redrawn. By selection of the appropriate command, it may be edited to correct specifications directly on the screen. The command name will vary depending on which submenu option is selected. Generally, however, the name is recognizable. The term used to EDIT a line, for example, may be called BREAK, EXTEND, or TRIM. Each term meaning refers to a revision. Line modification may be accomplished as follows:

1. A line on the screen (Fig. 13-3-2A) has been drawn longer than necessary. Select the command option to change its length (BREAK).
2. Select the line (point 1) to be changed. Be sure to select it at (OSNAP ENDPOINT) the end you wish altered.
3. Modify the line by picking new endpoint 2.

LINE EDITING

With CAD the answer to "Can it be done?" is not only a resounding "Yes" but also "Which method would you like to use?" Suppose, for example, you wish to change the part in Fig. 13-3-3A to Fig. 13-3-3B. One option is to erase and re-draw it. A second is to gap (or break) the segment and add the new lines as follows:

1. Select the BREAK (EDIT) command and the line you wish to alter.
2. Designate the break points 1 and 2 (Fig. 13-3-3C).

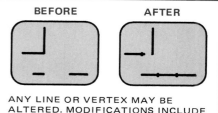

ANY LINE OR VERTEX MAY BE ALTERED. MODIFICATIONS INCLUDE ADDING OR DELETING A VERTEX AND JOINING, MOVING, STRETCHING EXTENDING, GAPPING, OR SHORTENING A LINE.

3. Select the LINE command.
4. With ORTHO on pick points 1, 3, 4 and 2. The part will appear as shown in Fig. 13-3-3B.

Other line-editing features are available including:

CHANGE — to change the endpoint location
OSNAP — to locate positions (e.g., NODE, QUADRANT) exactly on an object (Unit 6-2)
TRACE — to widen a line
OFFSET — to create parallel lines (Unit 6-1)
STRETCH — to change line positions yet retain original drawing form

To change top line entities in Fig. 13-3-4A for example:

1. Select the CHANGE command.
2. Select the lines 1 and 2 and press ENTER.
3. Select the change point 3. The result is shown in Fig. 13-3-4B.

The CHANGE command is very useful. It allows you to modify many entity characteristics including COLOR, LAYERS, and LINE TYPE. Simply select the appropriate sub-

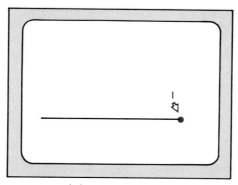

(A) ORIGINAL LINE

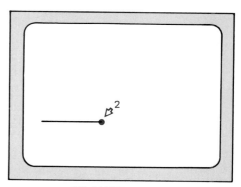

(B) ALTERED LINE

Fig. 13-3-2 Modify a line.

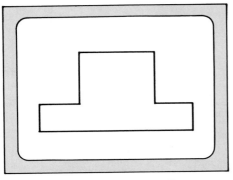

(A) ORIGINAL PART

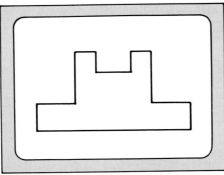

(B) DESIRED PART

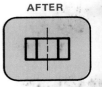

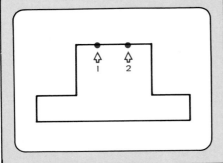

(C) SPECIFYING THE GAP

Fig. 13-3-3 Line editing.

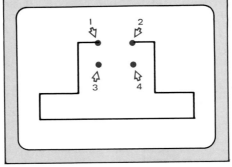

(D) GAPPED LINE

menu option, the lines that you wish to
change, and follow the prompts (e.g.,
COLOR and YELLOW).

The width of any line may be modified by using the TRACE (DRAW)
command as follows:

1. Select the TRACE command. (If

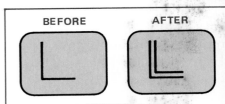

you want the line not to be drawn
solid, first select FILL and OFF.)
2. Key in the desired trace width (e.g.,
.50) and press ENTER.
3. Draw the trace pattern (points 1
through 5 in Fig. 13-3-5) and press
ENTER.

After an object has been drawn it is
possible to move several of the segments to another position by:

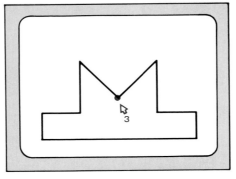

(A) ORIGINAL PART

Fig. 13-3-4 Changing entity characteristics.

(B) DESIRED PART

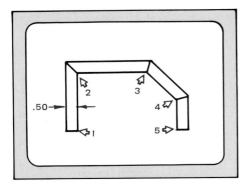

Fig. 13-3-5 Line widening.

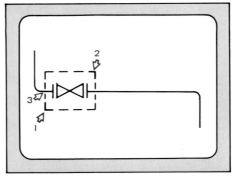

(A) ORIGINAL POSITION

Fig. 13-3-6 Changing the position of several lines.

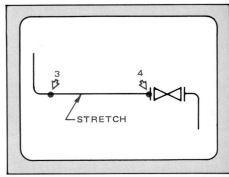

(B) NEW POSITION

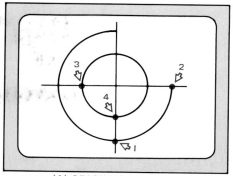

(A) ORIGINAL DRAWING

Fig. 13-3-7 Circle and arc editing.

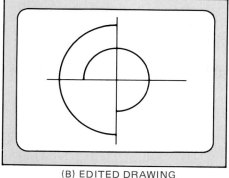

(B) EDITED DRAWING

circle and arc shown in Fig. 13-3-7, for example, may be altered by:

1. Select the EDIT command to BREAK the arc. (As an alternate, TRIM may also be used for this purpose using the center lines as intersections.)
2. Select the arc to modify at point 1.
3. Select the portion of the arc you wish modified (point 2).
4. Select the circle to modify at point 3.
5. Select the portion of the circle you wish modified (point 4). *Note:* Sometimes the incorrect part of the circle or arc may be deleted. In this case, immediately select UNDO and reverse the selection of the two points (default is CCW).

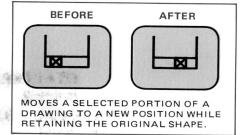

BEFORE   AFTER

MOVES A SELECTED PORTION OF A DRAWING TO A NEW POSITION WHILE RETAINING THE ORIGINAL SHAPE.

1. Select the STRETCH command.
2. Select the objects you wish to move (by window) as shown with points 1 and 2 in Fig. 13-3-6A.

3. Select the distance to move (point 3 to point 4).

As you can see, there are a multitude of options available that may be used to revise a drawing. It is not necessary to delete an object. Instead, decide which line-editing option can be used to modify the existing screen image.

ARC EDITING

The editing features are also available for the purpose of revising circles, arcs, and splines on a drawing. The

TEXT EDITING

Many text editing features exist, including:

Changing text size
Changing text style
Dragging text to a new position
Rotating text
Correcting mis-spelled words
Adding or replacing words
Changing the $X-Y$ size ratio
Fitting text into a confined space

The text shown in Fig. 13-3-8A may be revised to that shown in Fig. 13-3-8B by:

1. Select the CHANGE command.
2. Select the text to be changed (by window) and press ENTER twice.
3. Select the change point 1.
4. Follow the screen prompts keying ENTER, new HEIGHT (e.g., .25 and ENTER) and rotation angle (0 and press ENTER).
5. Key in the replacement text and press ENTER.
6. Repeat steps 3, 4, and 5 for the other row of text.

You may need to fit text into a specified location. To do this:

1. Select the TEXT and FIT option.

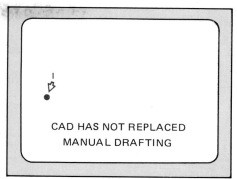

(A) ORIGINAL TEXT

Fig. 13-3-8 Text editing.

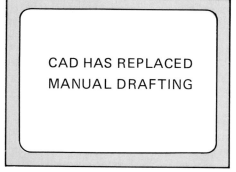

(B) MODIFIED TEXT

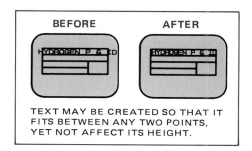

BEFORE   AFTER

TEXT MAY BE CREATED SO THAT IT FITS BETWEEN ANY TWO POINTS, YET NOT AFFECT ITS HEIGHT.

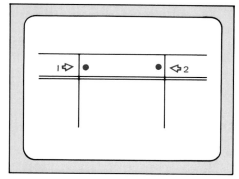

(A) SELECTING WIDTH

Fig. 13-3-9 Fit text into a confined space.

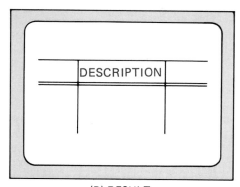

(B) RESULT

2. Select the specified location (points 1 and 2 in Fig. 13-3-9A).
3. Key in desired text height and press ENTER.
4. Key in desired text, DESCRIPTION and press ENTER. The result appears in Fig. 13-3-9B.

References

1. ANSI Y14.5M, *Dimensions and Tolerancing.*

ASSIGNMENT

See Assignment 7 for Unit 13-3 on page 250.

UNIT 13-4

Assembly Drawings

All machines and mechanisms are composed of numerous parts. A drawing showing the product in its completed state is called an *assembly drawing.*

Assembly drawings vary greatly in the amount and type of information they give, depending on the nature of the machine or mechanism they depict. The primary functions of the assembly drawing are to show the product in its completed shape, to indicate the relationship of its various components, and to designate these components by a part or detail number. Other information that might be given includes overall dimensions, capacity dimensions, relationship dimensions between parts (necessary information for assembly), operating instructions, and data on design characteristics.

DESIGN ASSEMBLY DRAWINGS

When a machine is designed, an assembly drawing or a design layout is first drawn to clearly visualize the performance, shape, and clearances of the various parts. From this assembly drawing, the detail drawings are made and each part is given a part number.

To assist in the assembling of the machine, part numbers of the various details are placed on the assembly drawing. The part number is attached to the corresponding part with a leader, as illustrated in Fig. 13-4-1. It is important that the detail drawing not use identical numbering schemes

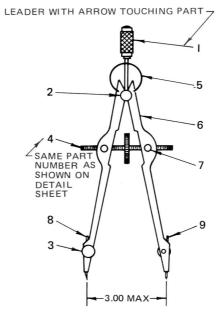

LEADER WITH ARROW TOUCHING PART

SAME PART NUMBER AS SHOWN ON DETAIL SHEET

3.00 MAX

Fig. 13-4-1 Identification numbers on assembly drawings.

when several item lists (bills of material) are used.

Often assembly drawings comprised of a multitude of different parts are difficult to interpret on the monitor. To improve this, many assemblies, especially those with complicated interiors, are developed sectioned (Chap. 8). CAD options may be used to even further remedy the situation. Two options in particular, color and layers, will be employed for this purpose. Modern CAD systems have color capability. Color may be used to enhance computer graphic images. While this is especially true for three-dimensional modeling (Chap. 17), it may be beneficial for two-dimensional application as well. Color displays offer a variety of user-definable contrasting colors to make it easier to discriminate among various groups of design elements on different layers of a complex design. Color speeds up the recognition of specific areas and subassemblies, helps the designer interpret complex surfaces, and highlights clearance and interference problems. If you have a color monitor, a colored image is generated directly on the screen. If not, an alternate method is available for the drafter to obtain the desired result. That is, by using the appropriate command(s) to a plotter, an original color drawing may be produced. (Great for checking results.) Different colored pens are used for this. Besides color,

line widths (Unit 4-6) may also be varied by the use of different pens. A multicolored result can be produced by:

1. Creating part of the object using the default color. This is shown by the shape description in Fig. 13-4-2.

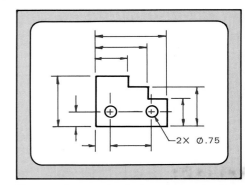

Fig. 13-4-2 Two-color display.

2. Selecting the COLOR option under LAYERS.
3. Responding to the prompts. Specify the desired color (e.g., RED, and press ENTER). *Note:* Change the layer before specifying color as this will provide additional flexibility and contribute to the simplification and preparation of assembly drawings.
4. Returning to the appropriate command, such as DIMENSIONING (DIM).
5. Finishing creation of the object. A two-color image similar to the screen display shown in Fig. 13-4-2 will be the result.

Additional colors may be added at any time by repeating the above procedure.

The concepts of color, pen, and layer, may be combined for various results. You may, for example, remove (turn off) any layer, and thus any color, whenever you wish. This will enhance the interpretation of the display. When plotting, each level is designated to a particular plotter pen. This way the original drawing may have any combination of colors and line widths.

INSTALLATION ASSEMBLY DRAWINGS

This type of assembly drawing is used when many unskilled people are employed to mass-assemble parts. Since these people are not normally trained to read technical drawings, simplified pictorial assembly drawings similar to the one shown in Fig. 13-4-3 are used.

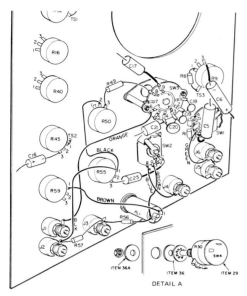

DETAIL A

Fig. 13-4-3 Installation assembly drawings.

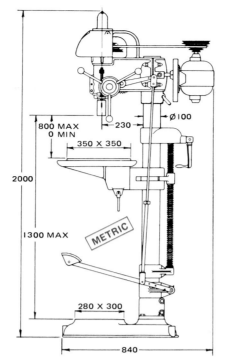

(A) DRILL PRESS

Fig. 13-4-4 Assembly drawings used in catalogs.

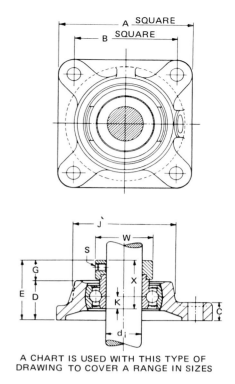

A CHART IS USED WITH THIS TYPE OF DRAWING TO COVER A RANGE IN SIZES

(B) PILLOW BLOCK

ASSEMBLY DRAWINGS FOR CATALOGS

Special assembly drawings are prepared for company catalogs. These assembly drawings show only pertinent details and dimensions that would interest the potential buyer. Often one drawing, having letter dimensions accompanied by a chart, is used to cover a range of sizes, such as the pillow block shown in Fig. 13-4-4.

ITEM LIST

An item list, often referred to as a bill of material, is an itemized list of all the components shown on an assembly drawing or a detail drawing. See Fig. 13-4-5. Often, an item list is placed on a separate sheet for ease of handling and duplicating. Since the item list is used by the purchasing department to order the necessary material for the design, it should show the raw material size rather than the finished size of the part.

For castings, a pattern number should appear in the size column in lieu of the physical size of the part.

Standard components, which are purchased rather than fabricated, such as bolts, nuts, and bearings, have the standard size or part number and

QTY	ITEM	MATL	DESCRIPTION	PT NO.
1	BASE	GI	PATTERN # A3154	1
1	CAP	GI	PATTERN # B7156	2
1	SUPPORT	AISI-1212	.38 X 2.00 X 4.38	3
1	BRACE	AISI-1212	.25 X 1.00 X 2.00	4
1	COVER	AISI-1035	.1345 (#10 GA USS) X 6.00 X 7.50	5
1	SHAFT	AISI-1212	Ø 1.00 X 6.50	6
2	BEARINGS	SKF	RADIAL BALL # 6200Z	7
2	RETAINING CLIP	TRUARC	N5000-725	8
1	KEY	STL	WOODRUFF # 608	9
1	SET SCREW	CUP POINT	HEX SOCKET .25UNC X 1.50	10
4	BOLT—HEX HD—REG	SEMI-FIN	.38UNC X 1.50 LG	11
4	NUT—REG HEX	STL	.38UNC	12
4	LOCK WASHER—SPRING	STL	.38 - MED	13
				14

(A) TYPICAL ITEM LIST   PARTS 7 TO 13 ARE PURCHASED ITEMS

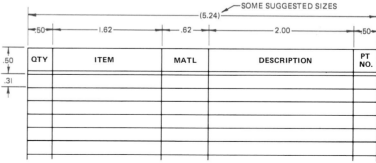

(B) SAMPLE SIZES

Fig. 13-4-5 Item list.

manufacturer on the item list. Information in the descriptive column should be sufficient for the purchasing agent to order these parts.

Item lists placed on the bottom of the drawing should read from bottom to top, while item lists placed on the top of the drawings should read from top to bottom. This practice allows additions to be made at a later date.

A drawing may be created by applying the various procedures outlined in this text. After completion, it may be desirable to specify material size. This may be accomplished either automatically or manually. The automatic option may be available through the use of additional software. Some pro-

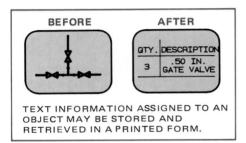

TEXT INFORMATION ASSIGNED TO AN OBJECT MAY BE STORED AND RETRIEVED IN A PRINTED FORM.

grams are capable of sizing individual parts, while others complete assemblies. If the prepared drawing is of a single part, for example, a sheet-metal pattern layout, the material size is easily determined. Select the AREA (IN-

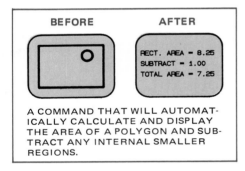

A COMMAND THAT WILL AUTOMATICALLY CALCULATE AND DISPLAY THE AREA OF A POLYGON AND SUBTRACT ANY INTERNAL SMALLER REGIONS.

QUIRY) and specify any number of points enclosing the pattern's perimeter. Follow the prompts to display both the required material area and the perimeter. An item list for an assembly

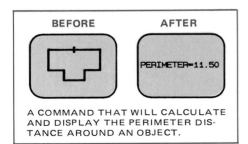

A COMMAND THAT WILL CALCULATE AND DISPLAY THE PERIMETER DISTANCE AROUND AN OBJECT.

drawing such as the one shown in Fig. 13-4-5 can be created by using symbolic representation. Symbols are used which correspond to the identities of certain parts. The symbol may represent any component. It may range from a piping elbow, to a PNP transistor, to a particular type of bolt. Each symbol will uniquely identify particular parts. It will serve to "flag" it on the drawing.

All blocks, attributes, etc., may acquire a unique identifier referred to as a HANDLE. Select HANDLES and ON. Use LIST (or DBLIST) to report the value of the entity's handle. Handles may assist preparation, however, a LISP program may be used to develop an item list.

Automatic item list generation may become complicated with networked systems. This is especially true for a large organization having many CAD employees. The problem arises that once a symbol has been selected, it must be maintained as such. This

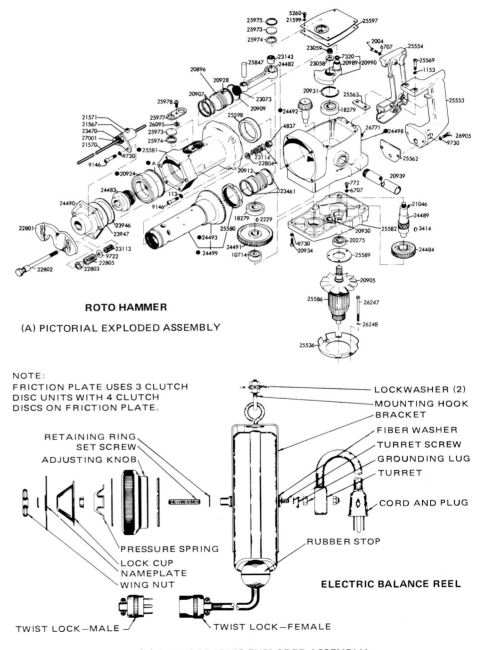

ROTO HAMMER

(A) PICTORIAL EXPLODED ASSEMBLY

NOTE:
FRICTION PLATE USES 3 CLUTCH DISC UNITS WITH 4 CLUTCH DISCS ON FRICTION PLATE.

(B) ORTHOGRAPHIC EXPLODED ASSEMBLY

Fig. 13-5-1 Exploded assembly drawings.

means it always must represent the same part and size identity. With so many employees using the same system, keeping this standardization may become difficult. A dedicated system, however, may not encounter the same problem, since control is localized. Since automatic item list generation is complicated and so specialized, it will not be used for the projects in this text. Use the TEXT command to key in each item specification in the same manner as you would letter it when drafting manually.

ASSIGNMENT

See Assignment 8 through 10 for Unit 13-4 on page 250.

Exploded Assembly Drawings

In many instances parts must be identified or assembled by persons unskilled in the reading of engineering drawings. Examples are found in the appliance-repair industry, which relies on assembly drawings for repair work and for reordering parts. Exploded assembly drawings, like that shown in Fig. 13-5-1, are used extensively in these cases, for they are easier to read. This type of assembly drawing is also used frequently by companies that manufacture do-it-yourself assembly kits, such as model-making kits. Item reference names in lieu of item reference numbers are usually used.

For this type of drawing, the parts are aligned in position. Frequently, shading using HATCH, FILL, or ASHADE (AUTOSHADE) makes the drawings appear more realistic.

ASSIGNMENT

See Assignment 11 for Unit 13-5 on page 251.

Detailed Assembly Drawings

Often these are made for fairly simple objects, such as pieces of furniture,

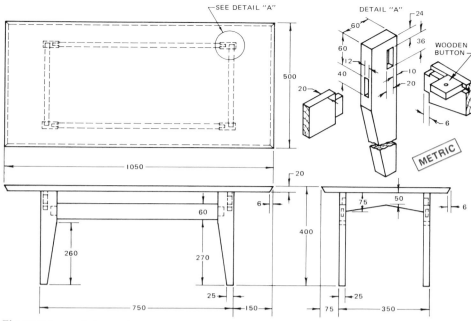

Fig. 13-6-1 Detailed assembly drawing.

when the parts are few in number and are not intricate in shape. All the dimensions and information necessary for the construction of each part and for the assembly of the parts are given directly on the assembly drawing. Separate views of specific parts, at a larger scale, may also be drawn in addition to the regular assembly drawing. Note that in Fig. 13-6-1 the enlarged views are drawn in picture form, not as regular orthographic views. This method is peculiar to architectural applications. On mechanical drawings DRAW details orthographically in full scale; then BLOCK and INSERT at the desired scale magnification.

ASSIGNMENT

See Assignment 12 for Unit 13-6 on page 252.

UNIT 13-7

Subassembly Drawings

Many completely assembled items, such as a car and a television set, are

assembled with many preassembled components as well as individual parts. These preassembled units are referred to as subassemblies. The assembly drawings of a transmission for an automobile and the "mother board" for a microcomputer are typical examples of subassembly drawings.

Subassemblies are designed to simplify final assembly as well as permit the item to be either assembled in a more suitable area or purchased from an outside source. This type of drawing shows only those dimensions which would be required for the completed assembly. Examples are size of the mounting holes and their location, shaft locations, and overall sizes. This type of drawing is found frequently in catalogs. The pillow block shown in Fig. 13-4-4B is a typical subassembly drawing.

ASSIGNMENT

See Assignment 13 for Unit 13-7 starting on page 253.

ASSIGNMENTS FOR CHAPTER 13

The projects in this chapter involve the preparation of engineering drawings using a combination of CAD commands. You are now at the point where CAD is used to "build drawings" not to "draw drawings." Prior to beginning a new drawing, you need to preplan your sequence as well as the limits. Determine whether you can use any of the time-saving features (MIRROR, COPY, ARRAY, BLOCK, FILLET, and so on) now available to you. Preplanning will help you to create the working and assembly drawings more accurately and rapidly.

Assignment for Unit 13-1, Working Drawings

1. Make a working drawing of one of the parts shown in Figs. 13-1-A, 13-1-B, or 13-1-C. Select appropriate views and dimensions and add to the drawing the information needed so that the parts can be completely manufactured.

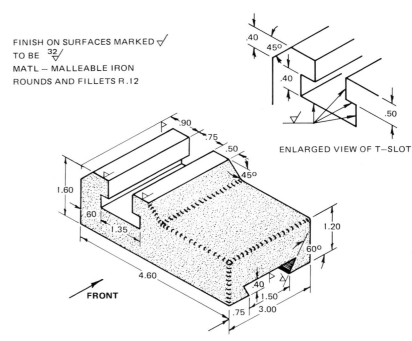

FINISH ON SURFACES MARKED ✓
TO BE 32/
MATL — MALLEABLE IRON
ROUNDS AND FILLETS R .12

ENLARGED VIEW OF T—SLOT

Fig. 13-1-A Cross slide.

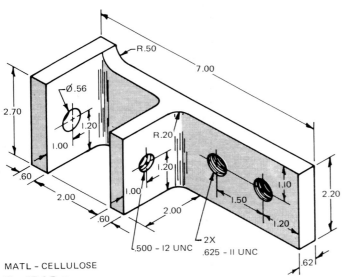

MATL - CELLULOSE

Fig. 13-1-B Connector.

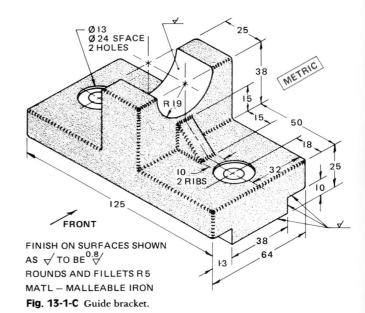

FINISH ON SURFACES SHOWN
AS ✓ TO BE 0.8/ ✓
ROUNDS AND FILLETS R 5
MATL — MALLEABLE IRON

Fig. 13-1-C Guide bracket.

2. Select one of the parts shown in Fig. 13-1-D or 13-1-E and make a three-view working drawing. Only the dovetail and T-slot dimensions are critical and units must be taken to an accuracy of three decimal places.

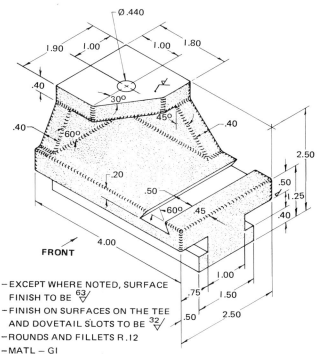

−EXCEPT WHERE NOTED, SURFACE
 FINISH TO BE ^{63}/
−FINISH ON SURFACES ON THE TEE
 AND DOVETAIL SLOTS TO BE ^{32}/
−ROUNDS AND FILLETS R.12
−MATL − GI

Fig. 13-1-D Guide rack.

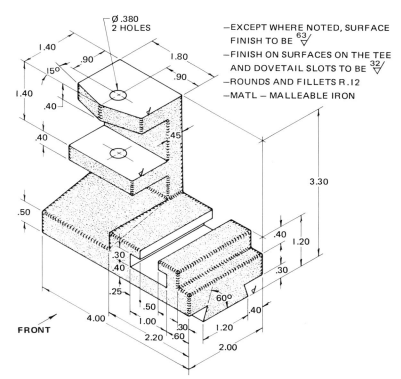

−EXCEPT WHERE NOTED, SURFACE
 FINISH TO BE ^{63}/
−FINISH ON SURFACES ON THE TEE
 AND DOVETAIL SLOTS TO BE ^{32}/
−ROUNDS AND FILLETS R.12
−MATL − MALLEABLE IRON

Fig. 13-1-E Locating stand.

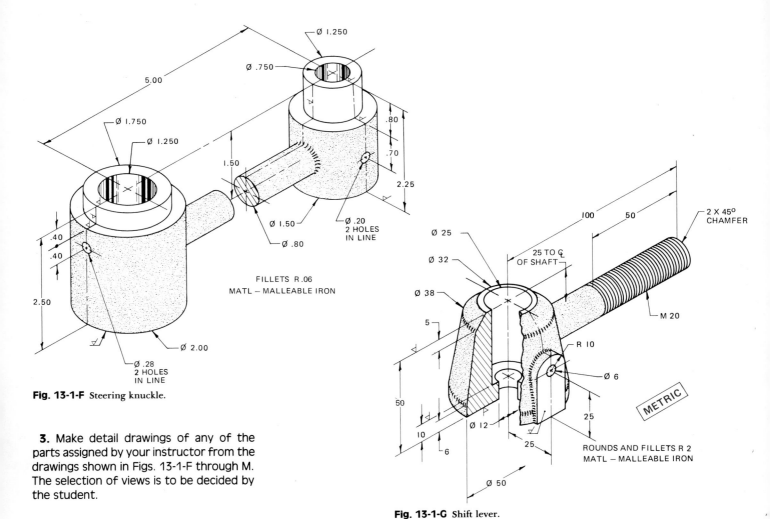

Fig. 13-1-F Steering knuckle.

Ø 1.250
Ø .750
5.00
Ø 1.750
Ø 1.250
1.50
Ø 1.50
Ø .80
.80
.70
2.25
Ø .20
2 HOLES
IN LINE
FILLETS R .06
MATL — MALLEABLE IRON
.40
.40
2.50
Ø 2.00
Ø .28
2 HOLES
IN LINE

3. Make detail drawings of any of the parts assigned by your instructor from the drawings shown in Figs. 13-1-F through M. The selection of views is to be decided by the student.

Ø 25
Ø 32
Ø 38
25 TO ₵
OF SHAFT
100
50
2 X 45°
CHAMFER
M 20
R 10
Ø 6
5
50
10
6
Ø 12
25
25
Ø 50
METRIC
ROUNDS AND FILLETS R 2
MATL — MALLEABLE IRON

Fig. 13-1-G Shift lever.

Ø 1.78
Ø .56
VIEW IN DIRECTION
OF ARROW "A"
.15
Ø 2.38
KEYSEAT FOR
SQ KEY
Ø .20
3 HOLES
EQL SPD
Ø 3.94
1.18
Ø .39
Ø .80
.20
.24
45°
.30
Ø 1.18
2.00
.56
3 LEGS
EQL SPD
.60
"A"
ROUNDS AND FILLETS R.06
MATL — CAST STEEL

Fig. 13-1-H Clutch.

Ø 100
Ø 60
Ø 25
30°
15°
3 JAWS
EQL SPD
Ø 6
3 HOLES
EQL SPD
13
10
KEYSEAT FOR
SQ KEY
63
10
Ø 50
Ø 40
5
3 RIBS EQL SPD
BETWEEN HOLES
METRIC
ROUNDS AND FILLETS R2
MATL — CAST STEEL

Fig. 13-1-J Mounting bracket.

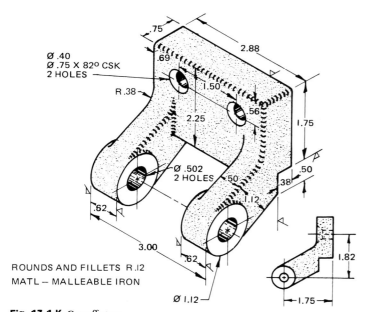

Ø .40
Ø .75 X 82° CSK
2 HOLES

R .38

ROUNDS AND FILLETS R .12
MATL — MALLEABLE IRON

Fig. 13-1-K Cut-off stop.

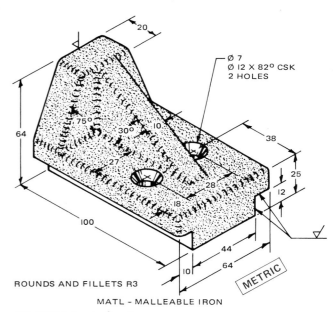

Ø 7
Ø 12 X 82° CSK
2 HOLES

ROUNDS AND FILLETS R3

MATL - MALLEABLE IRON

Fig. 13-1-L Sparker bracket.

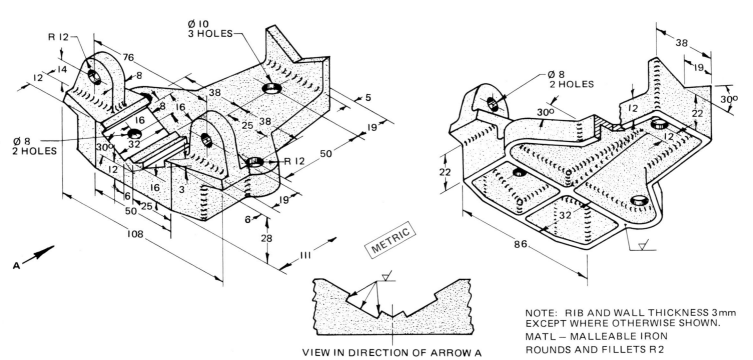

R 12

Ø 10
3 HOLES

Ø 8
2 HOLES

METRIC

VIEW IN DIRECTION OF ARROW A

Fig. 13-1-M Pipe vise base.

Ø 8
2 HOLES

NOTE: RIB AND WALL THICKNESS 3mm
EXCEPT WHERE OTHERWISE SHOWN.
MATL — MALLEABLE IRON
ROUNDS AND FILLETS R 2

4. Make detail drawings of any of the parts assigned by your instructor from the assembly drawings shown in Figs. 13-1-N or 13-1-N. The selection of views is to be decided by the student.

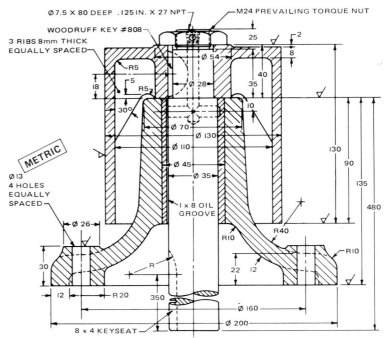

Fig. 13-1-N Pulley assembly.

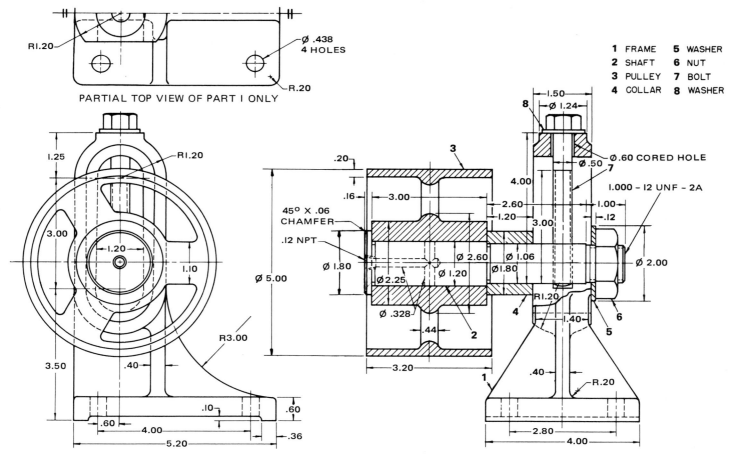

PARTIAL TOP VIEW OF PART I ONLY

1	FRAME	5	WASHER
2	SHAFT	6	NUT
3	PULLEY	7	BOLT
4	COLLAR	8	WASHER

Fig. 13-1-P Adjustable pulley.

Assignment for Unit 13-2, Multiple Detail Drawings

5. Make detail drawings of all the parts shown of one of the assemblies in Figs. 13-2-A or 13-2-B. Place the assembly and all parts on a single drawing. Since time is money, select only the views necessary to describe each part. Below each part show the following information: part number, name of part, material and number required. Illustrate details at a different scale than the assembly and prepare a mock-up sketch prior to booting the system.

6. Repeat assignment 5 for one of the assemblies shown in Figs. 13-2-C, 13-2-D, or 13-2-E.

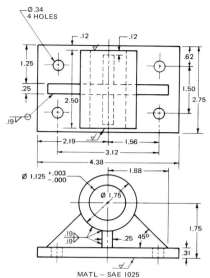

Fig. 13-2-A Shaft support.

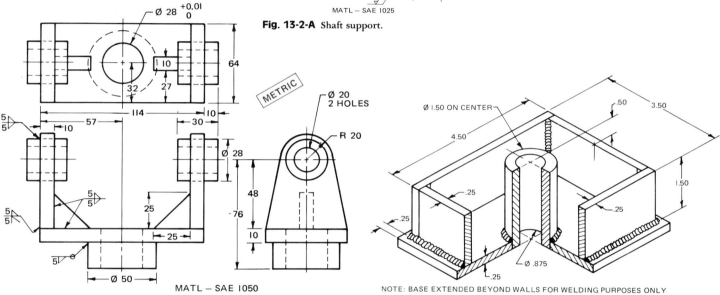

Fig. 13-2-B Shaft pivot support.

Fig. 13-2-C Shaft base.

NOTE: BASE EXTENDED BEYOND WALLS FOR WELDING PURPOSES ONLY

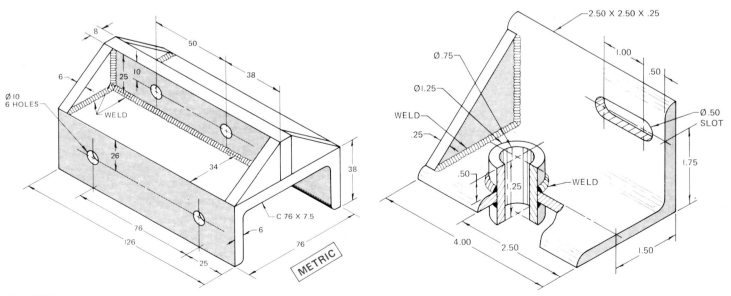

Fig. 13-2-D Caster frame.

Fig. 13-2-E Slide bracket.

Assignment for Unit 13-3, Drawing Revisions

7. Select one of the drawings shown in Fig. 13-3-A or 13-3-B and edit it with appropriate revisions to the drawing recording the changes in a drawing revision column.

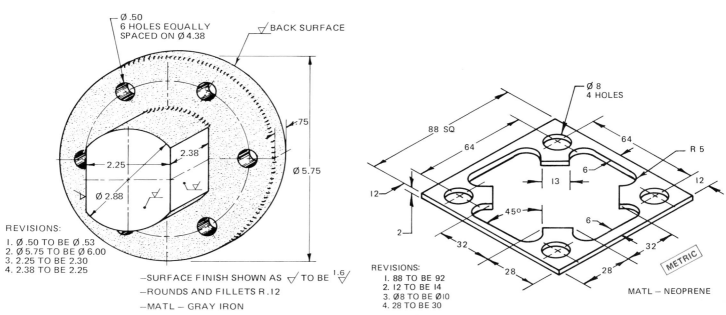

REVISIONS:
1. Ø .50 TO BE Ø .53
2. Ø 5.75 TO BE Ø 6.00
3. 2.25 TO BE 2.30
4. 2.38 TO BE 2.25

—SURFACE FINISH SHOWN AS ∇ TO BE 1.6∇
—ROUNDS AND FILLETS R .12
—MATL — GRAY IRON

Fig. 13-3-A Gasket.

REVISIONS:
1. 88 TO BE 92
2. 12 TO BE 14
3. Ø8 TO BE Ø10
4. 28 TO BE 30

MATL — NEOPRENE

Fig. 13-3-B Axle cap.

Assignment for Unit 13-4, Assembly Drawings

8. Make a one-view assembly drawing of one of the assemblies shown in Fig. 13-4-A or 13-4-B. For Fig. 13-4-B, show a round bar (Ø 25 mm) in phantom being held in position. Prepare the drawing with visible object lines using layer 1 and pen 1; other line styles layer 2, 5, 6 and pen 2; dimensions layer 3 and pen 3; text and item list layer 4 and pen 4.

Include on the drawing an item list and identification part numbers using the TEXT command.

9. Repeat assignment 8 for the assembly shown in Fig. 13-1-N.

10. Repeat assignment 8 for the assembly shown in Fig. 13-1-P.

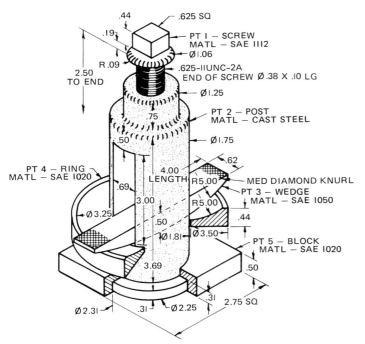

Fig. 13-4-A Tool post holder.

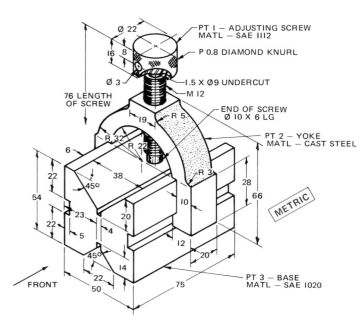

Fig. 13-4-B V-block clamp.

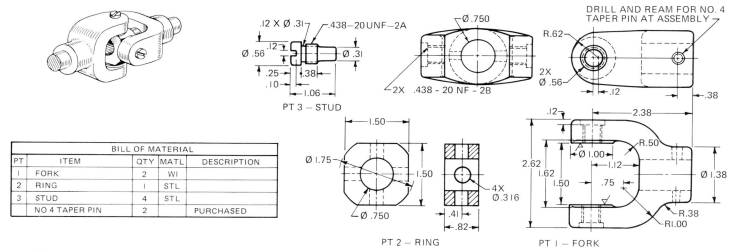

Fig. 13-5-A Universal joint.

BILL OF MATERIAL				
PT	ITEM	QTY	MATL	DESCRIPTION
1	FORK	2	WI	
2	RING	1	STL	
3	STUD	4	STL	
	NO 4 TAPER PIN	2		PURCHASED

Assignment for Unit 13-5, Exploded Assembly Drawings

11. Make an exploded assembly drawing in orthographic projection of one of the assemblies shown in Fig. 13-5-A or 13-5-B. Use center lines to align parts and holes. Change layers, pens and/or colors as assigned by your instructor.

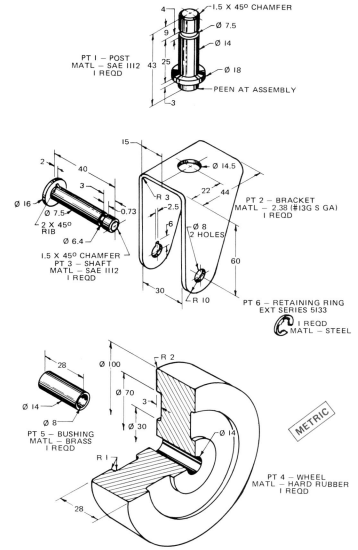

Fig. 13-5-B Caster.

Assignment for Unit 13-6, Detailed Assembly Drawings

12. Make a detailed orthographic assembly drawing of one of the assemblies shown in Fig. 13-6-A, or 13-6-B. Include on the drawing the method of assembly (i.e., nailing, wood screws, doweling, etc.) and an item list.

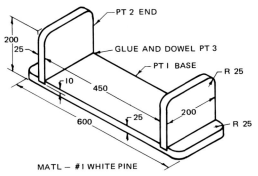

MATL — #1 WHITE PINE

Fig. 13-6-A Book rack.

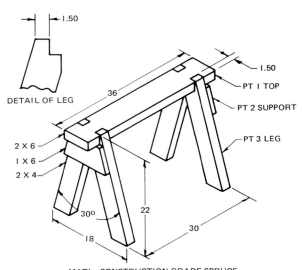

DETAIL OF LEG

MATL—CONSTRUCTION GRADE SPRUCE

NOTE: WOOD SIZES (THICKNESS AND WIDTH) ARE NOMINAL SIZES

Fig. 13-6-B Saw horse.

Assignment for Unit 13-7, Subassembly Drawings

13. Make a one-view orthographic subassembly drawing of one of the assemblies shown in Fig. 13-7-A or 13-7-B. A broken-out or partial section view is recommended to show the interior features. Include on the drawing pertinent dimensions, identification numbers on assembly drawing, an item list, and a phantom outline of the adjoining part or features. Change layers, and colors as assigned by your instructor.

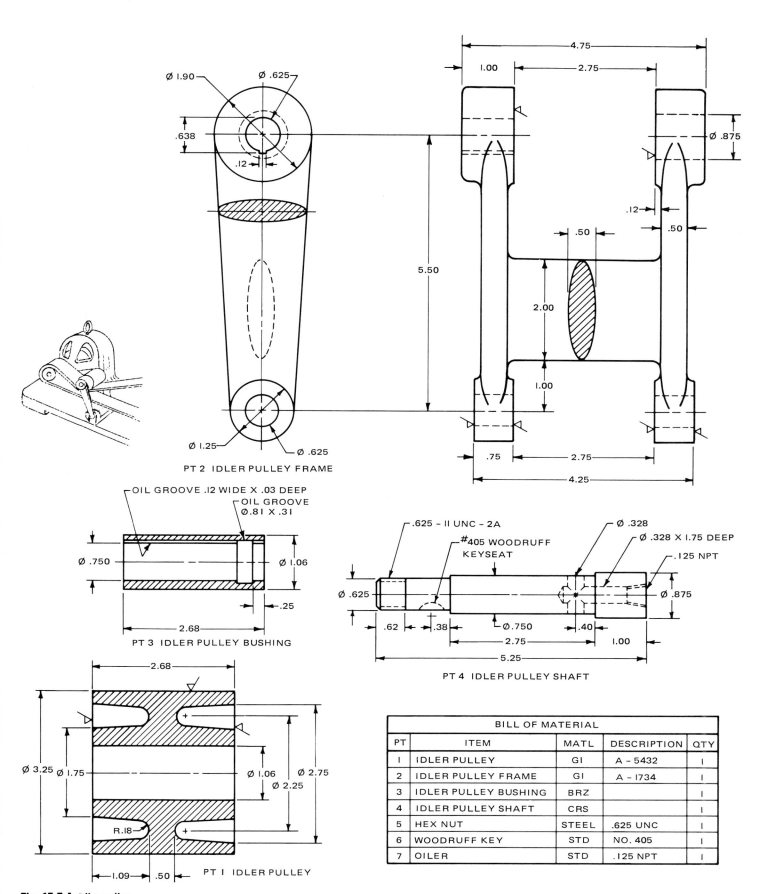

Ø 1.90   Ø .625

.638

.12

5.50

Ø 1.25   Ø .625

PT 2 IDLER PULLEY FRAME

4.75

1.00   2.75

Ø .875

.12   .50

.50

2.00

1.00

.75   2.75

4.25

OIL GROOVE .12 WIDE X .03 DEEP
OIL GROOVE
Ø.81 X .31

Ø .750   Ø 1.06

.25

2.68

PT 3 IDLER PULLEY BUSHING

.625 - 11 UNC - 2A

#405 WOODRUFF
KEYSEAT

Ø .328

Ø .328 X 1.75 DEEP

.125 NPT

Ø .625

Ø .875

Ø .750

.62   .38   .40

2.75   1.00

5.25

PT 4 IDLER PULLEY SHAFT

2.68

Ø 3.25 Ø 1.75   Ø 1.06   Ø 2.75

Ø 2.25

R.18

1.09   .50

PT 1 IDLER PULLEY

BILL OF MATERIAL				
PT	ITEM	MATL	DESCRIPTION	QTY
1	IDLER PULLEY	GI	A – 5432	1
2	IDLER PULLEY FRAME	GI	A – 1734	1
3	IDLER PULLEY BUSHING	BRZ		1
4	IDLER PULLEY SHAFT	CRS		1
5	HEX NUT	STEEL	.625 UNC	1
6	WOODRUFF KEY	STD	NO. 405	1
7	OILER	STD	.125 NPT	1

Fig. 13-7-A Idler pulley.

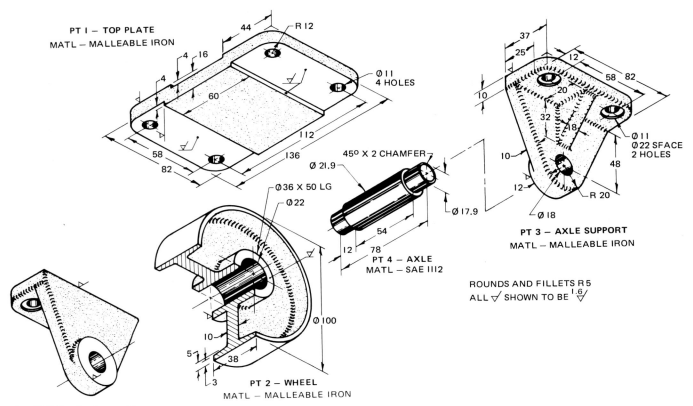

PT 1 — TOP PLATE
MATL — MALLEABLE IRON

44   R 12

4   16

4

60

58

82   136   112

Ø 11
4 HOLES

45° X 2 CHAMFER

Ø 21.9

Ø 36 X 50 LG

Ø 22

Ø 17.9

54

12   78

PT 4 — AXLE
MATL — SAE 1112

PT 3 — AXLE SUPPORT
MATL — MALLEABLE IRON

37

25   12

10   20   58   82

32

48   Ø 11
Ø 22 SFACE
2 HOLES

10

48

12

Ø 18   R 20

ROUNDS AND FILLETS R 5
ALL ▽ SHOWN TO BE ¹·⁶▽

Ø 100

10

5   38

3   PT 2 — WHEEL
MATL — MALLEABLE IRON

Fig. 13-7-B Wheel assembly.

14

CAD/CAM Drawings for Computer Numerical Control

■ UNIT 14-1

Two-Axis Control Systems

Interactive graphics programs are used to develop assemblies, item lists, three-dimensional models, and mathematical results. The results are considered to be working engineering drawings, yet the design may never be produced on paper. The data generated by a CAD system can be directly utilized by a CAM (computer-aided manufacturing) system. It may, for example, be transmitted to CNC (computer numerical control) programming routines used to produce parts as shown in Fig. 14-1-1. Thus the term *CAD/CAM* emerged. Generally, CAM is thought to be divided into CNC and robotics.

CAD/CAM deals with the automation of design and manufacturing and is in the developmental stage. Many schools and companies, for example, have CAD capability and/or CAM capability. Few, however, have true CAD/CAM capability. That is, a direct "hard-wire" connection between the two as represented by the slash. In the true CAD/CAM system, designers and engineers interact with the computer by means of a graphics terminal. They design and manufacture a part from start to finish. The design and drafting are accomplished electroni-

cally. A number and/or security system ensures that the latest copy of the design is available to all departments. Each design activity, as well as all models, is stored in an integrated CAD/CAM "data base." On the factory floor, the manufacturing staff is on the same network as the designers. Programs take the design information

and automatically convert it into other programs which run milling machines, multiple drill presses, assembly lines, and so forth. A series of computer-controlled machines perform a complete task to automatically fabricate parts by a flexible manufacturing system (FMS). This ideal system, as illustrated in Fig. 14-1-2, helps to epito-

Fig. 14-1-1 Fully automated industrial CAD/CAM. *(Computervision.)* Courtesy Computervision

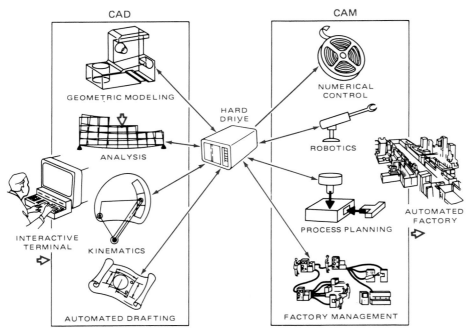

CAD

CAM

GEOMETRIC MODELING

NUMERICAL CONTROL

HARD DRIVE

ANALYSIS

ROBOTICS

INTERACTIVE TERMINAL

KINEMATICS

PROCESS PLANNING

AUTOMATED FACTORY

AUTOMATED DRAFTING

FACTORY MANAGEMENT

Fig. 14-1-2 Integrated computer-aided engineering (CAE) system.

mize the "total automated factory." Total automated factories, however, are a potential yet to be fully realized.

CNC, as with CAD, is a functioning component of automation. It is, however, connected to other manufacturing activities primarily by people and paperwork. For example, a design is created using a CAD system. Next, it is taken and reprogrammed (partial programming) by a parts programmer into the computer that controls the CNC equipment. The part is then automatically fabricated by creating the tool path. Thus you can see that the slash between CAD and CAM requires considerably more effort than pressing a button.

COMPUTER NUMERICAL CONTROL

CNC is a means of automatically directing some or all of the functions of a machine from instructions. The instructions are generally stored on tape and are fed to the controller through a tape reader. The controller interprets the coded instructions and directs the machine through the required operations.

It has been established that because of the consistent high accuracy of numerically controlled machines, and because human errors have been almost entirely eliminated, rejected parts have been considerably reduced.

Because both setup and tape preparation times are short, numerically controlled machines produce a part faster than manually controlled machines.

When changes become necessary on a part, they can easily be implemented by changing the original tapes. The process takes very little time and expense in comparison to the alteration of a jig.

Another area where numerically controlled machines are better is in the quality or accuracy of the work. In many cases a numerically controlled machine can produce parts more accurately at no additional cost, resulting in reduced assembly time and better

interchangeability of parts. This latter fact is especially important when spare parts are required.

Common guidelines have been established that enable dimensioning and tolerancing practices to be used effectively in delineating parts for CNC. Each object is prepared using baseline (or coordinate) dimensioning methods. First, the selection of an absolute (0, 0, 0) or (0, 0) coordinate origin is made depending on whether the control is three-axis or two-axis. All part dimensions would be referenced from that origin. After a multiview working drawing is produced, the information is transferred to manufacturing equipment. Most manufacturers use some sort of interactive (human) interface. This approach does not produce fully automated CAD/CAM. Partial information (partial programming) in the form of manufacturing data is generated. This allows the NC computer to compile instructions from programs stored within its memory. The result is a detailed program plan for tool-path generation. While not as automatic as hardwired CAD/CAM, much of the tedium has been removed. Easy-to-use instructions in partial programming require much less effort than by completely creating the program. The complete procedure is illustrated in Fig. 14-1-3. The partial programming portion of the process is shown within the dashed box. The machine tool automatically produces the finished part only after this has been accomplished. Fully automated CAD/CAM replaces the portion of the process within the dashed box by a hard wire. The procedures outlined in this chapter are valid for either process.

DIMENSIONING FOR A TWO-AXIS COORDINATE SYSTEM

The CNC concept is based on the system of rectangular or cartesian coordinates in which any position can be de-

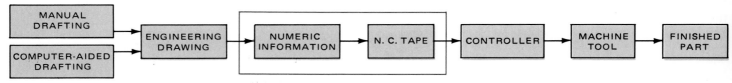

MANUAL DRAFTING

COMPUTER-AIDED DRAFTING

ENGINEERING DRAWING

NUMERIC INFORMATION

N. C. TAPE

CONTROLLER

MACHINE TOOL

FINISHED PART

Fig. 14-1-3 Numerical control sequence.

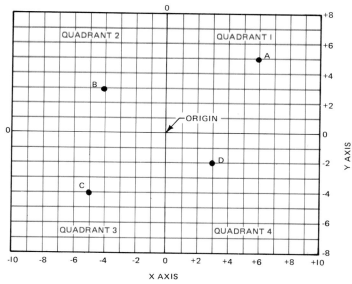

Fig. 14-1-4 Two-dimensional coordinates (*X* and *Y*).

scribed in terms of distance from an origin point along either two or three mutually perpendicular axes. Two-dimensional coordinates (*X*, *Y*) define points in a plane. See Fig. 14-1-4.

The *X* axis is horizontal and is considered the first and basic reference axis. Distances to the right of the *Y* axis are considered positive *X* values and to the left of the *Y* axis as negative *X* values.

The *Y* axis is vertical and perpendicular to the *X* axis in the plane of a drawing showing *XY* relationships. Distances above the *X* axis are considered positive *Y* values and below the *X* axis as negative *Y* values. The position where the *X* and *Y* axes cross is called the *origin*, or *zero point*.

For example, four points lie in a plane, as shown in Fig. 14-1-4. The plane is divided into four quadrants. Point *A* lies in quadrant 1 and is located at position (6, 5), with the *X* coordinate first, followed by the *Y* coordinate. Point *B* lies in quadrant 2 and is located at position (−4, 3). Point *C* lies in quadrant 3 and is located at position (−5, −4). Point *D* lies in quadrant 4 and is located at position (3, −2).

Designing for numerical control would be greatly simplified if all work were done in the first quadrant because all the values would be positive and the plus and minus signs would not be required. For that reason many CAD/CAM systems place the origin (0, 0) to the lower left. This way only positive values apply. However, any of the four quadrants may be used on a particular system, and, as such, programming in any quadrant should be understood.

Some numerically controlled machines are designed for locating points in only the *X* and *Y* directions. These are called *two-axis* machines. The function of these machines is to move the machine table or tool to a specified position in order to perform work, as shown in Fig. 14-1-5. With the fixed spindle and movable table as shown in Fig. 14-1-5B, hole *A* is drilled; then the table moves to the left, positioning point *B* below the drill. This is the most frequently used method. With the fixed table and movable spindle as shown in Fig. 14-1-5*C*, hole *A* is drilled; then the spindle moves to the right, positioning the drill above point *B*. This changes the direction of the motion, but the movement of the cutter as related to the work remains the same.

Origin

As previously mentioned, the origin is the point where the *X* and *Y* axes intersect. It is the point from which all coordinate dimensions are measured. Many systems have a fixed origin built in.

Two examples of fixed origins on machine tables are shown in Fig. 14-1-6. In Fig. 14-1-6A all points are located in the first quadrant, resulting in positive *X* and *Y* values. This is the most frequently used method. In Fig. 14-1-6B all points are located in the third quadrant, resulting in negative *X* and *Y* values.

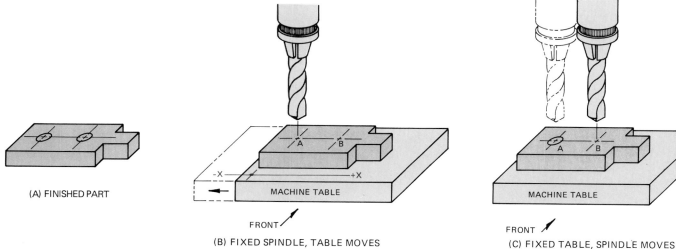

(A) FINISHED PART

(B) FIXED SPINDLE, TABLE MOVES

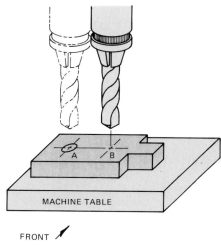

(C) FIXED TABLE, SPINDLE MOVES

Fig. 14-1-5 Positioning the work.

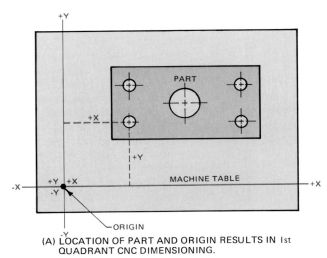

(A) LOCATION OF PART AND ORIGIN RESULTS IN 1st QUADRANT CNC DIMENSIONING.

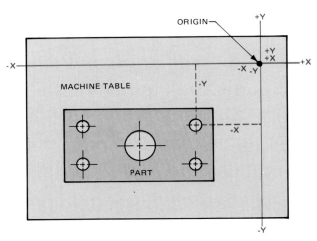

(B) LOCATION OF PART AND ORIGIN RESULTS IN 3rd QUADRANT CNC DIMENSIONING.

Fig. 14-1-6 Origin location.

Setup Point

The setup point is located on the part or the fixture holding the part. It may be the intersection of two finished surfaces, the center of a previously machined hole in the part, or a feature of the fixture. It must be accurately located in relation to the origin, as shown in Fig. 14-1-7.

Relative Coordinate (Point-to-Point) Programming

With CONTINUOUS linear dimensioning each new position is given from the last position. To compute the next position wanted, it is necessary to establish the sequence in which the work is to be done.

An example of this type of dimensioning is shown in Fig. 14-1-7A. The distance between the left edge of the part and hole 1 is given as .75 in. From hole 1 to hole 4 the dimension shown is 4.50 in. (X axis), and from hole 1 to hole 2 the dimension shown is 1.50 in. (Y axis). These dimensions give the distance from the last drilled hole to the next drilled hole. Assume the holes are to be drilled in the sequence shown in the figure. Hole 1 is located (2.75, 2.75) from the origin point. After hole 1 has been drilled, the drill spindle is positioned above the center of hole 2. Hole 2 has the same X-coordinate dimension as hole 1, making the X increment zero. Since the vertical distance between holes 1 and 2 is 1.50 in., the Y increment becomes +1.50.

After hole 2 is drilled, the drill spindle is positioned above the center of hole 3. Since the horizontal distance between holes 2 and 3 is 4.50 in., the X increment is +4.50. Hole 3 has the same Y-coordinate dimension as hole 2, making the Y increment zero.

From hole 3 the drill spindle is positioned above the center of hole 4. Hole 4 has the same X-coordinate dimension as hole 3, making the X increment zero. Since the vertical distance between hole 3 and hole 4 is 1.50 in., the Y increment is −1.50.

Figure 14-1-8 lists the distance between holes and indicates the direction of motion by plus and minus signs. It can be seen that each pair of coordinates shows the distance between each location in sequence.

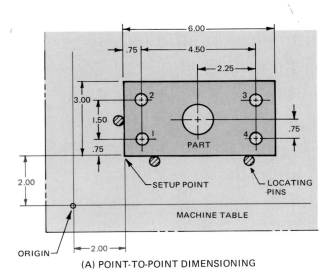

(A) POINT-TO-POINT DIMENSIONING

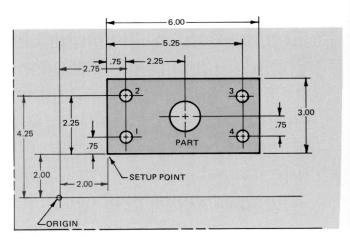

(B) BASE LINE DIMENSIONING

Fig. 14-1-7 Dimensioning for numerical control.

HOLE	X	Y
1	+ 2.75	+ 2.75
2	0	+ 1.50
3	+ 4.50	0
4	0	− 1.50

Fig. 14-1-8 Relative coordinate (point-to-point) dimensioning of holes shown in Fig. 14-1-7.

ABSOLUTE COORDINATE PROGRAMMING

Many systems now use absolute coordinate programming instead of the point-to-point method of dimensioning. With BASELINE dimensioning, all dimensions are taken from the origin, as such, baseline or datum dimensioning, as shown in Fig. 14-1-7B, is used. For example, after hole 1 is drilled, the drill spindle has to be positioned above the center of hole 2. The coordinates for hole 2 are (2.75, 4.25). Figure 14-1-9 shows the absolute coordinate dimensions of the holes shown in Fig. 14-1-7B.

HOLE	X	Y
1	+ 2.75	+ 2.75
2	+ 2.75	+ 4.25
3	+ 7.25	+ 4.25
4	+ 7.25	+ 2.75

Fig. 14-1-9 Absolute coordinate dimensioning of holes shown in Fig. 14-1-7.

ASSIGNMENTS

See Assignments 1 through 3 for Unit 14-1 starting on pages 269.

Three-Axis Control Systems

Many CNC machines operate in three directions, the table and carriage moving in the X and Y directions, and the tool spindle, such as a turret drill, traveling in an up-and-down direction. A vertical line taken through the center of the machine spindle is referred to as the Z axis and is perpendicular to the plane formed by the X and Y axes. See Fig. 14-2-1.

Thus, a point in space can be described by its X, Y, and Z coordinates. For example, $P1$ in Fig. 14-2-2 can be described by its (X, Y, Z) coordinates as $(4, 3, 5)$ and $P2$ as $(11, 2, 8)$. All dimensions of a machine part likewise would be referenced from the 0, 0, 0 origin. The part shown in Fig. 14-2-3, for example, illustrates a lower-right-rear position as 12, 10, 0. This means that the coordinate location for that corner is 12 units (inches) to the right $(+X)$ 10 units back $(+Y)$ and 0 units up $(+Z)$. All other positions are interpreted in the same manner. This coordinate location information is what is transmitted (either manually or automatically) to the CNC equipment.

A popular system used on many CNC machines, such as the turret drill, is to establish the Z zero reference plane above the workpiece. Each

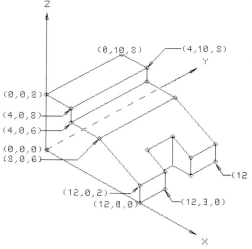

Fig. 14-2-3 Three-dimensional coordinates.

tool is then adjusted and calibrated to the Z zero reference plane.

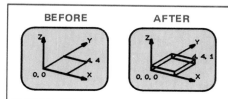

BEFORE **AFTER**

THREE-DIMENSIONAL MODELING COORDINATE POINTS ARE LOCATED AT A HORIZONTAL DISTANCE (X), A VERTICAL DISTANCE (Y), AND A DEPTH DISTANCE (Z), FROM AN 0, 0, 0 POINT (DRAWING ORIGIN).

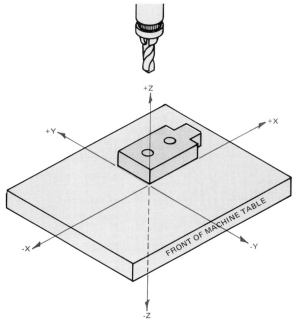

Fig. 14-2-1 X, Y, and Z axes.

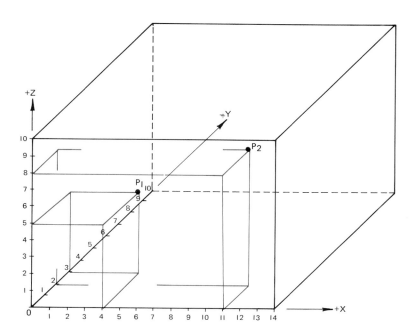

Fig. 14-2-2 Points in space.

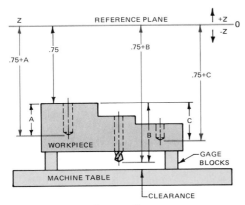

Fig. 14-2-4 Calculating Z distance.

For example, Fig. 14-2-4 shows a part requiring three drilled holes. As the center hole is drilled through, the part is raised by gage blocks so that the drill does not touch the machine table. The height of the gage blocks is determined by the distance the drill passes through the workpiece plus clearance, or .06 in. $+ 0.3D + .12$ in. See Fig. 14-2-5. If a .75 in. drill were used, the gage block height would be .06 $+$ .23 $+$ .12 $=$ .41 in.

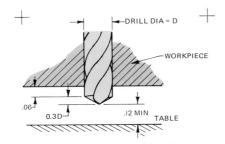

Fig. 14-2-5 Determining gage block height.

If the distance from the top of the workpiece to the Z zero reference plane is set at .75 in., the Z coordinates for the three holes shown are $-(.75 + A)$, $-(.75 + B)$, and $-(.75 + C)$.

DIMENSIONING AND TOLERANCING

Recommended guidelines for dimensioning and tolerancing practices for use in defining parts for numerical-control fabrication are:

1. When the basic coordinate system is established, the setup point should be placed at an appropriate location on the part itself.
2. Any number of subcoordinate

systems may be used to define features of a part as long as these systems can be related to the basic coordinate system of the given part.

3. Define part surfaces in relation to three mutually perpendicular reference planes. Establish these planes along part surfaces which parallel the machine axes if these axes can be predetermined.
4. Dimension the part precisely so that the physical shape can be readily determined. Dimension from the origin (0, 0, 0) to points on the part surfaces using BASE-LINE linear dimensions.
5. Regular geometric contours such as ellipses, parabolas, and hyperbolas, are shown as such on the drawing but are defined in the database by mathematical formulae. If necessary, the CNC machinery can easily be programmed to approximate these curves by linear interpolation, that is, as a series of short, straight lines whose endpoints are close enough together to ensure meeting the required tolerances for contour. In the case of arbitrary curves, the drawing should specify appropriate points on the curve by coordinate dimensions or a table of coordinates. Consideration should be given to the number of points needed to define the curve; however, one should keep in mind the fact that the tighter the tolerance or the smaller the radius of curvature, the closer together the points should be.
6. Changes in contour should be unambiguously defined with prime consideration for design intent.
7. Holes in a circular pattern should preferably be located with coordinate dimensions.
8. Where possible, express angular dimensions relative to the X axis in degrees and decimal parts of a degree.
9. Use plus and minus tolerances, not limit dimensions. Preferably, the tolerance should be equally divided bilaterally.
10. Positional tolerancing, form tolerancing, and datum referencing should be used where applicable. Datum features specified on the drawing in proper sequence will clearly indicate their usage for setup.

11. Where profile tolerances are specified, the geometric boundary should be equally disposed bilaterally along the true profile. Avoid profile tolerances applied unilaterally along the true profile. Include no less than four defined points along the profile.
12. Tolerances are specified only on the basis of actual design requirement. The accuracy capability of numerically controlled equipment is not a basis for specifying more restrictive tolerances than are functionally required.

FILE TRANSFER

After a drawing is complete you may want to "translate" it into a CAM system. UTILITY options allow drawings and files to be transferred either in or out. For example, better text manipulation may be obtained by using a word processing program with the system. It is also possible to transfer a drawing out to be used with a different CAD system.

UTILITY options such as DXF, DXB, or IGES will reduce non-compatible programs to a common denominator so that the best features of each may be utilized. With CAD/CAM the drawing must be converted to the desired CAM system. This may be accomplished by:

1. Select DXF/DXB (UTILITY)
2. Select DXFOUT (or DXFIN to transfer in)
3. Key in the filename (e.g., A: CAD-CAM)
4. Set the accuracy and END the program
5. Log on to the CAM system
6. Follow CAM instructions to MERGE DXF IN
7. Enter the drawing file name (A:CADCAM)
8. Follow CAM manufacturer instructions to create the CAM workfile and produce the part.

ASSIGNMENTS

See Assignments 4 and 5 for Unit 14-2 on page 270.

ASSIGNMENTS FOR CHAPTER 14

Assignments for Unit 14-1, Two-Axis Control Systems

1. Prepare two drawings of the cover plate shown in Fig. 14-1-A. One drawing is to use point-to-point or continuous (relative coordinate) dimensioning for the 10 holes; the other drawing is to use absolute coordinate (baseline) dimensioning. Only the dimensions locating the holes need be shown. The radial and angular dimensions are to be replaced with absolute coordinate dimensions and taken to two decimal places. Below each drawing prepare a chart listing each hole and their X and Y coordinates. The letters shown on the holes show the sequence in which they are to be drilled. Scale 1 : 1.

2. Prepare two drawings of the cover plate shown in Fig. 14-1-B. One drawing is to use continuous dimensioning for the holes; the other drawing is to use absolute coordinate dimensioning. Only the dimensions locating the holes need be shown. Below each drawing prepare a chart listing each hole and its X and Y coordinates. The

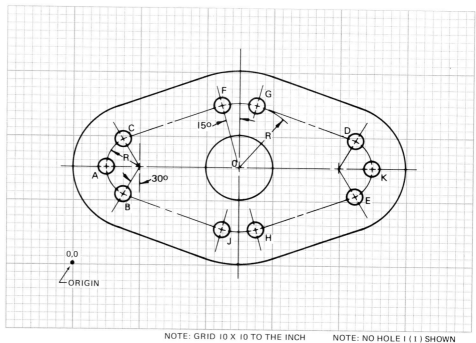

NOTE: GRID 10 X 10 TO THE INCH   NOTE: NO HOLE I (I) SHOWN

Fig. 14-1-A Cover plate.

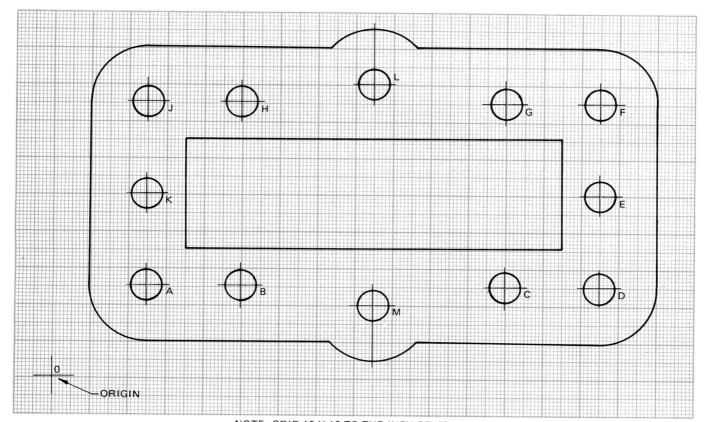

NOTE: GRID 10 X 10 TO THE INCH OR CENTIMETER   NOTE: NO HOLE I (I) SHOWN

Fig. 14-1-B Cover plate.

letters shown at the holes indicate the sequence in which they are to be drilled. Note the location of the origin. Scale 1 : 1.

3. Make a one-view drawing of the terminal board shown in Fig. 14-1-C. Convert the point-to-point dimensions to baseline programming to locate each hole. Below the drawing prepare a chart listing each hole and its *X* and *Y* coordinates. The letters on the holes show the sequence in which they are to be drilled. The origin for the *X* and *Y* coordinates is the lower left corner of the part.

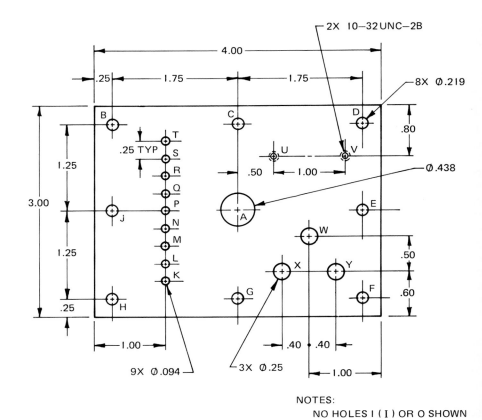

NOTES:
NO HOLES I (I) OR O SHOWN
MATL—.12 THK FIBER

Fig. 14-1-C Terminal board.

Assignments for Unit 14-2, Three-Axis Control Systems

4. Make a two-view drawing of the end plate shown in Fig. 14-2-A. Absolute (baseline) dimensioning is to be used, and only the dimensions locating the holes need be shown. The depth of the tap drill to be .12 in. below the last complete thread. Below the drawing prepare a chart listing each hole and its *X, Y,* and *Z* coordinates. Calculating the *Z* coordinate is to be done in the same manner as for the part shown in Fig. 14-2-4. Scale 1 : 1. *Note:* Programming will be for the tap-drill holes and the six through holes shown. Origin for the *X* and *Y* coordinates is the center of the end plate.

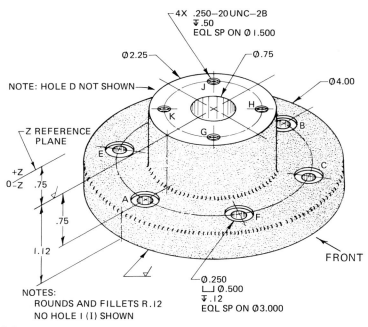

NOTES:
ROUNDS AND FILLETS R.12
NO HOLE I (I) SHOWN

Fig. 14-2-A End plate.

CHAPTER 15

Geometric Tolerancing

UNIT 15-1

Modern Engineering Tolerancing

An engineering drawing of a manufactured part is intended to convey information from the designer to the manufacturer and inspector. It must contain all information necessary for the part to be correctly manufactured. It must also enable an inspector to make a precise determination of whether the parts are acceptable.

Therefore each drawing must convey three essential types of information

1. The material to be used
2. The size or dimensions of the part
3. The shape or geometric characteristics

The drawing must also specify permissible variations for each of these aspects, in the form of tolerance or limits.

Materials are usually covered by separate specifications or supplementary documents, and the drawings need only make reference to these.

Size is specified by linear and angular dimensions. Tolerances may be applied directly to these dimensions or may be specified by means of a general tolerance note.

Shape and geometric characteristics, such as orientation and position, are described by views on the drawing, supplemented to some extent by dimensions.

In the past tolerances were often shown for which no precise interpretation existed, such as on dimensions which originated at nonexistent center lines. The specification of datum features was often omitted, resulting in measurements being made from actual surfaces when, in fact, datums were intended. There was confusion concerning the precise effect of various methods of expressing tolerances and of the number of decimal places used. While tolerancing of geometric characteristics was sometimes specified in the form of notes, no precise methods or interpretations were established. Straight or circular lines were drawn, without specifying how straight or round they should be. Square corners were drawn without specifying by how much the 90° angle could vary.

Modern systems of tolerancing, which include geometric and positional tolerancing, use of datum and datum targets, and more precise interpretations of linear and angular tolerances, provide designers and drafters with a means of expressing permissible variations in a very precise manner. Furthermore, the methods and symbols are international in scope and therefore help break down language barriers.

It is not necessary to use geometric tolerances for every feature on a part drawing. In most cases it is to be expected that if each feature meets all dimensional tolerances, form variations will be adequately controlled by the accuracy of the manufacturing process and equipment used.

This chapter covers the application of modern tolerancing methods on drawings.

National and International Standards References are made to technical drawing standards published by United States and ISO standardizing bodies. These bodies are generally referred to by their acronyms, as shown in Fig. 15-1-1.

ACRONYM	STANDARDIZING BODY	STANDARD FOR DIMENSIONING AND TOLERANCING
ANSI	AMERICAN NATIONAL STANDARDS INSTITUTE	ANSI YI4.5M
ISO	INTERNATIONAL ORGANIZATION FORI STANDARDIZATION	ISO RIIOI

Fig. 15-1-1 Standardizing bodies.

Most of the symbols in all these standards are identical, but there are some variations. These are chiefly in the methods of indicating datum features and of applying the symbols to drawings. In view of the exchange of drawings among the United States and other countries, it would be advantageous for drafters and designers to become acquainted with these different symbols.

For this reason whenever differences between United States and ISO standards occur, two methods are shown in some of the illustrations, and each is labeled with the acronym of the appropriate standardizing body, ANSI or ISO. However, differences in symbols or methods of application do not in any way affect the principles or interpretation of tolerances, unless specifically noted.

Illustrations

Most of the drawings in this chapter are not complete working drawings. They are intended only to illustrate a principle. Therefore, to avoid distraction from the information being presented, most of the details that are not essential to explain the principle have been omitted.

DEFINITIONS OF BASIC TERMS

Definitions of some of the basic terms used in dimensioning and tolerancing of drawings follow. While these terms are not new, their exact meanings warrant special attention in order that there be no ambiguity in the precise interpretation of tolerancing methods described in this chapter.

Dimension

A *dimension* is a geometric characteristic, of which the size is specified, such as diameter, length, angle, location, or center distance. The term is also used for convenience to indicate the magnitude or value of a dimension, as specified on a drawing. See Fig. 15-1-2.

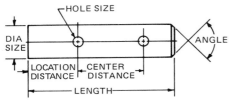

Fig. 15-1-2 Dimensions of a part.

Tolerance

The *tolerance* on a dimension is the total permissible variation in its size, which is equal to the difference between the limits of size. The plural term *tolerances* is sometimes used to denote the permissible variations from the specified size when the tolerance is expressed bilaterally.

For example, in Fig. 15-1-3A the tolerance on the center distance dimension 1.50 ± .04 is .08 in., but in common practice the values + .04 and − .04 are often referred to as the tolerances.

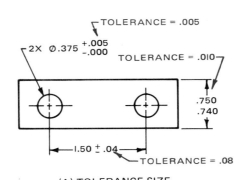

(A) TOLERANCE SIZE

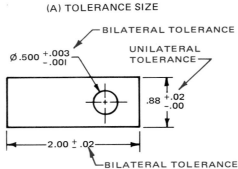

(B) TYPE OF TOLERANCE

Fig. 15-1-3 Tolerances.

A *bilateral tolerance* is a tolerance which is expressed as plus and minus values with respect to the specified size, where neither is zero, to denote permissible variations in both directions from the specified size.

A *unilateral tolerance* is one which applies in only one direction from the specified size, so that the permissible variation in the other direction is zero.

Size of Dimensions

In theory, it is impossible to produce a part to an exact size, because every part, if measured with sufficient accuracy, would be found to be a slightly different size. However, for purposes of discussion and interpretation, a number of distinct sizes for each dimension have to be recognized.

Actual Size *Actual size* simply means the measured size of an individual part.

Nominal Size The *nominal size* is the designation of size used for purposes of general identification.

The nominal size is used in referring to a part in an assembly drawing stocklist, in a specification, or in other such documents. It is very often identical to the basic size but in many instances may differ widely; for example, the external diameter of a .50 in. steel pipe is 0.84 in. (21.34 mm). The nominal size is .50 in.

Specified Size This is the size specified on the drawing when the size is associated with a tolerance. The specified size is usually identical to the design size or, if no allowance is involved, to the basic size.

Figure 15-1-4 shows two mating features with the tolerance and allowance zones exaggerated, to illustrate the sizes, tolerances, and allowances. This figure also illustrates the origin of tolerance block diagrams, as shown in Fig. 15-1-5, which are commonly used to show the relationships among part limits, gage or inspection limits, and gage tolerances.

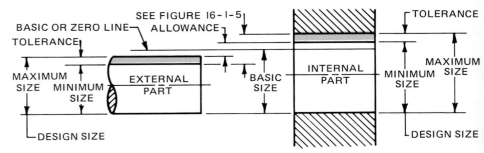

Fig. 15-1-4 Size of mating parts.

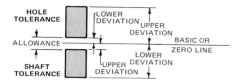

Fig. 15-1-5 Tolerance block diagram.

Design Size The *design size* of a dimension is the size in relation to which the tolerance for that dimension is assigned.

Theoretically, it is the size on which the design of the individual feature is based, and therefore it is the size which should be specified on the drawing. For dimensions of mating features it is derived from the basic size by the application of the allowance, but when there is no allowance, it is identical to the basic size.

Deviations

The differences between the basic, or zero, line and the maximum and minimum sizes are called the *upper* and *lower deviations,* respectively.

Thus in Fig. 15-1-6 the upper deviation of the external part is −.001, and the lower deviation is −.003. For the hole diameter, the upper deviation is +.002, and the lower deviation is +.001, whereas for the length of the pin the upper and lower deviations are +.02 and −.02, respectively.

Allowance A numerical value reflecting the difference between maximum and minimum sizes of mating parts, i.e., the minimum clearance or maximum interference. In Fig. 15-1-6 the allowance is .002.

Basic (Exact) Dimensions A *basic dimension* represents the theoretical exact size, profile, orientation, or location of a feature or datum target. It is the basis from which permissible variations are established by tolerances or other dimensions, in notes, or in feature control frames. See Fig. 15-1-7. They are shown without tolerances, and each basic dimension is enclosed in a rectangular frame to indicate that the tolerances in the general tolerance note do not apply.

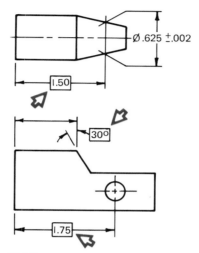

Fig. 15-1-7 Basic (exact) dimensions.

Feature

A *feature* is a specific, characteristic portion of a part, such as a surface, hole, slot, screw thread, or profile.

While a feature may include one or more surfaces, the term is generally used in geometric tolerancing in a more restricted sense, to indicate a specific point, line, or surface. Some examples are the axis of a hole, the edge of a part, or a single flat or curved surface, to which reference is being made or which forms the basis for a datum.

Axis

An *axis* is a theoretical straight line about which a part or circular feature revolves or could be considered to revolve. See Fig. 15-1-8.

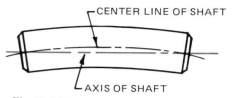

Fig. 15-1-8 Divergence of axis and center line when part is deformed.

INTERPRETATION OF DRAWINGS AND DIMENSIONS

It should not be necessary to specify the geometric shape of a feature, unless some particular precision is required. Lines which appear to be straight imply straightness; those that appear to be round imply circularity; those that appear to be parallel imply parallelism; those that appear to be square imply perpendicularity; center lines imply symmetry; and features that appear to be concentric about a common center line imply concentricity.

Therefore it is not necessary to add angular dimensions of 90° to corners of rectangular parts nor to specify that opposite sides are parallel.

However, if a particular departure from the illustrated form is permissible, or if a certain degree of precision of form is required, these must be specified. If a slight departure from the true geometric form or position is permissible, it should be exaggerated pictorially in order to show clearly where the dimensions apply. Figure 15-1-9 shows some examples. Dimensions which are not to scale should be underlined.

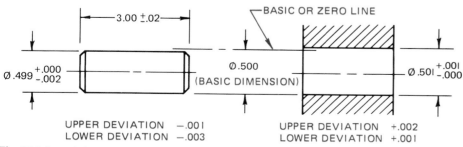

UPPER DEVIATION −.001
LOWER DEVIATION −.003

UPPER DEVIATION +.002
LOWER DEVIATION +.001

Fig. 15-1-6 Deviations.

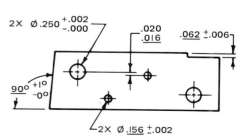

Fig. 15-1-9 Exaggeration of small dimensions.

Point-to-Point Dimensions

When datums are not specified, linear dimensions are intended to apply on a point-to-point basis, either between opposing points on the indicated surfaces or directly between the points marked on the drawing.

The examples shown in Fig. 15-1-10 should help to clarify this principle of point-to-point dimensions.

Location Dimensions with Datums

When location dimensions originate from a feature or surface specified as a datum, measurement is made from the theoretical datum, not from the actual feature or surface of the part.

There will be many cases where a curved center line, as shown in Fig. 15-1-10F, would not meet functional requirements or where the position of the hole in Fig. 15-1-10H would be required to be measured parallel to the base. This can easily be specified by referring the dimension to a datum feature, as shown in Fig. 15-1-11. This will be more fully explained in Unit 15-7, where the interpretation of coordinate tolerances is compared with geometric and positional tolerances.

Assumed Datums

There are often cases where the basic rules for measurements on a point-to-point basis cannot be applied, because the originating points, lines, or sur-

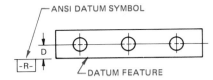

NOTE – DATUM PLANE R APPLIES TO ALL DIMENSIONS ORIGINATING FROM THIS SURFACE

(A) DRAWING CALLOUT

POINTS OF MEASUREMENT TO DATUM

(B) INTERPRETATION IF PART IS BOWED

Fig. 15-1-11 Dimensions referenced to a datum.

faces are offset in relation to the features located by the dimensions. See Fig. 15-1-12. It is then necessary to assume a suitable datum, which is usually the theoretical extension of one of the lines or surfaces involved.

The following general rules cover three types of dimensioning procedures commonly encountered.

1. If a dimension refers to two parallel edges or planes, the longer edge or larger surface, which has the greatest influence in the measurement is assumed to be the datum feature. For example, if the surfaces of the part shown in Fig. 15-1-12A were not quite parallel, as shown in the lower view, dimension D would be acceptable if the top surface were within limits when measured at a and b, but need not be within limits if measured at c.

2. If only one of the extension lines refers to a straight edge or surface, the extension of that edge or surface is assumed to be the datum. Thus in Fig. 15-1-12B measurement of dimension A is made to a datum surface as shown at a in the bottom view.

3. If both extension lines refer to offset points rather than to edges or surfaces, generally it should be assumed that the datum is a line running through one of these points and parallel to the line or surface to which it is dimensionally related. Thus in Fig. 15-1-12C dimension A is measured from the center of hole D to a line through the center of hole C which is parallel to the datum.

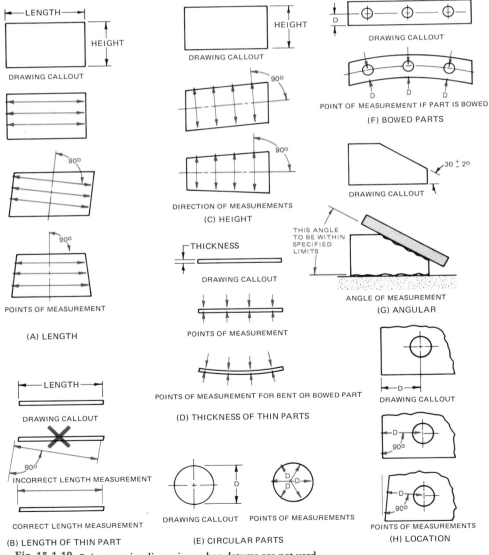

Fig. 15-1-10 Point-to-point dimensions when datums are not used.

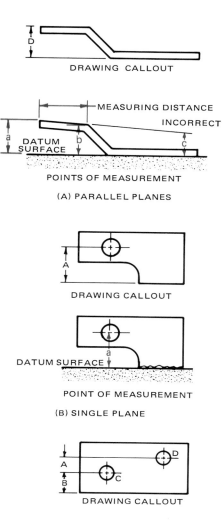

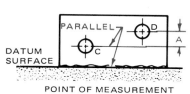

Fig. 15-1-12 Assumed datums.

Permissible Form Variations

The actual size of a feature must be within the limits of size, as specified on the drawing, at all points of measurement. This means that each measurement, made at any cross section of the feature, must not be greater than the maximum limit of size nor smaller than the minimum limit of size. See Fig. 15-1-13.

By themselves, toleranced linear dimensions, or limits of size, do not give specific control over many other variations of form, orientation, and, to some extent, position, such as errors of

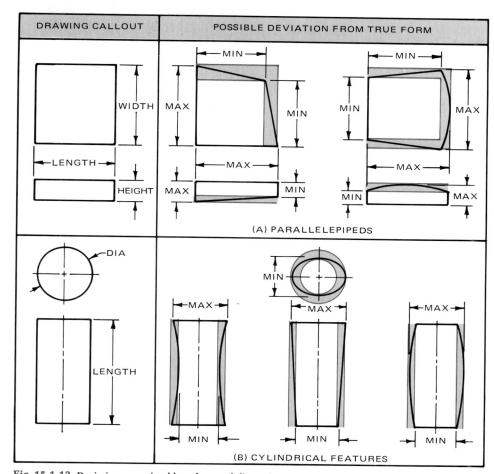

Fig. 15-1-13 Deviations permitted by toleranced dimensions.

squareness of related features or deviations caused by bending of parts, lobing, eccentricity, and the like. Therefore features may actually cross the boundaries of perfect form at the maximum material size.

In order to meet functional requirements, it is often necessary to control such deviations. This is done to ensure that parts are not only within their limits of size but also within specified limits of geometric form, orientation, and position. In the case of mating parts, such as holes and shafts, it is usually necessary to ensure that they do not deviate from perfect form at the maximum material size (envelope principle), by reason of being bent or otherwise deformed. This condition is shown in Fig. 15-1-14, where features conform to perfect form at the maximum material condition, but are permitted to deviate from perfect form at the minimum material condition.

If only size tolerances or limits of size are specified for an individual fea-

ture and no geometric tolerance is given, no element of the feature would extend beyond the maximum material boundary. Examples are shown in Fig. 15-1-15.

When geometric tolerances are applied the boundary of perfect form may be violated. Where it is desired to permit a surface of a feature to exceed the boundary of perfect form at MMC (maximum material condition), a note such as PERFECT FORM AT MMC NOT REQD is specified, exempting the pertinent size dimension from staying within the boundary of perfect form.

Reference and Source Material

1. ANSI Y14.5M, *Dimensioning and Tolerancing*.

ASSIGNMENTS

See Assignments 1 and 2 for Unit 15-1 starting on page 313.

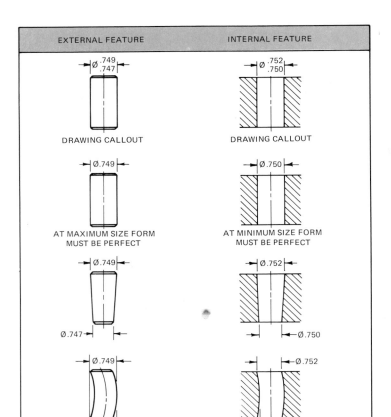

Fig. 15-1-14 Examples of deviation of form when perfect form at the maximum material condition is required.

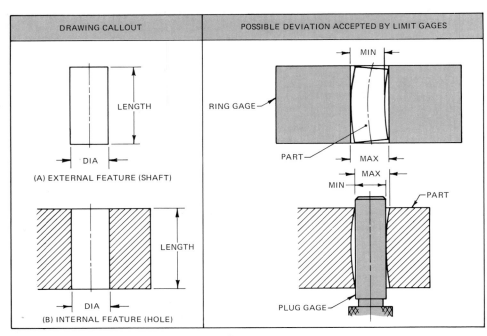

Fig. 15-1-15 Form variations accepted by gage limits.

Geometric Tolerancing

In principle, where only size tolerances or limits of size are specified for an individual feature, and no form tolerance is given, the maximum material limit of size could be expected to define an envelope of perfect form, and no element of the feature should extend beyond the boundary. However, this principle is not guaranteed unless suitable geometric tolerances are specified on the drawing. When perfect form at MMC for an individual feature is a critical functional requirement, i.e., where no element of the feature can be allowed to cross the boundary of perfect form at the maximum material size, a geometric tolerance of zero MMC (see Unit 15-3) must be specified.

A geometric tolerance is the maximum permissible variation of form, profile, orientation, location, and runout from that indicated or specified on the drawing. The tolerance value represents the width or diameter of the tolerance zone, within which the point, line, or surface of the feature shall lie.

From this definition it follows that a feature would be permitted to have any variation of form, or take up any position, within the specified geometric tolerance zone.

For example, a line controlled in a single plane by a straightness tolerance of .006 in. must be contained within a tolerance zone .006 in. wide. See Fig. 15-2-1.

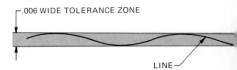

Fig. 15-2-1 Tolerance zone for straightness of a line.

Points, Lines, and Surfaces

The production and measurement of engineering parts deals, in most cases, with surfaces of objects. These surfaces may be flat, cylindrical, conical, or spherical or have some more or less irregular shape or contour.

Measurement, however, usually has to take place at specific points. A line or surface is evaluated dimensionally by making a series of measurements at various points along its length.

Therefore, geometric tolerances are chiefly concerned with points and lines, while surfaces are considered to be composed of a series of line elements running in two or more directions.

Points have position but no size, and therefore position is the only characteristic that requires control. Lines and surfaces have to be controlled for form, orientation, and location. Therefore geometric tolerances provide for control of these characteristics as shown in Fig. 15-2-2.

FEATURE CONTROL FRAME

Some geometric tolerances have been used for many years in the form of notes such as "PARALLEL WITH SURFACE *A* WITHIN .001" and "STRAIGHT WITHIN .12." While such notes are now obsolete, the reader should be prepared to recognize them on older drawings.

The current method is to specify geometric tolerances by means of the *feature control frame*. A feature control frame for an individual feature is divided into compartments containing the geometric characteristic symbol followed by the tolerance. See Fig. 15-2-3. Where applicable, the tolerance is preceded by the diameter symbol (see Unit 15-4) and may be followed by a material condition symbol (see Unit 15-3).

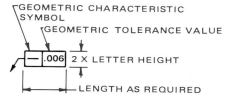

Fig. 15-2-3 Feature control frame for an individual feature.

The first compartment contains a symbol representing the geometric characteristic to be controlled. The second compartment contains the required tolerance value. When necessary, other compartments are added to contain datum references, as explained in Unit 15-5.

Geometric characteristic symbols used for form of a line are shown in Fig. 15-2-2. Other symbols will be introduced as required, but all are shown in this Unit for reference purposes.

SYMBOLS

Any geometric tolerance symbol may be created on a drawing. Use the LINE, CIRCLE, ARC, and/or LEADER commands to draw each one. If your drawing requires multiples of the same symbol, use the COPY command. It will be even faster and easier to place symbols on a drawing if a standard library is available. Simply access the desired symbol from the geometric tolerance library and place it where desired. One method is to draw and place in the library the complete feature control frame. More likely, however, the option to place each portion of the feature control frame individually will exist. In this way you will select the type of symbol(s), tolerance, relation to feature of

FEATURE	TYPE OF TOLERANCE	CHARACTERISTIC	SYMBOL	SEE UNIT
INDIVIDUAL FEATURES	FORM	STRAIGHTNESS	—	15-2, 15-4
		FLATNESS	▱	15-4
		CIRCULARITY (ROUNDNESS)	○	15-9
		CYLINDRICITY	⌭	
INDIVIDUAL OR RELATED FEATURES	PROFILE	PROFILE OF A LINE	⌒	15-10
		PROFILE OF A SURFACE	⌓	
RELATED FEATURES	ORIENTATION	ANGULARITY	∠	15-6
		PERPENDICULARITY	⊥	
		PARALLELISM	//	
	LOCATION	POSITION, SYMMETRY	⊕	15-7, 15-11
		CONCENTRICITY	◎	15-11
	RUNOUT	CIRCULAR RUNOUT	*↗	15-11
		TOTAL RUNOUT	*↗↗	
SUPPLEMENTARY SYMBOLS		MAXIMUM MATERIAL CONDITION	Ⓜ	15-3
		REGARDLESS OF FEATURE SIZE	Ⓢ	
		LEAST MATERIAL CONDITION	Ⓛ	
		PROJECTED TOLERANCE ZONE	Ⓟ	15-7
		ENVELOPE PRINCIPLE	Ⓔ **	15-1
		BASIC DIMENSION	XX	15-7, 15-8
		DATUM FEATURE	—A—	15-5
		DATUM TARGET	Ø.50 / A2	15-8

* MAY BE FILLED IN
** NOT USED IN ANSI STANDARDS

Fig. 15-2-2 Geometric characteristic symbols.

size, and datum surface identity prior to placement. Thus, by predefining the parameters, the library will be much smaller. It will not need every symbol in every possible combination to be predrawn and stored as individual symbols. In any case, if the library does not fit all of your applications, it may be modified. Also, if a geometric tolerance library is not standard, one can be created.

When necessary, other compartments are added to contain datum references, as explained in Unit 15-5.

Geometric characteristic symbols relating to lines (straightness, angularity, perpendicularity, profile of a line, parallelism position) are shown in Fig. 15-2-2. Other symbols will be introduced as required, but all are shown in the figure for reference purposes.

Application to Drawings

The feature control frame is related to the feature by one of the following methods (shown in Fig. 15-2-4):

1. Locating the frame below the size dimension to control the centerline, axis, or center plane of the feature.
2. Running a leader from the frame to the feature.
3. Attaching a side or end of the frame to an extension line extending from a plane surface feature.

4. Attaching a side or end of the frame to an extension of the dimension line pertaining to a feature of size. ISO practice is to attach the dimension line to the feature control frame and place the feature of size above or below the frame.

Application to Surfaces

The arrowhead of the leader from the feature control frame should touch the surface of the feature or the extension line of the surface.

The leader from the feature control frame should be directed at the feature in its characteristic profile. Thus, in Fig. 15-2-5 the straightness tolerance is directed to the side view, and the circularity tolerance to the end view. This may not always be possible,

and a tolerance connected to an alternative view, such as a circularity tolerance connected to a side view, is acceptable. When it is more convenient, or when space is limited, the arrowhead may be directed to an extension line, but not in line with the dimension line.

When two or more feature control frames apply to the same feature, they are drawn together with a single leader and arrowhead, as shown in Fig. 15-2-6.

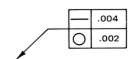

Fig. 15-2-6 Combined feature control frames directed to one surface.

CIRCULAR TOLERANCE ZONES

When the resulting tolerance zone is cylindrical, such as when straightness of the center line of a cylindrical feature is specified, a diameter symbol precedes the tolerance value in the feature control frame and the feature control frame is located below the dimension pertaining to the feature. See Fig. 15-2-7 and refer to Unit 15-4.

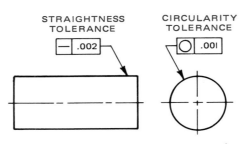

Fig. 15-2-5 Preferred location of feature control symbol.

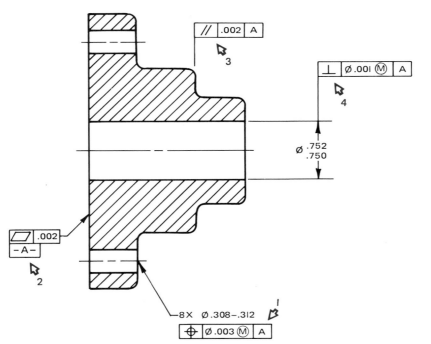

Fig. 15-2-4 Placement of feature control frame.

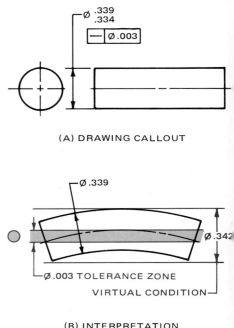

Fig. 15-2-7 Specifying straightness — RFS.

Form Tolerances

Form tolerances control straightness, flatness, circularity, and cylindricity. Orientation tolerances control angularity, parallelism, and perpendicularity.

Form tolerances are applicable to single (individual) features or elements of single features, therefore, form tolerances are not related to datums.

Form and orientation tolerances critical to function and interchangeability are specified where the tolerance of size and location do not provide sufficient control. A tolerance of form or orientation may be specified where no tolerance of size is given, e.g., the control of flatness.

STRAIGHTNESS

Straightness is a condition where the element of a surface or a center line is a straight line. A straightness tolerance specifies a tolerance zone within which the considered element of the surface or center line must lie. A straightness tolerance is applied in the view where the elements to be controlled are represented by a straight line. The straightness tolerance must be less than the size tolerance.

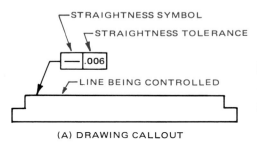

(A) DRAWING CALLOUT

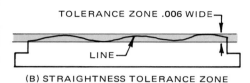

(B) STRAIGHTNESS TOLERANCE ZONE

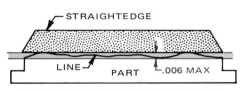

(C) CHECKING WITH A STRAIGHTEDGE

Fig. 15-2-8 Straightness symbol and application.

Straightness Controlling Surface Elements

Lines Straightness is fundamentally a characteristic of a line, such as the edge of a part or a line scribed on a surface. A straightness tolerance is specified on a drawing by means of a

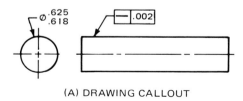

(A) DRAWING CALLOUT

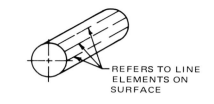

BENDING ERROR

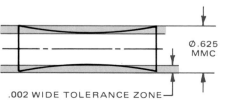

CONCAVE ERROR

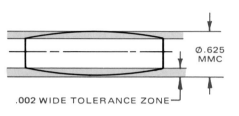

CONVEX ERROR

(B) INTERPRETATION

NOTE – NO PART OF THE CYLINDRICAL SURFACE MAY LIE OUTSIDE THE LIMITS OF SIZE

Fig. 15-2-9 Straightness errors in surface elements of a cylindrical part.

feature control frame, which is directed by a leader to the line requiring control, as shown in Fig. 15-2-8. It states in symbolic form that the line shall be straight within .006 in. This means that the line shall be contained within a tolerance zone consisting of the area between two parallel straight lines in the same plane, separated by the specified tolerance.

Theoretically, straightness could be measured by bringing a straightedge into contact with the line and determining that any space between the straightedge and the line does not exceed the specified tolerance.

Cylindrical Surfaces For cylindrical parts, or curved surfaces which are straight in one direction, the feature control frame should be directed to the side view, where line elements appear as a straight line, as shown in Figs. 15-2-9 and 15-2-10.

A straightness tolerance thus applied to the surface controls surface elements only. Therefore it would control bending or a wavy condition of the surface or a barrel-shaped part, but it would not necessarily control the straightness of the center line or the conicity of the cylinder.

Straightness of a cylindrical surface is interpreted to mean that each line element of the surface shall be contained within a tolerance zone consist-

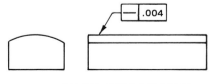

(A) DRAWING CALLOUT

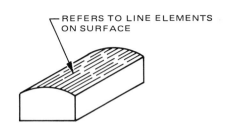

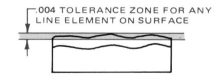

(B) INTERPRETATION

Fig. 15-2-10 Straightness of surface line elements.

ing of the space between two parallel lines, separated by the width of the specified tolerance, when the part is rolled along one of the planes. All circular elements of the surface must be within the specified size tolerance. When only limits of size (or a tolerance) are specified without other references to MMC, RFS, LMC (see Unit 15-3), no error in straightness would be permitted if the diameter were at its maximum material size. Since the limits of size must be respected, the full straightness tolerance may not be available for opposite elements in the case of waisting or barreling of the surface. See Fig. 15-2-9.

Conical Surfaces A straightness tolerance can be applied to a conical surface in the same manner as for a cylindrical surface, as shown in Fig. 15-2-11, and will ensure that the rate of taper is uniform. The actual rate of taper, or the taper angle, must be separately toleranced.

Flat Surfaces A straightness tolerance applied to a flat surface indicates straightness control in one direction only and must be directed to the line on the drawing representing the surface to be controlled and the direction in which control is required, as shown in Fig. 15-2-12A. It is then interpreted to mean that each line element on the surface in the indicated direction shall lie within a tolerance zone.

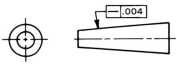

(A) DRAWING CALLOUT

DRAWING CALLOUT REFERS TO EACH LINE ON SURFACE

.004 TOLERANCE ZONE FOR ANY LINE ELEMENT ON SURFACE

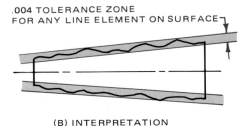

(B) INTERPRETATION

Fig. 15-2-11 Straightness of a conical surface.

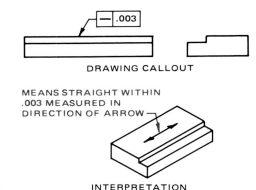

DRAWING CALLOUT

MEANS STRAIGHT WITHIN .003 MEASURED IN DIRECTION OF ARROW

INTERPRETATION

(A) STRAIGHTNESS IN ONE DIRECTION

SPECIFYING STRAIGHTNESS OF A FLAT SURFACE

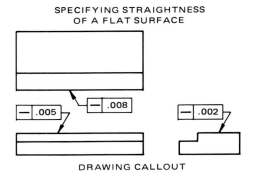

DRAWING CALLOUT

STRAIGHT WITHIN .002 MEASURED IN DIRECTION OF ARROWS

STRAIGHT WITHIN .005 MEASURED IN DIRECTION OF ARROWS

STRAIGHT WITHIN .008 MEASURED IN DIRECTION OF ARROWS

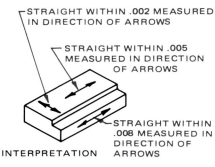

INTERPRETATION

(B) STRAIGHTNESS IN SEVERAL DIRECTIONS

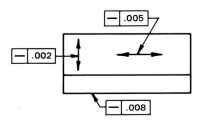

(C) THREE STRAIGHTNESS TOLERANCES ON ONE VIEW

Fig. 15-2-12 Three straightness tolerances on one view.

Different straightness tolerances may be specified in two or more directions when required, as shown in Fig. 15-2-12B. However, if the same straightness tolerance is required in

two coordinate directions on the same surface, a flatness tolerance rather than a straightness tolerance is used.

If it is not otherwise necessary to draw all three views, the straightness tolerances may all be shown on a single view by indicating the direction with short lines terminated by arrowheads, as shown in Fig. 15-2-12C.

Reference and Source Material

1. ANSI Y14.5M, *Dimensioning and Tolerancing.*

ASSIGNMENT

See Assignment 3 for Unit 15-2 on page 316.

■ UNIT 15-3

Relationship to Feature of Size

DEFINITIONS

Maximum Material Condition (MMC) When a feature or part is at the limit of size which results in it containing the maximum amount of material it is said to be at MMC. Thus it is the maximum limit of size for an external feature, such as a shaft, or the minimum limit of size for an internal feature, such as a hole. See Fig. 15-3-1.

Virtual Condition (Size) *Virtual condition* refers to the overall envelope of perfect form within which the feature would just fit. For an external feature such as a shaft, it is the maximum measured size plus the effect of permissible form variations, such as straightness, flatness, roundness, cylindricity, and orientation tolerances. For an internal feature such as a hole, it is the minimum measured size minus the effect of such form variations. See Fig. 15-3-1.

Least Material Condition (LMC) This term refers to that size of a feature which results in the part containing the minimum amount of material. Thus it is the minimum limit of size for an external feature, for example, a shaft, and the maximum limit of size for an internal feature, such as a hole. See Fig. 15-3-2.

Regardless of Feature Size (RFS) This term indicates that a geometric

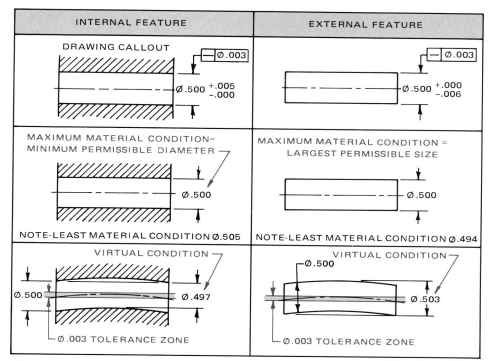

Fig. 15-3-1 Maximum material and virtual conditions.

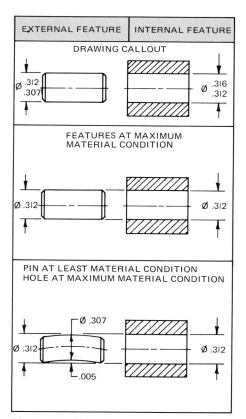

Fig. 15-3-2 Effect of form variation when only features of size are specified.

tolerance applies to any size of a feature which lies within its size tolerance.

MATERIAL CONDITION SYMBOLS

The symbols used to indicate "at maximum material condition,""regardless of feature size," and "at least material condition" are shown in Fig. 15-3-4. The United States is the only country to adopt the latter two symbols. The use of these symbols in local or general notes is prohibited.

Applicability of RFS, MMC, and LMC

Applicability of RFS, MMC, and LMC is limited to features subject to variations in size. They may be datum features or other features whose axes or center planes are controlled by geometric tolerances. In such cases, the following practices apply.

1. *Tolerance of position.* RFS, MMC, or LMC must be specified on the drawing with respect to the individual tolerance, datum reference, or both, as applicable.

2. *All other geometric tolerances.* RFS applies, with respect to the individual tolerance, datum reference, or both, where no modifying symbol is specified. MMC or LMC must be specified on the drawing where it is required.

FEATURES OF SIZE

Geometric tolerances which have so far been considered concern only lines, line elements, and single surfaces. These are features having no diameter or thickness, and tolerances applied to them cannot be affected by feature size.

Features of size are features which do have diameter or thickness. These may be cylinders, such as shafts and holes. They may be slots, tabs, or rectangular or flat parts, where two parallel, flat surfaces are considered to form a single feature. With features of size, the feature control frame is associated with the size dimension. See Figs. 15-3-1 and 15-3-7.

If freedom of assembly of mating parts is the chief criterion for establishing a geometric tolerance for a feature of size, the least favorable assembly condition exists when the parts are made to the maximum material condition. Further geometric variations can then be permitted, without jeopardizing assembly, as the features approach their least material condition.

EXAMPLE 1 The effect of a form tolerance is shown in Fig. 15-3-2, where a cylindrical pin of $\emptyset.307 - .312$ in. is intended to assemble into a round hole of $\emptyset.312 - .316$ in. If both parts are at their maximum material condition of $\emptyset.312$ in., it is evident that both would have to be perfectly round and straight in order to assemble. However, if the pin was at its least material condition of $\emptyset.307$ in., it could be bent up to .005 in. and still assemble in the smallest permissible hole.

EXAMPLE 2 Another example, based on the location of features, is shown in Fig. 15-3-3. This shows a part with two projecting pins required to assemble into a mating part having two holes at the same center distance.

The worst assembly condition exists when the pins and holes are at their maximum material condition, which is $\emptyset.250$ in. Theoretically, these parts would just assemble if their form, ori-

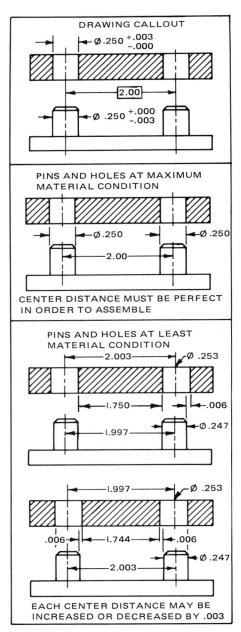

DRAWING CALLOUT

Ø.250 +.003 / -.000

2.00

Ø.250 +.000 / -.003

PINS AND HOLES AT MAXIMUM MATERIAL CONDITION

Ø.250

2.00

Ø.250

CENTER DISTANCE MUST BE PERFECT IN ORDER TO ASSEMBLE

PINS AND HOLES AT LEAST MATERIAL CONDITION

2.003

Ø.253

1.750

.006

1.997

Ø.247

1.997

Ø.253

.006

1.744

.006

2.003

Ø.247

EACH CENTER DISTANCE MAY BE INCREASED OR DECREASED BY .003

Fig. 15-3-3 Effect on location.

entation (squareness to the surface), and center distances were perfect. However, if the pins and holes were at their least material condition of Ø.247 and Ø.253 in., respectively, it is evident that one center distance could be increased and the other decreased by .003 in. without jeopardizing the assembly condition.

MAXIMUM MATERIAL CONDITION (MMC)

The symbol for MMC is shown in Fig. 15-3-4. The symbol sizes are based on percentages of the recommended letter height of dimensions.

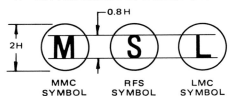

H = LETTER HEIGHT OF DIMENSIONS

0.8H

2H

M   **S**   **L**

MMC SYMBOL   RFS SYMBOL   LMC SYMBOL

Fig. 15-3-4 Modifying symbols.

If a geometric tolerance is required to be modified on an MMC basis, it is specified on the drawing by including the symbol Ⓜ immediately after the tolerance value in the feature control frame as shown in Fig. 15-3-5.

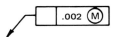

.002 Ⓜ

Fig. 15-3-5 Application of MMC symbol.

A form tolerance modified in this way can be applied only to a feature of size; it cannot be applied to a single surface. It controls the boundary of

the feature, such as a complete cylindrical surface, or two parallel surfaces of a flat feature. This permits the feature surface or surfaces to cross the maximum material boundary by the amount of the form tolerance unless it is required that the virtual condition be kept within the maximum material boundary in which case the form tolerance must be specified as zero at MMC, as shown in Fig. 15-3-6. However, a note such as PERFECT FORM AT MMC NOT REQD must be specified on the drawing. See Figs. 15-4-1 and 15-4-2.

.000 Ⓜ

NUMBER OF DIGITS SHOWN TO CORRESPOND WITH THE SIZE DIMENSION

(A) INCH APPLICATIONS

0 Ⓜ

(B) ALL METRIC APPLICATIONS

Fig. 15-3-6 MMC symbol with zero tolerance.

CHARACTERISTIC TOLERANCE		THE MAXIMUM MATERIAL CONDITION CONCEPT MAY BE APPLIED IF INDICATED BELOW, TO THE FEATURE BEING TOLERANCED AND/OR THE DATUM FEATURE ACCORDING TO THE DESIGN REQUIRED	
STRAIGHTNESS	—	**YES** FOR A FEATURE THE SIZE OF WHICH IS SPECIFIED BY A TOLERANCED DIMENSION, SUCH AS A HOLE, SHAFT OR A SLOT	**NO** FOR A PLANE SURFACE OR A LINE ON A SURFACE
PARALLELISM	//		
PERPENDICULARITY	⊥		
ANGULARITY	∠		
POSITION	⊕		
CONCENTRICITY	◎		
SYMMETRY	⊕		
FLATNESS	▱	**NO** FOR ALL FEATURES	
CIRCULARITY (ROUNDNESS)	○		
CYLINDRICITY	⌭		
PROFILE OF A LINE	⌒		
PROFILE OF A SURFACE	⌓		
CIRCULAR RUNOUT	↗		
TOTAL RUNOUT	↗↗		

Fig. 15-3-7 Application of maximum material condition to geometric symbols.

Application of MMC to geometric symbols is shown in Fig. 15-3-7.

Application with Maximum Value
It is sometimes necessary to ensure that the geometric tolerance does not vary over the full range permitted by the size variations. For such applications a maximum limit may be set to the geometric tolerance and this is shown in addition to that permitted at the maximum material condition, as shown in Fig. 15-3-8.

Fig. 15-3-8 Tolerance with a maximum specified value.

REGARDLESS OF FEATURE SIZE (RFS)

When MMC or LMC is not specified with a geometric tolerance for a feature of size, no relationship is intended to exist between the feature size and the geometric tolerance. In other words, the tolerance applies regardless of feature size.

In this case, the geometric tolerance controls the form, orientation, or location of the center line, axis, or median plane of the feature.

The regardless of feature size symbol shown in Fig. 15-3-4 is used only with a tolerance of position. See Unit 15-7 and Fig. 15-3-9.

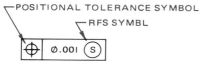

Fig. 15-3-9 Application of RFS symbol.

LEAST MATERIAL CONDITION (LMC)

The symbol for least material condition is shown in Fig. 15-3-4. It is the condition in which a feature of size contains the least amount of material within the stated limits of size. Specifying LMC is limited to positional tolerance applications where MMC does not provide the desired control and RFS is too restrictive. LMC is used to maintain a desired relationship between the surface of a feature and its true position at tolerance extremes. See Unit 15-7 and Fig. 15-3-10.

The symbols for RFS and LMC are used only in ANSI standards and have not been adopted internationally.

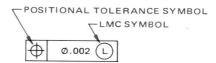

Fig. 15-3-10 Application of LMC symbol.

Reference and Source Material

1. ANSI Y14.5M, *Dimensioning and Tolerancing*.

ASSIGNMENTS

See Assignments 4 through 7 for Unit 15-3 on page 316.

■ UNIT 15-4

Straightness of a Feature of Size and Flatness

STRAIGHTNESS OF A FEATURE OF SIZE

Figures 15-4-1 and 15-4-2 show examples of cylindrical parts where all circular elements of the surface are to be within the specified size tolerance; however, the boundary of perfect form at MMC may be violated. This violation is permissible when the feature control frame is associated with the size dimension, or attached to an extension of the dimension line. In the two figures a diameter symbol precedes the tolerance value and the tolerance is applied on a RFS and a MMC basis respectively. Normally the straightness tolerance is smaller than the size tolerance but a specific design may allow the situation depicted in the figures. The collective effect of size and form variation can produce a virtual condition equal to the MMC size plus the straightness tolerance. See Fig. 15-4-2. The derived center line of the feature must lie within a cylindrical tolerance zone as specified.

Straightness — RFS

When applied on an RFS basis, as in Fig. 15-4-1, the maximum permissible

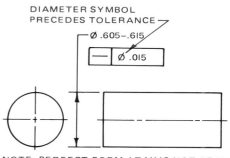

NOTE: PERFECT FORM AT MMC NOT REQD

(A) DRAWING CALLOUT

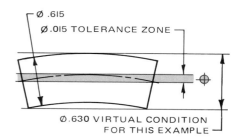

(B) INTERPRETATION

Fig. 15-4-1 Specifying straightness — RFS.

deviation from straightness is .015 in. regardless of the feature size. Note the absence of a modifying symbol indicates that RFS applies. The RFS symbol Ⓢ is shown only with a tolerance of position.

Straightness — MMC

If the straightness tolerance of .015 in. is required only at MMC, further straightness error can be permitted without jeopardizing assembly, as the feature approaches its least material size, Fig. 15-4-2. The maximum straightness tolerance is the specified tolerance plus the amount the feature departs from its MMC size. The center line of the actual feature must lie within the derived cylindrical tolerance zone such as given in the table of Fig. 15-4-2.

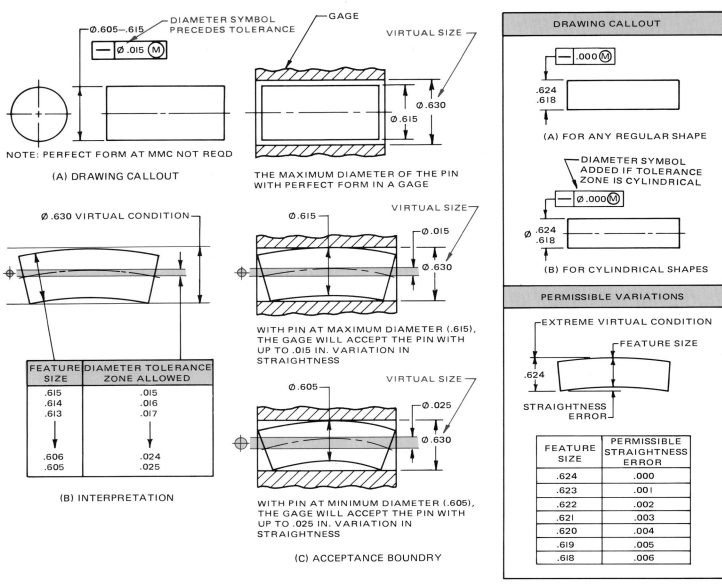

Fig. 15-4-2 Specifying straightness — MMC.

Fig. 15-4-3 Straightness — 0 MMC.

Straightness — Zero MMC

It is quite permissible to specify a geometric tolerance of zero MMC, which means that the virtual condition coincides with the maximum material size. See Fig. 15-4-3. Therefore, if a feature is at its maximum material limit everywhere, no errors of straightness are permitted.

Straightness on an MMC basis can be applied to any part or feature having straight-line elements in a plane which includes the diameter or thickness. This includes practically all the parts already shown on an RFS basis. However, it should not be used for features which do not have a uniform cross section.

Straightness with a Maximum Value

If it is desired to ensure that the straightness error does not become too great when the part approaches the least material condition, a maximum value may be added, as shown in Fig. 15-4-4.

Shapes Other Than Round

A straightness tolerance, not modified by MMC, may be applied to parts or features of any size or shape, provided they have a center plane, as in Fig. 15-4-5, which is intended to be straight in the direction indicated. Examples are parts having a hexagonal,

square, or rectangular cross section.

Tolerances directed in this manner apply to straightness of the center plane between all opposing line elements of the surfaces in the direction to which the control is directed. The width of the tolerance zone is in the direction of the arrowhead. If the cross section forms a regular polygon, such as a hexagon or square, the tolerance applies to the center plane between each pair of sides, without its being necessary to so state on the drawing.

Control in Specific Directions

As already stated, straightness of a center line applies only to center lines

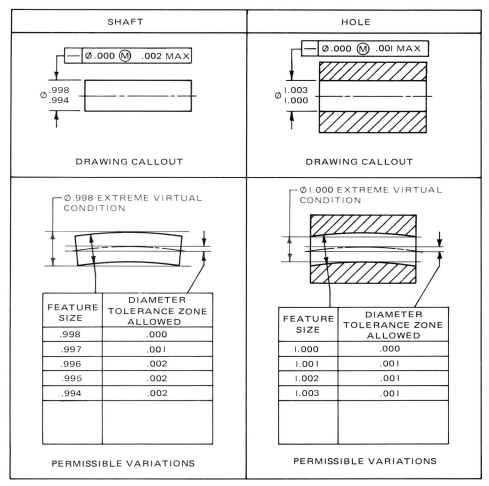

SHAFT	HOLE
— Ø.000 Ⓜ .002 MAX	— Ø.000 Ⓜ .001 MAX
Ø .998 / .994	Ø 1.003 / 1.000
DRAWING CALLOUT	DRAWING CALLOUT
⌐ Ø.998 EXTREME VIRTUAL CONDITION	⌐ Ø 1.000 EXTREME VIRTUAL CONDITION

FEATURE SIZE	DIAMETER TOLERANCE ZONE ALLOWED
.998	.000
.997	.001
.996	.002
.995	.002
.994	.002

FEATURE SIZE	DIAMETER TOLERANCE ZONE ALLOWED
1.000	.000
1.001	.001
1.002	.001
1.003	.001

PERMISSIBLE VARIATIONS   PERMISSIBLE VARIATIONS

Fig. 15-4-4 Straightness of a shaft and hole with a maximum value.

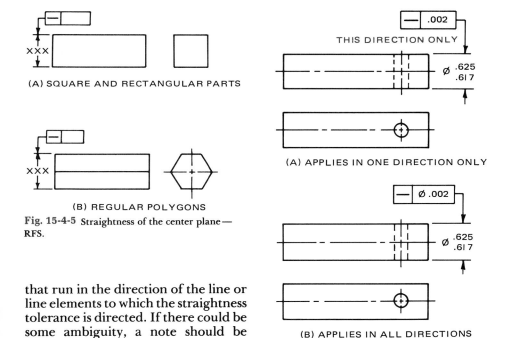

(A) SQUARE AND RECTANGULAR PARTS

(B) REGULAR POLYGONS

Fig. 15-4-5 Straightness of the center plane — RFS.

that run in the direction of the line or line elements to which the straightness tolerance is directed. If there could be some ambiguity, a note should be added, such as THIS DIRECTION ONLY, as shown in Fig. 15-4-6A. If

THIS DIRECTION ONLY — .002

Ø .625 / .617

(A) APPLIES IN ONE DIRECTION ONLY

— Ø .002

Ø .625 / .617

(B) APPLIES IN ALL DIRECTIONS

Fig. 15-4-6 Direction of application of straightness.

the part is circular and it is intended that the tolerance apply in all directions, a diameter symbol should precede the tolerance value, as shown in Fig. 15-4-6B.

If different tolerances apply in two directions, the tolerance zone is then a parallelepiped, as shown in Fig. 15-4-7.

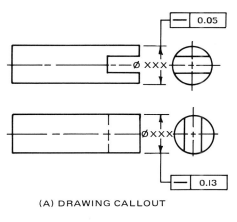

— 0.05

Ø XXX

Ø XXX

— 0.13

(A) DRAWING CALLOUT

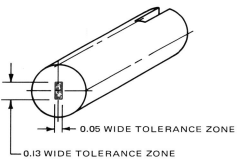

0.05 WIDE TOLERANCE ZONE

0.13 WIDE TOLERANCE ZONE

(B) TOLERANCE ZONE

Fig. 15-4-7 Straightness in two directions.

Straightness per Unit Length

Straightness may be applied on a unit length basis as a means of preventing an abrupt surface variation within a relatively short length of the feature. See Fig. 15-4-8. Caution should be exercised when using unit control without specifying a maximum limit for the total length because of the relatively large variations that may result if no such restriction is applied. This is because if the feature has a uniformly continuous bow throughout its length which just conforms to the tolerance applicable to the unit length then the overall tolerance may result in an unsatisfactory part. Figure 15-4-9 illustrates the possible condition if the

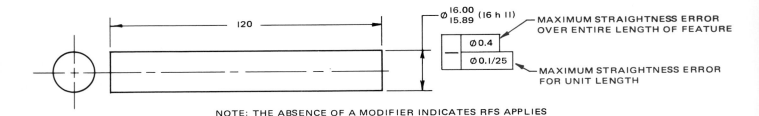

NOTE: THE ABSENCE OF A MODIFIER INDICATES RFS APPLIES

(A) DRAWING CALLOUT

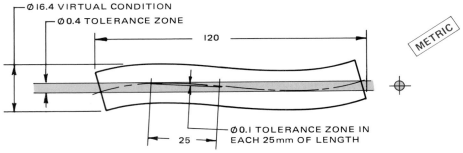

(B) INTERPRETATION

Fig. 15-4-8 Specifying straightness per unit length with specified total straightness, both RFS.

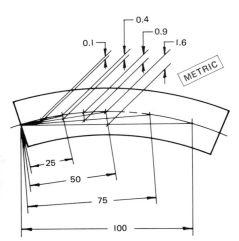

Fig. 15-4-9 Possible results of specifying straightness per unit length RFS with no maximum specified.

straightness per unit length given in Fig. 15-4-8 is used alone, that is, if straightness for the total length is not specified.

FLATNESS

The symbol for flatness is a parallelogram, with angles of 60° as shown in Fig. 15-4-10. The length and height are based on a percentage of the height of the lettering used on the drawing.

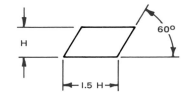

H = RECOMMENDED LETTER HEIGHT

Fig. 15-4-10 Flatness symbol.

Flatness of a Surface

Flatness of a surface is a condition in which all surface elements are in one plane. On such a surface all line elements in two or more directions are straight.

A flatness tolerance is applied to a line representing the surface of a part by means of a feature control frame, as shown in Fig. 15-4-11.

A flatness tolerance means that all points on the surface shall be contained within a tolerance zone consisting of the space between two parallel planes which are separated by the specified tolerance. These planes may be oriented in any manner to contain the surface; that is, they are not necessarily parallel to the base.

Where the considered surface is associated with a size dimension, the

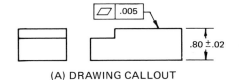

(A) DRAWING CALLOUT

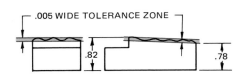

(B) INTERPRETATION

Fig. 15-4-11 Specifying flatness of a surface.

flatness tolerance must be less than the size tolerance.

If the same control is desired on two or more surfaces, a suitable note indicating the number of surfaces may be added instead of repeating the symbol, as shown in Fig. 15-4-12.

Flatness per Unit Area

Flatness may be applied, as in the case of straightness, on a unit basis as a means of preventing an abrupt surface variation within a relatively small area

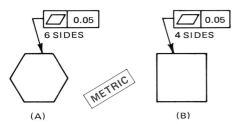

Fig. 15-4-12 Controlling flatness on two or more surfaces.

of the feature. The unit variation is used either in combination with a specified total variation, or alone. Caution should be exercised when using unit control alone for the same reason as was given to straightness.

Since flatness involves surface area, the size of the unit area, for example, 1.00×1.00 in., is specified to the right of the flatness tolerance, separated by a slash line. See Fig. 15-4-13.

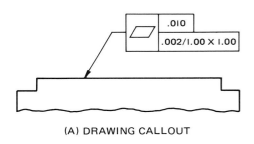

(A) DRAWING CALLOUT

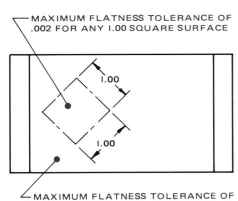

(B) INTERPRETATION

Fig. 15-4-13 Overall flatness tolerance combined with a flatness tolerance of a unit area.

Two or More Flat Surfaces in One Plane

Coplanarity is the condition of two or more surfaces having all elements in one plane. Coplanarity may be con-

trolled by form, orientation, or locational tolerancing, depending on the functional requirements.

Reference and Source Material

1. ANSI Y14.5M, *Dimensioning and Tolerancing*.

ASSIGNMENTS

See Assignments 8 through 12 for Unit 15-4 on page 317.

■ UNIT 15-5

Datums and the Three-Plane Concept

DATUMS

Datum A *datum* is a point, line, plane, or other geometric surface from which dimensions are measured when so specified or to which geometric tolerances are referenced. A datum has an exact form and represents an exact or fixed location, for purposes of manufacture or measurement.

Datum Feature A *datum feature* is a feature of a part, such as an edge or a surface, which forms the basis for a datum or is used to establish its location.

DATUMS FOR GEOMETRIC TOLERANCING

As defined, datums are exact geometric points, lines, or surfaces, each based on one or more datum features of the part. Surfaces are usually either flat or cylindrical, but other shapes are used when necessary. The datum features, being physical surfaces of the part, are subject to manufacturing errors and variations. For example, a flat surface of a part, if greatly magnified, will show some irregularity. If brought into contact with a perfect plane, it will touch only at the highest points, as shown in Fig. 15-5-1. The true datums are theoretical but are considered to exist, or to be simulated, by locating surfaces of machines, fixtures, and gaging equipment on which the part rests or with which it makes contact during manufacture and measurement.

DATUM PLANE

PART I

DATUM FEATURE

Fig. 15-5-1 Magnified section of a flat surface.

THREE-PLANE SYSTEM

Geometric tolerances, such as straightness and flatness, refer to unrelated lines and surfaces and do not require the use of datums.

Orientation and locational tolerances refer to related features; that is, they control the relationship of features to one another or to a datum or datum system. Such datum features must be properly identified on the drawing.

Usually only one datum is required for orientation purposes, but positional relationships may require a datum system consisting of two or three datums. These datums are designated as *primary*, *secondary*, and *tertiary*. When these datums are plane surfaces that are mutually perpendicular, they are commonly referred to as a *three-plane datum system*, or a *datum reference frame*.

Primary Datum If the primary datum feature is a flat surface, it could lie on a suitable plane surface, such as the surface of a gage, which would then become a primary datum, as shown in Fig. 15-5-2. Theoretically, there will be a minimum of three high spots on the flat surface which will come in contact with the surface of the gage.

Secondary Datum If the part, while lying on this primary plane, is brought into contact with a secondary plane, it will theoretically touch at a minimum of two points.

Tertiary Datum The part can now be slid along, while maintaining contact with the primary and secondary planes, until it contacts a third plane. This plane then becomes the tertiary datum, and the part will theoretically touch it at only one point.

These three planes constitute a datum system from which measurements can be taken. They will appear on the drawing, as shown in Fig. 15-5-3, except that the datum features will be identified in their correct se-

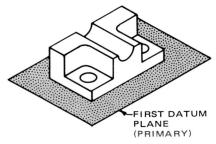

(A) PRIMARY DATUM

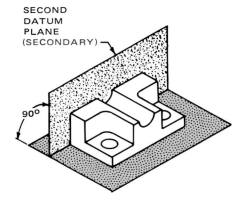

(B) SECONDARY DATUM

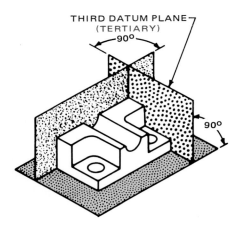

(C) TERTIARY DATUM

Fig. 15-5-2 The datum planes.

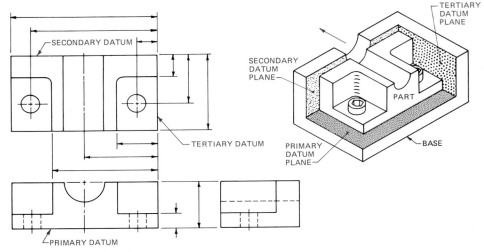

Fig. 15-5-3 Three-plane datum system.

quence by the methods described later in this unit.

It must be remembered that the majority of parts are not of the simple rectangular shape, and considerably more ingenuity may be required to establish suitable datums for more complex shapes.

Identification of Datums

Datum symbols are required to serve two purposes:

1. To indicate which is the datum surface or feature on the drawing
2. To identify, for reference purposes, the datum feature

There are two methods of datum symbolization in general use for such purposes: one is shown and used in ANSI standards; the other, the ISO method, is used in most other countries of the world.

ANSI Datum Feature Symbol

In the ANSI system, every datum feature is identified by a capital letter, enclosed in a rectangular box.

A dash is placed before and after the letter, to identify it as applying to a datum feature, as shown in Fig. 15-5-4.

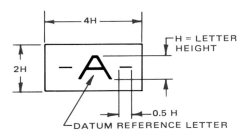

Fig. 15-5-4 ANSI datum feature symbol.

This identifying symbol may be directed to the datum feature in any one of the following ways.

1. By attaching a side, or end of the frame to an extension line from the feature, providing it is a plane surface

2. By running a leader with arrowhead from the frame to the feature
3. By adding the symbol to a note, a dimension, or a feature control frame pertaining to the feature
4. By attaching a side or end of the frame to an extension of the dimension line pertaining to a feature of size

These methods are illustrated in Fig. 15-5-5.

ISO Datum Feature Symbol

The ISO datum feature symbol is used by most other countries. The ISO datum feature symbol is a right-angled triangle, with a leader projecting from the 90° apex, as shown in Fig. 15-5-6. The base of the triangle should be slightly greater than the height of the lettering used on the drawing. The triangle may be filled in.

The datum is identified by a capital letter placed in a square frame and connected to the leader.

The ISO datum feature symbol may be directed to the datum feature in one of the following ways:

1. Placed on the outline of the feature or an extension of the outline (but clearly separated from the dimension line) when the datum feature is the line or surface itself
2. Shown as an extension of the dimension line when the datum feature is the axis or median plane
3. Placed on the axis or median plane when the datum is the axis or median plane of a single feature (e.g., a cylinder) or the common axis or

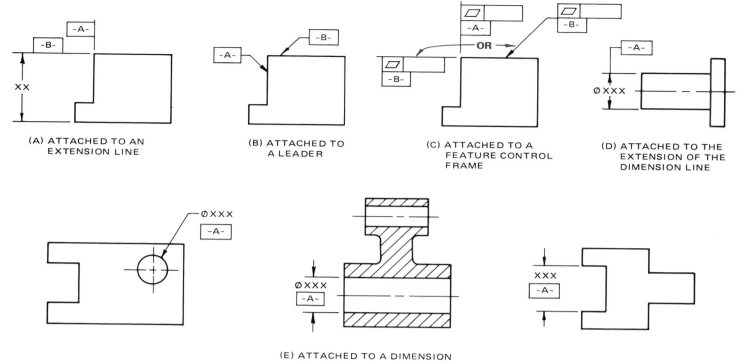

(A) ATTACHED TO AN EXTENSION LINE

(B) ATTACHED TO A LEADER

(C) ATTACHED TO A FEATURE CONTROL FRAME

(D) ATTACHED TO THE EXTENSION OF THE DIMENSION LINE

(E) ATTACHED TO A DIMENSION

Fig. 15-5-5 Placement of ANSI datum feature symbol.

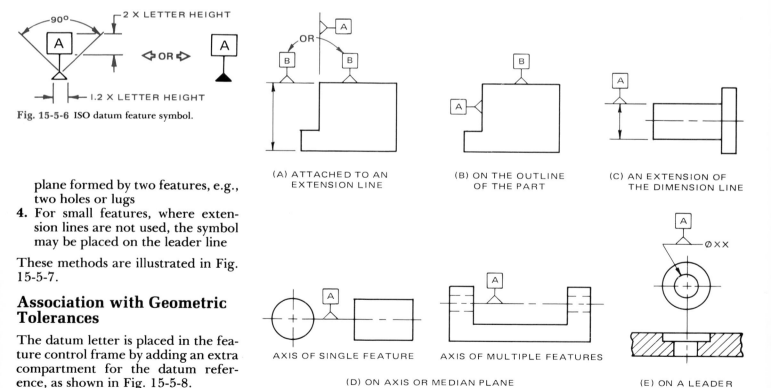

Fig. 15-5-6 ISO datum feature symbol.

(A) ATTACHED TO AN EXTENSION LINE

(B) ON THE OUTLINE OF THE PART

(C) AN EXTENSION OF THE DIMENSION LINE

AXIS OF SINGLE FEATURE

AXIS OF MULTIPLE FEATURES

(D) ON AXIS OR MEDIAN PLANE

(E) ON A LEADER

Fig. 15-5-7 Placement of ISO datum feature symbol.

plane formed by two features, e.g., two holes or lugs

4. For small features, where extension lines are not used, the symbol may be placed on the leader line

These methods are illustrated in Fig. 15-5-7.

Association with Geometric Tolerances

The datum letter is placed in the feature control frame by adding an extra compartment for the datum reference, as shown in Fig. 15-5-8.

If two or more datum references are involved, then additional frames are added and the datum references are placed in these frames in the correct order, that is, primary, secondary, and tertiary datums, as shown in Fig. 15-5-9.

Multiple Datum Features

If a single datum is established by two datum features, such as two ends of a

shaft, the features are each identified by separate letters. Both letters are then placed in the same compartment of the feature control symbol, with a

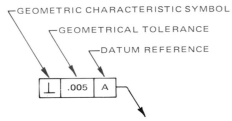

Fig. 15-5-8 Feature control symbol referenced to a datum.

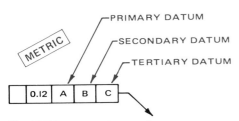

Fig. 15-5-9 Multiple datum references.

dash between them, as shown in Fig. 15-5-10A. The datum, in this case, is the common line between the two datum features.

Datums Based on Features of Size

When a feature of size is specified as a datum feature, such as diameters and widths, the datum has to be established from the full surface of the cylindrical feature or from two opposing surfaces of other features of size. These datums are subject to variations in size as well as form. Because variations are allowed by the size dimension, it becomes necessary to determine whether RFS or MMC applies in each case. For a tolerance of position, the datum reference letter is always followed by the appropriate modifying symbol in the feature control frame. For all other geometric tolerances, RFS is implied unless otherwise specified.

Datum Features — RFS

Where a datum feature of size is applied on a RFS basis, the datum is established by physical contact between the feature surface or surfaces and surfaces of the processing or measuring equipment.

Primary Datum Feature-Diameter
For an external feature, the datum is

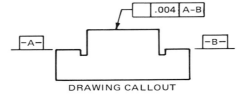

DRAWING CALLOUT

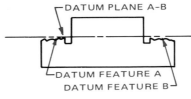

INTERPRETATION

(A) COPLANAR DATUM FEATURES

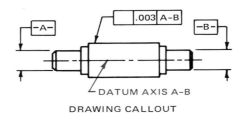

DATUM AXIS A-B

DRAWING CALLOUT

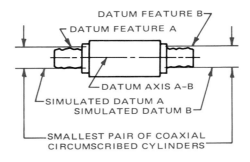

INTERPRETATION

(B) COAXIAL DATUM FEATURES

Fig. 15-5-10 Two datum features for one datum.

the axis of the smallest circumscribed cylinder which contacts the feature surface. For an internal feature, the datum is the axis of the largest inscribed cylinder which contacts the feature surface. See Fig. 15-5-11.

Primary Datum Feature-Width
For an external feature, the datum is the center plane between two parallel planes which, at minimum separation, contact the corresponding surfaces of the feature. For an internal feature, the datum is the center plane between two parallel planes which, at maximum separation, contact the corre-

sponding surfaces of the feature. See Fig. 15-5-12.

For both external and internal features, the secondary datum (axis or center plane) is established in the same manner as indicated above with an additional requirement: the contacting cylinder or parallel planes must be oriented perpendicular to the primary datum.

Datum Features — MMC

Where a datum feature of size is applied on an MMC basis, machine and gaging elements in the processing equipment, which remain constant in size, may be used to simulate a true geometric counterpart of the feature and to establish the datum. In this case, the size of the simulated datum is established by the specified MMC limit of size of the datum feature or its virtual condition, where applicable.

Where a datum feature of size is controlled by a specified tolerance of form, the size of the simulated datum is the MMC limit of size, with the exception that where a straightness tolerance is applied on an RFS or MMC basis, the size of the simulated datum is the virtual condition of the datum feature.

Datum features on an MMC basis always apply at their virtual condition. *Virtual condition* refers to the potential boundary of a feature, as specified on a drawing, derived from the collective effect of the maximum material limit of size and the specified form or orientation tolerance. These are added for external features, such as shafts, and subtracted for internal features, such as holes and slots.

If no form or orientation tolerance is specified, it is assumed, for datum reference purposes, that the tolerance is zero MMC.

The fact that a datum applies on an MMC basis is indicated in the feature control frame by the addition of the MMC symbol Ⓜ immediately following the datum reference, as shown in Fig. 15-5-13. When there is more than one datum reference, the MMC symbol must be added for each datum where this modification is required.

External Features with Regular Cross Sections — MMC
For external features having a cross section which is circular or which comprises a regular polygon, the datum will be of the same shape as the datum feature. The width

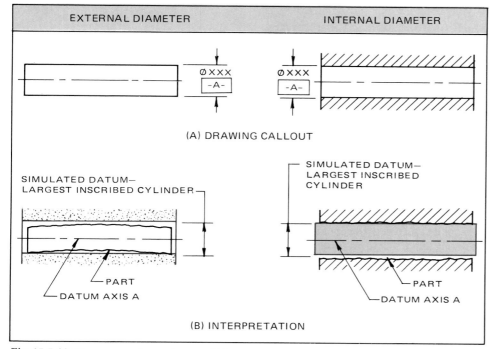

(A) DRAWING CALLOUT

(B) INTERPRETATION

Fig. 15-5-11 Diameter as primary datum — RFS.

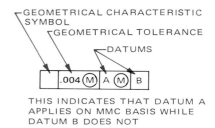

THIS INDICATES THAT DATUM A APPLIES ON MMC BASIS WHILE DATUM B DOES NOT

Fig. 15-5-13 References to datums — MMC.

or diameter of the datum will be equal to the maximum material limit of size, plus the specified form tolerance.

In Fig. 15-5-14, because no form tolerance is specified, the cylindrical gaging elements are made to the maximum material size of .565 in. This provides an exact location of the part when it is made to the maximum material condition. However, it allows a deviation of .003 in. in any direction from true position if the part is everywhere at the minimum material size of .559 in. and there are no form errors.

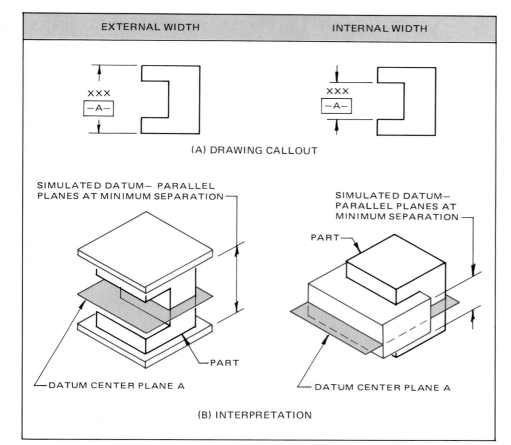

(A) DRAWING CALLOUT

(B) INTERPRETATION

Fig. 15-5-12 Width as primary datum RFS.

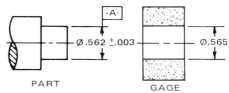

Fig. 15-5-14 Gage element for circular datum.

Rectangular Features — MMC If the specified datum feature consists of two flat surfaces and the cross section is not a regular polygon, then the datum consists of two parallel planes. These are separated by a distance equal to the maximum material condition, plus the specified form tolerance.

Figure 15-5-15A shows a flatness tolerance which applies separately to both datum feature surfaces. It should be noted that in such cases the form tolerance is not doubled in calculating the virtual condition. This is because if the part is everywhere at its maximum material condition, as shown in the gaging position, then a convex point on one side can only be offset by a concave point on the other side. If this were not true, the size dimension would be exceeded.

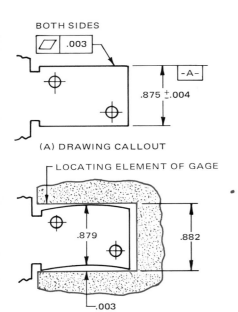

BOTH SIDES

.875 ±.004

-A-

(A) DRAWING CALLOUT

LOCATING ELEMENT OF GAGE

.879   .882

.003

(B) LOCATING ELEMENT OF GAGE

Fig. 15-5-15 Gage element for rectangular datum feature.

It should be noted that Fig. 15-5-15B shows the element of a gage which locates the datum on an MMC basis. It does not check the flatness requirement.

Reference and Source Material

1. ANSI Y14.5M, *Dimensioning and Tolerancing*

ASSIGNMENTS

See Assignments 13 through 16 for Unit 15-5 on page 318.

■ UNIT 15-6

Orientation

ANGULAR RELATIONSHIPS OF FLAT SURFACES

Orientation refers to the angular relationship which exists between two or more lines, surfaces, or other features. Angularity, parallelism, and perpendicularity are orientation tolerances applicable to related features.

There are three geometric symbols for these characteristics, as shown in

Fig. 15-6-1. The proportions are based on the height of the lettering used on the drawing.

Angularity is the condition of a surface or axis at a specified angle (other than 90°) from a datum plane or axis. An angularity tolerance specifies one of the following:

1. A tolerance zone the width of which is defined by two parallel planes at a specified basic angle from a datum plane, or axis, within which the surface of the considered feature must lie. See Fig. 15-6-2;
2. A tolerance zone defined by two parallel planes at the specified basic angle from a datum plane, or axis, within which the axis of the considered feature must lie. See Fig. 15-6-4A.

For geometric tolerancing of angularity, the angle between the datum and the controlled feature should be stated as a basic angle. Therefore it should be enclosed in a rectangular frame, as shown in Fig. 15-6-2, to indicate that the general tolerance note does not apply. However, the angle need not be stated for either perpendicularity (90°) or parallelism (0°).

Parallelism is the condition of a surface equidistant at all points from a datum plane or an axis equidistant along its length from a datum axis or plane. A parallelism tolerance specifies: (1) a tolerance zone defined by two planes or lines parallel to a datum plane, or axis, within which the line elements of the surface (Fig. 15-6-2) or axis of the considered feature must lie (see Fig. 15-6-4); or (2) a cylindrical tolerance, the axis of which is parallel to a datum axis within which the axis of the considered feature must lie (Fig. 15-6-10).

Perpendicularity is the condition of a surface, median plane, or axis at a right angle to a datum plane or axis. A perpendicularity tolerance specifies one of the following:

1. A tolerance zone defined by two parallel planes perpendicular to a datum plane, or axis, within which the surface, center line or median plane of the considered feature must lie (Figs. 15-6-2 and 15-6-12);
2. A tolerance zone defined by two parallel planes perpendicular to a datum axis within which the axis of the considered feature must lie (Fig. 15-6-13)
3. A cylindrical tolerance zone perpendicular to a datum plane or axis within which the center line of the considered feature must lie (Figs. 15-6-14 to 15-6-17)

ORIENTATION TOLERANCING OF FLAT SURFACES

Figure 15-6-2 shows three simple parts in which one flat surface is designated as a datum feature and another flat surface is related to it by one of the orientation tolerances.

Each of these tolerances is interpreted to mean that the designated surface shall be contained within a tolerance zone consisting of the space between two parallel planes, separated by the specified tolerance (.002 in.) and related to the datum by the basic angle specified (30, 90, or 0°).

Note that angularity, perpendicularity, and parallelism, when applied to plane surfaces, control flatness if a flatness tolerance is not specified.

Control in Two Directions

The measuring principles for angularity indicate the method of aligning the part prior to making angularity measurements. Proper alignment ensures that line elements of the surface perpendicular to the angular line elements are parallel to the datum.

For example, the part in Fig. 15-6-3 will be aligned so that line elements

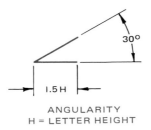

30°

1.5 H

ANGULARITY
H = LETTER HEIGHT

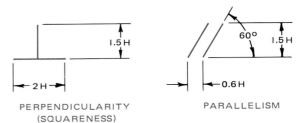

1.5 H

2 H

PERPENDICULARITY
(SQUARENESS)

60°   1.5 H

0.6 H

PARALLELISM

Fig. 15-6-1 Orientation symbols.

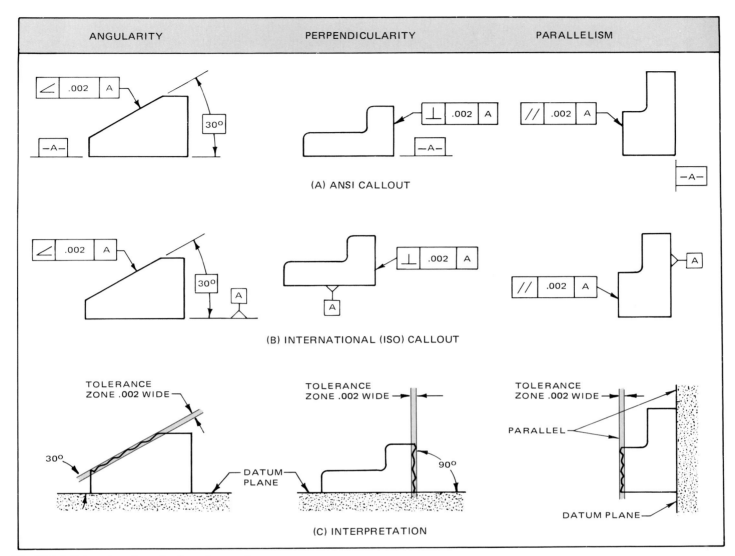

ANGULARITY	PERPENDICULARITY	PARALLELISM

(A) ANSI CALLOUT

(B) INTERNATIONAL (ISO) CALLOUT

TOLERANCE ZONE .002 WIDE

30°

DATUM PLANE

TOLERANCE ZONE .002 WIDE

90°

TOLERANCE ZONE .002 WIDE

PARALLEL

DATUM PLANE

(C) INTERPRETATION

Fig. 15-6-2 Orientation tolerancing for a plane surface.

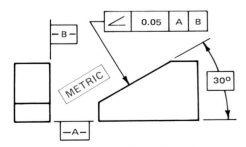

Fig. 15-6-3 Angularity referenced to a datum system.

running horizontally in the left-hand view will be parallel to the datum. However, these line elements will bear a proper relationship with the sides, ends, and top faces only if these surfaces are true and square with the primary datum.

It may be functionally more important to measure the angle in a direction parallel to a side or perpendicular to the front or back face. In this case, one side or face must be chosen as a secondary datum, as shown in Fig. 15-6-7.

Under these circumstances, the part is aligned on the angle or sine plate so that the secondary datum *B* is exactly parallel to the side of the angle plate.

ORIENTATION FOR AN AXIS OF CYLINDRICAL FEATURES

Tolerances intended to control orientation of the axis of a feature are applied to drawings as shown in Fig. 15-6-4.

The axis of the cylindrical feature must be contained within a tolerance zone consisting of the space between two parallel planes separated by the specified tolerance. The parallel planes are related to the datum by the basic angle of 45, 90, or 0°.

Since the tolerance planes for perpendicularity can be revolved around the feature axis, the tolerance zone effectively becomes a cylinder. The diameter of this cylinder is equal to the specified tolerance.

Internal Cylindrical Features

Figure 15-6-4 shows some simple parts in which the axis or center line of a hole is related by an orientation tolerance to a flat surface. The flat surface

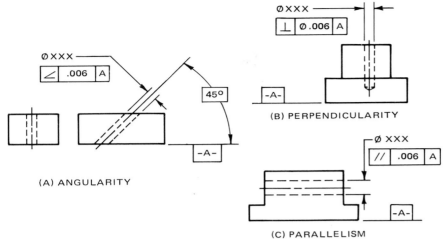

Fig. 15-6-4 Orientation of axis of holes with surfaces (feature RFS).

is designated as the datum feature.

The axis of the hole must be contained within a tolerance zone consisting of the space between two parallel planes. These planes are separated by a specified tolerance of .006 in. Figure 15-6-5 clearly illustrates the tolerance zone for angularity.

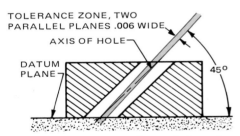

Fig. 15-6-5 Tolerance zone for angularity—Fig. 15-6-4A.

When the tolerance is one of perpendicularity, the tolerance-zone planes can be revolved around the feature axis without the angle being affected. The tolerance zone therefore becomes a cylinder. This cylindrical zone is perpendicular to the datum and has a diameter equal to the specified tolerance, as shown in Fig. 15-6-6.

Control of Parallelism in Two Directions The feature control symbol shown in Fig. 15-6-4C controls parallelism with a base only. If control with a side is also required, the side should be designated as a secondary datum, as shown in Fig. 15-6-8. The tolerance zone will be a parallelepiped, and two

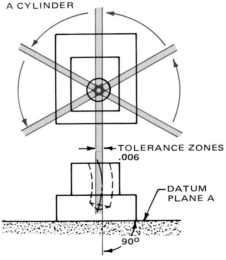

Fig. 15-6-6 Tolerance zone for perpendicularity —Fig. 15-6-4B.

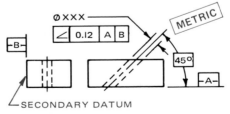

Fig. 15-6-7 Angularity referenced to two datums.

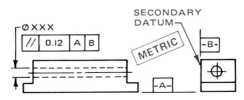

Fig. 15-6-8 Parallelism controlled in two directions.

separate measurements will have to be made.

Specifying Parallelism for an Axis Regardless of feature size, the feature axis shown in Fig. 15-6-9 must lie between two parallel planes .005 in. apart which are parallel to datum plane A. Additionally, the feature axis must be within any specified positional tolerance zone.

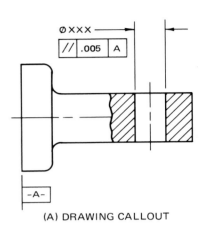

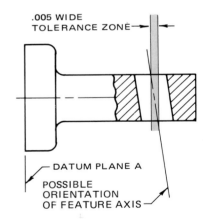

Fig. 15-6-9 Specifying parallelism for an axis (feature RFS).

Figure 15-6-10 specifies parallelism for an axis when both the feature and the datum feature are shown on a RFS basis. Regardless of feature size, the feature axis must lie within a cylindrical tolerance zone of .002 diameter whose axis is parallel to datum axis A. Additionally, the feature axis must be within any specified tolerance of location.

Figure 15-6-11 specifies parallelism for an axis when the feature is shown on an MMC basis and the datum fea-

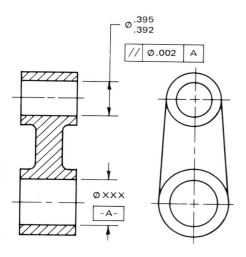

(A) DRAWING CALLOUT

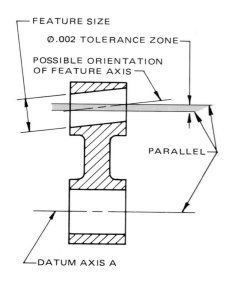

(B) INTERPRETATION

Fig. 15-6-10 Specifying parallelism for an axis (both feature and datum feature RFS).

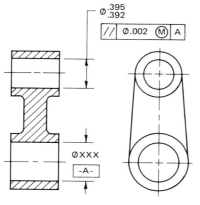

(A) DRAWING CALLOUT

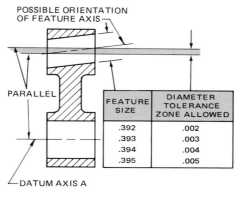

FEATURE SIZE	DIAMETER TOLERANCE ZONE ALLOWED
.392	.002
.393	.003
.394	.004
.395	.005

(B) INTERPRETATION

Fig. 15-6-11 Specifying parallelism for an axis (feature at MMC and datum feature RFS).

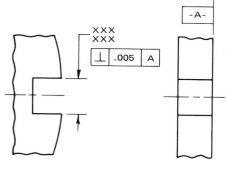

(A) DRAWING CALLOUT

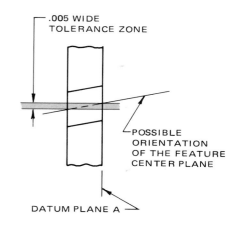

(B) INTERPRETATION

Fig. 15-6-12 Specifying perpendicularity for a median plane (feature RFS).

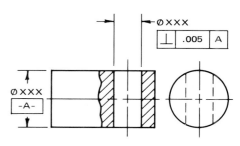

(A) DRAWING CALLOUT

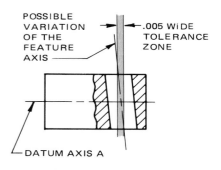

(B) INTERPRETATION

Fig. 15-6-13 Specifying perpendicularity for an axis (both feature and datum feature RFS).

ture is shown on a RFS basis. Where the feature is at the MMC (.392 in.), the maximum parallelism tolerance is .002 in. diameter. Where the feature departs from its MMC size, an increase in the parallelism tolerance is allowed which is equal to the amount of such departure. Additionally, the feature axis must be within any specified tolerance of location.

Perpendicularity for a Median Plane Regardless of feature size, the center plane of the feature shown in Fig. 15-6-12 must lie between two parallel planes .005 in. apart which are perpendicular to datum plane A. Additionally, the feature center plane must be within any specified tolerance of location.

Perpendicularity for an Axis (Both Feature and Datum RFS) Regardless of feature size, the feature axis shown in Fig. 15-6-13 must lie between two parallel planes .005 in. apart which are perpendicular to datum axis A. Additionally, the feature axis must be within any specified tolerance of location.

Perpendicularity for an Axis (Zero Tolerance at MMC) Where the feature shown in Fig. 15-6-14 is at the MMC (50.00 mm), its axis must be perpendicular to datum plane A. Where the feature departs from MMC, a perpendicularity tolerance is allowed which is equal to the amount of such departure. Additionally, the feature axis must be within any specified tolerance of location.

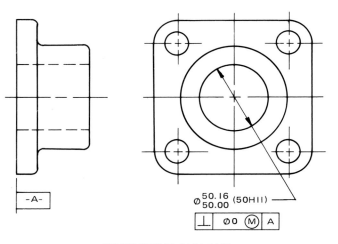

(A) DRAWING CALLOUT

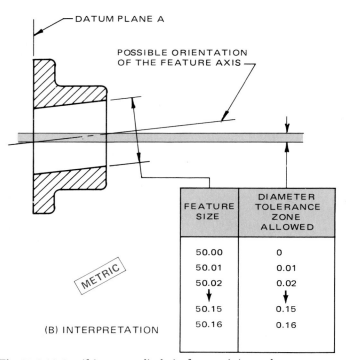

(B) INTERPRETATION

FEATURE SIZE	DIAMETER TOLERANCE ZONE ALLOWED
50.00	0
50.01	0.01
50.02	0.02
↓	↓
50.15	0.15
50.16	0.16

Fig. 15-6-14 Specifying perpendicularity for an axis (zero tolerance at MMC).

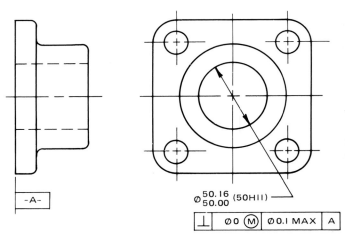

(A) DRAWING CALLOUT

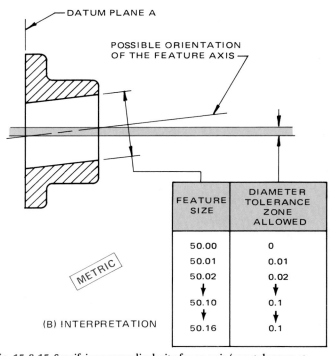

(B) INTERPRETATION

FEATURE SIZE	DIAMETER TOLERANCE ZONE ALLOWED
50.00	0
50.01	0.01
50.02	0.02
↓	↓
50.10	0.1
↓	↓
50.16	0.1

Fig. 15-6-15 Specifying perpendicularity for an axis (zero tolerance at MMC with a maximum specified).

Perpendicularity with a Maximum Tolerance Specified Where the feature shown in Fig. 15-6-15 is at MMC (50.00 mm), its axis must be perpendicular to datum plane *A*. Where the feature departs from MMC, a perpendicularity tolerance is allowed which is equal to the amount of such departure, up to the 0.1 mm maximum. Additionally, the feature axis must be within any specified tolerance of location.

External Cylindrical Features

Perpendicularity for an Axis (Pin or Boss RFS) Regardless of feature size, the feature axis shown in Fig. 15-6-16 must lie within a cylindrical zone 0.4 mm diameter which is perpendicular to and projects from datum plane *A* for the feature height. Additionally, the feature axis must be within any specified tolerance of location.

Perpendicularity for an Axis (Pin or Boss at MMC) Where the feature shown in Fig. 15-6-17 is at MMC (Ø15.984), the maximum perpendicularity tolerance is 0.05 diameter. Where the feature departs from its MMC size, an increase in the perpendicularity tolerance is allowed which is equal to the amount of such departure. Additionally, the feature axis must be within any specified tolerance of location.

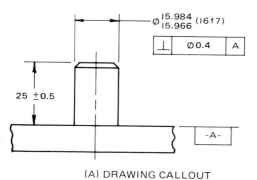

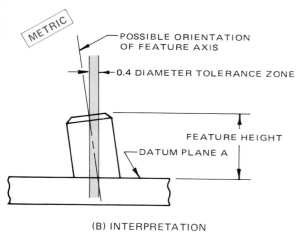

Fig. 15-6-16 Specifying perpendicularity for an axis (pin or boss RFS).

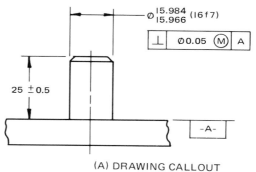

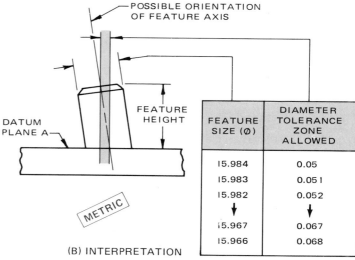

FEATURE SIZE (∅)	DIAMETER TOLERANCE ZONE ALLOWED
15.984	0.05
15.983	0.051
15.982	0.052
↓	↓
15.967	0.067
15.966	0.068

Fig. 15-6-17 Specifying perpendicularity for an axis (pin or boss at MMC).

Reference and Source Material

1. ANSI Y14.5M, *Dimensioning and Tolerancing.*

ASSIGNMENTS

See Assignments 17 through 21 for Unit 15-6 starting on page 319.

 UNIT 15-7

Positional Tolerancing

The location of features is one of the most frequently used applications of dimensions on technical drawings. Tolerancing may be accomplished either by *coordinate tolerances* applied to the dimensions or by *geometric (positional) tolerancing.*

Positional tolerancing is especially useful when applied on an MMC basis to groups or patterns of holes or other small features in the mass production of parts. This method meets functional requirements in most cases and permits assessment with simple gaging procedures.

Most examples in this unit are devoted to the principles involved in the location of small, round holes, because they represent the most commonly used applications. The same principles apply, however, to the location of other features, such as slots, tabs, bosses, and noncircular holes.

TOLERANCING METHODS

A single hole is usually located by means of rectangular coordinate dimensions, extending from suitable edges or other features of the part to the axis of the hole. Other dimensioning methods, such as polar coordinates, may be used when circumstances warrant.

There are two standard methods of tolerancing the location of holes, as illustrated in Fig. 15-7-1:

1. *Coordinate tolerancing,* which refers to tolerances applied directly to the coordinate dimensions or to applicable tolerances specified in a general tolerance note.
2. *(a) Positional tolerancing,* RFS (regardless of feature size).
(b) Positional tolerancing, MMC (maximum material condition).
(c) Positional tolerancing, LMC (least material condition).

These positional tolerancing methods are part of the system of geometric tolerancing.

Any of these tolerancing methods can be substituted one for the other, although with differing results. It is necessary, however, to first analyze the widely used method of coordinate

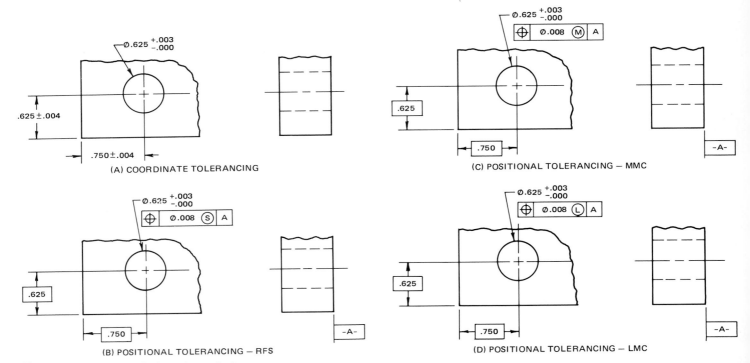

Fig. 15-7-1 Comparison of tolerancing methods.

tolerancing in order to explain and understand the advantages and disadvantages of the positional tolerancing methods.

COORDINATE TOLERANCING

Coordinate dimensions and tolerances may be applied to the location of a single hole, as shown in Fig. 15-7-2. They locate the hole axis and result in either a rectangular or a wedge-shaped tolerance zone within which the axis of the hole must lie.

If the two coordinate tolerances are equal, the tolerance zone formed will be a square. Unequal tolerances result in a rectangular tolerance zone. Where one of the locating dimensions is a radius, polar dimensioning gives a circular ring section tolerance zone. For simplicity, square tolerance zones are used in the analyses of most of the examples in this section.

It should be noted that the tolerance zone extends for the full depth of the hole, that is, the whole length of the axis. This is illustrated in Fig. 15-7-3 and explained in more detail in a later unit. In most of the illustrations, tolerances will be analyzed as they apply at the surface of the part, where the axis is represented by a point.

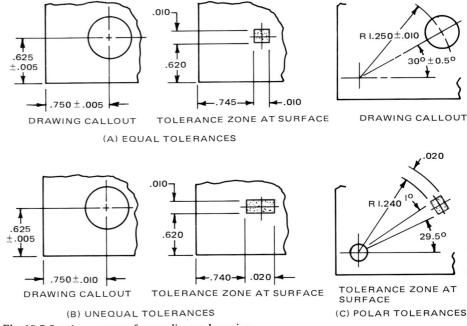

Fig. 15-7-2 Tolerance zones for coordinate tolerancing.

Maximum Permissible Error

The actual position of the feature axis may be anywhere within the rectangular tolerance zone. For square tolerance zones, the maximum allowable variation from the desired position occurs in a direction of 45° from the direction of the coordinate dimensions. See Fig. 15-7-4.

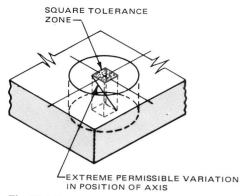

Fig. 15-7-3 Tolerance zone extending through part.

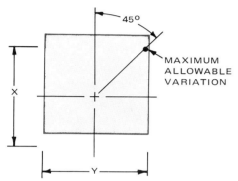

Fig. 15-7-4 Square tolerance zone.

For rectangular tolerance zones this maximum tolerance is the square root of the sum of the squares of the individual tolerances, or expressed mathematically

$$\sqrt{X^2Y^2}$$

For the examples shown in Fig. 15-7-2, the tolerance zones are shown in Fig. 15-7-5, and the maximum tolerance values are as shown in the following examples.

EXAMPLE A

$$\sqrt{.010^2 + .020^2} = .014$$

EXAMPLE B

$$\sqrt{.010^2 + .020^2} = .0224$$

EXAMPLE C For polar coordinates the extreme variation is

$$\sqrt{A^2 + T^2}$$

where $A = R \tan a$
T = tolerance on radius
R = mean radius
a = angular tolerance

Thus, the extreme variation in example C is

$$\sqrt{(1.25 \times .017\ 45)^2 + .020^2} = .03$$

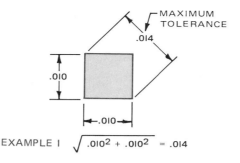

EXAMPLE 1 $\sqrt{.010^2 + .010^2} = .014$

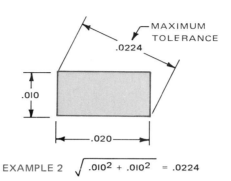

EXAMPLE 2 $\sqrt{.010^2 + .010^2} = .0224$

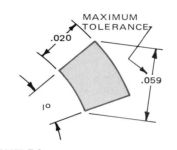

EXAMPLE 3

Fig. 15-7-5 Tolerance zones for parts shown in Fig. 15-7-2.

Note: Mathematically, A in the above formula should be $2R \tan a/2$, instead of $R \tan a$, and T should be $T \cos A/2$; but the difference in results is quite insignificant for the tolerances normally used.

Some values of tan A for commonly used angular tolerances are as follows:

A	tan a	A	tan a	A	tan a
0° 5'	0.00145	0° 25'	0.00727	0° 45'	0.01309
0° 10'	0.00291	0° 30'	0.00873	0° 50'	0.01454
0° 15'	0.00436	0° 35'	0.01018	0° 55'	0.01600
0° 20'	0.00582	0° 40'	0.01164	1° 0'	0.01745

Use of Chart

A quick and easy method of finding the maximum positional error permit- ted with coordinate tolerancing, without having to calculate squares and square roots, is by use of a chart like that shown in Fig. 15-7-6.

In Example A shown in Fig. 15-7-2, the tolerance in both directions is .010 in. The extensions of the horizontal and vertical lines of .010 in the chart intersect at point A, which lies between the radii of .013 and .014 in. When interpolated and rounded to three decimal places, the maximum permissible variation of position is .014 in.

In Example B shown in Fig. 15-7-2, the tolerances are .010 in. in one direction and .020 in. in the other. The extensions of the vertical and horizontal lines at .010 and .020 in., respectively, in the chart intersect at point B, which lies between the radii of .022 and .023 in. When interpolated and rounded to three decimal places, the maximum variation of position is .022 in. Figure 15-7-6 also shows a chart for use with tolerances in millimeters.

Advantages of Coordinate Tolerancing

The advantages claimed for direct co-ordinate tolerancing are as follows:

1. It is simple and easily understood, and, therefore, it is commonly used.
2. It permits direct measurements to be made with standard instruments and does not require the use of spe-cial-purpose functional gages or other calculations.

Disadvantages of Coordinate Tolerancing

There are a number of disadvantages to the direct tolerancing method:

1. It results in a square or rectangular tolerance zone within which the axis must lie. For a square zone this permits a variation in a 45° direc-tion of approximately 1.4 times the specified tolerance. This amount of variation may necessitate the speci-fication of tolerances which are only 70 percent of those that are functionally acceptable.
2. It may result in an undesirable ac-cumulation of tolerances when sev-eral features are involved, espe-cially when chain dimensioning is used.
3. It is more difficult to assess clear-ances between mating features and

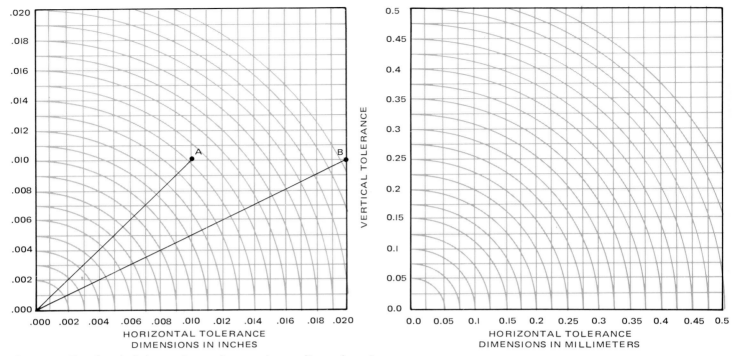

Fig. 15-7-6 Chart for calculating maximum tolerance using coordinate tolerancing.

components than when positional tolerancing is used, especially when a group or a pattern of features is involved.

4. It does not correspond to the control exercised by fixed functional "go" gages, often desirable in mass production of parts. This becomes particularly important in dealing with a group of holes. With direct coordinate tolerancing, the location of each hole has to be measured separately in two directions, whereas with positional tolerancing on an MMC basis one functional gage checks all holes in one operation.

POSITIONAL TOLERANCING

Positional tolerancing is part of the system of geometric tolerancing. It defines a zone within which the center, axis, or center plane of a feature of size is permitted to vary from true (theoretically exact) position. A positional tolerance is indicated by the position symbol, a tolerance, and appropriate datum references placed in a feature control frame. Basic dimensions represent the exact values to which geometric positional tolerances are ap-

plied elsewhere by symbols or notes on the drawing. They are enclosed in a rectangular frame (basic dimension symbol) as shown in Fig. 15-7-7. Where the dimension represents a diameter or a radius, the symbol ∅ or R is included in the rectangular frame. General tolerance notes do not apply to basic dimensions.

The frame size need not be any larger than that necessary to enclose the dimension. Permissible deviations

from the basic dimension are then given by a positional tolerance as described in this unit.

Formerly the word BASIC or the abbreviation TP was used to indicate such dimensions.

SYMBOL FOR POSITION

The geometric characteristic symbol for position is a circle with two solid center lines, as shown in Fig. 15-7-8.

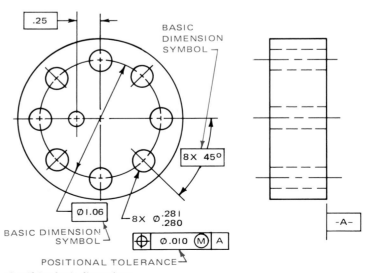

Fig. 15-7-7 Identifying basic dimensions.

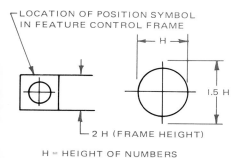

Fig. 15-7-8 Position symbol.

This symbol is used in the feature control frame in the same manner as for other geometric tolerances.

MATERIAL CONDITION BASIS

Positional tolerancing is applied on an MMC, RFS, or LMC basis. The appropriate symbol for the above follows the specified tolerance, and where required, the applicable datum reference in the feature control frame.

As positional tolerance controls the position of the axis of a cylindrical feature, the feature control frame is normally attached to the size of the feature, as shown in Fig. 15-7-9.

The positional tolerance represents the diameter of a cylindrical tolerance zone, located at true position as determined by the basic dimensions on the drawing, within which the axis or center line of the feature must lie.

Except for the fact that the tolerance zone is circular instead of square, a positional tolerance on this basis has exactly the same meaning as direct coordinate tolerancing but with equal tolerances in all directions.

It has already been shown that with rectangular coordinate tolerancing the maximum permissible error in location is not the value indicated by the horizontal and vertical tolerances, but rather is equivalent to the length of the diagonal between the two tolerances. For square tolerance zones this is 1.4 times the specified tolerance values. The specified tolerance can therefore be increased to an amount equal to the diagonal of the coordinate tolerance zone without affecting the clearance between the hole and its mating part.

It is quite practical, however, to replace coordinate tolerances with a positional tolerance having a value equal to the diagonal of the coordinate tolerance zone. This does not affect the clearance between the hole and its mating part, yet it offers 57 percent more tolerance area, as shown in Fig. 15-7-10. Such a change would most likely result in a reduction in the number of parts rejected for positional errors.

A simpler method is to make coordinate measurements and evaluate them

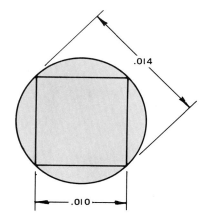

AREA OF CIRCUMSCRIBED CIRCULAR ZONE = 157% OF SQUARE TOLERANCE ZONE

Fig. 15-7-10 Relationship of tolerance zones.

on a chart, as shown in Fig. 15-7-11. For example, if measurements of four parts, made according to Fig. 15-7-9, are as shown in the table below, only two are acceptable using coordinate tolerancing. If positional tolerancing is used, three parts are acceptable. These positions are shown on the chart.

Part	Measurements		Acceptability
A	.565	.752	Rejected
B	.562	.754	Accepted
C	.557	.753	Accepted
D	.556	.754	Rejected

MMC as Related to Positional Tolerancing

The positional tolerance and MMC of mating features are considered in relation to each other. MMC by itself means a feature of a finished product contains the maximum amount of material permitted by the toleranced size dimension of that feature. Thus for holes, slots, and other internal features, maximum material is the condition where these features are at their minimum allowable sizes. For shafts, as well as for bosses, lugs, tabs, and other external features, maximum material is the condition where these are at their maximum allowable sizes.

A positional tolerance applied on a MMC basis may be explained in either of the following ways:

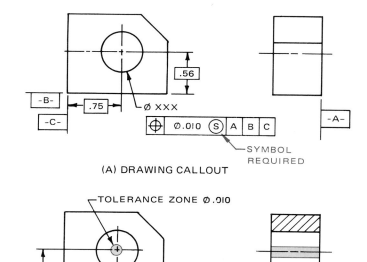

(A) DRAWING CALLOUT

(B) TOLERANCE ZONE

Fig. 15-7-9 Positional tolerancing — regardless of feature size.

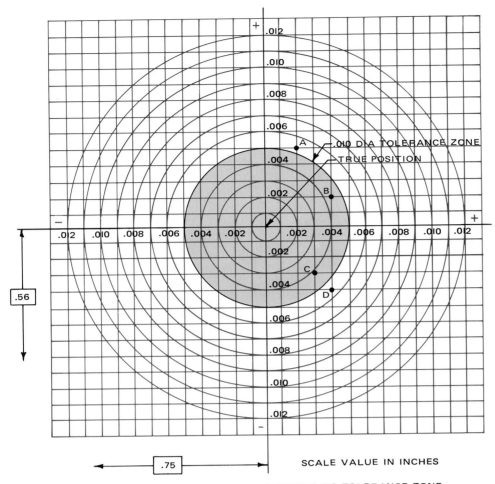

NOTE – DARK CIRCULAR AREA REPRESENTS ⌀.010 TOLERANCE ZONE

SCALE VALUE IN INCHES

Fig. 15-7-11 Chart for evaluating positional tolerancing — RFS.

1. *In terms of the surface of a hole.* While maintaining the specified size limits of the hole, no element of the hole surface shall be inside a theoretical boundary having a diameter equal to the minimum limit of size minus the positional tolerance located at true position. See Fig. 15-7-12.

2. *In terms of the axis of the hole.* Where a hole is at MMC (minimum diameter), its axis must fall within a cylindrical tolerance zone whose axis is located at true position. The diameter of this zone is equal to the positional tolerance. See Figs.15-7-13 holes A and B. This tolerance zone also defines the limits of variation in the attitude of the axis of the hole in relation to the datum surface. See Fig. 15-7-13 hole C. It is only when the feature is at MMC that the specified positional tolerance applies. Where the actual size of the feature is larger than MMC, additional positional tolerance re-

THEORETICAL BOUNDRY—
MINIMUM DIAMETER OF
HOLE (MMC) MINUS THE
POSITIONAL TOLERANCE

TRUE POSITION

HOLE POSITION MAY VARY BUT NO
POINT ON ITS SURFACE MAY BE
INSIDE THEORETICAL BOUNDRY

Fig. 15-7-12 Boundary for surface for a hole at MMC.

sults. See Fig. 15-7-15. This increase of positional tolerance is equal to the difference between the specified maximum material limit of size (MMC) and the actual size of the feature. The specified positional tolerance for a feature may be exceeded where the actual size is larger than MMC and still satisfy function and interchangeability requirements.

The problems of tolerancing for the position of holes are simplified when positional tolerancing is applied on an MMC basis. Positional tolerancing simplifies measuring procedures of functional "go" gages. It also permits an increase in positional variations as the size departs from the maximum material size without jeopardizing free assembly of mating features.

A positional tolerance on an MMC basis is specified on a drawing, on either the front or the side view, as shown in Fig. 15-7-14. The MMC symbol Ⓜ is added in the feature control frame immediately after the tolerance.

A positional tolerance applied to a hole on an MMC basis means that the boundary of the hole must fall outside a perfect cylinder having a diameter equal to the minimum limit of size minus the positional tolerance. This cylinder is located with its axis at true position. The hole must, of course, meet its diameter limits.

The effect is illustrated in Fig. 15-7-15, where the gage cylinder is shown at true position and the minimum and maximum diameter holes are drawn to show the extreme permissible variations in position in one direction.

Therefore, if a hole is at its maximum material condition (minimum diameter), the position of its axis must lie within a circular tolerance zone having a diameter equal to the specified tolerance. If the hole is at its maximum diameter (least material condition), the diameter of the tolerance zone for the axis is increased by the amount of the feature tolerance. The greatest deviation of the axis in one direction from true position is therefore

$$\frac{H + P}{2} = \frac{.004 + .008}{2} = .006$$

where H = hole diameter tolerance
P = positional tolerance

It must be emphasized that positional tolerancing, even on an MMC

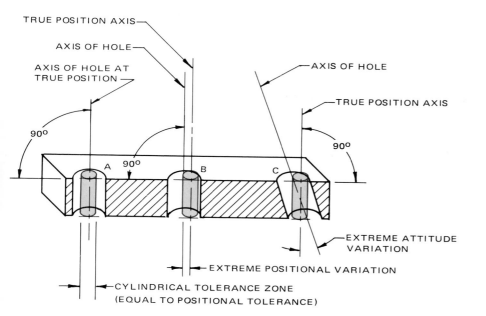

HOLE A — AXIS OF HOLE IS COINCIDENT WITH TRUE POSITION AXIS

HOLE B — AXIS OF HOLE IS LOCATED AT EXTREME POSITION TO THE LEFT OF TRUE POSITION AXIS (BUT WITHIN TOLERANCE ZONE)

HOLE C — AXIS OF HOLE IS INCLINED TO EXTREME ATTITUDE WITHIN TOLERANCE ZONE

NOTE — THE LENGTH OF THE TOLERANCE ZONE IS EQUAL TO THE LENGTH OF THE FEATURE, UNLESS OTHERWISE SPECIFIED ON THE DRAWING

Fig. 15-7-13 Hole axes in relationship to positional tolerance zones.

basis, is not a cure-all for positional tolerancing problems; each method of tolerancing has its own area of usefulness. In each application a method must be selected which best suits that particular case.

Positional tolerancing on an MMC basis is preferred when production quantities warrant the provision of functional "go" gages, because gaging is then limited to one simple operation, even when a group of holes is involved. This method also facilitates manufacture by permitting larger variations in position when the diameter departs from the maximum material condition. It cannot be used when it is essential that variations in location of the axis be observed regardless of feature size.

Zero Positional Tolerancing at MMC The application of MMC permits the tolerance to exceed the value specified, provided features are within size limits and parts are acceptable. This is accomplished by adjusting the minimum size limit of a hole to the absolute minimum required for the insertion of an applicable fastener located precisely at true position, and specifying a zero tolerance at MMC. See Fig. 15-7-17. In this case, the positional tolerance allowed is totally dependent on the actual size of the considered feature.

RFS as Related to Positional Tolerancing

In certain cases, the design or function of a part may require the positional tolerance or datum reference, or both, to be maintained regardless of actual feature sizes. RFS, where applied to the positional tolerance of circular features, requires the axis of each feature to be located within the specified positional tolerance regardless of the size of the feature. This requirement imposes a closer control of the features involved and introduces complexities in verification.

LMC as Related to Positional Tolerancing

Where positional tolerancing at LMC is specified, the stated positional tolerance applies when the feature contains the least amount of material permitted by its toleranced size dimension. Specification of LMC further requires perfect form at LMC. Perfect form at MMC is not required. Where the feature departs from its LMC size, an increase in positional tolerance is allowed, which is equal to the amount of such departure. See Fig. 15-7-18. Specifying LMC is limited to positional tolerancing applications where MMC does not provide the desired control and RFS is too restrictive.

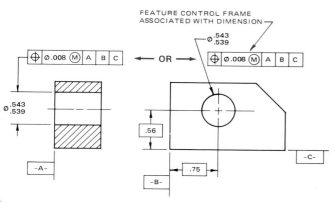

Fig. 15-7-14 Positional tolerancing — MMC.

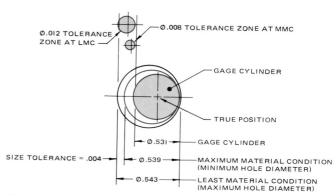

Fig. 15-7-15 Positional variations for tolerancing for Fig. 15-7-14.

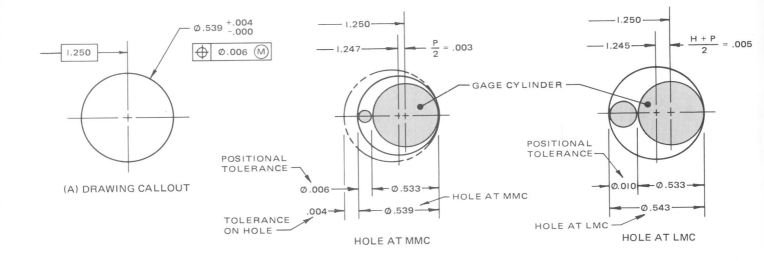

Fig. 15-7-16 Hole with an MMC positional tolerance.

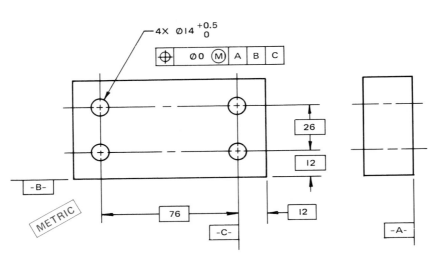

Fig. 15-7-17 Zero positional tolerance—MMC.

Positional Tolerancing a Group of Features

In many instances, a group of features (such as a group of mounting holes) must be positioned relative to a datum feature at MMC. See Fig. 15-7-19. Where datum feature *B* is at MMC, its axis determines the location of the pattern of features as a group. Where the datum feature B departs from MMC, its axis may be displaced relative to the location of the datum axis (datum *B* at MMC) by an amount equal to one-half the difference between its actual and MMC size.

Projected Tolerance Zone

The application of this concept is rec-

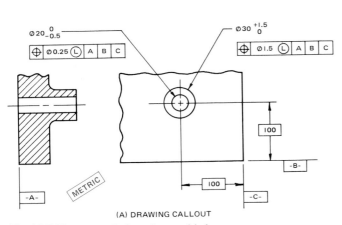

Fig. 15-7-18 LMC applied to a boss and hole.

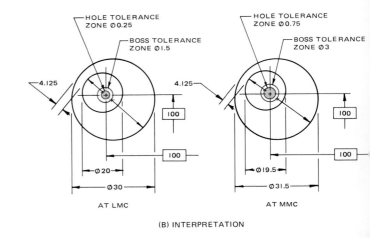

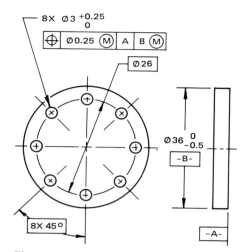

Fig. 15-7-19 Positional tolerancing a group of holes, datum feature at MMC.

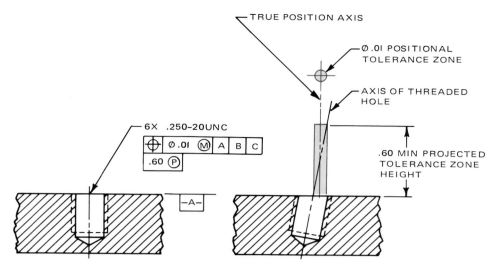

(A) DRAWING CALLOUT   (B) INTERPRETATION

Fig. 15-7-21 Specifying a projected tolerance zone.

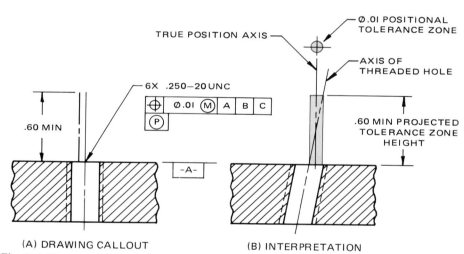

(A) DRAWING CALLOUT   (B) INTERPRETATION

Fig. 15-7-22 Projected tolerance zone indicated with a chain line.

ommended where the variation in perpendicularity of threaded or pressfit holes could cause fasteners, such as screws, studs, or pins, to interfere with mating parts, as shown in Fig. 15-7-20. Interference can occur where a positional tolerance is applied to the depth of a hole and the hole axis is inclined within allowable limits. Figure 15-7-21 illustrates the application of a positional tolerance using a projected tolerance zone. The specified length for the projected tolerance zone is the minimum value and represents the maximum permissible mating part thickness or installed length or height of components such as studs or dowel pins. For through holes, or in some situations, the direction of the projection from the datum surface may need further clarification. In such cases, the

projected tolerance zone may be indicated as illustrated in Fig. 15-7-22. The minimum extent and direction of the projected tolerance zone is shown on the drawing as a dimensioned value and a heavy chain line drawn closely adjacent to an extension of the center line of the hole.

Where design considerations require a closer control in the perpendicularity of a threaded hole than that allowed by the positional tolerance, a perpendicularity tolerance applied as a projected tolerance zone may be specified.

Reference and Source Material

1. ANSI Y14.5M, *Dimensioning and Tolerancing.*

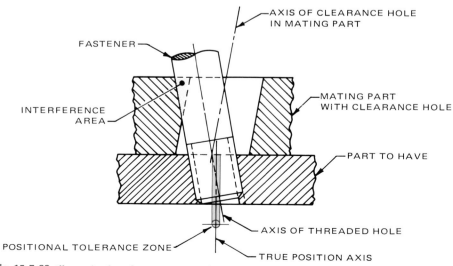

Fig. 15-7-20 Illustrating how fastener can interfere with mating part.

See Assignments 22 through 28 for Unit 15-7 on page 321.

■ UNIT 15-8

Datums for Positional Tolerancing

In the examples given so far, the position of the axis of the hole was established by using dimensions from the actual surfaces of the part. These surfaces were not designated as datums. The true or mean position of the axis was therefore a line parallel to a surface line element on each of the surfaces from which the dimensions were drawn, as illustrated in Fig. 15-8-1.

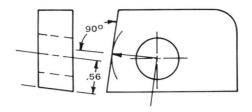

Fig. 15-8-2 Results when sides are off square.

In some applications this may be the desired requirement, but in most cases it is preferable to have the hole either related to other surfaces or features or related to a full side rather than a line on the surface. It is then necessary to specify the desired datum feature or features in the required order of priority.

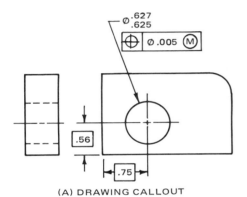

(A) DRAWING CALLOUT

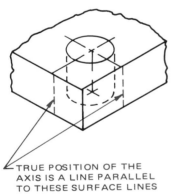

TRUE POSITION OF THE AXIS IS A LINE PARALLEL TO THESE SURFACE LINES

(B) INTERPRETATION OF TRUE POSITION

Fig. 15-8-1 Lines from which measurements are made.

If these sides are off-square with one another or with other surfaces of the part, the true position of the axis would be similarly off-square, as shown in a somewhat exaggerated format in Fig. 15-8-2.

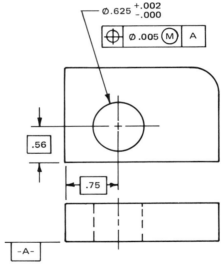

Fig. 15-8-3 Part with one datum feature specified.

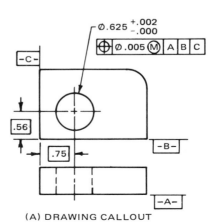

(A) DRAWING CALLOUT

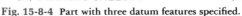

Fig. 15-8-4 Part with three datum features specified.

The first consideration in such applications is to decide on the primary datum feature. The usual course of action is to specify as the primary datum the surface into which the hole is produced. This will ensure that the true position of the axis is perpendicular to this surface or at the basic angle, if it is other than 90°. Secondary and tertiary datum features are then selected and identified, if required.

Figure 15-8-3 shows a part similar to that shown in Fig. 15-8-1 but with the addition of a primary datum feature and the MMC modifier. Figure 15-8-4 shows the same part with three datum features specified.

Long Holes It is not always essential to have the true position of a hole perpendicular to the face into which the hole is produced. It may be functionally more important, especially with long holes, to have it parallel to one of the sides. Figure 15-8-5 is a case in point. In this example the sides are designated as primary and secondary datums. A tertiary datum is not required.

Circular Datums Circular features, such as holes or external cylindrical features, can be used as datums just as readily as flat surfaces. In the simple part shown in Fig. 15-8-6, it is quite evident that the true position of the small hole is established from the axis of the large hole. In cases like these, it may not be necessary to specify one of the holes as a datum, although it would facilitate gaging if the datum were specified on an MMC basis.

In other cases, such as that shown in Fig. 15-8-7, it is essential to specify the datum; otherwise, the origin of the true-position dimension would be left in doubt. It could be either the axis of

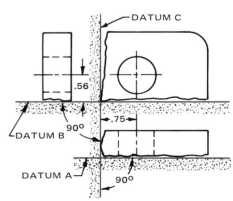

(B) INTERPRETATION OF TRUE POSITION

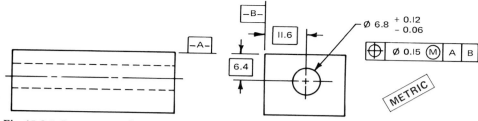

Fig. 15-8-5 Datum system for a long hole.

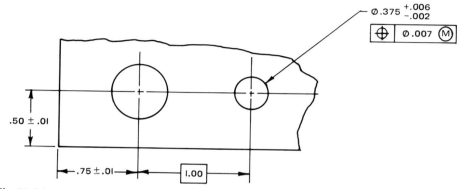

Fig. 15-8-6 Part where specification of the datum feature may not be required.

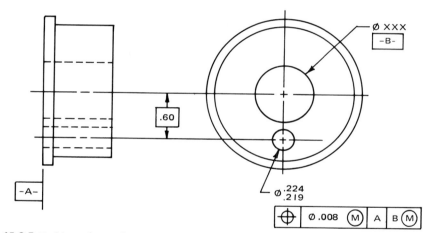

Fig. 15-8-7 Position referenced to a circular datum.

the hole or the axis of the outside cylindrical surface.

Multiple-Hole Datums The axis of holes is sometimes specified as a datum feature with MMC being specified for the datum reference. On an MMC basis, any number of holes or similar features which form a group or pattern may be specified as a single datum. All features forming such a datum must be related with a positional tolerance on an MMC basis. See Fig. 15-8-8.

COMPOSITE POSITIONAL TOLERANCING

Where design requirements permit the location of a pattern of features, as a group, to vary within a larger tolerance than the positional tolerance assigned to each feature within the pattern, composite positional tolerancing is used.

This provides a composite application for location of feature patterns as well as the inter-relation of features within these patterns. Requirements are annotated by the use of a composite feature control frame. Each complete horizontal entry in the feature control frame of Fig. 15-8-9 constitutes a separate requirement. The position symbol is entered once and is applicable to both horizontal entries. The upper entry is referred to as the pattern-locating control. It specifies the larger positional tolerance for the location of the pattern of features as a group. Applicable datums are specified in a desired order of precedence. The lower entry is referred to as the feature-relating control. It specifies the smaller positional tolerance for

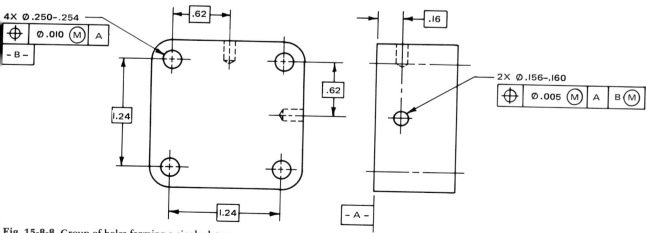

Fig. 15-8-8 Group of holes forming a single datum.

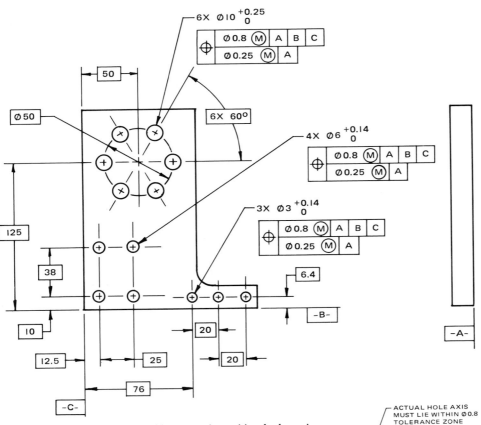

Fig. 15-8-9 Hole patterns located by composite positional tolerancing.

2. Functional requirements of the part may necessitate the use of only a portion of a surface as a datum feature, for example, the portion which contacts a mating part in assembly.

3. A surface selected as a datum feature may not be sufficiently true, and a flat datum feature may rock when placed on a datum plane, so that accurate and repeatable measurements from the surface would not be possible. This is particularly so for surfaces of castings, forgings, weldments, and some sheet-metal and formed parts.

A useful technique to overcome such problems is the datum target method. In this method certain points, lines, or small areas on the surfaces are selected as the bases for establishment of datums. For flat surfaces, this usually requires three target points or areas for a primary datum, two for a

each feature within the pattern and repeats the primary datum.

Each pattern of features is located from specified datums by basic dimensions. See Figs. 15-8-10 through 15-8-12. As can be seen from the sectional view of the tolerance zones in Fig. 15-8-10, the axes of both the large and small zones are parallel. The axes of the holes may vary obliquely only within the confines of the respective smaller positional tolerance zones. The axes of the holes must lie within the larger tolerance zones and also within the smaller tolerance zones.

DATUM TARGETS

The full feature surface was used to establish a datum for the features so far designated as datum features. This may not always be practical for the following reasons:

1. The surface of a feature may be so large that a gage designed to make contact with the full surface may be too expensive or too cumbersome to use.

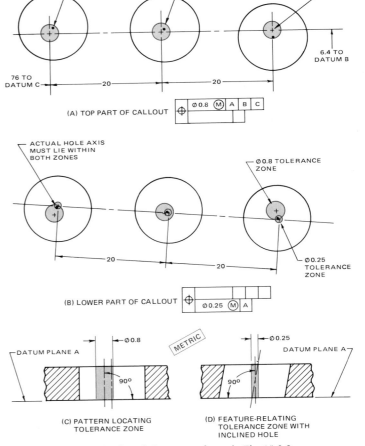

Fig. 15-8-10 Tolerance zones for the three-hole pattern shown in Fig. 15-8-9.

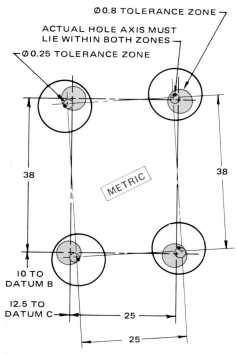

Fig. 15-8-11 Tolerance zones for the four-hole pattern shown in Fig. 15-8-9.

secondary datum, and one for a tertiary datum.

It is not necessary to use targets for all datums. It is quite logical, for example, to use targets for the primary datum and other surfaces or features

for secondary and tertiary datums if required; or to use a flat surface of a part as the primary datum and to locate fixed points or lines on the edges as secondary and tertiary datums.

Datum targets should be spaced as far apart from each other as possible to provide maximum stability for making measurements.

Datum Target Symbol

Points, lines, and areas on datum features are designated on the drawing by means of a datum target symbol. See Fig. 15-8-13. The symbol is placed outside the part outline with a radial (leader) line directed to the target point (indicated by an "X"), target line, or target area, as applicable. See Fig. 15-8-14. The use of a solid radial (leader) line indicates that the datum target is on the near (visible) surface. The use of a dashed radial (leader)

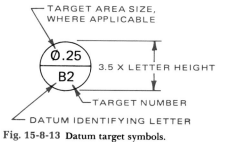

Fig. 15-8-13 Datum target symbols.

line, as in Fig. 15-8-19B, indicates that the datum target is on the far (hidden) surface. The leader, shown without an arrowhead, should not be shown in either a horizontal or vertical position. The datum feature itself is identified in the usual manner with a datum feature symbol.

The datum target symbol is a circle having a diameter approximately 3.5 times the height of the lettering used on the drawing. The circle is divided horizontally into two halves. The lower half contains a letter identifying the associated datum, followed by the target number assigned sequentially starting with 1 for each datum; for example, in a three-plane, six-point datum system, if the datums are A, B, and C, the datum targets would be A_1, A_2, A_3, B_1, B_2, and C_1. See Fig. 15-8-23. Where the datum target is an area, the area size may be entered in the upper half of the symbol, otherwise, the upper half is left blank.

Identification of Targets

Datum Target Points Each target point is shown on the surface, in its desired location, by means of a cross, drawn at approximately 45° to the coordinate dimensions. The cross is twice the height of the lettering used, as shown in Figs. 15-8-15 and 15-8-16A. Where there is no direct view, the point location is dimensioned on two adjacent views. See Fig. 15-8-16B.

Target points may be represented on tools, fixtures, and gages by spherically ended pins, as shown in Fig. 15-8-17.

Datum Target Lines A datum target line is indicated by the symbol "X" on

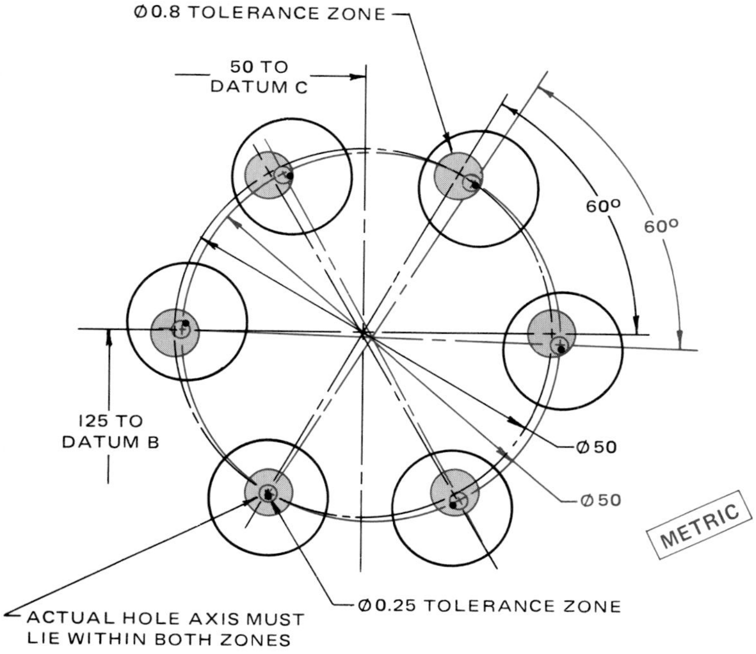

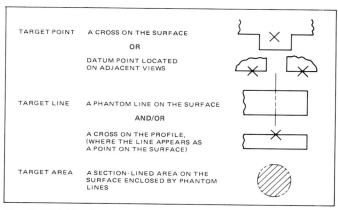

Fig. 15-8-14 Identification of datum targets.

Fig. 15-8-12 Tolerance zones for the six-hole pattern shown in Fig. 15-8-9.

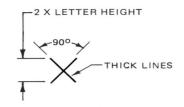

Fig. 15-8-15 Symbol for a datum target point.

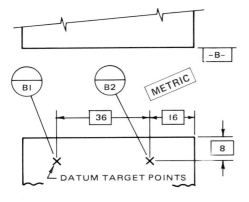

(A) DATUM POINTS SHOWN ON A SURFACE

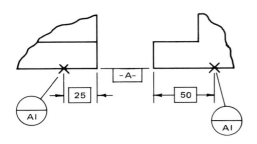

(B) DATUM POINT LOCATED BY TWO VIEWS
Fig. 15-8-16 Datum target point.

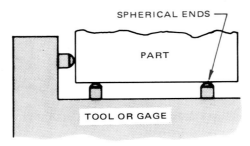

(A)

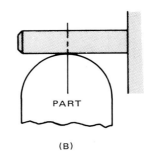

(B)

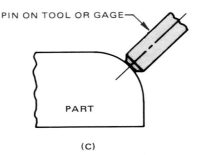

(C)
Fig. 15-8-17 Location of part on datum target points.

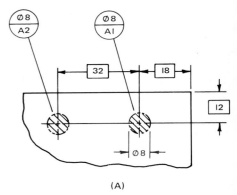

(A)

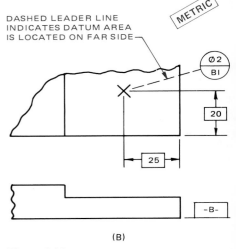

(B)
Fig. 15-8-19 Datum target areas.

an edge view of a surface, a phantom line on the direct view, or both. See Fig. 15-8-18. Where the length of the datum target line must be controlled, its length and location are dimensioned.

Datum Target Areas Where it is determined that an area or areas of flat contact is necessary to assure establishment of the datum (that is where spherical or pointed pins would be inadequate), a target area of the desired shape is specified. The datum target area is indicated by section lines inside a phantom outline of the desired shape, with controlling dimensions added. The diameter of circular areas is given in the upper half of the datum target symbol. See Fig. 15-8-19A.

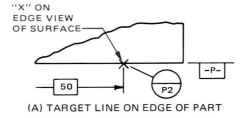

(A) TARGET LINE ON EDGE OF PART

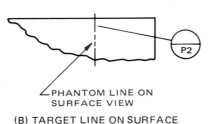

(B) TARGET LINE ON SURFACE
Fig. 15-8-18 Datum target line.

Where it becomes impractical to delineate a circular target area, the method of indication shown in Fig. 15-8-19B may be used.

Datum target areas may have any desired shape, a few of which are shown in Fig. 15-8-20. Target areas should be kept as small as possible, consistent with functional requirements, to avoid having large, crosshatched areas on the drawing.

Targets Not in the Same Plane

In most applications datum target points which form a single datum are all located on the same surface, as shown in Fig. 15-8-16A. However, this is not essential. They may be located on different surfaces, to meet functional requirements, as shown, for example, in Fig. 15-8-21. In some cases the datum plane may be located in space, that is, not actually touching the part, as shown in Fig. 15-8-22. In

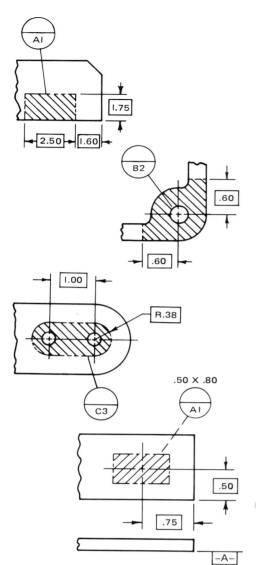

Fig. 15-8-20 Typical target areas.

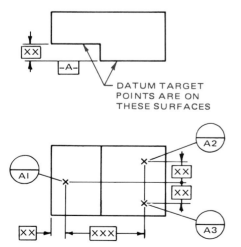

Fig. 15-8-21 Datum target points on different planes.

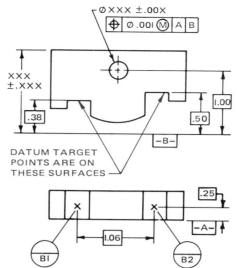

DATUM TARGET POINTS ARE ON THESE SURFACES

Fig. 15-8-22 Datum outside of part profile.

such applications the controlled features must be dimensioned from the specified datum, and the position of the datum from the datum targets must be shown by means of exact datum dimensions. For example, in Fig. 15-8-22 datum *B* is positioned by means of datum dimensions .38, .50, and 1.06. The top surface is controlled

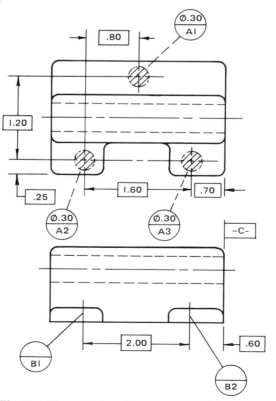

Fig. 15-8-23 Application of datum targets and dimensioning.

A1, A2, A3 TARGET AREAS
B1, B2 TARGET LINES
C1 TARGET POINT

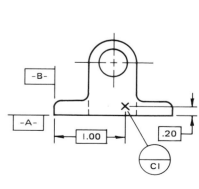

from this datum by means of a toleranced dimension, and the hole is positioned by means of the basic dimension 1.00 and a positional tolerance.

Dimensioning for Target Location

The location of datum targets is shown by means of basic dimensions. Each dimension is shown, without tolerances, enclosed in a rectangular frame, indicating that the general tolerance does not apply. Dimensions locating a set of datum targets should be dimensionally related or have a common origin.

Application of datum targets and datum dimensioning is shown in Fig. 15-8-23.

Reference and Source Material

1. ANSI Y14.5M, *Dimensioning and Tolerancing*

ASSIGNMENTS

See Assignments 29 and 30 for Unit 15-8 on page 322.

Circularity (Roundness) and Cylindricity

CIRCULARITY

Circularity refers to a condition of a circular line or the surface of a circular feature where all points on the line, or on the periphery of a plane cross section of the feature, are equidistant from a common axis or center point.

Examples of circular features would include disks, spheres, cylinders, and cones. The measurement plane for a sphere is any plane which passes through a section of maximum diameter. For a cylinder, cone, or other nonspherical feature, the measurement plane is any plane perpendicular to the axis or center line.

Errors of Circularity

Errors of circularity (out-of-roundness) of a circular line or the periphery of a cross section of a circular feature may occur as *ovality*, where differences appear between the major and minor

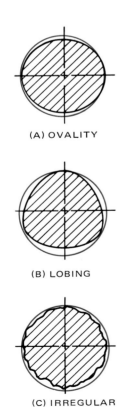

Fig. 15-9-1 Common types of circularity errors.

axes; as *lobing*, where in some instances the diametral values may be constant or nearly so; or as *random irregularities* from a true circle. All these errors are illustrated in Fig. 15-9-1. The geometric characteristic symbol for circularity is a circle, having a diameter equal to 1.5 times the height of letters on the drawing, as shown in Fig. 15-9-2.

Fig. 15-9-2 Circularity symbol.

Circularity Tolerance

A circularity tolerance may be specified by using this symbol in the feature control frame. It is expressed on an RFS basis.

A circularity tolerance specifies the width of an annular tolerance zone, bounded by two concentric circles in the same plane, within which the circular line or the periphery of the feature in that plane shall lie, as shown in Fig. 15-9-3. A circularity tolerance cannot be modified on an MMC basis since it controls surface elements only. The circularity tolerance must be less than the size tolerance.

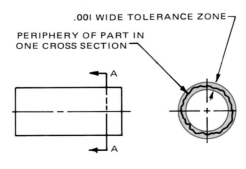

Fig. 15-9-3 Circularity tolerance.

Circularity of Noncylindrical Parts

Noncylindrical parts refer to conical parts and other features which are circular in cross section but which have variable diameters, such as those shown in Fig. 15-9-4. Since many sizes of circles may be involved, it is usually best to direct the circularity tolerance to the longitudinal surfaces as shown.

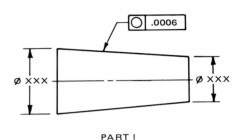

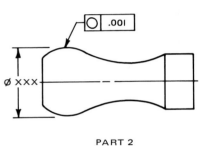

Fig. 15-9-4 Circularity tolerance on noncylindrical parts.

Cylindricity

Cylindricity is the condition of the surface which forms a cylinder where the surface elements in cross sections parallel to the axis are straight and parallel and in cross sections perpendicular to the axis are circular. The cylindricity tolerance is a composite control of form which includes circularity, straightness, and parallelism of the surface elements.

The geometric characteristic symbol for cylindricity consists of a circle with two tangent lines at 60°, as shown in Fig. 15-9-5.

A cylindricity tolerance specifies a tolerance zone bounded by two concentric cylinders within which the surface must lie. In the case of cylindricity, unlike that of circularity, the tolerance applies simultaneously to both circular and longitudinal ele-

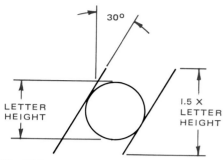

Fig. 15-9-5 Cylindricity symbol.

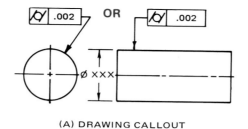

(A) DRAWING CALLOUT

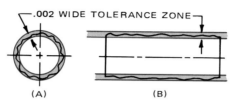

(A)　　　　(B)

Fig. 15-9-6 Cylindricity tolerance directed to either view.

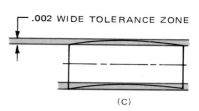

(C)

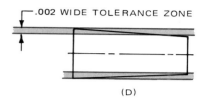

(D)

(B) PERMISSIBLE FORM ERRORS

ments of the surface, see Fig. 15-9-6. The leader from the feature control symbol may be directed to either view. The cylindricity tolerance must be less than the size tolerance.

Cylindricity tolerances can be applied only to cylindrical surfaces, such as round holes and shafts. No specific geometric tolerances have been devised for other circular forms, which require the use of several geometric tolerances. A conical surface, for example, must be controlled by a combination of tolerances for circularity, straightness, and angularity.

Errors of cylindricity may be caused by out-of-roundness, like ovality or lobing, by errors of straightness caused by bending or by diametral variation, by errors of parallelism like conicity or taper, and by random irregularities from a true cylindrical form.

Since cylindricity is a form tolerance controlling surface elements only, it cannot be modified on an MMC basis.

Reference and Source Material

1. ANSI Y14.5M, *Dimensioning and Tolerancing.*

ASSIGNMENTS

See Assignments 31 through 34 for Unit 15-9 on page 323.

ASSIGNMENTS FOR CHAPTER 15

As available, use a geometric tolerance library to place the required symbols onto the solutions to the assignments in this chapter.

Assignments for Unit 15-1, Modern Engineering Tolerancing

1. Parts may deviate from true form and still be acceptable provided the measurements lie within the limits of size. Show by means of a sketch with dimensions two acceptable form variations for each part shown in Fig. 15-1-A.

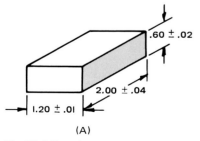

(A)

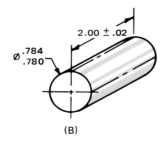

(B)

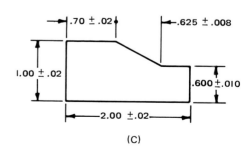

(C)

Fig. 15-1-A Assignments.

2. Prepare sketches from the drawings shown in Fig. 15-1-B or 15-1-C and the following information.

(a) Using illustration (A) make a tolerance block diagram similar to Fig. 15-1-5. Show the deviations and limits of size.

(b) Draw illustration (B) and indicate and dimension the tolerance zone.

(c) The exaggeration of sizes is used when it improves the clarity of the drawing. Draw illustration (C) and exaggerate the sizes which would improve the readability of the drawing. Dimension the exaggerated features.

(d) With reference to illustration (D), is the part acceptable? State your reason.

(e) With reference to the drawing callout shown in illustration (E), what parts would pass inspection?

(f) In the drawing callout in illustration (F), what parts in illustration (E) would pass inspection?

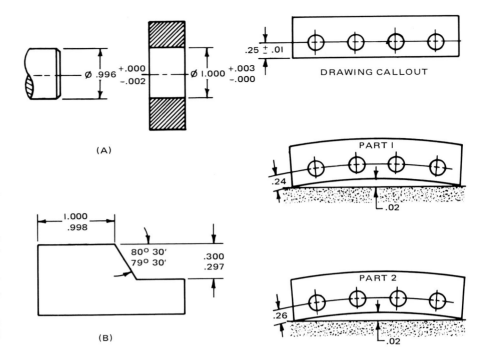

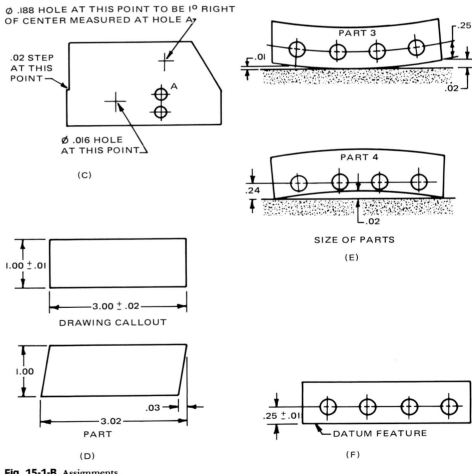

Fig. 15-1-B Assignments.

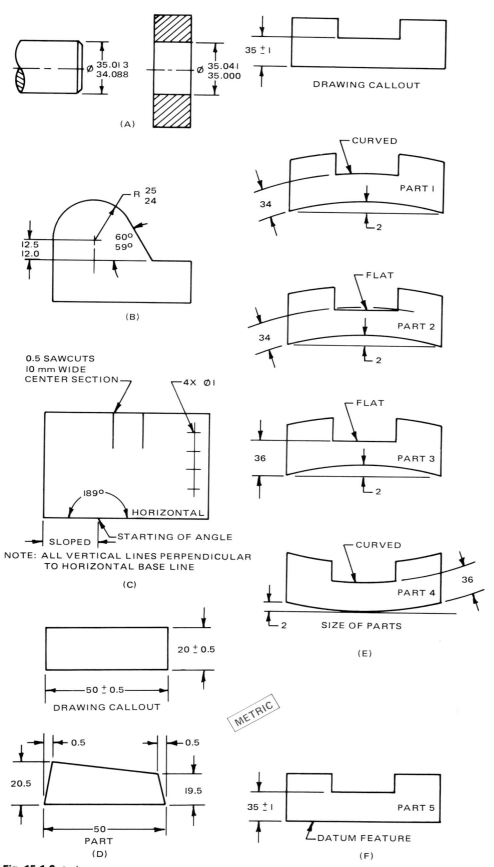

(A)

(B)

0.5 SAWCUTS
10 mm WIDE
CENTER SECTION

4X ⌀1

189°

HORIZONTAL

SLOPED

STARTING OF ANGLE

NOTE: ALL VERTICAL LINES PERPENDICULAR
TO HORIZONTAL BASE LINE

(C)

DRAWING CALLOUT

20 ± 0.5

50 ± 0.5

METRIC

0.5   0.5

20.5   19.5

50

PART

(D)

DRAWING CALLOUT

35 ± 1

CURVED

PART 1

34   2

FLAT

PART 2

34   2

FLAT

PART 3

36   2

CURVED

PART 4   36

2   SIZE OF PARTS

(E)

35 ± 1   PART 5

DATUM FEATURE

(F)

Fig. 15-1-C Assignments.

Assignment of Unit 15-2, Geometric Tolerancing

3. With reference to Fig. 15-2-A and the information given below, use symbols (or a library) to add the feature control frames to the following parts:

Part 1. Surface A to have a straightness tolerance of .004 in.

Part 2. Surface M to have a straightness tolerance of .006 in.
Surface N to have a straightness tolerance of .008 in.

Part 3. Surface R to be straight within .006 in. for direction *A* and straight within .002 in. for direction *B*.

Part 4. With straightness specified as shown, what is the maximum permissible deviation from straightness of the line elements if the radius is *(a)* .496 in., *(b)* .501 in., *(c)* .504 in.?

Part 5. Eliminate the top view and place the feature control frames on the front and side views.

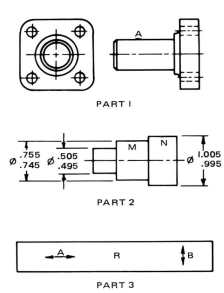

PART I

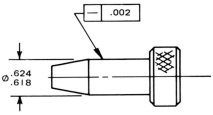

PART 2

PART 3

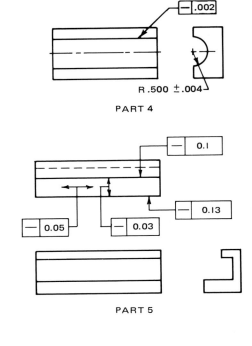

PART 4

PART 5

Fig. 15-2-A Assignments.

Assignments for Unit 15-3, Relationship to Feature of Size

4. With reference to Fig. 15-3-A, what is the maximum deviation permitted from straightness for the surface of the diameter if the shaft was *(a)* at MMC, *(b)* at LMC, *(c)* Ø.621?

5. With reference to Fig. 15-3-B, calculate the MMC, LMC, and extreme virtual condition of the hole and shaft. Refer to Fig. 15-3-1.

6. With reference to Fig. 15-3-B, if the hole was straight and at its MMC, how much could the shaft be bent and still assemble if the shaft diameter was *(a)* at MMC, *(b)* at LMC, *(c)* at Ø17.94?

7. With reference to Fig. 15-3-C, calculate the limits for the distances between the holes when the pins and holes are at *(a)* MMC, and *(b)* LMC.

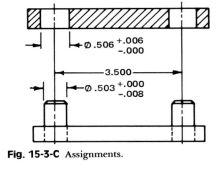

Fig. 15-3-A Assignments.

Fig. 15-3-C Assignments.

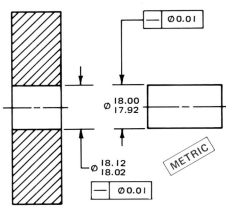

Fig. 15-3-B Assignment.

Assignments for Unit 15-4, Straightness of Features and Flatness

8. With reference to Fig. 15-4-A are parts A to E acceptable? State your reasons if part is not acceptable.

9. If Ⓜ was added to the straightness tolerance shown in Fig. 15-4-A, what parts would be acceptable? State your reasons if part is not acceptable.

10. Dimension the ring and snap gage shown in Fig. 15-4-B to check the pins shown. The ring gage should be of such a size as to check the entire length of pin. The two open ends of the snap gage should measure the minimum and maximum acceptable pin diameters.

11. In Fig. 15-4-C, part 1 is required to fit into part 2 so that there will not be any interference and the maximum clearance will never exceed .005 in. Show a flatness tolerance of .001 in. for both parts and a size with the largest size tolerance for part 2.

12. Show the tolerance zones and widths, for the two parts shown in Fig. 15-4-D.

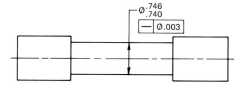

PART	FEATURE SIZE	STRAIGHTNESS DEVIATION	ACCEPTABLE
A	.747	.001	
B	.741	.004	
C	.742	.005	
D	.740	.006	
E	.740	.003	

Fig. 15-4-A Assignment.

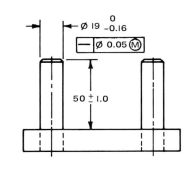

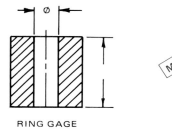

RING GAGE

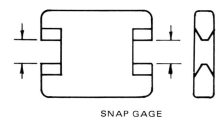

SNAP GAGE

Fig. 15-4-B Assignment.

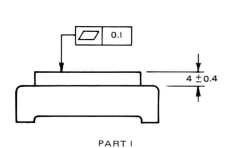

PART 1   PART 2

Fig. 15-4-C Assignments.

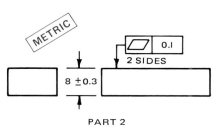

PART 1

PART 2

Fig. 15-4-D Assignment.

Assignments for Unit 15-5, Datums and the Three-Plane Concept

13. Draw the top and front views of Fig. 15-5-A and show the following information:
- Surface A is datum A.
- Surface B is datum B.
- Surfaces C and D are datum features which form a single datum.
- Using a symbol library add the geometric tolerances from the information shown on the drawing.

14. With reference to Fig. 15-5-B:
- The surface of the base plate to be datum A.
- Pins 1, 2, and 3 are used to establish the secondary and tertiary datums for the part shown.
- Make a two-view drawing of the part shown and identify the primary, secondary, and tertiary datum planes as A, B, and C, respectively.
- Add a flatness tolerance of 0.2 to the back of the slot.
- With reference to the slot and locational tolerances are the three parts shown acceptable?

15. With reference to Fig. 15-5-C: diameter M is to be used as datum A, the end face of diameter N is to be used as datum B, and the width of the slot at MMC on diameter N is to be used as datum C. Prepare two drawings, one with ANSI drawing standards the other with ISO drawing standards, which will identify these datums.

16. Prepare a three-view drawing showing the datums and feature control frames for Fig. 15-5-D.

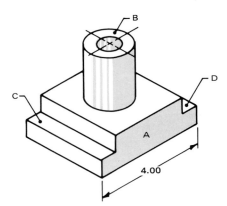

DATUM AND TOLERANCING INFORMATION

—A STRAIGHTNESS TOLERANCE OF .010 APPLIED TO THE CYLINDRICAL SURFACE

—THE BASE IS TO BE FLAT WITHIN .005

—DATUM A IS TO BE STRAIGHT WITHIN .008 FOR THE 4.00 LENGTH BUT THE STRAIGHTNESS ERROR NOT TO EXCEED .002 FOR ANY 1.00 LENGTH

—DATUM B IS TO BE FLAT WITHIN .004

—SURFACE B IS TO BE PARALLEL TO DATUM C–D WITHIN .006

Fig. 15-5-A Assignment.

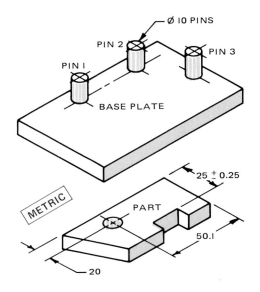

THE BACK OF THE SLOT IS TO HAVE A FLATNESS TOLERANCE OF 0.2

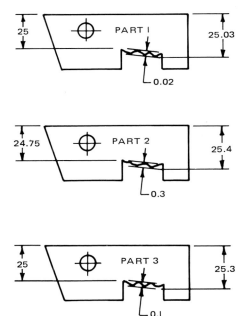

Fig. 15-5-B Assignment.

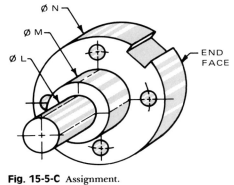

Fig. 15-5-C Assignment.

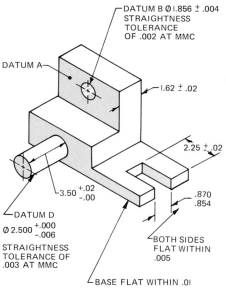

Fig. 15-5-D Assignment.

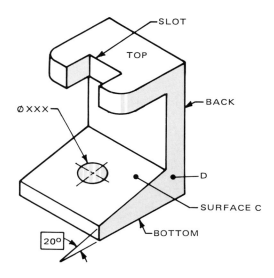

DATUM AND TOLERANCING INFORMATION

- BOTTOM TO BE DATUM A
- BACK TO BE DATUM B
- HOLE TO BE PERPENDICULAR TO BOTTOM WITHIN .003
- BACK TO BE PERPENDICULAR TO BOTTOM WITHIN .004
- TOP TO BE PARALLEL WITH BOTTOM WITHIN .005
- SURFACE C TO HAVE AN ANGULARITY TOLERANCE OF .006
  WITH THE BOTTOM. SURFACE D TO BE THE SECONDARY
  DATUM FOR THIS FEATURE.
- THE SIDES OF THE SLOT TO BE PARALLEL WITH EACH
  OTHER WITHIN .002
- BOTTOM TO HAVE A FLATNESS TOLERANCE OF .002
- BACK TO HAVE A FLATNESS TOLERANCE OF .004

Fig. 15-6-A Bracket.

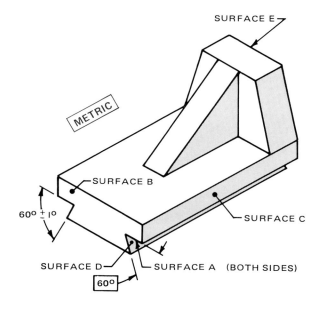

DATUM AND TOLERANCING INFORMATION

- SURFACE E TO HAVE A FLATNESS TOLERANCE OF 0.1 mm
- SURFACE D OF THE DOVETAIL MUST HAVE AN ANGULARITY
  TOLERANCE OF 0.05mm WITH DATUM A.
- SURFACE C SHOULD BE PERPENDICULAR TO DATUM A WITHIN
  0.03mm.
- SURFACE E MUST BE PERPENDICULAR TO DATUM A WITHIN
  0.02 mm.

Fig. 15-6-B Dovetail slide.

Assignments for Unit 15-6, Orientation

17. Today's drafters must be capable of interpreting and preparing drawings for use in other countries as well as in their own locality. From the information shown in Fig. 15-6-A prepare two three-view sketches, one showing the datums and geometric tolerancing symbols for use in the United States and the other sketch using ISO standards.

18. The surfaces shown in Fig. 15-6-B are required to be controlled in the following manner. Surfaces A, B, C, and D are datums A, B, C, D, respectively. Prepare a three-view drawing showing the datums and feature control symbols from the information supplied.

19. Prepare a two-view sketch of Fig. 15-6-C and from the information given show the datums and geometric tolerances. Given that the tangent of 0.5° is 0.0087, sketch the tolerance zone.

20. In Fig. 15-6-D it is functionally necessary that the shaft portion of the part not depart from perpendicularity with the holes by more than the tolerance specified. Show the drawing callout for this, and indicate the shape and size of the tolerance zone.

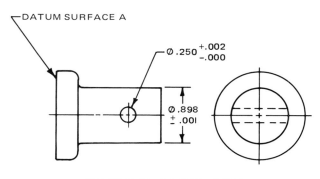

TOLERANCING INFORMATION

- HOLE TO BE PARALLEL WITH DATUM A WITHIN ± 0.5°

- THE Ø.898 SHAFT TO BE PERPENDICULAR TO DATUM A
  WITHIN .002 RFS

- DATUM A TO BE FLAT WITHIN .001

Fig. 15-6-C Cap.

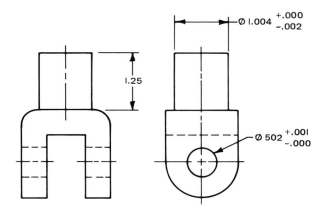

MAXIMUM PERPENDICULARITY TOLERANCE BETWEEN
HOLES AND SHAFT .005 IN 1.00 IN.

SHAFT TO BE DESIGNATED AS DATUM A

Fig. 15-6-D Bracket.

21. Complete the tables shown in Fig. 15-6-E showing the maximum allowable perpendicularity tolerances.

22. Draw the two views shown in Fig. 15-6-F and add the information shown with the drawing.

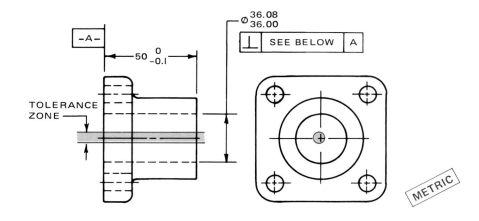

⊥ Ø0.03 A		⊥ Ø0 Ⓜ A		⊥ Ø0 Ⓜ Ø0.06 MAX A	
FEATURE SIZE	DIAMETER TOLERANCE ZONE ALLOWED	FEATURE SIZE	DIAMETER TOLERANCE ZONE ALLOWED	FEATURE SIZE	DIAMETER TOLERANCE ZONE ALLOWED
36		36		36	
36.01		36.01		36.01	
36.02		36.02		36.02	
36.03		36.03		36.03	
36.04		36.04		36.04	
36.05		36.05		36.05	
36.06		36.06		36.06	
36.07		36.07		36.07	
36.08		36.08		36.08	

Fig. 15-6-E Shaft support.

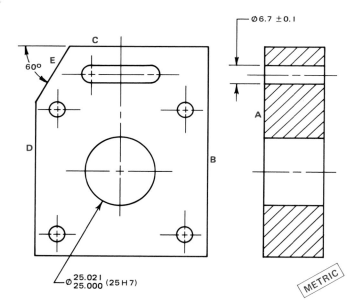

DATUM AND TOLERANCING INFORMATION

—SURFACES MARKED A, B, AND C ARE DATUMS A, B, AND C RESPECTIVELY

—SURFACE A IS PERPENDICULAR TO DATUMS B AND C WITHIN 0.2

—SURFACE D IS PARALLEL TO DATUM B WITHIN 0.1

—THE SLOT IS PARALLEL TO DATUM C WITHIN 0.2 AND PERPENDICULAR TO DATUM A WITHIN 0.3 AT MMC

—SURFACE E HAS AN ANGULARITY TOLERANCE OF 0.15 WITH DATUM C

—INDICATE THE BASIC DIMENSIONS ON THE DRAWING

Fig. 15-6-F Spacer.

Assignments for Unit 15-7, Tolerancing for Location of Features

23. If coordinate tolerances as shown in Fig. 15-7-A are given, what are the shapes of the tolerance zones and the distance between extreme permissible positions of the holes?

24. In Fig. 15-7-B add the largest equal tolerances so that if two such parts are assembled with the edges aligned, the distance between their hole centers could never be more than that shown.

25. If a tolerance shown in Fig. 15-7-C is specified for the vertical dimension, what tolerance should be added to the horizontal dimension to meet the same requirement as that required in Assignment 24?

26. In order to assemble correctly, the hole in the part in Fig. 15-7-D must not vary from its true position by more than that shown on the drawing when the hole is at its smallest size.

(a) Show suitable tolerancing to achieve this:
- By means of coordinate tolerancing
- By positional tolerancing without MMC
- By positional tolerancing on an MMC basis

(b) What would be the maximum permissible departure from true position if the hole were at its maximum diameter, using positional tolerancing RFS?

(c) What would be the maximum permissible departure from true position with a maximum-diameter hole and a positional tolerance on an MMC basis?

27. With reference to Fig. 15-7-D a projected tolerance zone of .60 in. is required for the Ø.502 in. hole. Show two methods of how this could be shown.

28. The part shown in Fig. 15-7-E is set on a revolving table, adjusted so that the part revolves about the true-position center of the large hole.

(a) If both indicators give identical readings and the results shown are obtained, which parts are acceptable?

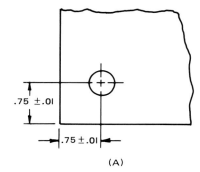

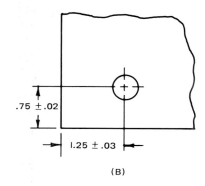

Fig. 15-7-A Assignments.

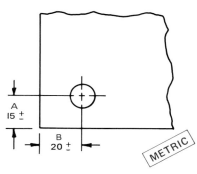

CALCULATE TOLERANCES
TO NEAREST 0.02
MAXIMUM DISTANCE BETWEEN
HOLE CENTERS = 0.5

Fig. 15-7-B Assignment.

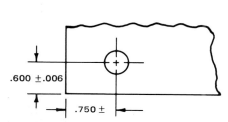

Fig. 15-7-C Assignment.

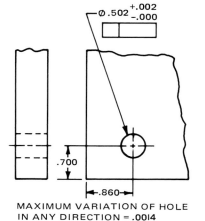

MAXIMUM VARIATION OF HOLE
IN ANY DIRECTION = .0014

Fig. 15-7-D Assignment.

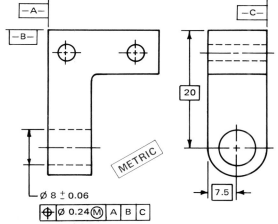

PART NO.	SIZE OF MANDREL	HIGHEST READING	LOWEST READING
1	8.00	1.54	1.32
2	8.06	0.18	−0.07
3	7.96	1.87	1.59
4	7.94	1.72	1.48
5	8.00	1.95	1.85
6	8.05	1.24	1.02

Fig. 15-7-E Assignment.

Assignments for Unit 15-8, Datums for Positional Tolerancing

29. Make a three-view drawing of the bearing housing shown in Fig. 15-8-A showing the datum features. Only the dimensions related to the datums need be shown. Scale 1:2.

30. Make a three-view drawing of the part shown in Fig. 15-8-B showing the datum features. Only the dimensions related to the datums need be shown. Scale 1:1. Datum information is as follows:

• *Primary datum A* (three areas-⌀3). A_1 and A_2 are located on center of surface *M*, one-fifth the depth distance from the front and back, respectively. A_3 is located on the center of surface *N* midway between the center of the hole and the right end.

• *Secondary datum B* is a datum line located at mid-height of surface *D*.

• *Tertiary datum C* is a datum point located on the center of surface *E*.

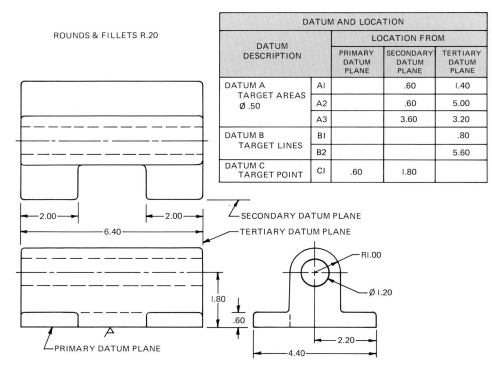

ROUNDS & FILLETS R.20

DATUM AND LOCATION				
DATUM DESCRIPTION		LOCATION FROM		
		PRIMARY DATUM PLANE	SECONDARY DATUM PLANE	TERTIARY DATUM PLANE
DATUM A TARGET AREAS ⌀ .50	A1		.60	1.40
	A2		.60	5.00
	A3		3.60	3.20
DATUM B TARGET LINES	B1			.80
	B2			5.60
DATUM C TARGET POINT	C1	.60	1.80	

Fig. 15-8-A Bearing housing.

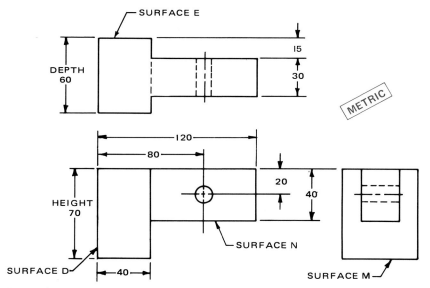

Fig. 15-8-B Assignment.

Assignments for Unit 15-9, Circularity (Roundness) and Cylindricity

31. Sketch the tolerance zone for the circularity tolerance in Fig. 15-9-A. If measurements made at cross sections *AA, BB,* and *CC,* indicate that all points on the periphery fall within the annular rings shown, would you conclude that the part met the specified circularity tolerance? If not, which cross section is not acceptable? State your reason.

32. Add circularity tolerances to the diameters shown in Fig. 15-9-B. The circularity tolerances are to be one-fifth of the size tolerances for each diameter.

33. Show on each part in Fig. 15-9-C a cylindrical tolerance. The size of the cylindrical tolerance is to equal one-quarter the size tolerance for each diameter.

34. Sketch the tolerance zone for the cylindrical tolerance in Fig. 15-9-D indicating its size and shape for the part shown.

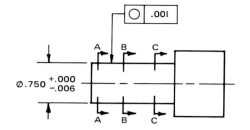

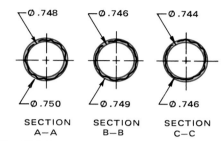

Fig. 15-9-A Assignments.

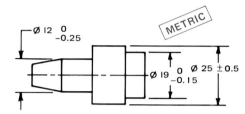

Fig. 15-9-B Assignments.

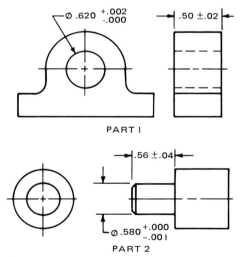

Fig. 15-9-C Assignments.

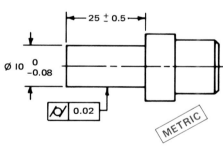

Fig. 15-9-D Assignments.

CHAPTER 16

Auxiliary Views

UNIT 16-1

Primary Auxiliary Views

Many machine parts have surfaces that are not perpendicular, or at right angles, to the plane of projection. These are referred to as *sloping* or *inclined* surfaces. In the regular orthographic views, such surfaces appear to be foreshortened, and their true shape is not shown. When an inclined surface has important characteristics that should be shown clearly and without distortion, an auxiliary view is used so that the drawing completely and clearly explains the shape of the object. In many cases, the auxiliary view will replace one of the regular views on the drawing, as illustrated in Fig. 16-1-1.

One of the regular orthographic views will have a line representing the edge of the inclined surface. The auxiliary view is projected from this edge line, at right angles, and is drawn parallel to the edge line.

LISP programming provides an option to have a primary auxiliary view automatically created perpendicular to the inclined surface. This, however, is not common to most systems. Thus, use projection lines and project at the specified angle. As an alternate, OFFSET and PERPENDICULAR lines option may be used separately, or in conjunction.

Only the true shape features on the views need be drawn, as shown in Fig. 16-1-2. Since the auxiliary view shows only the true shape and detail of the inclined surface features, a partial auxiliary view is all that is necessary. Likewise, the distorted features on the regular views may be omitted. Hidden lines are usually omitted except in cases where they are required for clarity. This procedure is recommended for production drafting where drafting costs are an important consideration. However, the drafter may be called upon to draw the complete views of the part. This type of drawing is often used for catalog and standard parts drawings.

The partial auxiliary view shown in Fig. 16-1-2 may easily be created by:

1. Select the OFFSET command.
2. Select the endpoint of the inclined surface (point 1), T (through), and a point where you want the first parallel line of identical length to the inclined line in the front view located (point 2).

NOTE: IN NONE OF THESE VIEWS DOES THE SLANTED (COLORED) SURFACE APPEAR IN ITS TRUE SHAPE.

(A) WEDGED BLOCK SHOWN IN THREE REGULAR VIEWS

NOTE: IN THIS EXAMPLE THE AUXILIARY PLANE REPLACED THE TOP PLANE IN ORDER THAT THE SLANTED (COLORED) SURFACE MAY BE SHOWN IN ITS TRUE SHAPE

(B) REPLACING THE TOP PLANE WITH AN AUXILIARY PLANE

Fig. 16-1-1 Relationship of the auxiliary plane to the three principle planes.

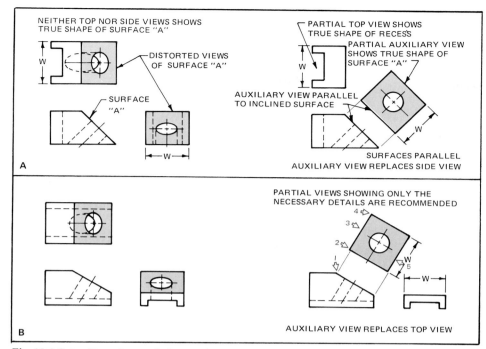

Fig. 16-1-2 Auxiliary views replacing regular views.

3. Repeat this procedure for the second parallel line except key in the width of the part (W) and press ENTER to position it (point 4).

4. The other two lines (3 and 5) forming the inclined surface may be created using the LINE and OSNAP-ENDPOINTS commands.

5. Finish the view using CIRCLE, LAYER, and CENTER lines commands.

Additional examples of auxiliary view drawings are shown in Fig. 16-1-3.

Figure 16-1-4 shows how to make an auxiliary view of a symmetrical object. Figure 16-1-4A shows the object in a pictorial view. In this illustration a center plane (X-Y) is used as a reference plane (Fig. 16-1-4B). It is drawn parallel (OFFSET) to the inclined surface shown in the front view. The edge view of this plane appears as a center line, line XY, on the top view. Number the points on the top view. Then transfer these numbers to the edge

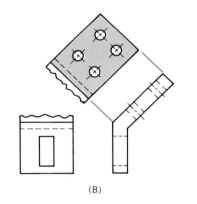

NOTE: CONVENTIONAL BREAK OR PROJECTED SURFACE ONLY NEED BE SHOWN ON PARTIAL VIEWS

Fig. 16-1-3 Examples of auxiliary view drawings.

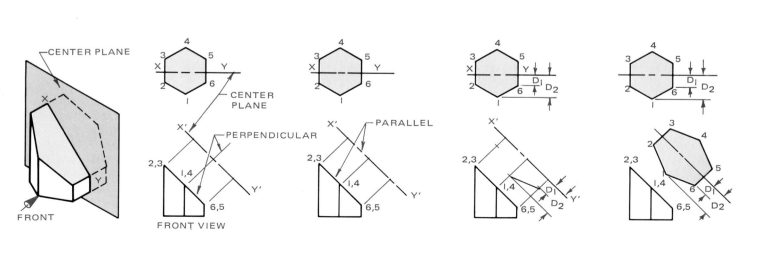

Fig. 16-1-4 To draw an auxiliary view using the center plane reference.

view of the inclined surface on the front view, as shown. Select LINE and OSNAP PER pen. Select the X-Y center plane and point 2,3 (front view). Repeat the procedure for points 1,4 and 6,5. The projection lines are created as shown in Fig. 16-1-4C. Now, in the top view, find the distances D1 and D2 from the numbered points to the center line using the DISTANCE option. These are the depth measurements. Transfer them to the auxiliary view using POLAR coordinate input with POINT measuring them off on one side of line X'Y', as shown in Fig. 16-1-4D. The result will be a set of three points on the projection lines. Connect these points and mirror the half-object about the X'Y' axis. Erase the projection lines. The result is shown in Fig. 16-1-4E showing the auxiliary view of the inclined surface that results.

Dimensioning Auxiliary Views

One of the basic rules of dimensioning is to dimension the feature where it can be seen in its true shape and size. Thus the auxiliary view will show only the dimensions pertaining to those features for which the auxiliary view was drawn. The view may be drawn using the procedure earlier described. The recommended method for the horizontal, vertical, and aligned dimensions is the unidirectional (text is horizontal) system. This method of dimensioning is easier to read. Be sure the unidirectional (DIMTOH, DIMTIH) text dimensional variable option is ON prior to placing ALIGNED LINEAR DIMENSIONS. Figure 16-1-5.

ASSIGNMENTS

See Assignments 1 through 5 for Unit 16-1 starting on page 329.

■ UNIT 16-2

Circular Features in Auxiliary Projection

As mentioned in Unit 16-1, at times it is necessary to show the complete views of an object. If circular features are involved in auxiliary projection, then the surfaces appear elliptical, not circular, in one of the views.

The method most commonly used to draw the true-shape projection of the curved surface is the plotting of a series of points on the line, the number of points being governed by the accuracy of the curved line required.

Figure 16-2-1 illustrates an auxiliary view of a truncated cylinder. The shape seen in the auxiliary view is an ellipse. This shape is easily drawn using the ELLIPSE command and specifying the major and minor axes or diameters. The minor axis is the diameter of the cylinder as seen by DK in the top view. The major axis is seen in the front view (AG). The result is shown in Fig. 16-2-1A. If the curved feature is not an ellipse, it must be drawn using the lengthy "lines of intersection" method and the FIT CURVE option. To accomplish this

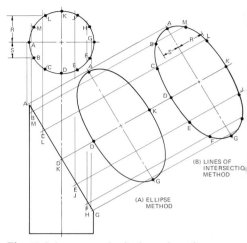

Fig. 16-2-1 Truncated cylinder and auxiliary views.

the circumference of the circle in the top view is divided to give a number of equally spaced points; in this case, 12 points, spaced 30° apart (360°/12 = 30°). These points are projected down to the edge line on the front view then at right angles to the edge line to the area where the auxiliary view will be drawn (Fig. 16-2-1B). A center plane for the auxiliary view (line AG) is drawn parallel to the edge line, and width settings taken from the top view are transferred to the auxiliary view. Note the width setting R for point L. Because the part is a true cylinder and the point divisions in the top view are all equal, the width setting R taken at L is also the correct width setting for C, E, and J. Width setting S for B is also the correct width setting for F, H, and M. When all the width settings have been transferred to the auxiliary view, the resulting points of intersection are connected by means of selecting PLINE, PEDIT, picking the line, then issuing the FIT CURVE option. ERASE the projection lines. As an alternate, create one-half and MIRROR the other half about center plane AG.

It is often necessary to construct the auxiliary view first in order to complete the regular views. This is shown in Fig. 16-2-2. Notice that the half ellipse option is used for the larger curved surface in the right side view. Either the ellipse or lines of intersection method may be used.

ASSIGNMENT

See Assignment 6 for Unit 16-2 on page 330.

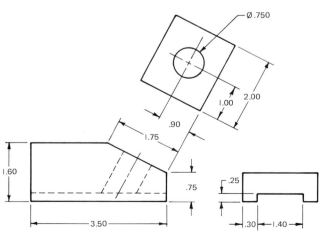

Fig. 16-1-5 Dimensioning auxiliary view drawings.

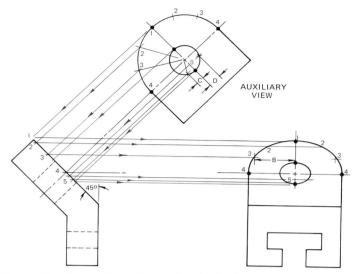

Fig. 16-2-2 Constructing the true shape of a curved surface by the ellipse or plotting method.

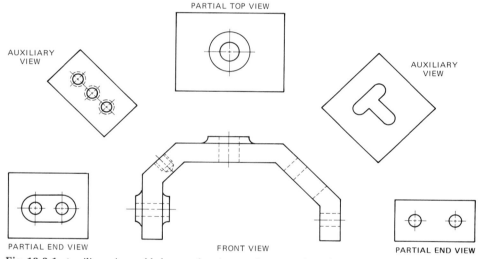

PARTIAL TOP VIEW

AUXILIARY VIEW

AUXILIARY VIEW

PARTIAL END VIEW

FRONT VIEW

PARTIAL END VIEW

Fig. 16-3-1 Auxiliary views added to regular views to show true shape features.

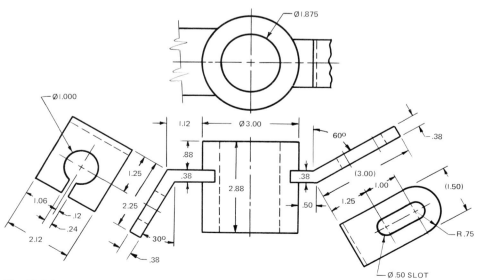

Ø1.875
Ø1.000
1.12
Ø3.00
60°
.38
.88
.38
(3.00)
2.88
1.00
.38
(1.50)
1.25
1.06
1.25
2.25
.50
.12
R.75
.24
2.12
30°
.38
Ø.50 SLOT

Fig. 16-3-2 Dimensioning a multi-auxiliary-view drawing.

■ UNIT 16-3

Multi-Auxiliary-View Drawings

Some objects have more than one surface not perpendicular to the plane of projection. In preparing working drawings of these objects, an auxiliary view may be required for each surface. Naturally, this would depend upon the amount and type of detail lying on these surfaces. This type of drawing is often referred to as a *multi-auxiliary-view* drawing. See Fig. 16-3-1.

One can readily see the advantage of using the unidirectional system of dimensioning for dimensioning an object such as shown in Fig. 16-3-2.

ASSIGNMENT

See Assignment 7 for Unit 16-3 on page 331.

■ UNIT 16-4

Secondary Auxiliary Views

Some objects, because of their shape, require a secondary auxiliary view to show the true shape of the surface or feature. See Fig. 16-4-1. The surface or feature is usually oblique to the principal planes of projection. In order to make a secondary auxiliary view, the primary auxiliary view is first projected parallel to a true-length line on the inclined surface (point 1, Fig. 16-4-1). Dimensions are taken from the second previous view. In this case, the second previous view is the front view and the dimensions to be taken from this view are height dimensions. (This is a very important concept to understand and is indispensible when studying descriptive geometry techniques.) The resulting primary auxiliary view of the oblique surface will always be shown as an edge view (Fig. 16-4-1). The secondary auxiliary view is projected from the primary auxiliary view, perpendicular to it. Take dimensions from the second previous view (top view). The resulting secondary auxiliary view is always shown in its true shape (Fig. 16-4-1). This means all lines, angles, circles, etc., are seen in their true size. Figure 16-4-2 shows

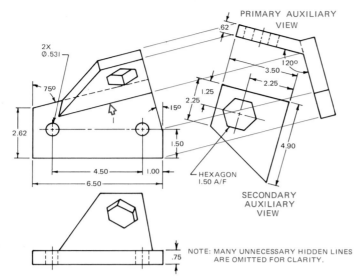

Fig. 16-4-1 Secondary auxiliary-view drawing.

the procedure for drawing a secondary auxiliary view. Remember always to take DISTANCES from the second previous view.

ASSIGNMENT

See Assignment 8 for Unit 16-4 on page 332.

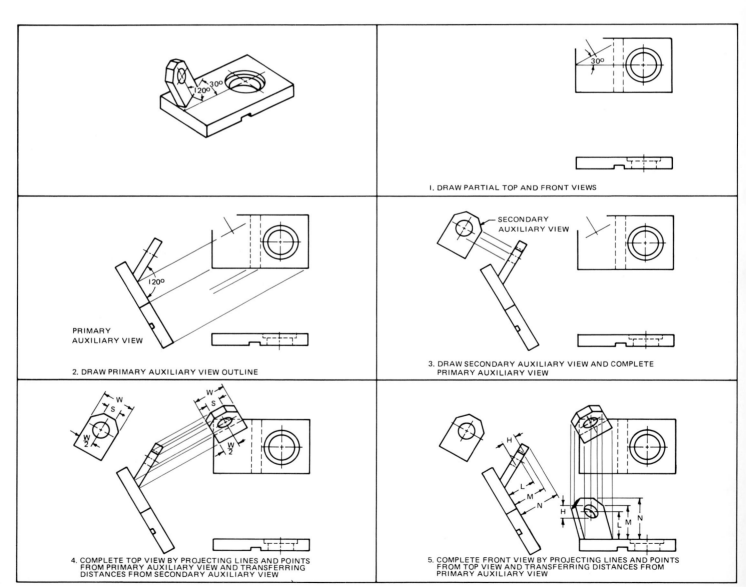

Fig. 16-4-2 Steps in drawing a secondary auxiliary view.

ASSIGNMENTS FOR CHAPTER 16

Assignments for Unit 16-1, Primary Auxiliary Views

1. Make a working drawing of the angle bracket shown in Fig. 16-1-A. Replace the top view with an auxiliary view. Scale 1:1.

2. Make a working drawing of the cross-slide bracket shown in Fig. 16-1-B. Replace the side view with an auxiliary view. Only partial views need be drawn, and hidden lines may be added to improve clarity. Scale 1:1.

3. Make a working drawing showing the top, front, and auxiliary views of the angle plate shown in Fig. 16-1-C. Only partial views are required for the auxiliary and front views. Hidden lines may be added to improve the clarity. Scale 1:1.

4. Make a working drawing showing the top, front, and partial auxiliary view of each of the two statue bases shown in Fig. 16-1-D. Scale 1:1.

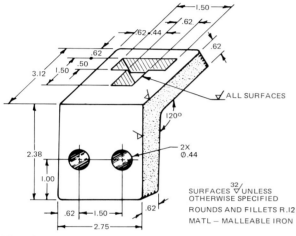

Fig. 16-1-A Angle bracket.

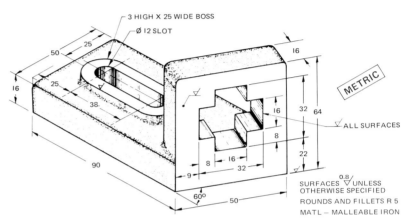

Fig. 16-1-B Cross-slide bracket.

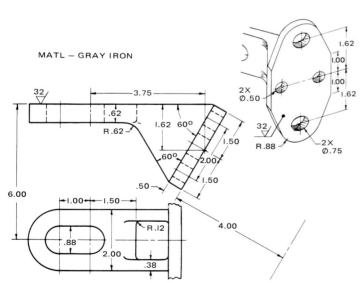

Fig. 16-1-C Angle plate.

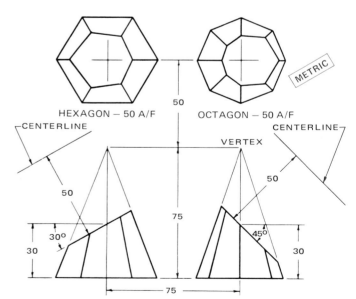

Fig. 16-1-D Status bases.

5. Select any two of the truncated prisms shown in Fig. 16-1-E, and show the top, front, and auxiliary views for each. All views are to be complete with hidden lines shown. Scale 1:1.

Assignment for Unit 16-2, Circular Features in Auxiliary Projection

6. Make a working drawing of one of the parts shown in Fig. 16-2-A or 16-2-B. Use the ellipse method in Fig. 16-2-A and the lines-of-intersection method for Fig. 16-2-B. Add hidden lines when required for clarity. Locational dimensions are to the center of auxiliary views. Scale 1:1.

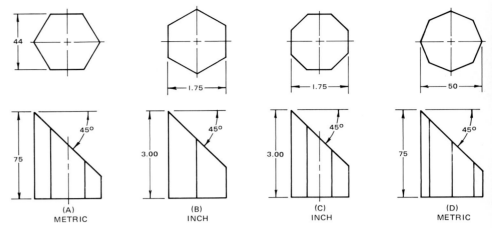

Fig. 16-1-E Truncated prisms.

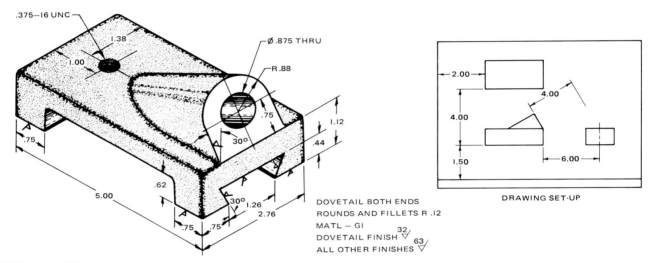

Fig. 16-2-A Control block.

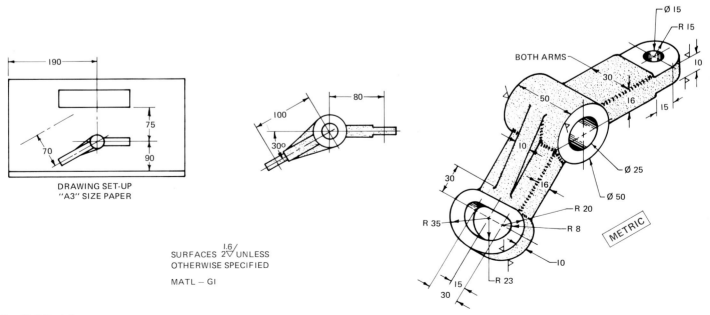

Fig. 16-2-B Link.

Assignment for Unit 16-3, Multi-Auxiliary-View Drawings

7. Make a working drawing of one of the parts shown in Figs. 16-3-A to 16-3-C. The selection and placement of views are shown. Only partial views need be drawn except where noted, and hidden lines may be added to improve clarity. Scale 1:1.

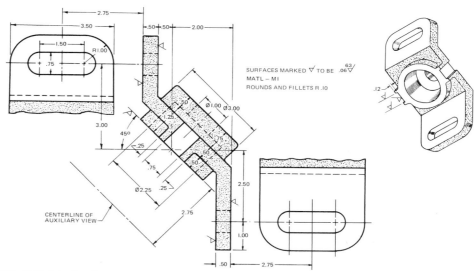

Fig. 16-3-A Inclined stop.

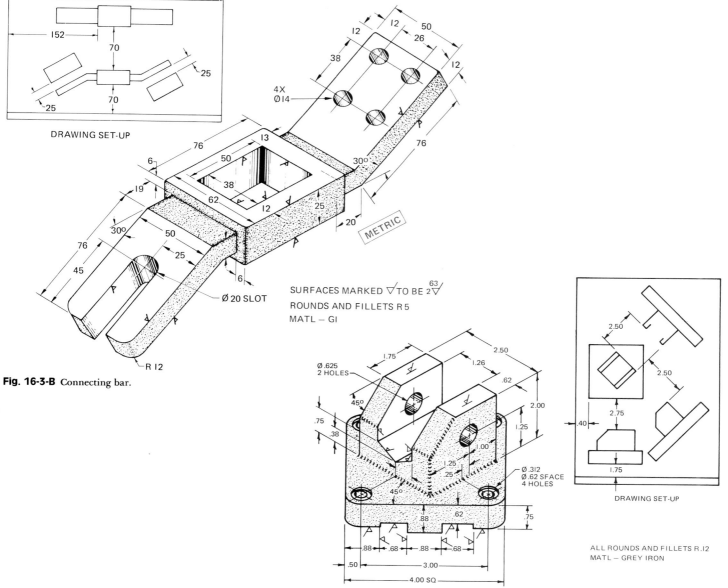

DRAWING SET-UP

Fig. 16-3-B Connecting bar.

SURFACES MARKED ▽ TO BE 2▽
ROUNDS AND FILLETS R 5
MATL — GI

Fig. 16-3-C Angle slide.

DRAWING SET-UP

ALL ROUNDS AND FILLETS R.12
MATL — GREY IRON

Assignment for Unit 16-4, Secondary Auxiliary Views

8. Make a working drawing of one of the parts shown in Fig. 16-4-A or 16-4-B. The selection and placement of views are shown beside the drawing. Only partial auxiliary views need be drawn, and hidden lines may be added to improve clarity. Scale 1 : 1.

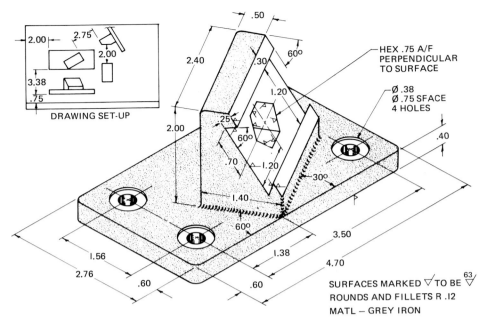

Fig. 16-4-A Dovetail bracket.

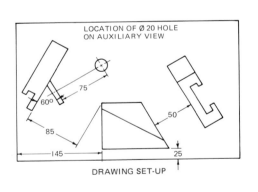

Fig. 16-4-B Pivot arm.

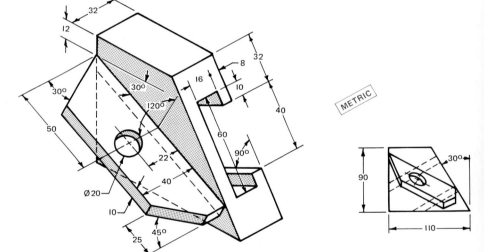

17

Pictorial Drawings

UNIT 17-1

Pictorial Drawings

Pictorial drawing is the oldest method of communication known, but the character of pictorial drawing has continually changed with the advance of civilization. In this text only those kinds of pictorial drawings commonly used by the engineer, designer, and drafter are considered. Pictorial drawings are useful in design, construction or production, erection or assembly, service or repairs, and sales. They are used to explain complicated engineering drawings to people who do not have the training or ability to read the conventional multiview drawings; to help the designer work out problems in space, including clearances and interferences; to train new employees in the shop; to speed up and clarify the assembly of a machine or the ordering of new parts; to transmit ideas from one person to another, from shop to shop, or from salesperson to purchaser; and as an aid in developing the power of visualization. The type of pictorial drawing used depends on the purpose for which it is drawn.

There are three general types into which pictorial drawings may be divided: axonometric, oblique, and perspective. These three differ from one another in the fundamental scheme of projection, as shown in Figs. 17-1-1 and 17-1-2.

A pictorial drawing may be created by using any two-dimensional (2D) CAD system. Generally, a grid pattern peculiar to the type of pictorial will be employed. Since isometrics are the most popular, an isometric grid option is found on every system. The grids serve as a guide to assist drawing along major axis lines. CAD systems also have an option for automatic genera-

tion of the pictorial. In this instance draw the multiview working drawing as usual (you will only be required to draw the plan view and key in the third dimension (Z-axis). Upon issuing the VIEWPOINT (VPOINT) command, the isometric pictorial may be automatically generated since the system has all X, Y, and Z endpoint position information. Automatic generation of

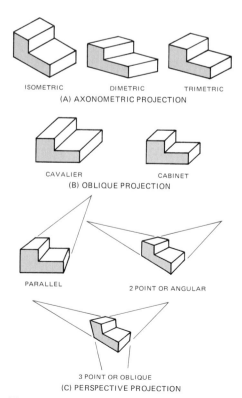

Fig. 17-1-1 Types of pictorial drawings.

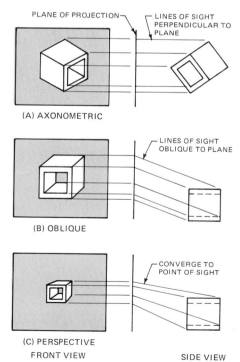

Fig. 17-1-2 Kinds of projections.

a pictorial is common to the axonometic and perspective types only.

AXONOMETRIC PROJECTION

A projected view in which the lines of sight are perpendicular to the plane of projection, but in which the three faces of a rectangular object are all inclined to the plane of projection, is called an *axonometric projection.* See Fig. 17-1-2. The projections of the three principal axes may make any angle with one another except 90°. Axonometric drawings, as shown in Figs. 17-1-3 and 17-1-4, are classified into three forms: *isometric drawings,* where the three principal faces and axes of the object are equally inclined to the plane of projection; *dimetric drawings,* where two of the three principal faces and axes of the object are equally inclined to the plane of projection; and *trimetric drawings,* where all three faces and axes of the object make different angles with the plane of projection. The most popular form of axonometric projection is the isometric.

ISOMETRIC DRAWINGS

This method is based on a procedure of revolving the object at an angle of 45° to the horizontal, so that the front corner is toward the viewer, then tipping the object up or down at an angle

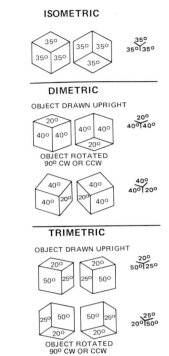

Fig. 17-1-4 Axonometric projection.

of 35°16′. See Fig. 17-1-5. When this is done to a cube, the three faces visible to the viewer appear equal in shape and size, and the side faces are at an angle of 30° to the horizontal. If the isometric view were actually projected from a view of the object in the tipped

position, the lines in the isometric view would be foreshortened and would, therefore, not be seen in their true length. To simplify the drawing of an isometric view, the actual measurements of the object are used. Although the object appears slightly larger without the allowance for foreshortening, the proportions are not affected. All isometric drawings are started by constructing the isometric axes, which are a vertical line for height and isometric lines to left and right, at an angle of 30° from the horizontal, for length and width. The three faces seen in the isometric view are the same faces that would be seen in the normal orthographic views: top, front, and side. Figure 17-1-5B illustrates the selection of the front corner (A), the construction of the isometric axes, and the completed isometric view. Note that all lines are drawn to their true length, measured along the isometric axes, and that hidden lines are usually omitted. Vertical edges are represented by vertical lines, and horizontal edges by lines at 30° to the horizontal. Two techniques can be used for making an isometric drawing of an irregularly shaped object, as illustrated in Fig. 17-1-6. In one method, the object is divided mentally into a number of sections and the sections are created one at a time in their proper relationship to one another. In the second method, a box is created with the maximum

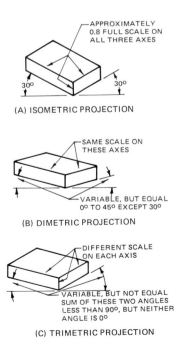

Fig. 17-1-3 Types of axonometric drawings.

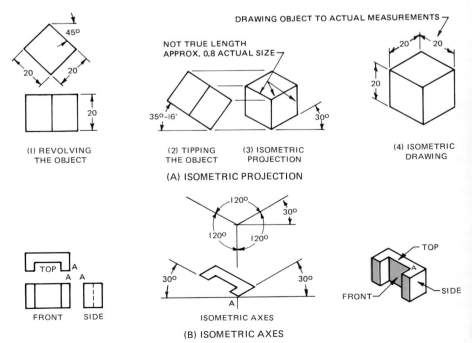

Fig. 17-1-5 Isometric axes and projection.

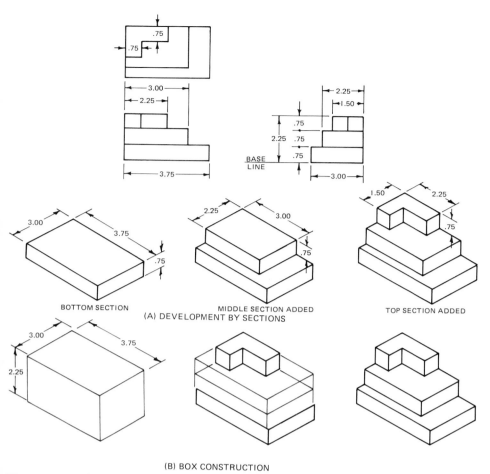

Fig. 17-1-6 Developing an isometric drawing.

the orthographic views. In isometric drawing, sloping surfaces appear as *nonisometric* lines. To create them, locate their endpoints, found on the ends of isometric lines, and join them with a straight line. Figures 17-1-7 and 17-1-8 illustrate examples in the construction of nonisometric lines.

Dimensioning Isometric Drawings

At times, an isometric drawing of a simple object may serve as a working drawing. In such cases, the necessary dimensions and specifications are placed on the drawing.

height, width, and depth of the object; then the parts of the box that are not part of the object are removed, leaving the pieces that form the total object.

Nonisometric Lines

Many objects have sloping surfaces that are represented by sloping lines in

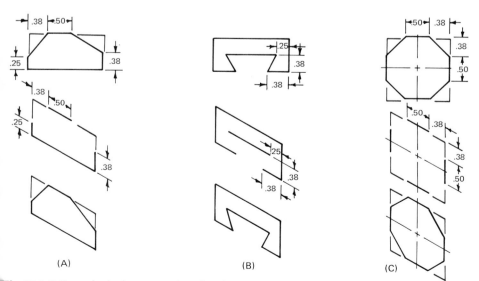

Fig. 17-1-7 Examples in the construction of nonisometric lines.

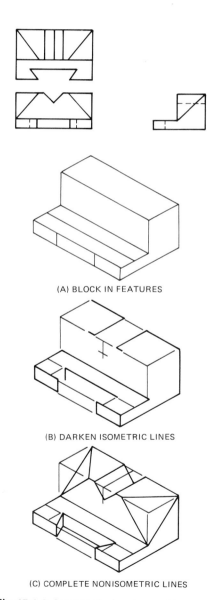

Fig. 17-1-8 Sequence in drawing an object having nonisometric lines.

Unidirectional dimensioning is the method of dimensioning isometric drawings. The letters and numbers are vertical and read from the bottom of the sheet. An example of this type of dimensioning is shown in Fig. 17-1-9.

To dimension a pictorial view, first draw two extension lines (or use existing centerlines). Next, select the ALIGNED (LINEAR-DIN) option. Select two points where you wish the dimension arrows to be placed. Select the text option (in line with the previous two points) and press ENTER.

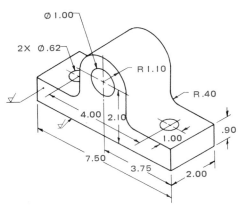

Fig. 17-1-9 Orienting the dimension line, arrowhead, and extension line.

Isometric Grid

With an isometric pattern the grids will appear at 30° angles rising to the left and right. Using this option, create the object in Fig. 17-1-6 by:

1. Select the SNAP command, STYLE (S), and the standard ISO-METRIC (I) option.
2. Key in a snap increment of .75. An isometric grid will appear. (For clarity, isometric lines are used in Fig. 17-1-10.)
3. Set the GRID to .75.
4. Select LINE and draw the top section as shown in Fig. 17-1-10-A.
5. Create the center section (Fig. 17-1-10-B). Use OBJECT SNAP-ENDPOINT to join lines from the top section.
6. Create the bottom section (Fig. 17-1-10-C).

More complicated drawings, with lines not on grid, will require the extensive use of polar coordinate input. Whenever possible, however, use the grid pattern. Isometric grids are particularly useful when developing certain schematics. Piping spool diagrams (Fig. 17-1-11) and plumbing riser dia-

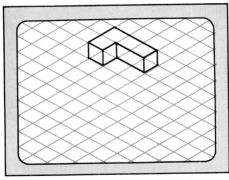

(A) ISOMETRIC PATTERN AND TOP SECTION

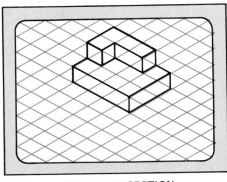

(B) CENTER SECTION

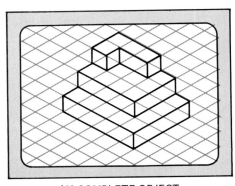

(C) COMPLETE OBJECT

Fig. 17-1-10 Isometric drawing.

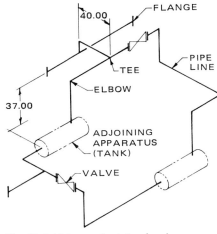

Fig. 17-1-11 Isometric piping drawing.

grams are two examples. The isometric circles are created by using ISO (ECLIPSE) and toggling the correct ISOPLANE (Unit 6-4).

Modeling

Thus far, all discussion has been confined to two-dimensional (2D) software. For the vast majority of engineering drawing applications, two-dimensional drafting will suffice. Multiview projection, which uses two or more two-dimensional views to describe a three-dimensional object is considered the standard operating procedure for many design offices. Occasionally, however, three-dimensional (axonometric) drawing capability is desirable. This can be accomplished as previously shown using a basic two-dimensional system. Lines are drawn inclined both to the right or left at 30° from the horizontal. These, with a vertical line, establish the three major axes of an isometric drawing.

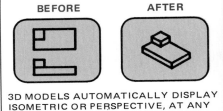

3D MODELS AUTOMATICALLY DISPLAY ISOMETRIC OR PERSPECTIVE, AT ANY VIEW POINT EITHER IN WIREFRAME (EDGE LINES) OR SOLID (SHADED) WHILE CONCEALING HIDDEN LINES.

This method, however, may become quite cumbersome requiring a considerable time expenditure. CAD systems provide a modeling option often referred to as *3D modeling*. With this option the model, isometric or otherwise, is automatically generated from the drawing. The method commonly used in modeling is to draw one view (often the plan or top view) and key in the third dimension (thickness or height). All X, Y, and Z coordinate information is provided to the system. The single-view (plan or top) method to create the object shown in Fig. 17-1-12A is

1. Display a .75-in. GRID and activate the SNAP.
2. Select the ELEVATION (SETTINGS) option.
3. Key in **0** for the elevation, which is

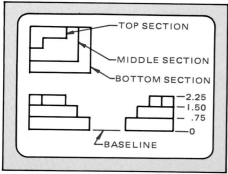

(A) THE PART TO BE MODELED

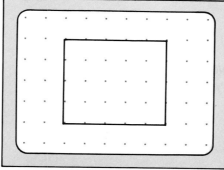

(B) PLAN VIEW OF BOTTOM SECTION

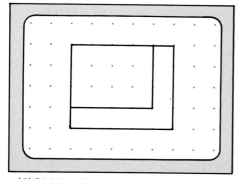

(C) PLAN VIEW WITH CENTER SECTION ADDED

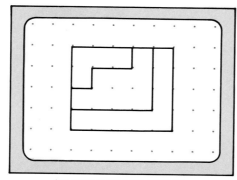

(D) TOP SECTION ADDED

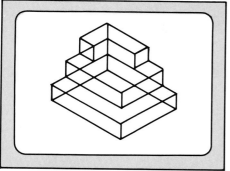

(E) WIRE-FRAME ISOMETRIC ILLUSTRATED WITH ALL LINES

(F) WIRE-FRAME ISOMETRIC ILLUSTRATED WITH HIDDEN LINE REMOVAL

Fig. 17-1-12 CAD model of Fig. 17-1-6.

the bottom of the object (referred to as the baseline), and **.75** for the THICKNESS (height) of the bottom section.

4. Select LINE and create the plan (top) view outline of the bottom section (Fig. 17-1-12B).
5. Select the ELEVATION (and THICKNESS) options.
6. Key .75 for the base elevation of the center section, which is .75 in. above the base line. Key .75 in. thickness (height) of the center section.
7. Create the complete plan view (four sides) outline for the center section (Fig. 17-1-12C).

8. Select the ELEVATION and THICKNESS options.
9. Key 1.50 for the base elevation of the top section and .75 thickness (height) of the top section.
10. Create the complete plan view outline for the top section (Fig. 17-1-12D).
11. Select the DISPLAY VIEWPOINT option VPOINT and AXES (use DVIEW for perspective applications).

Select a viewpoint (e.g., lower left quadrant). The model will be displayed as shown in Fig. 17-1-12E. This

type of model showing the perimeter of each plane is referred to as a *wire-frame* model. Notice that all lines of the object have been drawn. A system that only represents the result in this manner is not very useful. With every line shown, the display is cluttered, making it more difficult to interpret. If the object lines that are not visible were removed, it would be much more easily interpreted. At this point you may rotate the object about, viewing it from various points using VPOINT. Select PLAN (VPOINT) and ZOOM ALL to return to the original view. This is a powerful advantage of modeling. Once the object has been created, it can be viewed from any direction. This, of course, was not possible using the two-dimensional isometric grid method recently described.

CAD systems have more sophistication than the previous procedure illustrated. Their capability, for example, includes the ability to remove hidden lines. Simply select the HIDE option, YES, and the result will appear as shown in Fig. 17-1-12F.

There are several methods available to modify an existing model. Any elevation or thickness, for example, may be first determined using the LIST option. If it is not to correct specifications, you may CHANGE (UNIT 13-3) the PROPERTY (e.g., T). A 3-dimensional line may, at any time, be added using the coordinate input option 3DLINE (or 3DPOLY). A top plane for any object may be added by setting the elevation to the top value and a thickness of zero. Select 3DFACE (3D) option and draw the outline of the surface.

An example of a model that has been automatically generated using the multiple-viewport method is shown in Fig. 17-1-13. Viewports will allow you to simultaneously view both the multiview drawing and the model. CAD systems provide this option that

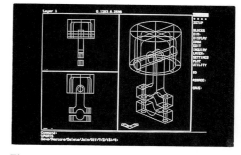

Fig. 17-1-13 Split-screen (viewports).

will generate the model as you are preparing the multiview drawing as follows:

1. Select VPORTS (under SETTINGS) and the number of views desired (2, 3, or 4).
2. Select the user coordinate system (UCS or DDUCS) for the view you wish to display in a particular direction. Suppose you wish to display the front view in the lower-left port. Select X (X axis), 90 (rotation), ENTER, SAVE, and the name (FRONT) of the view.
3. Set the cursor in the upper-left port to activate it.
4. Select PLAN, UCS, and the name of the view. Viewports may be displayed by DISPLAYING the PLAN, UCS and keying the view name. When you modify one view, the result will be seen in all views.

Surface model display yield yet another way to view a component or assembly. Surface model options are more sophisticated than wire-frame models since an "area fill" is used to represent each plane (or wall). The

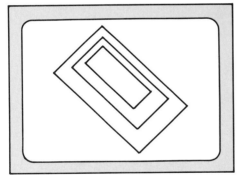
(A) PLAN VIEW OF OBJECT

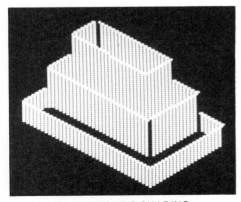
(B) AUTOMATIC SHADING

Fig. 17-1-14 Auto shader.

(A) WIRE FRAME

(B) SOLID SHADED

Fig. 17-1-15 Model comparison.

procedure to generate the display, however, is similar to wire frame. After creating the object (Fig. 17-1-14A), use the ASHADE command. A typical result is shown in Fig. 17-1-14B. A comparison between a wire-frame and surface model of the same object is shown in Fig. 17-1-15.

Nonisometric lines and planes may be expressed on a model. When creating the plan view (Fig. 17-1-16A) use the 3DFACE option and key the X, Y, Z positions for each endpoint. A resulting wire-frame model is shown in Fig. 17-1-16B. If you wish to change an existing entity but do not know its Z dimension, use the LIST option. It will list the current base elevation and thickness.

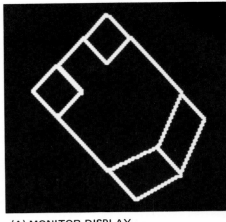
(A) MONITOR DISPLAY

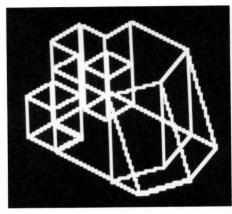
(B) WIRE FRAME ISOMETRIC

Fig. 17-1-16 Sloped 3D faces.

References and Source Material

1. ANSI Y14.4, *Pictorial Drawing*.
2. General Motors Corporation.

ASSIGNMENTS

See Assignments 1 through 4 for Unit 17-1 starting on page 344.

 **UNIT 17-2**

Curved Surfaces in Isometric

CIRCLES AND ARCS IN ISOMETRIC

A circle on any of the three faces of an object drawn in isometric has the shape of an ellipse. See Fig. 17-2-1.

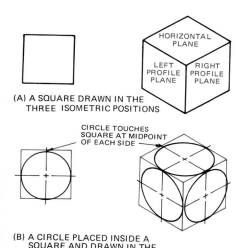

(A) A SQUARE DRAWN IN THE THREE ISOMETRIC POSITIONS

CIRCLE TOUCHES SQUARE AT MIDPOINT OF EACH SIDE

(B) A CIRCLE PLACED INSIDE A SQUARE AND DRAWN IN THE THREE ISOMETRIC POSITIONS

Fig. 17-2-1 Circles in isometric.

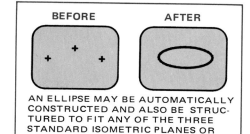

BEFORE   AFTER

AN ELLIPSE MAY BE AUTOMATICALLY CONSTRUCTED AND ALSO BE STRUCTURED TO FIT ANY OF THE THREE STANDARD ISOMETRIC PLANES OR FACES.

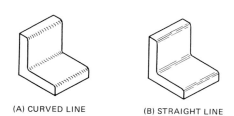

(A) CURVED LINE   (B) STRAIGHT LINE

Fig. 17-2-3 Illustrating fillets and rounds.

These may be created by specifying the ISOPLANE option, selecting the face (horizontal, left profile, or right profile), the diameter, and location. This allows the circle to be easily and accurately drawn. Figure 17-2-2 illustrates an application of isometric circles and arcs. Be sure to use BREAK to EDIT circles into arcs. If the object is created in the plan view using a thickness, use FILLET to produce the arcs prior to displaying the isometric model.

Fillets and Rounds

For most isometric drawings of parts having small fillets and rounds, the adopted practice is to draw the corners as sharp features. However, when it is desirable to represent the part, normally a casting, as having a more realistic appearance, the methods shown in Fig. 17-2-3 may be used. Remember to use the OFFSET command to produce the curved-line representations.

Irregular Curves in Isometric

Curves other than circles and arcs may be created isometrically.

1. Given the orthographic view (Fig. 17-2-4-A) display an isometric grid pattern so points on the curve may be located.
2. Create the outline using the LINE command (Fig. 17-2-4-B).
3. Select the PLINE (POLYLINE) command.
4. Locate points with the aid of the grid (Fig. 17-2-4-C).
5. Select PEDIT and FIT CURVE (Fig. 17-2-4-D).
6. Select the COPY command and follow the prompts.
7. Pick location for the identical second curve.

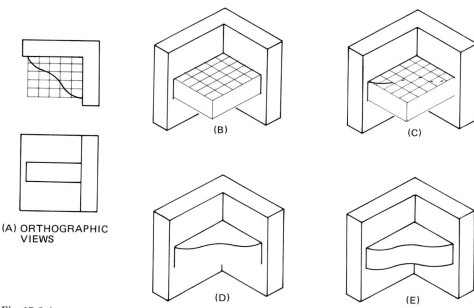

(A) ORTHOGRAPHIC VIEWS

Fig. 17-2-4 Drawing isometric arcs.

8. Remove the grid pattern.

The finished object will appear as shown in Fig. 17-2-4-E.

MODELING

As with lines, any curve can be modeled. This is easy to accomplish by the single-view method when the curved surface is seen from the plan view (Fig. 17-2-5). Remember to set the proper base elevation and thickness for each circle, arc, or spline. When the curved surface is perpendicular to the view you are drawing, however, the prob-

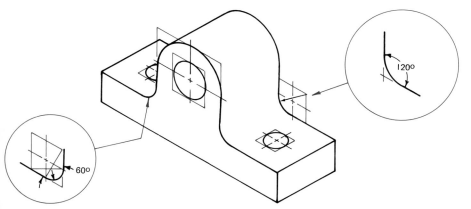

Fig. 17-2-2 Sequence in drawing isometric circles.

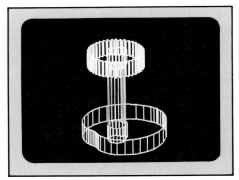

Fig. 17-2-5 Variable thicknesses and elevations. (Courtesy Auto Desk Inc.)

lem becomes more difficult. The view would have to be rotated 90°. This is accomplished by the use of VIEW-PORTS and UCS (Unit 17-1).

Multiple displays of a single model or several models may be viewed either manually or automatically. First, make a slide (MSLIDE) and place it into a library (SLIDLIB). Display slides manually using VSLIDE or automatically by developing a SCRIPT.

ASSIGNMENTS

See Assignments 5 through 8 for Unit 17-2 starting on page 346.

See Assignments 5 through 8 for Unit 17-2 starting on page 346.

 UNIT 17-3

Common Features in Isometric

ISOMETRIC SECTIONING

Isometric drawings are generally made showing exterior views, but sometimes a sectional view is needed. The section is taken on an isometric plane, that is, on a plane parallel to one of the faces of the cube. Figure 17-3-1 shows isometric full sections taken on a different plane for each of three objects. Use an isometric grid to create the objects. Section each surface by means of the HATCH command. Note the reference construction lines indicating the part that has been cut away. Isometric half-sections are illustrated in Fig. 17-3-2. Notice the outlines of the cut surfaces in A and B.

When an isometric drawing is sectioned, the section lines are shown at an angle of 60° with the horizontal or in a horizontal position, depending on

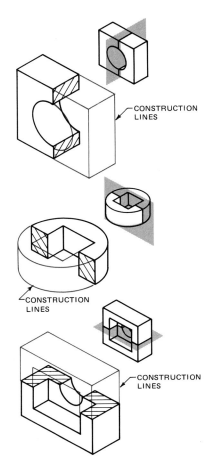

Fig. 17-3-1 Examples of isometric full sections.

where the cutting-plane line is located. In half-sections, the section lines are sloped in opposite directions, as shown in Fig. 17-3-2.

THREADS

The conventional method for showing threads in isometric is shown in Fig. 17-3-3. The threads are represented by a series of ellipses uniformly spaced along the center line of the thread. The spacing of the ellipses need not be the spacing of the actual pitch. Create one ellipse. Use COPY or OFFSET commands to create the others.

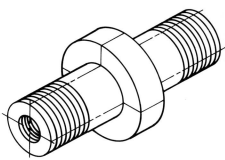

Fig. 17-3-3 Representation of isometric threads.

BREAK LINES

For long parts, break lines should be used to shorten the length of the drawing. Breaks using the SKETCH command is preferred, as shown in Fig. 17-3-4.

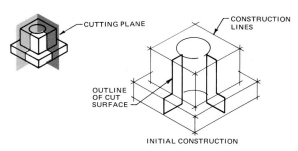

(A) PART 1

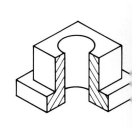

FINISHED DRAWING

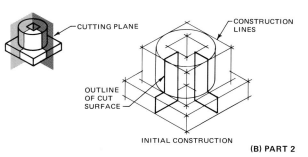

(B) PART 2

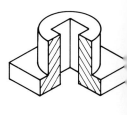

FINISHED DRAWING

Fig. 17-3-2 Examples of isometric half sections.

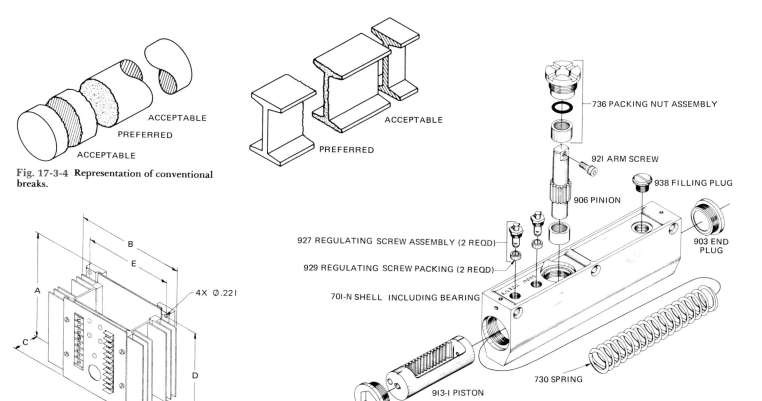

Fig. 17-3-4 Representation of conventional breaks.

Fig. 17-3-5 Isometric assembly drawing.

736 PACKING NUT ASSEMBLY

921 ARM SCREW

938 FILLING PLUG

906 PINION

903 END PLUG

927 REGULATING SCREW ASSEMBLY (2 REQD)

929 REGULATING SCREW PACKING (2 REQD)

70I-N SHELL INCLUDING BEARING

913-I PISTON

903 END PLUG

730 SPRING

Fig. 17-3-6 Exploded isometric assembly drawing.

ISOMETRIC ASSEMBLY DRAWINGS

Regular or exploded assembly drawings are frequently used in catalogs and sales literature, as illustrated by Figs. 17-3-5 and 17-3-6. Standard predrawn shapes or 3D objects may be useful here since they will not require re-creation. Select the 3D OBJECTS (3D) submenu command and follow the prompts to obtain the desired common shape (e.g., a box). Various modeling surfaces may also be automatically generated using 3DMESH, RULESURF, TABSURF, REVSURF, or EDGESURF.

ASSIGNMENTS

See Assignments 9 through 16 for Unit 17-3 starting on page 348.

■ UNIT 17-4

Oblique Projection

This method of pictorial drawing is based on the procedure of placing the object with one face parallel to the frontal plane and placing the other two faces on oblique (or receding) planes, to left or right, top or bottom, at a convenient angle. The three axes of projection are *vertical*, *horizontal*, and *receding*. Figure 17-4-1 illustrates a cube drawn in typical positions with the receding axes at 60°, 45°, and 30°. This form of projection has the advantage of showing one face of the object without distortion. The face with the greatest irregularity of outline or contour, or the face with the greatest number of circular features, or the face with the longest dimension, faces the front. See Fig. 17-4-2.

Two types of oblique projection are used extensively. In *cavalier oblique*, all lines are made to their true length,

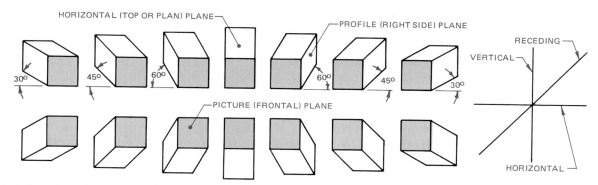

Fig. 17-4-1 Typical positions of receding axes for oblique projections.

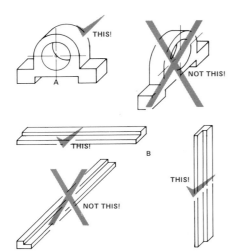

Fig. 17-4-2 Two general rules for oblique drawings.

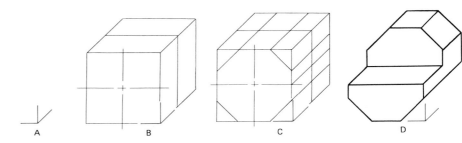

Fig. 17-4-4 Oblique construction by the box method.

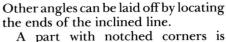

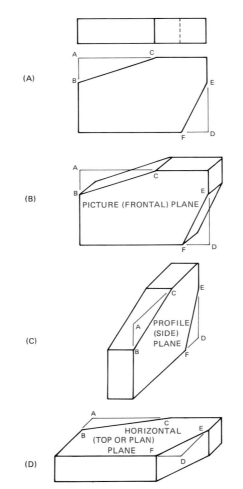

(A)

(B)

PICTURE (FRONTAL) PLANE

(C)

PROFILE (SIDE) PLANE

(D)

HORIZONTAL (TOP OR PLAN) PLANE

Fig. 17-4-5 Drawing inclined surfaces.

measured on the axes of the projection. In *cabinet oblique,* the lines on the receding axis are shortened by one-half their true length to compensate for distortion and to approximate more closely what the human eye would see. For this reason, and because of the simplicity of projection, cabinet oblique is a commonly used form of pictorial representation, especially when circles and arcs are to be drawn. Figure 17-4-3 shows a comparison of cavalier and cabinet oblique. Note that hidden lines are omitted unless required for clarity. Many of the techniques for isometric projection apply to oblique projection. Figure 17-4-4 illustrates the construction of an irregularly shaped object by the box method. Oblique modeling is presently not a CAD option.

INCLINED SURFACES

Angles which are parallel to the picture plane are drawn as their true size.

Other angles can be laid off by locating the ends of the inclined line.

A part with notched corners is shown in Fig. 17-4-5-A. An oblique drawing with the angles parallel to the picture plane is created using relative coordinate input (Fig. 17-4-5-B). In Fig. 17-4-5-C the angles are parallel to the profile plane. In Fig. 17-4-5-D the angles are parallel to the horizontal plane. In Figs. 17-4-5C and D the angle is created by polar coordinate input parallel to the oblique axes, as shown by the reference construction marking. Since the part, in each case, is drawn in cabinet oblique, the receding lines are shortened by one-half their true length.

OBLIQUE GRID

Specially designed (LISP) oblique lines or grids are available on some CAD systems (Fig. 17-4-6). Normally, however, use a rectangular pattern for the true-size front face. The rectangular pattern may also be used for the two 45° oblique faces.

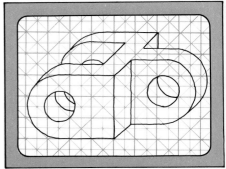

Fig. 17-4-6 Oblique sketching paper.

DIMENSIONING AN OBLIQUE DRAWING

Dimension lines are drawn parallel to the axes of projection. Extension lines are projected from the horizontal and

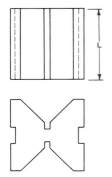

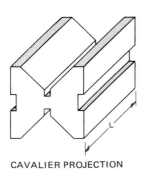

CAVALIER PROJECTION

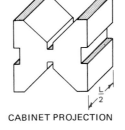

CABINET PROJECTION

Fig. 17-4-3 Types of oblique projection.

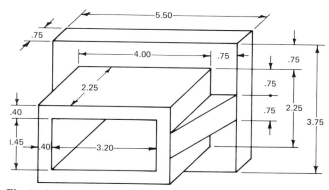

Fig. 17-4-7 Dimensioning an oblique drawing.

vertical object lines whenever possible.

The dimensioning of an oblique drawing is similar to that of an isometric drawing which is shown in Fig. 17-4-7. As in isometric dimensioning, usually it is necessary to first draw the extension lines.

ASSIGNMENTS

See Assignments 17 through 19 for Unit 17-4 on page 350.

◼ UNIT 17-5

Common Features in Oblique

CIRCLES AND ARCS

Whenever possible, the face of the object having circles or arcs should be selected as the *frontal* face so that the CIRCLE, ARC, and FILLET commands can be used. See Fig. 17-5-1. When circles or arcs must be drawn on one of the oblique faces, the ELLIPSE command (Fig. 17-5-2) can be used. The oblique circle should first be blocked in as an oblique square in order to locate the proper position of the circle. Blocking in the circle first also helps the drafter select the proper size and shape of the ellipse.

If the ELLIPSE command does not produce the desired result, a geometric construction can be used. This method is known as the *four-center method*. In Fig. 17-5-3-A a circle is shown as it would be drawn on the frontal plane, the profile plane, and the top plane.

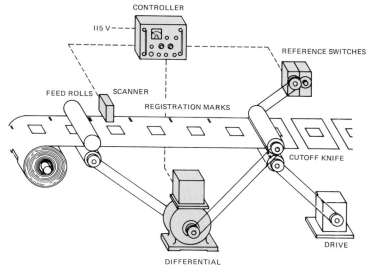

SCHEMATIC OF A COMPLETELY AUTOMATIC REGISTRATION CONTROL SYSTEM MAINTAINING THE LOCATION OF CUTOFF ON A CONTINUOUS PRINTED WEB.

Fig. 17-5-1 Application of oblique drawing.

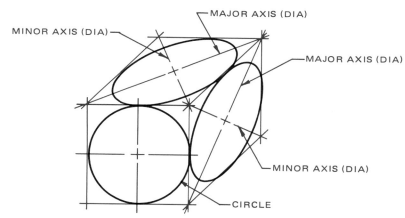

Fig. 17-5-2 Drawing oblique circles by means of offset measurements.

In Fig. 17-5-3-B, the oblique drawing has some arcs in a horizontal plane. In Fig. 17-5-3-C, the oblique drawing shown has some arcs in a profile plane. Circles not parallel to the picture plane when drawn by the approximate method are satisfactory for most purposes. The dimensioning of an oblique part is shown in Fig. 17-5-4.

OBLIQUE SECTIONING

Oblique drawings are generally made as outside views, but sometimes a sectional view is necessary. Using the HATCH command, the section is taken on a plane parallel to one of the faces of an oblique cube. Figure 17-5-5

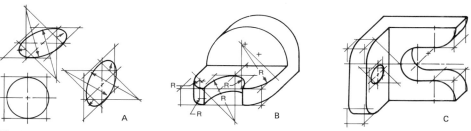

Fig. 17-5-3 Circles parallel to the picture plane are true circles; on other planes, ellipses.

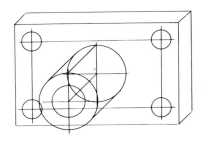

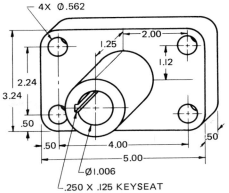

Fig. 17-5-4 Construction and dimensioning of an oblique object.

4X Ø.562
2.00
1.25
1.12
2.24
3.24
.50
.50
4.00
.50
5.00
Ø1.006
.250 X .125 KEYSEAT

shows an oblique full section and an oblique half-section. Construction lines show the part that has been cut away.

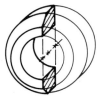

(A) FULL SECTION (B) HALF SECTION

Fig. 17-5-5 Oblique full and half sections.

TREATMENT OF CONVENTIONAL FEATURES

Fillets and Rounds Small fillets and rounds normally are drawn as sharp corners. When it is desirable to show the corners rounded, then the method shown in Fig. 17-5-6 is recommended.

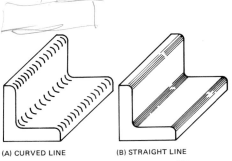

(A) CURVED LINE (B) STRAIGHT LINE

Fig. 17-5-6 Representing rounds and fillets.

Threads The conventional method of showing threads in oblique is shown in Fig. 17-5-7. The threads are represented by a series of circles uniformly spaced along the center line of the thread.

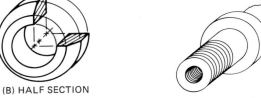

Fig. 17-5-7 Representation of threads in oblique.

The spacing of the circles need not be the spacing of the pitch and may quickly be created using the COPY or OFFSET command.

Breaks Figure 17-5-8 shows the conventional method for representing breaks.

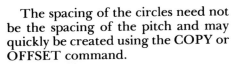

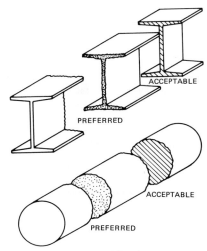

ACCEPTABLE
PREFERRED
ACCEPTABLE
PREFERRED

Fig. 17-5-8 Conventional breaks.

ASSIGNMENTS

See Assignments 20 and 21 for Unit 17-5 on page 351.

ASSIGNMENTS FOR CHAPTER 17

Assignments for Unit 17-1, Pictorial Drawings

1. Set up an isometric grid on the monitor and draw the four parts shown in Fig. 17-1-A. Do not show hidden lines. Each square shown on the drawing represents one isometric square on the grid.

2. Set up an isometric grid on the monitor and draw the four parts shown in Fig. 17-1-B. Do not show hidden lines. Each square shown on the drawing represents one isometric square on the grid.

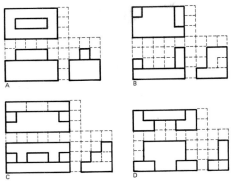

Fig. 17-1-A Isometric flat surface problems.

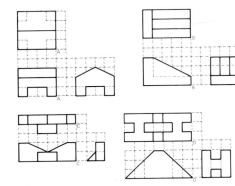

Fig. 17-1-B Isometric flat surface problems.

3. Prepare an isometric drawing of one of the parts shown in Fig. 17-1-C to 17-1-H. Plot scale 1:1 except for Fig. 17-1-G. Use 1:4.

4. Repeat Assignments 1, 2, and/or 3 using the modeling procedure. Use view ports as assigned by your instructor.

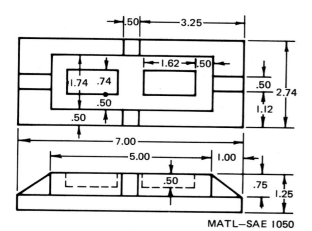

Fig. 17-1-C Base plate.

MATL—SAE 1050

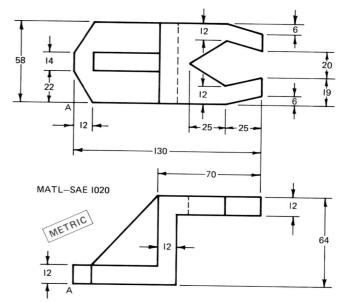

MATL—SAE 1020

METRIC

Fig. 17-1-D Support bracket.

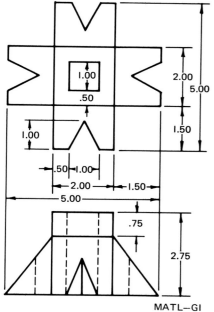

MATL—GI

Fig. 17-1-E Base plate.

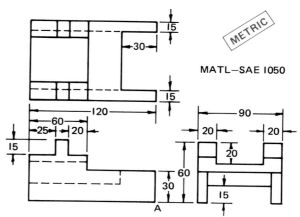

METRIC

MATL—SAE 1050

Fig. 17-1-F Step block.

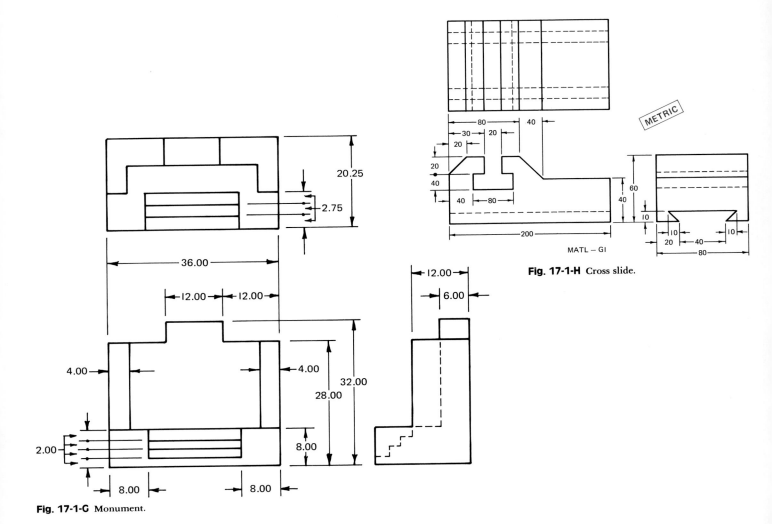

Fig. 17-1-G Monument.

Fig. 17-1-H Cross slide.

MATL — GI

METRIC

Assignments for Unit 17-2, Curved Surfaces in Isometric

5. Set up an isometric grid and draw the four parts shown in Fig. 17-2-A. Each square shown on the figure represents one square on the isometric grid. Hidden lines may be omitted for clarity.

6. Set up an isometric grid and draw the four parts shown in Fig. 17-2-B. Each square shown on the figure represents one square on the isometric grid. Hidden lines may be omitted for clarity. Use the option to select the appropriate isometric plane.

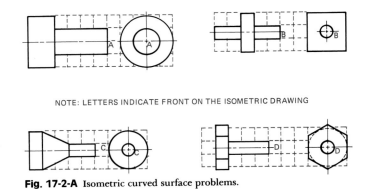

NOTE: LETTERS INDICATE FRONT ON THE ISOMETRIC DRAWING

Fig. 17-2-A Isometric curved surface problems.

Fig. 17-2-B Isometric curved surface problems.

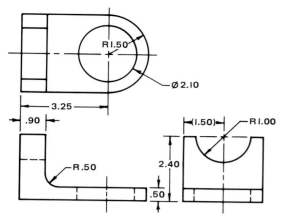

Fig. 17-2-C Cradle bracket.

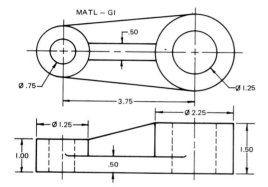

Fig. 17-2-E Link.

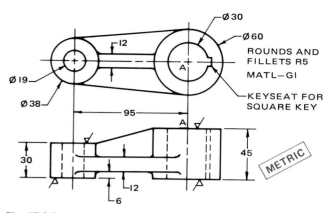

ROUNDS AND
FILLETS R5
MATL—GI

KEYSEAT FOR
SQUARE KEY

METRIC

Fig. 17-2-D Link.

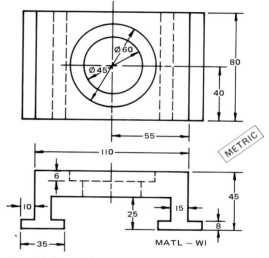

METRIC

MATL — WI

Fig. 17-2-F T-guide.

7. Using an isometric grid make an isometric drawing of one of the parts shown in Figs. 17-2-C to 17-2-H. Use scale 1 : 2 for Fig. 17-2-G. For all others use the scale 1 : 1.

8. Using the wire-frame modeling procedure repeat the above assignments for Figs. 17-2-A, 17-2-D, 17-2-E, and/or 17-2-F. Use four viewports for 17-2-G and three viewports for 17-2-H.

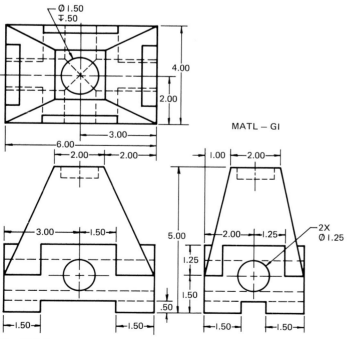

MATL — GI

Fig. 17-2-G Base.

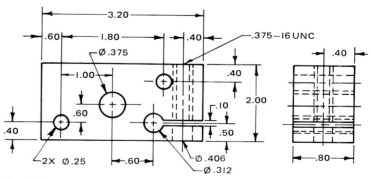

Fig. 17-2-H

Assignments for Unit 17-3, Common Features in Isometric

9. Prepare an isometric half-section view of one of the parts shown in Fig. 17-3-A or 17-3-B. Scale 1:1.

10. Prepare an isometric full section drawing of one of the parts shown in Fig. 17-3-C or 17-3-D. Scale 1:1.

11. Prepare an isometric drawing of the shaft shown in Fig. 17-3-E. Use a conventional break to shorten the length. Scale 1:1.

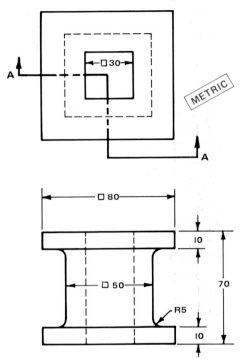

Fig. 17-3-A Guide block.

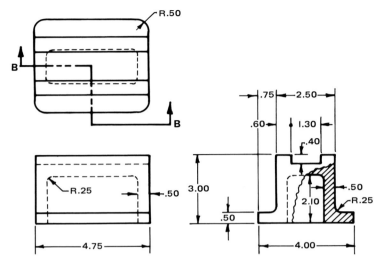

Fig. 17-3-B Base.

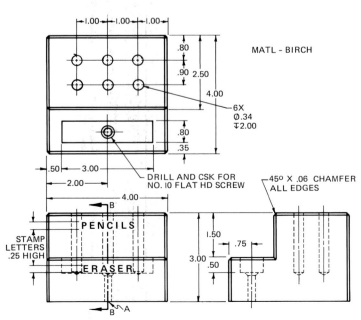

MATL – BIRCH

Fig. 17-3-C Pencil holder.

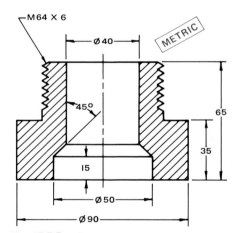

Fig. 17-3-D Adapter.

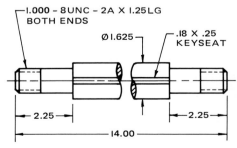

Fig. 17-3-E Shaft.

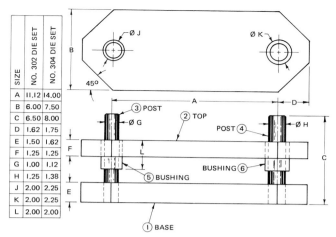

SIZE	NO. 302 DIE SET	NO. 304 DIE SET
A	11.12	14.00
B	6.00	7.50
C	6.50	8.00
D	1.62	1.75
E	1.50	1.62
F	1.25	1.25
G	1.00	1.12
H	1.25	1.38
J	2.00	2.25
K	2.00	2.25
L	2.00	2.00

Fig. 17-3-F Two-post die set.

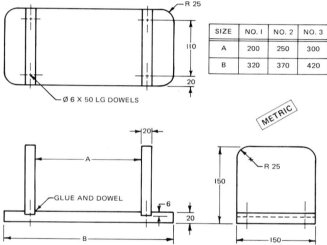

SIZE	NO. 1	NO. 2	NO. 3
A	200	250	300
B	320	370	420

METRIC

Fig. 17-3-G Book rack.

PT I – FORK – 2 REQD

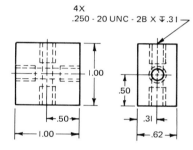

PT 2 – RING – I REQD
PT 3 – Ø .25 SPRING PIN – 2 REQD
PT 4 – .250 – 20 FHMS – .62 LG – 4 REQD

Fig. 17-3-H Universal joint.

12. Prepare an isometric assembly drawing of the two-post die set, model 302 or 304, shown in Fig. 17-3-F. Allow 2 in. between the top and base. Plot scale 1 : 2. Do not dimension. Include on the drawing an item list. Using part numbers, identify the parts on the assembly.

13. Using the wire-frame modeling procedure, repeat Assignment 12.

14. Prepare an isometric exploded assembly drawing of the book rack shown in Fig. 17-3-G. Choose book rack No. 2. Plot scale 1 : 2. Do not dimension. Include on the drawing an item list. Using part numbers, identify the parts on the assembly.

15. Using the wire-frame modeling procedure repeat Assignment 14.

16. Prepare an isometric exploded assembly drawing of the universal joint shown in Fig. 17-3-H or wheel puller Fig. 17-3-J. Scale 1 : 1. Do not dimension. Include on the drawing an item list. Using part numbers, identify the parts on the assembly.

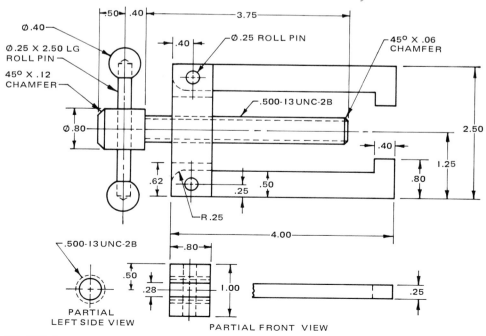

Fig. 17-3-J

Assignments for Unit 17-4, Oblique Projection

17. Using combined rectangular and 45° grids, prepare an oblique drawing of the three parts shown in Fig. 17-4-A. Each square shown on the figure represents one square on the monitor. Hidden lines may be omitted to improve clarity.

18. Using combined rectangular and 45° grids, prepare an oblique drawing of the three parts shown in Fig. 17-4-B. Each square shown on the figure represents one square on the monitor. Hidden lines may be omitted to improve clarity.

19. Prepare an oblique drawing of one of the parts shown in Fig. 17-4-C or 17-4-D. Scale 1:1.

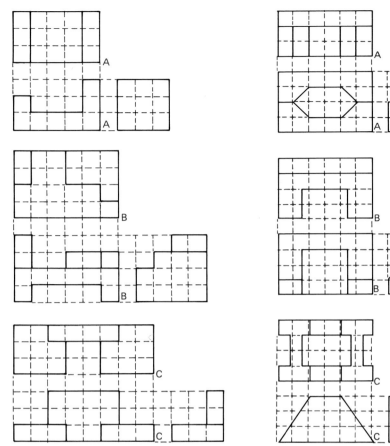

Fig. 17-4-A Oblique flat surface problems.   **Fig. 17-4-B** Oblique flat surface problems.

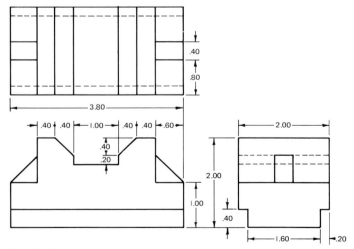

Fig. 17-4-C V-block rest.

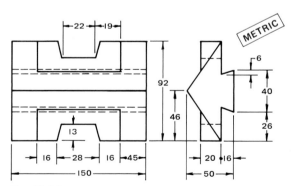

Fig. 17-4-D Dovetail guide.

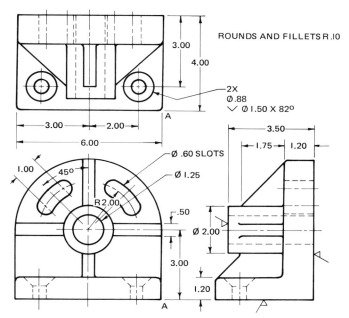

Fig. 17-5-A End bracket.

ROUNDS AND FILLETS R .10

2X
Ø .88
Ⅴ Ø 1.50 X 82°

3.00
4.00

3.00
2.00
6.00

1.00
45°
R 2.00

Ø .60 SLOTS
Ø 1.25

.50
Ø 2.00
3.00
1.20

3.50
1.75
1.20

Assignments for Unit 17-5, Common Features in Oblique

20. Prepare an oblique drawing of one of the parts shown in Fig. 17-5-A or 17-5-B. Scale 1 : 1.

21. Prepare an oblique drawing of one of the parts shown in Fig. 17-5-C, 17-5-D, or 17-5-E. Scale 1 : 1.

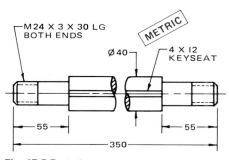

M24 X 3 X 30 LG
BOTH ENDS

METRIC

Ø 40
4 X 12
KEYSEAT

55
55
350

Fig. 17-5-B Shaft.

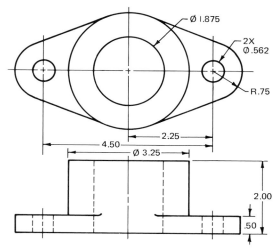

Ø 1.875
2X
Ø .562
R .75

2.25
4.50
Ø 3.25

2.00
.50

Fig. 17-5-C Bearing support.

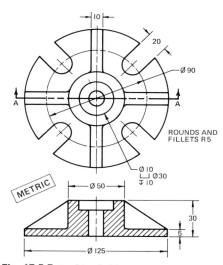

10
20
Ø 90

ROUNDS AND
FILLETS R 5

Ø 10
Ⅼ Ø 30
Ⅴ 10

METRIC

Ø 50
A
A

30
5
Ø 125

Fig. 17-5-D Bushing holder.

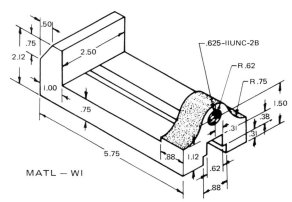

.50
.75
2.12
2.50
1.00
.75

.625–11UNC-2B
R .62
R .75
1.50
.38
.31
.31

5.75
.88
1.12
.62
.88

MATL — WI

Fig. 17-5-E Vise base.

A CAD ICON Glossary

Graphical representation and definition for each major command used in CAD.

BEFORE	AFTER	COMMAND	DESCRIPTION
		ABSOLUTE COORDINATE	A coordinate point located at a horizontal distance (X) and a vertical distance (Y) from the drawing origin (0,0). The origin is normally at the lower left of the monitor screen. See Unit 3-5.
		ARC	A partial circle may be created in several different ways including the selection of: (1) start/end/angle, (2) start/end/radius, (3) start/midpoint/end, (4) three points. See Unit 3-6.
		ARC TANGENT	A command option that will automatically create an arc tangent to two other arcs or circles. See Unit 6-2.
		AREA	A command that will automatically calculate and display the area of a polygon and subtract any internal smaller regions. See Unit 13-4.
		ARRAY (MINSERT, MULTIPLE COPIES)	A command that allows objects to be repeat-copied by keying in a specified X and Y distance (or angle) and number of copies. This pattern may be either rectangular or polar (circular). See Unit 6-6.
		AXIS (X and Y)	The X axis is the horizontal axis on the graphics monitor. The Y axis is vertical axis on the graphics monitor. The axes may be marked with a scale. See Unit 4-5.

BEFORE	AFTER	COMMAND	DESCRIPTION
		BASE POINT	The base point of a block or grouping of objects is the origin around which it will be inserted or placed. See Unit 5-9.
		BLOCK	Lines, arcs, and text may be assembled into a single drawing entity. Once blocked, they are treated as a single object. See Unit 5-9.
		BREAK	An edit command that will erase a portion of any object or break it into two with or without a gap. See Unit 3-2.
		CENTER LINE— AUTOMATIC	Determining the center of a circle or arc and automatically marking the center. See Unit 4-1.
		CHAMFER	A beveled edge may be created after the object has been drawn. This command may be used to create a hypotenuse (beveled edge) when its length is not known. See Unit 6-1.
		CHANGE	Properties of an entity such as layers, linetypes, pens, elevations, and so on may be altered. Any object need not be erased and redrawn but simply changed. See Unit 13-3.
		CIRCLE	A circle may be created in several different ways by selecting (1) center/radius, (2) center/key the size. (3) two opposite points on the circle, or (4) three points on the circumference. See Unit 3-6.
		CLOSE	Any perimeter or polygon may be "closed" by issuing the appropriate key stroke. See Unit 3-2.
		CONSTRUCTION LINES	Reference lines assist multiview drawing construction. This is especially useful when a grid pattern cannot be used. The lines are for reference purposes only and will be later erased. See Unit 3-4.
		COORDINATE	A point on the drawing that is designated by the horizontal and vertical distance from another point or the drawing origin. See Units 3-5 and 7-4.

BEFORE	AFTER	COMMAND	DESCRIPTION
		COPY	Entities or blocks of entities may be copied at any location. See Unit 6-6.
		CURSOR	An indicating mark on the monitor which is controlled by any of several types of input pointing devices such as, a joystick, puck, or stylus. See Unit 2-2.
		DIMENSION — ANGULAR	The automatic generation of a dimension indicating the angle between two nonparallel lines. See Unit 7-1.
		DIMENSION — ASSOCIATIVE (STRETCH)	Automatic revision of a dimension and text when an object is stretched, scaled, or rotated. The new dimension is created in its entirety according to the new size and orientation. See Unit 13-3.
		DIMENSION — BASE LINE	Linear dimensions continued from a common base line. The first extension line is common to teach dimension. See Units 7-4 and 14-1.
		DIMENSION — LINEAR	An automatic command that will calculate and place a dimension of an entity after it has been identified. See Unit 7-1.
		DIMENSION — RADIAL	The size of a selected circle or arc is calculated and the dimension is automatically placed. See Unit 7-2.
		DIMENSION VARIABLES	The values which determine the manner in which system dimensions are placed on the drawing may be varied. See Unit 7-1.
		DISTANCE/ANGLE (LIST, ID)	Describes spatial characteristics of a segment or between two points. The characteristics may include distance between end points, angle, the change in horizontal distance, the change in vertical distance, and location with respect to the origin. See Unit 3-5.
		DIVIDE (MEASURE)	An entity may be divided into any specified number of equal-length intervals. See Unit 6-1.

BEFORE	AFTER	COMMAND	DESCRIPTION
		DONUT	A solid (filled) circle, with or without a hole, may be automatically created. Elimination of the fill results in two circles concentric about a common center. See Unit 3-6.
		DRAG	The Dragmode option provides visual movement of an object. Each time the cursor is moved (dragged), the object will be redisplayed at the new position. See Units 3-2 and 5-9.
		EDIT-LINE (STRETCH, EXTEND, MODIFY, TRIM, GAP)	Any line or vertex may be altered. Modifications include adding or deleting a vertex and joining, moving stretching, extending, gapping, or shortening a line. See Unit 13-3.
		ELLIPSE (ISOPLANE)	An ellipse may be automatically constructed and also be structured to fit any of the three standard isometric planes or faces. See Units 6-4 and 17-2.
		END (QUIT)	When finishing work, deactivate and return to the main menu prior to logging off. Be careful to first save the drawing if it is to be used again. See Unit 3-1.
		ERASE	Any object or an identified rectangular window area may easily be erased. See Unit 3-2.
		ERASE LAST	Mistakes often are immediately recognized as such. Undo, oops, or back 1 will cancel the last command entered. See Unit 3-2.
		EXPLODE	Multiple entities blocked into a single object, as well as dimensions, may later be broken apart. Individual entities may then be altered without affecting the others. See Unit 5-9.
		FILING (FILES IN/OUT)	After a drawing is complete, it may be permanently stored. A common filing procedure involves "off-loading" the contents on to a floppy disk prior to storage. See Unit 4-7.
		FILLET	A command that will draw an arc tangent to two selected lines at a specified radius. See Unit 6-2.

BEFORE	AFTER	COMMAND	DESCRIPTION

BEFORE · **AFTER** · **COMMAND** · **DESCRIPTION**

FIT

Text may be created so that it fits between any two points yet not affect its height. See Unit 13-4.

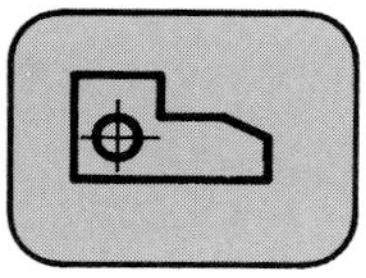

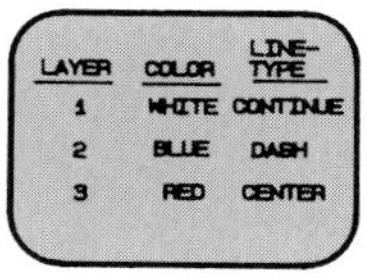

FLIPSCREEN

A single-screen system may be easily switched back and forth between the text and graphics display using a keystroke. See Unit 3-1.

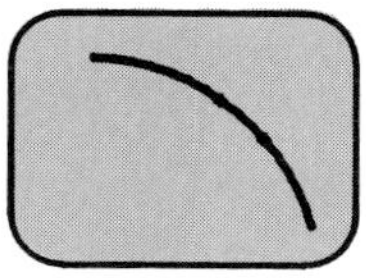

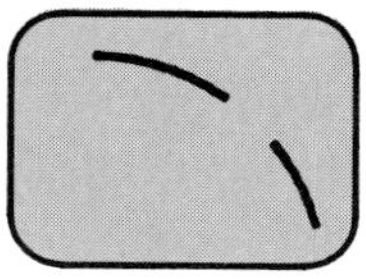

GAP

Any portion of a line, circle, or arc may be altered. See BREAK Unit 3-2.

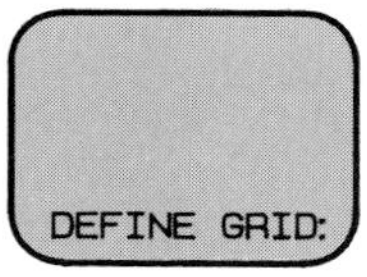

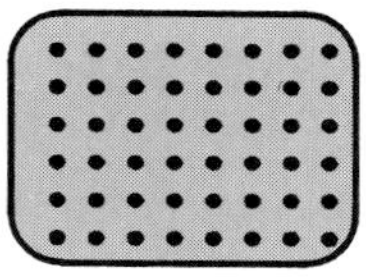

GRID

A network of equally spaced grid dots that can be used for reference. Grid spacing may be changed by keying in the horizontal and vertical distance. See Unit 3-3.

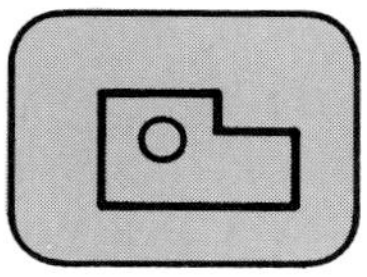

HATCH

A command that will automatically section or fill an area within an identified boundary. See Unit 8-1.

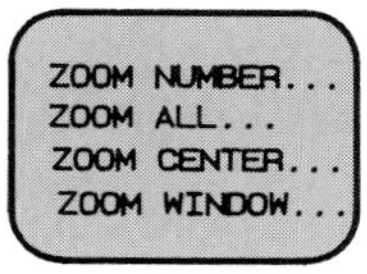

HELP (MENU)

The help option provides specified information regarding each command. It will explain each command option or define the method of execution. See Unit 3-1.

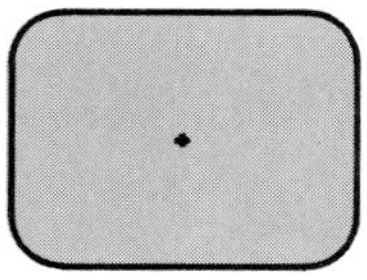

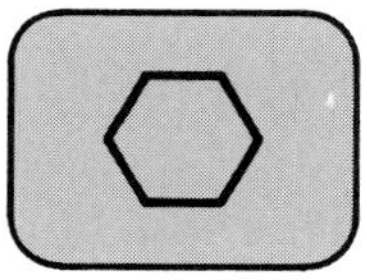

INSERT

A command that will scale up or down the size of a block of entities to be copied. See Unit 5-9.

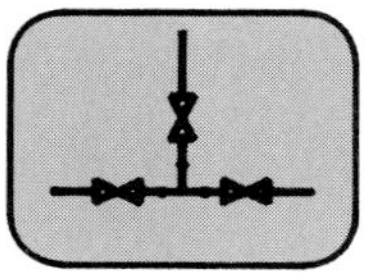

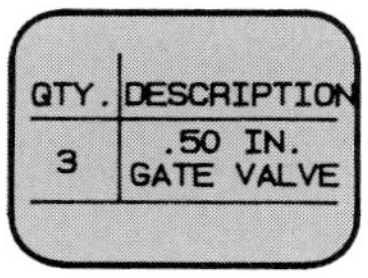

ITEM LIST (BILL OF MATERIAL)

Text information assigned to an object may be stored and retrieved in a printed form. See Unit 13-4.

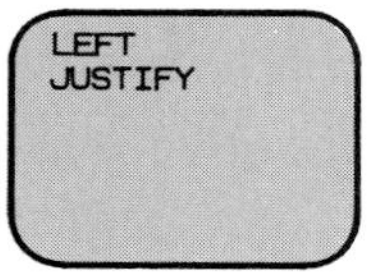

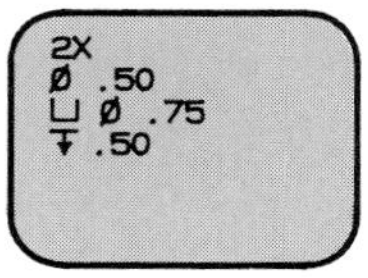

JUSTIFY

Rows of text may be "lined up" in any of several arrangements. Left justify, for example, will line the starting point for each row of text with respect to a vertical line. See Unit 3-7.

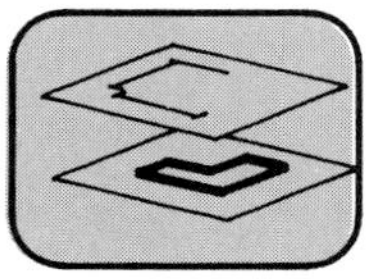

LAYER (LEVEL)

Different portions of a drawing may be created on different layers (or invisible planes). Layers may be "switched" on or off, allowing various combinations of a drawing to be displayed or plotted. See Unit 7-1.

BEFORE	AFTER	COMMAND	DESCRIPTION
		LEADER	The automatic creation of an arrow head located at the end of a line segment. See Unit 7-1.
		LIBRARY	A collection of stored groups of symbols that may be placed on any drawing. See Unit 7-2.
		LINES — CONTINUOUS	The creation of solid lines from point to point may be made either by using cursor or coordinate input. See Unit 3-2.
		LINE TANGENT (OSNAP-TAN)	A command option that will automatically draw a line tangent to two circles or arcs. See Unit 6-1.
		LINE THICKNESS	A line or curve may be widened after the desired width has been defined by the user. This option may be used to display a thick line on the monitor. See Unit 4-6.
		LINETYPE	Standard linetypes such as hidden, center, and phantom, may be created. See Unit 4-1.
		MIRROR	A process that results in a hinged, reflected, or mirrored image about a user-specified axis. See Unit 5-9.
		MODEL	Three-dimensional models automatically display isometric or perspective, at any view point either in wireframe (edge lines) or surface (shaded) while concealing hidden lines. See Unit 17-1.
		MOVE	A command that will move an object or group of objects to any location. See Unit 5-9.
		MOVE NEXT POINT	A gap between end points while in the LINE command. This allows separate lines to be created. See Unit 3-2.

BEFORE	AFTER	COMMAND	DESCRIPTION
		MULTISEGMENT LINE	Continuous line segments may be created from point to point. See Unit 3-2.
		OBJECT SNAP (OSNAP)	Entities may be "locked" to various positions of an object. Common positions include: endpoints, midpoints, tangent, center, nearest, quadrant, and perpendicular. See Unit 6-2.
		ORTHO-ON	This option automatically forces a line to be drawn on a horizontal or vertical axis only. See Unit 3-2.
		ORTHO-OFF	Allows the creation of diagonal lines at any angle. See Unit 3-2.
		PAN	A scan to a different portion of a drawing while zoomed in. See Unit 3-4.
		PARALLEL (OFFSET)	Identical lines or curves may be created from an existing line or curve at any offset distance. See Unit 6-1.
		PEN	Pen numbers refer to the plotting of a drawing to produce different line weights. A number 2 pen selection will be plotted with the pen that has been placed in the number 2 plotter position. See Units 2-2 and 4-1.
		PERIMETER	A command that will calculate and display the perimeter distance around an object. See Unit 13-4.
		PERPENDICULAR	An object snap option that will create a line at 90° to another line. See Unit 6-1.
		PLINE (SPLINE)	An irregular curve may be constructed after points along that curve have been identified. See Unit 6-5.

BEFORE	AFTER	COMMAND	DESCRIPTION
		PLOT	A plotter will create a finished drawing. Linework and lettering of professional quality will be produced. See Unit 4-6.
		POINT	Points may be located any place on the screen by either keying in the coordinates or picking a cursor position. See Unit 3-5.
		POLAR COORDINATES	A line or second point is located by keying its distance and angle from an existing point. See Unit 3-5.
		POLYGON	A polygon of any number of sides (greater than 2) may be inscribed or circumscribed about a circle of any radius. See Unit 6-3.
		POLYLINE	A series of connecting entities between cursor points and is considered a single object. See Unit 5-9.
		RECTANGLE	Creation of a rectangle by picking diagonal corners with the cursor or keying in the coordinates. See Unit 6-1 or POLYGON Unit 6-3.
		REDRAW	After deleting, the display often will appear messy. Redrawing will redisplay the objects on the screen, "cleaning up" the display. See Unit 3-2.
		REGENERATE (PACK)	Accumulated deletions and revision work utilize a significant amount of useless drawing storage (disk) space. Data packing will discard this from drawing memory, leaving more room for useful work. See Unit 3-2.
		RELATIVE COORDINATE	A coordinate position located at a horizontal and vertical distance from (relative to) the last point. See Unit 3-5.
		ROTATE	An object or group of objects may rotate about an origin at any specified angle. See Unit 5-9.

BEFORE	AFTER	COMMAND	DESCRIPTION
		RUBBERBAND	As the cursor moves across the screen, the entity (line, circle, arc) will be redisplayed. This provides an excellent visual guide for optimizing the entity size and position. See Unit 3-2.
	COMMAND: SAVE NAME: YOKE	**SAVE**	It is desirable to periodically update the drawing file to disk. This way in the event of a power failure or lock up, only work since the last save will be lost. See Unit 4-7.
		SCALE	A command that will scale up or down the size of an object or group of objects when specifying any scale factor. See Unit 5-9.
LIMITS X: 0, 11.00 Y: 0, 8.50 SCALE: FULL UNITS: DECIMAL	LIMITS X: 0, 34.00 Y: 0, 22.00 SCALE: HALF UNITS: DECIMAL	**SETUP**	When beginning a new drawing, the parameters such as drawing size, scale, and units may be selected. See Unit 3-1.
		SKETCH	This command permits freehand drawings to be created. It is used for irregular shape applications. See Units 4-4 and 6-5.
		SNAP-ON	A setting that will automatically snap the cursor to the nearest snap increment. The snap increment is often set to the grid spacing or half the grid spacing. See Unit 3-3.
		SNAP-OFF	A setting that will allow any point to be located at any position on the screen regardless of the grid pattern. See Unit 3-3.
	LIMITS X: 0, 11.00 Y: 0, 8.50 SCALE: FULL UNITS: DECIMAL	**STATUS (SETVAR)**	The established parameters for a particular drawing may be displayed on the monitor. See Unit 3-5.
		STRETCH	Moves a selected portion of a drawing to a new position while retaining the original shape. See Unit 13-3.
STANDARD FONT	ital font	**TEXT STYLE (FONT, SCRIPT)**	Various text-style options are available and may be selected for use on any drawing. See Unit 4-1.

BEFORE	AFTER	COMMAND	DESCRIPTION
		TEXT	Text is created using the keyboard and transferred to the drawing by cursor position select. See Units 3-7 and 7-1.
		TOLERANCE	Plus and minus limits may be independently specified. The tolerance will automatically be added next to the segment dimensioned. See Unit 7-5.
		TRACE	A command that will draw a single line as a double line after the desired width has been defined by the user. The spacing between the lines may be filled or left open. See Unit 13-3.
		TRIM (CLIP)	A command that will automatically trim or clip an object back to another object. See Unit 5-4.
		UNDO (OPPS, REDO)	This option is handy to use to immediately restore any portion of the drawing that had inadvertently been erased or altered. See Unit 3-2.
		Z AXIS	Three-dimensional modeling coordinate points are located at a horizontal distance (X), a vertical distance (Y), and a depth distance (Z), from an 0, 0, 0 point (drawing origin). See Unit 14-2.
		ZOOM	Any portion of a drawing may be temporarily magnified to more closely view small details or work to greater accuracy. See Unit 3-4.
		ZOOM ALL (FULL WINDOW)	A command that will display the complete drawing on the monitor. See Unit 3-4.

B Standard Parts and Technical Data

ANSI	Y1.1	**Abbreviations for Use on Drawings and in Text**

ANSI	Y14.1	Drawing Sheet Size and Format	ANSI	Y32.9	Graphic Electrical Wiring Symbols for Architectural and Electrical Layout Drawings
ANSI	Y14.2M	Line Conventions and Lettering	ANSI	B1.1	Unified Screw Threads
ANSI	Y14.3	Projections	ANSI	B4.2	Preferred Metric Limits and Fits
ANSI	Y14.4	Pictorial Drawing	ANSI	B17.1	Keys and Keyseats
ANSI	Y14.5M	Dimensioning and Tolerancing for Engineering Drawings	ANSI	B17.2	Woodruff Key and Keyslot Dimensions
ANSI	Y14.6	Screw Thread Representation	ANSI	B18.2.1	Square and Hex Bolts and Screws
ANSI	Y14.7	Gears, Splines, and Serrations	ANSI	B18.2.2	Square and Hex Nuts
ANSI	Y14.7	Gear Drawing Standards—Part 1, for Spur, Helical, Double Helical and Rack	ANSI	B18.3	Socket Cap, Shoulder, and Setscrews
ANSI	Y14.9	Forgings	ANSI	B18.6.2	Slotted-Head Cap Screws, Square-Head Setscrews, Slotted-Headless Setscrews
ANSI	Y14.10	Metal Stampings	ANSI	B18.6.3	Machine Screws and Machine Screw Nuts
ANSI	Y14.11	Plastics	ANSI	B18.21.1	Lock Washers
ANSI	Y14.14	Mechanical Assemblies	ANSI	B27.2	Plain Washers
ANSI	Y14.15	Electrical and Electronics Diagrams	ANSI	B46.1	Surface Texture
ANSI	Y14.15A	Interconnection Diagrams	ANSI	B94.6	Knurling
ANSI	Y14.17	Fluid Power Diagrams	ANSI	B94.11M	Twist Drills
ANSI	Y14.36	Surface Texture Symbols	ANSI	Z210.1	Metric Practice
ANSI	Y32.2	Graphic Symbols for Electrical and Electronics Diagrams			

Table 1   ANSI publications.

Quantity	Metric Unit	Symbol	Metric to Inch-Pound Unit	Inch-Pound to Metric Unit
Length	millimeter centimeter meter kilometer	mm cm m km	1 mm = 0.0394 in. 1 cm = 0.394 in. 1 m = 39.37 in. = 3.28 ft 1 km = 0.62 mile	1 in. = 25.4 mm 1 ft. = 30.5 cm 1 yd. = 0.914 m = 914 mm 1 mile = 1.61 km
Area	square millimeter square centimeter square meter	mm² cm² m²	1 mm² = 0.001 55 sq. in. 1 cm² = 0.155 sq. in. 1 m² = 10.8 sq. ft. = 1.2 sq. yd.	1 sq. in. = 6 452 mm² 1 sq. ft. = 0.093 m² 1 sq. yd. = 0.836 m²
Mass	milligram gram kilogram tonne	mg g kg t	1 g = 0.035 oz. 1 kg = 2.205 lb. 1 tonne = 1.102 tons	1 oz. = 28.3 g 1 lb. = 0.454 kg 1 ton = 907.2 kg = 0.907 tonnes
Volume	cubic centimeter cubic meter milliliter	cm³ m³ m	1 mm³ = 0.000 061 cu. in. 1 cm³ = 0.061 cu. in. 1 m³ = 35.3 cu ft = 1.308 cu. yd. 1 mℓ = 0.035 fl. oz.	1 fl. oz. = 28.4 cm³ 1 cu. in. = 16.387 cm³ 1 cu. ft. = 0.028 m³ 1 cu. yd. = 0.756 m³

Capacity	liter	L	U.S. Measure
			1 pt. = 0.473 L
			1 qt. = 0.946 L
			1 gal = 3.785 L
			Imperial Measure
			1 pt. = 0.568 L
			1 qt. = 1.137 L
			1 gal = 4.546 L
				U.S. Measure
				1 L = 2.113 pt.
				    = 1.057 qt.
				    = 0.264 gal.
				Imperial Measure
				1 L = 1.76 pt.
				    = 0.88 qt.
				    = 0.22 gal.

Temperature	Celsius degree	°C	$°C = \frac{5}{9}(°F\text{-}32)$	$°F = \frac{9}{5} \times °C + 32$

Force	newton
	kilonewton
		N
		kN
			1 N = 0.225 lb (f)
			1 kN = 0.225 kip (f)
			     = 0.112 ton (f)
				1 lb (f) = 4.45N
				        = 0.004 448 kN

Energy/Work	joule kilojoule megajoule	J kJ MJ	1 J = 0.737 ft · lb 1 J = 0.948 Btu 1 MJ = 0.278 kWh	1 ft · lb = 1.355 J 1 Btu = 1.055 J 1 kWh = 3.6 MJ
Power	kilowatt	kW	1 kW = 1.34 hp 1 W = 0.0226 ft · lb/min.	1 hp (550 ft · lb/s) = 0.746 kW 1 ft · lb/min = 44.2537 W

Pressure	kilopascal
	
	*kilogram per square centimeter
		kPa
		
		kg/cm²
			1 kPa = 0.145 psi
			      = 20.885 psf
			      = 0.01 ton-force per sq. ft.
			1 kg/cm² = 13.780 psi
				1 psi = 6.895 kPa
				1 lb-force/sq. ft. = 47.88 Pa
				1 ton-force/sq. ft. = 95.76 kPa

Torque	newton meter *kilogram meter *kilogram per centimeter	N · m kg/m kg/cm	1 N · m = 0.74 lb · ft 1 kg/m = 7.24 lb · ft 1 kg/cm = 0.86 lb · in	1 lb · ft = 1.36 N · m 1 lb · ft = 0.14 kg/m 1 lb · in = 1.2 kg/cm
Speed/Velocity	meters per second kilometers per hour	m/s km/h	1 m/s = 3.28 ft/s 1 km/h = 0.62 mph	1 ft/s = 0.305 m/s 1 mph = 1.61 km/h

*Not SI units, but included here because they are employed on some of the gages and indicators currently in use in industry.

Table 2   Metric conversion tables.

ONE HUNDREDTH OF AN INCH INCREMENTS TO ONE INCH

Inch	.00	.01	.02	.03	.04	.05	.06	.07	.08	.09
.00	0.00	0.25	0.51	0.76	1.02	1.27	1.52	1.78	2.03	2.29
.10	2.54	2.79	3.05	3.30	3.56	3.81	4.06	4.32	4.57	4.83
.20	5.08	5.33	5.59	5.84	6.10	6.35	6.60	6.86	7.11	7.37
.30	7.62	7.87	8.13	8.38	8.64	8.89	9.14	9.40	9.65	9.91
.40	10.16	10.41	10.67	10.92	11.18	11.43	11.68	11.94	12.19	12.45
.50	12.70	12.95	13.21	13.46	13.72	13.97	14.22	14.48	14.73	14.99
.60	15.24	15.49	15.75	16.00	16.26	16.51	16.76	17.02	17.27	17.53
.70	17.78	18.03	18.29	18.54	18.80	19.05	19.30	19.56	19.81	20.07
.80	20.32	20.57	20.83	21.08	21.34	21.59	21.84	22.10	22.35	22.61
.90	22.86	23.11	23.37	23.62	23.88	24.13	24.38	24.64	24.89	25.15

ONE TENTH OF AN INCH INCREMENTS TO TWENTY INCHES

Inches	0	.10	.20	.30	.40	.50	.60	.70	.80	.90
0	0.0	2.5	5.1	7.6	10.2	12.7	15.2	17.8	20.3	22.9
1	25.4	27.9	30.5	33.0	35.6	38.1	40.6	43.2	45.7	48.3
2	50.8	53.3	55.9	58.4	61.0	63.5	66.0	68.6	71.1	73.7
3	76.2	78.7	81.3	83.8	86.4	88.9	91.4	94.0	96.5	99.1
4	101.6	104.1	106.7	109.2	111.8	114.3	116.8	119.4	121.9	124.5
5	127.0	129.5	132.1	134.6	137.2	139.7	142.2	144.8	147.3	149.9
6	152.4	154.9	157.5	160.0	162.6	165.1	167.6	170.2	172.7	175.3
7	177.8	180.3	182.9	185.4	188.0	190.5	193.0	195.6	198.1	200.7
8	203.2	205.7	208.3	210.8	213.4	215.9	218.4	221.0	223.5	226.1
9	228.6	231.1	233.7	236.2	238.8	241.3	243.8	246.4	248.9	251.5
10	254.0	256.5	259.1	261.6	264.2	266.7	269.2	271.8	274.3	276.9
11	279.4	281.9	284.5	287.0	289.6	292.1	294.6	297.2	299.7	302.3
12	304.8	307.3	309.9	312.4	315.0	317.5	320.0	322.6	325.1	327.7
13	330.2	332.7	335.3	337.8	340.4	342.9	345.4	348.0	350.5	353.1
14	355.6	358.1	360.7	363.2	365.8	368.3	370.8	373.4	375.9	378.5
15	381.0	383.5	386.1	388.6	391.2	393.7	396.2	398.8	401.3	403.9
16	406.4	408.9	411.5	414.0	416.6	419.1	421.6	424.2	426.7	429.3
17	431.8	434.3	436.9	439.4	442.0	444.5	447.0	449.6	452.1	454.7
18	457.2	459.7	462.3	464.8	467.4	469.9	472.4	475.0	477.5	480.1
19	482.6	485.1	487.7	490.2	492.8	495.3	497.8	500.4	502.9	505.5
20	508.0	510.5	513.1	515.6	518.2	520.7	523.2	525.8	528.3	530.9

Table 3   Conversion of decimals of an inch to millimeters.

IN.	0	1/16	1/8	3/16	1/4	5/16	3/8	7/16	1/2	9/16	5/8	11/16	3/4	13/16	7/8	15/16
0	.0	1.6	3.2	4.8	6.4	7.9	9.5	11.1	12.7	14.3	15.9	17.5	19.1	20.6	22.2	23.8
1	25.4	27.0	28.6	30.2	31.8	33.3	34.9	36.5	38.1	39.7	41.3	42.9	44.5	46.0	47.6	49.2
2	50.8	52.4	54.0	55.6	57.2	58.7	60.3	61.9	63.5	65.1	66.7	68.3	69.9	71.4	73.0	74.6
3	76.2	77.8	79.4	81.0	82.6	84.1	85.7	87.3	88.9	90.5	92.1	93.7	95.3	96.8	98.4	100.0
4	101.6	103.2	104.8	106.4	108.0	109.5	111.1	112.7	114.3	115.9	117.5	119.1	120.7	122.2	123.8	125.4
5	127.0	128.6	130.2	131.8	133.4	134.9	136.5	138.1	139.7	141.3	142.9	144.5	146.1	147.6	149.2	150.8
6	152.4	154.0	155.6	157.2	158.8	160.3	161.9	163.5	165.1	166.7	168.3	169.9	171.5	173.0	174.6	176.2
7	177.8	179.4	181.0	182.6	184.2	185.7	187.3	188.9	190.5	192.1	193.7	195.3	196.9	198.4	200.0	201.6
8	203.2	204.8	206.4	208.0	209.6	211.1	212.7	214.3	215.9	217.5	219.1	220.7	222.3	223.8	225.4	227.0
9	228.6	230.2	231.8	233.4	235.0	236.5	238.1	239.7	241.3	242.9	244.5	246.1	247.7	249.2	250.8	252.4
10	254.0	255.6	257.2	258.8	260.4	261.9	263.5	265.1	266.7	268.3	269.9	271.5	273.1	274.6	276.2	277.8
11	279.4	281.0	282.6	284.2	285.8	287.3	288.9	290.5	292.1	293.7	295.3	296.9	298.5	300.0	301.6	303.2
12	304.8	306.4	308.0	309.6	311.2	312.7	314.3	315.9	317.5	319.1	320.7	322.3	323.9	325.4	327.0	328.6
13	330.2	331.8	333.4	335.0	336.6	338.1	339.7	341.3	342.9	344.5	346.1	347.7	349.3	350.8	352.4	354.0
14	355.6	357.2	358.8	360.4	362.0	363.5	365.1	366.7	368.3	369.9	371.5	373.1	374.7	376.2	377.8	379.4

Table 4   Conversion of fractions of an inch to millimeters.

Fraction	Decimal	Fraction	Decimal
$\frac{1}{64}$	0.015625	$\frac{33}{64}$	0.515625
$\frac{1}{32}$	0.03125	$\frac{17}{32}$	0.53125
$\frac{3}{64}$	0.046875	$\frac{35}{64}$	0.546875
$\frac{1}{16}$	0.0625	$\frac{9}{16}$	0.5625
$\frac{5}{64}$	0.078125	$\frac{37}{64}$	0.578125
$\frac{3}{32}$	0.09375	$\frac{19}{32}$	0.59375
$\frac{7}{64}$	0.109375	$\frac{39}{64}$	0.609375
$\frac{1}{8}$	0.1250	$\frac{5}{8}$	0.6250
$\frac{9}{64}$	0.140625	$\frac{41}{64}$	0.640625
$\frac{5}{32}$	0.15625	$\frac{21}{32}$	0.65625
$\frac{11}{64}$	0.171875	$\frac{43}{64}$	0.671875
$\frac{3}{16}$	0.1875	$\frac{11}{16}$	0.6875
$\frac{13}{64}$	0.203125	$\frac{45}{64}$	0.703125
$\frac{7}{32}$	0.21875	$\frac{23}{32}$	0.71875
$\frac{15}{64}$	0.234375	$\frac{47}{64}$	0.734375
$\frac{1}{4}$	0.2500	$\frac{3}{4}$	0.7500
$\frac{17}{64}$	0.265625	$\frac{49}{64}$	0.765625
$\frac{9}{32}$	0.28125	$\frac{25}{32}$	0.78125
$\frac{19}{64}$	0.296875	$\frac{51}{64}$	0.796875
$\frac{5}{16}$	0.3125	$\frac{13}{16}$	0.8125
$\frac{21}{64}$	0.328125	$\frac{53}{64}$	0.828125
$\frac{11}{32}$	0.34375	$\frac{27}{32}$	0.84375
$\frac{23}{64}$	0.359375	$\frac{55}{64}$	0.859375
$\frac{3}{8}$	0.3750	$\frac{7}{8}$	0.8750
$\frac{25}{64}$	0.390625	$\frac{57}{64}$	0.890625
$\frac{13}{32}$	0.40625	$\frac{29}{32}$	0.90625
$\frac{27}{64}$	0.421875	$\frac{59}{64}$	0.921875
$\frac{7}{16}$	0.4375	$\frac{15}{16}$	0.9375
$\frac{29}{64}$	0.453125	$\frac{61}{64}$	0.953125
$\frac{15}{32}$	0.46875	$\frac{31}{32}$	0.96875
$\frac{31}{64}$	0.484375	$\frac{63}{64}$	0.984375
$\frac{1}{2}$	0.5000	1	1.0000

Table 5   Decimal equivalents of common inch fractions.

ANGLE	SINE	COSINE	TAN	COTAN	ANGLE
0°	.0000	1.0000	.0000	θ	90°
1°	0.0175	0.9998	0.0175	57.290	89°
2°	0.0349	0.9994	0.0349	28.636	88°
3°	0.0523	0.9986	0.0524	19.081	87°
4°	0.0698	0.9976	0.0699	14.301	86°
5°	0.0872	0.9962	0.0875	11.430	85°
6°	0.1045	0.9945	0.1051	9.5144	84°
7°	0.1219	0.9925	0.1228	8.1443	83°
8°	0.1392	0.9903	0.1405	7.1154	82°
9°	0.1564	0.9877	0.1584	6.3138	81°
10°	0.1736	0.9848	0.1763	5.6713	80°
11°	0.1908	0.9816	0.1944	5.1446	79°
12°	0.2079	0.9781	0.2126	4.7046	78°
13°	0.2250	0.9744	0.2309	4.3315	77°
14°	0.2419	0.9703	0.2493	4.0108	76°
15°	0.2588	0.9659	0.2679	3.7321	75°
16°	0.2756	0.9613	0.2867	3.4874	74°
17°	0.2924	0.9563	0.3057	3.2709	73°
18°	0.3090	0.9511	0.3249	3.0777	72°
19°	0.3256	0.9455	0.3443	2.9042	71°
20°	0.3420	0.9397	0.3640	2.7475	70°
21°	0.3584	0.9336	0.3839	2.6051	69°
22°	0.3746	0.9272	0.4040	2.4751	68°
23°	0.3907	0.9205	0.4245	2.3559	67°
24°	0.4067	0.9135	0.4452	2.2460	66°
25°	0.4226	0.9063	0.4663	2.1445	65°
26°	0.4384	0.8988	0.4877	2.0503	64°
27°	0.4540	0.8910	0.5095	1.9626	63°
28°	0.4695	0.8829	0.5317	1.8807	62°
29°	0.4848	0.8746	0.5543	1.8040	61°
30°	0.5000	0.8660	0.5774	1.7321	60°
31°	0.5150	0.8572	0.6009	1.6643	59°
32°	0.5299	0.8480	0.6249	1.6003	58°
33°	0.5446	0.8387	0.6494	1.5399	57°
34°	0.5592	0.8290	0.6745	1.4826	56°
35°	0.5736	0.8192	0.7002	1.4281	55°
36°	0.5878	0.8090	0.7265	1.3764	54°
37°	0.6018	0.7986	0.7536	1.3270	53°
38°	0.6157	0.7880	0.7813	1.2799	52°
39°	0.6293	0.7771	0.8098	1.2349	51°
40°	0.6428	0.7660	0.8391	1.1918	50°
41°	0.6561	0.7547	0.8693	1.1504	49°
42°	0.6691	0.7431	0.9004	1.1106	48°
43°	0.6820	0.7314	0.9325	1.0724	47°
44°	0.6947	0.7193	0.9657	1.0355	46°
45°	0.7071	0.7071	0.0000	1.0000	45°
ANGLE	COSINE	SINE	COTAN	TAN	ANGLE

Table 6   Trigonometric functions.

NUM-BER	SQUARE	SQUARE ROOT	CIRCUM-FERENCE OF CIRCLE	AREA OF CIRCLE	NUM-BER	SQUARE	SQUARE ROOT	CIRCUM-FERENCE OF CIRCLE	AREA OF CIRCLE	NUM-BER	SQUARE	SQUARE ROOT	CIRCUM-FERENCE OF CIRCLE	AREA OF CIRCLE
1	1	1	3.14	0.78	36	1296	6.0000	113.10	1017.88	71	5041	8.4261	223.05	3959.19
2	4	1.41	6.28	3.14	37	1369	6.0828	116.24	1075.21	72	5184	8.4853	226.19	4071.50
3	9	1.73	9.43	7.07	38	1444	6.1644	119.38	1134.11	73	5329	8.5440	229.34	4185.39
4	16	2.00	12.57	12.57	39	1521	6.2450	122.52	1194.59	74	5476	8.6023	232.48	4300.84
5	25	2.34	15.71	19.64	40	1600	6.3246	125.66	1256.64	75	5625	8.6603	235.62	4417.88
6	36	2.4495	18.85	28.27	41	1681	6.4031	128.81	1320.25	76	5776	8.7178	238.76	4536.47
7	49	2.6458	21.99	38.48	42	1764	6.4807	131.95	1385.44	77	5929	8.7750	241.90	4656.64
8	64	2.8284	25.13	50.27	43	1849	6.5574	135.09	1452.20	78	6084	8.8318	245.04	4778.37
9	81	3.0000	28.27	63.62	44	1936	6.6332	138.23	1520.53	79	6241	8.8882	248.19	4901.68
10	100	3.1623	31.46	78.54	45	2025	6.7082	141.37	1590.43	80	6400	8.9443	251.33	5026.56
11	121	3.3166	34.56	95.03	46	2116	6.7823	144.51	1661.90	81	6561	9.0000	254.47	5183.01
12	144	3.4641	37.70	113.09	47	2209	6.8557	147.65	1734.94	82	6724	9.0554	257.61	5281.03
13	169	3.6056	40.84	132.73	48	2304	6.9282	150.80	1809.56	83	6889	9.1104	260.75	5410.62
14	196	3.7417	43.98	153.94	49	2401	7.0000	153.94	1885.74	84	7056	9.1652	263.89	5541.78
15	225	3.8730	47.12	176.72	50	2500	7.0711	157.08	1963.50	85	7225	9.2200	267.04	5674.52
16	256	4.0000	50.27	201.06	51	2601	7.1414	160.22	2042.82	86	7396	9.2736	270.18	5808.82
17	289	4.1231	53.41	226.98	52	2704	7.2111	163.36	2123.72	87	7569	9.3274	273.32	5944.69
18	324	4.2426	,.55	254.47	53	2809	7.2801	166.50	2206.18	88	7744	9.3808	276.46	6082.14
19	361	4.3589	59.69	283.53	54	2916	7.3485	169.65	2290.22	89	7921	9.4340	279.60	6221.15
20	400	4.4721	62.83	314.16	55	3025	7.4162	172.79	2375.83	90	8100	9.4868	282.74	6361.74
21	441	4.5826	65.97	346.36	56	3136	7.4833	175.93	2463.01	91	8281	9.5393	285.89	6503.90
22	484	4.6904	69.12	380.13	57	3249	7.5498	179.07	2551.76	92	8464	9.5917	289.03	6647.63
23	529	4.7958	72.26	415.48	58	3364	7.6158	182.21	2642.08	93	8649	9.6437	292.17	6792.92
24	576	4.8990	75.39	452.39	59	3481	7.6811	185.35	2733.97	94	8836	9.6954	295.31	6939.79
25	625	5.0000	78.54	490.87	60	3600	7.7460	188.50	2827.43	95	9025	9.7468	298.45	7088.24
26	676	5.0990	81.68	530.93	61	3721	7.8102	191.64	3922.47	96	9216	9.7979	301.59	7238.25
27	729	5.1962	84.82	572.56	62	3844	7.8740	194.78	3019.07	97	9409	9.8489	304.74	7389.83
28	784	5.2915	87.97	615.75	63	3969	7.9373	197.92	3117.25	98	9604	9.8995	307.88	7542.98
29	841	5.3852	91.11	660.52	64	4096	8.0000	201.06	3216.99	99	9801	9.9509	311.02	7697.71
30	900	5.4772	94.25	706.86	65	4225	8.0623	204.20	3318.31	100	10 000	10.000	314.16	7854.00
31	961	5.5678	97.39	754.77	66	4356	8.1240	207.35	3421.19	101	10 201	10.0499	317.30	8011.87
32	1024	5.6569	100.53	804.25	67	4489	8.1854	210.49	3525.65	102	10 404	10.0995	320.44	8171.30
33	1089	5.7446	103.67	855.30	68	4624	8.2462	213.63	3631.68	103	10 609	10.1489	323.58	8332.31
34	1156	5.8310	106.81	907.92	69	4761	8.3066	216.77	3739.28	104	10 816	10.1980	326.73	8494.89
35	1225	5.9161	109.96	962.113	70	4900	8.3666	219.91	3848.50	105	11 025	10.2470	329.87	8659.04

Table 7 **Function of numbers.**

Across Flats	ACRFLT	Machine Steel	MST
American National Standards Institute	ANSI	Machined	✓
And	&	Malleable Iron	MI
Angular	ANLR	Material	MATL
Approximate	APPROX	Maximum	MAX
Assembly	ASSY	Maximum Material Condition	Ⓜ or MMC
Basic	BSC	Meter	m
Bill of Material	B/M	Metric Thread	M
Bolt Circle	BC	Micrometer	μm
Brass	BR	Millimeter	mm
Brown and Sharpe Gage	B&S GA	Minimum	MIN
Bushing	BUSH	Module	MDL
Canada Standards Institute	CSI	Newton	N
Carbon Steel	CS	Nominal	NOM
Casting	CSTG	Not to Scale	x̲x̲
Cast Iron	CI	Number	NO
Center Line	CL or ℄	On Center	OC
Center to Center	C to C	Outside Diameter	OD
Centimeter	cm	Parallel	PAR
Chamfer	CHAM	Pascal	Pa
Circularity	CIR	Perpendicular	PERP
Cold-Rolled Steel	CRS	Pitch	P
Concentric	CONC	Pitch Circle	PC
Counterbore	⎍ or CBORE	Pitch Diameter	PD
Counterdrill	CDRILL	Plate	PL
Countersink	∨ or CSK	Radius	R
Cubic Centimeter	cm³	Reference or Reference Dimension	( ) or REF
Cubic Meter	m³	Regardless of Feature Size	Ⓢ
Datum	DAT	Revolutions per Minute	rev/min
Degree (Angle)	° or DEG	Right Hand	RH
Depth	DP or ⧾	Root Diameter	RD
Diameter	⌀ or DIA	Second (Arc)	(″)
Diametral Pitch	DP	Second (Time)	SEC
Dimension	DIM	Section	SECT
Drawing	DWG	Slotted	SLOT
Eccentric	ECC	Socket	SOCK
Equally Spaced	EQL SP	Spherical	SPHER
Figure	FIG	Spotface	⎍ or SFACE
Finish All Over	FAO	Square	□ or SQ
Flat	FL	Square Centimeter	cm²
Gage	GA	Square Meter	m²
Gray Iron	GI	Steel	STL
Head	HD	Straight	STR
Heat Treat	HT TR	Symmetrical	⊣⊢ or SYM
Heavy	HVY	Taper—Flat	▷
Hexagon	HEX	—Round	⊳
Hydraulic	HYDR	Taper Pipe Thread	NPT
Inside Diameter	ID	Thread	THD
International Organization for Standardization	ISO	Through	THRU
International Pipe Standard	IPS	Tolerance	TOL
Kilogram	kg	True Profile	TP
Kilometer	km	U.S. Gage	USG
Left Hand	LH	Watt	W
Length	LG	Wrought Iron	WI
Liter	L	Wrought Steel	WS

ISO Ⓐ   ANSI -A-

Table 8   Abbreviations and symbols used on technical drawings.

NUMBER OR LETTER SIZE DRILL	SIZE		NUMBER OR LETTER SIZE DRILL	SIZE		NUMBER OR LETTER SIZE DRILL	SIZE		NUMBER OR LETTER SIZE DRILL	SIZE	
	mm	INCHES		mm	INCHES		mm	INCHES		mm	INCHES
80	0.343	.014	50	1.778	.070	20	4.089	.161	K	7.137	.281
79	0.368	.015	49	1.854	.073	19	4.216	.166	L	7.366	.290
78	0.406	.016	48	1.930	.076	18	4.305	.170	M	7.493	.295
77	0.457	.018	47	1.994	.079	17	4.394	.173	N	7.671	.302
76	0.508	.020	46	2.057	.081	16	4.496	.177	O	8.026	.316
75	0.533	.021	45	2.083	.082	15	4.572	.180	P	8.204	.323
74	0.572	.023	44	2.184	.086	14	4.623	.182	Q	8.433	.332
73	0.610	.024	43	2.261	.089	13	4.700	.185	R	8.611	.339
72	0.635	.025	42	2.375	.094	12	4.800	.189	S	8.839	.348
71	0.660	.026	41	2.438	.096	11	4.851	.191	T	9.093	.358
70	0.711	.028	40	2.489	.098	10	4.915	.194	U	9.347	.368
69	0.742	.029	39	2.527	.100	9	4.978	.196	V	9.576	.377
68	0.787	.031	38	2.578	.102	8	5.080	.199	W	9.804	.386
67	0.813	.032	37	2.642	.104	7	5.105	.201	X	10.084	.397
66	0.838	.033	36	2.705	.107	6	5.182	.204	Y	10.262	.404
65	0.889	.035	35	2.794	.110	5	5.220	.206	Z	10.490	.413
64	0.914	.036	34	2.819	.111	4	5.309	.209			
63	0.940	.037	33	2.870	.113	3	5.410	.213			
62	0.965	.038	32	2.946	.116	2	5.613	.221			
61	0.991	.039	31	3.048	.120	1	5.791	.228			
60	1.016	.040	30	3.264	.129	A	5.944	.234			
59	1.041	.041	29	3.354	.136	B	6.045	.238			
58	1.069	.042	28	3.569	.141	C	6.147	.242			
57	1.092	.043	27	3.658	.144	D	6.248	.246			
56	1.181	.047	26	3.734	.147	E	6.350	.250			
55	1.321	.052	25	3.797	.150	F	6.528	.257			
54	1.397	.055	24	3.861	.152	G	6.629	.261			
53	1.511	.060	23	3.912	.154	H	6.756	.266			
52	1.613	.064	22	3.988	.157	I	6.909	.272			
51	1.702	.067	21	4.039	.159	J	7.036	.277			

Table 9   Number and letter-size drills.

METRIC DRILL SIZES		Reference Decimal Equivalent (Inches)	METRIC DRILL SIZES		Reference Decimal Equivalent (Inches)	METRIC DRILL SIZES		Reference Decimal Equivalent (Inches)
Preferred	Available		Preferred	Available		Preferred	Available	
—	0.40	.0157	—	2.7	.1063	14	—	.5512
—	0.42	.0165	2.8	—	.1102	—	14.5	.5709
—	0.45	.0177	—	2.9	.1142	15	—	.5906
—	0.48	.0189	3.0	—	.1181	—	15.5	.6102
0.50	—	.0197	—	3.1	.1220	16	—	.6299
—	0.52	.0205	3.2	—	.1260	—	16.5	.6496
0.55	—	.0217	—	3.3	.1299	17	—	.6693
—	0.58	.0228	3.4	—	.1339	—	17.5	.6890
0.60	—	.0236	—	3.5	.1378	18	—	.7087
—	0.62	.0244	3.6	—	.1417	—	18.5	.7283
0.65	—	.0256	—	3.7	.1457	19	—	.7480
—	0.68	.0268	3.8	—	.1496	—	19.5	.7677
0.70	—	.0276	—	3.9	.1535	20	—	.7874
—	0.72	.0283	4.0	—	.1575	—	20.5	.8071
0.75	—	.0295	—	4.1	.1614	21	—	.8268
—	0.78	.0307	4.2	—	.1654	—	21.5	.8465
0.80	—	.0315	—	4.4	.1732	22	—	.8661
—	0.82	.0323	4.5	—	.1772	—	23	.9055
0.85	—	.0335	—	4.6	.1811	24	—	.9449
—	0.88	.0346	4.8	—	.1890	25	—	.9843
0.90	—	.0354	5.0	—	.1969	26	—	1.0236
—	0.92	.0362	—	5.2	.2047	—	27	1.0630
0.95	—	.0374	5.3	—	.2087	28	—	1.1024
—	0.98	.0386	—	5.4	.2126	—	29	1.1417
1.00	—	.0394	5.6	—	.2205	30	—	1.1811
—	1.03	.0406	—	5.8	.2283	—	31	1.2205
1.05	—	.0413	6.0	—	.2362	32	—	1.2598
—	1.08	.0425	—	6.2	.2441	—	33	1.2992
1.10	—	.0433	6.3	—	.2480	34	—	1.3386
—	1.15	.0453	—	6.5	.2559	—	35	1.3780
1.20	—	.0472	6.7	—	.2638	36	—	1.4173
1.25	—	.0492	—	6.8	.2677	—	37	1.4567
1.3	—	.0512	—	6.9	.2717	38	—	1.4361
—	1.35	.0531	7.1	—	.2795	—	39	1.5354
1.4	—	.0551	—	7.3	.2874	40	—	1.5748
—	1.45	.0571	7.5	—	.2953	—	41	1.6142
1.5	—	.0591	—	7.8	.3071	42	—	1.6535
—	1.55	.0610	8.0	—	.3150	—	43.5	1.7126
1.6	—	.0630	—	8.2	.3228	45	—	1.7717
—	1.65	.0650	8.5	—	.3346	—	46.5	1.8307
1.7	—	.0669	—	8.8	.3465	48	—	1.8898
—	1.75	.0689	9.0	—	.3543	50	—	1.9685
1.8	—	.0709	—	9.2	.3622	—	51.5	2.0276
—	1.85	.0728	9.5	—	.3740	53	—	2.0866
1.9	—	.0748	—	9.8	.3858	—	54	2.1260
—	1.95	.0768	10	—	.3937	56	—	2.2047
2.0	—	.0787	—	10.3	.4055	—	58	2.2835
—	2.05	.0807	10.5	—	.4134	60	—	2.3622
2.1	—	.0827	—	10.8	.4252			
—	2.15	.0846	11	—	.4331			
2.2	—	.0866	—	11.5	.4528			
—	2.3	.0906	12	—	.4724			
2.4	—	.0945	12.5	—	.4921			
2.5	—	.0984	13	—	.5118			
2.6	—	.1024	—	13.5	.5315			

Table 10   Metric twist drill sizes.

THREADS PER INCH AND TAP DRILL SIZES

SIZE INCHES		Graded Pitch Series						Constant Pitch Series					
		Coarse UNC		Fine UNF		Extra Fine UNEF		8 UN		12 UN		16 UN	
Number or Fraction	Deci-mal	Threads per Inch	Tap Drill Dia.	Threads per Inch	Tap Drill Dia.	Threads per Inch	Tap Drill Dia.	Threads per Inch	Tap Drill Dia.	Threads per Inch	Tap Drill Dia.	Threads per Inch	Tap Drill Dia.
0	.060	—	—	80	3/64	—	—	—	—	—	—	—	—
2	.086	56	No. 50	64	No. 49	—	—	—	—	—	—	—	—
4	.112	40	No. 43	48	No. 42	—	—	—	—	—	—	—	—
5	.125	40	No. 38	44	No. 37	—	—	—	—	—	—	—	—
6	.138	32	No. 36	40	No. 33	—	—	—	—	—	—	—	—
8	.164	32	No. 29	36	No. 29	—	—	—	—	—	—	—	—
10	.190	24	No. 25	32	No. 21	—	—	—	—	—	—	—	—
1/4	.250	20	7	28	3	32	.219	—	—	—	—	—	—
5/16	.312	18	F	24	1	32	.281	—	—	—	—	—	—
3/8	.375	16	.312	24	Q	32	.344	—	—	—	—	UNC	—
7/16	.438	14	U	20	.391	28	Y	—	—	—	—	16	V
1/2	.500	13	.422	20	.453	28	.469	—	—	—	—	16	.438
9/16	.562	12	.484	18	.516	24	.516	—	—	UNC	—	16	.500
5/8	.625	11	.531	18	.578	24	.578	—	—	12	.547	16	.562
3/4	.750	10	.656	16	.688	20	.703	—	—	12	.672	UNF	—
7/8	.875	9	.766	14	.812	20	.828	—	—	12	.797	16	.812
1	1.000	8	.875	12	.922	20	.953	UNC	—	UNF	—	16	.938
1 1/8	1.125	7	.984	12	1.047	18	1.078	8	1.000	UNF	—	16	1.062
1 1/4	1.250	7	1.109	12	1.172	18	1.188	8	1.125	UNF	—	16	1.188
1 3/8	1.375	6	1.219	12	1.297	18	1.312	8	1.250	UNF	—	16	1.312
1 1/2	1.500	6	1.344	12	1.422	18	1.438	8	1.375	UNF	—	16	1.438
1 5/8	1.625	—	—	—	—	18	—	8	1.500	12	1.547	16	1.562
1 3/4	1.750	5	1.562	—	—	—	—	8	1.625	12	1.672	16	1.688
1 7/8	1.875	—	—	—	—	—	—	8	1.750	12	1.797	16	1.812
2	2.000	4.5	1.781	—	—	—	—	8	1.875	12	1.922	16	1.938
2 1/4	2.250	4.5	2.031	—	—	—	—	8	2.125	12	2.172	16	2.188
2 1/2	2.500	4	2.250	—	—	—	—	8	2.375	12	2.422	16	2.438
2 3/4	2.750	4	2.500	—	—	—	—	8	2.625	12	2.672	16	2.688
3	3.000	4	2.750	—	—	—	—	8	2.875	12	2.922	16	2.938
3 1/4	3.250	4	3.000	—	—	—	—	8	3.125	12	3.172	16	3.188
3 1/2	3.500	4	3.250	—	—	—	—	8	3.375	12	3.422	16	3.438
3 3/4	3.750	4	3.500	—	—	—	—	8	3.625	12	3.668	16	3.688
4	4.000	4	3.750	—	—	—	—	8	3.875	12	3.922	16	3.938

Note: The tap diameter sizes shown are nominal. The class and length of thread will govern the limits on the tapped hole size.

Table 11 Inch screw threads.

Table 12 Isometric screw threads.

Nominal Size DIA (mm) 2nd choice	Preferred	Coarse Thread Pitch	Coarse Tap Drill Size	Fine Thread Pitch	Fine Tap Drill Size	4 Thread Pitch	4 Tap Drill Size	3 Thread Pitch	3 Tap Drill Size	2 Thread Pitch	2 Tap Drill Size	1.5 Thread Pitch	1.5 Tap Drill Size	1.25 Thread Pitch	1.25 Tap Drill Size	1 Thread Pitch	1 Tap Drill Size	0.75 Thread Pitch	0.75 Tap Drill Size	0.5 Thread Pitch	0.5 Tap Drill Size	0.35 Thread Pitch	0.35 Tap Drill Size
	1.6	0.35	1.25																				
1.8		0.35	1.45																				
	2	0.4	1.6																				
2.2		0.45	1.75																				
	2.5	0.45	2.05																			0.35	2.15
	3	0.5	2.5																			0.35	2.65
3.5		0.6	2.9																			0.35	3.15
	4	0.7	3.3																	0.5	3.5		
4.5		0.75	3.7																	0.5	4.0		
	5	0.8	4.2																	0.5	4.5		
	6	1	5.0															0.75	5.2				
	8	1.25	6.7	1	7.0											1	7.0	0.75	7.2				
	10	1.5	8.5	1.25	8.7									1.25	8.7	1	9.0	0.75	9.2				
	12	1.75	10.2	1.25	10.8							1.5	10.5	1.25	10.7	1	11						
14		2	12	1.5	12.5							1.5	12.5	1.25	12.7	1	13						
	16	2	14	1.5	14.5							1.5	14.5			1	15						
18		2.5	15.5	1.5	16.5					2	16	1.5	16.5			1	17						
	20	2.5	17.5	1.5	18.5					2	18	1.5	18.5			1	19						
22		2.5	19.5	1.5	20.5					2	20	1.5	20.5			1	21						
	24	3	21	2	22					2	22	1.5	22.5			1	23						
27		3	24	2	25					2	25	1.5	25.5			1	26						
	30	3.5	26.5	2	28					2	28	1.5	28.5			1	29						
33		3.5	29.5	2	31					2	31	1.5	31.5										
	36	4	32	3	33					2	34	1.5	34.5										
39		4	35	3	36					2	37	1.5	37.5										
	42	4.5	37.5	3	39	4	38	3	39	2	40	1.5	40.5										
45		4.5	40.5	3	42	4	41	3	42	2	43	1.5	43.5										
	48	5	43	3	45	4	44	3	45	2	46	1.5	46.5										

SERIES WITH GRADED PITCHES · SERIES WITH CONSTANT PITCHES

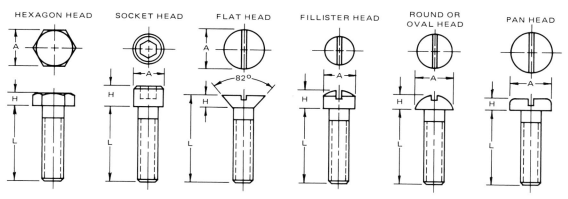

U.S. CUSTOMARY (INCHES)

Nominal Size	Hexagon Head		Socket Head		Flat Head		Fillister Head		Round or Oval Head	
	A	H	A	H	A	H	A	H	A	H
.250	.44	.17	.38	.25	.50	.14	.38	.17	.44	.19
.312	.50	.22	.47	.31	.62	.18	.44	.20	.56	.25
.375	.56	.25	.56	.38	.75	.21	.56	.25	.62	.27
.438	.62	.30	.66	.44	.81	.21	.62	.30	.75	.33
.500	.75	.34	.75	.50	.88	.21	.75	.33	.81	.35
.625	.94	.42	.94	.62	1.12	.28	.88	.42	1.00	.44
.750	1.12	.50	1.12	.75	1.38	.35	1.00	.50	1.25	.55

METRIC (MILLIMETERS)

Nominal Size	Hexagon Head		Socket Head		Flat Head		Fillister Head		Pan Head	
	A	H	A	H	A	H	A	H	A	H
M3	5.5	2	5.5	3	5.6	1.6	6	2.4	5.6	1.9
4	7	2.8	7	4	7.5	2.2	8	3.1	7.5	2.5
5	8.5	3.5	9	5	9.2	2.5	10	3.8	9.2	3.1
6	10	4	10	6	11	3	12	4.6	11	3.8
8	13	5.5	13	8	14.5	4	16	6	14.5	5
10	17	7	16	10	18	5	20	7.5	18	6.2
12	19	8	18	12						
14	22	9	22	14						
16	24	10	24	16						

Table 13   Common cap screws.

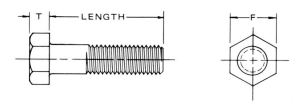

U.S. CUSTOMARY (INCHES)

Nominal Bolt Size	Width Across Flats F	Thickness T
.250	.438	.172
.312	.500	.219
.375	.562	.250
.438	.625	.297
.500	.750	.344
.625	.938	.422
.750	1.125	.500
.875	1.312	.578
1.000	1.500	.672
1.125	1.688	.750
1.250	1.875	.844
1.375	2.062	.906
1.500	2.250	1.000

METRIC (MILLIMETERS)

Nominal Bolt Size and Thread Pitch	Width Across Flats F	Thickness T
M5 x 0.8	8	3.9
M6 x 1	10	4.7
M8 x 1.25	13	5.7
M10 x 1.5	15	6.8
M12 x 1.75	18	8
M14 x 2	21	9.3
M16 x 2	24	10.5
M20 x 2.5	30	13.1
M24 x 3	36	15.6
M30 x 3.5	46	19.5
M36 x 4	55	23.4

Table 14   Hexagon-head bolts and cap screws.

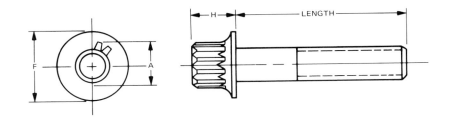

NOMINAL BOLT SIZE AND THREAD PITCH	HEAD SIZES		
	F	A	H
M5 x 0.8	9.4	5.9	5
M6 x 1	11.8	7.4	6.3
M8 x 1.25	15	9.4	8
M10 x 1.5	18.6	11.7	10
M12 x 1.75	22.8	14	12
M14 x 2	26.4	16.3	14
M16 x 2	30.3	18.7	16
M20 x 2.5	37.4	23.4	20

Table 15   Twelve-spline flange screws.

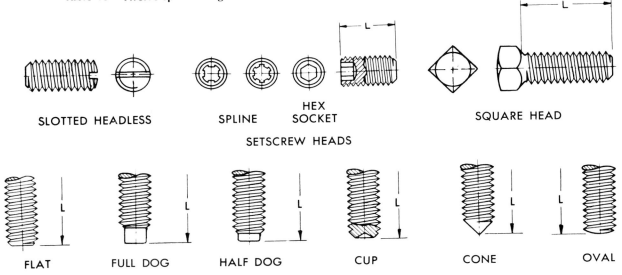

U.S. CUSTOMARY (INCHES)		METRIC (MILLIMETERS)	
Nominal Size	Key Size	Nominal Size	Key Size
.125	.06	M1.4	0.7
.138	.06	2	0.9
.164	.08	3	1.5
.190	.09	4	2
.250	.12	5	2
.312	.16	6	3
.375	.19	8	4
.500	.25	10	5
.625	.31	12	6
.750	.38	16	8

Table 16   Setscrews.

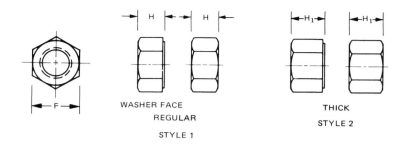

WASHER FACE
REGULAR
STYLE 1

THICK
STYLE 2

U.S. CUSTOMARY (INCHES)			
Nominal Nut Size	Distance Across Flats F	Thickness Max.	
		Style 1 H	Style 2 H₁
.250	.438	.218	.281
.312	.500	.266	.328
.375	.562	.328	.406
.438	.625	.375	.453
.500	.750	.438	.562
.562	.875	.484	.609
.625	.938	.547	.719
.750	1.125	.641	.812
.875	1.312	.750	.906
1.000	1.500	.859	1.000
1.125	1.688	.969	1.156
1.250	1.875	1.062	1.250
1.375	2.062	1.172	1.375
1.500	2.250	1.281	1.500

METRIC (MILLIMETERS)			
Nominal Nut Size and Thread Pitch	Distance Across Flats F	Thickness Max.	
		Style 1 H	Style 2 H₁
M4 x 0.7	7	—	3.2
M5 x 0.8	8	4.5	5.3
M6 x 1	10	5.6	6.5
M8 x 1.25	13	6.6	7.8
M10 x 1.5	15	9	10.7
M12 x 1.75	18	10.7	12.8
M14 x 2	21	12.5	14.9
M16 x 2	24	14.5	17.4
M20 x 2.5	30	18.4	21.2
M24 x 3	36	22	25.4
M30 x 3.5	46	26.7	31
M36 x 4	55	32	37.6

Table 17   Hexagon-head nuts.

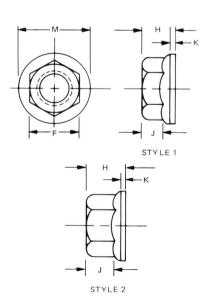

STYLE 1

STYLE 2

METRIC (MILLIMETERS)							
Nominal Nut Size and Thread Pitch	Width Across Flats F	Style 1				Style 2	
		H	J	K	M	H	J
M6 x 1	10	5.8	3	1	14.2	6.7	3.7
M8 x 1.25	13	6.8	3.7	1.3	17.6	8	4.5
M10 x 1.5	15	9.6	5.5	1.5	21.5	11.2	6.7
M12 x 1.75	18	11.6	6.7	2	25.6	13.5	8.2
M14 x 2	21	13.4	7.8	2.3	29.6	15.7	9.6
M16 x 2	24	15.9	9.5	2.5	34.2	18.4	11.7
M20 x 2.5	30	19.2	11.1	2.8	42.3	22	12.6

Table 18   Hex flange nuts.

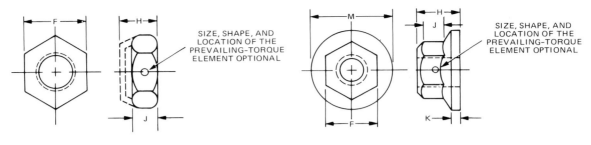

HEX NUTS   HEX FLANGE NUTS

NOMINAL NUT SIZE AND THREAD PITCH	WIDTH ACROSS FLATS F	HEX NUTS Style 1 H max.	HEX NUTS Style 1 J max.	HEX NUTS Style 2 H max.	HEX NUTS Style 2 J max.	HEX FLANGE NUTS Style 1 H	HEX FLANGE NUTS Style 1 J	HEX FLANGE NUTS Style 1 K	HEX FLANGE NUTS Style 1 M	HEX FLANGE NUTS Style 2 H	HEX FLANGE NUTS Style 2 J
M5 × 0.8	8.0	6.1	2.3	7.6	2.9						
M6 × 1	10	7.6	3	8.8	3.7	7.6	3	1	14.2	8.8	3.7
M8 × 1.25	13	9.1	3.7	10.3	4.5	9.1	3.7	1.3	17.6	10.3	4.5
M10 × 1.5	15	12	5.5	14	6.7	12	5.5	1.5	21.5	14	6.7
M12 × 1.75	18	14.2	6.7	16.8	8.2	14.4	6.7	2	25.6	16.8	8.2
M14 × 2	21	16.5	7.8	18.9	9.6	16.6	7.8	2.3	29.6	18.9	9.6
M16 × 2	24	18.5	9.5	21.4	11.7	18.9	9.5	2.5	34.2	21.4	11.7
M20 × 2.5	30	23.4	11.1	26.5	12.6	23.4	11.1	2.8	42.3	26.5	12.6
M24 × 3	36	28	13.3	31.4	15.1						
M30 × 3.5	46	33.7	16.4	38	18.5						
M36 × 4	55	40	20.1	45.6	22.8						

Table 19   Prevailing-torque insert-type nuts.

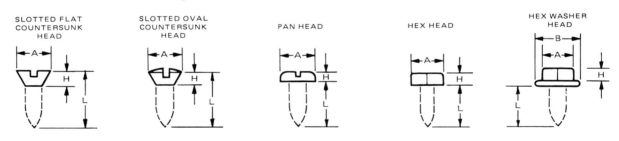

U.S. CUSTOMARY (INCHES)												METRIC (MILLIMETERS)												
NOMINAL SIZE		SLOTTED FLAT COUNTERSUNK HEAD		SLOTTED OVAL COUNTERSUNK HEAD		PAN HEAD		HEX HEAD		HEX WASHER HEAD			NOMINAL SIZE	SLOTTED FLAT COUNTERSUNK HEAD		SLOTTED OVAL COUNTERSUNK HEAD		PAN HEAD		Slot Recess	HEX HEAD		HEX WASHER HEAD		
No.	DIA.	A	H	A	H	A	H	A	H	A	B	H		A	H	A	H	A	H	H	A	H	A	B	H
2	.086	.17	.05	.17	.05	.17	.05	.12	.05	.12	.17	.05	2	3.6	1.2	3.6	1.2	3.9	1.4	1.6	3.2	1.3	3.2	4.2	1.3
4	.112	.23	.07	.23	.07	.22	.07	.19	.06	.19	.24	.06	2.5	4.6	1.5	4.6	1.5	4.9	1.7	2	4	1.4	4	5.3	1.4
6	.138	.28	.08	.28	.08	.27	.08	.25	.09	.25	.33	.09	3	5.5	1.8	5.5	1.8	5.8	1.9	1.3	5	1.5	5	6.2	1.5
8	.164	.33	.10	.33	.10	.32	.10	.25	.11	.25	.35	.11	3.5	6.5	2.1	6.5	2.1	6.8	2.3	2.5	5.5	2.4	5.5	7.5	2.4
10	.190	.39	.17	.39	.17	.37	.11	.31	.12	.31	.41	.12	4	7.5	2.3	7.5	2.3	7.8	2.6	2.8	7	2.8	7	9.2	2.8
													5	9.5	2.9	9.5	2.9	9.8	3.1	3.5	8	3	8	10.5	3
													6	11.9	3.6	11.9	3.6	12	3.9	4.3	10	4.8	10	13.2	4.8
													8	15.2	4.4	15.2	4.4	15.6	5	5.6	13	5.8	13	17.2	5.8
													10	1.9	5.4	19	5.4	19.5	6.2	7	15	7.5	15	19.8	7.5
													12	22.9	6.4	22.9	6.4	23.4	7.5	8.3	18	9.5	18	23.8	9.5

Table 20   Tapping screws.

KIND OF MATERIAL	THREAD-FORMING								THREAD-CUTTING			SELF DRILLING	
	Type A	Type B	Type AB	HEX HEAD B	SWAGE FORM*	SWAGE FORM* B	Type U	Type 21	Type F*	Type L	Type B-F*	DRIL-KWICK	TAPITS*
SHEET METAL .0156 to .0469in. thick (0.4 to 1.2mm) (Steel, Brass, Aluminum, Monel, etc.)	✓	✓	✓	✓	✓	✓		✓				✓	✓
SHEET STAINLESS STEEL .0156 to .0469in thick (0.4 to 1.2mm)	✓	✓	✓	✓	✓	✓		✓	✓			✓	✓
SHEET METAL .20 to .50in. thick (1.2 to 5mm) (Steel, Brass, Aluminum, etc.)		✓	✓	✓	✓		✓	✓	✓			✓	
STRUCTURAL STEEL .20 to .50in. thick (1.2 to .5mm)				✓	✓		✓		✓				
CASTINGS (Aluminum, Magnesium, Zinc, Brass, Bronze, etc.)		✓	✓	✓	✓	✓	✓		✓				
CASTINGS (Grey Iron, Malleable Iron, Steel, etc.)					✓		✓		✓				
FORGINGS (Steel, Brass, Bronze, etc.)					✓		✓		✓				
PLYWOOD, Resin Impregnated: Compreg, Pregwood, etc. **NATURAL WOODS**	✓	✓	✓	✓			✓		✓		✓	✓	✓
ASBESTOS and other compositions: Ebony, Asbestos, Transite, Fiberglas, Insurok, etc.	✓	✓	✓	✓		✓						✓	✓
PHENOL FORMALDEHYDE: Molded: Bakelite, Durez, etc. Cast: Catalin, Marblette, etc. Laminated: Formica, Textolite, etc.		✓	✓	✓		✓	✓		✓		✓		
UREA FORMALDEHYDE: Molded: Plaskon, Beetle, etc. **MELAMINE FORMALDEHYDE:** Melantite, Melamac						✓	✓				✓		
CELLULOSE ACETATES and NITRATES: Tenite, Lumarith, Plastacele Pyralin, Celanese, etc. **ACRYLATE & STYRENE RESINS:** Lucite, Plexiglas, Styron, etc.		✓	✓	✓	✓		✓				✓		
NYLON PLASTICS: Nylon, Zytel					✓	✓	✓			✓			

Table 21   Selector guide to thread cutting screws.

FLAT WASHER   LOCKWASHER   SPRING LOCKWASHER

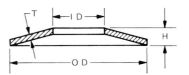

Table 22 — Common washer sizes.

U.S. CUSTOMARY (INCHES)

Bolt Size	Flat Washers Type A–N			Lockwashers Regular		
	ID	OD	Thick	ID	OD	Thick
#6	.156	.375	.049	.141	.250	.031
#8	.188	.438	.049	.168	.293	.040
#10	.219	.500	.049	.194	.334	.047
#12	.250	.562	.065	.221	.377	.056
.250	.281	.625	.065	.255	.489	.062
.312	.344	.688	.065	.318	.586	.078
.375	.406	.812	.065	.382	.683	.094
.438	.469	.922	.065	.446	.779	.109
.500	.531	1.062	.095	.509	.873	.125
.562	.594	1.156	.095	.572	.971	.141
.625	.656	1.312	.095	.636	1.079	.156
.750	.812	1.469	.134	.766	1.271	.188
.875	.938	1.750	.134	.890	1.464	.219
1.000	1.062	2.000	.134	1.017	1.661	.250
1.125	1.250	2.250	.134	1.144	1.853	.281
1.250	1.375	2.500	.165	1.271	2.045	.312
1.375	1.500	2.750	.165	1.398	2.239	.344
1.500	1.625	3.000	.165	1.525	2.430	.375

METRIC (MILLIMETERS)

Bolt Size	Flat Washers			Lockwashers			Spring Lockwashers		
	Id	Od	Thick	Id	Od	Thick	Id	Od	Thick
2	2.2	5.5	0.5	2.1	3.3	0.5			
3	3.2	7	0.5	3.1	5.7	0.8			
4	4.3	9	0.8	4.1	7.1	0.9	4.2	8	0.3 / 0.4
5	5.3	11	1	5.1	8.7	1.2	5.2	10	0.4 / 0.4 / 0.5 / 0.5
6	6.4	12	1.5	6.1	11.1	1.6	6.2	12.5	0.5 / 0.7
7	7.4	14	1.5	7.1	12.1	1.6	7.2	14	0.5 / 0.8
8	8.4	17	2	8.2	14.2	2	8.2	16	0.6 / 0.9
10	10.5	21	2.5	10.2	17.2	2.2	10.2	20	0.8 / 1.1
12	13	24	2.5	12.3	20.2	2.5	12.2	25	0.9 / 1.5
14	15	28	2.5	14.2	23.2	3	14.2	28	1.0 / 1.5
16	17	30	3	16.2	26.2	3.5	16.3	31.5	1.2 / 1.7
18	19	34	3	18.2	28.2	3.5	18.3	35.5	1.2 / 2.0
20	21	36	3	20.2	32.2	4	20.4	40	1.5 / 2.25 / 1.75
22	23	39	4	22.5	34.5	4	22.4	45	2.5
24	25	44	4	24.5	38.5	5			
27	28	50	4	27.5	41.5	5			
30	31	56	4	30.5	46.5	6			

Table 23 — Belleville washers. (Wallace Barnes Co. Ltd.)

U.S. CUSTOMARY (INCHES)

Outside Diameter Max.	Inside Diameter Min.	Stock Thickness T	H Approx.
.187	.093	.010	.015
.250	.125	.009	.017
		.013	.020
.281	.138	.010	.020
		.015	.023
.312	.156	.011	.022
		.017	.025
.343	.164	.013	.024
		.019	.028
.375	.190	.015	.027
		.020	.030
.500	.255	.018	.034
		.025	.038
.625	.317	.022	.042
		.032	.048
.750	.380	.028	.051
		.040	.059
.875	.442	.031	.059
		.045	.067
1.000	.505	.035	.067
		.050	.075
1.125	.567	.038	.073
		.056	.084
1.250	.630	.040	.082
		.062	.092
1.375	.692	.044	.088
		.067	.101

METRIC (MILLIMETERS)

Outside Diameter Max.	Inside Diameter Min.	Stock Thickness T	H Approx.
4.8	2.4	0.16	0.33
		0.25	0.38
6.4	3.2	0.22	0.44
		0.34	0.51
7.9	4	0.27	0.55
		0.42	0.64
9.5	4.8	0.38	0.69
		0.51	0.76
12.7	6.5	0.46	0.86
		0.64	0.97
		0.97	1.20
15.9	8.1	0.56	1.07
		0.81	1.22
19.1	9.7	0.71	1.3
		1.02	1.5
		1.42	1.8
22.2	11.2	0.79	1.5
		1.14	1.7
25.4	12.8	0.89	1.7
		1.27	1.9
		1.85	2.3
28.6	14.4	0.97	1.9
		1.42	2.1
31.8	16	1.02	2.1
		1.58	2.3
34.9	17.6	1.12	2.2
		1.70	2.6
38.1	19.2	1.14	2.4
		1.83	2.7
44.5	22.4	1.45	2.9
		2.16	3.3
50.8	25.4	1.65	3.3
		2.46	3.7
63.5	31.8	2.03	4.1
		3.05	4.6

| U.S. CUSTOMARY (INCHES) | | | | | | METRIC (MILLIMETERS) | | | | | |
| Diameter of Shaft | | Square Key Nominal Size | | Flat Key Nominal Size | | Diameter of Shaft | | Square Key Nominal Size | | Flat Key Nominal Size | |
From	To	W	H	W	H	Over	Up To	W	H	W	H
.500	.562	.125	.125	.125	.094	6	8	2	2		
.625	.875	.188	.188	.188	.125	8	10	3	3		
.938	1.250	.250	.250	.250	.188	10	12	4	4		
1.312	1.375	.312	.312	.312	.250	12	17	5	5		
1.438	1.750	.375	.375	.375	.250	17	22	6	6		
1.812	2.250	.500	.500	.500	.375	22	30	7	7	8	7
2.375	2.750	.625	.625			30	38	8	8	10	8
2.875	3.250	.750	.750			38	44	9	9	12	8
3.375	3.750	.875	.875			44	50	10	10	14	9
3.875	4.500	1.000	1.000			50	58	12	12	16	10

Table 24 Square and flat stock keys.

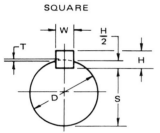

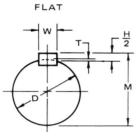

C = ALLOWANCE FOR PARALLEL KEYS = .005 in. OR 0.12 mm

$$S = D - \frac{H}{2} - T = \frac{D - H + \sqrt{D^2 - W^2}}{2} \qquad T = \frac{D - \sqrt{D^2 - W^2}}{2}$$

$$M = D - T + \frac{H}{2} + C = \frac{D + H + \sqrt{D^2 - W^2}}{2} + C$$

W = NOMINAL KEY WIDTH (INCHES OR MILLIMETERS)

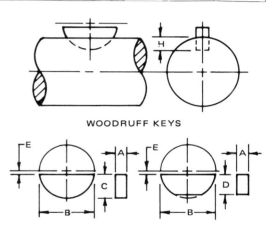

WOODRUFF KEYS

| U.S. CUSTOMARY (INCHES) | | | | | METRIC (MILLIMETERS) | | | | | |
| Nominal Size | Key | | | Keyseat | Key No. | Nominal Size | Key | | | Keyseat |
A × B	E	C	D	H		A × B	E	C	D	H
.062 × .500	.047	.203	.194	.172	204	1.6 × 12.7	1.5	5.1	4.8	4.2
.094 × .500	.047	.203	.194	.156	304	2.4 × 12.7	1.3	5.1	4.8	3.8
.094 × .625	.062	.250	.240	.203	305	2.4 × 15.9	1.5	6.4	6.1	5.1
.125 × .500	.049	.203	.194	.141	404	3.2 × 12.7	1.3	5.1	4.8	3.6
.125 × .625	.062	.250	.240	.188	405	3.2 × 15.9	1.5	6.4	6.1	4.6
.125 × .750	.062	.313	.303	.251	406	3.2 × 19.1	1.5	7.9	7.6	6.4
.156 × .625	.062	.250	.240	.172	505	4.0 × 15.9	1.5	6.4	6.1	4.3
.156 × .750	.062	.313	.303	.235	506	4.0 × 19.1	1.5	7.9	7.6	5.8
.156 × .875	.062	.375	.365	.297	507	4.0 × 22.2	1.5	9.7	9.1	7.4
.188 × .750	.062	.313	.303	.219	606	4.8 × 19.1	1.5	7.9	7.6	5.3
.188 × .875	.062	.375	.365	.281	607	4.8 × 22.2	1.5	9.7	9.1	7.1
.188 × 1.000	.062	.438	.428	.344	608	4.8 × 25.4	1.5	11.2	10.9	8.6
.188 × 1.125	.078	.484	.475	.390	609	4.8 × 28.6	2.0	12.2	11.9	9.9
.250 × .875	.062	.375	.365	.250	807	6.4 × 22.2	1.5	9.7	9.1	6.4
.250 × 1.000	.062	.438	.428	.313	808	6.4 × 25.4	1.5	11.2	10.9	7.9

Table 25 Woodruff keys.

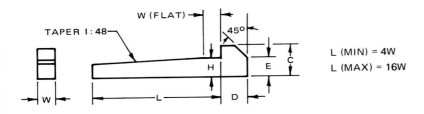

TAPER I:48

W (FLAT)

45°

H   E   C

L (MIN) = 4W
L (MAX) = 16W

W   L   D

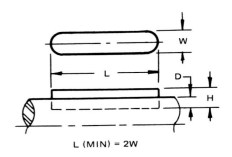

W
L
D
H

L (MIN) = 2W

U.S. CUSTOMARY (INCHES)										
Shaft Diameter	Square Type					Flat Type				
	W	H	C	D	E	W	H	C	D	E
.500–.562	.125	.125	.250	.219	.156	.125	.094	.188	.125	.125
.625–.875	.188	.188	.312	.281	.219	.188	.125	.250	.188	.156
.938–1.250	.250	.250	.438	.344	.344	.250	.188	.312	.250	.188
1.312–1.375	.312	.312	.562	.406	.406	.312	.250	.375	.312	.250
1.438–1.750	.375	.375	.688	.469	.469	.375	.250	.438	.375	.312
1.812–2.250	.500	.500	.875	.594	.625	.500	.375	.625	.500	.438
2.312–2.750	.625	.625	1.062	.719	.750	.625	.438	.750	.625	.500
2.875–3.250	.750	.750	1.250	.875	.875	.750	.500	.875	.750	.625

METRIC (MILLIMETERS)										
Shaft Diameter	Square Type					Flat Type				
	W	H	C	D	E	W	H	C	D	E
12–14	3.2	3.2	6.4	5.4	4	3.2	2.4	5	3.2	3.2
16–22	4.8	4.8	10	7	5.4	4.8	3.2	6.4	5	4
24–32	6.4	6.4	11	8.6	8.6	6.4	5	8	6.4	5
34–35	8	8	14	10	10	8	6.4	10	8	6.4
36–44	10	10	18	12	12	10	6.4	11	10	8
46–58	13	13	22	15	16	13	10	16	13	11
60–70	16	16	27	19	20	16	11	20	16	13
72–82	20	20	32	22	22	20	13	22	20	16

Note: Metric standards governing key sizes were not available at the time of publication. The sizes given in the above chart are "soft conversion" from current standards and are not representative of the precise metric key sizes which may be available in the future. Metric sizes are given only to allow the student to complete the drawing assignment.

Table 26   Square and flat gib-head keys.

U.S. CUSTOMARY (INCHES)				
Key No.	L	W	H	D
2	.500	.094	.141	.094
4	.625	.094	.141	.094
6	.625	.156	.234	.156
8	.750	.156	.234	.156
10	.875	.156	.234	.156
12	.875	.234	.328	.219
14	1.00	.234	.328	.234
16	1.125	.188	.281	.188
18	1.125	.250	.375	.250
20	1.250	.219	.328	.219
22	1.375	.250	.375	.250
24	1.50	.250	.375	.250
26	2.00	.188	.281	.188
28	2.00	.312	.469	.312
30	3.00	.375	.562	.375
32	3.00	.500	.750	.500
34	3.00	.625	.938	.625

METRIC (MILLIMETERS)				
Key No.	L	W	H	D
2	12	2.4	3.6	2.4
4	16	2.4	3.6	2.4
6	16	4	6	4
8	20	4	6	4
10	22	4	6	4
12	22	6	8.4	7
14	25	6	8.4	6
16	28	5	7	5
18	28	6.4	10	6.4
20	32	7	8	5
22	35	6.4	10	6.4
24	38	6.4	10	6.4
26	50	5	7	5
28	50	8	12	8
30	75	10	14	10
32	75	12	20	12
34	75	16	24	16

Table 27   Pratt and Whitney keys.

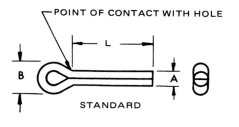

STANDARD

POINT OF CONTACT WITH HOLE

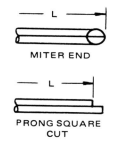

MITER END

PRONG SQUARE CUT

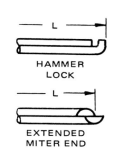

HAMMER LOCK

EXTENDED MITER END

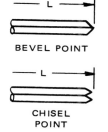

BEVEL POINT

CHISEL POINT

U.S. CUSTOMARY (INCHES)				METRIC (MILLIMETERS)			
Nominal Bolt or Thread Size Range	Nominal Cotter-Pin Size (A)	Cotter-Pin Hole	Min. End Clearance*	Nominal Bolt or Thread-Size Range	Nominal Cotter-Pin Size (A)	Cotter-Pin Hole	Min. End Clearance*
.125	.031	.047	.06	−2.5	0.6	0.8	1.5
.188	.047	.062	.08	2.5−3.5	0.8	1.0	2.0
.250	.062	.078	.11	3.5−4.5	1.0	1.2	2.0
.312	.078	.094	.11	4.5−5.5	1.2	1.4	2.5
.375	.094	.109	.14	5.5−7.0	1.6	1.8	2.5
.438	.109	.125	.14	7.0−9.0	2.0	2.2	3.0
.500	.125	.141	.18	9.0−11	2.5	2.8	3.5
.562	.141	.156	.25	11−14	3.2	3.6	5
.625	.156	.172	.40	14−20	4	4.5	6
1.000−1.125	.188	.203	.40	20−27	5	5.6	7
1.250−1.375	.219	.234	.46	27−39	6.3	6.7	10
1.500−1.625	.250	.266	.46	39−56	8.0	8.5	15
				56−80	10	10.5	20

*End of bolt to center of hole

Table 28   Cotter pins.

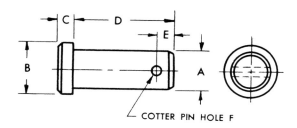

COTTER PIN HOLE F

U.S. CUSTOMARY (INCHES)						METRIC (MILLIMETERS)					
Pin Dia A	B	C	Min. D	E	Drill Size F	Pin Dia. A	B	C	Min. D	E	Drill Size F
.188	.31	.06	.59	.11	.078	4	6	1	16	2.2	1
.250	.38	.09	.80	.12	.078	6	10	2	20	3.2	1.6
.312	.44	.09	.97	.16	.109	8	14	3	24	3.5	2
.375	.50	.12	1.09	.16	.109	10	18	4	28	4.5	3.2
.500	.62	.16	1.42	.22	.141	12	20	4	36	5.5	3.2
.625	.81	.20	1.72	.25	.141	16	25	4.5	44	6	4
.750	.94	.25	2.05	.30	.172	20	30	5	52	8	5
1.000	1.19	.34	2.62	.36	.172	24	36	6	66	9	6.3

Table 29   Clevis pins.

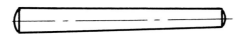

Taper pins

U.S. CUSTOMARY (INCHES)

NUMBER	7/0	6/0	5/0	4/0	3/0	2/0	0	1	2	3	4	5	6	7	8	9
SIZE (LARGE END)	.062	.078	.094	.109	.125	.141	.152	.172	.193	.219	.250	.289	.314	.409	.492	.591
LENGTH																
.375	X	X														
.500	X	X	X	X	X	X	X									
.625	X	X	X	X	X	X	X									
.750		X	X	X	X	X	X	X	X	X						
.875						X	X	X	X	X						
1.000			X	X	X	X	X	X	X	X	X	X	X			
1.250						X	X	X	X	X	X	X	X	X		
1.500							X	X	X	X	X	X	X	X		
1.750								X	X	X	X	X	X	X		
2.000								X	X	X	X	X	X	X	X	
2.250									X	X	X	X	X	X	X	
2.500									X	X	X	X	X	X	X	
2.750										X	X	X	X	X	X	X

METRIC (MILLIMETERS)

NUMBER	7/0	6/0	5/0	4/0	3/0	2/0	0	1	2	3	4	5	6	7	8	9
SIZE (LARGE END)	1.6	2	2.4	2.8	3.2	3.6	4	4.4	4.9	5.6	6.4	7.4	8	10.4	12.5	15
LENGTH																
10	X	X														
12	X	X	X	X	X	X	X									
16	X	X	X	X	X	X	X									
20		X	X	X	X	X	X	X	X	X						
22					X	X	X	X	X							
25			X	X	X	X	X	X	X	X	X	X				
30						X	X	X	X	X	X	X	X			
40							X	X	X	X	X	X	X			
45								X	X	X	X	X	X			
50								X	X	X	X	X	X	X	X	
55									X	X	X	X	X	X	X	
65									X	X	X	X	X	X	X	
70										X	X	X	X	X	X	X

Table 30 Taper pins.

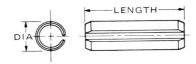

Spring pins

PIN DIAMETER (INCHES)

Length	.062	.094	.125	.156	.188	.250	.312
.250	X	X					
.375	X	X	X				
.500	X	X	X	X	X		
.625	X	X	X	X	X	X	
.750	X	X	X	X	X	X	X
.875	X	X	X	X	X	X	X
1.00	X	X	X	X	X	X	X
1.250		X	X	X	X	X	X
1.500		X	X	X	X	X	X
1.750		X	X	X	X	X	X
2.000		X	X	X	X	X	X
2.225			X	X	X	X	X
2.500				X	X	X	X
3.000						X	X
3.500						X	X

PIN DIAMETER (MILLIMETERS)

Length	1.5	2	2.5	3	4	5	6	8	10	12
5	X	X								
10	X	X	X	X						
15	X	X	X	X	X	X				
20	X	X	X	X	X	X	X			
25	X	X	X	X	X	X	X	X		
30		X	X	X	X	X	X	X	X	X
35		X	X	X	X	X	X	X	X	X
40		X	X	X	X	X	X	X	X	X
45			X	X	X	X	X	X	X	X
50			X	X	X	X	X	X	X	X
55				X	X	X	X	X	X	X
60				X	X	X	X	X	X	X
70							X	X	X	X
75							X	X	X	X
80							X	X	X	X

Table 31 Spring pins.

A		A3		B		C			D			E			U

	U.S. CUSTOMARY (INCHES)								METRIC (MILLIMETERS)								
	PIN DIAMETER									PIN DIAMETER							
Length	.09	.125	.188	.250	.312	.375	.500	Length	2	3	4	5	6	8	10	12
.250	X	X						5	X	X	X					
.375	X	X	X					10	X	X	X	X	X			
.500	X	X	X	X				15	X	X	X	X	X	X		
.625	X	X	X	X	X			20	X	X	X	X	X	X	X	
.750	X	X	X	X	X	X		25	X	X	X	X	X	X	X	X
.875	X	X	X	X	X	X		30	X	X	X	X	X	X	X	X
1.000	X	X	X	X	X	X	X	35		X	X	X	X	X	X	X
1.250	X	X	X	X	X	X	X	40			X	X	X	X	X	X
1.500		X	X	X	X	X	X	45				X	X	X	X	X
1.750			X	X	X	X	X	50				X	X	X	X	X
2.000			X	X	X	X	X	55					X	X	X	X
2.250			X	X	X	X	X	60					X	X	X	X
2.275				X	X	X	X	65					X	X	X	X
3.000				X	X	X	X	70						X	X	X
								75						X	X	X

Note: Metric size pins were not available at the time of publication. Sizes were soft converted to allow students to complete drawing assignments.

Table 32 Groove pins.

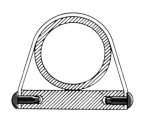

WIDELY USED FOR
FASTENING BRACKETS

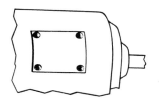

ATTACHING NAMEPLATES,
INSTRUCTION PANELS

	U.S. CUSTOMARY (INCHES)										METRIC (MILLIMETERS)							
STUD NUMBER	SHANK DIA.	DRILL SIZE	HEAD DIA.	STANDARD LENGTHS						STUD NUMBER	SHANK DIA.	DRILL SIZE	HEAD DIA.	STANDARD LENGTHS				
				.125	.188	.250	.312	.375	.500					4	6	8	10	12	14
0	.067	51	.130	●	●	●				0	1.7	1.7	3.3	●	●	●			
2	.086	44	.162	●	●	●				2	2.2	2.2	4.1	●	●	●			
4	.104	37	.211		●	●	●			4	2.6	2.6	5.4		●	●	●		
6	.120	31	.260			●	●	●		6	3.0	3.0	6.6			●	●	●	
7	.136	29	.309				●	●	●	7	3.4	3.4	7.8				●	●	●
8	.144	27	.309					●	●	8	3.8	3.8	7.8					●	●
10	.161	20	.359					●	●	10	4.1	4.1	9.1					●	●
12	.196	9	.408						●	12	5.0	5.0	10.4						●
14	.221	2	.457						●	14	5.6	5.6	11.6						●
16	.250	¼	.472						●	16	6.3	6.3	12						●

Note: Metric size studs were not available at the time of publication. Sizes were soft converted to allow students to complete drawing assignments.

Table 33 Grooved studs. (Drive-Lok)

Use these columns first to locate your correct GRIP LENGTH

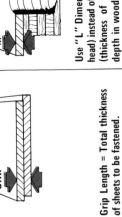

Grip = Total thickness of all sheets fastened together

Minimum Grip	Nominal Grip	Maximum Grip
1	2	3
2	3	4
4	5	6
5	6	7
7	8	9
9	10	11
11	12	13
13	14	15
15	16	17
19	20	21
23	24	25
27	28	29

.125in. (3mm) Dia Part Numbers

Length Under Head L	Universal Head	100° Csk Head	Full Brazier Head
5	✓	✓	✓
6	✓	✓	✓
8	✓	✓	✓
10	✓	✓	✓
12	✓	✓	✓
14	✓	✓	✓
16	✓		
18			
20			
24			
28			
32			

.156in. (4mm) Dia Part Numbers

Length Under Head L	Universal Head	100° Csk Head
5	✓	
6	✓	✓
8	✓	✓
10	✓	✓
12	✓	✓
14	✓	✓
16	✓	✓
18	✓	✓
20	✓	✓
24		
28		
32		

.188in. (5mm) Dia Part Numbers

Length Under Head L	Universal Head	100° Csk Head	Full Brazier Head	All Purpose Liner Head
5	✓		✓	✓
6	✓		✓	✓
8	✓	✓	✓	✓
10	✓	✓	✓	✓
12	✓	✓	✓	✓
14	✓	✓	✓	✓
16	✓	✓	✓	✓
18	✓	✓	✓	✓
20	✓	✓	✓	✓
24	✓	✓	✓	✓
28	✓		✓	
32	✓			

.250in. (6mm) Dia Part Numbers

Length Under Head L	Universal Head	100° Csk Head	Full Brazier Head
5	✓	✓	✓
6	✓	✓	✓
8	✓	✓	✓
10	✓	✓	✓
12	✓	✓	✓
14	✓	✓	✓
16	✓	✓	✓
18	✓	✓	✓
20	✓	✓	✓
24	✓	✓	✓
28	✓	✓	✓
32	✓	✓	✓

Note: Metric drive rivets were not available at the time of publication. Sizes were soft converted to allow students to complete drawing assignments.

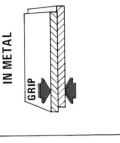

HIT THE PIN

Drive pin flush with rivet head

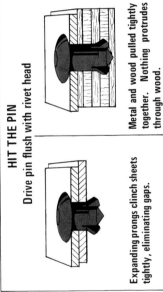

Expanding prongs clinch sheets tightly, eliminating gaps.

Metal and wood pulled tightly together. Nothing protrudes through wood.

IN METAL

GRIP

Grip Length = Total thickness of sheets to be fastened.

IN WOOD

Use "L" Dimension (length under head) instead of grip length. L = M (thickness of metal) + D (hole depth in wood).

Southco Lion Fasteners

Table 34 Aluminum drive rivets.

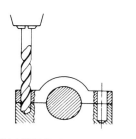

DRILL HOLE SLIGHTLY UNDERSIZE

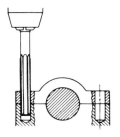

REAM FULL SIZE

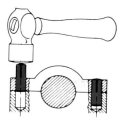

DRIVE OR PRESS LOK DOWELS INTO PLACE

LOK DOWELS LOCK SECURELY AND PARTS SEPARATE EASILY

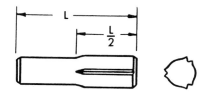

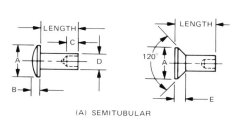

(A) SEMITUBULAR

(B) SPLIT

U.S. CUSTOMARY (INCHES)							METRIC (MILLIMETERS)						
	DIAMETER							DIAMETER					
LENGTH	.125	.188	.250	.312	.375	.500	LENGTH	4	6	8	10	12	14
.375	•						10	•					
.500	•	•	•	•			12	•	•	•			
.625	•	•	•	•			16	•	•	•	•		
.750	•	•	•	•	•		20	•	•	•	•	•	
.875	•	•	•	•	•		22	•	•	•	•	•	
1.000	•			•	•	•	26	•	•	•	•	•	•
1.250		•		•	•	•	32		•	•	•	•	•
1.500					•	•	38			•	•	•	•
1.750				•	•	•	44				•	•	•
2.000				•	•	•	50				•	•	•

Note: Metric size dowels were not available at the time of publication. Sizes were soft converted to allow students to complete drawing assignments.

Table 35   Lok dowels. (Drive-Lok)

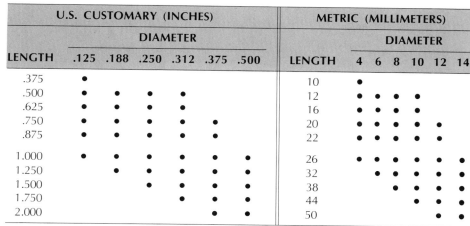

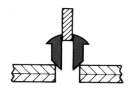

	D	A	B	C	E	MIN. LENGTH
U.S. CUSTOMARY (INCHES)	.062	.125	.031	.062	—	.062
	.094	.156	.031	.062	.031	.078
	.109	.188	.031	.078	—	.078
	.125	.218	.047	.109	.049	.109
	.141	.250	.047	.125	.049	.125
	.188	.312	.062	.141	.062	.156
	.219	.438	.062	.188	.062	.188
	.250	.500	.078	.219	.094	.219
	.312	.562	.109	.250		.250
METRIC (MILLIMETERS)	1.5	2.8	0.4	1.2		1.6
	2.2	3.7	0.6	1.6	0.8	2.0
	2.5	4.7	0.7	2.0		2.0
	3.1	5.5	0.9	2.4	1.0	2.4
	3.6	5.9	1.0	3.2	1.2	3.2
	4.7	7.9	1.5	3.9	1.6	4.0
	5.4	11.1	1.7	4.8	1.8	4.8
	6.3	12.7	2.0	5.6	2.2	5.6
	7.7	14.3	2.4	6.2		6.4

Table 36   Semi-tubular and split rivets.

U.S. CUSTOMARY (INCHES)				METRIC (MILLIMETERS)			
HOLE DIA.	PANEL RANGE	HEAD Dia.	Height	HOLE DIA.	PANEL RANGE	HEAD Dia.	Height
.125	.031–.140	.188	.047	3.18	0.8– 3.6	4.8	1.2
	.031–.125	.218	.062		0.8– 3.2	5.5	1.5
.156	.250–.375	.218	.047	4.01	5.9– 9.4	5.5	1.3
.188	.062–.156	.375	.125	4.75	1.6– 4.0	9.5	3.2
	.156–.281	.438	.094		4.0– 7.1	11.1	1.9
.219	.062–.125	.375	.094	5.54	1.6– 3.2	9.5	2.4
	.094–.312		.078		2.4– 8.0		2.0
.250	.094–.219	.625	.125	6.35	2.3– 5.6	16	3.2
	.125–.375	.750	.062		3.2– 9.5	19	1.3
.297	.140–.328	.500	.078	7.14	3.4– 8.1	12.3	1.9
.375	.250–.500	.438	.109	9.53	6.4–12.7	11.1	2.6
.500	.312–.375	.750	.109	12.7	8.1– 9.4	19	2.5

Table 37   Plastic rivets.

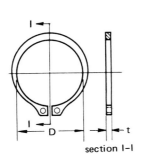

section I-I

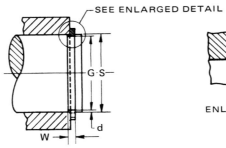

SEE ENLARGED DETAIL

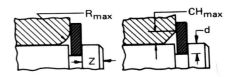

ENLARGED DETAIL OF GROOVE PROFILE
AND EDGE MARGIN (Z)

| | SHAFT DIA. | EXTERNAL SERIES | RETAINING RING DIMENSIONS | | GROOVE DIMENSIONS | | | | MAX. CORNER RADII AND CHAMFER OF RETAINED PARTS | | EDGE MARGIN | NOMINAL GROOVE DEPTH (REF) |
| | | | | | DIAMETER | | WIDTH | | | | | |
	S	Size—No.	D	t	G	Tol.	W	Tol.	R Max.	Ch. Max.	z	d
U.S. CUSTOMARY (INCHES)	.188	5100-18	.168	.015	.175	±.0015	.018	+.002	.014	.008	.018	.006
	.250	5100-25	.225	.025	.230	±.0015	.029	+.003	.018	.011	.030	.010
	.312	5100-31	.281	.025	.290	±.002	.029	+.003	.020	.012	.033	.011
	.375	5100-37	.338	.025	.352	±.002	.029	+.003	.026	.015	.036	.012
	.500	5100-50	.461	.035	.468	±.002	.039	+.003	.034	.020	.048	.016
	.625	5100-62	.579	.035	.588	±.003	.039	+.003	.041	.025	.055	.018
	.750	5100-75	.693	.042	.704	±.003	.046	+.003	.046	.027	.069	.023
	.875	5100-87	.810	.042	.821	±.003	.046	+.003	.051	.031	.081	.027
	1.000	5100-100	.925	.042	.940	±.003	.046	+.003	.057	.034	.090	.030
	1.125	5100-112	1.041	.050	1.059	±.004	.056	+.004	.063	.038	.099	.033
	1.250	5100-125	1.156	.050	1.176	±.004	.056	+.004	.068	.041	.111	.037
	1.375	5100-137	1.272	.050	1.291	±.004	.056	+.004	.072	.043	.126	.042
	1.500	5100-150	1.387	.050	1.406	±.004	.056	+.004	.079	.047	.141	.047
METRIC (MILLIMETERS)	4	M5100-4	3.6	0.25	3.80	−0.08	0.32	+0.05	0.35	0.25	0.3	0.10
	6	M5100-6	5.5	0.4	5.70	−0.08	0.5	+0.1	0.35	0.25	0.5	0.15
	8	M5100-8	7.2	0.6	7.50	−0.1	0.7	+0.15	0.5	0.35	0.8	0.25
	10	M5100-10	9.0	0.6	9.40	−0.1	0.7	+0.15	0.7	0.4	0.9	0.30
	12	M5100-12	10.9	0.6	11.35	−0.12	0.7	+0.15	0.8	0.45	1.0	0.33
	14	M5100-14	12.9	0.9	13.25	−0.12	1.0	+0.15	0.9	0.5	1.2	0.38
	16	M5100-16	14.7	0.9	15.10	−0.15	1.0	+0.15	1.1	0.6	1.4	0.45
	18	M5100-18	16.7	1.1	17.00	−0.15	1.2	+0.15	1.2	0.7	1.5	0.50
	20	M5100-20	18.4	1.1	18.85	−0.15	1.2	+0.15	1.2	0.7	1.7	0.58
	22	M5100-22	20.3	1.1	20.70	−0.15	1.2	+0.15	1.3	0.8	1.9	0.65
	24	M5100-24	22.2	1.1	22.60	−0.15	1.2	+0.15	1.4	0.8	2.1	0.70
	25	M5100-25	23.1	1.1	23.50	−0.15	1.2	+0.15	1.4	0.8	2.3	0.75
	30	M5100-30	27.9	1.3	28.35	−0.2	1.4	+0.15	1.6	1.0	2.5	0.83
	35	M5100-35	32.3	1.3	32.9	−0.2	1.4	+0.15	1.8	1.1	3.1	1.05
	40	M5100-40	36.8	1.6	37.7	−0.3	1.75	+0.2	2.1	1.2	3.4	1.15
	45	M5100-45	41.6	1.6	42.4	−0.3	1.75	+0.2	2.3	1.4	3.9	1.3
	50	M5100-50	46.2	1.6	47.2	−0.3	1.75	+0.2	2.4	1.4	4.2	1.4

Table 38 **Retaining rings—external.** (ⓒ 1965, 1958 Waldes Koh-i-noor, Inc. Reprinted with permission.)

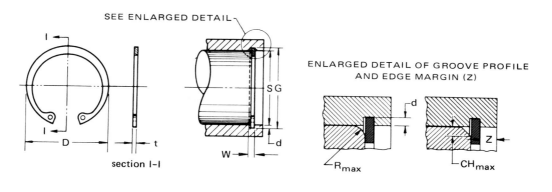

SEE ENLARGED DETAIL

section I-I

ENLARGED DETAIL OF GROOVE PROFILE
AND EDGE MARGIN (Z)

	HOUSING DIA.	INTERNAL SERIES	RETAINING RING DIMENSIONS		GROOVE DIMENSIONS				MAX. CORNER RADII AND CHAMFER OF RETAINED PARTS		EDGE MARGIN	NOMINAL GROOVE DEPTH
					DIAMETER		WIDTH					
	S	Size—No.	D	t	G	Tol.	W	Tol.	R Max.	Ch. Max.	z	d
U.S. CUSTOMARY (INCHES)	.250	N5000-25	.280	.015	.268	±.001	.018	+.002	.011	.008	.027	.009
	.312	N5000-31	.346	.015	.330	±.001	.018	+.002	.016	.013	.027	.009
	.375	N5000-37	.415	.025	.397	±.002	.029	+.003	.023	.018	.033	.011
	.500	N5000-50	.548	.035	.530	±.002	.039	+.003	.027	.021	.045	.015
	.625	N5000-62	.694	.035	.665	±.002	.039	+.003	.027	.021	.060	.020
	.750	N5000-75	.831	.035	.796	±.002	.039	+.003	.032	.025	.069	.023
	.875	N5000-87	.971	.042	.931	±.003	.046	+.003	.035	.028	.084	.028
	1.000	N5000-100	1.111	.042	1.066	±.003	.046	+.003	.042	.034	.099	.033
	1.125	N5000-112	1.249	.050	1.197	±.004	.056	+.004	.047	.036	.108	.036
	1.250	N5000-125	1.388	.050	1.330	±.004	.056	+.004	.048	.038	.120	.040
	1.375	N5000-137	1.526	.050	1.461	±.004	.056	+.004	.048	.038	.129	.043
	1.500	N5000-150	1.660	.050	1.594	±.004	.056	+.004	.048	.038	.141	.047
METRIC (MILLIMETERS)	8	MN5000-8	8.80	0.4	8.40	+0.6	0.5	+0.1	0.4	0.3	0.6	0.2
	10	MN5000-10	11.10	0.6	10.50	+0.1	0.7	+0.15	0.5	0.35	0.8	0.25
	12	MN5000-12	13.30	0.6	12.65	+0.1	0.7	+0.15	0.6	0.4	1.0	0.33
	14	MN5000-14	15.45	0.9	14.80	+0.1	1.0	+0.15	0.7	0.5	1.2	0.40
	16	MN5000-16	17.70	0.9	16.90	+0.1	1.0	+0.15	0.7	0.5	1.4	0.45
	18	MN5000-18	20.05	0.9	19.05	+0.1	1.0	+0.15	0.75	0.6	1.6	0.53
	20	MN5000-20	22.25	0.9	21.15	+0.15	1.0	+0.15	0.9	0.7	1.7	0.57
	22	MN5000-22	24.40	1.1	23.30	+0.15	1.2	+0.15	0.9	0.7	1.9	0.65
	24	MN5000-24	26.55	1.1	25.4	+0.15	1.2	+0.15	1.0	0.8	2.1	0.70
	25	MN5000-25	27.75	1.1	26.6	+0.15	1.2	+0.15	1.0	0.8	2.4	0.80
	30	MN5000-30	33.40	1.3	31.9	+0.2	1.4	+0.15	1.2	1.0	2.9	0.95
	35	MN5000-35	38.75	1.3	37.2	+0.2	1.4	+0.15	1.2	1.0	3.3	1.10
	40	MN5000-40	44.25	1.6	42.4	+0.2	1.75	+0.2	1.7	1.3	3.6	1.20
	45	MN5000-45	49.95	1.6	47.6	+0.2	1.75	+0.2	1.7	1.3	3.9	1.30
	50	MN5000-50	55.35	1.6	53.1	+0.2	1.75	+0.2	1.7	1.3	4.6	1.55

Table 39   Retaining rings—internal. (© 1965, 1958 Waldes Koh-i-noor, Inc. Reprinted with permission.)

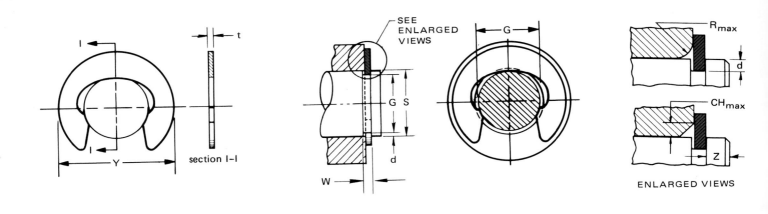

	SHAFT DIA.	EXTERNAL SERIES 11-410	RETAINING RING DIMENSIONS		GROOVE DIMENSIONS					MAXIMUM ALLOWABLE CORNER RADII AND CHAMFER OF RETAINED PARTS		EDGE MARGIN	NOMINAL GROOVE DEPTH (REF)
					Diameter		Width						
	S	Size—No.	Y	t	G	Tol.	W	Tol.	R Max.	Ch. Max.	z	d
U.S. CUSTOMARY (INCHES)	.250	11-410-25	.311	.025	.222	−.004	.029	+.003	.023	.018	.030	.015
	.312	11-410-31	.376	.025	.278	−.004	.029	+.003	.024	.018	.036	.018
	.375	11-410-37	.448	.025	.337	−.004	.029	+.003	.026	.020	.040	.020
	.500	11-410-50	.581	.025	.453	−.006	.039	+.003	.030	.023	.050	.025
	.625	11-410-62	.715	.035	.566	−.006	.039	+.003	.033	.025	.062	.031
	.750	11-410-75	.845	.042	.679	−.006	.046	+.003	.036	.027	.074	.037
	.875	11-410-87	.987	.042	.792	−.006	.046	+.003	.040	.031	.086	.043
	1.000	11-410-100	1.127	.042	.903	−.006	.046	+.003	.046	.035	.100	.050
	1.125	11-410-112	1.267	.050	1.017	−.008	.056	+.004	.052	.040	.112	.056
	1.250	11-410-125	1.410	.050	1.130	−.008	.056	+.004	.057	.044	.124	.062
	1.375	11-410-137	1.550	.050	1.241	−.008	.056	+.004	.062	.048	.138	.069
	1.500	11-410-150	1.691	.050	1.354	−.008	.056	+.004	.069	.053	.150	.075
	1.750	11-410-175	1.975	.062	1.581	−.010	.068	+.004	.081	.062	.174	.087
	2.000	11-410-200	2.257	.062	1.805	−.010	.068	+.004	.091	.070	.200	.100
METRIC (MILLIMETERS)	8	11-410-080	10	0.6	7	−0.1	0.7	+0.15	0.6	0.45	1.5	0.5
	10	11-410-100	12.2	0.6	9	−0.1	0.7	+0.15	0.6	0.45	1.5	0.5
	12	11-410-120	14.4	0.6	10.9	−0.1	0.7	+0.15	0.6	0.45	1.7	0.5
	14	11-410-140	16.3	1	12.7	−0.1	1.1	+0.15	1	0.8	2	0.65
	16	11-410-160	18.5	1	14.5	−0.1	1.1	+0.15	1	0.8	2.3	0.75
	18	11-410-180	20.4	1.2	16.3	−0.1	1.3	+0.15	1.2	0.9	2.6	0.85
	20	11-410-200	22.6	1.2	18.1	−0.2	1.3	+0.15	1.2	0.9	2.9	0.95
	22	11-410-220	25	1.2	19.9	−0.2	1.3	+0.15	1.2	0.9	3.2	1.05
	24	11-410-240	27.1	1.2	21.7	−0.2	1.3	+0.15	1.2	0.9	3.5	1.15
	25	11-410-250	28.3	1.2	22.6	−0.2	1.3	+0.15	1.2	0.9	3.6	1.2
	30	11-410-300	33.7	1.5	27	−0.2	1.3	+0.2	1.5	1.15	4.5	1.5
	35	11-410-350	39.4	1.5	31.5	−0.25	1.6	+0.2	1.5	1.15	5.3	1.75
	40	11-410-400	45	1.5	36	−0.25	1.6	+0.2	1.5	1.15	6	2
	45	11-410-450	50.6	1.5	40.5	−0.25	1.6	+0.2	1.5	1.15	6.8	2.25
	50	11-410-500	56.4	2	45	−0.25	2.2	+0.2	2	1.5	7.5	2.5

Table 40　**Retaining rings—radial assembly.** (© 1965, 1958 Waldes Koh-i-noor, Inc. Reprinted with permission.)

MORSE TAPERS

| No. of Taper | TAPER | |
	inches per Foot	mm per 100 mm
0	.625	5.21
1	.599	4.99
2	.599	4.99
3	.602	5.02
4	.623	5.19
5	.631	5.26
6	.626	5.22
7	.624	5.20

BROWN AND SHARPE TAPERS

| No. of Taper | TAPER | |
	inches per Foot	mm per 100 mm
1	.502	4.18
2	.502	4.18
3	.502	4.18
4	.502	4.18
5	.502	4.18
6	.503	4.19
7	.502	4.18
8	.501	4.18
9	.501	4.18
10	.516	4.3
11	.501	4.18
12	.500	4.17
13	.500	4.17
14	.500	4.17
15	.500	4.17
16	.500	4.17

Table 41 Machine tapers.

PRODUCT	OUTSTANDING FEATURES	APPLICATION METHOD	COLOR
1357	A high performance adhesive with long bonding range, excellent initial strength. Meets specification requirements of MMM-A-121 (supersedes MIL-A-1154 C), MIL-A-5092 B, Type II, and MIL-A-21366. Bonds rubber, cloth, wood, foamed glass, paper honeycomb, decorative plastic laminates. Also used with metal-to-metal for bonds of moderate strength.	Spray or Brush	Gray/ Green or Olive
2210	Fast drying, exhibits aggressive tack that allows coated surfaces to knit easily under hand roller pressure. Excellent water and oil resistance. Meets specification requirements of MMM-A-121 (supersedes MIL-A-1154 C), MIL-A-21366, and MMM-A-00130a. Bonds a wide range of materials including rubber, leather, cloth, aluminum, wood, hardboard. Used extensively for bonding decorative plastic laminates.	Brush, Roller, or Trowel	Yellow
2215	Fast drying and has a rapid rate of strength build-up. Its aggressive tack permits adhesive coated surfaces to bond easily with moderate pressure. Bonds decorative plastic laminates to metal, wood, and particle board. Also used for general bonding of rubber, leather, cloth, aluminum, wood, hardboard, etc.	Spray	Light Yellow
2218	Offers rapid strength build-up, high-ultimate strength. Has a high softening point and excellent resistance to plastic flow. Adhesion to steel is especially good. Meets specification requirements of MMM-A-121 (supersedes MIL-A-1154 C). Bonds high density decorative plastic laminates to metal or wood. Widely used to fabricate honeycomb and sandwich-type building panels with various face sheets, including porcelain enamel steel.	Spray	Green
2226	Water dispersed, has high immediate bond strength, long bonding range. Changes color from blue to green while drying. Used to bond foamed plastics, plastic laminate, wood, rubber, plywood, wallboard, wood veneer, plaster, and canvas to themselves and to each other.	Spray or Brush	Wet: Lt. Blue Dry: Green
4420	High performance, fast-drying adhesive designed for application by pressure curtain coating and mechanical roll coating. Bonds decorative plastic laminates to plywood or particle board and is suitable for conveyor line production of laminated panels of various types such as aluminum to wood or hardboard.	Roll Coating	Yellow
4488	Lower viscosity version of Cement 4420 for use specifically with flow-over or Weir-type curtain coaters. Bonds decorative plastic laminates to plywood or particle board and is suitable for conveyor line production of laminated panels of various types, such as aluminum to wood or hardboard.	Curtain and Roll Coating	Yellow
4518	Designed for spray application with automatic or production line equipment. Dries very fast, requires pressure from a niproll (rotary press) or platen press to assure proper bonding. Bonds decorative plastic laminates to plywood or particle board on both flat work and postforming. Also used for conveyor line production of laminated panels of various types such as aluminum to wood or hardboard. Meets requirements of MIL-A-5092 B, Type II.	Spray	Green
4729	Similar to Cement 2218 except that it is formulated with a nonflammable solvent. Requires force drying to prevent blushing.	Spray	Red
5034	Water dispersed, has high immediate bond strength and long bonding range. Bonds foamed plastics, plastic laminate, wood, rubber, plywood, wallboard, wood veneer, plaster, and canvas to themselves and to each other.	Spray or Brush	Neutral

Table 42 Physical properties and application data of adhesives. (3M Company.)

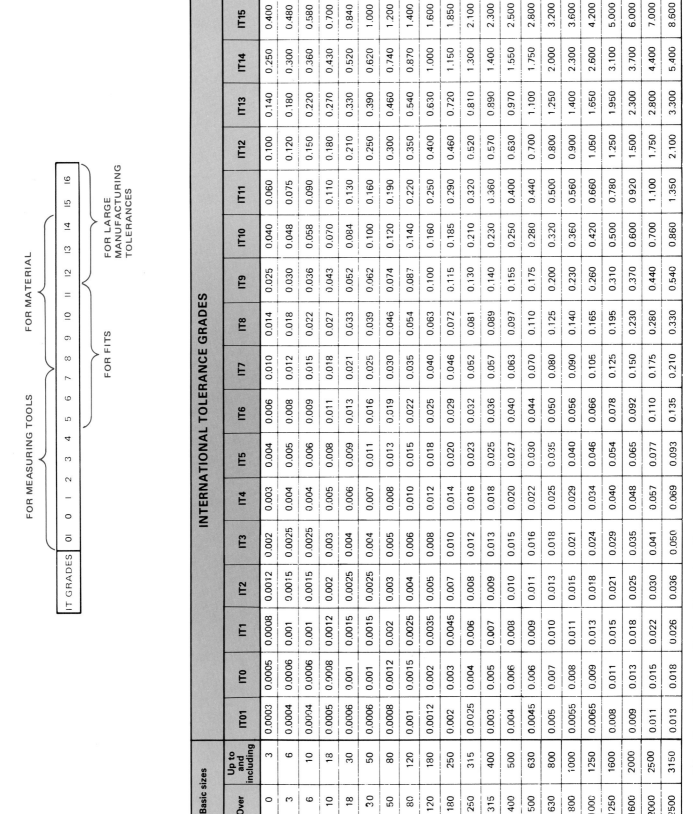

INTERNATIONAL TOLERANCE GRADES

IT GRADES	01	0	1	2	3	4	5	6	7	8	9	10	11	12	13	14	15	16

FOR MEASURING TOOLS — FOR FITS — FOR MATERIAL — FOR LARGE MANUFACTURING TOLERANCES

Basic sizes		IT01	IT0	IT1	IT2	IT3	IT4	IT5	IT6	IT7	IT8	IT9	IT10	IT11	IT12	IT13	IT14	IT15	IT16
Over	Up to and including																		
0	3	0.0003	0.0005	0.0008	0.0012	0.002	0.003	0.004	0.006	0.010	0.014	0.025	0.040	0.060	0.100	0.140	0.250	0.400	0.600
3	6	0.0004	0.0006	0.001	0.0015	0.0025	0.004	0.005	0.008	0.012	0.018	0.030	0.048	0.075	0.120	0.180	0.300	0.480	0.750
6	10	0.0004	0.0006	0.001	0.0015	0.0025	0.004	0.006	0.009	0.015	0.022	0.036	0.058	0.090	0.150	0.220	0.360	0.580	0.900
10	18	0.0005	0.0008	0.0012	0.002	0.003	0.005	0.008	0.011	0.018	0.027	0.043	0.070	0.110	0.180	0.270	0.430	0.700	1.100
18	30	0.0006	0.001	0.0015	0.0025	0.004	0.006	0.009	0.013	0.021	0.033	0.052	0.084	0.130	0.210	0.330	0.520	0.840	1.300
30	50	0.0006	0.001	0.0015	0.0025	0.004	0.007	0.011	0.016	0.025	0.039	0.062	0.100	0.160	0.250	0.390	0.620	1.000	1.600
50	80	0.0008	0.0012	0.002	0.003	0.005	0.008	0.013	0.019	0.030	0.046	0.074	0.120	0.190	0.300	0.460	0.740	1.200	1.900
80	120	0.001	0.0015	0.0025	0.004	0.006	0.010	0.015	0.022	0.035	0.054	0.087	0.140	0.220	0.350	0.540	0.870	1.400	2.200
120	180	0.0012	0.002	0.0035	0.005	0.008	0.012	0.018	0.025	0.040	0.063	0.100	0.160	0.250	0.400	0.630	1.000	1.600	2.500
180	250	0.002	0.003	0.0045	0.007	0.010	0.014	0.020	0.029	0.046	0.072	0.115	0.185	0.290	0.460	0.720	1.150	1.850	2.900
250	315	0.0025	0.004	0.006	0.008	0.012	0.016	0.023	0.032	0.052	0.081	0.130	0.210	0.320	0.520	0.810	1.300	2.100	3.200
315	400	0.003	0.005	0.007	0.009	0.013	0.018	0.025	0.036	0.057	0.089	0.140	0.230	0.360	0.570	0.890	1.400	2.300	3.600
400	500	0.004	0.006	0.008	0.010	0.015	0.020	0.027	0.040	0.063	0.097	0.155	0.250	0.400	0.630	0.970	1.550	2.500	4.000
500	630	0.0045	0.006	0.009	0.011	0.016	0.022	0.030	0.044	0.070	0.110	0.175	0.280	0.440	0.700	1.100	1.750	2.800	4.400
630	800	0.005	0.007	0.010	0.013	0.018	0.025	0.035	0.050	0.080	0.125	0.200	0.320	0.500	0.800	1.250	2.000	3.200	5.000
800	1000	0.0055	0.008	0.011	0.015	0.021	0.029	0.040	0.056	0.090	0.140	0.230	0.360	0.560	0.900	1.400	2.300	3.600	5.600
1000	1250	0.0065	0.009	0.013	0.018	0.024	0.034	0.046	0.066	0.105	0.165	0.260	0.420	0.660	1.050	1.650	2.600	4.200	6.600
1250	1600	0.008	0.011	0.015	0.021	0.029	0.040	0.054	0.078	0.125	0.195	0.310	0.500	0.780	1.250	1.950	3.100	5.000	7.800
1600	2000	0.009	0.013	0.018	0.025	0.035	0.048	0.065	0.092	0.150	0.230	0.370	0.600	0.920	1.500	2.300	3.700	6.000	9.200
2000	2500	0.011	0.015	0.022	0.030	0.041	0.057	0.077	0.110	0.175	0.280	0.440	0.700	1.100	1.750	2.800	4.400	7.000	11.000
2500	3150	0.013	0.018	0.026	0.036	0.050	0.069	0.093	0.135	0.210	0.330	0.540	0.860	1.350	2.100	3.300	5.400	8.600	13.500

Table 43   International Tolerance Grades. (Values in millimeters.)

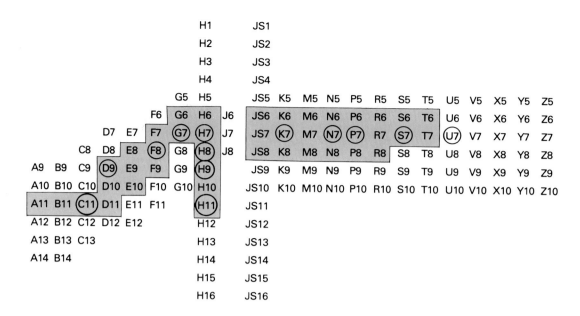

Legend: First choice tolerance zones encircled (ANSI B4.2 preferred)
Second choice tolerance zones framed (ISO 1829 selected)
Third choice tolerance zones open

TOLERANCE ZONES FOR INTERNAL DIMENSIONS (HOLES)

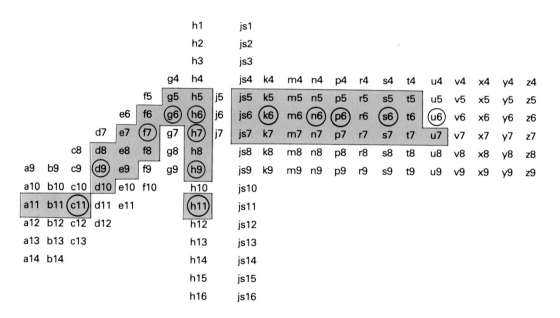

Legend: First choice tolerance zones encircled (ANSI B4.2 preferred)
Second choice tolerance zones framed (ISO 1829 selected)
Third choice tolerance zones open

TOLERANCE ZONES FOR EXTERNAL DIMENSIONS (SHAFTS)

Table 43 (cont'd.)   International Tolerance Grades.

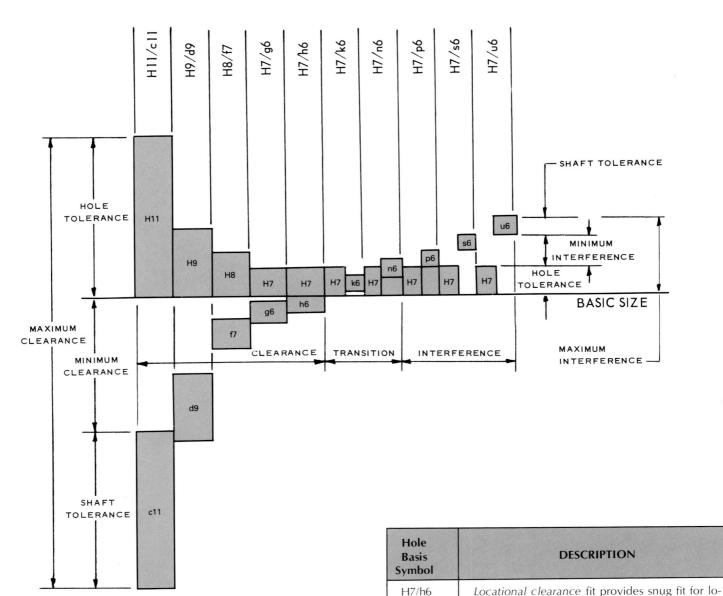

Hole Basis Symbol	DESCRIPTION
H11/c11	*Loose running* fit for wide commercial tolerances or allowances on external members.
H9/d9	*Free running* fit not for use where accuracy is essential, but good for large temperature variations, high running speeds, or heavy journal pressures.
H8/f7	*Close running* fit for running on accurate machines and for accurate location at moderate speeds and journal pressures.
H7/g6	*Sliding* fit not intended to run freely, but to move and turn freely and locate accurately.

Hole Basis Symbol	DESCRIPTION
H7/h6	*Locational clearance* fit provides snug fit for locating stationary parts; but can be freely assembled and disassembled.
H7/k6	*Locational transition* fit for accurate location, a compromise between clearance and interference.
H7/n6	*Locational transition* fit for more accurate location where greater interference is permissible.
H7/p6	*Locational interference* fit for parts requiring rigidity and alignment with prime accuracy of location but without special bore pressure requirements.
H7/s6	*Medium drive* fit for ordinary steel parts or shrink fits on light sections, the tightest fit usable with cast iron.
H7/u6	*Force* fit suitable for parts which can be highly stressed or for shrink fits where the heavy pressing forces required are impractical.

Table 44 Preferred hole basis fits description.

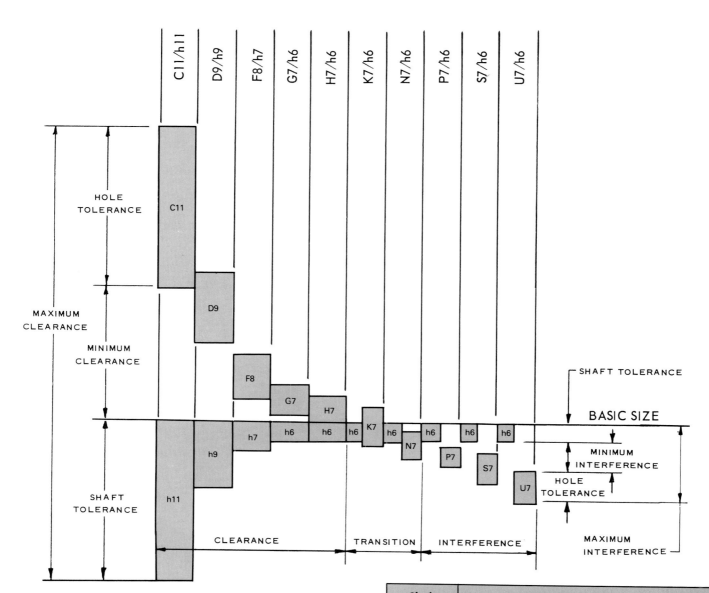

Shaft Basis Symbol	DESCRIPTION
C11/h11	*Loose running* fit for wide commercial tolerances or allowances on external members.
D9/h9	*Free running* fit not for use where accuracy is essential, but good for large temperature variations, high running speeds, or heavy journal pressures.
F8/h7	*Close running* fit for running on accurate machines and for accurate location at moderate speeds and journal pressures.
G7/h6	*Sliding* fit not intended to run freely, but to move and turn freely and locate accurately.
H7/h6	*Locational clearance* fit provides snug fit for locating stationary parts; but can be freely assembled and disassembled.

Shaft Basis Symbol	DESCRIPTION
K7/h6	*Locational transition* fit for accurate location, a compromise between clearance and interference.
N7/h6	*Locational transition* fit for more accurate location where greater interference is permissible.
P7/h6	*Locational interference* fit for parts requiring rigidity and alignment with prime accuracy of location but without special bore pressure requirements.
S7/h6	*Medium drive* fit for ordinary steel parts or shrink fits on light sections, the tightest fit usable with cast iron.
U7/h6	*Force* fit suitable for parts which can be highly stressed or for shrink fits where the heavy pressing forces required are impractical.

Table 45 **Preferred shaft basis fits description.**

EXAMPLE: RC2 SLIDING FIT FOR A
Ø1.50 NOMINAL HOLE DIAMETER — BASIC HOLE SYSTEM

Ø1.4996 — MAX SHAFT DIAMETER

SHAFT TOLERANCE .0004 — Ø1.4992 MIN SHAFT DIAMETER

MAX CLEARANCE .0014
MIN CLEARANCE .0004

HOLE TOLERANCE .0006 — Ø1.5000 — MIN HOLE DIAMETER
Ø1.5006 — MAX HOLE DIAMETER

Nominal Size Range Inches		Class RC1 Precision Sliding			Class RC2 Sliding Fit			Class RC3 Precision Running			Class RC4 Close Running		
		Hole Tol. GR5	Minimum Clearance	Shaft Tol. GR4	Hole Tol. GR6	Minimum Clearance	Shaft Tol. GR5	Hole Tol. GR7	Minimum Clearance	Shaft Tol. GR6	Hole Tol. GR8	Minimum Clearance	Shaft Tol. GR7
Over	To	−0		+0	−0		+0	−0		+0	−0		+0
0	.12	+0.15	0.1	−0.12	+0.25	0.1	−0.15	+0.4	0.3	−0.25	+0.6	0.3	−0.4
.12	.24	+0.2	0.15	−0.15	+0.3	0.15	−0.2	+0.5	0.4	−0.3	+0.7	0.4	−0.5
.24	.40	+0.25	0.2	−0.15	+0.4	0.2	−0.25	+0.6	0.5	−0.4	+0.9	0.5	−0.6
.40	.71	+0.3	0.25	−0.2	+0.4	0.25	−0.3	+0.7	0.6	−0.4	+1.0	0.6	−0.7
.71	1.19	+0.4	0.3	−0.25	+0.5	0.3	−0.4	+0.8	0.8	−0.5	+1.2	0.8	−0.8
1.19	1.97	+0.4	0.4	−0.3	+0.6	0.4	−0.4	+1.0	1.0	−0.6	+1.6	1.0	−1.0
1.97	3.15	+0.5	0.4	−0.3	+0.7	0.4	−0.5	+1.2	1.2	−0.7	+1.8	1.2	−1.2
3.15	4.73	+0.6	0.5	−0.4	+0.9	0.5	−0.6	+1.4	1.4	−0.9	+2.2	1.4	−1.4
4.73	7.09	+0.7	0.6	−0.5	+1.0	0.6	−0.7	+1.6	1.6	−1.0	+2.5	1.6	−1.6
7.09	9.85	+0.8	0.6	−0.6	+1.2	0.6	−0.8	+1.8	2.0	−1.2	+2.8	2.0	−1.8
9.85	12.41	+0.9	0.8	−0.6	+1.2	0.8	−0.9	+2.0	2.5	−1.2	+3.0	2.5	−2.0
12.41	15.75	+1.0	1.0	−0.7	+1.4	1.0	−1.0	+2.2	3.0	−1.4	+3.5	3.0	−2.2

Table 46 **Running and sliding fits.** (Values in thousandths of an inch.)

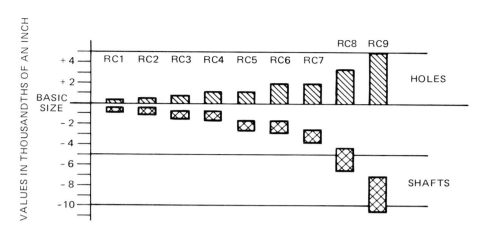

RUNNING AND SLIDING FITS
BASIC HOLE SYSTEM

Class RC5 Medium Running			Class RC6 Medium Running			Class RC7 Free Running			Class RC8 Loose Running			Class RC9 Loose Running		
Hole Tol. GR8	Minimum Clearance	Shaft Tol. GR7	Hole Tol. GR9	Minimum Clearance	Shaft Tol. GR8	Hole Tol. GR9	Minimum Clearance	Shaft Tol. GR8	Hole Tol. GR10	Minimum Clearance	Shaft Tol. GR9	Hole Tol. GR11	Minimum Clearance	Shaft Tol. GR10
−0		+0	−0		+0	−0		+0	−0		+0	−0		+0
+0.6	0.6	−0.4	+1.0	0.6	−0.6	+1.0	1.0	−0.6	+1.6	2.5	−1.0	+2.5	4.0	−1.6
+0.7	0.8	−0.5	+1.2	0.8	−0.7	+1.2	1.2	−0.7	+1.8	2.8	−1.2	+3.0	4.5	−1.8
+0.9	1.0	−0.6	+1.4	1.0	−0.9	+1.4	1.6	−0.9	+2.2	3.0	−1.4	+3.5	5.0	−2.2
+1.0	1.2	−0.7	+1.6	1.2	−1.0	+1.6	2.0	−1.0	+2.8	3.5	−1.6	+4.0	6.0	−2.8
+1.2	1.6	−0.8	+2.0	1.6	−1.2	+2.0	2.5	−1.2	+3.5	4.5	−2.0	+5.0	7.0	−3.5
+1.6	2.0	−1.0	+2.5	2.0	−1.6	+2.5	3.0	−1.6	+4.0	5.0	−2.5	+6.0	8.0	−4.0
+1.8	2.5	−1.2	+3.0	2.5	−1.8	+3.0	4.0	−1.8	+4.5	6.0	−3.0	+7.0	9.0	−4.5
+2.2	3.0	−1.4	+3.5	3.0	−2.2	+3.5	5.0	−2.2	+5.0	7.0	−3.5	+9.0	10.0	−5.0
+2.5	3.5	−1.6	+4.0	3.5	−2.5	+4.0	6.0	−2.5	+6.0	8.0	−4.0	+10.0	12.0	−6.0
+2.8	4.5	−1.8	+4.5	4.0	−2.8	+4.5	7.0	−2.8	+7.0	10.0	−4.5	+12.0	15.0	−7.0
+3.0	5.0	−2.0	+5.0	5.0	−3.0	+5.0	8.0	−3.0	+8.0	12.0	−5.0	+12.0	18.0	−8.0
+3.5	6.0	−2.2	+6.0	6.0	−3.5	+6.0	10.0	−3.5	+9.0	14.0	−6.0	+14.0	22.0	−9.0

Table 46 (cont'd.) **Running and sliding fits.** (Values in thousandths of an inch.)

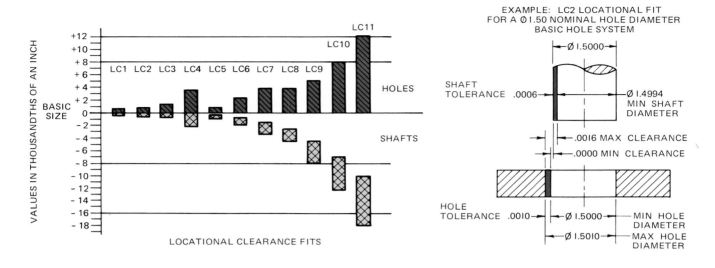

EXAMPLE: LC2 LOCATIONAL FIT
FOR A Ø 1.50 NOMINAL HOLE DIAMETER
BASIC HOLE SYSTEM

LOCATIONAL CLEARANCE FITS

Nominal Size Range Inches		Class LC1			Class LC2			Class LC3			Class LC4			Class LC5		
		Hole Tol. GR6	Minimum Clearance	Shaft Tol. GR5	Hole Tol. GR7	Minimum Clearance	Shaft Tol. GR6	Hole Tol. GR8	Minimum Clearance	Shaft Tol. GR7	Hole Tol. GR10	Minimum Clearance	Shaft Tol. GR9	Hole Tol. GR7	Minimum Clearance	Shaft Tol. GR6
Over	To	−0		+0	−0		+0	−0		+0	−0		+0	−0		+0
0	.12	+0.25	0	−0.15	+0.4	0	−0.25	+0.6	0	−0.4	+1.6	0	−1.0	+0.4	0.1	−0.25
.12	.24	+0.3	0	−0.2	+0.5	0	−0.3	+0.7	0	−0.5	+1.8	0	−1.2	+0.5	0.15	−0.3
.24	.40	+0.4	0	−0.25	+0.6	0	−0.4	+0.9	0	−0.6	+2.2	0	−1.4	+0.6	0.2	−0.4
.40	.71	+0.4	0	−0.3	+0.7	0	−0.4	+1.0	0	−0.7	+2.8	0	−1.6	+0.7	0.25	−0.4
.71	1.19	+0.5	0	−0.4	+0.8	0	−0.5	+1.2	0	−0.8	+3.5	0	−2.0	+0.8	0.3	−0.5
1.19	1.97	+0.6	0	−0.4	+1.0	0	−0.6	+1.6	0	−1.0	+4.0	0	−2.5	+1.0	0.4	−0.6
1.97	3.15	+0.7	0	−0.5	+1.2	0	−0.7	+1.8	0	−1.2	+4.5	0	−3.0	+1.2	0.4	−0.7
3.15	4.73	+0.9	0	−0.6	+1.4	0	−0.9	+2.2	0	−1.4	+5.0	0	−3.5	+1.4	0.5	−0.9
4.73	7.09	+1.0	0	−0.7	+1.6	0	−1.0	+2.5	0	−1.6	+6.0	0	−4.0	+1.6	0.6	−1.0
7.09	9.85	+1.2	0	−0.8	+1.8	0	−1.2	+2.8	0	−1.8	+7.0	0	−4.5	+1.8	0.6	−1.2
9.85	12.41	+1.2	0	−0.9	+2.0	0	−1.2	+3.0	0	−2.0	+8.0	0	−5.0	+2.0	0.7	−1.2
12.41	15.75	+1.4	0	−1.0	+2.2	0	−1.4	+3.5	0	−2.2	+9.0	0	−6.0	+2.2	0.7	−1.4

Table 47 Locational clearance fits. (Values in thousandths of an inch.)

Nominal Size Range Inches		Class LT1			Class LT2		
		Hole Tol. GR7	Maximum Interference	Shaft Tol. GR6	Hole Tol. GR8	Maximum Interference	Shaft Tol. GR7
Over	To	−0		+0	−0		+0
0	.12	+0.4	0.1	−0.25	+0.6	0.2	−0.4
.12	.24	+0.5	0.15	−0.3	+0.7	0.25	−0.5
.24	.40	+0.6	0.2	−0.4	+0.9	0.3	−0.6
.40	.71	+0.7	0.2	−0.4	+1.0	0.3	−0.7
.71	1.19	+0.8	0.25	−0.5	+1.2	0.4	−0.8
1.19	1.97	+1.0	0.3	−0.6	+1.6	0.5	−1.0
1.97	3.15	+1.2	0.3	−0.7	+1.8	0.6	−1.2
3.15	4.73	+1.4	0.4	−0.9	+2.2	0.7	−1.4
4.73	7.09	+1.6	0.5	−1.0	+2.5	0.8	−1.6
7.09	9.85	+1.8	0.6	−1.2	+2.8	0.9	−1.8
9.85	12.41	+2.0	0.6	−1.2	+3.0	1.0	−2.0
12.41	15.75	+2.2	0.7	−1.4	+3.5	1.0	−2.2

Table 48 Transition fits. (Values in thousandths of an inch.)

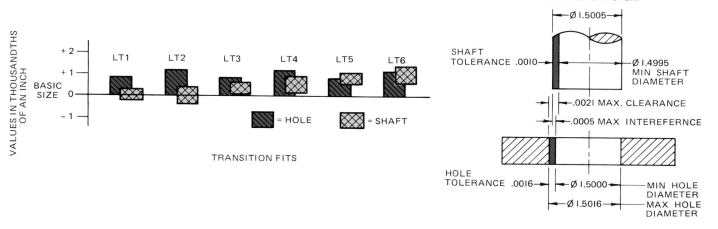

EXAMPLE: LT2 TRANSITION FIT
FOR A Ø1.50 NOMINAL HOLE DIAMETER
BASIC HOLE SYSTEM

TRANSITION FITS

Class LC6			Class LC7			Class LC8			Class LC9			Class LC10			Class LC11		
Hole Tol. GR9	Minimum Clearance	Shaft Tol. GR8	Hole Tol. GR10	Minimum Clearance	Shaft Tol. GR9	Hole Tol. GR10	Minimum Clearance	Shaft Tol. GR9	Hole Tol. GR11	Minimum Clearance	Shaft Tol. GR10	Hole Tol. GR12	Minimum Clearance	Shaft Tol. GR11	Hole Tol. GR13	Minimum Clearance	Shaft Tol. GR12
−0		+0	−0		+0	−0		+0	−0		+0	−0		+0	−0		+0
+1.0	0.3	−0.6	+1.6	0.6	−1.0	+1.6	1.0	−1.0	+2.5	2.5	−1.6	+4.0	4.0	−2.5	+6.0	5.0	−4.0
+1.2	0.4	−0.7	+1.8	0.8	−1.2	+1.8	1.2	−1.2	+3.0	2.8	−1.8	+5.0	4.5	−3.0	+7.0	6.0	−5.0
+1.4	0.5	−0.9	+2.2	1.0	−1.4	+2.2	1.6	−1.4	+3.5	3.0	−2.2	+6.0	5.0	−3.5	+9.0	7.0	−6.0
+1.6	0.6	−1.0	+2.8	1.2	−1.6	+2.8	2.0	−1.6	+4.0	3.5	−2.8	+7.0	6.0	−4.0	+10.0	8.0	−7.0
+2.0	0.8	−1.2	+3.5	1.6	−2.0	+3.5	2.5	−2.0	+5.0	4.5	−3.5	+8.0	7.0	−5.0	+12.0	10.0	−8.0
+2.5	1.0	−1.6	+4.0	2.0	−2.5	+4.0	3.6	−2.5	+6.0	5.0	−4.0	+10.0	8.0	−6.0	+16.0	12.0	−10.0
+3.0	1.2	−1.8	+4.5	2.5	−3.0	+4.5	4.0	−3.0	+7.0	6.0	−4.5	+12.0	10.0	−7.0	+18.0	14.0	−12.0
+3.5	1.4	−2.2	+5.0	3.0	−3.5	+5.0	5.0	−3.5	+9.0	7.0	−5.0	+14.0	11.0	−9.0	+22.0	16.0	−14.0
+4.0	1.6	−2.5	+6.0	3.5	−4.0	+6.0	6.0	−4.0	+10.0	8.0	−6.0	+16.0	12.0	−10.0	+25.0	18.0	−16.0
+4.5	2.0	−2.8	+7.0	4.0	−4.5	+7.0	7.0	−4.5	+12.0	10.0	−7.0	+18.0	16.0	−12.0	+28.0	22.0	−18.0
+5.0	2.2	−3.0	+8.0	4.5	−5.0	+8.0	7.0	−5.0	+12.0	12.0	−8.0	+20.0	20.0	−12.0	+30.0	28.0	−20.0
+6.0	2.5	−3.5	+9.0	5.0	−6.0	+9.0	8.0	−6.0	+14.0	14.0	−9.0	+22.0	22.0	−14.0	+35.0	30.0	−22.0

Table 47 (cont'd.)   Locational clearance fits. (Values in thousandths of an inch.)

Class LT3			Class LT4			Class LT5			Class LT6		
Hole Tol. GR7	Maximum Interference	Shaft Tol. GR6	Hole Tol. GR8	Maximum Interference	Shaft Tol. GR7	Hole Tol. GR7	Maximum Interference	Shaft Tol. GR6	Hole Tol. GR8	Maximum Interference	Shaft Tol. GR7
−0		+0	−0		+0	−0		+0	−0		+0
+0.4	0.25	−0.25	+0.6	0.4	−0.4	+0.4	0.5	−0.25	+0.6	0.65	−0.4
+0.5	0.4	−0.3	+0.7	0.6	−0.5	+0.5	0.6	−0.3	+0.7	0.8	−0.5
+0.6	0.5	−0.4	+0.9	0.7	−0.6	+0.6	0.8	−0.4	+0.9	1.0	−0.6
+0.7	0.5	−0.4	+1.0	0.8	−0.7	+0.7	0.9	−0.4	+1.0	1.2	−0.7
+0.8	0.6	−0.5	+1.2	0.9	−0.8	+0.8	1.1	−0.5	+1.2	1.4	−0.8
+1.0	0.7	−0.6	+1.6	1.1	−1.0	+1.0	1.3	−0.6	+1.6	1.7	−1.0
+1.2	0.8	−0.7	+1.8	1.3	−1.2	+1.2	1.5	−0.7	+1.8	2.0	−1.2
+1.4	1.0	−0.9	+2.2	1.5	−1.4	+1.4	1.9	−0.9	+2.2	2.4	−1.4
+1.6	1.1	−1.0	+2.5	1.7	−1.6	+1.6	2.2	−1.0	+2.5	2.8	−1.6
+1.8	1.4	−1.2	+2.8	2.0	−1.8	+1.8	2.6	−1.2	+2.8	3.2	−1.8
+2.0	1.4	−1.2	+3.0	2.2	−2.0	+2.0	2.6	−1.2	+3.0	3.4	−2.0
+2.2	1.6	−1.4	+3.5	2.4	−2.2	+2.2	3.0	−1.4	+3.5	3.8	−2.2

Table 48 (cont'd.)   Transition fits. (Values in thousandths of an inch.)

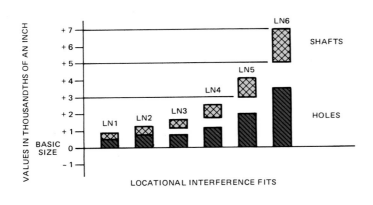

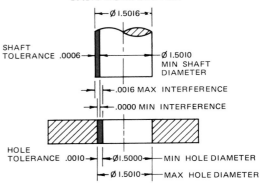

EXAMPLE: LN2 LOCATIONAL INTERFERENCE
FIT FOR A Ø1.50 NOMINAL HOLE DIAMETER
BASIC HOLE SYSTEM

Nominal Size Range Inches		Class LN1 Light Press Fit			Class LN2 Medium Press Fit		
		Hole Tol. GR6	Maximum Interference	Shaft Tol. GR5	Hole Tol. GR7	Maximum Interference	Shaft Tol. GR6
Over	To	−0		+0	−0		+0
0	.12	+0.25	0.4	−0.15	+0.4	0.65	−0.25
.12	.24	+0.3	0.5	−0.2	+0.5	0.8	−0.3
.24	.40	+0.4	0.65	−0.25	+0.6	1.0	−0.4
.40	.71	+0.4	0.7	−0.3	+0.7	1.1	−0.4
.71	1.19	+0.5	0.9	−0.4	+0.8	1.3	−0.5
1.19	1.97	+0.6	1.0	−0.4	+1.0	1.6	−0.6
1.97	3.15	+0.7	1.3	−0.5	+1.2	2.1	−0.7
3.15	4.73	+0.9	1.6	−0.6	+1.4	2.5	−0.9
4.73	7.09	+1.0	1.9	−0.7	+1.6	2.8	−1.0
7.09	9.85	+1.2	2.2	−0.8	+1.8	3.2	−1.2
9.85	12.41	+1.2	2.3	−0.9	+2.0	3.4	−1.2
12.41	15.75	+1.4	2.6	−1.0	+2.2	3.9	−1.4

Table 49 Locational interference fits. (Values in thousandths of an inch.)

Nominal Size Range Inches		Class FN1 Light Drive Fit			Class FN2 Medium Drive Fit		
		Hole Tol. GR6	Maximum Interference	Shaft Tol. GR5	Hole Tol. GR7	Maximum Interference	Shaft Tol. GR6
Over	To	−0		+0	−0		+0
0	.12	+0.25	0.5	−0.15	+0.4	0.85	−0.25
.12	.24	+0.3	0.6	−0.2	+0.5	1.0	−0.3
.24	.40	+0.4	0.75	−0.25	+0.6	1.4	−0.4
.40	.56	+0.4	0.8	−0.3	+0.7	1.6	−0.4
.56	.71	+0.4	0.9	−0.3	+0.7	1.6	−0.4
.71	.95	+0.5	1.1	−0.4	+0.8	1.9	−0.5
.95	1.19	+0.5	1.2	−0.4	+0.8	1.9	−0.5
1.19	1.58	+0.6	1.3	−0.4	+1.0	2.4	−0.6
1.58	1.97	+0.6	1.4	−0.4	+1.0	2.4	−0.6
1.97	2.56	+0.7	1.8	−0.5	+1.2	2.7	−0.7
2.56	3.15	+0.7	1.9	−0.5	+1.2	2.9	−0.7
3.15	3.94	+0.9	2.4	−0.6	+1.4	3.7	−0.9

Table 50 Force and shrink fits. (Values in thousandths of an inch.)

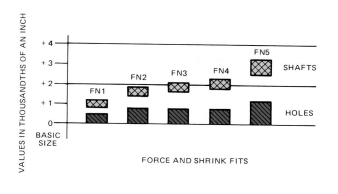

FORCE AND SHRINK FITS

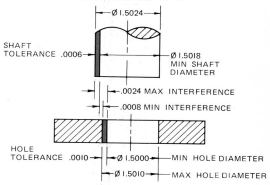

EXAMPLE: FN2 MEDIUM DRIVE FIT FOR A Ø 1.50 NOMINAL HOLE DIAMETER BASIC HOLE SYSTEM

Class LN3 Heavy Press Fit			Class LN4			Class LN5			Class LN6		
Hole Tol. GR7	Maximum Interference	Shaft Tol. GR6	Hole Tol. GR8	Maximum Interference	Shaft Tol. GR7	Hole Tol. GR9	Maximum Interference	Shaft Tol. GR8	Hole Tol. GR10	Maximum Interference	Shaft Tol. GR9
−0		+0	−0		+0	−0		+0	−0		+0
+0.4	0.75	−0.25	+0.6	1.2	−0.4	+1.0	1.8	−0.6	+1.6	3.0	−1.0
+0.5	0.9	−0.3	+0.7	1.5	−0.5	+1.2	2.3	−0.7	+1.8	3.6	−1.2
+0.6	1.2	−0.4	+0.9	1.8	−0.6	+1.4	2.8	−0.9	+2.2	4.4	−1.4
+0.7	1.4	−0.4	+1.0	2.2	−0.7	+1.6	3.4	−1.0	+2.8	5.6	−1.6
+0.8	1.7	−0.5	+1.2	2.6	−0.8	+2.0	4.2	−1.2	+3.5	7.0	−2.0
+1.0	2.0	−0.6	+1.6	3.4	−1.0	+2.5	5.3	−1.6	+4.0	8.5	−2.5
+1.2	2.3	−0.7	+1.8	4.0	−1.2	+3.0	6.3	−1.8	+4.5	10.0	−3.0
+1.4	2.9	−0.9	+2.2	4.8	−1.4	+4.0	7.7	−2.2	+5.0	11.5	−3.5
+1.6	3.5	−1.0	+2.5	5.6	−1.6	+4.5	8.7	−2.5	+6.0	13.5	−4.0
+1.8	4.2	−1.2	+2.8	6.6	−1.8	+5.0	10.3	−2.8	+7.0	16.5	−4.5
+2.0	4.7	−1.2	+3.0	7.5	−2.0	+6.0	12.0	−3.0	+8.0	19	−5.0
+2.2	5.9	−1.4	+3.5	8.7	−2.2	+6.0	14.5	−3.5	+9.0	23	−6.0

Table 49 (cont'd). Locational interference fits. (Values in thousandths of an inch.)

Class FN3 Heavy Drive Fit			Class FN4 Shrink Fit			FN5 Heavy Shrink Fit		
Hole Tol. GR7	Maximum Interference	Shaft Tol. GR6	Hole Tol. GR7	Maximum Interference	Shaft Tol. GR6	Hole Tol. GR8	Maximum Interference	Shaft Tol. GR7
−0		+0	−0		+0	−0		+0
			+0.4	0.95	−0.25	+0.6	1.3	−0.4
			+0.5	1.2	−0.3	+0.7	1.7	−0.5
			+0.6	1.6	−0.4	+0.9	2.0	−0.6
			+0.7	1.8	−0.4	+1.0	2.3	−0.7
			+0.7	1.8	−0.4	+1.0	2.5	−0.7
			+0.8	2.1	−0.5	+1.2	3.0	−0.8
+0.8	2.1	−0.5	+0.8	2.3	−0.5	+1.2	3.3	−0.8
+1.0	2.6	−0.6	+1.0	3.1	−0.6	+1.6	4.0	−1.0
+1.0	2.8	−0.6	+1.0	3.4	−0.6	+1.6	5.0	−1.0
+1.2	3.2	−0.7	+1.2	4.2	−0.7	+1.8	6.2	−1.2
+1.2	3.7	−0.7	+1.2	4.7	−0.7	+1.8	7.2	−1.2
+1.4	4.4	−0.9	+1.4	5.9	−0.9	+2.2	8.4	−1.4

Table 50 (cont'd). Force and shrink fits. (Values in thousandths of an inch.)

Example ⌀ 50H9/d9

Hole Size ⌀ 50.062 / 50.000

Shaft Size ⌀ 49.920 / 49.858

Clearance Max. 0.204 / Min. 0.080

Example ⌀ 70H7/g6
(Use values midway between 60 and 80.)

Hole Size ⌀ 70.030 / 70.000

Shaft Size ⌀ 69.990 / 69.971

Clearance Max. 0.059 / Min. 0.010

		PREFERRED HOLE BASIS CLEARANCE FITS															
		LOOSE RUNNING			FREE RUNNING			CLOSE RUNNING			SLIDING			LOCATIONAL CLEARANCE		
BASIC SIZE		Hole H11	Shaft c11	Fit	Hole H9	Shaft d9	Fit	Hole H8	Shaft f7	Fit	Hole H7	Shaft g6	Fit	Hole H7	Shaft h6	Fit
1	MAX	1.060	0.940	0.180	1.025	0.980	0.070	1.014	0.994	0.030	1.010	0.998	0.018	1.010	1.000	0.016
	MIN	1.000	0.880	0.060	1.000	0.955	0.020	1.000	0.984	0.006	1.000	0.992	0.002	1.000	0.994	0.000
1.2	MAX	1.260	1.140	0.180	1.225	1.180	0.070	1.214	1.194	0.030	1.210	1.198	0.018	1.210	1.200	0.016
	MIN	1.200	1.080	0.060	1.200	1.155	0.020	1.200	1.184	0.006	1.200	1.192	0.002	1.200	1.194	0.000
1.6	MAX	1.660	1.540	0.180	1.625	1.580	0.070	1.614	1.594	0.030	1.610	1.598	0.018	1.610	1.600	0.016
	MIN	1.600	1.480	0.060	1.600	1.555	0.020	1.600	1.584	0.006	1.600	1.592	0.002	1.600	1.594	0.000
2	MAX	2.060	1.940	0.180	2.025	1.980	0.070	2.014	1.994	0.030	2.010	1.998	0.018	2.010	2.000	0.016
	MIN	2.000	1.880	0.060	2.000	1.955	0.020	2.000	1.984	0.006	2.000	1.992	0.002	2.000	1.994	0.000
2.5	MAX	2.560	2.440	0.180	2.525	2.480	0.070	2.514	2.494	0.030	2.510	2.498	0.018	2.510	2.500	0.016
	MIN	2.500	2.380	0.060	2.500	2.455	0.020	2.500	2.484	0.006	2.500	2.492	0.002	2.500	2.494	0.000
3	MAX	3.060	2.940	0.180	3.025	2.980	0.070	3.014	2.994	0.030	3.010	2.998	0.018	3.010	3.000	0.016
	MIN	3.000	2.880	0.060	3.000	2.955	0.020	3.000	2.984	0.006	3.000	2.992	0.002	3.000	2.994	0.000
4	MAX	4.075	3.930	0.220	4.030	3.970	0.090	4.018	3.990	0.040	4.012	3.996	0.024	4.012	4.000	0.020
	MIN	4.000	3.855	0.070	4.000	3.940	0.030	4.000	3.978	0.010	4.000	3.988	0.004	4.000	3.992	0.000
5	MAX	5.075	4.930	0.220	5.030	4.970	0.090	5.018	4.990	0.040	5.012	4.996	0.024	5.012	5.000	0.020
	MIN	5.000	4.855	0.070	5.000	4.940	0.030	5.000	4.978	0.010	5.000	4.988	0.004	5.000	4.992	0.000
6	MAX	6.075	5.930	0.220	6.030	5.970	0.090	6.018	5.990	0.040	6.012	5.996	0.024	6.012	6.000	0.020
	MIN	6.000	5.855	0.070	6.000	5.940	0.030	6.000	5.978	0.010	6.000	5.988	0.004	6.000	5.992	0.000
8	MAX	8.090	7.920	0.260	8.036	7.960	0.112	8.022	7.987	0.050	8.015	7.995	0.029	8.015	8.000	0.024
	MIN	8.000	7.830	0.080	8.000	7.924	0.040	8.000	7.972	0.013	8.000	7.986	0.006	8.000	7.991	0.000
10	MAX	10.090	9.920	0.260	10.036	9.960	0.112	10.022	9.987	0.050	10.015	9.995	0.029	10.015	10.000	0.024
	MIN	10.000	9.830	0.080	10.000	9.924	0.040	10.000	9.972	0.013	10.000	9.986	0.005	10.000	9.991	0.000
12	MAX	12.110	11.905	0.315	12.043	11.950	0.136	12.027	11.984	0.061	12.018	11.994	0.035	12.018	12.000	0.029
	MIN	12.000	11.795	0.095	12.000	11.907	0.050	12.000	11.966	0.016	12.000	11.983	0.006	12.000	11.989	0.000
16	MAX	16.110	15.905	0.315	16.043	15.950	0.136	16.027	15.984	0.061	16.018	15.994	0.035	16.018	16.000	0.029
	MIN	16.000	15.795	0.095	16.000	15.907	0.050	16.000	15.966	0.016	16.000	15.983	0.006	16.000	15.989	0.000
20	MAX	20.130	19.890	0.370	20.052	19.935	0.169	20.033	19.980	0.074	20.021	19.993	0.041	20.021	20.000	0.034
	MIN	20.000	19.760	0.110	20.000	19.883	0.065	20.000	19.959	0.020	20.000	19.980	0.007	20.000	19.987	0.000
25	MAX	25.130	24.890	0.370	25.052	24.935	0.169	25.033	24.980	0.074	25.021	24.993	0.042	25.021	25.000	0.034
	MIN	25.000	24.760	0.110	25.000	24.883	0.065	25.000	24.959	0.020	25.000	24.980	0.007	25.000	24.987	0.000
30	MAX	30.130	29.890	0.370	30.052	29.935	0.169	30.033	29.980	0.074	30.021	29.993	0.041	30.021	30.000	0.034
	MIN	30.000	29.760	0.110	30.000	29.883	0.065	30.000	29.959	0.020	30.000	29.980	0.007	30.000	29.987	0.000
40	MAX	40.160	39.880	0.440	40.062	39.920	0.204	40.039	39.975	0.089	40.025	39.991	0.050	40.025	40.000	0.041
	MIN	40.000	39.720	0.120	40.000	39.858	0.080	40.000	39.950	0.025	40.000	39.975	0.009	40.000	39.984	0.000
50	MAX	50.160	49.870	0.450	50.062	49.920	0.204	50.039	49.975	0.089	50.025	49.991	0.050	50.025	50.000	0.041
	MIN	50.000	49.710	0.130	50.000	49.858	0.080	50.000	49.950	0.025	50.000	49.975	0.009	50.000	49.984	0.000
60	MAX	60.190	59.860	0.520	60.074	59.900	0.248	60.046	59.970	0.106	60.030	59.990	0.059	60.030	60.000	0.049
	MIN	60.000	59.670	0.140	60.000	59.826	0.100	60.000	59.940	0.030	60.000	59.971	0.010	60.000	59.981	0.000
80	MAX	80.190	79.850	0.530	80.074	79.900	0.248	80.046	79.970	0.106	80.030	79.990	0.059	80.030	80.000	0.049
	MIN	80.000	79.660	0.150	80.000	79.826	0.100	80.000	79.940	0.030	80.000	79.971	0.010	80.000	79.981	0.000
100	MAX	100.220	99.830	0.610	100.087	99.880	0.294	100.054	99.964	0.125	100.035	99.988	0.069	100.035	100.000	0.057
	MIN	100.000	99.610	0.170	100.000	99.793	0.120	100.000	99.929	0.036	100.000	99.966	0.012	100.000	99.978	0.000
120	MAX	120.220	119.820	0.620	120.087	119.880	0.294	120.054	119.964	0.125	120.035	119.988	0.069	120.035	120.000	0.057
	MIN	120.000	119.600	0.180	120.000	119.793	0.120	120.000	119.929	0.036	120.000	119.966	0.012	120.000	119.978	0.000
160	MAX	160.250	159.790	0.710	160.100	159.855	0.345	160.063	159.957	0.146	160.040	159.986	0.079	160.040	160.000	0.065
	MIN	160.000	159.540	0.210	160.000	159.755	0.145	160.000	159.917	0.043	160.000	159.961	0.014	160.000	159.975	0.000

Table 51   Preferred hole basis fits. (Dimensions in millimeters.)

Example ⌀ 10H7/n6

Hole Size ⌀ $^{10.015}_{10.000}$

Shaft Size ⌀ $^{10.019}_{10.010}$

Max. Clearance 0.015

Max. Interference 0.019

Example ⌀ 35H7/u6
(Use values midway between 30 and 40.)

Hole Size ⌀ $^{35.023}_{35.000}$

Shaft Size ⌀ $^{35.068}_{35.054}$

Min. Interference 0.031

Max. Interference 0.068

PREFERRED HOLE BASIS TRANSITION AND INTERFERENCE FITS															
BASIC SIZE	LOCATIONAL TRANSN.			LOCATIONAL TRANSN.			LOCATIONAL INTERF.			MEDIUM DRIVE			FORCE		
	Hole H7	Shaft k6	Fit	Hole H7	Shaft n6	Fit	Hole H7	Shaft p6	Fit	Hole H7	Shaft s6	Fit	Hole H7	Shaft u6	Fit
1 MAX	1.010	1.006	0.010	1.010	1.010	0.006	1.010	1.012	0.004	1.010	1.020	−0.004	1.010	1.024	−0.008
MIN	1.000	1.000	−0.006	1.000	1.004	−0.010	1.000	1.006	−0.012	1.000	1.014	−0.020	1.000	1.018	−0.024
1.2 MAX	1.210	1.206	0.010	1.210	1.210	0.006	1.210	1.212	0.004	1.210	1.220	−0.004	1.210	1.224	−0.008
MIN	1.200	1.200	−0.006	1.200	1.204	−0.010	1.200	1.206	−0.012	1.200	1.214	−0.020	1.200	1.218	−0.024
1.6 MAX	1.610	1.606	0.010	1.610	1.610	0.006	1.610	1.612	0.004	1.610	1.620	−0.004	1.610	1.624	−0.008
MIN	1.600	1.600	−0.006	1.600	1.604	−0.010	1.600	1.606	−0.012	1.600	1.614	−0.020	1.600	1.618	−0.024
2 MAX	2.010	2.006	0.010	2.010	2.010	0.006	2.010	2.012	0.004	2.010	2.020	−0.004	2.010	2.024	−0.008
MIN	2.000	2.000	−0.006	2.000	2.004	−0.010	2.000	2.006	−0.012	2.000	2.014	−0.020	2.000	2.018	−0.024
2.5 MAX	2.510	2.506	0.010	2.510	2.510	0.006	2.510	2.512	0.004	2.510	2.520	−0.004	2.510	2.524	−0.008
MIN	2.500	2.500	−0.006	2.500	2.504	−0.010	2.500	2.506	−0.012	2.500	2.514	−0.020	2.500	2.518	−0.024
3 MAX	3.010	3.006	0.010	3.010	3.010	0.006	3.010	3.012	0.004	3.010	3.020	−0.004	3.010	3.024	−0.008
MIN	3.000	3.000	−0.006	3.000	3.004	−0.010	3.000	3.006	−0.012	3.000	3.014	−0.020	3.000	3.018	−0.024
4 MAX	4.012	4.009	0.011	4.012	4.016	0.004	4.012	4.020	0.000	4.012	4.027	−0.007	4.012	4.031	−0.011
MIN	4.000	4.001	−0.009	4.000	4.008	−0.016	4.000	4.012	−0.020	4.000	4.019	−0.027	4.000	4.023	−0.031
5 MAX	5.012	5.009	0.011	5.012	5.016	0.004	5.012	5.020	0.000	5.012	5.027	−0.007	5.012	5.031	−0.011
MIN	5.000	5.001	−0.009	5.000	5.008	−0.016	5.000	5.012	−0.020	5.000	5.019	−0.027	5.000	5.023	−0.031
6 MAX	6.012	6.009	0.011	6.012	6.016	0.004	6.012	6.020	0.000	6.012	6.027	−0.007	6.012	6.031	−0.011
MIN	6.000	6.001	−0.009	6.000	6.008	−0.016	6.000	6.012	−0.020	6.000	6.019	−0.027	6.000	6.023	−0.031
8 MAX	8.015	8.010	0.014	8.015	8.019	0.005	8.015	8.024	0.000	8.015	8.032	−0.008	8.015	8.037	−0.013
MIN	8.000	8.001	−0.010	8.000	8.010	−0.019	8.000	8.015	−0.024	8.000	8.023	−0.032	8.000	8.028	−0.037
10 MAX	10.015	10.010	0.014	10.015	10.019	0.005	10.015	10.024	0.000	10.015	10.032	−0.008	10.015	10.037	−0.013
MIN	10.000	10.001	−0.010	10.000	10.010	−0.019	10.000	10.015	−0.024	10.000	10.023	−0.032	10.000	10.028	−0.037
12 MAX	12.018	12.012	0.017	12.018	12.023	0.006	12.018	12.029	0.000	12.018	12.039	−0.010	12.018	12.044	−0.015
MIN	12.000	12.001	−0.012	12.000	12.012	−0.023	12.000	12.018	−0.029	12.000	12.028	−0.039	12.000	12.033	−0.044
16 MAX	16.018	16.012	0.017	16.018	16.023	0.006	16.018	16.029	0.000	16.018	16.039	−0.010	16.018	16.044	−0.015
MIN	16.000	16.001	−0.012	16.000	16.012	−0.023	16.000	16.018	−0.029	16.000	16.028	−0.039	16.000	16.033	−0.044
20 MAX	20.021	20.015	0.019	20.021	20.028	0.006	20.021	20.035	−0.001	20.021	20.048	−0.014	20.021	20.054	−0.020
MIN	20.000	20.002	−0.015	20.000	20.015	−0.028	20.000	20.022	−0.035	20.000	20.035	−0.048	20.000	20.041	−0.054
25 MAX	25.021	25.015	0.019	25.021	25.028	0.006	25.021	25.035	−0.001	25.021	25.048	−0.014	25.021	25.061	−0.027
MIN	25.000	25.002	−0.015	25.000	25.015	−0.028	25.000	25.022	−0.035	25.000	25.035	−0.048	25.000	25.048	−0.061
30 MAX	30.021	30.015	0.019	30.021	30.028	0.006	30.021	30.035	−0.001	30.021	30.048	−0.014	30.021	30.061	−0.027
MIN	30.000	30.002	−0.015	30.000	30.015	−0.028	30.000	30.022	−0.035	30.000	30.035	−0.048	30.000	30.048	−0.061
40 MAX	40.025	40.018	0.023	40.025	40.033	0.008	40.025	40.042	−0.001	40.025	40.059	−0.018	40.025	40.076	−0.035
MIN	40.000	40.002	−0.018	40.000	40.017	−0.033	40.000	40.026	−0.042	40.000	40.043	−0.059	40.000	40.060	−0.076
50 MAX	50.025	50.018	0.023	50.025	50.033	0.008	50.025	50.042	−0.001	50.025	50.059	−0.018	50.025	50.086	−0.045
MIN	50.002	50.000	−0.018	50.000	50.017	−0.033	50.000	50.026	−0.042	50.000	50.043	−0.059	50.000	50.070	−0.086
60 MAX	60.030	60.021	0.028	60.030	60.039	0.010	60.030	60.051	−0.002	60.030	60.072	−0.023	60.030	60.106	−0.057
MIN	60.000	60.002	−0.021	60.000	60.020	−0.039	60.000	60.032	−0.051	60.000	60.053	−0.072	60.000	60.087	−0.106
80 MAX	80.030	80.021	0.028	80.030	80.039	0.010	80.030	80.051	−0.002	80.030	80.078	−0.029	80.030	80.121	−0.072
MIN	80.000	80.002	−0.021	80.000	80.020	−0.039	80.000	80.032	−0.051	80.000	80.059	−0.078	80.000	80.102	−0.121
100 MAX	100.035	100.025	0.032	100.035	100.045	0.012	100.035	100.059	−0.002	100.035	100.093	−0.036	100.035	100.146	−0.089
MIN	100.000	100.003	−0.025	100.000	100.023	−0.045	100.000	100.037	−0.059	100.000	100.071	−0.093	100.000	100.124	−0.146
120 MAX	120.035	120.025	0.032	120.035	120.045	0.012	120.035	120.059	−0.002	120.035	120.101	−0.044	120.035	120.166	−0.109
MIN	120.000	120.003	−0.025	120.000	120.023	−0.045	120.000	120.037	−0.059	120.000	120.079	−0.101	120.000	120.144	−0.166
160 MAX	160.040	160.028	0.037	160.045	160.052	0.013	160.040	160.068	−0.003	160.040	160.125	−0.060	160.040	160.215	−0.150
MIN	160.000	160.003	−0.028	160.000	160.027	−0.052	160.000	160.043	−0.068	160.000	160.000	−0.125	160.000	160.190	−0.215

Table 51 (cont'd.) Preferred hole basis fits.

Example ⌀ 100C11/h11

Hole Size ⌀ $^{100.390}_{100.170}$

Shaft Size ⌀ $^{100.000}_{99.780}$

Clearance Max. 0.610 Min. 0.170

Example ⌀ 11H7/h6
(Use values midway between 10 and 12.)

Hole Size ⌀ $^{11.016}_{11.000}$

Shaft Size ⌀ $^{11.000}_{10.990}$

Clearance Max. 0.026 Min. 0.000

		PREFERRED SHAFT BASIS CLEARANCE FITS															
		LOOSE RUNNING			FREE RUNNING			CLOSE RUNNING			SLIDING			LOCATIONAL CLEARANCE		
BASIC SIZE		Hole C11	Shaft h11	Fit	Hole D9	Shaft h9	Fit	Hole F8	Shaft h7	Fit	Hole G7	Shaft h6	Fit	Hole H7	Shaft h6	Fit
1	MAX	1.120	1.000	0.180	1.045	1.000	0.070	1.020	1.000	0.030	1.012	1.000	0.018	1.010	1.000	0.016
	MIN	1.060	0.940	0.060	1.020	0.975	0.020	1.006	0.990	0.006	1.002	0.994	0.002	1.000	0.994	0.000
1.2	MAX	1.320	1.200	0.180	1.245	1.200	0.070	1.220	1.200	0.030	1.212	1.200	0.018	1.210	1.200	0.016
	MIN	1.260	1.140	0.060	1.220	1.175	0.020	1.206	1.190	0.006	1.202	1.194	0.002	1.200	1.194	0.000
1.6	MAX	1.720	1.600	0.180	1.645	1.600	0.070	1.620	1.600	0.030	1.612	1.600	0.018	1.610	1.600	0.016
	MIN	1.660	1.540	0.060	1.620	1.575	0.020	1.606	1.590	0.006	1.602	1.594	0.002	1.600	1.594	0.000
2	MAX	2.120	2.000	0.180	2.045	2.000	0.070	2.020	2.000	0.030	2.012	2.000	0.018	2.010	2.000	0.016
	MIN	2.060	1.940	0.060	2.020	1.975	0.020	2.006	1.990	0.006	2.002	1.994	0.002	2.000	1.994	0.000
2.5	MAX	2.620	2.500	0.180	2.545	2.500	0.070	2.520	2.500	0.030	2.512	2.500	0.018	2.510	2.500	0.016
	MIN	2.560	2.440	0.060	2.520	2.475	0.020	2.506	2.490	0.006	2.502	2.494	0.002	2.500	2.494	0.000
3	MAX	3.120	3.000	0.180	3.045	3.000	0.070	3.020	3.000	0.030	3.012	3.000	0.018	3.010	3.000	0.016
	MIN	3.060	2.940	0.060	3.020	2.975	0.020	3.006	2.990	0.006	3.002	2.994	0.002	3.000	2.994	0.000
4	MAX	4.145	4.000	.0220	4.060	4.000	0.090	4.028	4.000	0.040	4.016	4.000	0.024	4.012	4.000	0.020
	MIN	4.070	3.925	0.070	4.030	3.970	0.030	4.010	3.988	0.010	4.004	3.992	0.004	4.000	3.992	0.000
5	MAX	5.145	5.000	0.220	5.060	5.000	0.090	5.028	5.000	0.040	5.016	5.000	0.024	5.012	5.000	0.020
	MIN	5.070	4.925	0.070	5.030	4.970	0.030	5.010	4.988	0.010	5.004	4.992	0.004	5.000	4.992	0.000
6	MAX	6.145	6.000	0.220	6.060	6.000	0.090	6.028	6.000	0.040	6.016	6.000	0.024	6.012	6.000	0.020
	MIN	6.070	5.925	0.070	6.030	5.970	0.030	6.010	5.988	0.010	6.004	5.992	0.004	6.000	5.992	0.000
8	MAX	8.170	8.000	0.260	8.076	8.000	0.112	8.035	8.000	0.050	8.020	8.000	0.029	8.015	8.000	0.024
	MIN	8.080	7.910	0.080	8.040	7.964	0.040	8.013	7.985	0.013	8.005	7.991	0.005	8.000	7.991	0.000
10	MAX	10.170	10.000	0.260	10.076	10.000	0.112	10.035	10.000	0.050	10.020	10.000	0.029	10.015	10.000	0.024
	MIN	10.080	9.910	0.080	10.040	9.964	0.040	10.013	9.985	0.013	10.005	9.991	0.005	10.000	9.991	0.000
12	MAX	12.205	12.000	0.315	12.093	12.000	0.136	12.043	12.000	0.061	12.024	12.000	0.035	12.018	12.000	0.029
	MIN	12.095	11.890	0.095	12.050	11.957	0.050	12.016	11.982	0.016	12.006	11.989	0.006	12.000	11.989	0.000
16	MAX	16.205	16.000	0.315	16.093	16.000	0.136	16.043	16.000	0.061	16.024	16.000	0.035	16.018	16.000	0.029
	MIN	16.095	15.890	0.095	16.050	15.957	0.050	16.016	15.982	0.016	16.006	15.989	0.006	16.000	15.989	0.000
20	MAX	20.240	20.000	0.370	20.117	20.000	0.169	20.053	20.000	0.074	20.028	20.000	0.041	20.021	20.000	0.034
	MIN	20.110	19.870	0.110	20.065	19.948	0.065	20.020	19.979	0.020	20.007	19.987	0.007	20.000	19.987	0.000
25	MAX	25.240	25.000	0.370	25.117	25.000	0.169	25.053	25.000	0.074	25.028	25.000	0.041	25.021	25.000	0.034
	MIN	25.110	24.870	0.110	25.065	24.948	0.065	25.020	24.979	0.020	25.007	24.987	0.007	25.000	24.987	0.000
30	MAX	30.240	30.000	0.370	30.117	30.000	0.169	30.053	30.000	0.074	30.028	30.000	0.041	30.021	30.000	0.034
	MIN	30.110	29.870	0.110	30.065	29.948	0.065	30.020	29.979	0.020	30.007	29.987	0.007	30.000	29.987	0.000
40	MAX	40.280	40.000	0.440	40.142	40.000	0.204	40.064	40.000	0.089	40.034	40.000	0.050	40.025	40.000	0.041
	MIN	40.120	39.840	0.120	40.080	39.938	0.080	40.025	39.975	0.025	40.009	39.984	0.009	40.000	39.984	0.000
50	MAX	50.290	50.000	0.450	50.142	50.000	0.204	50.064	50.000	0.089	50.034	50.000	0.050	50.025	50.000	0.041
	MIN	50.130	49.840	0.130	50.080	49.938	0.080	50.025	49.975	0.025	50.009	49.984	0.009	50.000	49.984	0.000
60	MAX	60.330	60.000	0.520	60.174	60.000	0.248	60.076	60.000	0.106	60.040	60.000	0.059	60.030	60.000	0.049
	MIN	60.140	59.810	0.140	60.100	59.926	0.100	60.030	59.970	0.030	60.010	59.981	0.010	60.000	59.981	0.000
80	MAX	80.340	80.000	0.530	80.174	80.000	0.248	80.076	80.000	0.106	80.040	80.000	0.059	80.030	80.000	0.049
	MIN	80.150	79.810	0.150	80.100	79.926	0.100	80.030	79.970	0.030	80.010	79.981	0.010	80.000	79.981	0.000
100	MAX	100.390	100.000	0.610	100.207	100.000	0.294	100.090	100.000	0.125	100.047	100.000	0.069	100.035	100.000	0.057
	MIN	100.170	99.780	0.170	100.120	99.913	0.120	100.036	99.965	0.036	100.012	99.978	0.012	100.000	99.978	0.000
120	MAX	120.400	120.000	0.620	120.207	120.000	0.294	120.090	120.000	0.125	120.047	120.000	0.069	120.035	120.000	0.057
	MIN	120.180	119.780	0.180	120.120	119.913	0.120	120.036	119.965	0.036	120.012	119.978	0.012	120.000	119.978	0.000
160	MAX	160.460	160.000	0.710	160.245	160.000	0.345	160.106	160.000	0.146	160.054	160.000	0.079	160.040	160.000	0.065
	MIN	160.210	159.750	0.210	160.145	159.900	0.145	160.043	159.960	0.043	160.014	159.975	0.014	160.000	159.975	0.000

Table 52 Preferred shaft basis fits. (Dimensions in millimeters.)

Example ⌀ 16N7/h6

Hole Size ⌀ 15.995 / 15.977

Shaft Size ⌀ 16.000 / 15.989

Max. Clearance 0.006

Max. Interference 0.023

Example ⌀ 45U7/h6
(Use values midway between 40 and 50.)

Hole Size ⌀ 44.944 / 44.919

Shaft Size ⌀ 45.000 / 44.984

Min. Interference 0.040

Max. Interference 0.081

		PREFERRED SHAFT BASIS TRANSITION AND INTERFERENCE FITS															
BASIC SIZE		LOCATIONAL TRANSN.			LOCATIONAL TRANSN.			LOCATIONAL INTERF.			MEDIUM DRIVE			FORCE		
		Hole K7	Shaft h6	Fit	Hole N7	Shaft h6	Fit	Hole P7	Shaft h6	Fit	Hole S7	Shaft h6	Fit	Hole U7	Shaft h6	Fit
1	MAX	1.000	1.000	0.006	0.996	1.000	0.002	0.994	1.000	0.000	0.986	1.000	−0.008	0.982	1.000	−0.012
	MIN	0.990	0.994	−0.010	0.986	0.994	−0.014	0.984	0.994	−0.016	0.976	0.994	−0.024	0.972	0.994	−0.028
1.2	MAX	1.200	1.200	0.006	1.196	1.200	0.002	1.194	1.200	0.000	1.186	1.200	−0.008	1.182	1.200	−0.012
	MIN	1.190	1.194	−0.010	1.186	1.194	−0.014	1.184	1.194	−0.016	1.176	1.194	−0.024	1.172	1.194	−0.028
1.6	MAX	1.600	1.600	0.006	1.596	1.600	0.002	1.594	1.600	0.000	1.586	1.600	−0.008	1.582	1.600	−0.012
	MIN	1.590	1.594	−0.010	1.586	1.594	−0.014	1.584	1.594	−0.016	1.576	1.594	−0.024	1.572	1.594	−0.028
2	MAX	2.000	2.000	0.006	1.996	2.000	0.002	1.994	2.000	0.000	1.986	2.000	−0.008	1.982	2.000	−0.012
	MIN	1.990	1.994	−0.010	1.986	1.994	−0.014	1.984	1.994	−0.016	1.976	1.994	−0.024	1.972	1.994	−0.028
2.5	MAX	2.500	2.500	0.006	2.496	2.500	0.002	2.494	2.500	0.000	2.486	2.500	−0.008	2.482	2.500	−0.012
	MIN	2.490	2.494	−0.010	2.486	2.494	−0.014	2.484	2.494	−0.016	2.476	2.494	−0.024	2.472	2.494	−0.028
3	MAX	3.000	3.000	0.006	2.996	3.000	0.002	2.994	3.000	0.000	2.986	3.000	−0.008	2.982	3.000	−0.012
	MIN	2.990	2.994	−0.010	2.986	2.994	−0.014	2.984	2.994	−0.016	2.976	2.994	−0.024	2.972	2.994	−0.028
4	MAX	4.003	4.000	0.011	3.996	4.000	0.004	3.992	4.000	0.000	3.985	4.000	−0.007	3.981	4.000	−0.011
	MIN	3.991	3.992	−0.009	3.984	3.992	−0.016	3.980	3.992	−0.020	3.973	3.992	−0.027	3.969	3.992	−0.031
5	MAX	5.003	5.000	0.011	4.996	5.000	0.004	4.992	5.000	0.000	4.985	5.000	−0.007	4.981	5.000	−0.011
	MIN	4.991	4.992	−0.009	4.984	4.992	−0.016	4.980	4.992	−0.020	4.973	4.992	−0.027	4.969	4.992	−0.031
6	MAX	6.003	6.000	0.011	5.996	6.000	0.004	5.992	6.000	0.000	5.985	6.000	−0.007	5.981	6.000	−0.011
	MIN	5.991	5.992	−0.009	5.984	5.992	−0.016	5.980	5.992	−0.020	5.973	5.992	−0.027	5.969	5.992	−0.031
8	MAX	8.005	8.000	0.014	7.996	8.000	0.005	7.991	8.000	0.000	7.983	8.000	−0.008	7.978	8.000	−0.013
	MIN	7.990	7.991	−0.010	7.981	7.991	−0.019	7.976	7.991	−0.024	7.968	7.991	−0.032	7.963	7.991	−0.037
10	MAX	10.005	10.000	0.014	9.996	10.000	0.005	9.991	10.000	0.000	9.983	10.000	−0.008	9.978	10.000	−0.013
	MIN	9.990	9.991	−0.010	9.981	9.991	−0.019	9.976	9.991	−0.024	9.968	9.991	−0.032	9.963	9.991	−0.037
12	MAX	12.006	12.000	0.017	11.995	12.000	0.006	11.989	12.000	0.000	11.979	12.000	−0.010	11.974	12.000	−0.015
	MIN	11.988	11.989	−0.012	11.977	11.989	−0.023	11.971	11.989	−0.029	11.961	11.989	−0.039	11.956	11.989	−0.044
16	MAX	16.006	16.000	0.017	15.995	16.000	0.006	15.989	16.000	0.000	15.979	16.000	−0.010	15.974	16.000	−0.015
	MIN	15.988	15.989	−0.012	15.977	15.989	−0.023	15.971	15.989	−0.029	15.961	15.989	−0.039	15.956	15.989	−0.044
20	MAX	20.006	20.000	0.019	19.993	20.000	0.006	19.986	20.000	−0.001	19.973	20.000	−0.014	19.967	20.000	−0.020
	MIN	19.985	19.987	−0.015	19.972	19.987	−0.028	19.965	19.987	−0.035	19.952	19.987	−0.048	19.946	19.987	−0.054
25	MAX	25.006	25.000	0.019	24.993	25.000	0.006	24.986	25.000	−0.001	24.973	25.000	−0.014	24.960	25.000	−0.027
	MIN	24.985	24.987	−0.015	24.972	24.987	−0.028	24.965	24.987	−0.035	24.952	24.987	−0.048	24.939	24.987	−0.061
30	MAX	30.006	30.000	0.019	29.993	30.000	0.006	29.986	30.000	−0.001	29.973	30.000	−0.014	29.960	30.000	−0.027
	MIN	29.985	29.987	−0.015	29.972	29.987	−0.028	29.965	29.987	−0.035	29.952	29.987	−0.048	29.939	29.987	−0.061
40	MAX	40.007	40.000	0.023	39.992	40.000	0.008	39.983	40.000	−0.001	39.966	40.000	−0.018	39.949	40.000	−0.035
	MIN	39.982	39.984	−0.018	39.967	39.984	−0.033	39.958	39.984	−0.042	39.941	39.984	−0.059	39.924	39.984	−0.076
50	MAX	50.007	50.000	0.023	49.992	50.000	0.008	49.983	50.000	−0.001	49.966	50.000	−0.018	49.939	50.000	−0.045
	MIN	49.982	49.984	−0.018	49.967	49.984	−0.033	49.958	49.984	−0.042	49.941	49.984	−0.059	49.914	49.984	−0.086
60	MAX	60.009	60.000	0.028	59.991	60.000	0.010	59.979	60.000	−0.002	59.958	60.000	−0.023	59.924	60.000	−0.057
	MIN	59.979	59.981	−0.021	59.961	59.981	−0.039	59.949	59.981	−0.051	59.928	59.981	−0.072	59.894	59.981	−0.106
80	MAX	80.009	80.000	0.028	79.991	80.000	0.010	79.979	80.000	−0.002	79.952	80.000	−0.029	79.909	80.000	−0.072
	MIN	79.979	79.981	−0.021	79.961	79.981	−0.039	79.949	79.981	−0.051	79.922	79.981	−0.078	79.879	79.981	−0.121
100	MAX	100.010	100.000	0.032	99.990	100.000	0.012	99.976	100.000	−0.002	99.942	100.000	−0.036	99.889	100.000	−0.089
	MIN	99.975	99.978	−0.025	99.955	99.978	−0.045	99.941	99.978	−0.059	99.907	99.978	−0.093	99.854	99.978	−0.146
120	MAX	120.010	120.000	0.032	119.990	120.000	0.012	119.976	120.000	−0.002	119.934	120.000	−0.044	119.869	120.000	−0.109
	MIN	119.975	119.978	−0.025	119.955	119.978	−0.045	119.941	119.978	−0.059	119.899	119.978	−0.101	119.834	119.978	−0.166
160	MAX	160.012	160.000	0.037	159.988	160.000	0.013	159.972	160.000	−0.003	159.915	160.000	−0.060	159.825	160.000	−0.150
	MIN	159.972	159.975	−0.028	159.948	159.975	−0.052	159.932	159.975	−0.068	159.875	159.975	−0.125	159.785	159.975	−0.215

Table 52 (cont'd.) Preferred shaft basis fits.

NORTH AMERICAN GAGES												EUROPEAN GAGES								
Ferrous metals, such as galvanized steel, tin plate						Nonferrous metals, such as copper, brass, aluminum			Steel and iron wire and bare copper piano wire			Galvanized steel, tin plate, copper, strip steel and steel, copper and aluminum tubes						Nonferrous		
U.S. Standard (USS)			U.S. Standard (Revised) Formerly Manufactures Standard			American Standard or Brown and Sharpe (B & S)			United States Steel Wire Gage			Birmingham (BWG)			New Birmingham (BG)			Imperial Wire Gage Imperial Standard (SWG)		
Gage	in.	mm	Gage	in.	mm	Gage	in.	mm	Gage	in.	mm	Gage	in.	mm	Gage	in.	mm	Gage	in.	mm
			3	.240	6.01	3	.229	5.83												
4	.234	5.95	4	.224	5.70	4	.204	5.19	4	.225	5.72	4	.238	6.05	4	.250	6.35	4	.232	5.89
5	.219	5.56	5	.209	5.31	5	.182	4.62	5	.207	5.26	5	.220	5.59	5	.223	5.65	5	.212	5.39
6	.203	5.16	6	.194	4.94	6	.162	4.12	6	.192	4.88	6	.203	5.16	6	.198	5.03	6	.192	4.88
7	.188	4.76	7	.179	4.55	7	.144	3.67	7	.177	4.50	7	.180	4.57	7	.176	4.48	7	.176	4.47
8	.172	4.37	8	.164	4.18	8	.129	3.26	8	.162	4.11	8	.165	4.19	8	.157	3.99	8	.160	4.06
9	.156	3.97	9	.149	3.80	9	.114	2.91	9	.148	3.77	9	.148	3.76	9	.140	3.55	9	.144	3.66
10	.141	3.57	10	.135	3.42	10	.102	2.59	10	.135	3.43	10	.134	3.40	10	.125	3.18	10	.128	3.25
11	.125	3.18	11	.120	3.04	11	.091	2.30	11	.121	3.06	11	.120	3.05	11	.111	2.83	11	.116	2.95
12	.109	2.78	12	.105	2.66	12	.081	2.05	12	.106	2.68	12	.109	2.77	12	.099	2.52	12	.104	2.64
13	.094	2.38	13	.090	2.78	13	.072	1.83	13	.092	2.32	13	.095	2.41	13	.088	2.24	13	.092	2.34
14	.078	1.98	14	.075	1.90	14	.064	1.63	14	.080	2.03	14	.083	2.11	14	.079	1.99	14	.080	2.03
15	.070	1.79	15	.067	1.71	15	.057	1.45	15	.072	1.83	15	.072	1.83	15	.070	1.78	15	.072	1.83
16	.063	1.59	16	.060	1.52	16	.051	1.29	16	.063	1.63	16	.065	1.65	16	.063	1.59	16	.064	1.63
17	.056	1.43	17	.054	1.37	17	.045	1.15	17	.054	1.37	17	.058	1.47	17	.056	1.41	17	.056	1.42
18	.050	1.27	18	.048	1.21	18	.040	1.02	18	.048	1.21	18	.049	1.25	18	.050	2.58	18	.048	1.22
19	.044	1.11	19	.042	1.06	19	.036	0.91	19	.041	1.04	19	.042	1.07	19	.044	1.19	19	.040	1.02
20	.038	0.95	20	.036	0.91	20	.032	0.81	20	.035	0.88	20	.035	0.89	20	.039	1.00	20	.036	0.91
21	.034	0.87	21	.033	0.84	21	.029	0.72	21	.032	0.81	21	.032	0.81	21	.035	0.89	21	.032	0.81
22	.031	0.79	22	.030	0.76	22	.025	0.65	22	.029	0.73	22	.028	0.71	22	.031	0.79	22	.028	0.71
23	.028	0.71	23	.027	0.68	23	.023	0.57	23	.026	0.66	23	.025	0.64	23	.028	0.71	23	.024	0.61
24	.025	0.64	24	.024	0.61	24	.020	0.51	24	.023	0.58	24	.022	0.56	24	.025	0.63	24	.022	0.56
25	.022	0.56	25	.021	0.53	25	.018	0.46	25	.020	0.52	25	.020	0.51	25	.022	0.56	25	.020	0.51
26	.019	0.48	26	.018	0.46	26	.016	0.40	26	.018	0.46	26	.018	0.46	26	.020	0.50	26	.018	0.46
27	.017	0.44	27	.016	0.42	27	.014	0.36	27	.017	0.44	27	.016	0.41	27	.017	0.44	27	.016	0.42
28	.016	0.40	28	.015	0.38	28	.013	0.32	28	.016	0.41	28	.014	0.36	28	.016	0.40	28	.015	0.38
29	.014	0.36	29	.014	0.34	29	.011	0.29	29	.015	0.38	29	.013	0.33	29	.014	0.35	29	.014	0.35
30	.013	0.32	30	.012	0.31	30	.010	0.25	30	.014	0.36	30	.012	0.31	30	.012	0.31	30	.012	0.32
31	.011	0.28	31	.011	0.27	31	.009	0.23	31	.013	0.34	31	.010	0.25	31	.011	0.28			
32	.010	0.26	32	.010	0.25	32	.008	0.20	32	.013	0.33	32	.009	0.23				32	.011	0.27
33	.009	0.24	33	.009	0.23	33	.007	0.18	33	.012	0.30	33	.008	0.20	33	.009	0.22	33	.010	0.25
34	.009	0.22	34	.008	0.21	34	.006	0.16	34	.010	0.26	34	.007	0.18	34	.008	0.20	34	.009	0.23
									35	.010	0.24	35	.005	0.13	35	.007	0.18	35	.008	0.21
36	.007	0.18	36	.007	0.17	36	.005	0.13	36	.009	0.23	36	.004	0.10	36	.006	0.16			
									37	.008	0.22							37	.007	0.17
38	.006	0.16	38	.006	0.15	38	.004	0.10	38	.008	0.20				38	.005	0.12	38	.006	0.15
									39	.008	0.19									
									40	.007	0.18				40	.004	0.10	40	.005	0.12
									41	.007	0.17							42	.004	0.10

Note: Metric standards governing gage sizes were not available at the time of publication. The sizes given in the above chart are "soft conversion" from current inch standards and are not meant to be representative of the precise metric gage sizes which may be available in the future. Conversions are given only to allow the student to compare gage sizes readily with the metric drill sizes.

Table 53 Wire and sheet-metal gages and thicknesses.

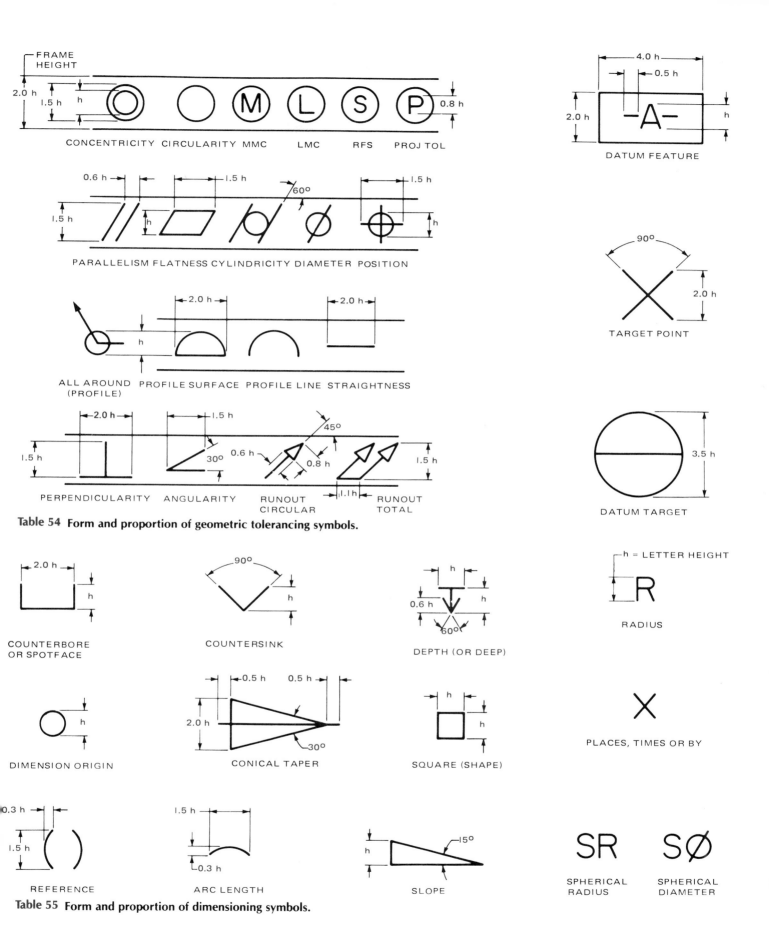

Table 54 Form and proportion of geometric tolerancing symbols.

Table 55 Form and proportion of dimensioning symbols.

SYMBOL FOR:	ANSI Y14.5	ISO
STRAIGHTNESS	—	—
FLATNESS	▱	▱
CIRCULARITY	○	○
CYLINDRICITY	⌭	⌭
PROFILE OF A LINE	⌒	⌒
PROFILE OF A SURFACE	⌓	⌓
ALL AROUND—PROFILE	⟲	NONE
ANGULARITY	∠	∠
PERPENDICULARITY	⊥	⊥
PARALLELISM	//	//
POSITION	⊕	⊕
CONCENTRICITY/COAXIALITY	◎	◎
SYMMETRY	NONE	≡
CIRCULAR RUNOUT	↗	↗
TOTAL RUNOUT	↗↗	↗↗
AT MAXIMUM MATERIAL CONDITION	Ⓜ	Ⓜ
AT LEAST MATERIAL CONDITION	Ⓛ	NONE
REGARDLESS OF FEATURE SIZE	Ⓢ	NONE
PROJECTED TOLERANCE ZONE	Ⓟ	Ⓟ
DIAMETER	∅	∅
BASIC DIMENSION	50	50
REFERENCE DIMENSION	(50)	(50)
DATUM FEATURE	-A-	⟋ OR ⟋Ⓐ
DATUM TARGET	(∅6/A1)	(∅6/A1)
TARGET POINT	✕	✕
DIMENSION ORIGIN	⊕→	NONE
FEATURE CONTROL FRAME	⊕ ∅0.5Ⓜ A B C	⊕ ∅0.5Ⓜ A B C
CONICAL TAPER	▷	▷
SLOPE	◁	◁
COUNTERBORE/SPOTFACE	⌴	NONE
COUNTERSINK	⌵	NONE
DEPTH/DEEP	↧	NONE
SQUARE (SHAPE)	□	□
DIMENSION NOT TO SCALE	15	15
NUMBER OF TIMES/PLACES	8X	8X
ARC LENGTH	⌒105	NONE
RADIUS	R	R
SPHERICAL RADIUS	SR	NONE
SPHERICAL DIAMETER	S∅	NONE

*MAY BE FILLED IN

Table 56   Comparison of ANSI and ISO symbols.

	Nominal Pipe Size Inches	Outside Diameter	Wall Thickness			Approx. Distance Pipe Enters Fitting	Weight (lbs/ft)		
			Sched. 40 (Standard)	Sched. 80 (Extra Strong)	Sched. 160		Sched. 40 (Standard)	Sched. 80 (Extra Strong)	Sched. 160
U.S. CUSTOMARY (INCHES)	⅛ (.125)	.405	.068	.095	—	.188	.24	.31	—
	¼ (.250)	.540	.088	.119	—	.281	.42	.54	—
	⅜ (.375)	.675	.091	.126	—	.297	.57	.74	—
	½ (.500)	.840	.109	.147	.188	.375	.85	1.09	1.31
	¾ (.750)	1.050	.113	.154	.219	.406	1.13	1.47	1.94
	1.00	1.315	.133	.179	.250	.500	1.68	2.17	2.84
	1.25	1.660	.140	.191	.250	.549	2.27	3.00	3.76
	1.50	1.900	.145	.200	.281	.562	2.72	3.63	4.86
	2	2.375	.154	.218	.344	.578	3.65	5.02	7.46
	2.5	2.875	.203	.276	.375	.875	5.79	7.66	10.01
	3	3.500	.216	.300	.438	.938	7.58	10.25	14.31
	3.5	4.000	.226	.318	—	1.000	9.11	12.51	—
	4	4.500	.237	.337	.531	1.062	10.79	14.98	22.52
	5	5.563	.258	.375	.625	1.156	14.62	20.78	32.96
	6	6.625	.280	.432	.719	1.250	18.97	28.57	45.34
	8	8.625	.322	.500	.906	1.469	28.55	43.39	74.71

Table 57   American Standard Wrought Iron Pipe.

INDEX